Contemporary Motivation Research

Contemporary
Motivation
Research

**From Global
to Local
Perspectives**

edited by
Marold Wosnitza
Stuart A. Karabenick
Anastasia Efklides
Peter Nenniger

HOGREFE

Library of Congress Cataloging in Publication

is available via the Library of Congress Marc Database under the
LC Control Number 2008938003

Library and Archives Canada Cataloguing in Publication

Contemporary motivation research : from global to local
perspectives / edited by Marold Wosnitza ... [et al.].

Includes bibliographical references.
ISBN 978-0-88937-356-3

1. Motivation (Psychology). I. Wosnitza, Marold

BF503.C66 2008   153.8   C2008-906311-2

© 2009 by Hogrefe & Huber Publishers

PUBLISHING OFFICES
USA: Hogrefe Publishing, 875 Massachusetts Avenue, 7th Floor, Cambridge, MA 02139
           Phone (866) 823-4726, Fax (617) 354-6875; E-mail info@hogrefe.com
EUROPE: Hogrefe & Huber Publishers, Rohnsweg 25, 37085 Göttingen, Germany
           Phone +49 551 49609-0, Fax +49 551 49609-88, E-mail hh@hogrefe.com

SALES & DISTRIBUTION
USA: Hogrefe Publishing, Customer Services Department,
           30 Amberwood Parkway, Ashland, OH 44805
           Phone (800) 228-3749, Fax (419) 281-6883, E-mail custserv@hogrefe.com
EUROPE: Hogrefe & Huber Publishers, Rohnsweg 25, 37085 Göttingen, Germany
           Phone +49 551 49609-0, Fax +49 551 49609-88, E-mail hh@hogrefe.com

OTHER OFFICES
CANADA: Hogrefe & Huber Publishers, 1543 Bayview Avenue, Toronto, Ontario M4G 3B5
SWITZERLAND: Hogrefe & Huber Publishers, Länggass-Strasse 76, CH-3000 Bern 9

Hogrefe Publishing
Incorporated and registered in the Commonwealth of Massachusetts, USA

Hogrefe & Huber Publishers
Incorporated and registered in Göttingen, Lower Saxony, Germany

Printed and bound in the USA
ISBN 978-0-88937-356-3

Contents

List of Contributors   vii

Preface   xi

Part 1: Global Perspective in Motivation

Motivation in School from Contextual and Longitudinal Perspectives
Marja Vauras, Pekka Salonen, Erno Lehtinen, & Riitta Kinnunen   1

Seeking Help: Generalizable Self-Regulatory Process and Social-Cultural
Barometer
Stuart A. Karabenick & Richard S. Newman   25

A Framework for Personal Goals in Collaborative Learning Contexts
Marold Wosnitza & Simone Volet   49

Motivational Aspects of Cognitive Load Theory
Wolfgang Schnotz, Stefan Fries, & Holger Horz   69

Global and Local Perspectives on Human Affect: Implications of the
Control-Value Theory of Achievement Emotions
Reinhard Pekrun   97

Metacognitive Experiences as the Link between Situational Characteristics,
Motivation, and Affect in Self-Regulated Learning
Fotini Dina & Anastasia Efklides   117

On a Differential Explanation of Self-Direction in Motivating Learning
Environments
Peter Nenniger, Katja van den Brink, & Dirk Bissbort   147

Linking Personality to Work Motivation and Performance: Individual
Differences Effects
Tanja Bipp   167

Mediators and Moderators of Approach-Performance and Avoidance-Performance
Relationships in Children: Theoretical and Experimental Aspects
Gunnar Bjørnebekk   185

Part 2: Situation and Context Effects in Motivation: Local Perspective

Interest and Efficacy Beliefs in Self-Regulated Learning: Does the Task
Make a Difference?
Mary Ainley, Sarah Buckley, & Joanne Chan   207

The Impact of Goal and Feedback Treatments on Self-Determined
Motivation and Situational Interest in a Computer-Based Learning Context
Doris Lewalter & Katrin Scholta   229

Specification Issues in the Use of Multilevel Modeling to Examine the
Effects of Classroom Context: The Case of Classroom Goal Structures
Tamera B. Murdock & Angela D. Miller   249

Motivation Development in Novice Teachers: The Development of
Utility Filters
Susan Bobbitt Nolen, Christopher J. Ward, Ilana Seidel Horn, Sarah Childers,
Sara Sunshine Campbell, & Karan Mahna   265

Students' Perceptions of Parental Attitudes toward Academic Achievement:
Effects on Motivation, Self-Concept and School Achievement
Francisco Peixoto & Raquel Carvalho   279

Influencing Students' Motivation for School: The Case of First-Year Students
from Different Ethnic Backgrounds in the Netherlands in the Lowest Level
of Secondary School
Thea Peetsma & Ineke van der Veen   299

Normative vs. Non-Normative Performance Goals: Effects on Behavioral
and Emotional Regulation in Achievement Situations
Georgios D. Sideridis   321

Incentives and Flow Experience in Learning Settings and the Moderating
Role of Individual Differences
Julia Schüler & Stefan Engeser   339

Striving for Personal Goals: The Role of Negative Mood and the Availability
of Mood-Regulation Strategies
Thomas A. Langens   359

List of Contributors

Mary Ainley
University of Melbourne
Psychology Department
Redmond Barry Building
VIC, 3010, Australia

Tanja Bipp
Eindhoven University of Technology
Department of Technology Management
Human Performance Management
Group
Pav U41, P.O. Box 513
5600 MB Eindhoven, Netherlands

Dirk Bissbort
University Koblenz-Landau
Campus Landau
Centre for Educational Research
Bürgerstr. 23
76829 Landau, Germany

Gunnar Bjørnebekk
University of Oslo
The Norwegian Centre for Studies of
Conduct Problems
P.O. Box 1565 Vika
NO-0118 Oslo, Norway

Sarah Buckley
University of Melbourne
Psychology Department
Redmond Barry Building
VIC, 3010, Australia

Sara Sunshine Campbell
University of Washington
Box 353600, Seattle
WA 98195-3600, USA

Joanne Chan
The Hong Kong Polytechnic University
Department of Applied Social Sciences
Hung Hom
Hong Kong

Sarah Childers
University of Washington
Box 353600, Seattle
WA 98195-3600, USA

Raquel Carvalho
I.S.P.A.
R. Jardim do Tabaco 34
1149-041 Lisbon, Portugal

Fotini Dina
Aristotle University of Thessaloniki
School of Psychology
541 24 Thessaloniki, Greece

Anastasia Efklides
Aristotle University of Thessaloniki
School of Psychology
541 24 Thessaloniki, Greece

Stefan Engeser
Technical University Munich
Department of Psychology
Lothstr. 17
80335 Munich, Germany

Stefan Fries
Bielefeld University
Universitätsstraße 25
33615 Bielefeld, Germany

Holger Horz
University of Koblenz-Landau
Thomas-Nast-Str. 44
76829 Landau, Germany

Ilana Seidel Horn
University of Washington
Box 353600, Seattle
WA 98195-3600, USA

Stuart A. Karabenick
Combined Program in Education and
Psychology
University of Michigan 1
400D School of Education
610E. University, Ann Arbor, MI 48109,
USA

Riitta Kinnunen
University of Turku
Deptartment of Teacher Education
and Centre for Learning Research
Assistentinkatu 5, 20014 Turku, Finland

Thomas A. Langens
University of Wuppertal
Department of Psychology
Gaußstraße 20
42097 Wuppertal, Germany

Erno Lehtinen
University of Turku
Deptartment of Teacher Education
and Centre for Learning Research
Assistentinkatu 5, 20014 Turku, Finland

Doris Lewalter
Technical University Munich
Fachgebiet Gymnasialpädagogik
Lothstr. 17
80335 Munich, Germany

Karan Mahna
University of Washington
Box 353600, Seattle
WA 98195-3600, USA

Angela D. Miller
University of Kansas
Schiefelbusch Life Span Institute
Lawrence, KS, 66045

Tamera B. Murdock
University of Missouri-Kansas City
Department of Psychology
Kansas City, MO, 64110-2499

Peter Nenniger
University Koblenz-Landau
Campus Landau
Centre for Educational Research
Bürgerstr. 23
76829 Landau, Germany

Richard S. Newman
University of California, Riverside
School Psychology
Graduate School of Education
Riverside, CA 92521, USA

Susan Bobbitt Nolen
University of Washington
Box 353600, Seattle
WA 98195-3600, USA

Thea Peetsma
University of Amsterdam
Faculty of Social and Behavioural Sciences
P.O. Box 94208
1090 GE Amsterdam, Netherlands

Francisco Peixoto
I.S.P.A.
R. Jardim do Tabaco 34
1149-041 Lisbon, Portugal

Reinhard Pekrun
University of Munich
Department of Psychology
Leopoldstrasse 13
80802 Munich, Germany

Pekka Salonen
University of Turku
Deptartment of Teacher Education
and Centre for Learning Research
Assistentinkatu 5, 20014 Turku, Finland

Wolfgang Schnotz
University of Koblenz-Landau
Thomas-Nast-Str. 44
76829 Landau, Germany

Katrin Scholta
RWTH Technical University Aachen
Institut for Education
Eilfschornsteinstr. 7
52056 Aachen, Germany

Julia Schüler
University of Zurich
Department of Psychology
Binzmühlestrasse 14/6
8050 Zurich, Switzerland

Georgios D. Sideridis
University of Crete
Department of Psychology
741 00 Rethimno, Greece

Katja van den Brink
University Koblenz-Landau
Campus Landau
Centre for Educational Research
Bürgerstr. 23
76829 Landau, Germany

Ineke van der Veen
University of Amsterdam
Faculty of Social and Behavioural Sciences
P.O. Box 94208
1090 GE Amsterdam, Netherlands

Marja Vauras
University of Turku
Deptartment of Teacher Education
and Centre for Learning Research
Assistentinkatu 5, 20014 Turku, Finland

Simone Volet
Murdoch University Perth
School of Education
Murdoch 6150, Western Australia

Christopher J. Ward
University of Washington
Box 353600, Seattle
WA 98195-3600, USA

Marold Wosnitza
Murdoch University Perth
School of Education
Murdoch 6150, Western Australia

Preface

**Marold Wosnitza, Stuart Karabenick,
Anastasia Efklides, & Peter Nenniger**

All social and behavioral sciences face the challenge of determining which theories and empirical findings are comprehensible and applicable only within given contexts or cultural confines and those that are generalizable, albeit with appropriate parametric adjustments. This emic versus etic distinction originated in linguistics (Pike, 1954), anthropology (Goodenough, 1970; Harris, 1980), and subsequently sociology and psychology exemplified in work by Triandis and colleagues (Triandis, Malpass, & Davidson, 1971). In the field of education, Cronbach (1982) framed the issue as the need to emphasize external as well as internal validity in research designs. The field of motivation is no exception. In fact, it is arguable that the nature of the subject renders motivation phenomena especially susceptible to the influences of context and culture. Motivation concerns the determinants of the direction, intensity, and persistence of behaviors, and includes their cognitive and affective concomitants. Motivation theories propose different ways to conceptualize those determinants, such as needs, motives, goals, self-beliefs, and differences in how individuals construe situations.

Contributions to the motivation literature vary in the degree of attention to issues of generality. At one end of the continuum are cross-cultural studies in which specificity takes center stage. Research that focuses on the influence of context also attends to issues of relative generality (to other contexts). Many studies, however, are conducted under highly localized conditions, and even if they tacitly assume generality (e.g., to other classrooms or schools) there are limiting conditions that often remain unexamined. This issue is very much at the center of current research and evaluation in education (Green, Camilli, & Elmore, 2006). Accordingly, there is clearly a need in the field of motivation to showcase the range of work in a way that recognizes contributions that are "snapshots" and those characterized as presenting a "global picture." Whereas each contribution to this volume has elements of both, it is divided into two parts that feature global and local perspectives to varying degrees.

Part 1: Global Perspective in Motivation

The first part presents several theoretical issues that reflect more global motivational processes and research. In their chapter "Motivation in School from Contextual and Longitudinal Perspective" *Vauras, Salonen, Lehtinen, and Kinnunen* focus on how motivational orientations, socio-emotional coping strategies and cognition are established and maintained in the classroom context over school years. Contrary to short-term changes, the emphasis is on the interactive, long-term development of cognition and motivation in multidirectional social interactions. They discuss how these interactions must be understood as embedded in complex social contexts and institutional-cultural frames of reference.

In "Seeking Help: Generalizable Self-Regulatory Process and Social-Cultural Barometer" *Karabenick and Newman* discuss how unlike other (cognitive and metacognitive) strategies, seeking help is a generalizable social-interactive process that renders it susceptible to specific motivation-related social and cultural influences. The social-interactive context in which help seeking takes place can influence comprehension monitoring, the perceived costs and benefits of seeking (and not seeking) help, from whom help is requested, and why.

In their chapter "A Framework for Personal Goals in Collaborative Learning Contexts" *Wosnitza and Volet* explicate the complex nature and characteristics of small group learning environments by proposing a generalizable systematic conceptual framework that incorporates both personal and group goals. Examples are provided that illustrate its application to tasks with different structures and demands.

Schnotz, Fries, and Horz then present "Motivational Aspects of Cognitive Load Theory" that begins with a rewiew of how cognitive load, defined in terms of mental effort, is integral to the process of learning and instruction. They then describe the challenges and complexities that arise when integrating motivation and cognitive load theory, especially given recent developments in motivation research that include effects of the learning context.

Pekrun links emotions with motivation in achievement settings. The emphasis of the chapter "Global and Local Perspectives on Human Affect: Implications of the Control-Value Theory of Achievement Emotions" is on proximal and distal antecedents of achievement emotions, ranging from situational to personal and to social and socio-historical contexts. The chapter discusses where research on achievement emotions is consistent with generalizable principles (conceptual, theoretical and methodological) and where it is limited by virtue of context or culture and ways that context, culture or other conditions constrain such generalizations.

In "Metacognitive Experiences as the Link between Situational Characteristics, Motivation, and Affect in Self-Regulated Learning", *Dina and Efklides* argue in favor of a Model of Self-Regulated Learning that takes into consideration both general person and situational factors in learning settings. Their approach features "metacognitive experiences" which have a cognitive and affective character and connect extrinsic feedback with students' representation of the learning situation, their competence and self-concept. Moreover, metacognitive experiences mediate the situational effects on state anxiety. This interaction of general person characteristics and situationally sensitive metacognitive experiences allows both stability and variation in behavior and renders self-regulation adaptive in the short as well in the long run.

Nenniger, van den Brink, and Bissbort's chapter "On a Differential Explanation of Self-Direction in Motivating Learning Environments" attempts to reconcile contradictory findings in research on self-directed/self-regulated learning. The concept they introduce involves "differential modes of self-direction" and their interactive dynamics with motivational processes. They follow the question whether motivation is global or must be treated locally using separately adapted partial theories and propose that a differential approach integrating complementary research traditions is more suitable for adequate explanations.

In "Linking Personality to Work Motivation and Performance: Individual Differences Effects" *Bipp* reviews the current literature that relates personality constructs of cross-cultural stability to motivational constructs, building a foundation for explaining their relation to achievement behavior. Especially, approaches to integrate personality factors into a comprehensive model of goal-oriented action, work motivation and performance are presented and supplemented by empirical data. She shows that the fact that goals and associated constructs such as goal orientations can serve as a missing link between personality traits and performance in different settings supports the generalizability of the notion that motivational constructs or self-regulatory processes mediate or transport the effects of personality traits on performance.

In the last chapter of this section, "An Investigation of Possible Mediators and Moderators of the Approach and Avoidance - Performance Relationship in Children: Theoretical and Experimental Aspects", Bjørnebekk seeks to expand the existing view of motivation in achievement theory by exploring how emotional processes directly and indirectly influence more situational specific cognition, affect during problem solving, and performance through individual variation in approach and avoidance tendencies and goal distance in time. The author proposed, therefore, that the generalized functional significance of achievement goals is overemphasized, and should be more properly conceived as context dependent. This chapter, thus, paves the way for a more local perspective to motivational phenomena as exemplified in the chapters of the second part.

Part 2: Situation and Context Effects in Motivation: Local Perspective

In Part 2 of this book, situation and context effects are emphasized. Interest and feedback are two situation- and context-specific factors that affect motivation. In "Interest and Efficacy Beliefs in Self-Regulated Learning: Does the Task Make a Difference?", *Ainley, Buckley, and Chan* focus on the motivational variables of interest and self-efficacy, and provide snapshots of relationships between interest and self-efficacy as they occur while students work on specific problems in classrooms. These snapshots gain added dimensionality as instantiations of motivational variables that have well-researched roles in the global picture.

In the chapter "The Impact of Goal and Feedback Treatments on Self-Determined Motivation and Situational Interest in a Computer Based Learning Context" *Lewalter and Scholta* describe how motivation and interest develop in relation to extrinsic feedback; thus the authors contribute to our understanding of the mechanism of motivational development and change. Specifically, they propose that the way people handle goals and feedback depends very much on the situation and prior learning experiences in similar contexts. According to the authors, research programs combining local and global focuses of investigation promise to provide a more complete understanding of the complex ways in which motivational processes are affected by personal and situational characteristics on different levels depending on the specific learning context.

Murdock and Miller then present "Specification Issues in the Use of Multilevel Modeling to Examine the Effects of Classroom Context: The Case of Classroom Goal Structures" that determine global and specific motivational factors that influence student cheating in school. Their analysis considers teasing apart the role of individual goals from classroom goal structure by comparing and contrasting the various structural models that have been specified and tested in the motivation literature. In particular, the authors address variation in the sources of data used to assess goal structures, and hypothesized relations between personal goals and classroom goal structures.

Nolen, Ward, Horn, Childers, Campbell, and Mahna argue in their chapter "Motivation Development in Novice Teachers: The Development of Utility Filters" that general descriptions of motivation do not adequately capture preservice teachers' motivation. They describe how understanding teachers' motivation to learn prompted practices in a graduate level, secondary pre-service teacher education program, and how it developed in multiple social contexts. The authors introduce the concept of "motivational filters", and in particular the utility filter, to describe how preservice teachers make decisions about learning. Further, they propose that we should not focus on local snapshots nor a global picture but rather a narrative in which processes of development and change can be documented and analyzed.

Peixoto and Carvalho then focus on "Students' Perceptions of Parental Attitudes toward Academic Achievement: Effects on Motivation, Self-Concept and School Achievement". Particular attention is paid to relationships with motivational orientations. In particular the authors show that perceived parental attitudes towards learning as a process or as performance have direct and indirect effects on students' motivational orientation and school achievement. In their chapter, motivational orientations are considered as global predispositions, in the sense that they can be considered as a trait, more or less stable, but that specific school tasks determine how these orientations are actualized.

In the next chapter "Influencing Students' Motivation for School: The Case of First-Year Students from Different Ethnic Background in the Netherlands in the Lowest Level of Secondary School" *Peetsma and van der Veen* show that what are considered unfavorable motivational tendencies in a specific context can be transformed into more positive, long-term goals. Furthermore, differences between specific groups of students, such as girls and students from ethnic minorities, are considered. The utilized motivation theories can be seen as more global, at least for the western world, but aspects of motivation and context seem to have different outcomes for different groups of students.

In "Normative vs. Non-Normative Performance Goals: Effects on Behavioral and Emotional Regulation in Achievement Situations" *Sideridis* describes the affective experiences of students with and without learning problems when motivated for different reasons. The connection between emotional and motivational processes when performing specific tasks and the generalizability of these processes across different populations is discussed. Motives at the task level are examined, along with tests of the proposition that performance-approach goals, which represent situation-specific motives, can be further differentiated into normative and non-normative components.

The following chapter "Incentives and Flow Experience in Learning Settings and the Moderating Role of Individual Differences" by *Schüler and Engeser* provides a snapshot of motivational processes in terms of the experience of "flow", which is connected to general motivational frameworks. Their analysis delineates how the motivation to engage in behavior is determined by an interaction between personal motives and goals and the situation, with its incentives and affordances.

Finally, *Langens*, in the last chapter, investigates the effects of negative mood and mood-regulation strategies on long-term goal striving. Two general principles that specify the effect of mood and mood regulation on goal striving are outlined, and three studies that empirically test these principles are presented in the chapter "Striving for Personal Goals: The Role of Negative Mood and the Availability of Mood-Regulation Strategies". In addition to general principles, results indicate ways that effects of mood-regulation strategies on goal striving are moderated by cultural and contextual factors.

To conclude, the present volume provides a wealth of perspectives in the conceptualization of and research on motivational phenomena. The global or local perspectives theme adopted here arises particularly when motivation is seen in relation to affect and self-regulation, both of which are tied to situation and context factors. From this point of view, the complexity and diversity of motivational phenomena are shown, and the challenges for research and theory are highlighted, because "snapshots" require an understanding of the interaction of general mechanisms as they confront local conditions. The development and change of motivation is another prominent theme, which while closely related to global/local perspectives, adds a temporal dimension in human motivation that continues to be a challenge for future research.

References

Cronbach, L. J. (1982). *Designing evaluations of educational and social programs.* San Francisco: Jossey-Bass.

Goodenough, W. (1970). *Description and comparison in cultural anthropology.* Cambridge, UK: Cambridge University Press.

Green, J. L., Camilli, G., & Elmore, P. B. (2006). *Handbook of complementary methods in education research.* Mahwah, NJ: Erlbaum.

Harris, M. (1980). *Cultural Materialism: The Struggle for a Science of Culture.* New York: Random House.

Pike, K. L. (1967). *Language in relation to a unified theory of structure of human behavior* (2nd ed.). The Hague, The Netherlands: Mouton.

Triandis, H. C., Malpass, R. S., & Davidson, A. R. (1971). Cross-Cultural Psychology. *Biennial Review of Anthropology, 7,* 1-84.

Motivation in School from Contextual and Longitudinal Perspectives

Marja Vauras, Pekka Salonen, Erno Lehtinen, & Riitta Kinnunen

The focus of this chapter is on how motivational orientations and socio-emotional coping strategies in relation to cognition are established and maintained in the classroom context over the school years. Contrary to short-term changes, the emphasis is on interactive, long-term development of cognition and motivation in multidirectional social interactions, which must be understood as embedded in complex social contexts and institutional-cultural frames (e.g. Lehtinen, Vauras, Salonen, Olkinuora, & Kinnunen, 1995; Olkinuora & Salonen, 1992). In our studies, the primary focus has been on the sub-performing students, that is, students who experience multiple cognitive and motivational problems in school. In order to unveil the behavior-in-context, mirroring the complexity of dynamic and socially embedded human motivation, emotion and learning, a multi-method research approach has been applied, with a strong emphasis on observations in real-life situations. In this chapter, we argue on the basis of the evidence from multiple observations and measurements in varying (local) contexts that there is a strong tendency for gradual formation of more generalized, relatively stable motivational (global) dispositions that are resistant to change, particularly, in the case of students with learning difficulties.

Our chapter is structured in three sections. We start by presenting our theoretical perspective on motivation, and a relational model that describes learners' basic alternatives for orienting and adapting to interpersonal learning contexts. The second section discusses the problem of general versus specific motivation in terms of stability of the learner's motivational dispositions, and variability and modifiability of motivation-related behaviors in school contexts. Evidence from our longitudinal studies is used to illustrate the accretion and generalization of motivational tendencies over the school years. Motivationally and cognitively diverging developmental paths are intimately linked to the discussion on inertia in learning, for example, how some students show strong resistance to instruction. Intervention studies and case analyses are used to illustrate resistance patterns and the dynamics of resistance. We argue that resilience is linked to interpersonal dynamics between the students and the teachers shaping the transactions and instructional scaffolding in school settings, which is compatible with more general notions of the person-environment fit theory (see Hunt, 1975) and educational match vs. mismatch in terms of motivation and emotion (see, e.g., Eccles & Midgley, 1989; Roeser, Eccles, & Sameroff, 2000; Wigfield, Eccles, & Rodriguez, 1998). In the third section, we present a revised conceptualization of micro-genetic and long-term developmental dynamics of learning-related interactions. Balanced versus biased interpersonal cycles in generalization and stagnation of motivation patterns are discussed in this connection, and demonstrated by a case example. Brief remarks on multimodal person-situation transaction cycles and contextual variability conclude the chapter.

Adaptive Learning: Systemic Motivational Orientation and Coping Perspective

A large body of research evidence exists on different motivational constructs (interest, goals, values, orientations), which have been used to depict individual differences (for reviews, see Urdan & Maehr, 1995) and have strong relevance to students' educational outcomes (see review, e.g., Wigfield et al., 1998). These constructs and their concomitants undoubtedly deserve conceptual and empirical attention in the future. However, we argue that when the ultimate goal is to reconstruct learning environments to fit all learners, and to help modify social, learning-related interactions among participants in these environments, a more holistic understanding on motivation in learning is also necessary. Individuals learn and develop over a long periods of time in social and cultural contexts, sharing fundamental experiences and learning outcomes, but they also have unique roles, perspectives, and interpretations in these situations that cannot be reduced to socially shared cultural experiences (e.g., Volet, Vauras, & Salonen, submitted). Along with socio-constructivist views, the recognition of the importance of social influences on learning and motivation has increased (e.g., Eccles, Wigfield, & Schiefele, 1998), and a growing number of scholars have incorporated social constructs into models of motivation (e.g., McCaslin & Good 1996; McCaslin, 2004) and made serious attempts to understand motivation in context (e.g., Volet & Järvelä, 2001; see also Vauras, Salonen, & Kinnunen, 2008).

The aim to understand individuals' complex long-term and socially embedded development, behavior and behavioral outcomes challenges researchers to constantly reassess and refine their methodologies. Conventional methodological approaches addressing "static", unidirectional or linear relationships between isolated variables cannot provide a sufficient basis for understanding the complexity and bidirectional, non-linear dynamics and cumulative processes of behavior-in-context. In particular, when the long-term goal is to reconstruct learning environments to fit all learners, and to help modify social, learning-related interactions among participants, methodologies that help us to gain a more holistic understanding on motivation in learning is needed.

Integration of Theoretical Views and Multi-Method Approach as a Basis of Orientation and Coping Model

At the end of 1970's, Salonen, Lehtinen and Olkinuora (e.g., Olkinuora & Salonen, 1992; Salonen, 1988) conceptualized a triadic, integrated model of motivational orientations comprising basic motivational orientation dimensions and corresponding sets of coping strategies. These orientations (*task, ego defensive , and social dependence*) were derived from three adaptive goal dimensions, which are established during children's learning and social reward or control histories, and they all can be characterized by their focal adaptive focus (task, self, and guiding other, respectively) and the constellation of self-efficacy beliefs a person assigns either to situational or learning features. Since early development of the model, Salonen and his colleagues have gradually elaborated the model to better cover the developmental, multimodal, contextual and interpersonal dynamics in learning situations (see, e.g., Lehtinen et al., 1995; Salonen, Lehtinen, & Olkinuora, 1998; Vauras, Salonen, Lehtinen, & Lepola, 2001; Vauras et al., 2008). The orientation and coping model described the learner's fundamental alternatives for orienting and adapting to interpersonal learning settings (e.g., Olkinuora & Salonen, 1992; Salonen, 1988; Salonen et al, 1998). This original triadic orientation and coping model was based on: (1) classic *psychological theories* of K. Lewin and A. R. Luria focusing on the motivational-emotional tensions and conflicts contributing to the dynamic organization and disorganization of behavior in learning situations (Barker, Dembo, & Lewin, 1941; Lewin, 1935; Luria, 1932); (2) *social psychological* (communication) theories of co-orientation, such as ethno methodological conceptualizations by H. Garfinkel (1967) and A. Cicourel (1973), models of interpersonal balance by T. Newcomb (1953), F. Heider (1958) and R. D. Laing (Laing, Phillipson, & Russell, 1966) or consensus by T. Scheff (1967; for a review see Siegrist, 1970); and (3) conceptualizations of *motivation and coping* distinguishing between task-focused / mastery oriented (intrinsically motivated), ego-focused / helpless, and socially focused (extrinsically motivated) modes of motivation and coping behaviors (see, e.g., Diener & Dweck, 1978; Harter, 1978; Lazarus, Averill, & Opton, 1974; Nicholls, 1979; White, 1959).

Our basic intention was to understand cognitive, motivational and emotional processes within a wider context of interpersonal relationships and adaptations (learner – guidance giver – learning task), and to explain the situational organization versus disorganization (progressions vs. regressions) of learning activity as a function of task-oriented and non-task-oriented adaptive goal structures and motivational-emotional tension systems. Balanced dyadic co-orientation and motivational interpersonal symmetry were assumed to maintain the learner's organized task-focused activity, whereas lack of dyadic co-orientation and rigid interpersonal motivational asymmetries or emotional tensions (e.g., the learner's excessive tendency to appeal the guidance giver and/or to protect his/her own ego) were hypothesized to yield to the disorganization of task-focused behavior (for more details and empirical evidence, see Lepola, Salonen, Vauras, & Poskiparta, 2004; Olkinuora & Salonen, 1992; Salonen et al., 1998; Vauras et al., 2001).

The construction of the model resulted from an interplay between the above mentioned theoretical ideas and empirical research. Although theoretical and technological developments from 1970's to the present have allowed us to adopt gradually more sophisticated and economical research methods, we have, right from the beginning, employed a multi-method research approach. This includes instruments and methods to tap the complexity of real-life, dynamic and socially embedded human motivation, emotion and learning. There have been three main qualitative focuses of our methodological approach: (1) learners' in multiple relations (e.g., teachers, parents, peers, types of tasks, subject-matter domains) and contexts of activity (e.g., learning, problem-solving, individual, collaborative); (2) change of learner's behavior across different contexts and behavioral changes as related to contextual factors; and (3) multimodal intrapersonal dynamic relationships, for example, between motivational, affective and behavioral processes.

Through a rigorous multi-method approach, we better understand the learner as a whole- person-in-context (for concept, see e.g., Boekaerts, 1993), that is, as a person with learning processes and outcomes strongly dependent not only on cognitive and metacognitive skills but also on socio-emotional goals, motivations and coping tendencies interacting with the affordances and constraints of the learning environments. This approach is appropriate for an integrative and context-driven theoretical approach, which embeds learning and learning problems in a broader context of adaptation and functional relationships between person and learning environment. As examples, in our early studies these methods could consist of: (1) conventional "static" measurements of and motivational and emotional dispositions (e.g., scales for sense of control and self-concept of attainment; Nicholls, 1978) intended to reveal motivational and socio-emotional dispositions and long–term developmental changes; (2) dynamic on-line assessments of motivational and emotional changes during extended series of task performances leading to recurrent experiences of failure (or success) resembling typical school practice and test task sequences and supposing to reveal differential motivational regulation patterns in vulnerable and resilient children (e.g., applications of Lewinian level of aspiration test; Hoppe, 1930); and (3) dynamic on-line assessments of behavioral stability and variation across varying performance contexts (special needs teaching, parent guidance, test-taking), aiming to reveal recurrent affect- or motivation-related micro-genetic transaction patterns in different student-adult-task settings leading to "regressive" disorganization or "progressive" organization of cognitive performance and to determine how generalized or restricted such dynamic patterns are across different tasks and interaction contexts. Our online assessment procedure was a modern application of the pioneering work of Luria (1932) and Lewin and his colleagues (e.g., Barker, Dembo, & Lewin, 1941) addressing affect- and motivation-related changes in the dynamic organization versus disorganization of cognitive activity.

In sum, we have used both on- and off-line methods in combination, which may include a variety of mixed methods, such as observations, interviews, measurements and scales from multiple perspectives, competence assessments, psychological tests, and experiments (e.g., eye-movement studies). We have also aimed at quantifying the qualitative data to empower analyses and generalization of outcomes and to manage complex relationships with either larger numbers of participants or observations (e.g., pattern units in interaction). Often our studies have been conducted within longitudinal and (quasi-experimental) intervention designs. Today, there is a promise of approaching methodologies (e.g., Anolli, Duncan, Magnusson, & Riva, 2005; Hollenstein, 2007; Steenbeek & van Geert, 2007) and digital technologies (e.g., Koch & Zumbach, 2002; Lamey, Hollenstein, Lewis, & Granic, 2004; Nummenmaa & Nummenmaa, 2008), which importantly widen possibilities for in-depth analyses of real-life motivation and emotion and offer faster and more economic solutions to otherwise laborious dynamic multi-method research attempting to reconstruct and model the real-life situations.

Triadic Motivational Orientation and Coping Model in Socially Shared Learning Contexts

The basic triadic relational orientation and coping model consists of core elements of the socially guided or joint learning situation: the learner, the instructor (e.g., teacher, parent or peer) and the learning task with a curriculum-based learning goal. The three modes of motivational orientation, Task Orientation, Ego-Defensive Orientation and Social Dependence Orientation, describe the different ways learners may become motivationally and emotionally sensitized or "attuned" to different aspects of the learning situation, and their different ways of coping with such demands. Each orientation can be characterized by its adaptive focus (Task, Self, Instructor), its activated major functional system (Approach, Avoidance) and its constellation of self-efficacy beliefs and emotional indications (Lepola et al., 2004; Salonen et al., 1998; Vauras et al., 2001; Vauras et al., 2008). In Figure 1, the basic activity structures in these orientations are captured.

Figure 1. Basic activity structures of motivational orientations.

In our triadic model of motivational orientation and coping (for details and developments, see Lehtinen et al., 1995; Lepola et al., 2004; Olkinuora & Salonen, 1992; Salonen, 1988; Salonen et al., 1998; Vauras et al., 2001; Vauras et al., 2008), a distinction is made between task-oriented versus two types of non-task-oriented behavior, ego-defensiveness and social dependence. These three groups of behavior with distinctive motivational foci and approach/avoidance characteristics represent different dispositions to cope with learning and performance situations. In task-oriented coping activity, the learning task and task-related novelties and challenges have a strong positive valence for the student engaging in persistent mastery efforts (see Figure 1, panel A). In social dependence-oriented coping, the student has no genuine motivational relation to the learning task, as his or her main focus is to seek social approval as a means for reinforcing social affiliation. The guiding adult and often peers possess a strong positive valence inducing, for example, excessive help seeking and imitativeness (see Figure 1, panel B). In ego-defensive coping, the task (and often the guidance-giver) possesses a negative valence as the student tries to protect his or her self from threats and the loss of well-being, for example, through engaging in avoidance behavior or substitute activities directed toward some substitute goal with a strong positive valence (see Figure 1, panel C).

Like dichotomized conceptualizations of motivational orientations, which we have ourselves criticized (e.g., Vauras et al., 2001), our triadic model has often been interpreted as representing trait-like entities despite efforts to underline its dynamic features (see, e.g., Lehtinen et al., 1995). This interpretation is easy to understand, though, particularly from the point of view of the teacher. It is evident that experiences in home and traditional school environment may result in a limited set of more or less generalized and stabilized motivational tendencies, which are further reinforced in succeeding situations, finally becoming stagnated. In the school context, many students' coping behaviors have, thus, become repetitive in nature, manifesting as a certain more or less generalized orientation to learning. It must be marked that this does not indicate that these tendencies are trait-like, but essentially *interactionist and dynamic*. They characteristically mirror the strength of the coping and orientation tendency, and are not exclusive but may fluctuate within and across situations and contexts. However, this common (from our point of view, mistaken) interpretation and criticism has forced us to more distinctly analyze the manifestation of motivational coping and orientations across contexts and over time and link them to long-term developmental, situational interaction dynamics (i.e., micro-genesis) and contextual and institutional-cultural (macro-level) factors (e.g., Lehtinen et al., 1995; Olkinuora & Salonen, 1992; Salonen et al., 1998; Vauras et al., 2001, 2008).

Observation and intervention studies have provided evidence for tracking micro-genetic fluctuations in students' coping efforts and possibilities to modify the situational interpretations and coping efforts, which eventually are expected to lead to changes in orientations as well. Failure to powerfully influence, in particular, some highly vulnerable students' interpretations and coping behavior, have further forced us to scrutinize the actual dyadic or polyadic interactions between a student, peers and a guiding adult (parent or teacher) in learning and instructional settings. Next, we briefly describe the evidence from our studies to give empirical grounds for the elaborated integrative model, which illustrates our current conceptualization of micro-genetic (situational) and long-term developmental dynamics of learning-related multimodal person-situation interactions.

Generalization, Variability and Modifiability of Motivational Coping and Orientations

We have proposed that the disposition toward any of the three orientation and coping tendencies discussed above is formed during children's learning and social control/reward histories in family, day-care contexts and early school years (Vauras et al., 2001; see also Lepola et al., 2004), and is actualized in certain sets of forthcoming learning situations with similar cues (Salonen et al, 1998; Salonen, Lepola & Vauras, 2007). Recent dynamic systems conceptualizations strongly support this assumption (e.g., Dumas, Lemay, & Dauwalder, 2001; Hollenstein, Granic, Stoolmiller, & Snyder, 2004; Lewis, Lamey, & Douglas, 1999; Martin, Fabes, Hanish, & Hollenstein, 2005). Further, theories of interpersonal or relational control (e.g., Rogers & Escudero, 2004) shed light upon the situational and developmental mechanisms contributing to the gradual formation of inter-individual differences in motivational orientations and socio-emotional coping patterns (Salonen et al., 2007). The dynamic systems view suggests that cumulatively differentiating developmental trajectories of motivationally-emotionally vulnerable (low-achieving) and resilient (high-achieving) children are based on early parent-child and, later, teacher-child dyadic regulations which have become repetitive (see Fagot & Gauvain, 1997; Gauvain & DeMent, 1991; Granic & Dishion, 2003; Hollenstein et al., 2004; Salonen et al., 2007). Gradually these interactions build up different developmental trajectories for the dyads, as well as differentiating socio-cognitive and motivational-emotional developmental paths and outcomes for the children.

Long-Term Cognitive-Motivational Development: Stabilization and Accretion

Individuals differ as regards their resources to cope with environmental challenges, complexity and change (Cowan, Cowan, & Schultz, 1996; Murphy & Moriarty, 1976). Individual differences, which can be detected on early age, between at risk (or 'vulnerable') and resilient students are hypothesized to contribute to the educational *polarization phenomenon* manifested in the vastly diverging developmental trajectories of steadily progressing and retarding student groups. A wide and hard-to-reduce gap between high- and low-achieving students—in terms of cognitive competence, motivation, self-beliefs and school attitudes—evidencing of cumulative diverging developmental courses is reported, not only within tracked school settings (as originally tested; see, e.g., Berends, 1995; Urdan, Midgley, & Wood, 1995) but importantly also in mainstream, desegregated and heterogeneous classrooms (e.g., Fuchs & Fuchs 1994; Semmel, Gerber, & MacMillan 1994; see Stanovich 1986 on the 'Matthew effect'). In line with this, our own earlier work presents empirical evidence for cognitive-motivational and socio-emotional development and, further, interactions underlying the polarization phenomenon within the school context (Lehtinen et al., 1995; Salonen et al., 1998; Vauras et al., 2001). Our evidence stems, primarily, from longitudinal studies of reading and text comprehension skills in elementary school, as illustrated below.

Vauras, Kinnunen and Kuusela (1994) followed high-, average-, and low-achieving students for two years from grade 3 to grade 5 (i.e., from age 9-10 to age 11-12), during which time their text-processing skills were measured. Already at the start, an extensive gap between low-achieving and other students' text comprehension was observed. This differential development in students' comprehension skills seemed to create a widening achievement gap, most strikingly between low- and high-achieving students. It was concluded that, when low-achieving students are confronted with rapidly increasing task and learning demands, they have accumulating difficulties in responding to these demands successfully because of their inadequately developed text-processing and metacognitive strategies. Converging evidence came from the study by Lepola, Vauras and Poskiparta (2002; see Lepola et al., 2004), in which the polarization phenomenon between the reading groups was observed across the school years (from grade 2 to grade 8). This phenomenon was portrayed as a growing achievement gap between prospective good and poor readers. In fact, poor, average, and good reading careers started clearly to diverge from grade 3 and onwards. The intervention studies, aimed to empower low-achieving students' mathematical and reading competences, tell the same story when we compared control and all other students' development (e.g., Kajamies, Vauras, & Kinnunen, in press; Vauras et al., 1999a, b).

The long-term relative regress observed in low-achieving students' competencies is multimodal in nature, evident on top of cognitive competences in emotional responses to learning and performance situations, and in coping efforts and motivational dispositions, entrapping students into a vicious developmental cycle. Lepola et al. (2002, see Lepola et al., 2004) showed the strong relatedness of motivational tendencies to the reading achievement of prospective reading groups. The results revealed that the poor readers had a significantly weaker task orientation and higher non-task-orientation (ego- and/or social dependence) already in grade 1 than the prospective good readers. Increasing and stabilizing differences in task-orientation were observed from grade 1 to grade 8.[1] The opposite motivational patterns interacting with reading comprehension differences across school years seemed to co-determine favorable and unfavorable learning trajectories (Schneider, Stefanek, & Dotzler, 1997, as cited in Lepola et al., 2004; Schultz & Switzky, 1990).

Although it must be kept in mind that these results concerning longitudinal development reveal average cognitive-motivational paths, for many, in particular low- and high-achieving students' prior to school and early school years, patterns are strongly predictive as regards later development. The problem of generalizing motivational dispositions and cognitive deficiencies become even more unwavering in the light of results indicating strong co-morbidity, indicated as multimodal accumulation effects. For example, early reading and writing problems may later manifest also as difficulties in reading comprehension, composition, foreign language learning and mathematics. Vauras, Junttila, Iiskala, Kajamies, Kinnunen and Kaukiainen (2003; for measure, see Junttila, Kaukiainen, Voeten, & Vauras, 2006) presented results on accretion of higher order learning difficulties in the follow-up of over 1000 elementary school students, showing how linguistic (decoding and reading comprehension) and mathematical (number, arithmetic and word problem solving skills) were intimately linked in the groups of low- and high-achievers from grade 3 onwards. The results concerning the same students in the study by Vauras and Junttila (2007) showed, further, strong relationships between social competence and cognitive school performance in reading and mathematics. The profiles of the manifold proficient and unskilled students formed a mirror image in terms of social skills (such as co-operation skills, empathy, control of impulsive and disruptive behavior), and loneliness of the students with linguistic and mathematical difficulties. These results are in accordance with evidence in the research literature showing how cognitive competence is associated not only with students' motivational competence, but has also wider social dimensions, such as loneliness, self-esteem and social skills, which contribute to learning and motivation processes (see e.g., meta-analysis by Kavale & Forness, 1996).

Scaffolding and Interpersonal Transactions in Teaching-Learning Contexts: Modifiability of the Motivation-Related Behaviors

In light of the evidence implicating a widening cognitive-motivational gap between different student groups over the school years, possibilities of intervening accumulating learning problems and emotional-motivational vulnerability become pertinent. Along with increased educational demands, the observed distinctive developmental paths have intensified the discussion on resilience or resistance in learning. When we consider the possibilities of influencing predicted cognitive-motivational development, it is important to keep in mind that although coping and orientation tendencies may become highly

---

[1] In the light of increasing learning demands and increasing negative school attitudes, it is interesting to note, though, that general increase of ego-defensiveness from 6th to 8th grade washed out differences in this respect at the 8th grade.

dominant they are not exclusive. Considerable fluctuation between task- and non-task-oriented coping behaviors can be found even among vulnerable low-achieving students. Therefore, an analysis of frequency of task-oriented behaviors and features triggering task-oriented behaviors helps us to form a basis for remedial instruction. Although as such this is almost an impossible research task due to demands for numerable observations in different learning tasks and contexts, the mere information on occurrence of task-orientation in low-achieving students' learning-related behavior have proven to be of key importance.

Teacher scaffolding is assumed to provide learners with unique opportunities to remedy their cognitive-metacognitive deficits in specific domains of learning. Scaffolded instruction (Wood, Bruner, & Ross, 1976) is strongly congruent with the Vygotskian theoretical framework (Vygotsky 1962, 1978). In an optimal instructional interaction, the teacher determines the student's "region of sensitivity to instruction" and, through graduated intervention, "adjusts the scaffolding to the child's developing capabilities" (Rogoff & Gardner, 1984, p. 101). In each phase of skill development, the learner is given appropriate supportive tools, which, building on the already formed capabilities, provide a sufficient framework for reaching the next skill level and closing the gap between the actual developmental level and task requirements. The process of scaffolding is essentially interactive and reciprocal. Participation in this social form of regulation is particularly useful to enrich the range of strategies that learners can use, and to power their capacity to use them strategically and autonomously. We have earlier hypothesized (e.g., Vauras Rauhanummi, Kinnunen, & Lepola, 1999b) that low-achieving students need carefully designed, innovative, flexible and adaptive special support environments to dismantle their maladaptive beliefs and interpretations and to strengthen their competence. Therefore, the first steps should be taken in environments not resembling the typical contexts where negative anticipations and interpretations are automatically triggered. The effectiveness data from our intervention studies, embedded, for example, in game-like environments, have supported this assumption. The cognitive domains in our intervention studies have been reading comprehension and/or mathematical word problem solving.

In the study by Vauras, Lehtinen, Kinnunen and Salonen (1992; see also Lehtinen et al., 1995), a 32-hr cognitive-motivational intervention program for fourth-grade, 10- to 11-year-old students with learning difficulties was applied. After the small-group intervention, an experimental classroom program was designed to examine the post-intervention conditions for the attained skills. Significant average improvement was obtained, and in the condition where both cognitive-metacognitive and emotional-motivational coping strategies were explicitly trained, long-term transfer effects were also found. The group-level results from later intervention studies with third-grade (Vauras et al., 1999a, b) and fourth-grade (Kajamies et al., in press) low-achieving students have yielded similar, highly significant training effects.

However, despite the use of ideas behind transactional dialogue (e.g., Pressley et al., 1992) and, in general, powerful learning environments and apprenticeship models (e.g., for discussions, see De Corte, Verschaffel, Entwistle, & van Merriënboer, 2003) in designing and carrying out special needs intervention programs and typically a rather long time alloted to instructional efforts, some students still show strong resistance to instruction and often fail to benefit from teacher (or peer) scaffolding. The recurring resistance patterns in some sub-groups have caused us puzzlement since they are apparently persistent even in circumstances where, for example learning takes place at a relaxed pace in small groups, the learning environment is appealing, including age-relevant attractors such as game-like contexts, students are willing and to participate in the activities and to invest their efforts, systematic, well-organized cognitive-metacognitive, yet personalized, training is offered, and constant teacher scaffolding is available.

In all of our intervention studies, we have found a group of students with no evident progress in their cognitive-motivational competencies. For example, in the study by Vauras et al. (1992) long-term maintenance and transfer were dependent on the students' motivational coping tendencies; some initial task orientation required for these effects. Weakest training effects were achieved in students who displayed dominantly ego-defensive tendencies, and only short-term effects were achieved in students with strong tendencies to cope in learning situations through social dependence. However, when prolonged classroom training was provided, even students with low initial task orientation and maladaptive coping tendencies began to show more lasting training effects and transfer of learning. In the study by Vauras et al. (1999a, b), developmental data showed that the resistant and responsive groups differed significantly in two crucial aspects prior-to-training, that is, already at the first grade two years before: metacognition (particularly comprehension monitoring) and non-task orientation (particularly social dependence). All in all, we have been able to conclude that long-term, stabilized motivational and emotional vulnerability accompanied with social and self-regulatory ineffectiveness severely interfere with students' ability to benefit from instruction. We will illustrate the interaction and motivational vulnerability dynamics contributing to this kind failure with three cases from the intervention study by Vauras et al. (1992).

Case Examples: Vulnerability in Resistance Dynamics

As a part of the intervention study by Vauras et al. (1992), we analyzed students' on-line behavior, and behavioral fluctuations and changes in relation to scaffolding. Since these results are not reported in Vauras et al. (1992), we give an account of the main results relevant to the discussion in this chapter, concentrating on three representative cases. The two boys, *Pasi* and *Sauli*, performed poorly on cognitive and metacognitive measures (in most, below average among struggling learners), and showed ego-defensive avoidance behavior in many performance situations, manifesting as tension, anxiety and restlessness. The girl, *Pia*, showed both social dependence and ego-defensive coping behaviors in the face of academic tasks, and performed similarly very poorly in cognitive and metacognitive measures.

Our analysis was targeted on the phase where practicing and teacher scaffolding took place. In this phase, first, the given skills were practiced by a series of exercises, progressing from relatively familiar contents and simple text structures to more unfamiliar contents and complex structures. Thus, the task demands increased progressively both within each session and along the intervention. In some exercises, either self-guided or collaborative practicing was enhanced by role-taking instructions to increase task involvement. In some tasks, thinking aloud while performing an exercise was encouraged. After a series of short exercises or after one complex task, the students were stimulated to verbally describe the procedures and strategies they had used. This articulation of a student's own task performance and solutions served as a basis on which the scaffolding dialogue was initiated. The student's spontaneous ability to perform a task and to verbalize solution strategies determined the level of adult guidance. The teacher reworked the task with the students and reconstructed the reasoning and comprehension processes involved in the task solution in scaffolded discussions. With increasing student ability, the gradual fading of assistance and simulation by others was aimed at fostering the growth of self-regulation.

The scaffolding dialogue was initiated by the teacher most frequently in the situations where the student's spontaneous verbalizations were reasonably low; that is, the student gave impulsive, mindless descriptions or inexact descriptions of his/her own task solution. In general, the scaffolding dialogues had a beneficial impact on the students' understanding of the strategies. It was evident, though, that the scaffolding could not always be accomplished to the optimal or even satisfactory level (see Figure 2). *Pia* manifested patterns where scaffolding gains were evident already in the beginning phases of the training, whereas *Pasi* and, even more pronounced, *Sauli*, showed very poor scaffolding results in the first training phase and began to improve slowly only in the second phase, that is, after approximately 10 hours of training.

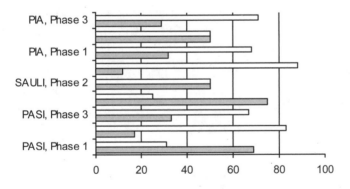

□ failed or weak; □ sufficient or optimal

Figure 2. The percentages of successful and failed scaffolding dialogues.

The success of scaffolding importantly coincided with the degree of non-task-oriented behavior. As shown in Figure 3, the students, when demonstrating weak or failing scaffolding, typically manifested a high degree of ego-defensive (EO) behavior. In instances where the teacher failed (or failed to start) the instructional discussion, the students often showed a high degree of ego-defensive behavior. Successful scaffolding took place, when the students' level of ego-defensiveness was low. Most strikingly this can be seen in the case of *Sauli*. This finding is in accordance with the assumption that low-achieving students' socio-emotional vulnerability inhibits or slows down cognitive progression.

Finally, the above on-line observational data can be contrasted with the immediate effects of training, assessed by the summarization task, measuring vertical transfer of training (see Figure 4). The students were asked to write a good summary of comparable, unfamiliar texts on history before and immediately after the training. These results are highly in accordance with the data obtained by the process analyses, showing most pronounced improvements in the skills of *Pia*, and low gains for *Pasi* and *Sauli*. Thus, slow process in instructional discussion was strongly associated with low cognitive gains.

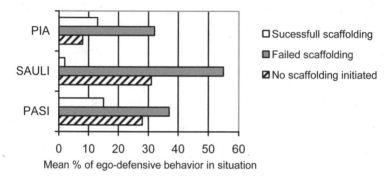

Figure 3. Mean percentages of ego-defensive coping behavior during failed and successful scaffolding and in instances when no scaffolding was initiated with the student.

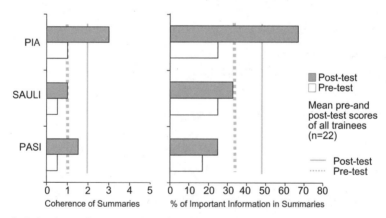

Figure 4. Gains in reading comprehension skills as a function of intervention.

Towards Analysis of Interacting Participants as a Way to Understand Motivational Stability and Resistance Patterns

The results of our process-oriented analysis throughout different stages of the scaffolding process evidence a sequence of cognitive – socio-emotional interactions, that is, a microgenesis indicating difficulties in scaffolding. The general results concerning the resistance patterns of multiply vulnerable students have shifted our attention more closely to the problem: What actually happens between the interacting participants in teaching-learning settings, and how do guiding adults / teachers perceive and react in these interpersonal transactions? This question is also important in elaborating the yet-to-be-found answers to general versus specific motivation.

Modern models of guided and joint learning (such as scaffolding, reciprocal teaching, and collaborative learning) which aim to foster a learner's self-regulation and collaborative learning skills, share some "required" social features, such as reciprocal regulatory processes, flexible shifts of agency, modulation of negative emotions and sharing and transfer of responsibility between the participants. These features implicate group dynamics that rule out unidirectional, rigid control and adaptation relations or reciprocal attempts to establish competitive dominance (Vauras et al., 2008; Volet et al., submitted). However, despite the innovative and well-structured instructional designs and best intentions of the guiding adults, empirical observations indicate how interacting teachers, students and student teams actually often engage in more or less optimal interpersonal transactions, leading to poor learning outcomes and even unintended, negative affective and motivational outcomes. In the case of low-achieving students, we can assume that less optimal interpersonal transactions and group dynamics in instructional dialogue and joint peer learning become pronounced due to the empirical evidence showing, for example, weaker self-regulatory and social competences (as well as higher emotional vulnerability) compared to the other peers (e.g., Al-Yagon, 2003; Al-Yagon & Mikulincer, 2004; Kavale & Forness, 1996). Since we have discussed interpersonal dynamics and group processes more thoroughly in other recent publications (e.g., Salonen, Vauras, & Efklides, 2005; Salonen & Vauras, 2006; Salonen et al., 2007; Vauras et al., 2008), we intend not do it here. Instead, in the concluding section, we outline a modified conception of situational and developmental dynamics of motivational-emotional dispositions and cognitive active (see Lehtinen et al., 1995) on the basis of the conceptual analyses of the recent research literature and empirical findings.

Micro-Genetic and Long-Term Developmental Dynamics of Learning-Related Interactions

The following integrative model illustrates our current conceptualization of micro-genetic (situational) and long-term developmental dynamics of learning-related multimodal person-situation interactions (cf. the earlier model, Lehtinen et al., 1995). We assume that cognitive functions and motivational-emotional tendencies are formed during an individual's adaptation and learning history (i.e., long-term development), along with the learner's repeated encounters with different physical and social learning environments. The integrative model underscores the following relational and dynamic aspects of behavior: (1) interpersonal organization and dynamics, (2) behavior-in-context (in relation to objects, co-actors, situation factors), (3) multimodal (cognitive, metacognitive, emotional, motivational, social) co-ordinations, and (4) (bidirectional) transactions between micro-genetic (situational) on-line changes and developmental trajectories across longer time spans.

Balanced and Biased Interpersonal Cycles in Generalization and Stagnation of Motivation Patterns

Figure 5 illustrates how the learner's adaptation history, formed during long-term development, contributes to generalized dispositions and tendencies to act across a variety of situations and to respond to certain sets of situational conditions described in the successive panes (triangles). Each pane displays a series of consecutive learning or task-performance episodes during which "micro-genetic", short-term situational interaction processes take place. Generalized cognitive and motivational-emotional dispositions, together with interpretations that arise in specific situations, anticipations, affects, motives, and coping and regulatory efforts, determine the kind person-situation interaction processes that are actualized during the episodes. A typical situational episode is described at three levels: (1) the learner's real-time process of approaching the task, starting the task-performance, performing, and terminating the task-performance, (2) the learner's intrapersonal consecutive cycles of cognitive, emotional and motivational interpretations and adjustments to situational and task cues (depicted as vertical arrows), and (3) interpersonal motivational and emotional co-ordinations within the triangular learner - guiding person /co-learner – task -system in terms of "balanced" (egalitarian) or "biased" (non-egalitarian) relationship patterns.

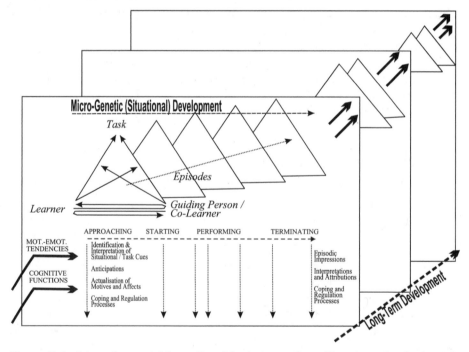

Figure 5. An integrative model for multimodal micro-genetic and long-term developmental interactions.

Balanced patterns are characterized by dyadic power-equivalence (or only slight domineering-submissiviness – complementarity) and neutral or positive affect symmetry, whereas biased constellations typically comprise high-domineering acts responded to either with highly submissive behaviors or strong (counter-) domineering efforts accompanied with negative affectivity of both participants (Salonen et al., 2005; Vauras et al., 2008). The core assumption of the model is that the dyadic power and affiliation relationship patterns (level 3) essentially contribute to the learner's intrapersonal cognitive, emotional and motivational processes (levels 1 and 2). On the other hand, intrapersonal cumulative changes are assumed to restructure interpersonal patterns. We have argued that balanced power and affiliation relationship patterns create preconditions for consistent mutual task-orientation (shared task-focus and task goals) (Salonen et al., 2005; Vauras et al., 2008), successful scaffolding with dyadic synchrony and flexible shifting of agency between participants (Salonen et al., 2005; Salonen et al., 2007), and continued task-focused self-regulations in the learner (Vauras et al., 2008; Volet et al., submitted). The balanced constellation is described as the learner's and guidance giver's / co-learner's strong focus on the task (arrows directed toward the task) and takes into account each other's way to interpret the task (arrows directed toward other participant's task-assimilation). In the balanced constellation, the participants do not experience mutual negativity or their own ego as a potential object of social threat or, for example, that the assimilations represented by curved "ego-mirroring" arrows do not actualize.

The biased interpersonal constellation implies the absence or weakness of the learner's self-governed focus on the task, and a pronounced directedness either to the partner's expectations and wishes (i.e., social dependence orientation) or to the learner's own internal states and situational cues suggesting threat to well-being (i.e., ego-defensive orientation). Under such conditions the learner becomes increasingly sensitized to situational cues indicating loss of personal control and / or social threat (e.g., task-difficulty cues, guidance-giver's directiveness, evaluative pressures) and, instead of continuing task-oriented, self- and co-regulated task-focused efforts, engages in dependence-type (e.g., clinging, seeking favors, transferring responsibility to the authority figure) or ego-defensive (e.g., substitute activity, withdrawal, acting out) coping behaviors. The guidance-giver or co-learner usually responds to the learner's submissiveness and dependence-type coping efforts with increased directiveness or intrusiveness which reinforces rigidly complementary non-egalitarian interpersonal constellation. On other hand, the learner's ego-defensive avoidance behaviors, substitute activities, acting-out behaviors and signs of negativity are likely to induce mutual negativity and exaggerated domineering efforts in the guidance-giver / co-learner (mutually activated "ego-mirroring" arrows). A rigid, negatively charged dominance-submission pattern or escalatory cycle of mutual domineering efforts is formed. The biased patterns of power and affective relationships in dyads (or in small-groups) essentially distort the situational formation of learner's task-focused goals, undermine and self- and co-regulatory responses in front of difficulties, and lead to the disorganization of the learner's task-focused activity (Salonen et al., 2005; Salonen et al., 1998; Salonen et al., 2007; Vauras et al., 2008).

If we interpret this in Lewinian terms, while in balanced constellations the goal of activity creates a unitary motivational-affective tension field (reaching from past to future episodes) that integrates the elements or modules of the activity into a hierarchically organized system of action, biased constellations create competing or conflicting goal structures yielding conflict-charged tension field that will "regress" or disorganize the activity into a series of disconnected and incoherent elements (Barker et al., 1941; Salonen, 1988; Salonen et al., 1998; Vauras et al., 2001).

The repeated interactions between the learner and the task and between the participants (parents and children, teachers and students, collaborating peers) are building blocks for the established dyadic relationship patterns and the resulting relationship patterns provide the dynamic context for participants' subsequent interactions with the learning environment (see Lollis & Kuczynski, 1997). As task-performance episodes and intrapersonal processes recur cyclically they not only build diverging socio-cognitive and motivational-emotional developmental paths and outcomes for the learners, but also lead to differentiating interpersonal constellations and role positions for guidance givers and learners with differential learning histories (Sroufe, 1989).

A Case Illustration: Micro-Genetic and Long-Term Developmental Dynamics

Last, we demonstrate some key ideas in this model with a case description. *Heli* (a female student, followed from third to sixth grade) typically approached new learning situations with a rather generalized low sense of self-efficacy, weak self-concept of attainment, and fear of failure (see Lehtinen et al., 1995; Salonen et al., 1998). She responded to even slight task difficulty cues or teacher prompts with avoidance behaviors (e.g., passivity, inhibited staring, averting gaze from the task) or with acting-out behaviors (e.g. extreme restlessness, substitute activities, whining, or tantrums). Symptoms of motivational-emotional tension and conflict typically increased after only one or two experienced difficulties or task-approach requests from a guiding adult. The intensity of negative emotional signs increased rapidly during such situations. "Short-cut" behaviors with a low level of organization emerged. After a recent failure, the depressive emotional state was often indicated by self-deprecatory causal attributions and the negative mood was transferred to the next task-performance episodes. Interestingly, when she realized that the teacher gave a series of routine school-tasks and no longer asked difficult questions, she shifted almost immediately to social dependence coping.

To reconstruct possible antecedents and recurrent interpersonal constellations contributing to situational behavior, *Heli* was observed in learning situations with her father (who had actually "controlled" her home-work for years) as guidance-giver. The recurrent interaction patterns suggested the interpersonal origins of *Heli's* motivational and emotional problems in learning situations, and were strikingly similar to interaction between *Heli* and special needs teachers. When facing *Heli's* usual task-avoidance behavior the father (apparently incapable to adequate scaffolding) tried to demand or "force" *Heli* to concentrate on task through negatively charged verbal prompts and exertion of power (e.g., harsh commands, threatening gestures of physical punishment, and even actual physical punishment). *Heli* consistently showed increased avoidance behaviors, restlessness, sobbing, and crying (and threatening "I'll tell mother!)".

We observed dozens of situations where Heli, after confronting task-difficulty cues, slight obstacles, and father prompts, engaged in avoidance and conflict behaviors that escalated rapidly and culminated in open social conflict. The father, then, apparently having a bad conscience, gave up his demands and worked on the task for the daughter. *Heli*, in turn, almost immediately took the role of a "good girl," and the father responded with positive emotional signs. Despite the socio-emotional "resolution," the biased interpersonal constellation remained and continued to distort the self- and co-regulation processes in subsequent guided learning episodes. In an interview, the father showed awareness that *Heli* was "playing a social game" in which she entered into an alliance with her emotionally more sensitive mother against the occasionally stern father. According to the father, *Heli* manipulated the mother to provide unnecessary help in homework situations in which he would require more independent work. The father admitted that he, too, has the tendency to relent in the face of the daughter's extreme frustration. Both parents reported that such episodes had been rather frequent during the first school years.

The case of *Heli* provides evidence that the cyclic processes leading to cumulative reinforcing of non-task-oriented coping tendencies are interactively formed during long-term development and maintained by situational conditions. The observed dyadic patterns with special needs teachers were strikingly similar to the patterns *Heli* showed with her father. With time, interaction with the remedial teacher resulted, with increasing frequency, in extreme forms of avoidance and conflict behavior. The frustrated teacher sometimes gave up efforts to elicit the independent task-related activity required at *Heli's* grade level. Having just responded with extreme avoidance, conflict behavior, and disorganization of action (tantrums), she shifted almost immediately to social dependence coping when she realized that the teacher had given a series of routine school-tasks and was no longer asking difficult questions. *Heli*, now appealing, smiling, and chatting, completed the series without a sign of fatigue or frustration. This demonstrates how changing interpersonal power and affect constellations may induce profound changes in intrapersonal processes and person-situation interactions. It seemed that such episodes increased the teacher's tendency to balance the social situation through allowing a very low level of aspiration. After such a tension-reducing change, *Heli* tried to maintain the established comfortable situation through working cheerfully on easy tasks.

Concluding Remarks

A powerful theme emerging from the research is the difficulty in balancing early parental (and later teacher) support and demands, as well as behavior control processes, with children with attentional problems, learning disabilities, emotional-behavioral disorders, and inadequate social skills. During the guidance process, children at risk (being, e.g., extremely distractible, avoidant, hostile, helpless, security-seeking) are likely to be over-controlled, over-demanded or over-supported. This usually means an increasing mismatch in cognitive, motivational or socio-emotional domains. Therefore either the *attachment* (comfort and proximity seeking tendency) or *avoidance systems* are likely to be activated in learning situations under the conditions of "felt insecurity" instead of task-exploration from a secure base (Maslin-Cole & Spieker, 1990).

Although the multimodal person-situation transaction cycles often cumulatively reinforce established interpersonal patterns, and often lead to the reinforcement of existing intrapersonal cognitive and motivational-emotional tendencies, dynamic systems are essentially not deterministic but "multi-deterministic" (Lewis, 1995). They often produce non-linear developmental outcomes and emergent patterns. Sometimes even slight initial changes, for instance, in task difficulty cues, learner and/or guidance giver appraisals, or affective responses may launch cumulative interaction cycles which may lead to the formation of "new" recurrent interpersonal behavioral patterns (i.e., alternative attractor states), as well as to the weakening of existing intrapersonal dispositions, or to the formation of new behavioral tendencies. Such "determination" can, however, be reversed for instance through reorganizing situational cues and person-situation constellations.

We refer once more to the case of Heli, which nicely illustrates the reversal of the determination. We studied Heli's behavior across a variety of situational contexts in order to find situational cues that might promote more organized, task-oriented activity. We had observed that formal "symbolic" mathematical problems (e.g., addition and subtraction equations with an "x") almost immediately launched non-task-oriented behaviors. When we constructed fully analogous "enactive" concrete representations (Bruner, 1966), for example, through using paper clip chains to solve equations, Heli built, counted and compared long chains several times, as long as she got an invariant result ("metacognitive control"!). The activity was fully task-oriented, highly organized, and very persistent for 15-20 minutes. Also other contexts with a sufficient amount of familiar cues and routine activities were found to promote the actualization of task-orientation and hierarchically integrated task-focused activity. Thus, despite partially successful reorganization of person-situation interaction patterns, a multitude of powerful unfavorable person – task - guidance giver attractor states (e.g., "negative" motivational-emotional response tendencies to task difficulty cues, teacher prompts and corrective feedback) still seemed to pull Heli and guidance giver towards "regressive" interaction patterns. Our integrative model highlights the multimodal and multilevel complexity of the situational and developmental processes underlying Heli's treatment resistance and the difficulties in overcoming it. The model suggests that not only should we support the learner's cognitive-metacognitive skills and reorganize the biased cognitive and emotional interpretations of the task and, guidance giver and a student, but simultaneously restructure the biased social prompt and feedback patterns into more neutral and egalitarian ones. For instance, utilizing communication and feedback scripts and learning tasks atypical of school might dampen confrontations (regressive attractor states) and redirect interactions repeatedly toward more progressive encounters (emerging progressive attractor states). As soon as a learner's sense of agency, coping strategies and cognitive self- and co-regulation skills are reinforced, challenging aspects typical of more school-like tasks and interaction patterns could be stepwise introduced.

We have tried to argue that in order to find answers for local (situational and contextual) fluctuations as well as to understand developmental dynamics leading to possible global, generalized and even stagnated, motivational coping behaviors and orientation in learning situations, we have to more deeply understand the multimodal and multi-deterministic dynamic systems formed during the learning-teaching sequences between the participants (cf., Vauras et al., 2008). These interaction patterns must be analyzed.

from the perspective of all significant participants in these situations. Students' and teachers' interaction behavior in a classroom or special-needs education groups is affected by reciprocated communication. For example, our observations clearly indicate that students can lure the teacher to behaviors that strengthen maladaptive situational orientation in students, and may even result in prolonged inadequate coping of the teacher in subsequent encounters (Salonen et al., 1998). In low-achieving students, the global nature of motivation is mirrored in more or less generalized (over contexts, tasks, domains, or even over the whole schooling) motivational and emotional tendencies, which repeatedly trigger similar diffusion in learning activities. These tendencies are stagnated and global, because the environments have not been responsive enough or have responded in a way which increases maladaptive behavior, as in the example given above. The evidence from intervention studies and classroom observations show how maladaptive behaviors of the low-achieving students, particularly in later school years, cannot be reversed by changing distinct individual interpretations or isolated aspects of learning environments.

Most of our previous analyses in school contexts concern long-term development in so-called traditional learning environments. This is true also for research underlying the main motivational constructs and theories in general. However, some features of emerging learning environments may importantly change the transactive nature of school learning and, thus, have consequences on formation and generalization of inter-individual cognitive-motivational differences and trajectories. Our intention is to understand motivation across today's widely differing learning contexts and environments. In this way, motivation can be dealt with as an inherent part of a socially and culturally embedded activity system (e.g., Vauras et al., 2001). This underlines, further, the need to unveil the role of interpersonal coordination or macro-patterns of social interaction as co-determinants of learners' and teachers' regulatory activity and motivational and emotional coping in dyadic or polyadic learning (Vauras et al., 2008).

Acknowledgements

The research was supported by Grants no. 201782 to the first author and no. 205658 from the Council of Cultural and Social Science Research, The Academy of Finland, to the third author.

References

Al-Yagon, M. (2003). Children at risk for learning disorders: Multiple perspectives. *Journal of Learning Disabilities, 36*, 318-335.

Al-Yagon, M., & Mikulincer, M. (2004). Socioemotional and academic adjustment among children with learning disorders: The meditational role of attachment-based factors. *Journal of Special Education, 38*, 111-123.

Anolli, L., Duncan, S., Magnusson, M. S., & Riva, G. (Eds.). (2005). *The hidden structure of interaction. From neurons to culture patterns.* Amsterdam: IOS Press.

Barker, R., Dembo, T., & Lewin, K. (1941). Frustration and regression: An experiment with young children. *University of Iowa Studies in Child Welfare. Vol. 18*, No. 1.

Berends, M. (1995). Educational stratification and students' social bonding to school. *British Journal of Sociology of Education, 16*, 327-351.

Boekaerts, M. (1993). Being concerned with well-being and with learning. *Educational Psychologist, 28*, 149-167.

Bruner, J. S. (1966). *Towards a theory of instruction.* New York: Norton.

Cicourel, A. V. (1973). *Cognitive sociology: Language and meaning in social interaction.* Middlesex: Penguin.

Cowan, P. A., Cowan, C. P., & Schulz, M. S. (1996). Thinking about risk and resilience in families. In E. M. Hetherington & E. A. Blechman (Eds.), *Stress, coping, and resiliency in children and families* (pp. 1–38). Mahwah, NJ: Erlbaum.

De Corte, E., Verschaffel, L., Entwistle, N., & van Merriënboer, J. (2003). *Powerful learning environments: Unravelling basic components and dimensions.* Oxford: Pergamon.

Diener, C., & Dweck, C. (1978). An analysis of learned helplessness: Continuous changes in performance, strategy, and achievement cognitions following failure. *Journal of Personality and Social Psychology, 36*, 451-462.

Dumas, J. E., Lemay, P., & Dauwalder, J.- P. (2001). Dynamic analyses of mother-child interactions in functional and dysfunctional dyads: A synergetic approach. *Journal of Abnormal Child Psychology, 29*, 317-329.

Eccles, J., & Midgley, C. (1989). Stage/environment fit: Developmentally appropriate classrooms for early adolescents. In R. E. Ames & C. Ames (Eds.), *Research on motivation in education* (5 thed., Vol. 3, pp. 139-186). New York: Academic Press.

Eccles, J. S., Wigfield, A., & Schiefele, U. (1998). Motivation. In N. Eisenberg (Ed.) *Handbook of child psychology* (5th ed., Vol. 3, pp. 1017-1095). New York: Wiley.

Fagot, B. I., & Gauvain, M. (1997). Mother-child problem solving: Continuity through the early childhood years. *Developmental Psychology, 33*, 480-488.

Fuchs, D., & Fuchs, L. S. (1994). Inclusive schools movement and the radicalization of special education reform. *Exceptional Children, 60*, 294-309.

Garfinkel, H. (1967). *Studies in ethnomethodology.* Englewood Cliffs: Prentice-Hall.

Gauvain, M., & DeMent, T. (1991). The role of shared social history in parent-child cognitive activity. *Quarterly Newsletter of the Laboratory of Comparative Human Cognition, 13*, 58-66.

Granic, I., & Dishion, T. J. (2003). Deviant talk in adolescent friendships: A step toward measuring a pathogenic attractor process. *Social Development, 12*, 314-334.

Harter, S. (1978). Effectance motivation reconsidered: Toward a developmental model. *Human Development, 21*, 34-64.

Heider, F. (1958). *The psychology of interpersonal relations.* New York: Wiley.

Hollenstein, T. (2007). State space grids: Analyzing dynamics across development. *International Journal of Behavioral Development, 31*, 384-396.

Hollenstein, T., Granic, I., Stoolmiller, M., & Snyder, J. (2004). Rigidity in parent-child interactions and the development of externalizing and internalizing behavior in early childhood. *Journal of Abnormal Child Psychology, 32*, 595-607.

Hoppe, F. (1930). Erfolg und Misserfolg [Success and failure]. *Psychologische Forschung, 14*, 1–62.

Hunt, D. E. (1975). Person-environment interaction: A challenge found wanting before it was tried. *Review of Educational Research, 45*, 209-230.

Junttila, N., Kaukiainen, A., Voeten, M., & Vauras, M. (2006). Multisource assessment of children's social competence. *Educational and Psychological Measurement, 66*, 874-895.

Kajamies, A., Vauras, M., & Kinnunen, R. (in press). Instructing students with learning difficulties in mathematical problem solving. *Scandinavian Journal of Educational Research.*

Kavale, K. A., & Forness, S. R. (1996). Social skill deficits and learning disabilities: A meta-analysis. *Journal of Learning Disabilities, 29*, 226-237.

Koch, S. C., & Zumbach, J. (2002). The use of video analysis software in behavior observation research: Interaction patterns in task-oriented small groups. *Forum Qualitative Sozialforschung [Forum: Qualitative Social Research]* [On-line Journal], *3*. Retrieved October 13, 2007, from http://www.qualitative-research.net/fqs-texte/2-02/2-02kochzumbach-e.htm.

Laing, R. D., Phillipson, M., & Russell, L. (1966). *Interpersonal perception: A theory and a method of research.* London: Methuen.

Lamey, A., Hollenstein, T., Lewis, M.D., & Granic, I. (2004). *GridWare* (Version 1.1). [Computer software]. Retrieved August 22, 2007, from http://statespacegrids.org.

Lazarus, R. S., Averill, J. R., & Opton, E. M. (1974). The psychology of coping: Issues of research and assessment. In G. V. Coelho, D. A. Hamburg, & J. E. Adams (Eds.) *Coping and adaptation* (pp. 249-315). New York: Basic Books.

Lehtinen, E., Vauras, M., Salonen, P., Olkinuora, E., & Kinnunen, R. (1995). Long-term development of learning activity: Motivational, cognitive, and social interaction. *Educational Psychologist, 30,* 21-35.

Lepola, J., Vauras, M., & Poskiparta, E. (2002). Pitkittäistutkimus lukutaidon ja motivaation kehityksestä esikoulusta kahdeksannelle luokalle [A longitudinal study of reading and motivation from preschool to the eight grade]. *Psykologia. Journal of the Finnish Psychological Society, 37,* 33-44

Lepola, J., Salonen, P., Vauras, M., & Poskiparta, E. (2004). Understanding the development of subnormal performance in children from a motivational-interactionist perspective. In H. Switzky (Ed.), *International Review of Research in Mental Retardation: Personality and motivational systems in mental retardation. Personality and motivational systems in mental retardation* (Vol. 28, pp. 145-189). San Diego: Elsevier Academic Press.

Lewin, K. (1935). *A dynamic theory of personality.* New York: McGraw-Hill.

Lewis, M. D. (1995). Cognition-emotion feedback and the self-organization of developmental paths. *Human Development, 38,* 71-102.

Lewis, M. D., Lamey, A. V., & Douglas, L. (1999). A new dynamic systems method for the analysis of early socioemotional development. *Developmental Science, 2,* 457-475.

Lollis, S., & Kuczynski, L. (1997). Beyond one hand clapping: Seeing bidirectionality in parent-child relations. *Journal of Social and Personal Relationships, 14,* 441-461.

Luria, A. R. (1932). *The nature of human conflicts.* New York: Liveright.

Martin, C. L., Fabes, R. A., Hanish, L. D., & Hollenstein, T. (2005). Social dynamics in the preschool. *Developmental Review, 25,* 299-327.

Maslin-Cole, C., & Spieker, S. (1990). Attachment as a basis for independent motivation. A view from risk and nonrisk samples. In M. T. Greenberg, D. Cicchetti, & E. M. Cummings (Eds.), *Attachment in the preschool years: Theory, research and intervention* (pp. 245-271). Chicago: University of Chicago Press.

McCaslin, M. (2004). Coregulation of opportunity, activity, and identity in student motivation. In D. M. McInerney & S. Van Etten (Eds.), *Big theories revisited* (Volume 4, pp. 249-274). Greenwich, CT: Information Age.

McCaslin, M., & Good, T. (1996). The informal curriculum. In D. Berliner & R. Calfee (Eds.), *Handbook of educational psychology* (pp. 622-673). New York: Macmillan.

Murphy, L. B., & Moriarty. A. E. (1976). *Vulnerability, coping, and growth: From infancy to adolescence.* London: Yale University Press.

Newcomb, T. (1953). An approach to the study of communicative acts. *Psychological Review, 60,* 393-304.

Nicholls, J. (1978). The development of the concepts of effort and ability, perception of academic attainment, and the understanding that difficult tasks require more ability. *Child Development, 49,* 800-814.

Nicholls J. (1979). Quality and equality in intellectual development: The role of motivation in education. *American Psychologist, 34,* 1071-1084.

Nummenmaa, M., & Nummenmaa, L. (2008). Emotions and interest in visible and invisible web based learning activities. *British Journal of Educational Psychology, 78,* 163-178.

Olkinuora, E., & Salonen, P. (1992). Adaptation, motivational orientation, and cognition in a subnormally-performing child: A systemic perspective for training. In B. Wong (Ed.), *Intervention research in learning disabilities: An international perspective* (pp. 190-213). New York: Springer-Verlag.

Pressley, M., Beard El-Dinary, P., Gaskins, I., Schuder, T., Bergman, J.L., Almasi, J., & Brown, R. (1992). Beyond direct explanation: Transactional instruction in reading comprehension strategies. *Elementary School Journal, 92,* 511-554.

Roeser, R. W., Eccles, J. S., & Sameroff, A. J. (2000). School as a context of early adolescents' academic and social-emotional development: A summary of research findings. *Elementary School Journal, 100,* 443-471.

Rogers, L. E., & Escudero, V. (Eds.). (2004). *Relational communication: An interactional perspective to the study of process and form.* Mahwah, NJ: Erlbaum.

Rogoff, B., & Gardner, W. (1984). Adult guidance of cognitive development. In B. Rogoff & J. Lave (Eds.), *Everyday cognition: Its development in social context* (pp. 95-116). Cambridge: Harvard University Press.

Salonen, P. (1988). Learning disabled children's situational orientations and coping strategies. *Nordisk Pedagogik, 8,* 70-75.

Salonen, P., Lehtinen, E., & Olkinuora, E. (1998). Expectations and beyond: The development of motivation and learning in a classroom context. In J. Brophy (Ed.), *Advances in research on teaching: Expectations in the classroom* (Vol. 7, pp. 111-150). Greenwich, CT.: JAI Press.

Salonen, P., Lepola, J., & Vauras, M. (2007). Scaffolding interaction in task oriented and non-task oriented parent-child dyads. *European Journal of Psychology of Education, 22,* 77-94.

Salonen, P., & Vauras, M. (2006). Von der Fremdregulation zur Selbstregulation: Die Rolle von sozialen Makrostrukturen in der Interaktion zwischen Lehrenden und Lernenden [From other-regulation to self-regulation: The role of social macro-patterns in teacher-learner interaction]. In M. Baer, M. Fuchs, P. Füglister, K. Reusser, & H. Wyss (Eds.,) *Didaktik auf psychologischer Grundlage: Von Hans Aebli's kognitionspsychologischer Didaktik zur modernen Lehr- und Lernforschung* (pp. 207-217). Bern: h.e.p. Verlag.

Salonen, P., Vauras, M., & Efklides, A. (2005). Social interaction - What can it tell us about metacognition and co-regulation in learning? *European Psychologist, 10,* 199-208.

Scheff, T. J. (1967). Towards a sociological model of consensus. *American Sociological Review, 32,* 32-46.

Schneider, W., Stefanek, J., & Dotzler H. (1997). Erwerb des Lesens und des Rechtschreibens: Ergebnisse aus dem SCHOLASTIK-Projekt. [Achievement in reading and spelling: Results from SCHOLASTIK Project]. In F. E. Weinert & A. Helmke (Eds.), *Entwicklung im Grundschulalter* (pp. 113-129). Weinheim: PsychologieVerlagsUnion.

Schultz, G. F., & Switzky, H. N. (1990). The development of intrinsic motivation in students with learning problems. *Preventing School Failure, 34,* 14-20.

Semmel, M. I., Gerber, M. M., & MacMillan, D. L. (1994). Twenty-five years after Dunn's article: A legacy of policy analysis research in special education. *Journal of Special Education, 27,* 481-495.

Siegrist, J. (1970). *Das Consensus-Modell. Studien zur Interaktionstheorie und zur kognitiven Sozialisation.* [The consensus-model. Studies on interaction theory and cognitive socialisation]. Stuttgart: F. Enke Verlag.

Sroufe, L. A. (1989). Relationships and relationship disturbances. In A. J. Sameroff & R. N. Emde (Eds.), *Relationships and relationship disturbances in early childhood. A developmental approach* (pp. 97-124). New York: Basic Books.

Stanovich, K. E. (1986). Matthew effects in reading: Some consequences of individual differences in the acquisition of literacy. *Reading Research Quarterly, 21,* 360-406.

Steenbeek, H. W., & van Geert, P. L. (2007). A theory and dynamic model of dyadic interaction: Concerns, appraisals, and contagiousness in a developmental context. *Developmental Review, 27,* 1- 40.

Urdan, T. C., & Maehr, M. L. (1995). Beyond a two-goal theory of motivation and achievement: A case for social goals. *Review of Educational Research, 65,* 213-244.

Urdan, T., Midgley, C., & Wood, S. (1995). Special issues in reforming middle level schools. *Journal of Early Adolescence, 15,* 9-37.

Vauras, M., & Junttila, N. (2007). Children's loneliness, social competence and school success: The role of the family. *Scientific Annals of the Psychological Society of Northern Greece, 5,* 1-16.

Vauras, M., Junttila, N., Iiskala, T. Kajamies, A., Kinnunen, R., & Kaukiainen, A. (2003). Learning difficulties, social competence, and loneliness. *Scientific Annals of the Psychological Society of Northern Greece, 1,* 1-9.

Vauras, M. Kinnunen, R., & Rauhanummi, T. (1999a). The role of metacognition in the context of integrated strategy intervention. *European Journal of Psychology of Education, 14,* 555-569.

Vauras, M., Rauhanummi, T., Kinnunen, R., & Lepola, J. (1999b). Motivational vulnerability as a challenge for educational interventions. *International Journal of Educational Research, 31,* 515-531.

Vauras, M., Kinnunen, R., & Kuusela, L. (1994). Development of text-processing skills in high-, average-, and low-achieving primary school children. *Journal of Reading Behavior, 26,* 361-389.

Vauras, M., Lehtinen, E., Kinnunen, R., & Salonen, P. (1992). Socio-emotional coping and cognitive processes in training learning-disabled children. In B. Wong (Ed.) *Intervention research in learning disabilities: An international perspective* (pp. 163-189). New York: Springer-Verlag.

Vauras, M., Salonen, P., Lehtinen, E., & Lepola, J. (2001). Long-term development of motivation and cognition in family and school contexts. In Volet, S. & Järvelä, S. (Eds.) *Motivation in learning contexts: Theoretical and methodological implications* (pp. 285-305). Amsterdam: Pergamon.

Vauras, M., Salonen, P., & Kinnunen, R. (2008). Influences of group processes and interpersonal regulation on motivation, affect and achievement. In M. Maehr, S. Karabenick & T. Urdan (Eds.), *Advances in Motivation and Achievement. Social Psychological Perspective on Motivation and Achievement* (Vol. 15, pp. 275-314). London: Emerald Group Publishing.

Volet, S. E., & Järvelä, S. (Eds.). (2001). *Motivation in learning contexts: Theoretical advances and methodological implications.* Amsterdam: Elsevier Science.

Volet, S., Vauras, M., & Salonen, P. (submitted). Integrating the psychological and social nature of self- and other forms of regulation in learning contexts. ´

Vygotsky, L. S. (1962). *Thought and language.* New York: Wiley.

Vygotsky, L. S. (1978). *Mind in society. The development of higher psychological processes.* Cambridge, MA: Harvard University Press.

White, R. (1959). Motivation reconsidered: The concept of competence. *Psychological Review, 66,* 297-333.

Wigfield, A., Eccles, J. S., & Rodriguez, D. (1998). The development of children's motivation in school contexts. *Review of Research in Education, 23,* 73-118.

Wood, D., Bruner, J. S., & Ross, G. (1976). The role of tutoring in problem solving. *Journal of Child Psychology and Psychiatry, 17,* 89-100.

Seeking Help

Generalizable Self-Regulatory Process and Social-Cultural Barometer

Stuart A. Karabenick & Richard S. Newman

Introduction

In 1978, the Perkin-Elmer Corporation won the NASA contract to manufacture the mirror for the Hubble Space Telescope. The success of Hubble Space Telescope rested on Perkin-Elmer's ability to create a one-of-a-kind mirror with maximum smoothness and precise curvature – a technological challenge for the team of engineers entrusted with the Hubble project. To ensure the success of the project, Perkin-Elmer hired renowned technical experts and optical engineers as consultants to assist the Hubble team. However, even though the Hubble team faced many problems during the mirror production process, they resisted seeking help from the experts. For example, when one of the consultants, Roderic Scott, would come by, team members said to each other, «Hey, Rod is out there. Don't let him in. Turn up the radio.» (Capers & Lipton, 1993, p. 51). As a result of not seeking help, the engineers failed to resolve serious problems that emerged from the production of the mirror, which in turn led to the installation of a seriously flawed mirror into the telescope (Sandoval & Lee, 2006, p. 151).

The poor judgment described above is not uncommon. It is indeed a global phenomenon. Groups and individuals often fail to seek help that is so plainly needed. So, why didn't the Perkin-Elmer engineers accept the expert help that was readily available? The temptation is to invoke person characteristics, charging that the engineers were just incompetent or lazy. In so doing, we hold them individually and collectively accountable for the flawed mirror. Sandoval and Lee (2006) point out, however, that organizational cultures and norms are also influential. Instead of placing the blame on character flaws, the explanation for such actions is more complex—both person and situation factors must be taken into consideration. In addition, seeking help is a multi-faceted process that is often rife with ambiguity and involves more than the decision to seek help. As with engineers in organizational settings, dire consequences can result when students fail to get the help they need. For students, the help-seeking process involves answering such questions as: Do I understand what I'm reading? Do I need help? What will others think of me if I ask? Who should I approach? For what purpose? As presented in this chapter, although the help seeking process is a global phenomenon, answers to these questions are a function of the cultural and social conditions that exist in local contexts.

Examining why students do or do not seek help and the complexity of the process is due in part to the social-interactive nature of the act (Newman, 2000). Seeking help involves approaching others, with all of its attendant consequences. Doing so usually takes time and effort, and it can render one indebted to those providing it. Most of all, however, is the risk of being judged less capable by teachers or peers, which could be embarrassing (Shapiro, 1983) and generally threatening to one's self-worth (Covington, 1992). In combination, these costs can completely discourage students and other learners from seeking needed help (Fisher, Nadler, & Whitcher-Alagna, 1982). Thus early research on help seeking focused on why students are so reluctant to ask questions (e.g., Dillon, 1988) and why their passivity becomes more pervasive as they progress through the grades (Good, Slavings, Harel, & Emerson, 1987).

The Legacy of Dependence

One reason for the low rate of help seeking is its identification with the stigma of dependency, especially in Western societies (Fischer & Torney, 1976; Sears, Maccoby, & Levin, 1957; Triandis, 1994). Beller (1955), for example, advanced the notion that seeking help is a component of a general dependency drive in children, and Winterbottom (1958) focused on the importance of child-rearing practices that foster independent adults. Independence was incorporated into early theories of achievement motivation (McClelland, 1961), such that reliance on others was considered anathema to the development of an achievement motive. Affiliation imagery was generally viewed as counter-indicative of achievement in projective (TAT) coding systems. Although Nurturant press (Nup), which consisted of personal sources in TAT imagery that aided the story character, was recognized in such systems, it was eventually eliminated. In Feather's (1961, 1963) classic studies of persistence following continuous failures, assistance from outside resources was never an option.

Despite the common observation that many human endeavors are undertaken cooperatively, independence remains firmly embedded as a Western and particularly American cultural icon. The instructional implications of this view are straightforward: students should do their own work; teachers should not reinforce requests for help; and asking others for help should be considered cheating (see Anderman & Murdoch, 2007). Under the burden of such admonitions it is no wonder that students often avoid seeking help. This view has prevailed even in the face of social-cultural perspectives—such as Vygotsky's (1978) "zone of proximal development"—in which seeking help is not only desirable but essential to the development of skills and intellectual functioning.

The Shift in Perspective

As described in recent reviews (Karabenick, 1998; Karabenick & Newman, 2006, in press-a, in press-b), the critical shift in help seeking research followed Nelson-Le Gall's (1981, 1987) explication of the reasons why students seek help, with some reasons considered more adaptive than others. According to her analysis, continued dependence on others could result from engaging in what Nelson-Le Gall termed executive (also referred to as *expedient, excessive,* or *less adaptive*) help seeking, which is effort-avoidant and unnecessary (Nelson-Le Gall, 1981, 1987), and which can be as non-adaptive as avoiding seeking help entirely (see Marchand & Skinner, 2007; Newman, 2007). Learners who ask for the answers to math problems, often without much initial effort, may immediately benefit by completing an assignment, but they would be no less dependent on help when encountering difficulty on subsequent occasions. It would make sense, therefore, to discourage executive help seeking. It would not, however, be prudent to discourage seeking help that is more adaptive.

Nelson-Le Gall identified more adaptive help as "instrumental" in that it is designed to obtain just enough assistance to overcome difficulties, with the ultimate objective of increasing learning and understanding, for example, by asking for hints or explanations instead of direct help (Nelson-Le Gall, 1981, 1985; Nelson-Le Gall, Gumerman, & Scott-Jones, 1983). Rather than maintain dependency, instrumental help seeking (also referred to as *adaptive, strategic, appropriate,* or *autonomous*; Butler, 1998; Karabenick, 1998; Nelson-Le Gall, 1981; Newman, 2000; Ryan, Patrick, & Shim, 2005) can decrease dependency by increasing students' knowledge and skills. Accordingly, the distinction between more and less adaptive forms (or goals) of help seeking is necessary to understand its function in the learning process.

Help Seeking as a Strategy

There is general agreement that seeking help can be classified as a form of behavioral, or social, self-regulation (Pintrich & Zusho, 2002), which is part of the "tool kit" of cognitively, behaviorally, and emotionally engaged learners (Boekaerts, Pintrich, & Zeidner, 2000; Butler, 1998, 2006; Karabenick, 1998, 2003, 2004; Karabenick & Newman, 2006; Nelson-Le Gall & Resnick, 1998; Newman, 2000; Skinner & Zimmer-Gembeck, 2007; Zimmerman & Martinez-Pons, 1990; Zusho, Karabenick, Bonney, & Sims, 2007). Ames (1983) was one of the first to view help seeking as a strategy from an achievement-attribution-theory perspective. He found that college students with "help-relevant" attributions for failure (internal, unstable, deficit specific) rather than "help-irrelevant" attributions for failure (internal, stable, general) were more likely to seek help by attending remedial sessions. And Kuhl and Fuhrmann (1998) considered help seeking an example of volitional control over the environment. If help seeking is a strategy of self-regulated learners then students who seek help should also be those more likely to use other strategies; this conjecture has received considerable support (Karabenick & Knapp, 1991).

Seeking help is positioned at the intersection of cognitive and metacognitive strategies and the social-cultural learning context. Cognitive strategies such as rehearsal and elaboration could involve social interaction (e.g., reciting a poem to others), but not necessarily. Metacognitive planning, monitoring, and regulating also need not involve interactions with others, although they could in some instances (e.g., checking with others to determine one's level of comprehension). Seeking help does, however, involve others because others are part of the process, often with a high degree of intensity and interactivity, as when others are asked to explain complex ideas. The student-teacher relationship is a prime example. It is an extended relationship, with multiple instances of bids for assistance and responses to those requests that, whether used adaptively or not, is what makes help seeking unique among self-regulated learning strategies.

A Multi-Step (Global) Process

Several models of the help-seeking process have been proposed (e.g., Aleven, McLaren, & Koedinger, 2006; Gross & McMullen, 1983; Nelson-Le Gall, 1981; Newman, 1990, 1998a, 1998b). Although varying somewhat, they generally include several steps at which learners: (a) determine whether there is a problem; (b) determine whether help is needed/wanted; (c) decide whether to seek help; (d) decide on the type of help (goal); (e) decide on whom to ask; (f) solicit help; (g) obtain help; and (h) process the help received. It should be noted there is no claim that the sequence of steps in the help-seeking process is necessarily linear or completely mindful. Learners may often survey sources of help, for example, before deciding on whether to seek it, and decisions to seek help may bypass an awareness of need. No research thus far has systematically examined this issue.

Determining whether there is a problem is an often overlooked but important initial condition to begin the process, which can involve a precipitating event such as an unsolved problem, an unfinished paper, or receiving a failing grade. It can also depend on such factors as social comparison processes (e.g., the grade your friends received) and levels of aspiration (e.g., whether a "C" in algebra is just fine). A learner's comprehension criterion—the level of understanding one is willing to accept—can start the process as well. Social influences may even enter into determining whether there is a problem. Evidence indicates, for example, that information about others' levels of comprehension can influence one's own comprehension monitoring processes. This may occur when individuals who are simultaneously receiving information (e.g., listening to a lecture) signal their lack of comprehension (e.g., by asking a question), which in turn influences others. An experimental study examined this phenomenon by controlling the number of questions that a co-learner asked while watching video presentations manipulated to create ambiguity (Karabenick, 1996). Figure 1 shows the number of times learners indicated they were "confused" while watching the video. Compared to a control condition in which no co-learner was present, learners' own levels of confusion increased when co-learners asked more questions. Also intriguing is that the learner's level of confusion was somewhat less when co-learners failed to ask questions; this finding suggests that the absence of others' questions could lead learners to believe they, too, comprehend, even when they do not.

Recognition of a problem could lead to other remedies (e.g., the use of other strategies). When these are ineffective, however, help seeking can be the solution. The level of need for help in large part determines its use. However, the relationship between need and help seeking is not always monotonic, nor is need always transparent to an observer. Karabenick and Knapp (1988b) had college students in several large introductory psychology classes report the help sought during the term for academic reasons (e.g., from teachers, other students, advisors) and their level of need for help and expected grade in the course.

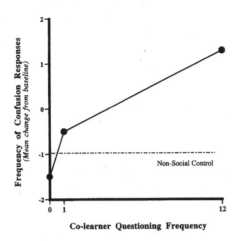

Figure 1. Social influences on comprehension monitoring evidenced by the level of experienced confusion as a function of the frequency of co-learner questioning (from Karabenick, 1996).

As shown in Figure 2, those doing well in the course needed little help, which was reflected in their equally low levels of help seeking. Help seeking increased until moderate levels (the C– to B+ range). Instead of increasing monotonically, however, as indicated by the dashed lines in the figure, students performing very poorly in the course reported seeking less help. Apparently they were sufficiently discouraged, helpless or disengaged from the learning process that even approaching others for assistance was considered useless, or even threatening, lending support to the adage that those who need help the most are least likely to seek it.

The low level of help seeking by higher performing students should not be taken to indicate they would not do so should the need arise. In fact, evidence demonstrates that "better" learners—those who are more self-regulating in their use of other learning strategies—are more, rather than less, likely to seek help *when needed* (Karabenick & Knapp, 1991). That study found, for example, that there was no correlation between students who used more metacognitive strategies (i.e., planning, monitoring and regulating) and help seeking. However, as might be expected, students who employed metacognitive strategies were less likely to need help. The association between strategy use and help seeking emerged only after statistically controlling for differences in students' reports of their need for help. A second way to show that self-regulated learners are more likely to seek help is by asking them to indicate what they would do if they needed it. Thus metacognition use was directly related to the level of agreement with contingently phrased survey items (similar to likelihood statements) in the Karabenick and Knapp (1991) study (e.g., "If I needed help with my classes, I would ask my teacher") to a degree that was almost identical to that between metacognition use and reported help seeking after controlling students' stated level of need. In sum, better, more self-regulated students are more likely to seek help, *when needed.*

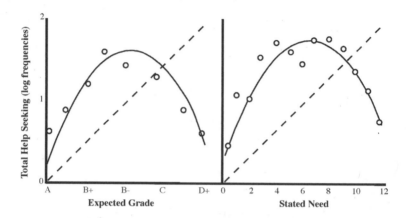

Figure 2. Help seeking as a function of the severity of need both in terms of reported need and expected course grade (adapted from Karabenick & Knapp, 1988b).

The foregoing analysis raises the question of the extent that observers are capable of judging the adequacy of help seeking. For example, just knowing whether learners have sought help, without additional information, is insufficient to understand the adaptive significance of that behavior. First-time observers are sometimes placed in that circumstance (e.g., substitute teachers). Students who sit quietly may be help avoidant, but they may also understand the material. Those who ask questions may not understand the material, even after some attempts, or they may ask with little effort. After sufficient interactions with students, however, observers can acquire the information necessary to become well-calibrated and reliable judges. Ryan, Patrick, and Shim (2005) demonstrated this by having teachers identify their middle school students as having appropriate, avoidant, or dependent help-seeking tendencies. That these judgments were consistent with students' self-reports, as well as the differences between the groups on other measures, suggests that informed observers (teachers in this instance) are capable of such differentiations.

Assuming help is needed, or in some cases even in its absence, whether help is wanted depends on such factors as whether other strategies have been exhausted and, as discussed earlier, the attributions students employ for their difficulties or failures (Ames, 1983). At that point, the decision to seek help, the subject of most of the research to be discussed subsequently, is a function of the perceived benefits and costs of seeking and not seeking it. Determining the sources of assistance (the target of requests), such as friends (informal sources), teachers (formal sources), or hybrids (e.g., student peer advisors) can follow the decision to seek help, although it is frequently taken into consideration simultaneously as well. For example, teachers are typically considered sources of higher quality assistance than are friends but may cost more in terms of threatened evaluation apprehension. Friends may provide lower quality help but cost less (e.g., are more accessible) (Knapp & Karabenick, 1988). Having identified the source of help there remains the task of knowing how to approach the source, and finally, once obtaining the help, to process it for maximum benefit.

Adaptive Help Seeking

Describing the resources of self-regulated learners who seek help in the most adaptive manner most generally involves how they would negotiate each step in the process to maximize immediate and long-term gains (Karabenick & Newman, in press-a, in press-b; Newman, 2008). This process is shown schematically in Figure 3. The steps include: (1) well-calibrated comprehension monitoring and an awareness of when help is needed to overcome difficulties; (2) affective-motivational resources, which include having the academic and social goals and self-beliefs that facilitate opting to seek (and not to avoid seeking) help (e.g., not feeling threatened by what teachers or peers might think; (3) the ability to determine the appropriate help required, which in most instances is instrumental help, although in some circumstances could be direct help; (4) social competencies, which include knowing whom to approach for the desired help in ways that are socially desirable and do not disrupt existing relationships; and (5) the skills and strategies to process the help received in a manner that increases the likelihood of achieving desired goals (e.g., solving problems, completing assignments, or performing well on exams). We now turn to the characteristics of learners and the contexts that influence whether learners engage in those adaptive, *and other*, forms of help seeking.

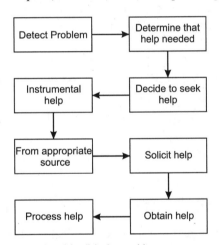

Figure 3. Adaptive (i.e., normative, ideal) help-seeking sequence.

Patterns of Help Seeking

In addition to specifying, a priori, the components of adaptive help seeking, we can also ask how they go together, specifically whether learners: (a) feel threatened about seeking help; (b) intend to seek help, (c) seek instrumental or executive help, and (d) prefer to obtain help from formal (teachers) or informal sources (e.g., other students). These components and their association were assessed in Karabenick (2004). Importantly, the different phases of the help-seeking process were assessed conditionally. For example, college students were asked about the likelihood they would seek instrumental or executive help when needed, and whether they would approach teachers or peers *if they did*. A variable-centered (factor) analysis revealed two patterns of help seeking: (a) an approach pattern consisting of students' tendencies to seek instrumental help from teachers, and (b) an avoidance pattern consisting of help-seeking threat, intentions to avoid seeking help, and executive help seeking. The link between avoidance and contingent executive help seeking was especially important as it indicates that threatened and avoidant students would seek help, albeit in a way that is less adaptive.

Furthermore, a person-centered (cluster) analysis (Karabenick, 2003) suggested that there were four differentiable groups of students. (a) Strategic/Adaptive Formal students had relatively high levels of seeking instrumental help from teachers; (b) Strategic/Adaptive Informal students were similarly high in instrumental help seeking but less likely to seek help from teachers (and more from peers). Students in both of these groups had low levels of threat, avoidance, and executive help seeking. (c) An Avoidant group, by contrast, was relatively high in threat, help-seeking avoidance, and executive help seeking and moderate on the other indicators. (d) A Non-Strategic group was low on all indicators. Interestingly, the proportion of students in the avoidant cluster (23%) was almost identical to the proportion of middle school students classified as avoidant by their teachers (Ryan et al., 2005). The person-centered analysis provided information not readily apparent based on a variable-centered analysis (Niemivirta, 2002), especially regarding the difference between formal and informal Strategic/Adaptive help-seeking groups.

Person and Contextual Influences

Person Characteristics

Research has consistently shown that students who are more likely to seek help in a strategic manner can also be characterized as having a more adaptive motivational profile. Specifically, they are more self-efficacious, highly value and have greater intrinsic interest in their courses, and have higher global self-esteem and less test anxiety (Karabenick & Knapp, 1991). Their achievement goals are also more motivationally adaptive, given consistent evidence that instrumental/adaptive help seeking is more likely among students with higher mastery achievement goal orientations; that is, students who construe seeking help within the broader goal of understanding and self-improvement (Arbreton, 1998; Butler, 1998; Butler & Neuman, 1995; Karabenick, 2003, 2004; Newman, 2002; Pintrich, 2000; Ryan, Hicks, & Midgley, 1997; Ryan et al., 2005; Ryan & Pintrich, 1997, 1998; Skaalvik & Skaalvik, 2005). Students who are more concerned about appearing incompetent (i.e., are more performance-avoidance orientated), however, are less likely to seek needed help. If performance-oriented students do seek help, it is often in the form of expedient or executive help seeking (Karabenick, 2004; Karabenick, Zusho, & Kempler, 2005).

Table 1 summarizes the association (correlations) between the five segments of the help-seeking process described earlier and achievement goals (mastery and performance-approach and performance-avoid), based on data from middle and high school (Karabenick et al., 2005) and college students (Karabenick, 2004). Only statistically significant correlations are shown. Clear patterns are present across the two studies and age groups. Instrumental help seeking is related only to middle, high school and college students' endorsement of mastery goals. Seeking help from teachers (i.e., formal help seeking) is also associated with performance approach goals, that is, students' concerns about their ability and desires to perform better than their peers. Threat, avoidance and executive help seeking (i.e., an avoidance pattern) are related only to mastery avoidance goals (i.e., concerns about not learning or mastering material; Elliot & Thrash, 2002) and both performance approach and avoidance goals. Thus, students whose goals reflect greater concerns about their ability, not mastering material, or performing poorly in comparison to peers, are less likely to seek help, or to seek executive (i.e., work-avoidant) help if they do, as described above. In addition to the evidence regarding achievement goals, there is also evidence of associations between help seeking and students' social goals. In particular, Ryan et al. (1997) assessed elementary school students' intimacy goals (their interest in developing meaningful friendships), which were considered the social equivalent of mastery achievement goals, and social status goals (concern about one's social image, similar to performance or ability goals). As predicted, intimacy goals were related inversely to perceived threat and avoiding help seeking, whereas social status goal endorsement was related to the avoidance of help seeking.

Table 1. Relations between middle and high school (Grades 6-12) and college student help seeking and personal achievement goal orientations.

Help-seeking component	Mastery approach		Mastery avoidance		Performance approach		Performance avoidance	
	6-12	College	6-12	College	6-12	College	6-12	College
Instrumental	.26	.32	--					
Formal	.45	.16	--		.13	.12		
Threat			--	.25	.21	.32	.33	.53
Avoid			--	.25		.20	.19	.41
Executive			--	.17	.24	.20	.30	.41

Note: Based on data from Karabenick, Zusho, & Kempler (2005) and Karabenick (2004). Only significant (p < .001) correlations are shown. Cells with -- indicate goal was not assessed.

Butler (2007) has recently extended research on students' goals by developing measures to assess teachers' goals for teaching, which consisted of mastery, ability approach, ability avoidance, and work avoidance. The frequency of teachers' reported help seeking for several problem areas (assessed in a manner that could be considered to control for need) was related directly to their level of mastery goals endorsement and inversely to ability-avoidance goal endorsement. Perceived benefits and threats of help seeking were also related in ways that were consistent with their goal endorsement. Teachers who approached their work as an opportunity for learning (e.g., "class made me want to learn more") were more likely to seek help for problems related to teaching, as well as viewing seeking help as more beneficial and less threatening. Those who were concerned about their lack of ability (e.g., that their classes did not do worse on an exam) were less likely to seek help. Thus, the associations between teachers' and students' achievement goals and help seeking are quite consistent. Subsequent work (see below) has examined whether teachers' goals for teaching translate into differences in help seeking by the students in their classes.

Teacher, Classroom and School Contextual Influences

As emphasized previously, help seeking is a social/interactive process (Newman, 1998a). Teachers who respond to requests for help by giving students hints and taking advantage of such occasions as teachable moments are likely to not only help students overcome their difficulties, but also to learn that seeking help, often in the form of asking questions, is a valuable academic strategy. In contrast, teachers and others who respond to requests in a perfunctory or directive manner are more likely to reinforce overly dependent executive/expedient help seeking. Furthermore, students exposed to teachers and others who create learning environments that tolerate exploration and uncertainty are more likely to conclude that all problems need not be solved independently and that it is acceptable to engage others in the learning process (McCaslin & Good, 1996). When teachers scaffold learning experiences and socialize the normalcy of academic difficulty, need for collaboration, and expectation of responses to their questions that contain explanations rather than just answers, students internalize a personal sense of empowerment and "voice" (Nelson-Le Gall & Resnick, 1998).

Classes can also differ according to the achievement goals that teachers emphasize, that is, their achievement goal structures (Ames & Archer, 1988; Midgley, 2002), and student help seeking is sensitive to such classroom characteristics (Church, Elliot, & Gable, 2001; Midgley, 2002; Urdan, Ryan, Anderman, & Gheen, 2002). The pattern is very consistent with students' personal goal orientations but in this instance represents the level of students' aggregated classroom perceptions as estimates of goal structures. Students in elementary school classes, which students collectively judge as more focused on mastery, are less likely to avoid seeking needed help (Turner et al., 2002). For middle school students, tendencies to seek or to avoid seeking help are related both to performance as well as classroom mastery goals (Karabenick et al., 2005; Newman, 2002; Ryan, Gheen, & Midgley, 1998). And for college students, available evidence suggests that performance rather than classroom mastery goals are critical. Specifically, students in classes they (collectively) perceive to be more focused on avoiding demonstrations of incompetence (performance-avoidance goals) display a help-seeking avoidance pattern; that is, they are more threatened and are less likely to seek needed help. If they do, it would be for expedient rather than instrumental purposes (Karabenick, 2004). In general, then, help seeking is more influenced by concerns about evaluation as the instructional context becomes increasingly focused on evaluation in the later grades, and especially at the post-secondary level.

Studies have also examined the influence of students' perceptions of classroom climate, teacher support, and academic press. Turner et al. (2002) reported that elementary school students in classes in which teachers provided and promoted opportunities for collaboration (among other instructional and motivational teacher practices) were less likely to avoid seeking help. Higher levels of students' reported help-seeking approach intentions are also related to teachers' respect for students and promotion of respect among classmates (Stipek et al., 1998). Classes that middle and high school students judged more supportive (using a combined index of teacher support that included teacher caring, teacher promotion of respect and collaboration) are more likely to elicit approach and less likely to elicit help-seeking avoidance (Karabenick, et al., 2005). That study also found that students in classes rated higher in academic press (i.e., higher standards and press for understanding) reported more approach help seeking, but press was unrelated to avoidance. Similarly, classes in which students perceived their teachers as more concerned about their social and emotional well-being are less likely to avoid seeking help (Ryan, Pintrich, & Midgley, 2001). Most recently, Butler and Shibaz (in press) examined associations between teachers' mastery and ability (i.e., performance) goals for teaching (Butler, 2007) and student help seeking. Teacher mastery orientation directly (and teacher avoidance orientation inversely) predicted the extent their students' perceived them as supportive of question asking and help seeking. Students of teachers with higher ability avoidance goals were also more likely to engage in cheating, although teacher goals did not predict the level of student help seeking in their classes.

Tracking is another way that context influences help seeking. Butler (2007) reasoned that by virtue of their emphasis on individual differences, schools that employ tracking would engender higher levels of students' performance achievement goal orientations. As a consequence of concerns about demonstrating ability, students in tracked schools should, accordingly, be more help-seeking avoidant. It was further predicted that students in upper tracks would be disadvantaged due to greater concerns about demonstrating low ability by seeking help, as would low ability students in mixed ability classes. Results supported the predicted differences between tracked and non-tracked schools and the lower rate of help seeking in high ability tracked classes. Tracking, therefore, is yet another pathway for the context to focus students on their ability by exacerbating social comparisons, engendering self-threat, and making it less likely that they will seek needed help.

In addition to evidence from elementary and secondary students, college students' intentions to seek help in the form of question asking are related to their perceptions of teacher support for questioning (Karabenick & Sharma, 1994). Teacher support in that study was assessed in response to students' class-aggregated perceptions of whether teachers: gave specific instructions to ask, provided opportunities to ask (e.g., wait time), gave informative responses to questions, rewarded or punished students for asking, reacted with positive or negative emotions to questions, and stated that questions were valuable. Evidence supported a structural model, in which the influence of teacher support on the likelihood students would ask questions was mediated by the level of student inhibition to ask. Thus teachers who were collectively judged by their students to be more supportive were less inhibited, which in turn inversely predicted the likelihood of asking. Analyses of the Support of Questioning scale in that study also suggested that providing students with the opportunity to ask questions (e.g., wait time), and how elaborate the teachers' responses were to questions were particularly important in students' judgments of instructors' support of question asking.

Social Comparison and the Influence of Peers

As long as social comparisons do not engender performance-avoidance goals, comparing their performances and understanding with that of others can have a positive influence on help seeking because of the information provided about the student's strengths and weaknesses. That information can help children evaluate their peers' capacity to be effective helpers (Ruble & Frey, 1991). It also helps students make realistic judgments about whether they personally have tried enough before turning to others. With development, children are increasingly able to judge when assistance is truly necessary so they can request the right amount of help. There are also changes in how children conceptualize ability, and social comparisons help students classify their peers' abilities (who's smart and who's dumb), as well as perceiving those who need help as not very "smart" (Nicholls & Miller, 1984).

Adaptive help seeking requires that students skillfully approach their peers as well as their teachers, for example, by knowing whom to approach (e.g., the student who may know the answer) and how to initiate requests that are direct, sincere, polite, and clear about what exactly is being requested (Cooper, Marquis, & Ayers-Lopez, 1982). Children are most likely to learn how to ask for—and receive—elaborated help (e.g., explanations rather than direct answers) in a constructive fashion (Webb & Palincsar, 1996). Especially at upper-elementary and middle school levels, collaborative activities are opportunities for students to ask—and be asked—questions, which allow an exchange of perspectives among individuals who are working on relatively equal footing. As students observe the effectiveness of peers' questions in resolving difficulties, they are likely to learn that different individuals contribute unique skills and knowledge. They may learn how, in the future, to choose helpers according to both their own needs and others' competencies (Webb, Ing, Kersting, & Nemer, 2006).

Friends assist and support one another (Berndt & Keefe, 1996), and high quality friendships are especially characterized by mutual support and other features that influence peer help seeking. In close, communal relationships (Mills, Clark, Ford, & Johnson, 2004), children would not be as concerned about self-disclosure, threat to self-esteem, and indebtedness to those who help them. In a friendly context, children find it easier to manage and negotiate social demands of interactions and focus their shared efforts on learning and problem solving. Children in conflictual relationships, by contrast, are more reluctant to disclose difficulties to one another and are thus less likely to expect help even when requested.

Peer help seeking also depends on students' social goals. As noted earlier, the more strongly they strive for goals of social affiliation (i.e., desire for friendship and intimacy), the more students value and use help seeking as a strategy for dealing with academic difficulties (Ryan et al., 1997). The more strongly students strive for goals of social status (i.e., desire for peer approval and popularity), the more embarrassed they are to ask for help in the classroom (Ryan et al., 1997). At the transition to middle school, when students typically are increasingly concerned about their self-image in addition to the increase in evaluation pressures, social status goals are likely to inhibit help seeking, especially if an individual's self-esteem is easily threatened and his or her peer group does not value academic success. More important, however, inhibition is likely to be minimized if the student has a strong sense of self and a peer group that does value learning. Such influences may also play a role when students transition to college contexts. If nothing else, their peers during that time are a convenient and even preferred source of assistance (Knapp & Karabenick, 1988).

Influences of Culture

In addition to the context of classrooms (and schools), broader cultural factors can facilitate or constrain whether and how students and others seek help. As noted earlier, the Western cultural stress on individualism is the value most directly relevant for help seeking. It follows that students in more collectivist cultures should be less concerned with violations of individualistic norms (see Triandis, 1994) and seek help more readily. However, the influence is often more complex and interactive than general essentialist views would suggest (Nisbett, 2003). For example, Japanese college students' collectivistic acculturation, which stresses cooperation, dependency and empathy, facilitates their seeking help from peers outside of the classroom (Shwalb & Sukemune, 1998). Yet cultural norms in Japanese society also prescribe considerable deference to authority. As a consequence, cultural norms dictate that students not interrupt their instructors in class to ask questions. The same deference to authority occurs in other relatively collectivist societies as well, such as in Malaysia (Hashim, Yaakub, Hashim, Othman, & Ali, 2003).

Nadler (1998) was able to examine this cultural dimension within the same country by comparing rates of help seeking by Israeli students raised in collectivist-oriented kibbutz societies with those socialized in individualistic-oriented cities. As predicted, kibbutz students indicated they would seek more help in a variety of situations than did city dwellers. Exemplifying situational moderation, however, kibbutz dwellers sought help more on group than on individual tasks, whereas city dwellers did so more on individual than group tasks. This underscores the importance of taking into consideration characteristics of tasks, specific learning contexts, or even whether the help is sought in public (as in classrooms) or privately (e.g., after class or in faculty offices) (Karabenick & Knapp, 1988a)—an instance of local conditions moderating the global help-seeking process.

Another manifestation of cultural influences occurs as students interact in multicultural settings, specifically the psychological distance that students perceive between each other, which can influence the likelihood that students will seek help from their peers. In a direct study of cultural distance, Volet and Karabenick (2006) measured U.S. and Australian college students' intentions to seek help from peers that differed from them in terms of their socio-cultural background. As shown in Figure 4, the more students were culturally unlike other students, the less likely they would approach peers for needed assistance with their studies. The relation between distance and help seeking was similarly monotonic for monocultural students (e.g., U.S. students in the U.S.), mixed culture (e.g., non-Australians raised in Australia), and other cultural students (e.g., non-U.S. citizens). Significantly, the effect of cultural difference between those in need of assistance and help providers was influenced by whether their teachers created a classroom that supported intergroup acceptance—the more support, the less the effect of cultural distance. This suggests that attempts to ameliorate barriers between students that impede the fruitful exchange of skills and knowledge can benefit learners who need assistance.

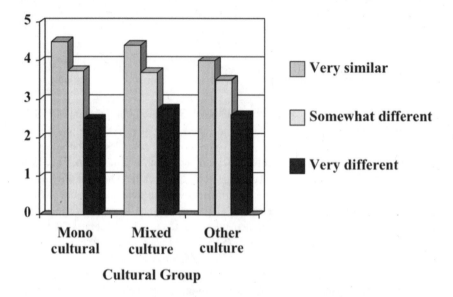

Figure 4. Intention of U.S. and Australian students in different cultural groups to seek help from peers that differ from them by degrees of cultural distance.

Help Seeking in and by Groups

Although it frequently occurs as part of the collaborative process, such as cooperative learning and work in groups in general, help seeking has not been isolated for examination. Recently, however, Webb et al. (2006) reanalyzed studies of small group collaboration in classrooms in order to examine relationships between giving and receiving help, subsequent activity that processed the help received, and the influence of help seeking on students' learning outcomes. Among their conclusions were: (a) that negative group process (e.g., put-downs, insults) was linked to reduced help seeking, and (b) that help seeking in groups is influenced by the classroom culture within which collaboration occurs—that it would be difficult for facilitative collaboration in general, and help seeking in particular, to occur in performance-focused classrooms. Therefore, consistent with previously cited studies of the influences of classroom context (Karabenick, 2004; Ryan et al., 1998; Turner et al., 2002), seeking help when collaborating is more likely when the overall instructional context emphasizes understanding rather than just correct answers, that fosters communication and the acceptability of error, and that encourages the sharing of ideas (Wood, Cobb, & Yackel, 1991). There are other strategies for increasing students' ability and willingness to ask questions in groups, such as reciprocal questioning (King, 1989, 1990, 1991) and other practices that reduce the risks of help seeking (Schofeld, 1995). In other words, the overall classroom context and collaborative experiences can be mutually reinforcing or conflict, rather than isolated and discontinuous, and features of both determine whether groups in those settings facilitate or impede adaptive help seeking.

As described in the introduction to this chapter, in addition to help seeking by individuals within groups, groups seek (or fail to seek) assistance from an external source, a frequent necessity in organizational settings (Sandoval & Lee, 2006) as well as schools, which if not utilized effectively can have unfortunate consequences. The likely resource for groups in K-12 school settings is the classroom teacher, and in college work groups, other knowledgeable students (Volet & Ang, 1998). As with any group decision, whether and in what form to seek help involves many of the within-group processes discussed above. It would also depend on the individuals' characteristics (e.g., their achievement goal orientations) and tendencies to seek or avoid help as individuals. We could expect that groups of students who were inclined to seek adaptive help individually should be similarly inclined when in groups, and that help seeking by such groups would reflect individuals' tendencies. Groups of students with avoidance tendencies should likewise reflect individual help seeking tendencies. The consequences for groups with mixed approaches to help seeking would be more difficult to predict, and as noted above, characteristics of the learning context would also matter.

These predictions were tested in an experimental analog of group help seeking in the classroom. Karabenick and Newman (2004) assigned college students, pre-assessed for their individual tendencies to avoid seeking help, to dyads instructed to solve word problems that were difficult and resulted in a series of failure experiences. Pairs of students performed either under mastery or performance achievement goal conditions. Students were permitted to ask for assistance from an external source. In general, help seeking was more prevalent under mastery achievement goal conditions, which stressed the importance of learning and improvement, than under performance goal conditions, which emphasized ability and competition with other dyads. In addition, achievement goal conditions and individuals' tendencies to avoid seeking help interacted to determine the incidence of group help seeking. Most intriguing was that dyads in which both members were classified as high in help-seeking threat asked for just as much help under performance as under mastery achievement goal conditions. When one dyad member was high in threat, however, group help seeking was less frequent under performance than under mastery conditions. This suggested that, when conditions emphasized that performance was diagnostic of ability, the threat posed by students who sought help as individuals was mitigated when shared with similarly threatened others (Amoroso & Walters, 1969). The frequency of group help seeking, as well as discourse analysis of the dyads as they performed the task, provided support for a diffusion of threat model of collaborative help seeking. Further studies of this phenomenon are warranted given how often collaborative learning is employed in higher education instructional settings, which would predict that highly threatened students working collaboratively would be more likely to ask their instructors or other outside sources for help than the students would when working alone.

New Directions

Communication and Information Rich Contexts

Information and computer technologies (ICT) have had a profound influence on the dynamics of help seeking by virtue of learners' expanded access to archival sources (Wikipedia, Google), other individuals, and increasingly, intelligent systems (Keefer & Karabenick, 1998). Computer-mediated communication (CMC) makes available myriad individuals and virtual communities as potential sources of assistance. And the cost (time, effort) of seeking help via CMC from these sources has considerably decreased. In addition to decreased cost, CMC contexts can facilitate help seeking by the reduction of self-threat that comes from increased anonymity and the elimination of social status cues. Karabenick and Knapp (1988b) demonstrated this phenomenon by allowing one group of students to seek help while performing a disjunctive concept formation task to receive help in one condition from a computer program designed to provide it, and another group from an assistant (actually simulated) who was ostensibly monitoring the session. More than twice as many students requested help from the computer (86%) than from the assistant (36%) and four times the average number of requests from the computer compared to the assistant (3.5 vs. .8, respectively). Despite the fact that the participants were aware their performance and help seeking was recorded, the knowledge that another person was involved in delivering the help was apparently sufficient to depress help seeking. Or, from the other perspective, the automated help received removed the perceived self-consequences of asking for help from another individual.

Since then, automated learning systems that are capable of providing help have become more ubiquitous and sophisticated. Adaptive, intelligent interactive learning environments (ILEs) that respond to changing learner characteristics are becoming increasingly available. Intelligent tutoring systems have been developed that use performance information both to adjust task difficulty (as in adaptive testing) and provide online tutoring and help. Recent innovations are based on comprehensive models of the help-seeking process (Aleven et al., 2006; Aleven, Stahl, Schworm, Fischer, & Wallace, 2003). With these systems, not only is the help offered context-dependent, learners can also select different types of help (e.g., answers or hints consisting of explanation). One version of the model is shown in Figure 5.

The tutoring system has been somewhat successful, in that it predicted help-seeking behavior and errors and improved some aspects of help-seeking behavior. In early tests, students did not learn more with the tutor at the domain level, and students did not learn help-seeking skills. Further developments, however, have been designed to target help seeking as one of the learning goals, to increase the amount of instruction in help seeking by having students practice prior to their performance sessions, and to improve students' metacognitive skills and self-assessment of their understanding (Roll, Aleven, McLaren, & Koedinger, 2007).

Evidence thus far indicates that students using such systems over use expedient help (abuse of the system) by opting to obtain direct hints rather than indirect instrumental help (e.g., access to a glossary of definitions). Explanations for such behavior include the belief that clicking through hints may be desirable and adaptive, something that medical students do (Yudelson et al., 2006), and that doing so may be considered self-instructional, that is, students learn from the hints. Yet to be examined, however, are the broader instructional conditions in which the tutor is used. As noted earlier with regard to help seeking in collaborative groups, the tutor is not isolated from the broader motivational context, and not enough is known about students' perceptions that context or how use of the tutor(s) is influenced by those conditions. Also unexplored are the different motivation goals that students bring to the task and whether, for example, students with higher mastery-approach and lower performance-avoidance goal orientations would, as the reviewed research suggests, be less likely to deviate from normative help seeking.

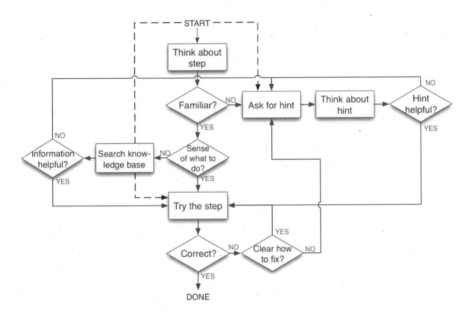

Figure 5. Model of the Help-Seeking Tutor used with the Cognitive Tutoring program (Roll, Aleven, McLaren, & Koedinger, 2007).

One issue as yet to be examined is whether help seeking that involves CMC, ILEs and other intelligent systems poses conceptual challenges regarding the very definition of help seeking itself (Keefer & Karabenick, 1998). If we assume that help seeking is a social-interactive process, then how do we classify seeking "help" from intelligent systems rather than other individuals? One resolution entails a functional analysis to determine whether an intelligent system is implicitly social according to the criteria of whether the presence of "others" is real (e.g., a teacher in a classroom), imagined (e.g., what would your mother think), or implied (e.g., someone will know that I sought help). Thus it may not matter whether the others are present at the time learners seek artificial help but rather whether traces of that act—what is potentially disclosable—would be subject to social influences. In the case of ILEs the issue is whether learners construe their actions as seeking help, that is, whether ILEs alter the very identification of such actions as help seeking when they solicit help from artificial sources (Keefer & Karabenick, 1998; Vallacher &

Wegner, 1987). In addition, what becomes critical to understand are the broader motiva-tion-related characteristics and consequences of the learning contexts in which artificial systems are situated (Schofield, 1995). As stated previously, whether learning occurs in mastery- versus performance-focused instructional setting may be just as important when seeking help from cognitive tutors in ILEs as it is when asking teachers questions in class. And finally, we may question the ease of access to resources, which as the ILE research suggests, may lead to an over-reliance on executive help seeking.

Non-Academic Threats

Thus far the focus of help seeking has been confined to learning and instruction. There are, however, other arenas in schools in which seeking help is relevant. Recently, New-man and his colleagues (Newman, 2006, 2008; Newman & Murray, 2005; Newman, Murray, & Lussier, 2001; Newman & Sanchez, 2007) have begun to examine student and teacher responses to peer-related incidents such as teasing, threats and physical aggres-sion, which place students at risk. What should students do when such incidents take place and the teacher, or another responsible party is not present? How should teachers view such requests, and would the characteristics of students matter (e.g., gender, more vs. less popular)? Newman has analyzed the costs and benefits of seeking and not seeking help when students are the victims of bullying by applying the concepts of adaptive help seeking and the matrix used for academic difficulties. There are benefits and costs both of seeking help and not seeking help. Asking the teacher for help, for example, can alleviate the problem (benefit) but also results in reprisals from the perpetrator (cost). Not seeking help can result in physical or psychological pain (cost) but also stature among peers for not "tattling" (benefit). For their part, teachers view such threats differently depending on who asks them to intercede and how they should respond. It is already evident that the help-seeking framework provides a unique perspective, which will benefit teachers as well *as* students.

Concluding Comments

Help seeking is a social and behavioral strategy of self-regulated learning that most often involves a social transaction with teachers, classmates, and parents, but increasingly other resources that may be technologically mediated. However, its social dimension renders seeking help more complex than other regulation strategies such as rehearsing, organiz-ing, self-checking, and self-testing, strategies that students can carry out independently. Whereas the process of seeking help is a global phenomenon, its expression is moderated by local social and other factors that influence how that process unfolds, which renders it a social-cultural barometer of the conditions in which it occurs.

The present review has emphasized that help seeking does not necessarily signify de-pendency, and that independence is not the same as autonomy. Adaptive help seeking involves knowing when help is needed (good calibration); adopting instrumen-tal/autonomous help-seeking goals; seeking appropriate sources of help; the skills to ac-quire the help; and effectively processing the help received. It can be an important self-regulated learning strategy that is responsive to conditions that promote the use of other forms of SRL (e.g., achievement goals, self-determination needs). More adaptively motivated and strategic learners are more likely to seek help when needed. Focusing on ability, ego, competition, and ability tracking is detrimental to effective help seeking, as it is with other facets of the learning process. ICT and ILE technology can have a dramatic influence on help seeking (e.g., lower cost), but it also raises questions about the very definition of help seeking as necessarily social.

Teachers and peers play important roles in students becoming self-regulated learners by fostering mastery goals of understanding and improvement that facilitate, rather than ability related performance goals that inhibit adaptive help seeking. When teachers stress the intrinsic value of learning in their classrooms rather than just getting good grades (or avoiding bad grades), students tend to ask task-related questions in order to truly understand their work. Knowing how one is doing in relation to classmates can have both positive (e.g., "it's 'normal' to need help") and negative consequences (e.g., concerns about social status). Sensitive and responsive teachers can moderate the effects of anticipated negative consequences, such as embarrassment, that discourage students from seeking needed assistance. They can also play an instrumental role in the development of students' personal beliefs about the costs and benefits of help seeking. Teachers can help establish cooperative classroom norms that facilitate the degree to which peer involvement provides children opportunities to experience beneficial social aspects of learning. Teachers increasingly need to be aware of how technology, in the form of communications or online tutoring, can facilitate student help seeking by reducing its cost (time, effort, embarrassment), while cautioning students about the potential for its excessive misuse. Finally, learners must develop more effective help-seeking strategies, which would be important for teachers and other providers of help to nurture as they would cognitive and metacognitive learning strategies, in the classroom as well as in increasingly ubiquitous technology-supported contexts. Considerable evidence indicates that whether such efforts are successful depends on understanding the local social and cultural conditions that influence facets of the general help-seeking process. There are substantial challenges to transforming research into pedagogical practice, but also many rewards in the form of better learning, and perhaps even higher quality space telescope mirrors.

Acknowledgments
Portions of the research reported herein were supported by a grant from the Math and Science Partnership Program of the National Science Foundation (Award No. 0335369). Any opinions, findings and conclusions or recommendations expressed are the presenter's and do not necessarily reflect those of the National Science Foundation.

References

Aleven, V., McLaren, B., & Koedinger, K. (2006). Toward computer-based tutoring of help-seeking skills. In S. A. Karabenick & R. S. Newman (Eds.), *Help seeking in academic settings: Goals, groups and contexts* (pp. 259-296). Mahwah, NJ: Erlbaum.

Aleven, V., Stahl, E., Schworm, S., Fischer, F., & Wallace, R. M. (2003). Help seeking and help design in interactive learning environments. *Review of Educational Research, 73(2)*, 277-320.

Ames, C., & Archer, J. (1988). Achievement goals in the classroom: Students' learning strategies and motivation processes. *Journal of Educational Psychology, 80*, 260-267.

Ames, R. (1983). Help seeking and achievement orientation: Perspectives from attribution theory. In B. M. DePaulo, A. Nadler, & J. D. Fisher (Eds.), *New directions in helping: Help seeking* (Vol. 2, pp. 165-186). New York: Academic.

Amoroso, D., & Walters, R. (1969). Effects of anxiety and socially mediated anxiety reduction on paired-associate learning. *Journal of Personality and Social Psychology, 11*, 388-396.

Anderman, E. M., & Murdoch, T. B. (2007). *The psychology of academic cheating*. Burlington, MA: Elsevier.

Arbreton, A. (1998). Student goal orientation and help-seeking strategy use. In S. A. Karabenick (Ed.), *Strategic help seeking: Implications for learning and teaching* (pp. 95-116). Mahwah, NJ: Erlbaum.

Beller, E. (1955). Dependency and autonomous achievement striving related to orality and anality in early childhood. *Child Development, 28*, 287-315.

Berndt, T. J., & Keefe, K. (1996). Friends' influence on school adjustment: A motivational analysis. In J. Juvonen & K. R. Wentzel (Eds.), *Social motivation: Understanding children's school adjustment* (pp. 248-278). Cambridge, MA: Cambridge University Press.

Boekaerts, M., Pintrich, P. R., & Zeidner, M. (2000). *Handbook of self-regulation*. San Diego, CA: Academic.

Butler, R. (1998). Determinants of help seeking: Relations between perceived reasons for classroom help-avoidance and help-seeking behaviors in an experimental context. *Journal of Educational Psychology, 90*, 630-644.

Butler, R. (2006). An achievement goal perspective on student help seeking and teacher help giving in the classroom: Theory, research, and educational implications. In S. A. Karabenick & R. S. Newman (Eds.), *Help seeking in academic settings: Goals, groups, and contexts* (pp. 15-44). Mahwah, NJ: Erlbaum.

Butler, R. (2007). Teachers' achievement goal orientations and associations with teachers' help seeking: Examination of a novel approach to teacher motivation. *Journal of Educational Psychology, 99*, 241-252.

Butler, R., & Neuman, O. (1995). Effects of task and ego achievement goals on help-seeking behaviors and attitudes. *Journal of Educational Psychology, 87*, 261-271.

Butler, R., & Shibaz, L. (in press). Achievement goals for teaching as predictors of students' perceptions of teachers' behaviors and student help seeking and cheating. *Learning and Instruction*.

Capers, C., & Lipton, C. (1993). The Hubble space telescope disaster. *Academy of Management Executive, 7*, 23-37.

Church, M. A., Elliot, A. J., & Gable, S. L. (2001). Perceptions of classroom environment, achievement goals, and achievement outcomes. *Journal of Educational Psychology, 93*, 43-54.

Cooper, C. R., Marquis, A., & Ayers-Lopez, S. (1982). Peer learning in the classroom: Tracing developmental patterns and consequences of children's spontaneous interactions. In L. C. Wilkinson (Ed.), *Communicating in the classroom* (pp. 69-84). New York: Academic.

Covington, M. V. (1992). *Making the grade: A self-worth perspective on motivation and school reform*. Cambridge, MA: Cambridge University Press.

Dillon, J. T. (1988). The remedial status of student questioning. *Journal of Curriculum Studies, 20*, 197-210.

Elliot, A. J., & Thrash, T. M. (2002). Approach-avoidance motivation in personality: Approach and avoidance temperaments and goals. *Journal of Personality & Social Psychology, 82*, 804-818.

Feather, N. T. (1961). The relationship of persistence at a task to expectations of success and achievement-related motives. *Journal of Abnormal and Social Psychology, 63*, 552–561.

Feather, N. T. (1963). Persistence at a difficult task with an alternative task of intermediate difficulty. *Journal of Abnormal and Social Psychology, 66*, 604-609.

Fischer, P. L., & Torney, J. V. (1976). Influence of children's stories on dependency: A sex-typed behavior. *Developmental Psychology, 12*, 489-490.

Fisher, J. D., Nadler, A., & Whitcher-Alagna, S. (1982). Recipient reactions to aid. *Psychological Bulletin, 91*, 27-54.

Good, T. L., Slavings, R. L., Harel, K. H., & Emerson, H. (1987). Student passivity: A study of question-asking in K-12 classrooms. *Sociology of Education, 60*, 181-199.

Gross, A. E., & McMullen, P. A. (1983). Models of the help-seeking process. In J. D. Fisher, N. Nadler, & B. M. DePaulo (Eds.), *New directions in helping: Help seeking* (Vol. 2, pp. 45-61). New York: Academic.

Hashim, R. A., Yaakub, N. F., Hashim, H. J., Othman, A. H., & Ali, R. M. (2003, August). *Correlates of academic help-seeking behaviours among adolescents: Insights from a cognitive-motivational perspective.* Paper presented at the Biennial Meeting of the European Association for Research on Learning and Instruction, Padova, Italy.

Karabenick, S. A. (1996). Social influences on metacognition: Effects of co-learner questioning on comprehension monitoring. *Journal of Educational Psychology, 88*, 689-703.

Karabenick, S. A. (Ed.). (1998). *Strategic help seeking: Implications for learning and teaching.* Mahwah, NJ: Erlbaum.

Karabenick, S. A. (2003). Help seeking in large college classes: A person-centered approach. *Contemporary Educational Psychology, 28*, 37-58.

Karabenick, S. A. (2004). Perceived achievement goal structure and college student help seeking. *Journal of Educational Psychology, 96*, 569-581.

Karabenick, S. A., & Knapp, J. R. (1988a). Effects of computer privacy on help-seeking. *Journal of Applied Social Psychology, 18*, 461-472.

Karabenick, S. A., & Knapp, J. R. (1988b). Help-seeking and the need for academic assistance. *Journal of Educational Psychology, 80*, 406-408.

Karabenick, S. A., & Knapp, J. R. (1991). Relationship of academic help seeking to the use of learning strategies and other instrumental achievement behavior in college students. *Journal of Educational Psychology, 83*, 221-230.

Karabenick, S. A., & Newman, R. S. (2004, April). *Should we seek help: An unexplored aspect of group collaboration.* Paper presented at the Annual meeting of the American Educational Research Association, San Diego, California.

Karabenick, S. A., & Newman, R. S. (Eds.). (2006). *Help seeking in academic settings: Goals, groups, and contexts.* Mahwah, NJ: Erlbaum.

Karabenick, S. A., & Newman, R. S. (in press-a). Seeking help as an adaptive response to learning difficulties: Person, situation, and developmental influences. In B. McGaw, P. L. Peterson, & Eva Baker (Eds.), *International encyclopedia of education* (3rd ed.). Amsterdam: Elsevier.

Karabenick, S. A., & Newman, R. S. (in press-b). Help seeking as a behavioral strategic learning strategy. In E. Anderman & L. Anderman (Eds.), *Psychology of classroom learning: An encyclopedia.* Farmington Hills, MI: Thompson Gale.

Karabenick, S. A., & Sharma, R. (1994). Perceived teacher support of student questioning in the college classroom: Its relation to student characteristics and role in the classroom questioning process. *Journal of Educational Psychology, 86*, 90-103.

Karabenick, S. A., Zusho, A., & Kempler, T. M. (2005, August). *Help seeking and perceived classroom context.* Paper presented at the biennial meeting of the European Association for Research on Learning and Instruction. Nicosia, Cyprus.

Keefer, J. A., & Karabenick, S. A. (1998). Help seeking in the information age. In S. A. Karabenick (Ed.), *Strategic help seeking: Implications for learning and teaching* (pp. 219-250). Mahwah, NJ: Erlbaum.

King, A. (1989). Effects of self-questioning training on college student's comprehension of lectures. *Contemporary Educational Psychology, 14*, 366-381.

King, A. (1990). Reciprocal peer questioning: A strategy for teaching students how to learn through lectures. *The Clearing House, 64*, 131-135.

King, A. (1991). Enhancing peer interaction and learning in the classroom through reciprocal questioning. *American Educational Research Journal, 27*, 664-687.

Knapp, J. R., & Karabenick, S. A. (1988). Incidence of formal and informal academic help-seeking in higher education. *Journal of College Student Development, 29*, 223-227.

Kuhl, J., & Fuhrmann, A. (1998). Decomposing self-regulation and self-control: The theoretical and empirical basis of the Volitional Components Checklist. In J. Heckhausen & C. Dweck (Eds.), *Motivation and self-regulation across the life-span* (pp. 15-49). New York: Cambridge University Press.

McCaslin, M., & Good, T. L. (1996). The informal curriculum. In D. C. Berliner & R. C. Calfee (Eds.), *Handbook of educational psychology* (pp. 622-670). New York: Simon & Schuster Macmillan.

McClelland, D. C. (1961). *The achieving society*. New York: The Free Press.

Marchand, G., & Skinner, E. (2007). Motivational dynamics of children's academic help seeking and concealment. *Journal of Educational Psychology, 99*, 65-82.

Midgley, C. (Ed.). (2002). *Goals, goal structures, and patterns of adaptive learning*. Mahwah, NJ: Erlbaum.

Mills, J., Clark, M. S., Ford, T., & Johnson, M. (2004). Measuring communal strength. *Personal Relationships, 11*, 213-230.

Nadler, A. (1998). Relationship, esteem, and achievement perspectives on autonomous and dependent help seeking. In S. A. Karabenick (Ed.), *Strategic help seeking: Implications for learning and teaching* (pp. 61-93). Mahwah, NJ: Erlbaum.

Nelson-Le Gall, S. (1981). Help seeking: An understudied problem-solving skill in children. *Developmental Review, 1*, 224-246.

Nelson-Le Gall, S. (1985). Help seeking behavior in learning. *Review of research in education* (Vol. 12, pp. 55-90). Washington, DC: American Educational Research Association.

Nelson-Le Gall, S. (1987). Necessary and unnecessary help-seeking in children. *Journal of Genetic Psychology, 148*, 53-62.

Nelson-Le Gall, S., Gumerman, R. A., & Scott-Jones, D. (1983). Instrumental help-seeking and everyday problem-solving: A developmental perspective. In B. DePaulo, A. Nadler, & J. Fisher (Eds.), *New directions in helping: Help seeking* (Vol. 2, pp. 265-284). New York: Academic.

Nelson-Le Gall, S., & Resnick, L. (1998). Help seeking, achievement motivation, and the social practice of intelligence in school. In S. A. Karabenick (Ed.), *Strategic help seeking: Implications for learning and teaching* (pp. 39-60). Hillsdale, NJ: Erlbaum.

Newman, R. S. (1990). Children's help-seeking in the classroom: The role of motivational factors and attitudes. *Journal of Educational Psychology, 82*, 71-80.

Newman, R. S. (1998a). Adaptive help seeking: A role of social interaction in self-regulated learning. In S. A. Karabenick (Ed.), *Strategic help seeking: Implications for learning and teaching* (pp. 13-37). Mahwah, NJ: Erlbaum.

Newman, R. S. (1998b). Students' help seeking during problem solving: Influences of personal and contextual achievement goals. *Journal of Educational Psychology, 90*, 644-658.

Newman, R. S. (2000). Social influences on the development of children's adaptive help seeking: The role of parents, teachers, and peers. *Developmental Review, 20*, 350-404.

Newman, R. S. (2002). What do I need to do to succeed...when I don't understand what I'm doing!?: Developmental influences on students' adaptive help seeking. In A. Wigfield & J. Eccles (Eds.), *Development of achievement motivation* (pp. 285-306). San Diego, CA: Academic.

Newman, R. S. (2006). Students' adaptive and nonadaptive help seeking in the classroom: Implications for the context of peer harassment. In S. A. Karabenick & R. S. Newman (Eds.), *Help seeking in academic setting: Goals, groups, and contexts* (pp. 225-258). Mahwah, NJ: Erlbaum.

Newman, R. S. (2007). The motivational role of adaptive help seeking in self-regulated learning. In D. Schunk & B. Zimmerman (Eds.), *Motivation and self-regulated learning: Theory, research, and application* (pp. 315-337). Mahwah, NJ: Erlbaum.

Newman, R. S. (2008). Adaptive and non-adaptive help seeking with peer harassment: An integrative perspective of coping and self-regulation. *Educational Psychologist, 43*, 1-15.

Newman, R. S., & Murray, B. J. (2005) How students and teachers view the seriousness of peer harassment: When is it appropriate to seek help? *Journal of Educational Psychology, 97*, 347-365.

Newman, R. S., Murray, B., & Lussier, C. (2001). Confrontation with aggressive peers at school: Students' reluctance to seek help from the teacher. *Journal of Educational Psychology, 93*, 398-410.

Newman, R. S., & Sanchez, V. (2007, April). *Coping with peer harassment: Teachers' sensitivity to elementary-school students' requests for help.* Paper presented at the Annual Meeting of American Educational Research Association, Chicago, Illinois.

Nicholls, J. G., & Miller, A. (1984). Reasoning about the ability of self and others: A developmental study. *Child Development, 55*, 1990-1999.

Niemivirta, M. (2002). Individual differences and developmental trends in motivation: Integrating person-centered and variable-centered methods. In P. R. Pintrich & M. L. Maehr (Eds.), *Advances in motivation and achievement: New directions in measures and methods* (Vol. 12, pp. 241-275). Amsterdam: Elsevier.

Nisbett, R. (2003). *The geography of thought.* New York: Simon & Schuster.

Pintrich, P. R. (2000). An achievement goal theory perspective on issues in motivation terminology, theory, and research. *Contemporary Educational Psychology, 25*, 92-104.

Pintrich, P. R., & Zusho, A. (2002). Student motivation and self-regulated learning in the college classroom. In J. C. Smart & W. G. Tierney (Eds.), *Higher education: Handbook of theory and research* (Vol. XVII, pp. 731-810). New York: Agathon.

Roll, I., Aleven, V., McLaren, B., & Koedinger, K. (2007, August). *Modeling and tutoring help seeking with a cognitive tutor.* Paper presented at the Biennial Meeting of the European Association for Research on Learning and Instruction, Budapest, Hungary.

Ruble, D. N., & Frey, K. S. (1991). Changing patterns of comparative behavior as skills are acquired: A functional model of self-evaluation. In J. Suls & T. A. Wills (Eds.), *Social comparison: Contemporary theory and research* (pp. 79-113). Hillsdale, NJ: Erlbaum.

Ryan, A. M., Gheen, M., & Midgley, C. (1998). Why do some students avoid asking for help? An examination of the interplay among students' academic efficacy, teachers' social-emotional role, and classroom goal structure. *Journal of Educational Psychology, 90*, 528-535.

Ryan, A. M., Hicks, L., & Midgley, C. (1997). Social goals, academic goals, and avoiding help in the classroom. *Journal of Early Adolescence, 17*, 152-171.

Ryan, A. M., Patrick, H., & Shim, S. O. (2005). Differential profiles of students identified by their teacher as having avoidant, appropriate or dependent help-seeking tendencies in the classroom. *Journal of Educational Psychology, 97*, 275-285.

Ryan, A. M., & Pintrich, P. R. (1997). "Should I ask for help?" The role of motivation and attitudes in adolescents' help seeking in math class. *Journal of Educational Psychology, 89*, 329-341.

Ryan, A. M., & Pintrich, P. R. (1998). Achievement and social motivational influences on help seeking in the classroom. In S. A. Karabenick (Ed.), *Strategic help seeking: Implications for learning and teaching* (pp. 117-139). Mahwah, NJ: Erlbaum.

Ryan, A. M., Pintrich, P. R., & Midgley, C. (2001). Avoiding help seeking in the classroom: Who and why? *Educational Psychology Review, 13*, 93-114.

Sandoval, B. A., & Lee, F. (2006). When is seeking help appropriate? How norms affect help seeking in organizations. In S. A. Karabenick & R. S. Newman (Eds.), *Help seeking in academic settings: Groups, goals, and contexts* (pp. 151-173). Mahwah, NJ: Erlbaum.

Schofield, J. W. (1995). *Computers and classroom culture.* Cambridge, MA: Cambridge University Press.

Sears, R. R., Maccoby, E. E., & Levin, H. (1957). *Patterns of child rearing.* Oxford, England: Row, Peterson.

Shwalb, D. W., & Sukemune, S. (1998). Help seeking in the Japanese college classroom: Cultural, developmental, and social-psychological influences. In S. A. Karabenick (Ed.), *Strategic help seeking: Implications for learning and teaching* (pp. 141-170). Mahwah, NJ: Erlbaum.

Shapiro, E. G. (1983). Embarrassment and help seeking. In B. M. DePaulo, A. Nadler, & J. D. Fisher (Eds.), *New directions in helping: Help Seeking* (Vol. 2, pp. 143–163). New York: Academic.

Skaalvik, S., & Skaalvik, E. M. (2005). Self-concept, motivational orientation and help-seeking behavior in mathematics: A study of adults returning to high school. *Social Psychology of Education, 8*, 285-302.

Skinner, E., & Zimmer-Gembeck, M. (2007). The development of coping. *Annual Review of Psychology, 58*, 119-144.

Stipek, D., Salmon, J. M., Givvin, K. B., Kazemi, E., Saxe, G., & MacGyvers, V. L. (1998). The value (and convergence) of practices suggested by motivation research and promoted by mathematics education reformers. *Journal for Research in Mathematics Education, 29*, 465-488.

Triandis, H. (1994). Theoretical and methodological approaches to the study of collectivism and individualism. In U. Kim, H. Triandis, C. Kagitcibasi, S.-C. Choi, & G. Yoon (Eds.), *Individualism and collectivism: Theory, method and applications: Cross-cultural research and methodology series* (pp. 41-51). Thousand Oaks, CA: Sage.

Turner, J. C., Midgley, C., Meyer, D. K., Gheen, M., Anderman, E. M., Kang, Y., & Patrick, H. (2002). The classroom environment and students' reports of avoidance strategies in mathematics: A multimethod study. *Journal of Educational Psychology*, 94, 88-106.

Urdan, T., Ryan, A. M., Anderman, E. M., & Gheen, M. H. (2002). Goals, goal structures, and avoidance behaviors. In C. Midgley (Ed.), *Goals, goal structures, and patterns of adaptive learning* (pp. 55-84). Mahwah, NJ: Erlbaum.

Vallacher, R. R., & Wegner, D. M. (1987). What do people think they're doing? Action identification and human behavior. *Psychological Review, 94*, 3-15.

Volet, S. E., & Ang, G. (1998). Culturally mixed groups on international campuses: An opportunity for intercultural learning. *Higher Education Research & Development, 17*, 5-23.

Volet, S., & Karabenick, S. A. (2006). Help seeking in cultural context. In S. A. Karabenick & R. S. Newman (Eds.), *Help seeking in academic settings: Groups, goals, and contexts* (pp. 117-150). Mahwah, NJ: Erlbaum.

Vygotsky, L. S. (1978). *Mind in society. The development of higher psychological processes*. Cambridge, MA: Harvard University Press.

Webb, N. M., Ing, M., Kersting, N., & Nemer, K. M. (2006). Help seeking in cooperative learning groups. In S. A. Karabenick & R. S. Newman (Eds.), *Help seeking in academic settings: Goals, groups, and contexts* (pp. 65-121). Mahwah, NJ: Erlbaum.

Webb, N. M., & Palincsar, A. S. (1996). Group processes in the classroom. In D.C. Berliner & R. C. Calfee (Eds.), *Handbook of educational psychology* (pp. 841-873). New York: Simon and Schuster Macmillan.

Wood, T., Cobb, P., & Yackel. E. (1991). Change in teaching mathematics: A case study. *American Educational Research Journal, 28*, 587-616.

Winterbottom, M. R. (1958). The relation of need for achievement to learning experiences in independence and mastery. In J. W. Atkinson (Ed.), *Motives in fantasy, action, and society* (pp. 453-478.). New York: Van Nostrand.

Yudelson, M., Medvedeva, O., Legowski, E., Castine, M., Jukic, D., & Crowley, R. S. (2006, December). *Mining student learning data to develop high level pedagogic strategy in a medical ITS.* Paper presented at the Workshop on Educational Data Mining at The Twenty-First National Conference on Artificial Intelligence (AAAI 2006), Boston, Massachusetts.

Zimmerman, B. J., & Martinez-Pons, M. (1990). Student differences in self-regulated learning: Relating grade, sex, and giftedness to self-efficacy and strategy use. *Journal of Educational Psychology, 82*, 51-59.

Zusho, A., Karabenick, S. A., Bonney, C. R., & Sims, B. C. (2007). Contextual determinants of motivation and help seeking in the college classroom. In R. P. Perry & J. C. Smart (Eds.), *The scholarship of teaching and learning in higher education: An evidence-based perspective* (pp. 611-659). Dordrecht, The Netherlands: Springer.

A Framework for Personal Content Goals in Collaborative Learning Contexts

Marold Wosnitza & Simone Volet

Personal goals as representing direction and meaning for individual behavior and conceptualised as *achievement goal orientation* (e.g. Ames, 1992; Dweck, 1986; Pintrich, 2000) or *content goals* (Ford & Nichols, 1991; Pintrich, 2000; Wentzel, 1994) have been central concepts in research on motivation in learning contexts for several decades. In the last 20 years, however, personal goals have evolved from a relatively stable notion of global direction to a more, specific, situated and dynamic construction. Part of the argument for this shift, is the view that the explanatory power of goals would be improved if they were considered as an integral part of the learning process. This development has been particularly useful for understanding the significance of goals in real-life learning situations because it goes beyond an emphasis on individual achievement goal orientations. In this chapter, we focus on *personal content goals* generated in collaborative learning contexts. We discuss their complex nature and characteristics and present a conceptual framework that integrates several ideas related to goals in such environments. This approach is consistent with the overall shift towards more situated and local perspectives on personal content goals. Data from three studies are presented to support the conceptual usefulness of the framework.

Our framework for personal content goals in collaborative learning contexts is based on two theoretical traditions related to immediate goals (Anderman, 1999) in learning and motivation. It builds upon achievement goal orientation research, which has identified two types of achievement goals, performance and mastery, and their further development into a multiple goal approach that distinguishes furthermore between approach and avoidance dimensions (Elliott, 1999; Pintrich, 2000). It also incorporates recent work grounded in a broader perspective on multiple and more holistic goals. Boekaerts (2002), for example, claimed that academic goals could only be understood in interaction with socio-emotional goals that emerge in real-life learning situations. This perspective recognises the range of personal, academic and non-academic goals (e.g., social, well-being) that individuals can pursue concurrently and dynamically in real-life learning situations (Boekaerts, 2002; Boekaerts, de Koning & Veder, 2006; Ford & Nichols, 1991; Harackiewicz, Barron, Pintrich, Elliot & Trash, 2002; Harackiewicz & Linnenbrink, 2005; Roeser, 2004; Wentzel, 1991).

Research on personal content goals and achievement goal orientations emerging in collaborative learning contexts is still limited. Overall, these goal concepts have mainly been investigated in the context of individual self-directed learning tasks and classroom learning situations. On the grounds that collaborative learning creates some interdependence between participants, it is reasonable to expect that personal content goals would reflect the social context in which they are embedded and which they constitute. In order to study goals in collaborative learning settings, a more comprehensive conceptual approach is required. The aim of this chapter is to discuss a conceptual framework for personal content goals in collaborative learning contexts that integrates prior research on the origin of action, goal orientation, and multiple goals with several theoretical ideas emerging from research related to social forms of learning and contextual dimensions and influences.

Definition and Function of Personal Content Goals

The proposed focus on personal content goals to explain the source of actions can be traced back to Flavell''s definition of goals as "the tacit or explicit objectives that instigate and maintain the cognitive enterprise" (1981, p. 40). Yet while the directive and driving function of goals to steer and give meaning to self-regulating processes is well recognised and documented (e.g. Boekaerts, 2002; Boekaerts, de Koning, & Vedder, 2006; Ford, 1992; Ford & Nichols, 1991; Lawrence & Volet, 1991), their monitoring and evaluative function has generally received less attention (Lawrence & Volet, 1991). Lawrence and Volet (1991) argued that the sources of goals can be within the self or the environment and, furthermore, that goals can be oriented towards the self or the task. This distinction has received little attention in empirical research on goals. Only relatively recently has research started to examine how students simultaneously pursue multiple goals and the importance of considering students' perceptions of their personal goal achievement (Karoly, Boekaerts, & Maes, 2005; Lemos, 1999). Finally, most of the empirical research on personal goals has been framed in terms of students' learning on their own within a classroom learning situation. The nature of students' goals in learning environments that are explicitly designed for social forms of learning, however, has received less attention. A more complete and global perspective, therefore, would be a conceptual framework capable of incorporating multiple personal content goals as well as their direction within social, and in particular collaborative, learning settings.

Multiple Goals

Following Boekaerts, Ford, Harackiewicz, Pintrich, Wentzel, and colleagues, we argue that individuals can pursue several goals concurrently within a collaborative learning activity and that different configurations of personal content goals can be identified. As discussed by many researchers, some personal content goals may not focus on achievement, such as learning and performance, but refer to well-being or social strivings. Another approach is Ford and colleagues' (Ford, 1992; Ford & Nichols, 1991) comprehensive taxonomy of personal human goals, grounded in developmental theory. They describe a range of possible personal content goals, organised at the most abstract level into two broad categories, namely goals representing desirable outcomes within the individual and alternatively, goals representing desirable outcomes with respect to the relationship between people and their environment. Ford (1992), Wentzel (1991, 1994, 1996) and Boekaerts (2002; Boekaerts, de Koning, & Vedder, 2005) claimed that individual behaviour is often guided by multiple personal content goals simultaneously, and the more goals that can be achieved by the same action, the higher the level of motivation to achieve these goals. The notion of multiple personal content goals naturally leads to the notion of individual configurations of goals and possibly a hierarchy of goals in real-life situations, as suggested by Carver and Scheier (2000). Measuring how multiple personal content goals not only inter-relate and acquire or lose saliency during an activity but ultimately affect behaviour is challenging.

The notion of the multiplicity of goals has attracted even less attention in research on collaborative learning. Recent work by Boekaerts and colleagues, however, has investigated the goal preferences of students from different ethno-cultural backgrounds and whether such differences had an impact on their perception of the quality of collaborative learning (Boekaerts & Hijzen, 2007; Hijzen, Boekaerts, & Vedder, 2006). For example, in one study they compared the goal preferences of students in more effective versus less effective collaborative learning teams. Their mixed methods investigations of goal preferences and goal profiles across diverse contexts have provided empirical support for a multiple goal perspective. Our own empirical work related to multiple goals has adopted a different approach. Instead of investigating multiple goals as an outcome (or dependent variable) in specific situations or in particular groups, we have examined how different configurations of goals, or goal profiles generated in particular situations, provide the driving force for subsequent regulatory processes. This conceptualisation will be further discussed in combination with the direction of goals.

Direction of Goals

The second proposed characteristic of personal content goals in collaborative learning contexts is direction. The idea is that goals in such contexts can be predominantly directed towards oneself or may include others; in other words, goals can be directed at achieving desired outcomes for the self or, alternatively, outcomes for others or the whole group. A dominant self or social direction is assumed to reflect the social identity of the individual, in Markus and Kitayama's (1991) sense of representing an independent or interdependent construal of the self, although intra-individual differences that reflect context sensitivity are also expected. Our conceptualisation of social direction in goals is distinct from the notion of social goals found in the literature (e.g. Boekaerts, 2002; Lemos, 1999; Dowson & McInerney, 2003). While social goals, like achievement goals refer to the content of personal goals, our proposal is that any personal content goal can display a social direction. Goals with a social direction are assumed to be particularly salient in collaborative learning activities. These can be found, for example, when an individual's goals seem to be confounded with the group's goals, suggesting an underlying assumption that the group operates with a single social identity. This would be illustrated in a situation in which an individual's stated goal implies that all peers share the same goal and are engaged in genuine shared regulation (e.g., Vauras, Iiskala, Kajamies, Kinnunen, & Lehtinen, 2003). In self-report data, for example, indicators of a social direction may include the use of collective terms such as "we", "us" or "our".

Alternatively, personal content goals can reflect social instrumental or social altruistic directions. As argued in relation to emotions in social online learning (Wosnitza & Volet, 2005), we propose that in collaborative learning situations, some goals with a self-direction may reflect expectations that the group can be instrumental in achieving self-endeavours. Examples would be a student wanting to become more confident with the support of the group or wanting to ensure that the group works effectively so *they* are not penalised by getting a lower mark. Both examples represent goals with a self-direction, with the group being seen as the means for their achievement. Conversely, some content goals with a social direction may not represent the symbiosis of personal and group goals but refer to personal goals aimed at benefiting others (Anderman, 1999). Examples of such altruistic orientations would be individuals' determination to contribute the best they can to the group effort, or to help any peer who needs assistance during the group activity. Both examples represent goals with a social direction, where the self is instrumental to their achievement.

Consistent with Boekaerts' view that individuals' cognitions and dispositions are sensitive to salient aspects of local learning contexts, it is argued that social identity can be influenced by salient local conditions and thus display context-sensitive adaptations. In the case of social learning contexts, and keeping in mind that students can pursue multiple goals simultaneously, one could imagine a student with a dominant interdependent self-construal and typically socially directed goals, who adopts some goals reflecting a self-direction. This may happen, for example, if their peers' goals are perceived as incompatible with their own values and priorities. Reciprocally, a student with a dominant independent self-construal and typically self-directed goals may endorse goals with a social direction if they experience genuinely shared aspirations with their group members.

Combining Multiple Goals with Directions of Goals

Table 1 integrates the two characteristics of personal content goals in social learning contexts: multiple goals and directions of goals, within a two-dimensional matrix. *Reading across columns* (right hand side) is the notion of multiple goals, represented here by three broad types of personal content goals that can be generated before and during a collaborative learning activity, namely, *performance, learning* and *well-being*. As mentioned above, researchers like Boekaerts (2002), Dowson and McInerney (2003), and Lemos (1999), have included social goals as a separate goal category to refer to a disparate range of personal social endeavours, for example, making new friends, enjoying each other's company, developing a social network or, more broadly, serving the community that supports them. Following Anderman's (1999) idea that academic and social goals can interact, the latter were incorporated within the three categories of personal content goals (performance, learning, well-being) in our own research. This made it possible to make the social dimension of goals a key component of the whole conceptual framework. This position is based on the assumption that personal content goals are located within the collaborative learning context, and must therefore take into consideration the social nature of the environment.

Performance goals can refer to the completion of a group learning activity, with a focus on the outcome or the process. In regard to outcome, the goal could be simply to complete the activity, or, alternatively, to strive for the highest possible mark. In regard to process, the goal could be to try to have minimal work to do or, alternatively, for the group to work effectively as a team. In contrast, *learning goals* refer to skills, knowledge and understanding that could be developed from participating in a group learning activity. Finally, *well-being goals* refer to emotional or affective aspects of participating in a group learning activity, for example, a goal to be accepted in the group, or peers not being upset, or for the group learning experience to be enjoyable.

Table 1. Matrix combining multiple content goals and direction of goals in collaborative learning contexts.

Directions of goals	Role of self & others	Multiple goals		
		Performance	Learning	Well-being
Self-direction	**Self** Dominant	A	B	C
	Self using Others for own benefits	D	E	F
Social direction	**Others** benefiting from Self	G	H	I
	Others & Self confounded (single entity)	J	K	L

Reading down the rows is the notion of direction of goals. The top two rows represent personal content goals with a predominant self-direction and the bottom two rows goals with a predominantly social direction. At the very top (first row), goals that are conceived as mainly self-directed (although the social environment is always present) are represented, for example, a personal drive to get the highest possible mark (cell A, performance), or to better understand the material (cell B, learning), or to enjoy the group experience (cell C, well-being). Goals with a dominant self-direction are typically those found in the existing literature on personal and achievement goals (e.g. Ames, 1992; Elliot, 1999; Ford & Nichols, 1991; Wentzel, 1991). Given the focus on social learning contexts, our conceptual framework includes a second type of self-directed goals. Unlike those represented in the first row, the goals represented in the second row take into account the presence of others, and they display an intention or expectation to use others to gain personal benefits; thus the self-direction. For example, a student may generate a goal of getting a better mark because of the group (cell D, performance), or of learning a lot from others (cell E, learning), or that peers will accept them (cell F, well-being). The bottom two rows represent goals with a social direction. Like those represented in the second row, the goals represented in the third row also take into account the presence of others, but this time, they represent the·pursuit of goals that will benefit others. For example, a student may express a commitment to contribute the best they can and to not let the group down (cell G, performance), or that peers will be able to learn from them (cell H, learning), or that they will not do anything that may upset others (cell I, well-being). Mentions of altruistic types of goals are not common in the existing literature (Anderman, 1999), yet some students are forthcoming in wanting to take personal responsibility and display pro-social orientations in collaborative learning activities (e.g., Volet & Mansfield, 2006).

The bottom row in the framework represents personal content goals, which suggest that the group is operating as a team, with the self and others confounded as a single social entity. This would be the case when a person spontaneously refers to personal goals as group goals; for example, that the group gets the highest possible mark (cell J, performance), or that 'we' all learn from each other (cell K, learning), or that 'our' group develops a good learning atmosphere (cell L, well-being). The notion of shared goals has not been given much attention in the educational psychology literature on goals, but has emerged in recent work on collaborative learning and self-regulation of learning (Järvelä, Häkkinen, Arvaja, & Leinonen, 2003; Vauras et al., 2003).

In combination, these two characteristics of personal content goals in collaborative learning contexts, multiple goals and goal direction, generate twelve distinctive types of goals that reflect different foci and different roles given to oneself and others. From the literature, it is clear that goals with a self-direction have been over-represented, while those with a social direction have received minimal attention. In the following section, we present results from several studies using the propose goal matrix as the conceptual framework.

Empirical Support

Study 1: Establishing the Conceptual Relevance of the Framework in Spontaneously Expressed Goals

We have investigated the conceptual relevance of the framework to represent the range of goals spontaneously expressed by students in social learning environments. Examples from two studies (1a and 1b) are used to illustrate these different types of goals in real life group work activities at university. Both studies elicited students' personal content goals for a group project that was carried out in the students' own time and over a period of several weeks. A significant feature of both studies was the fact that the outcome of the project resulted in a group mark which contributed to each student's Grade Point Average. The survey question eliciting students' goals for the group project was open-ended and thus allowed expressions of single or multiple goals. All goals were double-coded based on the framework. Inter-judge agreement was acceptable (over 75%) across all the data.

Study 1a was conducted in Germany with 44 information technology students enrolled in a third-year unit on web design. The group project required them to work in small groups of 4-5 students on the development of a website for an existing company. The students had to present the outcome of their project to the company and their teacher at the end of the unit. The group mark was based on the quality of the final product. In this study, goals were elicited only at the beginning of the project.

For most of the students (83%), performance was one of their main goals (get a good mark, pass the assignment, etc.). Some performance goals, however, included several components, for example, "My main goals are to adhere to the timetable (cell A, cf. table 1), to finish the assignment (cell A) and to get a good final grade (cell A)". A majority of the students (65%) reported multiple goals, which typically combined performance and learning goals, but also well-being. As with performance, learning goals could contain several aspects, for example, "My main goals are to learn something new (cell B), get to know new fields within the scopes of our studies (cell, B), deepen old familiar fields of our studies (cell B), improve my ability to work in groups (cell, B) and achieve good grades (cell, A)" or "My main goals are to personally get a further education through new knowledge (cell, B) and exchanging ideas with the other group members (cell K)". A few students also included well-being goals as their main goals, for example, "My main goals are to achieve the task (cell A), to take pleasure in the work (cell C) and have a good atmosphere in the group (cell L)" or "My main goals are to gain practical experience and new competencies (cell B) and to develop a good cooperation within the group (cell J)". As illustrated in the examples above, some goals had a predominant self-direction and others a social direction that combined others and self. In this study, we did not find expressions of goals with a social instrumental or social altruistic direction.

Study 1b was carried out in Australia with 81 second-year students enrolled in a physiology unit part of a highly competitive and demanding veterinary sciences programme. The students had to work in groups of six on an authentic clinical case that was quite challenging due to their limited prior knowledge and clinical experience. Their task was to generate several group learning objectives based on the case, to try to achieve them and to present their findings to the class at the end. As with the IT students, the group mark was based on the final product, the presentation. In the study with veterinary students, goals were elicited both at the beginning and the end of the group activity.

Not surprisingly, given the perceived difficulty of the task and the competitive and academically demanding nature of the veterinary programme as a whole, there was a predominance of self-directed goals (performance, learning or well-being), though more so at the beginning (97%) than at the end (83%). The types of self-directed goals focusing on performance (cell A), learning (cell B), and well-being (cell C) tended to be similar in nature to those expressed by the IT students in Germany. Whereas performance goals were typically generic and related to achievement and marks, learning goals typically focused on specific aspects of the task and what could be learned from it. In the study with veterinary students, however, some self-directed goals reflected intentions to use others for own benefits (cell E), though this was found only in regard to learning goals, for example, "to gain knowledge by working in a group that I wouldn't have gained independently" or "work as a team member and be able to identify my weaknesses". As with the IT students, there were no performance or well-being goals with a social instrumental direction, that is, where the self would use others for own benefits, were found. Since all group members were getting the same mark for the group activity, the absence of personal content goals involving using others to achieve a better performance was expected.

The increased proportion of goals with a social direction at the end of the project in the study with veterinary students provided further support for the view that goals are dynamic and can change over the duration of an activity. Many veterinary students were anxious about the group project at the start because it was perceived as too time-consuming given their multiple competing academic demands. At the end, however, the students appeared generally positive about the experience, which was reflected in the higher proportion of their goals with a social direction. The students' goals with a social direction, where others and self are confounded (cells J, K), were similar in nature to those found with the IT students. For example, performance goals with a genuine social direction (cell J) typically referred to group achievement, for example, "making sure group achieved goals" or "work as a group and to make a presentable presentation", whereas learning goals with a genuine social direction (cell K) reflected the importance of socially shared learning processes: "teach others what we have found out for ourselves from our own research" or "we all learnt from what the others had researched". Examples of goals where others benefited from the self (cell G) also were found, for example, "work as a team member" or "being able to work effectively in a group, being beneficial to every member". As in the study with IT students, there was no evidence of well-being and learning goals with a social direction where others benefited from the self (cells H, I), nor of performance and well-being goals with a self-direction where the self used others for own benefits (cells D, F).

Overall, the goals related to well-being appeared to be dichotomous in nature and reflected either a focus on the individual and concerns for personal well-being (cell C) or, alternatively, a focus on the team and development of a positive group atmosphere (cell L). Furthermore, and as could be expected in a formal learning environment, well-being goals always appeared along with another goal, typically learning, occasionally performance, sometimes both. The presence of well-being goals systematically appearing along with other goals appears to reflect the instructional purpose of the group learning activities, that is, for students to learn and to perform well. Yet well-being goals can be equally important, sometimes even more important. This could be the case for students who feel that personal well-being and a team atmosphere are indispensable to achieve the main learning objectives. This raises the critical issue of the context in which goals are generated.

Study 2: Examining the Context-Sensitive Nature of Multiple Goals and Goal Direction in an Unpopular Unit

A second study examined the assumption that immediate personal content goals are context-sensitive and can change over the duration of an activity. More specifically, it explored the context-sensitivity of different types of goals and goal direction. The study was carried out in Germany with 98 fourth-year education students enrolled in a research method unit that had been unpopular among students for a number of years given the perception that the content of the unit was not directly relevant to classroom practice. In that unit, students were required to work together in groups of 4-5 over a 12-week period and to work on six successive small tasks, each taking two weeks. These involved, for example, discussing the results of educational research studies or conducting a small empirical study themselves and discussing challenges related to methodology, data collection, and data analysis. Unlike the veterinary students and the IT students in Study 1, these education students did not receive a numerical mark for their work. They simply had to submit their group outcomes every two weeks, and their assignments were assessed on a "pass" or "revise" basis. In order to pass the unit, a student had to be a member of a group that obtained a "pass" for all six assignments.

This unit was perceived as suitable for an examination of the context-sensitivity of goals for two reasons. First, it was expected that in such a challenging unit, students' goals would be more likely to change over time. Second, since the students had to undertake several tasks with their group of peers, it was expected that a greater proportion of goals with a social direction may emerge over time, due to students having to cope as a group in order to pass the unit.

In this study, the data were collected in a questionnaire form both at the beginning and the end of the unit. On both occasions, the students were presented with a list of 12 goal statements and were asked to select their two main goals for the unit. Each goal represented one cell of the conceptual framework (e.g., A-self-performance, "My main goal is it to achieve the best possible result"). Table 2 shows the distribution of goals selected at the beginning (t1) and the end (t2) of the unit.

Table 2. Study 2: Distribution of goal nominations for Education students.

	Role of self & others	**Multiple goals**				
		Performance	Learning	Well-being		
self-direction	**Self** Dominant	A T1: 19.3% T2: 26.9%	B T1: 4.5% T2: 1.2%	C T1: 5.7% T2: 4.2%	T1: 29.5% T2: 32.3%	T1: 40.3% T2: 44.3%
	Self using Others for own benefits	D T1: 9.6% T2: 10.2%	E T1: 0.6% T2: 0.6%	F T1: 0.6% T2: 1.2%	T1: 10.8% T2: 12.0%	
social direction	**Others** benefiting from Self	G T1: 13.6% T2: 18.0%	H T1: ------- T2: 1.2%	I T1: 0.6% T2: 3.0%	T1: 14.2% T2: 22.2%	T1: 59.7% T2: 55.7%
	Others & Self confounded (single entity)	J T1: 25.0% T2: 23.9%	K T1: 2.3% T2: 2.4%	L T1: 18.2% T2: 7.2%	T1: 45.5% T2: 33.5%	
		T1: 67.5% T2: 79.0%	T1: 7.4% T2: 5.4%	T1: 25.1% T2: 15.6%	100%	

Reading across columns shows that students overwhelmingly selected performance goals. This was the case at both the beginning and the end. At the end nearly 80% of all goals selected by the students were performance-related. Only a small proportion of students selected a learning goal either at the beginning or at the end. Furthermore, and unlike Study 1 that was based on students' spontaneous goals, well-being goals appeared more important than learning goals, with about 25% at the beginning and 16% at the end.

The dominance of performance goals and minimal commitment to learning goals could be interpreted in light of the students' negative appraisals of that unit. As mentioned earlier, that unit was unpopular and mandatory, which students perceived as irrelevant preparation for their future profession (Stark & Mandl, 2000). "Grit your teeth and get it over with" was very often the students' motto. The data reflected these perceptions: High proportion of performance goals, low proportion of learning goals and some well-being goals. The decrease in well-being goals in favour of performance goals at the end of the unit may have been caused by some problems related to group dynamics. These were mentioned in the final evaluation of the unit by the university administration.

Reading down the columns shows the dominance of goals with a social direction both at the beginning (59.7%) and the end of the unit (55.7%). Furthermore, a comparison between the top two rows reveals that goals with a dominant self-direction (t1: 29.5%, t2: 32.3%) were chosen nearly three times as often as goals focusing on "self using others for own benefits" (t1: 10.8%, t2: 12.0%), a ratio that was consistent across the two measurement points. In regard to socially directed goals, goals referring to "others and self as a single entity" predominated. At the first measurement point, there were more than three times as many selections of this type of goal (t1: 45.5%) than goals focusing on "others benefiting from self" (t1: 14.2%). The preference for goals focusing on "self and others as a single entity" did not change between the two measurement points. What changed over time was the ratio, which increased from 1 to 3 to 2 to 3. This was due to the fact that, at the second measurement point, goals with a social direction referring to "others benefiting from self" increased (from 14.2% to 22.2%) while goals focusing on "self and others as a single entity" had decreased (from 45.5% to 33.3%).

The higher proportion of goals with a social direction in this study compared with Study 1 can be explained in relation to the nature of the unit, including its unpopular nature, the succession of tasks and the interdependence of group members with regard to passing the unit. As mentioned above, students had to submit all their assignments as a group, and in order to pass the unit a student had to be a member of a group of which all six assignments were assessed as passed. It is possible that the interdependency of group members contributed to students seeing themselves as part of a group, hence the strong social direction in their goals. The change over time could also reflect the students' growing awareness that if some peers needed help because they were not willing or able to participate in the assignments, then the students' had to do something about it. Furthermore, the finding that 10% (beginning) and 20% (end) of the students' selected goals directed at benefiting others contrasts sharply with Study 1 where hardly any such goals were found. Two explanations can be proposed. One is based on the nature of the specific group learning situation. Another may be the fact that the participants in this study were teacher education students who were preparing themselves for a profession directed towards helping others. In any case, this study supported the assumption of context-sensitivity of goals, and, in particular, the conceptual usefulness of distinguishing between goals with a self- and a social direction.

Study 3: Identifying Meaningful Groups of Students Based on Individual Goal Profiles

The purpose of the third study was to establish whether distinct, meaningful groups of students could be identified based on their individual goal profiles. Individual goal profiles were conceptually grounded in the framework of multiple goals and goals with a self- or a social direction. In turn, the meaningfulness of groups was examined using the relationship between students' goals and their appraisals of a particular group assignment.

A total of 313 students enrolled in a veterinary science (26.5 %) or business (73.5 %) undergraduate unit in which they had to carry out a small group project in their own time and over several weeks participated in this third study. The students completed a questionnaire at the beginning and the end of their group activity. As in Study 2, students were presented with a list of 12 goal statements, each representing one cell of the framework. The wording of each goal statement was contextualised to the particular group activity that students had to undertake. At the beginning and the end of the group assignment, students were asked to rate each statement according to the extent to which it represented an important goal for them in that group assignment ('something you will try hard/ tried hard to achieve in the group assignment'). The 4-point Likert scale ranged from 1 = not very important for me to 4 = a top priority for me.

In the analysis of the data, we endorsed Linnenbrink & Pintrich's (2001) suggestion that external or objective aspects of the context needed to be taken into account alongside subjective perceptions. In the present study, students' performance in the group assignment was not assessed individually but as a group, each student receiving the same group mark. Therefore, a distinction between a student's self- and socially directed performance goals for this task would be meaningless. Accordingly, it was decided that the questionnaire items which accessed self- and socially directed performance goals should be treated as forming a single factor (*performance goals*).

Secondly, and based on the results of the first study, it was reasonable to expect that in a formal academic learning situation, well-being goals would not form an independent factor but be associated with learning goals. Well-being and learning goals were therefore combined as a single factor for this investigation. In contrast, the distinction between self- and social direction was expected to be highly relevant, which led to the consideration of two separate constellations of goals, l*earning/well-being goals with a self-direction*, and *learning/well-being goals with a social direction*.

Overall, these context-derived considerations led to three distinct goal constellations in this study.

1. *Performance goals* – a combination of self- and socially focused performance goals (Table 1, cells A, D, G and J)
2. *Learning/well-being goals with a self-direction* (Table 1, cells B, C, E and F)
3. *Learning/well-being goals with a social direction* (Table 1, cells H, I, K and L)

The internal consistency reliabilities for each goal constellation, treated as scales and assessed by Cronbach's alpha, ranged from acceptable (beginning) to good (end). Table 3 displays the Cronbach's alphas, means, and standard deviations for each scale (or goal constellation) on the pre- and post-task questionnaires. As can be seen in the table, all means were above the scale midpoint of 2.5.

Table 3. Study 3: Descriptive statistics and internal consistency reliability coefficients for each goal constellation at the beginning and end of the group assignment.

		Beginning			End		
	N items	α	M	SD	α	M	SD
Performance	4	0.65	3.46	0.19	0.74	3.36	0.16
Learning/Well-being Goals with a self-direction	4	0.69	3.24	0.19	0.75	3.02	0.57
Learning/Well-being Goals with a social direction	4	0.68	3.09	0.91	0.70	2.90	0.19

The examination of meaningful groupings of students based on their individual goal profiles was undertaken using cluster analysis. This was considered a suitable procedure in order to maximise between-group heterogeneity and within-group homogeneity (Fortunato & Goldblatt, 2006; Linnenbrink & Pintrich, 2001). Cluster analysis of the performance goals, learning/well-being goals with a self-direction and learning/well-being with a social direction data from the pre-task questionnaires revealed two clearly distinct groups of students. Cluster 1 (Cl1) comprises 138 students with a lower goal profile, meaning that they scored significantly lower on all three subscales than the students in Cluster 2 (Cl2) (*Performance*: M_{CL1}=3.32, SD_{CL1}=.49, M_{CL2}= 3.57, SD_{CL2}=.39, $F(1, 311)$=24.70, p<.001; *Learning/Well-being-self*: M_{CL1}=2.80, SD_{CL1}=.41, M_{CL2}= 3.59, SD_{CL2}=.28, $F(1, 311)$=388.65, p<.001; *Learning/Well-being-social*: M_{CL1}=2.67, SD_{CL1}=.39, M_{CL2}= 3.42, SD_{CL2}=.35, $F(1, 311)$=312.75, p<.001), though the difference between Clusters 1 and 2 with respect to *Performance* goals was rather small (M_Δ=.25). Cluster 2 consists of 175 students with a higher goal profile – i.e., this cluster scored significantly higher on all three subscales than Cluster 1 (see Figure 1).

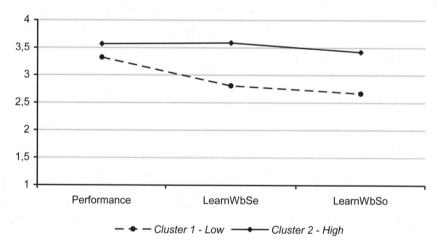

Figure 1. Study 3: Clusters of goal profiles.

Appraisal data were obtained using the contextualised version of the Students' Appraisals of Group Assignments (SAGA) instrument (Volet, 2001a). This instrument was designed to break down the construct of appraisals of group work into distinct aspects on the grounds that this was necessary to do justice to the complexity to such learning activities. Empirical support for distinguishing between various appraisals of group assignments is reported in Volet (2001a). The six SAGA scales measure students' appraisals of, respectively, *the cognitive benefits, motivating influence, group assessment, affect, management and interpersonal aspects of a specific group assignment.*

Data on the three types of goals (performance goals, learning/well-being goals with a social direction, learning/well-being goals with a self-direction) and the six types of appraisals were subjected to a canonical correlation analysis. In order to explore the meaningfulness of the goal clusters based on individuals' goal profiles, this was done separately for each of the two clusters. The results are shown in Figure 2.

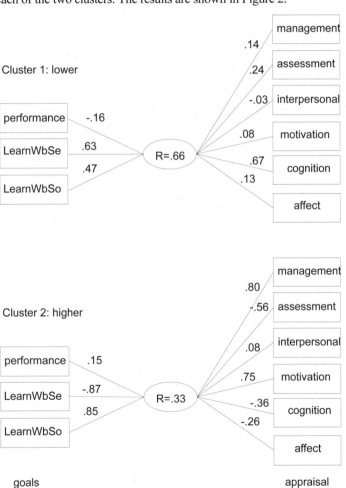

Figure 2. Study 3: Canonical correlational analysis for Clusters 1 and 2.

For Cluster 1 (a group of students with a low goal profile overall), the analysis revealed one significant root (R=.66, X^2=85.34, df=18, p<.001), which explained 43,6% of variance between the two sets. In contrast, for cluster 2 (a group of students with a high goal profile), the analysis also revealed one significant root between the sets, but only with a very low correlation of R=.33 which explained only 11% of variance (X^2=37.64, df=18, p<.001).

For Cluster 1, the resulting weights in the canonical correlation showed that the correlation between the two sets of variables was mainly carried by the variables learning/well-being goals with a self-direction (.63) and learning/well-being goals with a social direction (.47) on the goal side and by the variable cognition (.67) on the appraisal side. This means that for this particular group of students, the higher their learning/well-being goals with a self-direction and their learning/well-being goals with a social direction, the higher their perception of the cognitive benefit of the group assignment.

For Cluster 2, and keeping in mind the low amount of explained variance, the resulting weights in the canonical correlation indicate that the correlation between the two sets of variables are also mainly carried by the variables learning/well-being goals with a self-direction (-.87) and learning/well-being goals with a social direction (.85) on the goal side. In contrast, on the appraisal side, the correlation is carried by the variables management (.80), motivation (.75), and assessment (-.56). Explaining these relationships is more complex due to some correlations being negative and others positive. Overall, this means that the more the learning/well-being goals with a social direction and the less the learning/well-being goals with a self-direction are present, the more management (.80) and motivating influence appraisals (.75) and the less the appraisal of group assessment (-.56) can be found.

A tentative meaning can now be extracted from these analyses. Cluster 1 (see Figure 1) represents a group of students who may want to do well in this group assignment, but their learning/well-being goals (whether self- or socially directed) are only moderately important. Completing the task and getting a good grade is what is most important to them. Learning as much as possible with their peers and enjoying that experience is not their top priority. The relationship between their goals and their anticipation of the cognitive benefits of the group assignment suggests that variation in their goals is associated with variation in their expectations of the instrumental benefit of the group assignment to achieve what they want. Since their learning/well-being goals with a self- and a social direction are relatively low overall, this means that whatever variation exists within that group of students is closely related to their expectation of cognitive benefits. The other appraisals of the group assignment, such as its motivating influence, affect, management, group assessment and interpersonal aspects, do not contribute to explaining the level of their goals.

In contrast, Cluster 2 represents a group of students who may also want to do well in this group assignment, but their learning/well-being goals (both self- and socially directed) are more important to them. Learning as much as possible with their peers and enjoying that experience are important as well. Interestingly, the canonical correlation analyses show that students' learning/well-being goals with a self- and social direction contribute in opposite way to the relationship with their appraisals of the forthcoming group assignment, and, reciprocally, that some appraisals of their group assignments also contribute in opposite ways. Since the overall SAGA instrument represents a single underlying construct (appraisals of group assignments broken down into six different aspects) and, similarly, goals also represent a single underlying construct (intentions to invest energy into a group assignment, broken down into different foci and directions), these findings highlight the importance of breaking down goals and appraisals into a range of components, as these can play out differently with each other. For this group of students, learning/well-being goals with a self- and social direction did not appear to contribute to appraisals in the same way. In fact, each type of goal related to a different appraisal aspect in a different way. More specifically, learning/well-being goals with a self- and social direction did not seem to relate to appraisals of management, motivation and assessment in the same way. Overall, these findings highlight not only the importance of identifying multiple goals, but also the significance of paying attention to goal profiles. In this study, the learning goals of the group of students who displayed relatively low-level goals were affected in a similar way by their perceptions of the cognitive benefits of the forthcoming activity, regardless of whether their learning/well-being goals were self- or socially directed. And this relationship was of significance. In contrast, the self- and socially directed learning/well-being goals of the group of students who displayed relatively high-level goals did not play out with their appraisal processes in a similar way, and, reciprocally, different appraisals did not show consistent patterns of relationship with goals.

The complex patterns of relationship between goals and appraisals for students with high and low overall levels of personal content goals call for more research on the nature and respective role of goals with a particular focus, and, in particular, on the role of goal direction in social learning contexts.

Conclusion

In this chapter, it has been argued that research on personal content goals and goal orientations emerging in collaborative learning settings is still limited and that the specific context of such settings has to be taken into account in order to establish the significance of goals. According to Boekaerts et al. (2006), poor definitions and operationalisations of goal content, as well as a lack of subjective, context-sensitive measures of goals have contributed to limited insight into what drives students' goal-directed behaviours. The framework for personal content goals in collaborative learning contexts presented in this chapter was developed to address this issue. The framework combines the notions of multiplicity and direction of goals into a two-dimensional matrix. Data from several quantitative as well as qualitative oriented studies on university students' personal content goals for specific group activities were provided as support for the conceptual usefulness of the framework.

A unique feature of the framework is the proposal that performance, learning, and well-being goals can all have a self-direction or a social direction, which reflects the underlying interdependence between the learner and the other group members in collaborative learning contexts. An additional proposal is that since personal content goals are assumed to be context-sensitive, their operationalisation in empirical work should reflect that characteristic. Our empirical studies adopted this perspective by combining performance goals with a self- and a social direction as a single type of performance goal when all students received the same mark for a group activity.

Although it is possible for learners participating in a collaborative learning setting to be driven by one single goal, it is more likely that they will display complex profiles of multiple goals. These configurations of goal profiles could be related to at least the following two aspects. The first refers to students' perceptions of the context in which the collaborative learning process takes place, and the strong possibility that they will develop different goal profiles in different contexts. The studies presented in this chapter support the view that studying this relationship requires a multi-level context approach (Gurtner, Monnard, & Genoud, 2001; Volet, 2001b; Wosnitza, 2007). For example, students studying teacher education in Germany have to enrol in a number of subject-matter units (e.g., mathematics and English) alongside their education units. It is reasonable to expect that the goal profiles of these students may be quite different in their subject-matter units and their education units, even if the type of group assignment is similar across units. Furthermore, students' goal profiles could also develop differently depending on the structure of the task (e.g., whether the group product was assessed or not), and this independently of the programme in which the student is enrolled. Finally, students' personal content goal profiles could also vary depending on their small group membership, with different group compositions yielding different goal profiles. The second aspect is the personal background that students bring to a specific social learning environment. Study 3 revealed that individuals' prior experience, overall view of group work, as well as appraisals of the forthcoming group activity all contributed to the generation of qualitatively different goal profiles for the same collaborative learning activity. Students with negative appraisals of the cognitive benefits of their forthcoming collaborative learning task tended to display a more self-directed goal profile, whereas students with more positive perceptions of the same activity tended to display a more socially directed goal profile. A related aspect at the individual level is the notion of a hierarchy of goals (Anderman, 1999; Boekaerts, 2002; Carver & Scheier, 2000). The focus of our framework was on the immediate goals pursued by students in actual collaborative learning activities, and did not incorporate higher-order goals. Future research may also examine how immediate goals with self- and social direction may be instrumental to each other within a hierarchical perspective.

Another issue, only partially addressed in this chapter, is the dynamic nature of personal content goals. The importance of this issue was highlighted in the re-adjustments of goals over the duration of a group activity. Changes in goals appeared to be related to perceived changes in the context, as indicated by consistently high correlations between goals and appraisals on both occasions. One could expect that the dynamic nature of goals would be most obvious in a small group, where social dynamics are expected to be emotionally salient, and the consequence for students' commitment more immediate. For example, if a student approaches a collaborative learning environment with a socially dominated goal profile and joins a group of students mainly interested in their individual advancement, there is strong likelihood that this student will change his or her personal content goals for this particular group assignment. However, this may not necessarily affect other upcoming group assignments. In contrast, if that student accumulates negative experiences in several group assignments with different group members, it is most likely that his or her goals for future group assignments will change as a result. These issues are highly relevant for educators and will need to be examined in future research. Overall, this chapter provides further support for the view that goals represent a highly complex construct. The proposed framework for personal content goals in collaborative learning contexts, and the empirical studies that support the usefulness of the two underlying dimensions, extend our understanding of the significance of goals in learning environments. This research also highlights the value of using multiple research methodologies, where traditional surveys involving multi-level designs, group-centred and learner-centred analysis can be combined with repeated experience sampling, learning journals, and small group observations, as well as with more inductive approaches.

Acknowledgements

Part of the research reported in this chapter was supported by a grant from the Australian Research Council (Grant DP0666993).

References

Ames, C. (1992). Classrooms: Goals, structures, and student motivation. *Journal of Educational Psychology, 84*, 261-271.

Anderman, L. H. (1999). Expanding the discussion of social perceptions and academic outcomes: Mechanism and contextual influences. In T. Urdan (Ed.), *Advances in motivation and achievement: The role of content* (Vol. 11, pp 303-336). Stanford, CT: JAI Press.

Boekaerts, M. (2002). Bringing about change in the classroom: Strengths and weaknesses of the self-regulated learning approach – EARLI Presidential Address, 2001. *Learning and Instruction, 12*, 589-604.

Boekaerts, M., & Hijzen, D. (2007). Understanding the effect of culture on the pursuit of multiple goals, perception of learning conditions and the quality of cooperative learning. In F. Salili & R. Hoosain (Eds.), *Culture, motivation and learning: A multicultural perspective* (pp. 115-129). Information Age Publishing.

Boekaerts, M., de Koning, E., & Vedder, P. (2006). Goal-directed behavior and contextual factors in the classroom: An innovative approach to the study of multiple goals. *Educational Psychologist, 41*, 33-51.

Carver, C. S., & Scheier, M. F. (2000). On the structure of behavioural self-regulation. In M. Boekaerts, P. R. Pintrich, & M. Zeidner (Eds.), *Handbook of self-regulation* (pp. 41-84). San Diego. CA: Academic Press.

Dowson, M., & McInerney, D. M. (2003). What do students say about their motivational goals? Towards a more complex and dynamic perspective on student motivation. *Contemporary Educational Psychology, 28*, 91-113.

Dweck, C. (1986) Motivational processes affecting learning. *American Psychologist, 41(10)*, 1040-1048.

Elliot, A. J. (1999). Approach and avoidance motivation and achievement goals. *Educational Psychologist, 34*, 169-189.

Flavell, J. H. (1981). Cognitive monitoring. In W. Dickson (Ed.), *Children's oral communication skills* (pp. 35-60). New York: Academic Press.

Ford, M. E. (1992). *Motivation humans: Goals emotions, and personal agency beliefs.* London: Newbury: Sage Publications.

Ford, M. E., & Nichols, C. W. (1991). Using goal assessment to identify motivational patterns and facilitate behavioural regulation and achievement. In M. Maehr & P. R. Pintrich (Eds.), *Advances in motivation and achievement: Goals and self-regulatory processes* (Vol. 7, pp. 61-84). Greenwich, CT: JAI Press.

Fortunato, V. J., & Goldblatt, A. M. (2006). An examination of goal orientation profiles using cluster analysis and their relationships with dispositional characteristics and motivational response patterns. *Journal of Applied Social Psychology, 36*, 2150-2183.

Gurtner, J.-L., Monnard, I.,& Genoud, P. A. (2001). Towards a multilayer model of context and its impact on motivation. In S. Volet & S. Järvelä (Eds.), *Motivation in learning contexts: Theoretical advances and methodological implications* (pp. 189-208). Amsterdam: Pergamon.

Harackiewicz, J.M., Barron, K.E., Pintrich, P.R., Elliot, A.J., & Thrash T.M. (2002). Predicting success in college: A longitudinal study of achievement goals and ability measures as predictors and performance from freshman year through graduation. *Journal of Educational Psychology, 94*, 562-575.

Harackiewicz, J. M., & Linnenbrink, E. A. (2005). Multiple achievement goals and multiple pathways for learning: The agenda and impact of Paul R. Pintrich. *Educational Psychologist, 40*, 75-84.

Hijzen, D., Boekaerts, M., & Vedder, P. (2006). The relationship between the quality of cooperative learning, students' goal preferences, and perceptions of contextual factors in the classroom. *Scandinavian Journal of Psychology, 47*, 9-21.

Järvelä, S., Häkkinen, P., Arvaja, M., & Leinonen, P. (2003). Instructional support in CSCL. In P. Kirchner, J-W. Strijbos, & R. Martens (Eds.), *What we know about CSCL in higher education* (pp.115-139). New York: Kluwer Academic Publishers.

Karoly, P., Boekaerts, M., & Maes, S. (2005). Toward consensus in psychology of self-regulation: How far have we come? How far do we have yet to travel? *Applied Psychology, 54*, 300-311.

Lawrence, J.A., & Volet, S.E. (1991). The significance and function of students' goals: Adjustment in academic study. In L. Oppenheimer & J. Valsiner (Eds.), *The origins of action: Interdisciplinary and international perspectives* (pp.133-157). New York: Springer-Verlag.

Lemos, M. S. (1999). Students' goals and self-regulation in the classroom. *International Journal of Educational Research, 31*, 471-485.

Linnenbrink, E. A., & Pintrich, P. A. (2001). Multiple goals, multiple contexts. The dynamic interplay between personal goals and contextual goal stresses. In S. Volet & S. Järvelä (Eds.), *Motivation in learning contexts: Theoretical advances and methodological implications* (pp. 251-269). Amsterdam: Pergamon.

Markus, H.R., & Kitayama, S. (1991). Culture and the self: Implications for cognition, emotion and motivation. *Psychological Review, 98*, 224-253.

Pintrich, P. R. (2000). An achievement goal theory perspective on issues in motivation terminology, theory and research. *Contemporary Educational Psychology, 25*, 92-104.

Roeser, R. W. (2004). Competing schools of thought in achievement goal theory. In P. R. Pintrich & M. L. Maehr (Eds.), *Advances in Motivation and achievement: Motivating students, improving schools* (Vol. 13, pp 265-300).Oxford, UK: Elsevier.

Stark, R., & Mandl, H. (2000). *Probleme in der Methodenausbildung: Analyse und Intervention aus motivationstheoretischer Perspektive* (Forschungsbericht Nr. 116). [Problems in methodological training: Analysis and intervention from a motivational theoretical perspective (Research report no. 116)]. München: Ludwig-Maximilians-Universität, Lehrstuhl für Empirische Pädagogik und Pädagogische Psychologie.

Vauras, M., Iiskala, T., Kajamies, A., Kinnunen, R., & Lehtinen, E. (2003). Shared regulation and motivation of collaborating peers. A case study. *Psychologia, 46*, 19-37.

Volet, S.E. (2001a). Significance of cultural and motivational variables on students' appraisals of group work. In F. Salili, C.Y. Chiu, & Y.Y. Hong (Eds*). Student motivation: The culture and context of learning* (pp. 309-334). New York: Plenum.

Volet, S.E. (2001b). Understanding learning and motivation in context: A multi-dimensional and multi-level cognitive-situative perspective. In S. Volet & S. Järvelä (Eds.), *Motivation in learning contexts: Theoretical advanced and methodological implications* (pp. 57-82). Amsterdam: Pergamon.

Volet, S.E. (2007, August). *Studying motivational dynamics within and across socially challenging learning activities: Grappling with methodological issues.* Paper presented at the Biannual Meeting of the European Association for Research on Learning and Instruction. Budapest, Hungary.

Volet, S.E., & Mansfield, C. (2006). Group work at university: Significance of personal goals in the regulation strategies of students with positive and negative appraisals. *Higher Education, Research and Development, 25,* 341-356.

Wentzel, K.R. (1991). Social and academic goals at school: Motivation and achievement in context. In M. L. Maehr & P. R. Pintrich (Eds.), *Advances in motivation and achievement: Goals and self-regulatory processes* (Vol. 7., pp. 185-212). Greenwich, CT: JAI Press.

Wentzel, K.R. (1994). Relations of social goal pursuit to social acceptance, classroom behaviour, and perceived social support. *Journal of Early Adolescence, 13,* 4-20.

Wentzel, K.R. (1996). Social and academic motivation in middle school: Concurrent and long-term relations to academic effort. *Journal of Early Adolescence, 16,* 390-406.

Wosnitza, M. (2007). *Lernumwelt Hochschule und akademisches Lernen. Die subjektive Wahrnehmung sozialer, formaler und materiell-physischer Aspekte der Hochschule als Lernumwelt und ihre Bedeutung für das akademische Lernen.* [University learning environment and academic learning. The subjective perception of social, formal, and material aspects of universities as a learning environment and its relevance for academic learning]. Landau: VEP.

Wosnitza, M., & Volet, S. (2005). Origin, direction and impact of emotions in social online learning. *Learning and Instruction, 15,* 449-464.

Motivational Aspects of Cognitive Load Theory

Wolfgang Schnotz, Stefan Fries, & Holger Horz

Learning and instruction has undergone important changes during the last years, which were among others stimulated by technological innovations. The new technologies enable the construction of learning environments that allow presentation of information through computers, information networks and electronic displays by different representational formats in a very flexible way. Although the technical aspect is fundamental for the functioning of these learning environments, it is by itself not very interesting from a psychological or instructional science perspective. Important psychological and instructional aspects refer to the use of different representational formats, the perceptual as well as higher cognitive processes that occur when learners interact with learning environments, but also the motivation of the learner and his/her interests.

Most research on learning from spoken or written texts and from static or animated pictures has been performed from a cognitive perspective (e.g., Ainsworth & Labeke, 2004; Mayer, 2001, 2005; Schnotz, 2001, 2005). General research questions were: What goes on in the mind of the learner when spoken or written texts with or without static or animated pictures or graphs is presented to him or her? How can the displayed information be adapted to the limitations of the cognitive system? How should information be presented to influence learners' motivation in an adaptive way? The necessity of adapting instruction to the constraints of the learner's cognitive system has been the main concern of cognitive load theory, which has been developed by John Sweller and his colleagues and which has become increasingly influential in instructional psychology (cf. Paas, Renkl, & Sweller, 2003, 2004; Paas & Van Gog, 2006; Sweller, 1999, 2003, 2005; Sweller & Chandler, 1994; Sweller, van Merriënboer, & Paas, 1998). The fundamental claim of this theory is that without knowledge about the human cognitive architecture the effectiveness of instructional design is likely to be random. More specifically, cognitive load theory argues that many traditional instructional techniques do not adequately take into account the limitations of the human cognitive architecture, as they unnecessarily overload the learner's working memory, the central "bottleneck" of his/her cognitive system. Accordingly, cognitive load theory tries to integrate knowledge about the structure and functioning of the human cognitive system with principles of instructional design.

However, these considerations become only relevant if a fundamental condition is met sufficiently: Learners' motivation. As has been mentioned in the introduction to this volume, motivation concerns the determinants of the direction, intensity and persistence of behavior. Accordingly, learning and instruction is not only influenced by the architecture of the cognitive system, but also by motivation, which influences the persistence of learning (Driscoll, 1994; Vollmeyer & Rheinberg, 2000), the depth of text comprehension, and the use of learning strategies (Schiefele, 1991). Of course, one should not expect a theory, which clearly defines itself as cognitive to include motivational aspects. However, a closer look reveals striking similarities between research on cognitive load and research on motivation with regard to theoretical constructs and the corresponding measurement procedures. One kind of similarity is represented by procedures of measuring cognitive load. Among the various ways to measure cognitive load (Brünken, Plass, & Leutner, 2003), the most frequently used method is using self-reports. For example, Paas, van Merriënboer, and Adam (1994) asked students to judge the amount of effort they have invested in learning or in solving specific tasks on a nine-point scale ranging from "very, very low mental effort" (1) to "very, very high mental effort" (9). Whereas this measurement procedure is meant to grasp cognitive load, another very similar measurement procedure is meant to grasp motivation. Rheinberg, Vollmeyer, and Burns (2001) developed the questionnaire of actual motivation (QAM). The instrument is based on the idea that in order to show relations of motivation and learning one should tap the actual motivation for the learning task about to be initiated. Accordingly, the QAM is designed to measure the motivational status of individuals just before they start learning. In their model on self-regulated learning, Rheinberg, Vollmeyer, and Rollett (2000) assume that actualized motivation remains activated during the following process of learning. Hence, they tapped not only actualized motivation before learning, but also presented motivational items during the course of learning (see Vollmeyer & Rheinberg, 2006). One of these items refers to the learner's currently invested effort ("I am investing a lot of effort in the present task"). The semantics of this item are nearly the same as the mental effort item used by cognitive load researchers.

Rheinberg and colleagues do not intend to measure cognitive load, as this concept is not a part of their theoretical framework. Asking students about their invested effort is meant to estimate the intensity of behavior as a central variable to be explained by motivation. Paas and colleagues intend to measure cognitive load. The two measurement procedures are embedded into different theoretical frameworks, which in turn assume different variables to predict effort. Rheinberg and colleagues assume that mental effort is determined by the present state of motivation. Paas and colleagues assume that mental effort is a function of the learning task and the expertise of the learner. Empirical research provides ample evidence for both assumptions (for an overview on actualized motivation see Vollmeyer & Rheinberg, 2006; for an overview on cognitive load see Sweller, et al., 1998; Schnotz & Kürschner, 2007). Both theoretical frameworks agree that mental effort is a mediating variable related to learning outcome. Given these similarities, the question arises regarding how cognitive load and motivation are interrelated.

In the following chapter, we will elaborate on some (obvious or hidden) motivational aspects of cognitive load theory. In a first step, we will outline the basic assumptions of the theory. In a second step, we analyze some relations between motivation and the functioning of the human cognitive system with a focus on the relation between cognitive load, motivational persistence, and learning. More specifically, we will analyze the motivational aspects of learning related to intrinsic load, to extraneous load, and to germane load. In a third step, we will point out some basic relations between the concept of cognitive load and a fundamental concept of learning and development, the zone of proximal development. In a fourth step, we will draw some conclusions for instructional practice and further research in this domain.

Basic Assumptions of Cognitive Load Theory

According to cognitive load theory, humans possess a cognitive architecture that consists of sensory registers, a working memory, and a long-term memory (Sweller, et al., 1998). In the traditional view of multi-storage theories of memory, information was assumed to enter the cognitive system from the environment via sensory organs like the ear or the eye and to be briefly stored in the corresponding sensory register (e.g., the auditory register or the visual register). The information is then transmitted to short-term or working memory, where it is further processed and elaborated. Finally, the information can (with some likelihood) be transferred from working memory to long-term memory (cf. Atkinson & Shiffrin, 1971; Baddeley, 1986, 2000). A more modern and elaborated view of the cognitive functioning assumes that the information from the sensory registers is combined with information from long-term memory in working memory, where both kinds of information are further processed in order to construct mental representations such as propositional representations and mental models (Mayer, 2001, 2005; Schnotz & Bannert, 2003; Schnotz, 2005).

Adapting Instruction to the Human Cognitive Architecture

The basic problem of instruction according to cognitive load theory is as follows: Whereas long-term memory has a practically unlimited capacity, the capacity of working memory is highly limited. This limitation applies especially to the storage and processing of new information, which is the typical situation when instruction is given for learning. Instruction generally aims at learning, and learning is a process that results in changes of long-term memory. However, in order to create these changes, instruction has to trigger cognitive processing in working memory such as constructing mental representations, generally referred to as 'comprehension', or operating with these representations, generally referred to as 'thinking'. Only if this cognitive processing leads to changes in long-term memory can the whole process be referred to as 'learning'. Because working memory has a highly limited capacity, it is considered as the bottleneck for learning or changes in long-term memory, respectively. According to cognitive load theory, any kind of cognitive processing puts a 'cognitive load' on working memory, because it draws on its storage and processing capacity. It follows that whenever instruction triggers cognitive processing, it also puts a cognitive load on working memory. Accordingly, cognitive load theory argues that because working memory capacity is limited, instruction has to be adapted to this capacity (Chandler & Sweller, 1991; Paas, et al., 2004; Sweller, 1999; Sweller & Chandler, 1994; Sweller, et al., 1998).

Learning environments can manipulate cognitive load in different ways, and these manipulations can have different effects on an individual's comprehension, thinking, and learning. More specifically, one can distinguish an enabling effect, a facilitating effect, and an inhibiting effect of instructional manipulations. The enabling effect means that due to a reduction of cognitive load, processes become possible which otherwise would have remained impossible. The facilitating effect means that due to a reduction of cognitive load processes that were already possible, but still required high mental effort, become possible with less effort. Both the enabling effect (impossible processes become possible) and the facilitating effect (possible but difficult processes become easier) result from a reduction of cognitive load. Of course, there is also the possibility of an unintended increase in cognitive load. In this case, processes would become more difficult or even impossible, and the instructional manipulation would have an inhibiting effect on comprehension and learning.

Various effects of instructional manipulations can be considered as variants of an enabling or facilitating effect. In the field of multimedia learning, for example, Mayer (2001) has identified a number of instructional principles that can be considered from a cognitive load perspective. Mayer assumes that active learning from multimedia implies that learners select relevant words, select relevant images, organize the selected words into a verbal mental model, organize the selected images into a pictorial mental model, and finally integrate the verbal model and the pictorial model with prior knowledge into a coherent mental representation. Based on the assumption that this integrative processing requires the verbal and the pictorial information to be held in working memory at the same time, that channel capacity is limited, and that decay rates in working memory are high, Mayer derives various principles of multimedia learning. These principles include (among others) the multimedia principle, the temporal contiguity principle, the spatial contiguity principle, and the modality principle. The multimedia principle says that students learn better from words and pictures than from words alone provided the verbal and the pictorial information are simultaneously available in working memory. Pictures obviously provide additional support that enables mental model construction for learners who would otherwise be unable to construct the corresponding mental model, or they facilitate the construction of mental models. The temporal contiguity principle means that when pictures are presented with spoken words, students learn better if words and pictures are presented simultaneously. Simultaneous presentation of words and pictures facilitates integrative processing of both kinds of information. If pictures are presented with written words, then a split of visual attention is required because the eye has to switch between words and pictures, which prevent full temporal contiguity. However, one can maximize temporal contiguity if written words and pictures are presented close to each other. Accordingly, the spatial contiguity principle says that students learn better from written text and pictures when both information sources are spatially close than when they are far apart from each other. Spatial contiguity also facilitates the integrative processing of verbal and pictorial information. The modality principle assumes that students learn better when words are presented as spoken text simultaneously with pictures rather than as printed text, even under the condition of maximal spatial contiguity, because two sensory channels provide more capacity than one channel. The higher processing capacity enables or facilitates the cognitive processes involved in multimedia learning.

The rationale for these principles is that integrative processing requires that both verbal and pictorial information are simultaneously in working memory. If the multimedia learning principles mentioned are not taken into account in the design of a learning environment, the learner has to invest extra effort to hold the corresponding verbal and the pictorial information simultaneously in working memory despite unfavorable conditions. The required extra effort corresponds to an additional cognitive load resulting from the disregard of the multimedia learning principles. These principles seem to follow the guideline of reducing cognitive load, which is documented in publications that specifically aim to achieve that objective (Mayer & Moreno, 2003). The general view that cognitive load should be reduced as far as possible is closely related to the idea of effortless learning. Although this view can often be found, it is not justified by the recent and more elaborated version of cognitive load theory (Sweller, et al., 1998). Instead, a distinction is made between three kinds of cognitive load combined with the assumption that one kind of load will have a negative effect, whereas another kind of load will have a positive effect on learning.

Kinds of Cognitive Load

Cognitive load theory distinguishes three different kinds of cognitive load: Intrinsic, extraneous load, and germane. The intrinsic load is determined by the intellectual complexity of the instructional content or the task to be performed, related to the degree of expertise of the learner. The complexity of the instructional content or task corresponds to the required element interactivity. Any interactions between elements to be held in working memory require working memory capacity. Intrinsic cognitive load, therefore, corresponds to the number of related elements to be held and coordinated simultaneously in working memory. For a specific task in a specific learning situation, the intrinsic load cannot be manipulated. The extraneous load, on the contrary, is determined by the instructional format. More specifically, it is generated by an inappropriate instructional format: By the way the information is structured and presented to the learner. Extraneous load reflects the effort to process poorly designed instruction. Instructional design should aim to decrease extraneous cognitive load. The germane load reflects the effort of schema abstraction and schema automation. The process of schema abstraction corresponds to the formation of a new cognitive schema that represents the invariants and regularities within the experienced stimuli. Schema automation occurs through the repeated application of a schema. Automation means that the activation of the schema requires less and less working memory capacity. Thus, the cognitive load needed for schema application is reduced more and more. These processes change the content of long-term memory, and therefore result in learning. Individuals should be encouraged to engage in cognitive processing that triggers schema construction and increases the learners' level of expertise. Appropriate instructional design should direct the learner's attention to processes that are relevant for learning by the construction of schemata. Germane load should, therefore, not be reduced but rather increased if the total cognitive load stays within the limits of working memory capacity. To summarize, according to the traditional view of cognitive load theory, instructional design should reduce extraneous load, whereas germane load should be increased as far as possible to enhance learning.

Cognitive load theory provides guidelines for the optimization of instruction. These guidelines address the question of how information is to be presented in order to allow for optimal processing. However, successful learning does not only depend on the presenting of information and the adaptation the human cognitive architecture (Pintrich, 2000). In their comprehensive prescriptive theory of teaching, Klauer and Leutner (2007) identified six functions optimal instruction needs to fulfill. The first main step within the model is the establishment of motivation, followed by presenting and receiving information, processing of information, storage and retrieval of information and transfer of information. Together these five functions represent the general function of regulating optimal instruction. It should be evident that cognitive load theory does not tackle all these different functions. Klauer and Leutner (2007) discuss cognitive load theory when addressing the function of optimal information presentation. Most importantly, cognitive load theory does not attend to the question on how learners become motivated to learn and stay motivated during learning.

It comes as no surprise that there are also instructional models focusing on the role of motivation within the instructional process. Most prominently, Keller (1979; Keller & Kopp, 1987) has suggested an instructional theory of motivational design named ARCS with the following main components: attention (A: perceptual arousal, inquiry arousal, variability), relevance (R: familiarity, goal orientation, motive matching), confidence (C: expectancy for success, challenge setting, attribution molding), and satisfaction (S: natural consequences, positive consequences, equity). It might therefore be obvious that the design of learning environments should focus not only on cognitive aspects, but also on motivational aspects.

To sum up, cognitive load theory addresses the question of how constraints of the human cognitive architecture need to be taken into account when designing optimal instruction. However, optimal instruction must also consider the question of how energy is provided for using the cognitive system. The supply of energy for an individual's behavior is a basic topic of motivational theory.

Cognitive Load and Motivation

Motivation can be defined as a hypothetical construct, which is used to explain the choice, the intensity and the persistence of behavior (Rheinberg, 2006). As such, motivational theories address questions of the selection, orientation and energization of human behavior (Schultheiss & Brunstein, 2005). Furthermore, the subjective experience of actions can be explained by motivational variables (McClelland, 1987). Thus, theories of motivation to learn aim at explaining why a student starts learning or not, how concentrated he/she will learn and how persistent he/she will be. Because the kind of learning activity, its intensity and persistence influences learning outcomes, motivation is an important predictor of the extent to which learning will be successful. This is most evident when considering cumulative learning (Gagné, 1965), where the comprehension of some learning material is necessary for understanding succeeding material. Because persistence is needed, successful cumulative learning presupposes sufficient learner motivation.

Motivation and the Architecture of the Human Cognitive System

As we have seen, cognitive load theory addresses the question of how instruction can be adapted to the human cognitive architecture. One should not expect that motivation is capable of modifying the cognitive structure of a learner. Most cognitive theories consider working memory as the entity for storing and processing information with a specific limited capacity, which may vary among individuals but is more or less constant within an individual (cf. Baddeley, 1986; Miller, 1956; Miyake & Shah, 1999). Nevertheless, there are reasons to assume that motivation can influence working memory capacity within some limits. Anderson (1983) has assumed in his ACT* model of the human architecture, that working memory is not a store with a fixed capacity, but rather a part of declarative long-term memory. More specifically, he assumed that memory nodes in long-term memory can be activated to a lower or higher extent. Memory nodes with activation beyond some threshold level are assumed by definition to be the content of working memory. In other words, what is in working memory depends on which and how many memory nodes are sufficiently activated. Activation enters declarative long-term memory, which is considered as a propositional network, through specific nodes through perception of the outside world or through setting behavioral aims, and the activity spreads across this network to other nodes.

Working memory is limited insofar as a node, which is activated by a spread of activation, loses its activity rather quickly if no further activation is added. It follows that working memory capacity is limited, because due to the fading activity, only some limited set of memory nodes can be kept sufficiently active in order to be available for cognitive processing due to their sufficiently high level of activation. However, it also follows that if more activation is fed into the network at a specific time of processing, more units would be activated beyond the critical level of activity and, thus, working memory capacity increases. In other words, if a learner is very much concentrating his/her thoughts on a task, we may assume that more activation will be fed into the semantic network and, accordingly, more nodes will be sufficiently activated, compared to a situation in which his/her concentration is low. Considering that motivational variables are addressing the question of the energization of the human behavior, high energization may result in higher activation. Accordingly, high motivation can result in a temporary increase of working memory capacity.

Persistence, Cognitive Load and Learning

A behavioral outcome predicted by motivation that is highly relevant for learning is persistence. The higher the motivation of an individual, the longer he/she will be willing to deal with a learning task (Vollmeyer & Rheinberg, 2000). The necessity of persistence in order to learn successfully within a given learning environment has been largely neglected by cognitive load theory. The amount of cognitive load is usually derived from the element of interactivity required by a task during cognitive processing: It refers to the number of cognitive elements that have to be kept simultaneously in working memory in order to perform the next cognitive operations required by the task at hand. Thus, one might argue that cognitive load theory considers only snapshots during the learner's cognitive processing. However, learning is a process that takes time. Successful learning takes place only if the learner uses his/her limited working memory capacity for a sufficiently long time in order to grasp the content at hand. Just as Klauer and Leutner (2007) claim in their prescriptive theory of teaching, instructors need to address the motivation of the learner. Success of learning not only depends on whether he/she can handle the material at a given moment in time, but also on the persistence shown by the individual. This is where motivation goes on stage. Higher motivation leads to greater persistence in learning. A learner who is highly motivated will be ready to invest his/her mental effort for a longer time into learning and, thus, be more persistent than a learner with low motivation. The higher persistence, in turn, will result in better learning outcomes. In other words, highly motivated learners can be assumed to invest more total mental energy into the process of learning, and it will take more time until they are exhausted by a specific kind of learning task.

Schnotz and Kürschner (2007) have pointed out that although cognitive load theory generally considers cognitive load as derived from element-interactivity in working memory, researchers have implicitly argued that cognitive load can also be caused by a waste of time and effort even with low element-interactivity. This describes an important conceptual shift in cognitive load theory, because there are two kinds of limited resources in learning. One resource is working memory capacity, as pointed out by cognitive load theory. The other limited resource is a kind of processing energy, which can be exhausted during the process of learning and then needs to be recharged. This latter resource is determined by the motivation of the learner. The higher the motivation of a learner, the more energy he/she is willing to invest into learning (Vollmeyer & Rheinberg, 2000). If we accept the analogy of a truck, which has some amount of fuel, we can say that the greater the load on the truck and the longer the truck is going, the more fuel will be used (and the sooner it needs to be refueled). Similarly, the higher the average cognitive load and the longer the process of learning goes on, the more mental energy will be used and the sooner the individual will be exhausted.

One can assume that successful learning requires successful task performance as well as practice. This assumption corresponds to two well-known laws of learning: The law of effect and the law of exercise (Thorndike & Gates, 1930). The two laws are closely related to cognitive load theory and to motivation theory: Cognitive load of learning tasks should not be too high not only due to the necessity of successful performance (according to the law of effect). It should also not be too high in order to avoid using up too much mental energy and make learners too exhausted. As we will argue subsequently, cognitive load should also be not too low as a result very easy tasks. Schnotz and Rasch (2005) found that students invested less cognitive effort in performance and learning-relevant cognitive processes when learning from animation compared to learning from static pictures. The animation made cognitive processing (i.e., a mental simulation) too easy and in fact sub-challenged the learners. In other words, a reduction of cognitive load is not always helpful for learning. Although a very easy task requires only low element interactivity and as a consequence imposes only a low cognitive load, it still requires some mental energy and after some time will make the individual exhausted. This is exactly what is meant by the term 'waste of time and effort', which was often referred to as a kind of (extraneous) cognitive load.

Intrinsic Load and Motivation

What is Intrinsic Load?

As mentioned previously, intrinsic load is considered to be dependent on the task to be learned, whereas extraneous load is seen as resulting from inadequate instruction. The two kinds of load seem, therefore, to be conceptually clearly distinct. A closer look makes obvious, however, that the empirical distinction between intrinsic and extraneous load can be rather difficult. On the one hand, the distinction also depends on the learner's expertise (more specifically, on the alignment between learner's expertise and the difficulty of the task). On the other hand, the distinction depends on the instructional objectives. This will be explained subsequently with regard to text difficulty and with regard to the multimedia versus the redundancy effect.

If learners have low expertise, text difficulty has to be low as well. In such an easy text, many details and interrelations have to be made explicit instead of leaving them implicit and expecting that the learners will make the corresponding inferences by themselves. As the learner is expected to construct a mental model of the subject matter, this task defines the unavoidable intrinsic cognitive load. If text difficulty is low, that is, if the text requires as little cognitive processing as possible to construct the corresponding mental model from learners with low expertise, it includes only intrinsic load for these learners. If learners with low expertise were to receive a difficult text that leaves many details and interrelations implicit, the learners would be required to draw the corresponding inferences from their prior knowledge, which would be difficult for them due to their low expertise. Accordingly, the difficult text would result in an extraneous load for these learners, which would be added to the intrinsic load.

McNamara, Kintsch, Songer, and Kintsch (1996) have shown that a more difficult text due to lower text coherence can result in deeper text comprehension with higher prior knowledge learners than can an easier text. It follows that if learners' expertise is high, text difficulty should also be higher. This means that many details and interrelations remain implicit, because the learners are able to make the corresponding inferences by themselves. Accordingly, for learners with higher expertise, the more difficult text would include only intrinsic load. If learners with high expertise would receive an easy text that makes all the details and interrelations explicit, the learners would have to process much text information, which they have already inferred by themselves due to their higher expertise. Processing this text information would provide only redundant information, which would not go beyond what the learners have inferred already from their prior knowledge. One can refer to this as an intra-textual redundancy-effect. Paradoxically, the easy text would result in an extraneous load for learners with higher expertise, which adds to the intrinsic load. It follows that the distinction between intrinsic load and extraneous load is related to the individual's level of expertise.

The same point can be made with regard to the combination of text with pictures. In numerous studies researchers have found that students learn better from text and pictures than from text alone (Levie & Lentz, 1982; Levin, Anglin, & Carney, 1987; Mayer, 2001; Moreno & Mayer, 2002). This so-called *multimedia effect* occurs when learners have relatively low expertise about the subject matter (Mayer, 2001). When learners have higher expertise, they are often able to construct a mental model of the subject matter from the text alone (Mayer, 2001).

From the perspective of cognitive load theory, adding or deleting pictures to or from a text can be considered a manipulation of extraneous cognitive load. As the learner is expected to construct a mental model of the subject matter, this task defines the unavoidable intrinsic cognitive load. Any kind of instruction that imposes a higher load than the unavoidable intrinsic load causes an extraneous cognitive load on the learner's working memory. When learners have low expertise, constructing a mental model from text and pictures is easier than constructing the model from text alone. Combining text and pictures would be an appropriate instructional format, because it would result only in intrinsic load. Presenting a text without pictures to these learners would be an inappropriate instructional format, because mental model construction would be too difficult for them. In other words, the instructional format would impose an additional, extraneous cognitive load on their working memory. Thus presenting a text without pictures would result in intrinsic load plus extraneous load for this group of learners.

When learners have higher expertise, however, adding pictures to a text can have just the opposite effect. As Sweller and his colleagues have shown, multiple sources of information are sometimes not needed. Instead, one source can be self-contained, if it provides all the required information to construct a mental model of the subject matter (Chandler & Sweller, 1996; Sweller, et al., 1998). In this case, combining text and pictures would be an inappropriate instructional format, because the pictures would require working memory capacity without the benefit of better learning: The learner unnecessarily wanders between text and pictures, interrupts repeatedly ongoing processes of coherence formation, and looses time with unproductive search for unneeded information. The pictures would provide only redundant information, which would not go beyond what the student has learned already from the text. Sweller and his collaborators call this the *redundancy effect* or the expertise reversal effect (Sweller, et al., 1998; Kalyuga, Chandler, & Sweller, 1998, 2000). Due to the redundancy effect, adding a picture to a text or a text to a picture can have an inhibiting effect on learning, because the additional source of information increases extraneous cognitive load. In other words, a picture can be a needed help for learners with low expertise, but can become an unneeded help when expertise is higher. For learners with high expertise, combining a text with pictures would result in intrinsic load plus extraneous load, whereas presenting a text without pictures would be the appropriate instructional format including only intrinsic load. Again, it turns out that the distinction between intrinsic load and extraneous load is related to the learner's level of expertise.

Alignment of Task Difficulty and Expertise

The examples mentioned above have shown that the distinction between intrinsic load and extraneous load is influenced by the learner's expertise. More specifically, they have made obvious that cognitive load is intrinsic when the difficulty of the learning task is well aligned with the learner's level of expertise. If the learner's expertise is low, and if the difficulty of cognitive processing the learning material is also low (as, for example, when text comprehension requires only few inferences or when texts are combined with pictures), the cognitive load imposed by the learning material can be considered as intrinsic. If the learner's expertise is high and if the difficulty of cognitive processing the learning material is also high (as, for example, when text comprehension requires many inferences or when texts are presented alone without pictures), the cognitive load imposed by the learning material can also be considered as intrinsic. In both cases, the task difficulty is well aligned with the learner's expertise.

On the contrary, if the learner's expertise is low, but the difficulty of the learning material is high (as, for example, when text comprehension requires many inferences or when texts are presented alone without pictures), the cognitive load imposed by the learning material includes an extraneous component. Under the opposite conditions, namely if the learner's expertise is high, but the difficulty of the learning material is low (as, for example, when text comprehension requires only few inferences or when texts are combined with pictures), the cognitive load imposed by the learning material includes also an extraneous component. The reason for this seemingly paradox result is that the learner's working memory capacity is occupied by unneeded cognitive processing without the benefit of deeper comprehension and better learning. In these cases, the task difficulty is misaligned with the learner's expertise.

The distinction between intrinsic load and extraneous load and its relation to the learning material's difficulty as well as the learner's expertise is visualized in Figure 1. If the combination of difficulty and expertise falls into some middle area indicated by the diagonal lines, difficulty and expertise are well aligned, and the cognitive load of the task can be considered as intrinsic. If the task difficulty exceeds the learner's expertise, the learner is overwhelmed, and the instruction imposes extraneous load in addition to the intrinsic load. If the learner's expertise exceeds the task difficulty, the learner is subchallenged and his/her working memory capacity is occupied by unneeded cognitive processing. In this case, the instruction also includes extraneous load, which adds to the intrinsic load.

In their modified version of cognitive load theory, Schnotz and Kürschner (2007) have therefore replaced the traditional idea that intrinsic load is fixed, that is, cannot be manipulated, by the idea that the intrinsic load has to be adapted to the learner's level of expertise or to his/her zone of proximal development, respectively.

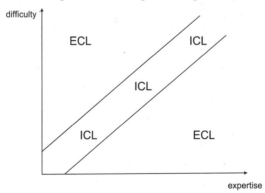

Figure 1. Relations between intrinsic load (ICL) as a result of adequate alignment of learning task difficulty with learner's expertise and additional extraneous load (+ECL) as a result of misalignment of task difficulty with expertise. Learning increases expertise.

Such an interpretation of cognitive load theory assumes the idea of optimal functioning that occurs whenever individual capabilities and task requirements are aligned to each other. Such reasoning on optimal functioning can also be found within motivational theories. Many theories predict high motivation whenever there is an optimal fit of task difficulty and ability level.

Flow

Csikszentmihaly has proposed in his flow theory (1990), that individuals function best if there is a fit of task difficulty and abilities. Flow is experienced if high abilities are met by high demands of the task. According to Csikszentmihaly (1990), a flow state is characterized by the following elements (see also Rheinberg, 2008):

- Task demands and feedback are perceived as clear and self-evident.
- Persons perceive optimally demanding task whilst being in total control of their actions.
- All actions are perceived as interrelated and smooth.
- Concentration is effortless.
- The experience of time is altered ("hours passed like minutes").
- There is a fusion of activity and the self.

A good example of a flow state is a pianist who is lost in exercising a piece of music. The pianist will enjoy this situation even he/she is highly concentrated, plays at the limit of own abilities and experiences a maximum cognitive load.

This example clarifies the contradiction between flow theory and cognitive load theory. If a learner is in a flow-state, he/she will perceive nearly no cognitive load following the flow theory, although the learners' working memory capacity is totally used. This aspect points out a weakness of measuring cognitive load by subjective ratings. Learners would report a low cognitive load in case of a flow state, whereas they actually have a high cognitive load during the flow state. Because flow is a motivational state that is perceived as an optimal motivational state, the cognitive load may be not perceived as effort but rather as a part of a subjective flow state. One may argue that experiencing flow during an experiment of a cognitive load seems to be rather unlikely. We agree to this, but at a closer look this is an argument against the ecologic validity of experiments concerning cognitive load theory: In real life most persons will experience flow-like states quite often during challenging tasks.

Besides, there are other motivational theories considering the importance of a fit of task difficulty and ability. For example, the risk-taking model of achievement motivation (Atkinson, 1957) assumes the highest activation of the achievement motive for tasks that are of an intermediate level for learners whose tendency to approach success is higher than their tendency to avoid failure, whereas learners whose tendency to avoid failure is higher than their tendency to approach success are more motivated to avoid such tasks (Karabenick & Youssef, 1968). Accordingly, when instructors want to motivate success-oriented learners they should present tasks that are aligned to the ability of the learner on an intermediate level, whereas learners who primarily fear failure will probably need tasks of a somewhat lower level. Adequate alignment of task difficulty and the learner's expertise level does not only allow for an appropriate cognitive processing but sustains motivation to learn.

Extraneous Load and Motivation

What is Extraneous Load?

Whereas intrinsic load is caused by the task-intrinsic aspects of the learning material, extraneous load is caused entirely by the format of the instruction (Sweller, 2005; Sweller, et al., 1998). More specifically, extraneous load is an unnecessary load caused by the design and organization of the learning material (Kalyuga, et al., 1998). Extraneous load requires an extra effort due to an inappropriate instructional format. Cognitive load theory has defined extraneous load in different ways, which are not fully equivalent. One definition considers extraneous load as resulting from an unnecessarily high degree of element interactivity in working memory due to the instructional format. For example, if a diagram is presented with integrated explanatory text, it is very hard to ignore the text even if the learner does not need the text for understanding. The learner is forced to assimilate simultaneously multiple elements of information, which imposes a heavy extraneous load on working memory. Another definition considers extraneous load as resulting from irrelevant cognitive activities. Activities are seen as irrelevant if they are not directed to schema acquisition and schema automation (Sweller & Chandler, 1994; Sweller, 2005). The two definitions are not equivalent, because cognitive activities that are irrelevant for learning do not necessarily include high element interactivity. In any case, however, the theory assumes that extraneous load interferes with learning and, thus, should be reduced as far as possible by eliminating irrelevant cognitive activities (Leung, Low, & Sweller, 1997; Sweller, et al., 1998).

Motivation and Extraneous Load

As extraneous load derives directly from features of the learning material; the motivation of the learner does not influence extraneous load. However, from a motivational perspective, one might argue against the necessity of always reducing extraneous load to a minimum. If all elements of a learning environment are cut back to the basic as design principles derived from CLT recommend it (e.g., Mayer & Moreno, 2002), the resulting instructional material may have lost all (unnecessary) details that made the task interesting beforehand. For example relating to a so-called universal interest may increase the interestingness of a text (Schank, 1979), although this may not be relevant for the topic to be learned. Thus, decreasing extraneous load may result in an instructionally optimized learning material that is no longer sufficiently interesting to catch the interest of a learner (Hidi & Harackiewicz, 2000), and no longer optimally activating from a motivational perspective. Figures 2a and 2b illustrate our hypothesis.

Learning environments, which are optimized in respect to a reduced extraneous load (Figure 2a), may not be sufficiently motivating because they are not optimally activating. Such low activation may result in lower persistence and eventually in worse learning results than learning material that imposes some extraneous load for the learner. This situation is depicted in Figures 2a und 2b. Figure 2a illustrates a case where extraneous load was reduced successfully, but in comparison to Figure 2b, learners show lower persistence due to a non-optimal activation by the learning task. A very simple presentation will sometimes leave a boring impression on learners if it contains no additional motivating elements. The assumption is that those motivating but not essential elements ("seductive details") will increase the persistence of learning. In an experimental study with a complex learning environment, students persisted significantly longer (one up to three hours) when situated instructions were integrated compared to a learning environment with instructions that were reduced to basic information only (Horz, Fries, & Winter, in press). Furthermore, students rated the situated instructions as additionally motivating and attractive. This result indicates that situational motivation is generated by motivating elements in a learning environment and leads to a higher persistence in learning.

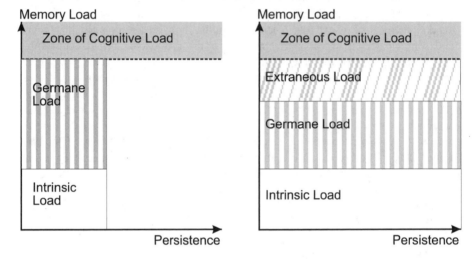

Figure 2a and 2b. Schematic illustration of possible positive motivational effect of extraneous but motivating learning materials. Figure 2a learning without extraneous but motivating learning materials; Figure 2b learning with extraneous but motivating materials.

However, other experiments showed that seductive details might interrupt the learning process in an inadequate way, so that lowered learning outcomes resulted (Garner, Gillingham, & White, 1989; Harp & Mayer, 1997; Hidi & Baird, 1986). All of these experiments with negative outcomes due to seductive details had two important limits. First, the seductive details had no or only very weak additional motivating effect. Second, the learning times overall were relatively short (noticeably less than one hour) and/or were held constantly in these experiments. Hence, the chance of a positive effect on persistence was lowered substantially in these experiments. Therefore, it is plausible that no positive effects of seductive details could be observed.

Germane Load and Motivation

What is Germane Load?
We have mentioned above that the germane load reflects the effort of schema abstraction and schema automation. However, it is not easy to predict whether a specific instructional

manipulation will actually affect the germane load instead of the extraneous load. For example, animations can be expected to reduce extraneous load, if they remove the necessity of drawing dynamic inferences. However, Schnotz and Rasch (2005) found that such animations could hinder rather than enhance learning. One could argue that the animation unintentionally increased extraneous load instead of reducing it. This seems to make sense at first sight. Learners were obviously able to perform the required mental simulations on their own. Thus, the simulation pictures provided process information that was in fact no longer required by the learner and therefore redundant. Providing redundant information is generally considered as an increase of extraneous cognitive load, because learners have to process additional unneeded information. Such redundancy can result in an expertise reversal effect, when individuals with higher learning prerequisites perform better without, rather than with additional information (Kalyuga, et al., 1998, 2000). However, this pattern does not correspond to the results of the studies mentioned above, because the negative effects of animation were found primarily when students had low learning prerequisites rather than high learning prerequisites. Therefore, the negative facilitating effect seems a function of something different than an increase of extraneous cognitive load, according to the expertise reversal effect. Another possibility seems to make sense as well: That the germane load was reduced instead of the extraneous one. If we rule out the view that the extraneous load was increased, and if we would further assume that the intrinsic load is fixed, then the decrease of germane load is the only remaining possibility to account for the impaired learning. However, there is a third possibility of interpreting the results; namely the assumption of an erroneous reduction of the intrinsic load, which created a misalignment with the learner's zone of proximal development. In other words, there is not only the problem of a distinction between germane load and extraneous load, but also the problem of a distinction between germane load and intrinsic load.

Paas and van Merriënboer (1994) have studied learning with worked-out examples that were designed to reduce extraneous load. Students profited from these worked-out examples only when the presented problems included sufficient variability. In these examples, arithmetic problems were embedded into contexts of high and low variability. When the problems were embedded into varying contexts, learning results were better than when the same problems were embedded into uniform contexts. Paas and van Merriënboer attributed the better learning results to an additional load caused by the variability of the problem contexts, and they considered this load to be germane. However, one can also argue that the worked-out examples required both the understanding of the embedding context and the understanding of arithmetic problems. In this case, the processing of information about the embedding context is part of the task and therefore part of the intrinsic load. If a learner has to solve problems embedded into variable contexts, he/she has to perform repeatedly new comprehension processes and has also to map repeatedly arithmetic problems onto different contexts. This is of course a more demanding task than if the embedding context would remain always the same. It follows that the problems with high context variability had a higher intrinsic (not germane!) load than the problems with low context variability.

As the working memory requirements of schema abstraction are considered as germane load, and as schema abstraction is considered as the basis of knowledge acquisition, one can assume that germane load is a requirement for learning. However, this assumption has important implications: The higher the germane load, the more learning should occur; whereas if there is no germane load, there should be no learning at all. Thus, in the case of an individual solving a task with a maximum of intrinsic load there would be no learning: The task would be so difficult that it would require all the available working memory capacity would be required just to cope with the task. Accordingly, there would be no capacity left for any germane load and, thus, no learning should occur. As we will see in the following, however, this assumption is highly questionable.

Studies of implicit learning indicate that humans are able to acquire knowledge without consciousness or awareness of the content of the knowledge. Individuals are able to grasp co-variations and invariances without becoming aware of these co-variations and invariants and, thus, are not able to describe them. From an evolutionary perspective, this is not surprising: It is very likely that phylogenetically primitive systems had developed before the emergence of conscious functioning and that these primitive systems also allowed learning from experiences even when the experiences were not processed consciously, because something like working memory did not exist yet (Reber, Walkenfeld, & Hernstadt, 1991). Perrig (1996) stressed that we talk about implicit learning if a behavioral change can be observed with a person in a situation, which can be deduced from a (single or multiple) experience of this situation without any report of insight or knowledge with the person that would be due to the experience (i.e., participants cannot report anything by introspection). Implicit learning is an unconscious way to acquire knowledge about complex regularities (knowledge that is not described and that the learner is not aware of, but which becomes obvious in a change of behavior). Implicit learning involves changes to the perceptual, cognitive or behavioral (regulatory) system, that is, changes to the functional architecture of continuously learning systems (such as neural networks). The abstraction of schemata (Bartlett, 1932; Schank & Abelson, 1977) is therefore not necessarily a conscious process that needs working memory capacity. Learners can profit from previous experiences when they have to perform tasks even without explicit memory of the experience. As Wenger (1998) has put it: Learning is everywhere; it is as natural as breathing and eating; individuals are therefore 'condemned' to learn.

We therefore assume that germane load is not necessarily required for learning, because learning can take place also without or very limited resources of working memory. There are possibilities of a non-conscious acquisition of information, which also implies that working memory is not the only way of getting information into long-term memory. Even in the case of a task with the possible maximum of intrinsic load some learning would still occur, although no working memory capacity is left for any germane load.

There are three points to be made for a further specification of germane cognitive load: First, germane load requires working memory capacity – otherwise, there would be no cognitive load. Second, germane load is beneficial for learning – otherwise, the load would not be germane. Third, according to the distinction between performance and learning, it is the cognitive processing in working memory, not the learning as a change in long-term memory that creates (germane) cognitive load. These points suggest the following tentative definition: Germane load is cognitive load due to cognitive activities in working memory that aim at intentional learning and that go beyond simple task performance. If these activities would not take place in working memory, they would not cause a cognitive load. If they would not aim at learning, they would not be germane. If they would not go beyond task performance, they would simply be part of the intrinsic load. The following cognitive activities would qualify for this characterization of germane cognitive load:

- Conscious application of learning strategies (i.e. strategies which are not automated yet),
- Conscious search for patterns in the learning material in order to deliberately abstract cognitive schemata (i.e. mindful abstraction),
- Restructuring of problem representations in order to solve a task more easily (i.e., by 'insight'), and
- Metacognitive processes that monitor cognition and learning.

All these kinds of activities explicitly aim at promoting learning. They require additional working memory capacity beyond the requirements of the task performance itself and can therefore be considered as an additional cognitive load component. Therefore, they correspond to our definition of germane cognitive load. However, in this case, germane load is no longer the prerequisite for any learning. It is also no longer equal to any cognitive load related positively to learning. Instead, germane load is the cognitive load of some specific cognitive activities that are performed in addition to the ordinary performance of a learning task and which aim at the further improvement of learning. Learning can occur even without germane load, but germane load can further enhance learning.

Motivation for Strategic Learning

Applying learning strategies resulting in germane cognitive load is also closely related to motivation. Many studies have shown that highly motivated learners tend to apply more sophisticated and elaborated learning strategies (e.g., Artelt, 2000; Schiefele, 1991). Furthermore, learners with certain motivationally relevant dispositions, as for example a learning goal orientation, show more strategic learning (for an overview see Pintrich, 2000). Based on both areas of research it seems reasonable to assume that motivation is related to germane load. Using elaborated learning strategies results in higher germane load. Highly motivated learners seem to have a tendency to increase their germane load within the learning environment. Whereas cognitive load theory only addresses issues of designing instruction in such a way as to have maximum germane load within the limits given, such self-induced germane load resulting from high motivation is not a topic in cognitive load theory. Furthermore, the idea of motivation influencing germane load provides ways for optimizing instructions that were so far neglected within cognitive load research. Just as proposed by Klauer and Leutner (2007) in their comprehensive model of instructional functions, establishing and maintaining motivation is a prerequisite for germane load to occur.

   Research on learning and motivation has investigated many motivationally relevant dispositions such as goal orientations, academic self-concept or the achievement motive. Among these dispositions, goal orientations play a prominent role. Researchers distinguish between learning goal orientation (mastery orientation) and a performance goal orientation (e.g., Dweck & Leggett, 1988). Goal orientations describe preferences for different types of goals. Individuals preferring learning goals are focused on experiencing an increase in knowledge or abilities. Individuals preferring performance goals are satisfied whenever they outperform others. In many studies, the relation of goal orientations and strategic learning was analyzed. Results show positive relations of learning goal orientations and strategic learning. Hence, it is reasonable to assume that learners high in learning goal orientation also should tend to increase their own germane load within the existing constraints. To our knowledge there have been no studies so far in which such motivational dispositions are measured and their influence on the learning success within different learning environments in which cognitive load is manipulated and analyzed.

Cognitive and Motivational Constraints on Germane Load

Instructional design influenced by cognitive load theory usually follows the idea that germane load should be as high as possible (cf. Paas, et al., 2004). Of course, it is important to know what *really is* possible under the specific conditions at hand. Germane load seems to be constrained in multiple ways: By working memory capacity, by the nature of the task (and, thus, by its intrinsic load), and by the learner's motivation. First, germane load is constrained, as any other kind of cognitive load, by the available working memory capacity. If the intrinsic load of a task is very high and uses most of the learner's working memory capacity, there is not much capacity left for any germane load even in the absence of extraneous load. Second, the germane load seems to be constrained by the nature of the task, and thus by the intrinsic load. Remember that we have defined above germane load as the part of working memory capacity occupied by cognitive processes as, for example, using specific learning strategies, schema abstraction, cognitive restructuring or metacognitive monitoring, which exceed the task requirements and are therefore additional cognitive processes aiming intentionally at improving learning. These additional cognitive processes are of course closely related to (i.e., are based on or refer to) the processing of the task requirements. In other words: Task performance serves as an information base or source of experience for these additional cognitive processes. It therefore seems plausible to assume that the germane load is constrained by the intrinsic load. Whereas it is possible to solve very difficult tasks (high intrinsic load) without deep metacognitive reflection (low germane load), it is not possible to reflect deeply (high germane load) about a very easy task (low intrinsic load). Thus far, we assume an asymmetric relation between germane load and intrinsic load: The intrinsic load can exceed the germane load, but the germane load cannot exceed the intrinsic load. It follows that a high amount of free working memory capacity due to a low intrinsic load is not beneficial for learning, because the free capacity can be used for germane load only to a limited extent. For example, reducing intrinsic load by the use of animation instead of static pictures can impair learning rather than improve it, because due to the facilitated task performance there is no longer stimulation for deeper cognitive processing.

A third constraint of germane load results from motivational aspects, that is, from the learner's willingness to use his/her available mental resources for additional strategic cognitive processing to enhance learning. Students do not automatically invest all their available cognitive capacity, which is not used for intrinsic or extraneous load, into learning. Instead, they decide whether or not to engage in specific learning activities and the amount of cognitive resources to invest in it. Germane cognitive load therefore depends also on general learning orientations, on affective and on motivational aspects of learning, including individual interest. For example, learners who follow a deep approach to learning will more likely adopt a higher germane load than will learners who follow a surface approach of learning (Entwistle & Ramsden, 1983; Marton & Säljö, 1984). Similarly, learners with high interest in the learning content will more likely adopt a higher germane load than learners with low interest (Renninger, Hidi, & Krapp, 1992).

Schiefele (1991) provided evidence for learners with high interest using strategies of deeper processing than will learners who are not interested in the material to be learned. The willingness to use mental resources for additional strategic cognitive processing may also depend from the cultural background of the learner. For example Hoppe-Graff and Kim (2004) showed that Korean pupils tend to see access to academic learning not only as a right but feel a duty towards their parents in being successful learners. This may result in higher effort and eventually in higher self-induced germane loads. Germane load is, therefore, not only a function of the quality of instruction but also an aspect of the learner's self-regulation (Winne & Hadwin, 1998) that may be influenced by its cultural background. Thus, it is not sufficient to provide learning environments that allow learners to have cognitive resources available for germane load. It is necessary to take care as far as possible that learners engage in this kind of processing, that they invest their available working memory resources into the corresponding learning activities.

To sum up, we have presented some conceptual clarifications regarding the basic concepts in cognitive load theory. We have shown how these concepts are related to basic assumptions of motivational theory. Whereas cognitive load theory allows for an adaptation of instruction to human cognitive architecture, motivational theory explains the energizational processes necessary for successful learning.

Cognitive Load and the Zone of Proximal Development

Cognitive load theory assumes that the intrinsic load is determined by the intellectual complexity of the task to be performed, related to the degree of expertise of the learner. Figure 3 shows the assumed relation between different levels of learners' expertise, learners' performance on a specific hypothetical task X and the intrinsic load imposed by this task on working memory. The upper part of Figure 3 shows how the learner's expertise (represented on the abscissa of the figure) determines the likelihood of the learner's successful performance (represented on the ordinate of the figure) on a task X. Learning as an increase of ability would be represented in this figure as a movement on the abscissa from left to right. Within the area of low expertise on the left hand, the likelihood of successful performance remains at 0% up to the expertise level L1. Between the expertise level L1 and the expertise level L2, the likelihood of successful performance increases from 0% to100%. Beyond the expertise level L2, the likelihood of successful performance remains at 100%. In other words: If the learner's expertise level is below L1, then the task is too difficult for the learner. If the learner's expertise level becomes higher than L1, then the task becomes easier for the learner. At the expertise level L2 and beyond, the task is so easy that performance is likely to be perfect.

The lower part of Figure 3 shows how the intrinsic cognitive load created by task X varies with the learner's level of expertise. Up to L1, the cognitive load (CL) of task X exceeds the learner's working memory capacity (WMC). The learner is therefore unable to perform the task successfully. Between L1 and L2, the cognitive load of the task is lower than the learner's working memory capacity. This means that the learner is able to perform the task, and there is free capacity of working memory left which can be used for germane cognitive load activities (GCL). At L2, the cognitive load of task X drops down to zero, because task performance becomes automated and does not need working memory capacity any more. Therefore, the available working memory capacity can be used for other activities in principle.

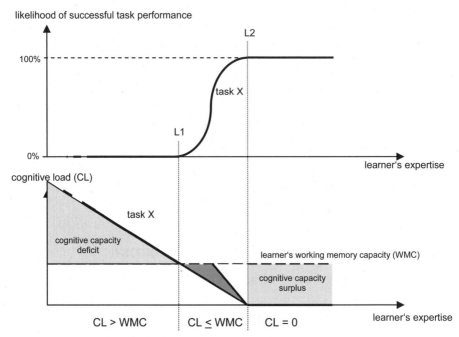

Figure 3. Task performance (top) and cognitive load (bottom) of a hypothetical task X for learners with different levels of expertise.

If we also consider our previous assumption, namely that the germane load is constrained by the intrinsic load, it follows that the possible germane load is not just the free working memory capacity, but also a portion of the free capacity constrained by the intrinsic load. The darker shaded area in Figure 3 signifies the possible amount of germane load, which is possible at a specific level of expertise. Beyond this area, no germane load can be created.

Whereas Figure 3 has shown the learner's performance on one hypothetical task X and the cognitive load in relation to the learner's expertise, Figure 4 shows the same dependencies for two different hypothetical tasks A and B. Task A is easier, whereas task B is more difficult. Both tasks can be performed without additional help or with additional help. If a task has to be performed without help, this is indicated in Figure 4 by the symbol '-'. If help is available during task performance, this is indicated by the symbol '+'. For a student who has reached learning state L3, task A would be very easy, when help is provided (A+). The likelihood of successful performance would be 100% under this condition. Even without help, the student's performance would be relatively good (A-). For the same student, task B would be unsolvable, if no help is provided (B-). Its likelihood of successful performance would be 0% under this condition. With help, however, the likelihood would increase considerably and the student would have a real chance to perform the task successfully (B+).

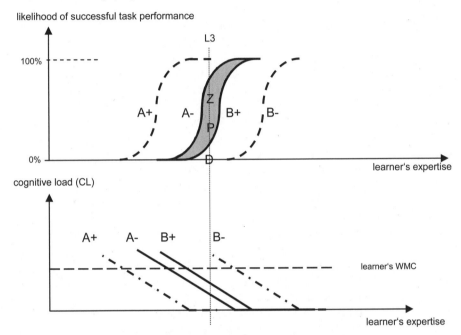

Figure 4. Task performance (top) and cognitive load (bottom) of an easy task A which can be solved by a learner at expertise level L3 without help as well as task performance (top) and cognitive load (bottom) of a difficult task B which can be solved by learner at expertise level L3 only with help. The range of difficulty between the two tasks is known as the zone of proximal development (ZPD).

The increase in performance because of instructional help is the core of the zone of proximal development (ZPD). The zone of proximal development has been defined by Vygotsky (1963) as the difference between an upper limit of task difficulty that the learner can accomplish without help and an upper limit of task difficulty that the learner can accomplish with help. The lower limit of the ZPD is defined as the most difficult task the learner can perform successfully without help. For a student at learning state L3 as shown in Figure 4, the most difficult task the learner can perform successfully without help would be task A. As can be seen from function A-, the learner could still perform this task with a reasonable likelihood, whereas a higher task difficulty would decrease performance tremendously when no help is provided. The upper limit of the ZPD is defined as the most difficult task that the learner can perform successfully with the best possible help available for this task. For the student at learning state L3 in Figure 4, the most difficult task the learner can perform successfully with help would be task B. The curve B+ shows the performance characteristics of the most difficult task that the learner can perform successfully with a still reasonable likelihood under optimal help. A further increase of task difficulty would decrease performance to a very low level even with optimal help. In Figure 4, the ZPD is represented by the shaded area between these two tasks: The easier task A performed without help and the more difficult task B performed with help.

Any instruction that aims at promoting learning should include learning tasks within the limits of the ZPD. If the task difficulty would be higher than the ZPD, the learner's cognitive capacity would be overwhelmed, because the cognitive load would exceed the learner's working memory capacity. If the task difficulty would be lower than the ZPD, the learner would be sub-challenged and a great deal of the available cognitive capacities would remain unused for the learning process. Learning environments that reduce requirements to the basic may reduce cognitive load but might not be optimal with respect to the learner's motivation, because a sub-challenge would be experienced as boring by the learner.

According to our analysis, three essential points have to be made. First, instruction does not only manipulate extraneous load. Instructional means can also manipulate intrinsic load. Second, the intrinsic load of a learning task cannot only be manipulated. It should be manipulated according to the learner's zone of proximal development in order to align the task with the learner's abilities. Third, although a decrease of cognitive load due to the facilitating function of instructional manipulations increases the free working memory capacity, this free capacity is not necessarily used for cognitive activities that would result in a germane load that enhances learning. Learners often do not engage in higher order cognitive processing that would lead them to a deeper comprehension leaving part of their working memory capacity unused. In these cases, learners need to be motivated, that is, stimulated to invest their available working memory capacity into additional cognitive activities that impose germane load and enhance learning.

Conclusions and Further Perspectives

Cognitive load theory has made so far an important contribution in the field of learning and instruction. It has stimulated numerous empirical studies about the relation of working memory and learning, deeper reflections about what is going on in the mind of the learner during the process of teaching, and it has changed the views of practitioners such as teachers and media designers about instruction and learning. However, our analysis has also shown that there are still weaknesses in the theory, which need further conceptual clarification, further empirical research and further thinking about practical applications. In particular, an adequate consideration of motivational aspects is missing in research based on cognitive load theory. Regarding our previous considerations, we want to draw now some conclusions with regard to cognitive load theory in respect to motivational theories and further empirical research related to the concepts of cognitive load.

Cognitive Load Theory

According to the standard view of cognitive load theory, working memory is a prerequisite for any kind of learning. The theory further assumes that the intrinsic load is fixed and, thus, cannot be manipulated, whereas the extraneous load should be minimized and the germane load should be maximized. Our analysis has led us to an alternative view. Accordingly, working memory is only required for explicit learning but not for implicit learning. Instead of considering the intrinsic load as fixed, we assume that the intrinsic load can be manipulated and that it has to be adapted to the learner's zone of proximal development. Moreover, successful learning depends on learners' adequate and persistent use of his/her limited working memory capacity. Learning does not only depend on a momentary usage of working memory's cognitive capacity, but also by learners' persistence.

We agree that extraneous load should be minimized in learning environments from cognitive load theory's perspective. However, extraneous load should be minimized only to the point, where the reduction of extraneous load hampers learners' motivation because of a boring and/or demotivating instructional design since motivating illustrative elements are missing.

We do not agree with most researchers in the field of cognitive load theory that germane load should be as high as possible under all circumstances. Instead, we consider germane load as subject to multiple constraints, which have to be taken into account in instructional design. Germane load is not only constrained by the available working memory capacity, it is also constrained by the nature of the learning task (i.e., by its intrinsic load) and learners' motivation. Additionally, germane load is constrained by the learner's willingness to invest his/her available working memory resources into specific learning-oriented activities and to perform these activities over a sufficient time, which depends on learners' persistence. Thus, germane cognitive load cannot be increased to any degree whatever within the limits of available working memory capacity. Instead, germane load should be balanced within the available working memory capacity with the intrinsic load of the learning task, which in turn has to be adapted to the learner's zone of proximal development and learners motivational prerequisites concerning his/her persistence to learn or to use learning strategies.

Our analysis has also shown that the different kinds of cognitive load and their relation to motivation need further clarification. Even cognitive load theory's central variable, the cognitive capacity of working memory, might be influenced on the learners' motivational state via the spread of activation in declarative memory (cf. Anderson, 1983).

A further problem results from different predictions made by flow theory and cognitive load theory regarding learners' experiences of cognitive load. That is because learners in flow state, compared to those not in flow state, may not experience (and hence not report) high cognitive load despite their investment of high effort and persistence. Thus the same amount of objective cognitive load may result in different behavioral outcomes depending on the motivational (flow) state of the learner.

In addition, theories of motivation to learn would profit from a closer look at cognitive load theory. There are motivational theories that claim to be related to cognition and motivation (Eccles & Wigfield, 2002); for example, the model of self-regulated learning proposed by Pintrich (2000). However, such theories fail to tackle the interplay of motivation and cognition within actual situations.

The following points summarize our theoretical analysis of cognitive load theory. Cognitive load theory oversimplifies the idea of lowering extraneous load and increasing germane load to foster learning processes. A high amount of free working memory capacity due to a full reduction of extraneous load and a low intrinsic load is not beneficial for learning per se, because the free capacity can be used for germane load only to a limited extent. Learners do not automatically invest all their cognitive resources, which are not used for intrinsic or extraneous load, into learning. Instead, they decide whether or not to engage in specific learning activities and the amount of cognitive resources to invest. Germane cognitive load, therefore, depends also on general learning orientations, on affective and on motivational aspects of learning. It is hard to tell which theories of motivation are best suited for developing a comprehensive cognitive-motivational theory tailored to explain the interplay of motivation, cognitive load, effort and learning outcome. Developing such a comprehensive model is beyond the scope of our current contribution. Nevertheless, it is a challenging task to integrate motivational theories and cognitive load theory to describe learning processes more exactly.

Such a comprehensive theory will have to be build from a global perspective on human cognition and motivation. A central question will be how such a theory can be scaled down to be applicable also to local perspectives. Cognitive load theory is a general theory that applies to all kind of domains and contexts. The conclusions drawn from this theory for instructional practice are the same independent of the cultural background of the learner. Contrary to cognitive load theory, however, many motivational theories consider content and context as crucial variables (e.g., the Expectancy-Value Model of Eccles und Wigfield, 2000). From this perspective, motivational phenomena are best understood if analyzed in relation to the content domain in which learning takes place. On the one hand, as researchers on cognitive load do not follow such a line of reasoning, looking at cognitive load theory from a motivational perspective may sensitize cognitive load theorists to have a closer look of the content being taught. In order to understand the interrelations between cognitive load and motivation, the context of learning and cultural background need to be taken into account. On the other hand, the generality of cognitive load theory may remind motivational researchers striving for local perspectives that also in motivational theories that pinpoint content and context as crucial variables, generality with respect to the motivational mechanisms being involved is (and should be) assumed too (cf. Krapp, 2003).

Further Empirical Research

Besides conceptual clarifications in cognitive load theory, further research is needed that investigates more closely the relation between different kinds of cognitive load, motivational state and persistence. Research should also discriminate between results of cognitive load manipulations and the motivational state of learners: Especially the phenomenon of flow state, which is the state of most efficient learning from a motivational perspective, needs to be experimentally investigated more precisely. Furthermore the research concerning motivating learning materials, which are only extraneous load from cognitive load theory's perspective, should take into account that motivational effects can be compassed in a better way if learners persistence plays a crucial role for learning success in experiments too. Moreover, experiments based on cognitive load theory do not realize the influence of high motivation during learning, as in flow state, up to now. Most learning experiments allow neither capturing effects of persistence nor effects of flow state during learning. We assume that research about reducing extraneous load did not take into account the necessity of persistence in order to learn successfully within a given learning environment. Persistence or different motivational states are largely neglected by cognitive load theory.

A further missing aspect or research concerning cognitive load theory concerns the assumption that learners high in learning goal orientation and with high metacognitive abilities also should tend to increase their own germane load within the existing constraints. Concerning strategies of research, cognitive load theory might learn from a typical research design used in studies on the relation of motivation and strategic learning. In research on motivation to learn and on self-regulated learning, a common procedure is to ask about their learning strategies. Given that germane load implies the usage of elaborated learning strategies a similar account might be used in cognitive load research. After completing some learning environment, researchers might simply ask for the strategies being used. This report should be indicative for germane load.

As our analysis has emphasized, simple rules-of-thumb regarding the reduction of cognitive load are inadequate. The different kinds of cognitive load are subject to multiple constraints, which have to be well balanced in teaching and learning. Instead of applying simple rules-of-thumb, we need a better understanding of how people learn under instructional guidance in respect to their motivational prerequisites. In other words, we need further theory driven empirical research on learning integrating theories on working memory and motivation. Cognitive load theory has made an important contribution to this field of research but an integration of important motivational aspects is missing. Therefore, understanding the role of working memory and its interplay with motivational variables in learning and instruction is still at its beginning.

Acknowledgments
We are grateful to John Sweller for various intensive discussions about fundamental issues of cognitive load theory. We also thank Eric Wiebe for suggesting the graphical display of our assumption of a constrained germane load in Figure 3.

References

Ainsworth, S., & van Labeke, N. (2004). Multiple forms of dynamic representation. *Learning and Instruction, 14*, 241-255.

Anderson, J. R. (1983). *The architecture of cognition.* Cambridge: Harvard University Press.

Atkinson, C., & Shiffrin, R. M. (1971). The control of short-term memory. *Scientific American, 225*, 82-90.

Artelt, C. (2000). Wie prädiktiv sind retrospektive Berichte für den Gebrauch von Lernstrategien für strategisches Lernen? [How predictive are retrospective reports on the use of learning strategies for strategic learning?]. *Zeitschrift für Pädagogische Psychologie, 14*, 72-84.

Atkinson, J. W. (1957). Motivational determinants of risktaking behavior. *Psychological Review, 64*, 359-372.

Baddeley, A. D. (1986). *Working memory.* Oxford: Clarendon Press.

Baddeley, A. D. (2000). The episodic buffer: A new component of working memory? *Trends in Cognitive Science, 4*, 417-423.

Bartlett, F. C. (1932). *Remembering: A study in experimental and social psychology*. London: Cambridge University Press.

Brünken, R., Plass, J. L., & Leutner, D. (2003). Direct measurement of cognitive load in multimedia learning. *Educational Psychologist, 38*, 53–61.

Chandler, P., & Sweller, J. (1991). Cognitive load theory and the format of instruction. *Cognition and Instruction, 8*, 293-332.

Chandler, P., & Sweller, J. (1996). Cognitive load while learning to use a computer program. *Applied Cognitive Psychology, 10*, 151-170.

Csikszentmihaly, M. (1990). *Flow*. New York: Harper & Row.

Driscoll, M. P., (1994). *Psychology of Learning for Instruction*. Needham Heights: Allyn & Bacon.

Dweck, C.S., & Leggett, E. L. (1988). A social-cognitive approach to motivation and personality. *Psychological Review, 95*, 256-273.

Eccles, J. S., & Wigfield, A. (2002). Motivational beliefs, values, and goals. *Annual Review of Psychology, 53*, 109–132.

Entwistle, N. J., & Ramsden, P. (1983). *Understanding student learning*. London: Croom Helm.

Gagné, R.M. (1965). *The conditions of learning*. New York: Holt, Rinehart & Winston.

Garner, R., Gillingham, M. G., & White, C.S. (1989). Effects of "seductive details" on macroprocessing and microprocessing in adults and children. *Cognition and Instruction, 6*, 41-57.

Harp, S., & Mayer, R. (1997). The role of interest in learning from scientific text and illustrations. On the distinction between emotional interest and cognitive interest. *Journal of Educational Psychology, 89*, 92–101.

Hidi, S., & Baird, W. (1986). Interestingness — a neglected variable in discourse processing. *Cognitive Science, 10*, 179–194.

Hidi, S., & Harackiewicz, J.M. (2000). Motivating the academically unmotivated: A critical issue for the 21st century. *Review of Educational Research, 70*, 151-179.

Hoppe-Graff, S., & Kim, H.-O. (2004). Understanding rights and duties in different cultures and contexts: Observations from German and Korean adolescents. In N.J. Finkel & F.M. Moghaddam (Eds.), *Human rights and duties: Empirical contributions and normative commentaries* (pp. 49–73). Washington: APA Press.

Horz, H., Winter C., & Fries, S. (in press). Differential Benefits of Situated Instructions. *Computer in Human Behavior.*

Kalyuga, S., Chandler, P., & Sweller, J. (1998). Levels of expertise and instructional design. *Human Factors, 40*, 1-17.

Kalyuga, S., Chandler, P., & Sweller, J. (2000). Incorporating learner experience into the design of multimedia instruction. *Journal of Educational Psychology, 92*, 1-11.

Karabenick, S. A., & Youssef, Z. I. (1968). Performance as a function of achievement motive level and perceived difficulty. *Journal of Personality and Social Psychology, 10*, 414-419.

Keller, J.M. (1979). Motivation and instructional design: A theoretical perspective. *Journal of Instructional Development, 2*, 26-34.

Keller, J.M., & Kopp, T.W. (1987). An application of the ARCS model of motivational design. In C.M. Reigeluth (Ed.), *Instructional theories in action. Lessons illustrating selected theories and models* (pp. 289-320). Hillsdale: Lawrence Erlbaum.

Klauer, K. J., & Leutner, D. (2007). *Lehren und Lernen. Einführung in die Instruktionspsychologie.* [Teaching and learning. An introduction to instructional psychology]. Weinheim: Beltz, PVU.

Krapp, A. (2003). Interest and human development: An educational-psychological perspective. *British Journal of Educational Psychology. Monograph Series II (2) Development and Motivation: Joint Perspectives*, 57-84.

Leung, M., Low, R., & Sweller, J. (1997). Learning from equations or words. *Instructional Science, 25*, 37-70.

Levie, W. H., & Lentz, R. (1982). Effects of text illustrations: A review of research. *Educational Communication and Technology Journal, 30*, 195-232.

Levin, J. R., Anglin, G. J., & Carney, R. N. (1987). On empirically validating functions of pictures in prose. In Willows, D. M. & Houghton, H. A. (Eds.). *The psychology of illustration* (Vol. 1: Basic research, pp. 51-85). New York: Springer.

Marton, F., & Säljö, R. (1984). Approaches to learning. In F. Marton, D. Hounsell, & D. Entwistle (Eds.), *The experience of learning* (pp. 39-58). Edinburgh: Scottish Academic Press.

Mayer, R. E. (2001). *Multimedia learning.* New York: Cambridge University Press.

Mayer, R. E. (Ed.) (2005). *The Cambridge Handbook of Multimedia Learning.* Cambridge: Cambridge University Press.

Mayer, R. E., & Moreno, R. (2002). Aids to computer-based multimedia learning. *Learning and Instruction, 12*, 107-119.

Mayer, R. E., & Moreno, R. (2003). Nine ways to reduce cognitive load in multimedia learning. *Educational Psychologist, 38*, 43-52.

McClelland, D. C. (1987). *Human motivation.* New York: Cambridge University Press.

McNamara, D.S., Kintsch, E., Songer, N.B., & Kintsch, W. (1996). Are good texts always better? Text coherence , background knowledge, and levels of understanding in learning from text. *Cognition and Instruction, 14*, 1-43.

Miller, G.A. (1956). The magical number seven, plus or minus two: Some limits on our capacity for processing information. *Psychological Review, 63*, 81-97.

Miyake, A., & Shah, P. (1999). *Models of working memory. Mechanisms of active maintenance and executive control.* Cambridge: University Press.

Moreno, R., & Mayer, R. E. (2002). Verbal redundancy in multimedia learning: When reading helps listening. *Journal of Educational Psychology, 94*, 156–163.

Paas, F., Renkl, A., & Sweller, J. (2003). Cognitive load theory and instructional design: Recent developments. *Educational Psychologist, 38*, 1–4.

Paas, F., Renkl, A., & Sweller, J. (2004). Cognitive load theory: Instructional implications of the interaction between information structures and cognitive architecture. *Instructional Science, 32*, 1–8.

Paas, F., & van Gog, T. (2006). Optimising worked example instruction: Different ways to increase germane cognitive load. *Learning and Instruction, 16*, 87-91.

Paas, F., & van Merriënboer, J.J.G. (1994) Variability of worked examples and transfer of geometrical problem-solving skills: A cognitive-load approach. *Journal of Educational Psychology, 86*, 122–133.

Paas, F., van Merriënboer, J. J. G., & Adam, J. J. (1994). Measurement of cognitive load in instructional research. *Perceptual and Motor Skills, 79*, 419-430.

Perrig, W. J. (1996). Implizites Lernen [Implicit learning]. In J. Hoffmann & W. Kintsch (Eds.), *Enzyklopädie der Psychologie* (pp. 203-234). Göttingen: Hogrefe.

Pintrich, P. R. (2000). The role of goal orientation in self-regulated learning. In M. Boekaerts, P. R. Pintrich, & M. Zeidner (Eds.), *Handbook of self-regulation* (pp. 452–502). San Diego, CA: Academic Press.

Reber, S., Walkenfeld, F. F., & Hernstadt, R. (1991). Implicit and explicit learning: Individual differences and IQ. *Journal of Experimental Psychology: Learning, Memory and Cognition, 17*, 888–896.

Renninger, K. A., Hidi, S., & Krapp, A. (Eds.) (1992). *The role of interest in learning and development.* Hillsdale: Erlbaum.

Rheinberg, F. (2006). *Motivation* (6th ed.). Stuttgart, Germany: Kohlhammer.

Rheinberg, F. (2008). Intrinsic motivation and flow. In H. Heckhausen & J. Heckhausen (Eds.), *Motivation and Action* (pp. 323-348). Cambridge: Cambridge University Press.

Rheinberg, F., Vollmeyer, R., & Burns, B. D. (2001). FAM: Ein Fragebogen zur Erfassung aktueller Motivation in Lern- und Leistungssituationen [FAM: A questionnaire to measure actual motivation in learning- and achievement situations]. *Diagnostica, 47*, 57-66.

Rheinberg, F., Vollmeyer, R., & Rollett, W. (2000). Motivation and action in self-regulated learning. In M. Boekaerts, P. R. Pintrich, & M. Zeidner (Eds.), *Handbook of self-regulation* (pp. 503–531). San Diego, CA: Academic Press.

Schank, R. C. (1979). Interestingness: Controlling inferences. *Artificial Intelligence, 12*, 273-297.

Schank, R. C., & Abelson, R. P. (1977). *Scripts, plans, goals and understanding.* Hillsdale: Erlbaum.

Schiefele, U. (1991). Interest, learning, and motivation. *Educational Psychologist, 26,* 299–323.

Schnotz, W. (2001). Sign systems, technologies, and the acquisition of knowledge. In J. F. Rouet, J. Levonen, & A. Biardeau (Eds.), *Multimedia Learning? Cognitive and Instructional Issues* (pp. 9-29). Amsterdam: Elsevier.

Schnotz, W. (2005). An integrated model of multimedia learning. In R. E. Mayer (Ed.), *The Cambridge Handbook of Multimedia Learning* (pp. 49-69). Cambridge: Cambridge University Press.

Schnotz, W., & Bannert, M. (2003). Construction and interference in learning from multiple representation. *Learning and Instruction, 13,* 141-156.

Schnotz, W., & Kürschner, C. (2007). A reconsideration of cognitive load theory. *Educational Psychology Review, 19,* 469-508.

Schnotz, W., & Rasch, T. (2005). Enabling, facilitating, and inhibiting effects of animations in multimedia Learning: Why reduction of cognitive load can have negative results on learning. *Educational Technology: Research and Development, 53,* 47-58.

Schultheiss, O. C., & Brunstein, J. C. (2005). An implicit motive perspective on competence. In A. J. Elliot & C. S. Dweck (Eds.), *Handbook of competence and motivation* (pp. 31–51). New York: Guilford Press.

Sweller, J. (1999). *Instructional design in technical areas.* Camberwell: ACER Press.

Sweller, J. (2003). Evolution of human cognitive architecture. In B. Ross (Ed.), *The psychology of learning and motivation* (Volume 43, pp. 215-266). San Diego: Academic Press.

Sweller, J. (2005). Implications of cognitive load theory for multimedia learning. In R. E. Mayer (Ed.), *The Cambridge handbook of multimedia learning* (pp. 19-30). New York: Cambridge University Press.

Sweller, J., & Chandler, P. (1994). Why some material is difficult to learn. *Cognition and Instruction, 12,* 185-233.

Sweller, J., van Merriënboer, J. J. G., & Paas, F. G. W. C. (1998). Cognitive architecture and instructional design. *Educational Psychology Review, 10,* 251-296.

Thorndike, E. L., & Gates, A. I. (1930). *Elementary Principals of Education.* New York: MacMillan.

Vollmeyer, R., & Rheinberg, F. (2000). Does motivation affect performance via persistence? *Learning and Instruction, 10,* 293–309.

Vollmeyer, R., & Rheinberg, F. (2006). Motivational effects on self-regulated learning with different tasks. *Educational Psychology Review, 18,* 239–253.

Vygotski, L. S. (1963). Learning and mental development at school age In B. Simon & J. Simon (Eds.), *Educational psychology in the U.S.S.R.* (pp. 21-34). London: Routledge & Kegan Paul.

Wenger, E. (1998). *Communities of Practice: Learning, Meaning, and Identity.* Cambridge: Cambridge University Press.

Winne, P. H., & Hadwin, A. F. (1998). Studying as self-regulated learning. In D. J. Hacker, J. Dunlosky, & A. C. Graesser (Eds.), *Metacognition in educational theory and practice* (pp. 277-304). Mahwah: Lawrence Erlbaum Associates.

Global and Local Perspectives on Human Affect

Implications of the Control-Value Theory of Achievement Emotions

Reinhard Pekrun

Introduction

Ever since scientific research has contributed to human endeavors of explaining empirical reality, it has sought to do so by reducing complex phenomena to simple laws. Along with criteria such as internal consistency, testability, and empirical validity, the parsimony achieved by scientific explanations served as a premier standard for judging their quality and practical utility. From such a perspective, explaining local phenomena by use of global, generalizable laws should be preferable to "local theories" (Schibeci & Grundy, 1987) that apply to a limited number of local phenomena only. However, while universal laws offer the advantage of explaining many phenomena (provided they are valid), it may be that they do not describe any of these phenomena in sufficient depth, implying that there may be a trade-off between parsimony and depth of explanation. Furthermore, there may be phenomena for which more global laws do not apply at all, so that describing them makes it necessary to construct a locally-specific set of laws or descriptive guidelines.

The frictions between global and local perspectives on empirical reality have long been recognized by philosophers of science, and have been used to group different sciences (including the humanities) according to the relative globality of the descriptions they offer. The terms "nomothetic" and "idiographic" have been proposed by German philosopher W. Windelband (1884) to describe global versus local approaches. Sciences such as physics or chemistry define the nomothetic endpoint of a continuum of relative globality, whereas history, literature, or ethnography are regarded as idiographic sciences. It should be noted, however, that the dichotomy of nomothetic and idiographic sciences is not equivalent to the distinction of natural sciences versus social sciences and the humanities, but is orthogonal to it. Natural sciences such as astronomy or disciplines within the earth sciences often serve idiographic rather than nomothetic purposes, and social and behavioral sciences such as economics, sociology, or cognitive psychology traditionally ascribe to nomothetic standards. Importantly, the distinction of nomothetic versus idiographic sciences also is not equivalent to the distinction of quantitative and qualitative approaches. Many nomothetic disciplines, such as psychology, make use of qualitative methodology (e.g., qualitative interviews), and many idiographic disciplines, such as astronomy, use quantitative methodology.

Accordingly, where should the psychology of motivation and emotion be located on the continuum from nomothetic (global) to idiographic (local)? Is it more appropriate to describe human feelings and reasons for human action by universal laws purportedly holding for all members of our species, or rather to do so in a way that is specific for sociohistorical contexts; for nations, institutions, and communities within these contexts; for different genders; or even for single individuals? This question is far from trivial. There is no all-or-none answer that would give clear priority for either of the two perspectives for all affective phenomena, and it likely cannot be answered by philosophical considerations of normative criteria defining good science, or simply by theoretical speculation about the usefulness of different paradigms. Rather, the answer likely depends on the phenomenon under consideration, and can only be reached by means of empirical investigation and empirically grounded construction of theories.

Studies testing the generalizability of laws of human affect across cultures, genders, life domains, and individuals may be of specific usefulness in this respect. Such studies may be helpful for answering questions like: Does test anxiety impair individual performance on exams across cultures, or are the effects of this emotion culture-specific? Do achievement goals exert similar motivational effects in male and female employees? Do appraisals of moral values have the same functional significance for social behavior in all human individuals? To the extent that the answer to such questions on generalizability is yes, global perspectives are preferable, since they provide answers that are not only valid, but also parsimonious. To the extent that the answer is no, it would be necessary to provide local explanations, and it would be necessary to do so for multiple instances as defined by different cultures, situations, genders, or individuals, thus multiplying the effort needed.

In this chapter, I will attempt to derive preliminary answers concerning the relative usefulness of global versus local perspectives for one important affective domain, namely, achievement emotions experienced by students. As a theoretical framework for deriving assumptions, the control-value theory of achievement emotions (Pekrun, 2006; Pekrun, Frenzel, Goetz, & Perry, 2007) will be used. I will first summarize the assumptions of the theory, and will then describe recent research that examined the generalizability of assumptions across cultures, genders, subject domains, and individuals. In all of the studies addressed, two different aspects of generalizability were considered: (a) Do the distributions of achievement emotions differ across cultures, domains, genders, or individuals? For example, are there significant mean level differences? (b) Do the functional properties of achievement emotions differ? That is, are there different relations with antecedents and outcomes across cultures, genders, domains, or individuals?

Positive answers to the second question (i.e., heterogeneity of functions) would likely entail positive answers to the first question (i.e., heterogeneity of distributions), and would imply that idiographic science and locally specific, non-generalizable descriptions are needed. Negative answers to the second question (i.e., homogeneity of functions) would suggest that nomothetic science is possible, even if combined with positive answers to the first question. In this case (i.e., functional homogeneity combined with heterogeneity of distributions), it would be possible to use generalizable laws for explaining functional properties of achievement emotions, but these laws would have to be enriched by knowledge about individual parameters of achievement emotions in order to make inferences about antecedents and outcomes in specific cultures, genders, domains, or individuals.

Overview of the Control-Value Theory of Achievement Emotions

Emanating from different research traditions, various theoretical accounts of achievement emotions have evolved, including attributional theories (Weiner, 1985), models of stress-related emotions in achievement settings (Folkman & Lazarus, 1985), expectancy-value approaches to emotions (Pekrun, 1992b; Turner & Schallert, 2001), and theories of test anxiety (see Zeidner, 1998). Sharing common basic assumptions, these various approaches are compensatory rather than mutually exclusive. In this context, the control-value theory provides a framework that attempts to integrate and extend assumptions from these different approaches (for an overview of the theory, see Figure 1; for more complete treatments, see Pekrun, 2006; Pekrun et al., 2007).

Addressing both activity-related and outcome-related achievement emotions, the theory is based on the premise that subjective appraisals of ongoing achievement activities, and of their past and future outcomes, are of primary importance for the arousal of these emotions. More specifically, the theory posits that *control appraisals* and *value appraisals* are the proximal determinants of achievement emotions. It is proposed that individuals experience achievement emotions when they experience being in control of, or out of control of, achievement activities and outcomes that are subjectively important to them.

Definition and Dimensions of Achievement Emotions

In past research on achievement emotions, studies typically focused on emotions relating to the success and failure outcomes of achievement activities, such as pride, anxiety, or shame (see Weiner, 1985; Zeidner, 2007). The control-value theory not only addresses these outcome emotions, but also activity-related emotions such as enjoyment of learning, boredom during instruction, or anger about task demands. Within the three-dimensional taxonomy of achievement emotions proposed by Pekrun (2006; Pekrun et al., 2007; see Table 1), the differentiation of activity emotions versus outcome emotions pertains to the *object focus* of achievement emotions. In addition, achievement emotions are grouped according to their *valence* (positive versus negative, or pleasant versus unpleasant), and to the degree of *activation* implied (activating versus deactivating, such as excitement versus pleasant relaxation [positive], or anger and anxiety versus hopelessness and boredom [negative]; also see Linnenbrink, 2007). By using the dimensions valence and activation, the taxonomy is consistent with circumplex models of affect (Feldman Barrett, & Russell, 1998).

In the three-dimensional taxonomy, achievement emotions are grouped according to their modal properties, thus providing a somewhat simplified classification. Some emotions may take multiple forms. For example, anxiety can imply freezing rather than activation, and shame involves physiological activation (as manifested in facial expression, e.g., flushing) that typically is combined with postural motoric inhibition. Also, some emotions may function in relation to both achievement activities and achievement outcomes. An important example is anger which can relate to task demands and the aversiveness of effort in ongoing activities, or to failure outcomes of these activities. Accordingly, it is classified being either an activity emotion or an outcome emotion (Table 1).

Table 1. Three-dimensional taxonomy of achievement emotions.

	Positive		Negative	
Object focus	Activating	Deactivating	Activating	Deactivating
Activity	Enjoyment	Relaxation	Anger Frustration	Boredom
Outcome	Joy Hope Pride Gratitude	Contentment Relief	Anxiety Shame Guilt Anger	Sadness Disappointment Hopelessness

Control and Value Appraisals as Proximal Antecedents

As noted, appraisals of control and value are posited to be proximal determinants of achievement emotions. *Control appraisals* pertain to the perceived controllability of achievement-related actions and outcomes. Appraisals of control, or of factors contributing to control, are implied by causal expectations (self-efficacy expectations and outcome expectancies), causal attributions of achievement, and competence beliefs (e.g., self-concepts of ability). *Value appraisals* relate to the subjective importance of achievement activities and their outcomes. Value appraisals are part of individuals' interest in the subject matter of achievement activities, and of their achievement goals involving the desire to attain success or to avoid failure.

Different kinds of control and value appraisals are assumed to instigate different kinds of emotions. Regarding *outcome emotions*, hope and anxiety are assumed to be aroused when there is some amount of perceived control or lack of control, respectively, the focus of attention being on the positive valences of anticipated success in the case of hope, and on the negative valences of anticipated failure in the case of anxiety. For example, if a student anticipates that he might fail an exam given that performance attainment on the exam is not sufficiently controllable, and if the exam is subjectively important, then anxiety is induced; if failure is not anticipated or if s/he does not care, there is no need to be anxious. Anticipatory joy is experienced when achievement outcomes are fully controllable and success is subjectively certain, and hopelessness when control is perceived to be completely absent. Retrospective outcome emotions like pride and shame are seen to be induced by attributions of success and failure as being caused by oneself or other persons, respectively.

Achievement-related *activity emotions* are also posited to depend on appraisals of control and values. Enjoyment of achievement activities is seen to depend on a combination of positive competence appraisals, and positive appraisals of the intrinsic qualities of the activity and its objects. For example, if a student doing homework assignments feels competent to master the learning material and is interested in the material, then studying is enjoyable. Anger and frustration are aroused when the incentive values of the activity are negative (e.g., when studying difficult problems takes too much effort which is experienced as being aversive). When the activity lacks any incentive values, boredom is deemed to be experienced.

Beliefs and Goals as Distal Individual Antecedents

Since control and value appraisals are regarded as proximal antecedents, any factors influencing these appraisals are posited to influence achievement emotions as well, over and above physiologically-bound temperament. Two such factors are achievement-related beliefs and goals. Competence beliefs underlie appraisals of control over achievement activities and their outcomes, while value beliefs underlie appraisals of the valence of these activities and outcomes, thereby influencing the arousal of achievement emotions. With reference to goals, it is assumed that pursuit of mastery goals focuses attention on the controllability and positive values of achievement activities, thus fostering positive activity emotions like enjoyment, and reducing negative activity emotions such as boredom and anger. In contrast, performance-approach goals are expected to focus attention on positive outcome related appraisals, and performance-avoidance goals on negative outcome-related appraisals, thus facilitating positive and negative outcome emotions, respectively (Pekrun, Elliot, & Maier, 2006).

Environments and Tasks as Antecedents

The control-value theory implies that environmental factors shaping perceived control and achievement values are also of critical importance for the arousal of achievement emotions. One important factor is the *cognitive quality* of environments and tasks at school or work, as implied by clearly structured, cognitively activating problems and learning materials. Cognitive quality is expected to exert positive effects on individuals' perceived competence and control, and on their valuing of tasks, thus positively influencing their achievement emotions. The relative difficulty of task demands should be important as well, since difficulty influences control, and since the match between task demands and individual competence can influence the subjective value of tasks. If demands are too high or too low, the incentive value of tasks may be reduced to the extent that boredom is experienced.

Furthermore, the *motivational quality* of environments and tasks is posited to be important, including both direct messages concerning the value of achievement as communicated by supervisors, teachers, or parents, and more indirect messages implied by their behavior. Examples of indirect messages are the task-related enthusiasm of teachers, colleagues, or supervisors that can fuel processes of emotional contagion (Hatfield, Cacioppo, & Rapson, 1994), and reactions to achievement outcomes such as support, praise, or criticism. Also, environments that meet basic needs (e.g., social needs) may indirectly influence the adoption of achievement values.

Environments that provide *support of autonomy and self-regulation* can increase an individual's sense of control, thus facilitating positive achievement emotions. In addition, by meeting needs for autonomy, such environments can increase the value of achievement activities. However, these beneficial effects likely depend on the match between individual competencies and need for autonomy, on the one hand, and the demands of these environments, on the other. In case of a mismatch, loss of control and negative emotions may result.

Finally, the *goal structures* provided by environments, as well as the *expectations* and *feedback* of achievement provided by others within these environments, are of critical importance for achievement emotions. Goal structures, expectations, and feedback can be based on mastery standards pertaining to absolute criteria or intra-individual competence gain, on normative standards based on competitive social comparison of individual performance, or on standards pertaining to cooperative group performance rather than individual performance. These different standards can influence individual achievement goals and any emotions mediated by these goals as outlined above. Furthermore, standards determine the relative opportunities of individuals for experiencing success and perceiving control, thus influencing control-dependent emotions. For example, normative standards involving competitive goal structures imply, by definition, that some individuals will experience success, whereas others will experience failure, thus increasing failure expectancies and failure-related emotions such as anxiety, hopelessness, and shame (Frenzel, Pekrun, & Goetz, 2007a).

Effects of Achievement Emotions on Learning and Performance

In addition to the determinants of achievement emotions, the control-value theory also addresses their functions for learning and performance. Specifically, it is posited that positive emotions like enjoyment, hope, and pride positively influence task absorption and engagement, use of flexible cognitive strategies such as organization and elaboration of learning material, and self-regulation of achievement activities. Activating negative emotions like anger, anxiety, and shame are expected to reduce cognitive resources and the use of flexible strategies and self-regulation. The motivational effects of these emotions are thought to be more complex, since they reduce intrinsic motivation, but can also evoke motivation to invest effort in order to avoid failure. Nevertheless, the overall influence of these emotions on performance at cognitively challenging tasks is likely to be negative, as suggested by the available evidence (Pekrun, Goetz, Titz, & Perry, 2002b; Zeidner, 2007). Finally, deactivating negative emotions such as boredom and hopelessness are expected to uniformly impair motivation, use of learning strategies, self-regulation, and the availability of cognitive resources, suggesting that these emotions have a negative influence on academic performance.

Reciprocal Causation of Achievement Emotions, Antecedents, and Effects

Emotions are assumed to influence achievement, but achievement outcomes are expected, in turn, to act on individual emotions, their appraisal antecedents, and social environments. By implication, antecedents, emotions, and their effects are thought to be linked by reciprocal causation over time. In line with perspectives of dynamical systems theory (Turner & Waugh, 2007), it is assumed that reciprocal causation can take different forms and can extend over fractions of seconds (e.g., in linkages between appraisals and emotions), days, weeks, months, or years. Positive feedback loops likely are quite typical (e.g., supervisors' and employees' anger reciprocally reinforcing each other), but negative feedback loops can also be important (e.g., failure inducing anxiety in a student, and anxiety motivating the student to successfully avoid failure on the next exam).

Regulation and Treatment of Achievement Emotions

Assumptions on reciprocal causality imply that achievement emotions can be regulated by targeting any of the elements involved in the cyclic feedback processes between emotions, antecedents, and outcomes (see Figure 1). Regulation and treatment of these emotions can address the emotion itself (emotion-oriented regulation and treatment; e.g., using relaxation techniques or taking drugs); the appraisals underlying emotions (appraisal-oriented regulation and treatment; e.g., reappraisals and cognitive therapy); the competencies determining individual agency and performance attainment (competence-oriented regulation and treatment; e.g., skills training); and the environment and the tasks within the environment (e.g., by career selection or task design; see Goetz, Frenzel, Pekrun, & Hall, 2006; Zeidner, 1998).

Socio-Cultural Context, Gender, Domain, and the Individual: Relative Universality of Achievement Emotions

In Pekrun's control-value theory, it is assumed that the functional mechanisms of human emotion are bound to universal, species-specific characteristics of our mind. In contrast, specific contents of emotions, as well as specific values of process parameters such as the intensity of emotions, may be specific to different cultural contexts, content domains, genders, and individuals. For example, it follows from the theory that relations between control and value appraisals, on the one hand, and achievement emotions, on the other, should be structurally equivalent for male and female students, even if mean values for these variables differ between genders. Similarly, relations between appraisals and emotions are assumed to be structurally equivalent across cultures, task domains, and individuals. In the same vein, the links between more distal antecedents and achievement emotions, and between achievement emotions and their outcomes, are posited to be universal. It is this assumption of *relative universality* that will be explored in the next sections.

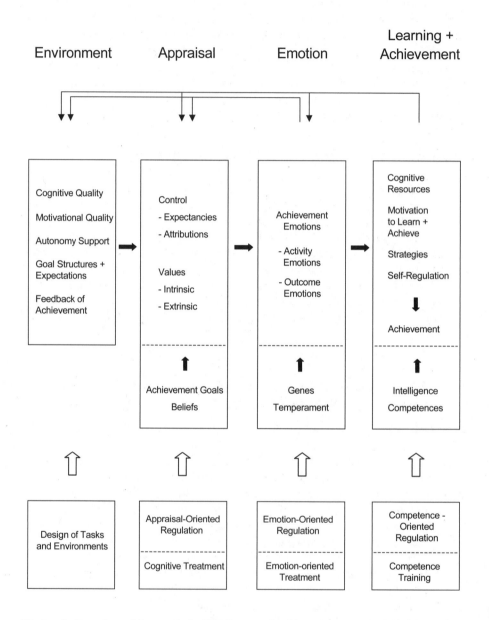

Figure 1. Overview of the control-value theory of achievement emotions (adapted from Pekrun, 2006).

Culture and Emotion

In two recent investigations, assumptions of the control-value theory were tested with samples from different cultures. In the first investigation, relationships between achievement goals and achievement emotions were analyzed in samples of American and German university students (Pekrun et al., 2006). In the second study, middle school students' emotions in mathematics were compared across German and Chinese student samples, and related to causal achievement attributions, parental expectations, and math achievement in these samples (Frenzel, Thrash, Pekrun, & Goetz, 2007).

Achievement Goals and Achievement Emotions: North America and Germany

In the Pekrun et al. (2006) research, we analyzed the predictive influence of university students' achievement goals assessed early in the semester on their course-related achievement emotions experienced several months later in the semester. The samples consisted of German (Study 1) and North American (Study 2) university students enrolled in introductory-level psychology courses. In both studies, a version of the Achievement Goals Questionnaire (AGQ; Elliot & McGregor, 2001) was used to assess the goals of the trichotomous achievement goal framework (mastery, performance-approach, and performance-avoidance goals; Elliot & Church, 1997). The Achievement Emotions Questionnaire (AEQ; Pekrun et al., 2002b; Pekrun, Goetz, & Perry, 2005a) was used to assess eight emotions frequently endorsed in undergraduate college classrooms (enjoyment, hope, pride, boredom, anger, anxiety, hopelessness, and shame). The studies were based on the control-value theory assumptions described above: Mastery goals predict activity emotions; performance-approach goals predict positive outcome emotions; performance-avoidance goals predict negative outcome emotions.

The two studies differed regarding course content (personality-social psychology in the American sample, statistics in the German sample). Therefore, it comes as no surprise that parameters of the emotion distributions also differed between the two samples, with the German participants reporting equivalent levels of pride and shame, but less enjoyment, hope, and boredom, and more anger, anxiety, and hopelessness, than their American counterparts. Given the differences between course contexts, these differences in emotion scores cannot provide any clear evidence on cultural differences.

In contrast to the mean level differences, the predictive relationships between achievement goals and achievement emotions showed an impressive equivalence across samples. As expected, mastery goals positively predicted students' enjoyment of learning, and negatively predicted their boredom and anger during the course, in both samples. In addition, mastery goals positively predicted students' hope and pride, suggesting that mastery goals not only promote activity emotions, but also induce students to think about future competence gains, as well as competence gains already acquired, thus promoting hope and pride. Performance-approach goals showed a trend for positively predicting pride which was significant in the American sample. Performance-avoidance goals positively predicted students' anxiety and showed trends towards positively predicting hopelessness and shame in both samples. All trends that were marginally significant in the single studies became fully significant when integrating the results across the two studies meta-analytically. Except the lack of a link between performance-approach goals and students' hope, these findings are fully consistent with the assumptions of the control-value theory. Furthermore, they indicate that the predictive relationships between achievement-related goals and emotions were equivalent across cultures, suggesting functional homogeneity of the relations between achievement emotions and their goal antecedents.

Achievement Emotions in Mathematics: Germany and China

While the Pekrun et al. (2006) research was of limited value for cross-cultural analysis due to the variation of course contents, Frenzel, Thrash, et al. (2007) made an explicit attempt to establish cross-cultural equivalence of samples, context, and measures in an investigation of mathematics emotions experienced by German and Chinese students. The students of both the German and the Chinese samples were from grade 8 and came from a mix of socio-economic backgrounds, and the achievement emotions assessed (enjoyment, pride, anger, anxiety, and shame) related to the same subject domain (mathematics) in both samples. Furthermore, the cross-cultural equivalence of the German and Chinese versions of the Achievement Emotions Questionnaire-Mathematics (AEQ-M; Pekrun, Goetz, & Frenzel, 2005b) used in this study was corroborated by mean and co-variance structure (MACS) analysis (Little, 1997).

The analysis of mean levels of emotion scores showed clear differences between cultures. Chinese students reported higher levels of enjoyment, pride, anxiety, and shame, whereas German students reported higher levels of anger. These differences are consistent with previous research that found higher scores for achievement anxiety in students from East Asian countries, as compared to students from Western countries (e.g., Organization for Economic Cooperation and Development [OECD], 2004), and extends these findings to achievement emotions other than anxiety. The findings are also consistent with existing evidence that anger is more avoided in collectivistic cultures, as compared to individualistic cultures (Grimm, Church, Katigbak, & Reyes, 1999; Matsumoto, Kudoh, Scherer, & Wallbott, 1988).

In contrast to mean-level differences, the relationships of achievement emotions with attributions, parental expectations, and math achievement were reasonably similar across countries. In both samples, students' subjective control, as indicated by high ability attributions for success in mathematics, correlated positively with their enjoyment and pride, and negatively with their anxiety, anger, and shame. As indicated by low ability attributions for failure, lack of control correlated negatively with enjoyment and pride and positively with the negative emotions. Furthermore, expectations by parents that their child was able to do well in mathematics correlated positively with the two positive emotions, and negatively with the three negative emotions, in both samples. Finally, enjoyment and pride correlated positively, and anger, anxiety, and shame negatively, with students' math achievement in both samples.

These findings are consistent with the control-value theory positing that subjective control over achievement, as well as parental expectations fostering control, promote achievement emotions such as enjoyment and pride, and reduce anger, anxiety, and shame. They also are consistent with the assumption that pleasant achievement emotions typically exert positive effects, and unpleasant achievement emotions negative effects, on students' academic achievement. In addition, the data show that these relationships were uniformly found across cultures in the present investigation.

Summary

While the data from the Pekrun et al. (2006) studies cannot be used to assess cross-cultural differences between distributions of achievement emotions, the investigation by Frenzel, Thrash, et al. (2007) clearly showed that mean levels of achievement emotions can differ substantially across cultures, in line with findings of previous investigations. In contrast, as implied by the findings of both sets of studies, the relationships of achievement emotions with achievement goals, perceived control, parental expectations, and academic achievement proved to be largely equivalent across cultures. The findings suggest cross-cultural functional homogeneity of these relationships.

Gender and Emotion: Mathematics Emotions Experienced by Female and Male Students

Gender differences in mathematics are an issue of considerable practical importance. While differences in mathematics achievement between females and males are small and declining, there are substantial differences in the affective domain world-wide (OECD, 2004). These differences are likely one important reason why females are underrepresented in careers in mathematics and computer science. In the OECD countries, only 30% of the university graduates in these disciplines are female on average (OECD, 2004). Affective variables in mathematics for which gender differences are documented include control-related variables such as competence beliefs and self-efficacy expectations, value-related variables such as the perceived usefulness of mathematics, and generalized attitudes towards mathematics (Bandura, 1997; Eccles, Wigfield, & Schiefele, 1998; OECD, 2004).

Regarding achievement emotions in mathematics, the one single emotion that has attracted researchers' interest was mathematics anxiety. Scores for anxiety in this domain are consistently higher for female, as compared to male, individuals (Hyde, Fennema, & Lamon, 1990; OECD, 2004). Achievement emotions other than anxiety, however, have been neglected by research, despite the fact that mathematics is a domain that can elicit a wide range of different feelings.

Using scales of the AEQ-M, Frenzel, Pekrun, and Goetz (2007b) explored gender differences in five mathematics emotions (enjoyment, pride, anxiety, hopelessness, and shame). The representative sample of this study consisted of over 2,000 German students in grade 5 (49.5% female). Primary research questions pertained to gender differences in mean levels of emotions, to the mediation of these differences by differences in control and value beliefs, and to the equivalence of the links between appraisals and emotions across genders. Students' competence beliefs in mathematics ("I am a good student in mathematics") were employed as an indicator of perceived control, and the intrinsic value of this domain ("Mathematics is my favorite subject") as well as the value of achievement in the domain ("It is very important for me to get good grades in mathematics") as indicators of subjective values. Using assumptions from the control-value theory, it was hypothesized that competence beliefs would be a positive predictor of enjoyment and pride, and a negative predictor of anxiety, hopelessness, and shame; that domain value would be a positive predictor of enjoyment; and that achievement value would be a positive predictor of pride, anxiety, hopelessness, and shame.

The findings suggest that there are clear differences between the mathematics emotions experienced by the two genders. Female students reported less enjoyment and pride in mathematics, and more anxiety, hopelessness, and shame, even after partialling out prior achievement. These differences were congruent with the differences found for control- and value-related beliefs. Girls had lower scores for competence beliefs and domain value, whereas the scores for achievement value in mathematics did not differ.

The findings of mediational regression analysis corroborated that gender was a significant predictor of all five emotions. After additionally including the competence belief and value variables in the regression equation, however, gender was no longer a significant predictor of pride, anxiety, hopelessness, and shame, and remained only a weak predictor of enjoyment, thus indicating substantial mediation of gender effects on mathematics emotions by control and values appraisals. More specifically, as expected, competence belief positively mediated gender effects on enjoyment and pride, and negatively mediated gender effects on anxiety, hopelessness, and shame. Domain value positively mediated gender effects on enjoyment, and achievement value positively mediated gender effects on pride, anxiety, hopelessness, and shame. This pattern of predictive links corroborates that students' mathematics emotions can be explained by their appraisals, and that gender differences in mathematics emotions are largely mediated by differences in these appraisals.

In addition, the equivalence of relationships between appraisals and emotions across genders was explored by multiple-group SEM analyses. The findings showed that these relationships were largely equivalent. For each of the five emotions, the appraisal-emotion relationships had the same sign, were equally significant, and had similar size across genders.

In sum, these findings indicate that there are substantial differences between the mathematics emotions experienced by female and male students, with female students showing a debilitating pattern of lower enjoyment and pride, combined with higher anxiety, hopelessness, and shame in mathematics. In line with assumptions of the control-value theory, these gender differences were largely mediated by students' competence and value appraisals. However, the links between these appraisals and all five emotions were demonstratively equivalent for female and male students, thus corroborating assumptions on the relative universality of relationships between appraisals and achievement emotions across genders.

Content Domain and Emotion: The Relative Domain Specificity of Achievement Emotions

In traditional approaches to achievement emotions, an underlying assumption was that these emotions are generalized across situations and task domains. Specifically, in test anxiety research, most studies regarded this emotion as a general personality trait predisposing individuals to experience anxiety whenever confronted with an evaluative situation (Zeidner, 1998). However, a few studies have empirically investigated the validity of this assumption, and found that achievement-related anxiety can show considerable variation across academic domains, as indicated by low cross-domain correlations of anxiety scores (Marsh, 1988). Furthermore, research on achievement-related subjective control and values has suggested that these variables are organized in domain-specific ways as well (self-concepts of ability, self-efficacy, and task values; Bong, 2001). By implication, it can be assumed that emotions other than anxiety should also show domain specificity.

In a series of three studies, we found evidence corroborating this assumption. The first two of these studies (Goetz, Pekrun, Hall, & Haag, 2006; Pekrun, Goetz, Titz, & Perry, 2002a) used single-item indicators for students' emotions experienced in different domains. In the Pekrun et al. (2002a) study, between-domain correlations were found to be non-significant for middle school students' enjoyment in mathematics, languages (German and English), music, and sports, and low for their anxiety in these domains. In the Goetz et al. (2006) investigation, enjoyment, anxiety, and boredom experienced by students (grades 7 to 10) showed weak between-domain relations across six different subject domains.

In the third study, Goetz, Frenzel, Pekrun, Hall, and Lüdtke (2007) explored both the domain specificity of levels of emotions, and the universality of their interrelations and links with academic achievement across domains. The study used multi-item measures derived from the Achievement Emotions Questionnaire (Pekrun et al., 2005a) to analyze 8th and 11th graders' enjoyment, pride, boredom, anger, and anxiety experienced in mathematics, physics, German, and English.

As expected, the findings showed that mean levels of emotions differed across domains. Students reported more enjoyment and pride, and less boredom, in English than in the other three subjects, and less anger and anxiety in both English and German, as compared with mathematics and physics. In addition to these mean-level differences, there were substantial interindividual differences of the domain-related emotion scores, as indicated by their correlations across domains. With the exception of correlations between emotions in the adjacent domains of mathematics and physics, and in the adjacent domains of German and English, all coefficients were below $r = .35$ in the sample of 8th graders, and below $r = .20$ in the sample of 11th graders. Taking into account that coefficients were corrected for unreliability of measures in this study, thus representing relationships at the latent level, these findings clearly showed that students' emotional experiences can be quite different across academic domains.

However, the domain specificity of students' emotions notwithstanding, their interrelations and links with academic achievement proved to be similar across domains. The size of these correlations was somewhat lower in German than in the other three domains. Nevertheless, in all four domains, enjoyment and pride showed substantial positive intercorrelations, as did boredom, anger, and anxiety. All correlations between the two positive emotions, on one hand, and the three negative emotions, on the other hand, were substantially negative in all four domains. Furthermore, the correlations of enjoyment and pride with students' academic achievement were consistently positive within all four domains, and the correlations of anxiety with achievement were consistently negative in all four domains. For boredom, all eight different correlations with achievement scores were negative, with seven of them reaching significance; for anger as well, all eight correlations were negative, with six of them reaching significance.

These findings suggest that achievement emotions show considerable domain specificity, in contrast to traditional approaches assuming that emotions such as test anxiety are generalized across situations. Domain specificity is indicated by the differences of mean levels of emotions, as well as the low correlations of emotions, across domains. This variation notwithstanding, the interrelations between different emotions, and between emotions and students' achievement, proved to be rather consistent, suggesting universality of structural and functional relationships across subject domains.

The Individual and Emotion: Achievement Emotions Within and Across Students

In the psychology of motivation and emotion, inferences about within-person functional relationships are typically derived from sample statistics pertaining to differences between experimental groups in experimental designs, or to covariation between variables in non-experimental studies. For example, in test anxiety research, negative relationships between anxiety and achievement over time are typically interpreted as indicating that anxiety exerts negative effects on achievement within individuals. Any use of sample statistics may be misleading, however, when wanting to draw inferences about intra-individual psychological functioning, since one and the same sample statistic may be produced by quite different patterns of underlying individual parameters.

A case in point is the use of correlations: It may happen that an inter-individual correlation between two variables does not represent the intra-individual relation between these two variables in any single person under study. Generally, inter-individual and intra-individual covariations between variables are statistically independent (Robinson, 1950; Schmitz & Skinner, 1993). An example of diverging inter-individual and intra-individual correlations is the relation between duration of sleep and frequency of migraine headaches (Schmitz & Skinner, 1993). At the population level (inter-individual correlation), these two variables are typically positively correlated, which seemingly implies that sleeping late can lead to headaches (or vice versa). At the individual level (intra-individual correlation), however, the two variables correlate *negatively*, implying that headaches are associated with *shorter* duration of sleep.

To analyze the intra-individual functions of motivation and emotion, intra-individual analysis is needed (e.g., analysis of the covariation of two variables over time within individuals). Such an analysis provides an idiographic perspective on the psychological functioning of individuals. When repeating such an analysis for each individual within a sample, the generalizability of intra-individual findings across individuals can be tested, making it possible to analyze the validity of nomothetic universality assumptions with a series of idiographic analyses.

Such a combined idiographic-nomothetic strategy was employed in a diary study of student-teachers' achievement emotions experienced over a period of six weeks before and during students' final university exams (Pekrun & Hofmann, 1996). The study included daily assessments of exam emotions and related variables, such as motivation to prepare for the exam. The findings showed that the average levels of different emotions varied widely across the 69 students included in the sample. Furthermore, the developmental trajectories of these emotions over the six-week period also showed considerable variation. For example, while average scores for anxiety increased until the beginning of the exam period (i.e., during the first three weeks) and decreased afterwards (during the remaining three weeks), the scores of individual students showed strikingly different patterns. Some students reported little anxiety throughout the six weeks, others experienced high levels of anxiety throughout; some students showed an increase followed by a decrease of scores, others a decrease followed by an increase, etc. The distribution of average scores over time was not well suited to describe any of the single students of the sample.

When analyzing the relationships between daily emotions and students' current motivation to learn, on average the intra-individual correlations were substantially positive for enjoyment, hope, and pride, negative for anger, boredom, hopelessness, and shame, and zero for anxiety. For most emotions, these relationships were consistent across students, although correlations varied in strength. For example, correlations over time between enjoyment and motivation to learn were positive for all students, without exception. For anxiety, however, a different picture emerged. While the relationship between anxiety and motivation was zero in some students, consistent with the average correlation in the sample, it was positive or negative in others, with many of these intra-individual correlations reaching substantial size ($r > .40$).

These different correlations may have been due to ambiguous motivational effects of anxiety, as suggested by the control-value theory. Negative effects of anxiety on intrinsic motivation and positive effects on motivation to avoid failure may be balanced differently in different individuals, explaining why the overall correlations between anxiety and motivation can differ as well. If so, the differences we found may well fit into a nomothetical framework of explaining the functional relationships of students' achievement-related anxiety. However, since data on different types of motivation were not available in the study, this interpretation remains speculative.

In sum, the findings of this diary study demonstrated that levels and trajectories of daily achievement emotions vary across individuals. Furthermore, they showed that relationships of most of these emotions with students' motivation to learn were equivalent across individuals. However, anxiety was an exception. Intra-individual relationships between anxiety and motivation to learn were positive, negative, or zero in different students, suggesting that functional relationships of achievement emotions need not always be the same for all individuals.

Summary and Conclusions

In four sets of studies, we explored the relative universality of distributional parameters and functional relationships of achievement emotions across cultures, genders, content domains, and individuals. Regarding culture, the comparative analysis of achievement emotions experienced in university courses by American and German university students showed that mean levels of emotions differed, whereas relationships with achievement goals adopted early in the semester were largely equivalent across samples. Similarly, our findings for German and Chinese middle school students' emotions in mathematics showed substantial differences of emotion profiles across cultures, whereas the links of mathematics emotions with variables of perceived control, parental expectations, and academic achievement were largely equivalent across the two cultures.

In the analysis of gender differences in mathematics emotions, mean levels of mathematics emotions differed between the two genders, with female students showing a more debilitative pattern of emotions than male students. This pattern was well explained by gender-linked differences in appraisals, in line with assumptions from the control-value theory. Female students had lower competence beliefs and domain values in mathematics, but similarly high subjective values of achievement in this domain, explaining their lower scores for enjoyment and pride, and higher scores for anxiety, hopelessness, and shame. However, the relationships between emotions and control-value appraisals were largely consistent across female and male students.

Regarding content domains as well, we found considerable differences in levels of emotions. Both generally and within individuals, emotions differed between academic subjects such as mathematics, physics, German, and English, suggesting that students' achievement emotions are organized in domain-specific ways. Nevertheless, the interrelations of different emotions, as well as their links with academic achievement, proved to be similar across these different domains. In German, the relationships between different emotions were structurally the same as in the other domains, but were less strong. This may have been due to the fact that German is a domain constituted of different subdomains (such as grammar, literature, and essay writing) that may evoke different feelings, thus making relationships between emotions more fuzzy than in other domains.

Finally, in our diary study we used a strategy combining idiographic and nomothetical elements to analyze distributions and functional relationships of students' daily emotions experienced before and during their final university exams. The findings showed that emotions differed between individuals, and that the development of these emotions over time also differed between individuals; any description of this development based on average scores would not be suited to describe how emotions unfolded in the individual student. Regarding functional relationships, the links of students' exam-related emotions with their motivation to learn were consistent across individuals for most emotions. However, anxiety was an exception. All kinds of intraindividual relationships (positive, negative, or zero) were present in the sample, maybe due to interindividual differences in the balance of positive and negative effects of anxiety on various types of intrinsic and extrinsic motivation.

Taken together, these findings suggest that the answer to the first question posed at the outset (do the distributions of achievement emotions differ?) is uniformly positive: Achievement emotions differ across cultures, genders, content domains, and individuals. The answer to the second question (do the functional properties of achievement emotions differ?), however, is largely negative. With few exceptions, the interrelations between different achievement emotions, as well as their relationships with outcomes and antecedents, were structurally equivalent across cultures, genders, content domains, and individuals, consistent with the view that a nomothetic psychology of human motivation and emotion is viable. Furthermore, the findings not only show that explanations of human affect can be parsimonious; they also document that nomothetic principles can be useful for explaining a wide range of phenomena, including appraisal and goal antecedents, environmental antecedents, and performance outcomes of achievement emotions as addressed by the control-value theory.

A number of limitations should be kept in mind, however, when interpreting the findings summarized in this chapter. The studies described here related to a select array of achievement emotions, used specific measures assessing these emotions, involved samples of K-12 and university students from selected countries, and were situated in academic contexts. It remains to be tested if the conclusions reached would hold with additional emotions, different measures, different samples, and other kinds of contexts such as work and sports. Furthermore, and more importantly, contemporary approaches to the relative universality of functional relationships may more generally be limited, in at least two ways.

First, even with strong empirical relations between achievement emotions, outcomes, and antecedents (such as $r = .50$, or $d = 1.00$), a major part of the variance is left unexplained. It seems that the nomothetic psychology of motivation and emotion is not yet able to unravel the multitude of interacting factors influencing affective processes. To do so, it will likely be necessary to more fully endorse process-oriented strategies using real-time estimates of motivation and emotion, as well as dynamic modeling of processes (Atkinson & Birch, 1970; Wehrle & Scherer, 2001), in future research.

Second, while nomothetic principles may be suited to describe and explain affective phenomena across a wide range of individuals and contexts, their value for describing the individual, contextualized contents of motivation and emotion likely is limited. To quite an extent, these contents depend on the specifics of individual autobiographical memories and life situations. In our own research on achievement emotions, we used qualitative interviews with K-12 and university students to acquire knowledge about the contents of achievement emotions (Pekrun, 1992a; Pekrun et al., 2002b), and found both generalizable structures and more idiosyncratic components specific to single individuals. The generalizable structures we found were used for constructing the Achievement Emotions Questionnaire (AEQ; Pekrun et al., 2005a). Variants of this instrument were employed in the research summarized herein, implying that achievement emotions were assessed in terms of components for which universality can reasonably be assumed, at the cost of disregarding more specific contents that characterize single individuals and contexts. To fully describe the diversity of these contents, approaches involving both nomothetic and idiographic elements are needed.

In sum, the research reported here strongly suggests that a global (i.e., nomothetic) approach to achievement emotions can provide evidence-based conclusions on the structures and functions of these emotions that are both valid and parsimonious. At the same time, however, it may be useful to complement global approaches by local (i.e., idiographic) approaches in order to get broader evidence on the specific distributions and contents of achievement emotions that characterize specific cultures, contexts, and individuals.

References

Atkinson, J. W., & Birch, D. (1970). *A dynamic theory of action*. New York: Wiley.

Bandura, A. (1997). *Self-efficacy: The exercise of control*. New York: Freeman.

Bong, M. (2001). Between- and within-domain relations of academic motivation among middle and high school students: Self-efficacy, task-value and achievement goals. *Journal of Educational Psychology, 93*, 23-34.

Eccles, J. S., Wigfield, A., & Schiefele, U. (1998). Motivation to succeed. In W. Damon (Series Ed.) & N. Eisenberg (Vol. Ed.), *Handbook of child psychology: Social, emotional, and personality development* (5th ed.,Vol.3, pp. 1017-1095). Hoboken, NJ: Wiley.

Elliot, A. J., & Church, M. A. (1997). A hierarchical model of approach and avoidance achievement motivation. *Journal of Personality and Social Psychology, 72*, 218-232.

Elliot, A. J., & McGregor, H. A. (2001). A 2 x 2 achievement goal framework. *Journal of Personality and Social Psychology, 80*, 501-519.

Feldman Barrett, L., & Russell, J. A. (1998). Independence and bipolarity in the structure of current affect. *Journal of Personality and Social Psychology, 74*, 967-984.

Folkman, S., & Lazarus, R. S. (1985). If it changes it must be a process: Study of emotion and coping during three stages of a college examination. *Journal of Personality and Social Psychology, 48*, 150-170.

Frenzel, A. C., Pekrun, R., & Goetz, T. (2007a). Perceived learning environments and students' emotional experiences: A multilevel analysis of mathematics classrooms. *Learning and Instruction, 17*, 478-493.

Frenzel, A. C., Pekrun, R., & Goetz, T. (2007b). Girls and mathematics – a "hopeless" issue? A control-value approach to gender differences in emotions towards mathematics. *European Journal of Psychology of Education, 22*, 497-514.

Frenzel, A. C., Thrash, T. M., Pekrun, R., & Goetz, T. (2007). Achievement emotions in Germany and China: A cross-cultural validation of the Academic Emotions Questionnaire-Mathematics (AEQ-M). *Journal of Cross-Cultural Psychology, 38*, 302-309.

Goetz, T., Frenzel, A., Pekrun, R., & Hall, N. (2006). Emotional intelligence in the context of learning and achievement. In R. Schulze & R. D. Roberts (Eds.), *Emotional intelligence: An international handbook* (pp. 233-253). Cambridge, MA: Hogrefe & Huber.

Goetz, T., Frenzel, A. C., Pekrun, R., Hall, N. C., & Lüdtke, O. (2007). Between- and within-domain relations of students' academic emotions. *Journal of Educational Psychology, 99*, 715-733.

Goetz, T., Pekrun, R., Hall, N. C., & Haag, L. (2006). Academic emotions from a socio-cognitive perspective: Antecedents and domain specificity of students' affect in the context of Latin instruction. *British Journal of Educational Psychology, 76*, 289-308.

Grimm, S. D., Church, A. T., Katigbak, M. S., & Reyes, J. A. S. (1999). Self-described traits, values, and moods associated with individualism and collectivism. *Journal of Cross-Cultural Psychology, 30*, 466-500.

Hatfield, E., Cacioppo, J. T., & Rapson, R. L. (1994). *Emotional contagion*. New York: Cambridge University Press.

Hyde, J. S., Fennema, E., & Lamon, S. J. (1990). Gender differences in mathematics performance: A meta-analysis. *Psychological Bulletin, 107*, 139-155.

Linnenbrink, E. A. (2007). The role of affect in student learning: A multi-dimensional approach to considering the interaction of affect, motivation, and engagement. In P. A. Schutz & R. Pekrun (Eds.), *Emotion in education* (pp. 107-124). San Diego, CA: Academic Press.

Little, T. D. (1997). Mean and covariance structures (MACS) analyses of cross-cultural data: Practical and theoretical issues. *Multivariate Behavioral Research, 32*, 53-76.

Marsh, H. W. (1988). The content specificity of math and English anxieties: The high school and beyond study. *Anxiety Research, 1*, 137-149.

Matsumoto, D., Kudoh, T., Scherer, K. R., & Wallbott, H. (1988). Antecedents and reactions to emotions in the United States and Japan. *Journal of Cross-Cultural Psychology, 19*, 267-285.

Organization for Economic Cooperation and Development (OECD) (2004). *Learning for tomorrow's world: First results from PISA 2003*. Paris: Author.

Pekrun, R. (1992a). Kognition und Emotion in studienbezogenen Lern- und Leistungssituationen: Explorative Analysen [Cognition and emotion of university students in achievement settings: An exploratory analysis]. *Unterrichtswissenschaft, 20,* 308-324.

Pekrun, R. (1992b). The expectancy-value theory of anxiety: Overview and implications. In D. G. Forgays, T. Sosnowski, & K. Wrzesniewski (Eds.), *Anxiety: Recent developments in self-appraisal, psychophysiological and health research* (pp. 23-41). Washington, DC: Hemisphere.

Pekrun, R. (2006). The control-value theory of achievement emotions: Assumptions, corollaries, and implications for educational research and practice. *Educational Psychology Review, 18,* 315-341.

Pekrun, R., Elliot, A. J., & Maier, M. A. (2006). Achievement goals and discrete achievement emotions: A theoretical model and prospective test. *Journal of Educational Psychology, 98,* 583-597.

Pekrun, R., Frenzel, A., Goetz, T., & Perry, R. P. (2007). The control-value theory of achievement emotions: An integrative approach to emotions in education. In P. A. Schutz & R. Pekrun (Eds.), *Emotions in education* (pp. 13-36). San Diego, CA: Academic Press.

Pekrun, R., Goetz, T., & Perry, R. P. (2005a). *Achievement Emotions Questionnaire (AEQ). User's manual.* Department of Psychology, University of Munich, Germany.

Pekrun, R., Goetz, T., & Frenzel, A. C. (2005b). *Achievement Emotions Questionnaire – Mathematics (AEQ-M). User's manual.* Department of Psychology, University of Munich, Germany.

Pekrun, R., Goetz, T., Titz, W., & Perry, R. P. (2002a, April). *A social cognitive, control-value theory of achievement emotions: Social antecedents and achievement effects of students' domain-related emotions.* Paper presented at the annual meeting of the American Educational Research Association, New Orleans.

Pekrun, R., Goetz, T., Titz, W., & Perry, R. P. (2002b). Academic emotions in students' self-regulated learning and achievement: A program of quantitative and qualitative research. *Educational Psychologist, 37,* 91-106.

Pekrun, R., & Hofmann, H. (1996, April). *Affective and motivational processes: Contrasting interindividual and intraindividual perspectives.* Paper presented at the annual meeting of the American Educational Research Association, New York.

Robinson, W. S. (1950). Ecological correlations and the behavior of individuals. *American Sociological Review, 15,* 351-356.

Schibeci, R. A., & Grundy, S. (1987). Local theories. *Journal of Educational Research, 81,* 91-96.

Schmitz, B., & Skinner, E. (1993). Perceived control, effort, and academic performance: Interindividual, intraindividual, and multivariate time series analyses. *Journal of Personality and Social Psychology, 64,* 1010-1028.

Turner, J. E., & Schallert, D. L. (2001). Expectancy-value relationships of shame reactions and shame resiliency. *Journal of Educational Psychology, 93,* 320-329.

Turner, J. E., & Waugh, R. M. (2007). A dynamical systems perspective regarding students' learning processes: Shame reactions and emergent self-organizations. In P. A. Schutz & R. Pekrun (Eds.), *Emotion in education* (pp. 125-145). San Diego, CA: Academic Press.

Wehrle, T., & Scherer, K. R. (2001). Toward computational modeling of appraisal theories. In K. R. Scherer, A. Schorr, & T. Johnstone (Eds.), *Appraisal processes in emotion* (pp. 350-365). New York: Oxford University Press.

Weiner, B. (1985). An attributional theory of achievement motivation and emotion. *Psychological Review, 92,* 548-573.

Windelband, W. (1884). *Geschichte und Naturwissenschaft* [History and science]. Tübingen, Germany: Mohr.

Zeidner, M. (1998). *Test anxiety: The state of the art.* New York: Plenum.

Zeidner, M. (2007). Test anxiety in educational contexts: Concepts, findings, and future directions. In P. A. Schutz & R. Pekrun (Eds.), *Emotion in education* (pp. 165-184). San Diego, CA: Academic Press.

Metacognitive Experiences as the Link between Situational Characteristics, Motivation, and Affect in Self-Regulated Learning

Fotini Dina & Anastasia Efklides

Introduction

Self-regulated learning (SRL) is a theoretical framework that has gained a prominent place in educational research in the last 20 years (Pintrich & DeGroot, 1990; Zimmerman, 1998). This theoretical framework is very broad and integrative, and stresses the synergy of cognition, motivation, metacognition, and volition in the learning process (Boekaerts, 1999). It posits the self and its priorities at the center of students' decisions and actions that pertain to their learning and school achievement. According to Zimmerman (1998) SRL is a cyclic process having three basic phases: forethought, performance/volitional control, and self-reflection. At the Forethought phase, motivation and self-efficacy beliefs play a very important role because they determine the goals to be set and the engagement with learning activities. At the Performance/Volitional Control phase cognition (knowledge, skills) and metacognition (planning, monitoring, and control of cognition) along with volitional strategies for the control of action and for surpassing the obstacles faced are the major determinants of learning behaviors. At the Self-Reflection phase, self-evaluations, self-reactions, and attributions about learning outcomes take place leading to adaptation of performance, of self-evaluations as well as of the goals set. These self-reflections and adaptations feed onto the next Forethought phase of the SRL process and influence the decisions to be made, thus starting another SRL cycle.

Although the SRL theoretical framework has been very successful in showing how students develop as learners and in which ways successful self-regulators differ from less successful ones, it is less informative on issues like the following: (a) Do, and how, the various components of SRL, which are operating in each phase, interact with each other within and across the various phases of SRL? An example of such interactions is between general person characteristics, such as motivation, cognitive ability, and affect (e.g., attitudes) at the Forethought phase; one could assume that these person characteristics impact the Performance/Volitional Control phase as well, because they have a bearing on cognition, on effort investment, and on affect experienced during task processing. (b) Another issue pertains to the role of affect in SRL. (c) A third issue regards if and how the components of the various phases of SRL that function at a person or macro-level (e.g., self-efficacy, ability, etc.) adapt to the task and situational level, that is, to the micro-level.

The above three issues, in essence, challenge the SRL theoretical framework with respect to its ability to move from the general to the specific level, from the context-free to the situational, from global relations to local dynamics developed because of situational and task features. Local dynamics involve cognitive, metacognitive, and affective reactions which impact the interactions between the various components of SRL and the self-regulation process itself.

In this chapter we present a study related to the issues listed above. Specifically, we will approach motivation as a process that is part of the Forethought phase and interacts with other components of the Performance/Volitional Control phase that takes place within a specific learning situation. We posit that motivational factors impact not only performance but affect as well, such as state anxiety or interest in and liking of the task. In this respect, we examine motivation as a person characteristic as well as a feature of the learning situation in the form of goal orientation instructions. As person characteristic (i.e., students' achievement goal orientations) motivation interacts with other general student characteristics such as cognitive ability, self-concept, test anxiety, and attitude toward the learning domain. These general personal characteristics that are operating at the Forethought phase establish the initial conditions for cognition, metacognition, and affect during problem solving in the Performance/Volitional Control phase, which is bound to specific learning situations.[1] In their turn, cognitive and metacognitive processes at the task level as well as another situational factor, namely extrinsic feedback (EF) to task performance, impact students' emotions (specifically, interest, liking, and state anxiety). However, since SRL does not take place on one occasion (i.e., a snapshot) but in multiple ones that share situational characteristics, the effects of one SRL cycle (e.g., in our study the first testing occasion) can carry over to subsequent SRL cycles as well (i.e., the second testing occasion).

In the present study, the learning situation involved mathematical tasks and resembled normal classrooms in which teachers promote achievement goals and provide feedback on students' performance. We claim that the effects of students' motivation, as a person characteristic, on their performance and emotions (such as state anxiety) are not tied to the specific learning situation students find themselves in nor to the SRL cycle (first or second testing occasion). The situational factors have their own effects on performance, on metacognition, and on affect, which are beyond those of students' general person characteristics. Also, since metacognition monitors cognitive processing and its outcome (Efklides, 2006), the effects of EF regarding the outcome of cognitive processing on students' state anxiety are mediated by metacognition. However, metacognition will not mediate the effect of situational motivation, namely goal instructions, on students' state anxiety because goal instructions do not provide information about cognitive processing and its outcome. Moreover, the SRL component that will mediate the effects of EF on state anxiety is metacognitive experiences, one of the facets of metacognition. In this way the question posed by the topic of this volume, that is, whether motivation can be best understood through a global approach or through snapshots, will be highlighted, albeit by embedding motivation within the theoretical framework of SRL and by differentiating its

---

[1] Learning situations vary in many respects; one of them is motivational instructions, namely the achievement goal instructions conveyed to students. They also set the learning tasks.

effects from other factors also involved in SRL.

In what follows, we shall refer, first, to affect and metacognitive experiences in learning situations and then to the relations of achievement goal orientations with emotions. Following that, we shall introduce other person characteristics that are present in learning situations, which may interact with task processing in the specific learning situation that we studied. Then an experimental study that tested the interactions between the various person and situational characteristics will be presented. Finally, the implications of the study's findings as regards the global or local perspective to motivation will be discussed.

Affect and Metacognitive Experiences

The role of affect in learning has always been considered important, with considerable emphasis on anxiety and interest. A theoretical framework that has been formulated to integrate motivation and emotions in learning contexts is Pekrun's control-value theory of achievement emotions (Pekrun, Elliot, & Maier, 2006; Pekrun, Goetz, Titz, & Perry, 2002). The theory proposes a taxonomy of emotions based on two dimensions: valence (positive or negative) and object focus (activity or outcome). Outcome-related emotions can be prospective (e.g., hope, anxiety, hopelessness) or retrospective (e.g., pride, shame). Activity-related emotions are enjoyment and boredom.

There are, however, other affective states that can be experienced during the learning process and have an impact on the self-regulation process during task processing (Efklides & Petkaki, 2005). These are metacognitive experiences (ME; Efklides, 2001, 2006), such as feeling of difficulty, feeling of satisfaction, feeling of confidence, estimate of effort, and others. Specifically, ME, and particularly metacognitive feelings, have a positive or negative affective character (valence) and inform the person about the task demands, the fluency of cognitive processing, and the quality of the outcome of processing. They are of critical importance for online control decisions and the self-regulation of task processing as well as for long-term motivation and SRL through their impact on self-concept (Efklides & Tsiora, 2002) and on causal attributions (Metallidou & Efklides, 2001).

Metacognitive experiences are manifested before (prospective), during, and after (retrospective) cognitive processing (Efklides, 2001, 2006). Yet, they are distinct from achievement-related emotions because they provide information on task and cognitive-processing features as well as on the quality of the outcome of processing rather than on features of the stimuli to which the various discrete emotions respond (e.g., eminent threat in the case of anxiety). We posit, however, that ME themselves can be stimuli that trigger appraisals about one's competence and can impact achievement-related emotions. For instance, confidence in the answer or solution produced to a problem is a subjective indicator of the success or failure of one's learning activity and this may trigger state anxiety, if it suggests that the threat of eminent failure is probable. Therefore, in achievement situations emotions and metacognitive feelings are important components of SRL, particularly because they are sensitive to person as well as to situation characteristics. Emotions, however, may also be associated with motivation, especially with achievement goal orientations, as we shall see in what follows.

Achievement Goal Orientations and Emotions

Achievement goal orientations are considered generalizable person characteristics that reflect students' concerns when they are involved in learning situations, but which can change depending on features of the learning context. Two main goal orientations were originally proposed: (a) mastery goal orientation (also known as task or learning goal orientation) and (b) ego or performance goal orientation (Ames, 1992; Dweck & Elliott, 1983; Nicholls, 1984). Mastery goals aim at learning and mastering the task and, thus, developing one's competence; performance goals promote the demonstration of one's ability or not appear worse than others. According to the normative goal orientation theory (Harackiewicz, Barron, Pintrich, Elliot, & Thrash, 2002), mastery goal orientation is associated with interest and positive affect, with effort investment and persistence on learning activities even if errors are made during the process of learning. On the other hand, performance goal orientation is associated with beliefs that ability rather than effort is necessary for academic success because, through success, one shows one's competence and superiority over the others; accordingly, failure endangers one's position in the social comparison process and should be avoided. For performance goal orientation, it is the normative criteria and the outcome of one's learning activity that are crucial rather than the activity itself. Thus when errors occur, the person experiences negative affect (Turner, Thorpe, & Meyer, 1998), and this may lead to maladaptive behaviors, such as effort withdrawal, task avoidance, or self-handicapping, so that one does not appear incompetent (Midgley & Urdan, 2001).

However, performance goals can also be associated with high performance and adaptive learning outcomes (Harackiewicz et al., 2002). This led to the distinction between performance-approach and performance-avoidance goals (Elliot & Church, 1997), with only the latter being maladaptive. Thus, performance goal orientation may take two forms: (a) an approach form that endorses competition with others as a means to prove one's ability to the self and to the others, and (b) an avoidance form that leads to avoidance of competition or task involvement so that others do not judge the person as incompetent (Urdan & Mestas, 2006).

Research on the tripartite model of achievement goal orientations has supported Pekrun's theory of achievement-related emotions (Pekrun et al., 2002, 2006) in the sense that students' mastery goal orientation has been found to be associated with interest and positive affect rather than with anxiety (Linnenbrink, 2005; Turner et al., 1998; see also Efklides & Dina, 2007). Performance-approach goal orientation is not necessarily associated with activity-related emotions, such as interest, but it is rather associated with positive affect following success on a learning task (Linnenbrink, 2005; Pekrun et al., 2006). Also, it may be associated with anxiety (Linnenbrink, 2005), although Pekrun et al. (2006) found no such relationship. It is possible that students with performance-approach orientation have a high sense of competence and self-esteem, which are components of self-concept (Dermitzaki & Efklides, 2000), and this high sense of competence is not threatened by competition and potential failure (Jagacinski & Strickland, 2000; Kavussanu, 2007; Turner et al., 1998). Finally, performance-avoidance goal orientation is not associated with interest because the emphasis is on the outcome of the learning activity; however, it is associated with anxiety because failure is conceived as a threat to one's self-esteem particularly for students with low perceived ability (Elliot & McGregor, 1999; Jagacinski & Strickland, 2000; McGregor & Elliot, 2002).

Person Characteristics and Anxiety

Studies on the relations of achievement goal orientations with anxiety often refer to trait anxiety—as measured with *test anxiety* (Linnenbrink, 2005)—rather than to state anxiety, which is associated with intervening thoughts regarding one's competence and self-efficacy as well as the implications of failure to the self and others (McLeod & Mathews, 1988; Sarason, 1975). State anxiety tends to be increased in individuals with high test anxiety when they are found in evaluative situations (Zeidner, 1995). Therefore, students' state anxiety in a testing situation can be predicted by their test anxiety and by situational factors. Elliot and McGregor (1999) tested the relations of trait and state anxiety with achievement goal orientations and found that test anxiety, as a trait, was an antecedent of performance-approach and performance-avoidance goal orientations, but was unrelated to mastery goal orientation. Moreover, only performance-avoidance goal orientation was related to state anxiety.

Attitude towards Mathematics

Another factor that may have an effect on state anxiety is students' attitude towards the learning domain—in our study, attitude towards mathematics. Achievement goal theory does not directly associate students' goal orientation with attitudes. Nevertheless, considering that attitudes have an affective component besides the cognitive and behavioral one (Rajecki, 1982), one can assume that mastery-oriented students will also have positive attitude because they are open to and have positive affect as regards learning in a specific domain. Moreover, positive attitude can act as a counter-force to test anxiety, ameliorating its effect on state anxiety.

Cognitive Ability and Self-Concept

Cognitive ability has been also associated with test anxiety, in the sense that lack of ability can be a source of test anxiety (Birenbaum & Nasser, 1994). However, there is no association of cognitive ability with achievement goal orientations (Chen, Gully, Whiteman, & Kilcullen, 2000; Elliot & McGregor, 1999). The same regards the associations of achievement goal orientations with subjective ability, that is, perception of one's competence (Elliot & McGregor, 1999). Perception of one's competence is a component of one's self-concept, which has been shown to be associated with cognitive ability (Dermitzaki & Efklides, 2000). On the other hand, cognitive ability and the respective self-concept are associated with ME (Efklides & Tsiora, 2002). This implies that cognitive ability and self-concept may exert their effects on state anxiety either through test anxiety or through ME, rather than directly.

Goal instructions and Extrinsic Feedback

Students' achievement goal orientations may be fostered by a classroom climate that matches their goals. The impact of goal instructions on students' goal orientations has been studied in the past with mixed results. Ames (1984, 1992) found that teachers' goals, and particularly emphasis on competition, fostered ability attributions by the students. On the contrary, noncompetitive instructions stressing mastery goals led to effort attributions, engagement to self-instructions, and self-monitoring (see also Graham & Golan, 1991). However, Newman (1998) found that students do not necessarily adopt the goals of the experimental condition, and Linnenbrink (2005), after an extended intervention, found no significant effect of classroom goals on students' goal orientation, although there was a tendency of students' goals to come closer to the goals stressed by the teacher (i.e., the classroom goal condition).

It should be also noted that in the Linnenbrink (2005) study classroom goal condition was not related to most of the outcomes measured in the study, except for the mastery goal condition that was beneficial for achievement. The combined mastery and performance-approach goal condition was supportive of both help seeking and achievement. Therefore, although classroom goal condition was not effective in changing students' achievement goal orientation, there was an effect on students' achievement, possibly because classroom goal condition interacted with students' personal goal orientation. Support for such an explanation comes from Efklides and Dina (2007) who found that performance goal instructions enhanced task performance more than did mastery instructions. Moreover, in the performance instruction groups, task performance was associated with students' mastery and performance-approach goal orientations, whereas in the mastery instruction groups there was also an association with performance-avoidance goal orientation.

When it comes to students' affect, goal instructions seem to have an effect, although not very strong. Jagacinski and Strickland (2000) found that task (i.e., mastery) orientation predicted anticipated positive affect, namely satisfaction, in the context of outstanding performance instructions (i.e., performance goal orientation) but not in an enjoyment context. Therefore, the evidence for the effects of goal instructions on students' goal orientations, performance, and affect, is not conclusive. It seems that goal instructions interact with students' personal goal orientations and possibly with other situational factors such as extrinsic feedback.

Indeed, students' ME and affect is influenced by extrinsic feedback (EF) given in response to their task performance. Efklides and Dina (2004) found that positive EF increased students' feelings of confidence and satisfaction, that is, retrospective ME related to the outcome of cognitive processing. On the contrary, negative EF led to lower ratings of the respective feelings when EF was repeated for a second time on the same tasks. Tauer and Harackiewicz (1999) found that positive EF increased positive affect, particularly in competitive conditions, whereas negative EF in a competitive context was detrimental to positive affect and intrinsic motivation. Nevertheless, persons with high achievement motivation enjoy competition and continue to be engaged with a task, even if they receive negative EF or no EF (Tauer & Harackiewicz, 1999).

The above findings suggest that situational factors, such as goal instructions and EF, can impact students' affect. Moreover, the mechanism through which goal instructions and EF influence students' performance and emotions may differ, since EF implicates students' ME while goal instructions do not necessarily do so.

The Present Study

The present study investigated the effects of achievement goal orientations, as personal and situational characteristics, and of EF on students' emotions, particularly their state anxiety. The study was designed to simulate an actual classroom context in which students self-regulate their learning. Specifically, students enter a learning situation with person characteristics such as cognitive ability, self-concept, test anxiety, attitudes towards the learning domain, and achievement goal orientations. They encounter situational factors such as task requirements, goal instructions, EF (positive or negative), and they experience affect (emotions) and ME that may enhance or undermine their sense of competence. The contribution of each of the above factors on state anxiety is far from clear, particularly because in such multi-factorial situations there can be mediational or even suppressing effects of one factor over others. In our study we aimed at depicting such effects so that the general mechanism associating achievement motivation with emotions can be enriched with components such as ME that bridge the general with the specific.

Research Questions – Hypotheses

The research questions posed were the following:
(1) In SRL, how are students' cognitive and affective person characteristics related to test (i.e., trait) and state anxiety? The prediction was that positive attitude towards mathematics, cognitive ability in mathematics, and self-concept in mathematics will be negatively related to both test anxiety and state anxiety, whereas test anxiety will be positively related to state anxiety (Hypothesis 1).
(2) Are students' achievement goal orientations related to test anxiety and state anxiety? The prediction was that students' goal orientations will be differentially related to test and state anxiety: mastery goal orientation will not be related to either test anxiety or state anxiety; performance-approach goal orientation *may be* positively related to both of them; performance-avoidance goal orientation will be positively related to both test anxiety and state anxiety. Moreover, the contribution of students' test anxiety to state anxiety will be both direct and indirect through performance-approach and performance-avoidance goal orientations (Hypothesis 2).
(3) Do situational factors, such as goal instructions, influence students' emotions, such as interest in and liking of the task, or state anxiety? The prediction was that mastery and performance instructions would be associated with interest and liking. However, mastery instructions, unlike performance instructions, will not contribute to students' state anxiety. Furthermore, considering the possible interaction of students' personal goal orientations with goal instructions, it was expected that goal instructions will mediate the effect of personal goal orientations on state anxiety (Hypothesis 3).

(4) Does EF as a situational factor influence students' emotions? The prediction was that positive EF would increase interest in and liking of tasks whereas negative EF will increase state anxiety. However, considering the effect of EF on students' ME (i.e., feeling of confidence) it was expected that the effect of EF on state anxiety will be mediated by students' ME (Hypothesis 4).

(5) Are the effects of person characteristics and goal instructions on state anxiety also mediated by students' ME? The prediction was that students' ME would mediate the effect of EF but not the effect of person characteristics and goal instructions; the latter would contribute to state anxiety independently from EF (Hypothesis 5).

Method

Design and Participants

The design of the study is shown in Figure 1. The sample (N = 870) comprised 388 students of Grade 7 (Mean age = 12.6 years, SD = .26) and 482 students of Grade 9 (Mean age = 14.5 years, SD = .44) of both genders (females = 430 and males = 440). They were students of various schools in a major Greek city. Six groups of students (see Figure 1) were formed in terms of goal instructions (mastery, performance, no goal instructions) and EF (positive, negative, no EF). The control group received neither goal instructions nor EF. Students were tested on two consecutive occasions. The measures used in the study and the order in which they were collected are given in Appendix A. The same order of testing was followed for all groups of students. All students, except the control group, received EF individually after they had completed each task.

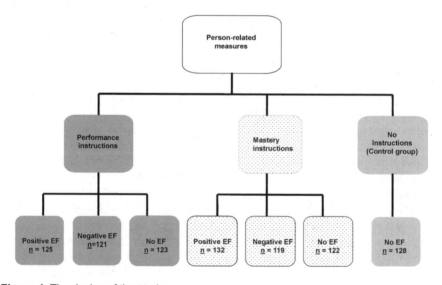

Figure 1. The design of the study.

Instructions

The instructions and EF given to the seven groups are given in Appendix B. The wording of EF matched that of the instructions so that there is consistency between goal instructions and the success or failure framing of EF.

Measures

Mathematical Ability Test

A battery of three tests involving simple equations, arithmetic operations, and comparison of fractions was used; there were 14 items in total: 4, 4, and 6, respectively (Demetriou, Platsidou, Efklides, Metallidou, & Shayer, 1991). A total score based on the sum of the scores on the three tests represented mathematical ability. Cronbach's alpha for this test was .76. Examples of items are:

- Simple equations: $m = 3n + 1$, $n = 4$, $m = \ldots$
- Arithmetic operations: $(12 \ \square \ 3) \circ 2 = 8$ (Please replace the symbols with an operator.)
- Comparison of fractions: Two jars presumably containing a mixture of two fluids were presented to the students. For each jar, the ratio of the two fluids of the mixture was denoted with a set of cups (different for each jar), each cup containing either a colored or a non-colored fluid. For example, the fluid in one cup was colored and in the other two was non-colored. The students had to indicate which jar would have darker color if the fluid of the respective cups for each jar were emptied inside it.

Self-Concept in Mathematics Questionnaire

The Self-Concept in Mathematics questionnaire is a self-report instrument constructed by Dermitzaki and Efklides (2000), which comprises 22 items tapping self-perception, self-efficacy, self-esteem, and perception of others' conception of one's math ability. Responses were given on a 5-point Likert scale. Example items are: "I think I am good in Mathematics," "I am pleased with my math ability," "I am expecting to do well in mathematics this year," "My classmates recognize my abilities in mathematics". A total score based on the sum of the responses on the 22 items represented math self-concept. The higher the score, the more positive the self-concept is. Cronbach's alpha in the present sample was .95.

Mathematics Attitude Scale (Aiken, 1996)

The Mathematics Attitude Scale consists of 20 items measuring positive and negative attitude towards mathematics. It was adapted to Greek by Dina (2000). Responses were given on a 5-point Likert scale. Example items for positive and negative attitude are the following: "Mathematics is very interesting to me, and I enjoy math classes" and "I do not like mathematics, and it scares me to have to take it", respectively. A total score representing positive attitude towards mathematics was computed, after conversion of the scoring of the items tapping negative attitude. Cronbach's alpha in the present sample was .93.

Goal Orientations Scale (Midgley et al., 1998)

It comprises 18 items, 6 for each of the three subscales measuring mastery goal orientation, performance-approach goal orientation, and performance-avoidance goal orientation, respectively. Responses were on a 5-point Likert scale. The three-factor structure was verified in the Greek adaptation, which emphasized mathematics rather than subject-free goal orientation in school (Dina, 2006). Example items are: For mastery goal orientation "An important reason why I do my school work is because I like to learn new things". For performance-approach goal orientation "I would feel successful in mathematics if I did better than most of the other students". For performance-avoidance goal orientation "It's very important to me that I don't look stupid in my math classes". Cronbach's alpha in the present sample for each subscale was .81, .79, .66, respectively.

Test Anxiety Inventory (TAI; Spielberger, 1980)

The TAI is a 20-item inventory that measures test anxiety as trait anxiety. Responses were on a 4-point Likert scale. The Greek adaptation confirmed the two-factor structure, namely worry and emotionality. Cronbach's alpha in the present sample for the whole inventory was .90. For the needs of the study, a total score representing test anxiety was used.

Cognitive Interference Questionnaire (CIQ; Sarason, 1975)

The CIQ was used to measure state anxiety. It is a self-report questionnaire. Of the 20 CIQ items, 10 were used to tap intervening thoughts during mathematical problem solving in our study. Responses were on a 5-point Likert scale. The Greek adaptation confirmed a single-factor structure. Cronbach's alpha in the present sample for the 10 items was .78.

Metacognitive Experiences Questionnaire (MEQ; Efklides, 2002) and Emotions

There were two sets of items on the MEQ, measuring retrospective and prospective ME as well as interest in and liking of the task, respectively. They comprised single item measures for each ME and each of the above two activity-related emotions, namely interest in and liking of the task, before and after problem solving. Responses were on a 4-point Likert scale. The MEQ included items that assessed the feeling of difficulty (FOD), estimate of effort (EOE), estimate of solution correctness (EOC), feeling of confidence

(FOC), and feeling of satisfaction (FOS). The last two ME were measured only after problem solving. The items were the following:

- Interest: How interesting is (was) the task?
- Liking: How much do (did) you like the task?
- Feeling of difficulty: How much difficulty do (did) you feel?
- Estimate of effort: How much effort do (did) you need to invest on the task?
- Estimate of solution correctness: How correctly do you think you can (did you) solve this task?
- Feeling of confidence: How confident are you that you solved correctly the task?
- Feeling of satisfaction: How satisfied are you with the task solution you provided?

Mathematical Tasks

Students had to solve three mathematical tasks of increasing difficulty, namely, Task 1, Task, 2, and Task 3. Objective task difficulty was determined in terms of the conceptual demands of each task.Task 1 required knowledge of fractions, specifically comparison of fractions. Students were presented with 5 fractions having different numerators and denominators and were asked to place them in order of magnitude. Task 2 required knowledge of the concept of area (measurement of the area of a triangle with or without conversion of measurement units, i.e., from dm to cm or m). Task 3 required knowledge of the concept of area as well as of percentage. Students were presented with a complex figure, comprising of orthogonal parts, with two squares embedded in it covering part of its whole area. Students were asked to calculate the orthogonal figure's area as well as the percentage of area covered by the two squares embedded in it.

Procedure

Students were tested in their classrooms. Goal instructions were given orally and were the same for all students in a classroom. As soon as a student of the EF groups finished working on a mathematical task, she/he notified the experimenter who gave EF on the student's task performance. The first phase of the first testing occasion, when person-related measures were administered, and the second phase, in which the mathematical tasks and ME were measured, were completed on the same day with a break between the two phases. The second testing, when the same mathematical tasks were administered for a second time, took place about three weeks after the first.

Results and Discussion

Before presenting the analyses that investigated the effects of person and situational factors on state anxiety as well as the role of ME, we will present the effects of goal instructions and EF on task performance as well as on ME and activity-related emotions, that is, interest and liking.

Effects on Task Performance

To test the effect of goal instructions and EF on students' task performance a repeated measures ANCOVA was performed on the two mean task performance scores (one for each of the two testing occasions). Mathematical ability, self-concept in mathematics, attitude towards mathematics, and students' goal orientations were the covariates in order to control for the effects of individual differences factors on task performance; group (7 groups of the study) was the between subjects factor, and testing (two testing occasions) was the within subjects factor. Table 1 shows the mean task performance scores. The analysis showed that the main effect of group was significant, $F(6, 846) = 4.722$, $p < .001$, partial $\eta^2 = .03$. The main effect of testing was nonsignificant and so was the interaction between group and testing.

Post hoc comparisons, following the Bonferroni method, showed that the Performance-No EF group and the Performance-Positive EF group significantly differed from the Mastery-Negative EF group and the Control group (no instruction, no EF) at $p < .05$. Moreover, the Performance-Positive EF group significantly differed from the Mastery-No EF group but not from the Mastery-Positive EF group (see Table 1). These findings support previous research showing the beneficial effects of performance instructions on task performance. Moreover, they also show that mastery instructions do not guarantee high performance if there is no positive EF. In other words, mastery instructions interact with EF, and performance is maintained at a relatively high level only when there is positive EF. On the contrary, performance instructions support achievement even in the absence of positive EF.

Table 1. Mean task performance (and standard error) for each testing occasion as a function of goal instructions and EF group.

Group	1st testing occasion	2nd testing occasion
Mastery-Positive EF	1.10 (.05)	1.03 (.06)
Mastery-Negative EF	.90 (.06)	.95 (.06)
Performance-Positive EF	1.20 (.06)	1.28 (.06)
Performance-Negative EF	1.06 (.06)	1.09 (.06)
Mastery-No EF	1.00 (.06)	.95 (.06)
Performance-No EF	1.13 (.06)	1.27 (.06)
Control group	.90 (.06)	.92 (.06)

Note: EF = extrinsic feedback.

Effects on ME and Activity-Related Emotions

A mean score of students' self-reports of their ME before and after each task across the three tasks was computed for each testing occasion in order to simplify and generalize findings. Thus, a MANCOVA was performed on the ME scores of each testing occasion as well as on interest and liking scores with mathematical ability, self-concept in mathematics, attitude towards mathematics, and students' goal orientations as the covariates and group (7 groups of the study) as the independent variable.

In the *first* testing occasion the main effect of group was significant, Pillai's = .145, $F(42, 5118) = 3.023$, $p < .001$, partial $\eta^2 = .02$. The univariate F values showed that the main effect of group was significant for all ME except for liking and interest. This implies that all students found the learning situation interesting regardless of goal instructions and EF, possibly because it was a new situation for them.

Post hoc comparisons of the retrospective ME, namely estimate of solution correctness, feeling of confidence, and feeling of satisfaction, were significantly higher ($p < .001$) in the Mastery-Positive EF, the Performance-Positive EF, the Performance-No EF groups and the Control group as compared to the Mastery-Negative EF group. The latter had the lowest scores of all groups on the above ME, although interest and liking were comparable to those of the other groups (see Table 2). These findings suggest that negative EF can attract students' interest in a new learning situation that stresses mastery goals but is detrimental for performance as well as for feelings of confidence and satisfaction.

As regards the feeling of difficulty and estimate of effort, the post hoc comparisons showed that the Performance-Negative EF group had higher scores on both of them as compared to the Positive EF groups (both Mastery and Performance) and the Performance-No EF groups ($p < .01$). This finding probably reflects an attribution of negative EF to task difficulty; yet, despite the increased self-reported estimate of effort in both Mastery- and Performance-Negative EF groups ($p < .05$), performance did not increase accordingly. Moreover, the Mastery-No EF group reported similar levels of feeling of difficulty and estimate of effort as the Mastery-Negative EF group. This finding underscores the importance of positive EF for mastery goal orientations to be able to support effort and performance.

Table 2. Mean scores (and standard error) of ME and activity-related emotions on the 3 mathematical tasks as a function of Instructions and EF group and testing occasion.

Group	Liking	Interest	FOD	EOE	EOC	FOC	FOS
			1st testing occasion				
Mastery-Pos. EF	2.24 (.05)	2.34 (.05)	2.29 (.05)	2.41 (.05)	2.70 (.05)	2.59 (.06)	2.69 (.06)
Mastery-Neg. EF	2.13 (.06)	2.20 (.05)	2.52 (.05)	2.65 (.05)	2.32 (.05)	2.05 (.06)	2.20 (.06)
Performance-Pos. EF	2.26 (.05)	2.28 (.05)	2.34 (.05)	2.51 (.05)	2.63 (.05)	2.54 (.06)	2.60 (.06)
Performance-Neg. EF	2.17 (.05)	2.30 (.05)	2.61 (.05)	2.65 (.05)	2.42 (.05)	2.14 (.06)	2.23 (.06)
Mastery-No EF	2.12 (.05)	2.27 (.05)	2.50 (.05)	2.61 (.05)	2.54 (.05)	2.28 (.06)	2.43 (.06)
Performance-No EF	2.19 (.05)	2.16 (.05)	2.35 (.05)	2.43 (.05)	2.72 (.05)	2.60 (.06)	2.59 (.06)
Control group	2.25 (.05)	2.32 (.05)	2.32 (.05)	2.39 (.05)	2.68 (.05)	2.53 (.06)	2.55 (.06)
			2nd testing occasion				
Mastery-Pos. EF	2.01 (.05)	2.15 (.05)	2.24 (.05)	2.32 (.05)	2.64 (.05)	2.54 (.06)	2.60 (.06)
Mastery-Neg. EF	1.83 (.06)	1.90 (.06)	2.53 (.06)	2.58 (.06)	2.21 (.06)	2.02 (.07)	2.12 (.06)
Performance-Pos. EF	2.17 (.06)	2.23 (.06)	2.36 (.06)	2.44 (.05)	2.68 (.06)	2.61 (.06)	2.64 (.06)
Performance-Neg. EF	1.95 (.06)	2.05 (.06)	2.67 (.06)	2.66 (.05)	2.25 (.06)	1.98 (.06)	2.04 (.06)
Mastery-No EF	2.13 (.06)	2.18 (.06)	2.39 (.06)	2.46 (.05)	2.47 (.06)	2.34 (.06)	2.34 (.06)
Performance-No EF	1.95 (.06)	1.98 (.06)	2.32 (.06)	2.42 (.05)	2.58 (.06)	2.45 (.06)	2.51 (.06)
Control group	2.06 (.05)	2.12 (.05)	2.39 (.05)	2.41 (.05)	2.56 (.05)	2.52 (.06)	2.45 (.06)

Note: EF = extrinsic feedback. FOD = Feeling of difficulty; EOE = Estimate of effort; EOC = Estimate of solution correctness; FOC = Feeling of confidence; FOS = Feeling of satisfaction.

In the *second* testing occasion, the main effect of group was significant, Pillai's = .159, $F(42, 5464) = 3.280$, $p < .001$, partial $\eta^2 = .02$, for all ME as well as for interest and liking. Interest and liking remained high when there was positive EF regardless of goal instructions. The Mastery-No EF and the Performance-Positive EF groups reported higher liking of and interest in the tasks than the Mastery-Negative EF group ($p < .01$). Therefore, repetition of a learning situation in which there is continuous failure, decreases interest in and liking of it mainly in the context of mastery instructions leading, thus, to disengagement from it.

As regards retrospective ME, the Positive EF groups (both Mastery and Performance) and the Performance-No EF group reported the highest estimate of solution correctness, feeling of confidence and feeling of satisfaction ($p < .001$) compared to the Negative EF groups (both Mastery and Performance). Regarding feeling of difficulty and estimate of effort, the Negative EF groups (both Mastery and Performance) gave higher scores compared to the Mastery-Positive EF group ($p < .01$).

Synopsis Regarding Group Differences

Overall, the results showed that performance instructions along with positive EF, even with no EF, promoted performance in mathematics and led to high retrospective ME in both testing occasions. This finding is congruent with the emphasis of performance goal orientation on achievement and feeling of satisfaction from it even in the absence of EF. The students self-evaluated their performance based on their estimate of solution correctness, and feeling of confidence, and this self-evaluation supported their feeling of satisfaction. Moreover, performance and retrospective ME continued to be high in the second testing occasion; liking of and interest in the task, however, was high mainly in the presence of positive EF.

On the other hand, the Mastery-No EF group, and the Control group maintained liking of and interest in the task although task performance was low. Thus, interest did not enhance performance. This finding suggests that situational interest in a mastery context does not by itself guarantee that students will exert effort on the tasks to increase performance unless there is positive EF. On the contrary, the expectation that task performance can be diagnostic of ability can lower interest but enhance performance and the corresponding retrospective ME as in the Performance-No EF group. What is most important, though, is that repeated negative EF, particularly in the Mastery-Negative EF group, had detrimental effects on performance, interest and liking and the retrospective ME. This implies that mastery instructions do not fortify students against negative affect when there is repeated failure-related EF.

Effects on State Anxiety

A repeated measures ANCOVA was also performed in order to compare the state anxiety scores in the two testing occasions between the groups of the study. Mathematical ability, test anxiety, attitude towards mathematics, self-concept in mathematics, and students' goal orientations were the covariates. Testing was the within subjects factor. The effect of testing was nonsignificant, but the Testing x Group interaction was significant, $F(6, 845)$ = .02, $p < .008$, partial $\eta^2 = .02$. As shown in Table 3, the Performance-Negative EF group had the highest state anxiety scores in both testing occasions. Furthermore, the reported state anxiety in this group increased in the second testing occasion unlike the other groups. Thus, performance instructions can have a side effect, that is, state anxiety, but only when there is repeated failure as indicated by negative EF.

Table 3. Mean scores (and standard error) of state anxiety as a function of instructions and EF group and testing occasion.

	State anxiety	
Group	1st testing occasion	2nd testing occasion
Mastery-Positive EF	25.54 (.58)	24.00 (.63)
Mastery-Negative EF	27.12 (.61)	25.53 (.66)
Performance-Positive EF	25.38 (.60)	25.31 (.66)
Performance-Negative EF	28.95 (.60)	29.60 (.65)
Mastery-No EF	27.03 (.60)	26.20 (.66)
Performance-No EF	25.80 (.60)	25.85 (.65)
Control group	25.43 (.58)	23.20 (.64)

Note: EF = extrinsic feedback.

Predictors of State Anxiety

The correlations between the person variables and state anxiety are given in Table 4.

Table 4. Pearson's r correlation coefficients between students' person-related characteristics.

	1	2	3	4	5	6	7	8
1. Mathematical ability								
2. Test Anxiety	-.20**							
3. Attitude towards mathematics	.23**	-.29**						
4. Self-concept in mathematics	.24**	-.13**	.62**					
5. Mastery goal orientation	.19**	-.08*	.65**	.59**				
6. Performance-approach goal orientation	-.01	.15**	.14**	.27**	.30**			
7. Performance-avoidance goal orientation	-.14**	.24**	-.17**	.00	.01	.45**		
8. State anxiety of 1st testing occasion	-.07*	.34**	-.14**	-.07*	.01	.09**	.08*	
9. State anxiety of 2nd testing occasion	-.08*	.31**	-.07*	-.05	.05	.05	.10**	.58**

Note: * $p < .05$; ** $p < .01$.

To investigate the extent to which person and situational factors predict state anxiety and whether situational effects are mediated by ME and emotions, a hierarchical regression analysis was conducted for each testing occasion. Eight successive models were tested as follows: Control variables (age and gender) were entered first (Model 1). Cognitive ability in mathematics and self-concept in mathematics were added in Model 2. Test anxiety, as an antecedent of achievement goal orientations, and attitude towards mathematics were added in Model 3. The next model (Model 4) additionally contained students' personal goal orientations (mastery, performance-approach, performance-avoidance). In Model 5 the first situational factor, namely goal instructions (mastery and performance instructions) was added. In Model 6 the second situational factor, namely extrinsic feedback variables (positive EF, negative EF)[2] were added. Model 7 additionally contained task performance.[3] Finally, Model 8 contained, besides all the previous variables, ME and activity-related emotions (namely liking, interest, feeling of difficulty, estimate of effort, estimate of solution correctness, feeling of confidence, and feeling of satisfaction).

The results of the analysis of the first testing occasion are shown in Table 5. The final model predicted 21.6% of the variance of state anxiety. The R^2 change in six of the eight models was significant. Specifically, cognitive ability in mathematics and self-concept in mathematics did not significantly add to the explained variance of state anxiety when entered in the analysis. The same happened when goal instructions were added to the predictors. On the contrary, the addition of EF did have a significant effect. What is worth noting in the final model (Model 8) is that of the 21 predictors the significant ones were gender (girls reported higher state anxiety than boys), test anxiety, attitude towards mathematics, students' mastery goal orientation, task performance, and of the ME only feeling of difficulty, estimate of solution correctness, and feeling of confidence. Moreover, attitude towards mathematics, task performance, and feeling of confidence were negatively related to state anxiety.

Regarding the mediation effects of ME, the comparison of Models 7 and 8 shows that once ME were entered in the model, EF no longer predicted state anxiety. This means that the effect of EF on state anxiety was fully mediated by ME (see Barron & Kenny, 1986).

These findings supported Hypothesis 1 as regards the effect of test anxiety and attitude towards mathematics on state anxiety. However, the effects of cognitive ability in mathematics and self-concept in mathematics were not significant. Moreover, the effect of test anxiety was direct and was not mediated by achievement goal orientations contrary to Hypothesis 2.

Contrary to Hypothesis 2 was also the finding that mastery goal orientation was a positive predictor of state anxiety. This finding is in total disagreement with goal orientation theory and unlike the correlations shown in Table 4, suggesting a possible suppression effect. For this reason, we further explored this finding with a series of regression analyses. First of all, the collinearity of goal orientation with the attitude toward mathematics was ruled out, since the highest correlation between them was .65 (see Table 1), much lower than the .80 threshold (Allison, 1999) above which both variables should not

---

[2] Goal instructions had three levels (mastery, performance, no instructions), and extrinsic feedback had three levels (positive EF, negative EF, and no EF). They were recoded into two new variables with two levels each (mastery – performance for goal instructions, and positive EF – negative EF for extrinsic feedback, coded with 1 and 0, respectively), following the suggestion for the use of categorical variables with more than two levels in regression analysis by Meyers, Gamst, and Guarino (2006). In this way these two variables in the regression show the effects of each of the two levels on the dependent variable compared to the reference groups (no instructions and no EF).

[3] Task performance score was a variable representing the mean of the three task performance scores separately in each testing occasion.

Table 5. Hierarchical regression analysis for state anxiety of the first testing occasion.

Predictors / Models	M1 (control variables)		M2 (cognitive ability and self-concept)		M3 (person factors)		M4 (goal orientations)		M5 (goal instructions)		M6 (extrinsic feedback)		M7 (task performance)		M8 (metacognitive experiences)	
	Beta	Sig.	Beta	Sig.	Beta	Sig.	Beta	Sig.	Beta	Sig.	Beta	Sig.	Beta	Sig.	Beta	Sig.
					Model 1											
Age	.06	.07	.06	.11	.04	.00	.02	.50	.03	.48	.02	.54	.02	.67	-.04	.27
Gender	.17	.00	.16	.00	.12	.00	.12	.00	.12	.00	.11	.00	.11	.00	.11	.00
					Model 2											
Cognitive ability in mathematics			-.03	.38	.02	.58	.01	.79	.01	.79	.00	.99	.04	.37	.02	.52
Self-concept in mathematics			-.05	.13	.00	.93	-.04	.40	-.04	.40	-.03	.42	-.03	.54	-.00	.92
					Model 3											
Test anxiety					.31	.00	.29	.00	.29	.00	.29	.00	.29	.00	.27	.00
Attitude towards mathematics					-.05	.22	-.11	.02	-.12	.01	-.12	.01	-.13	.01	-.12	.01
					Model 4											
Mastery goal orientation							.12	.01	.12	.01	.12	.01	.12	.01	.10	.02
Performance-approach goal orientation							.06	.14	.05	.17	.06	.12	.06	.10	.07	.07
Performance-avoidance goal orientation							-.03	.44	-.02	.52	-.02	.65	-.02	.64	-.01	.84
					Model 5											
Mastery instructions									.08	.08	.08	.14	.08	.11	.07	.21
Performance instructions									.08	.07	.08	.14	.09	.09	.08	.14
					Model 6											
Negative feedback											.09	.02	.09	.02	.06	.11
Positive feedback											-.07	.06	-.07	.08	-.04	.23
					Model 7											
Task performance													-.08	.02	-.08	.02
					Model 8											
Liking															-.02	.72
Interest															.09	.17
Feeling of difficulty															.18	.00
Estimate of effort															.01	.82
Estimate of solution correctness															.15	.03
Feeling of confidence															-.14	.04
Feeling of satisfaction															-.04	.52
R^2	.033		.038		.135		.145		.149		.166		.171		.216	
R^2c	.033		.005		.097		.010		.004		.018		.005		.045	
Fc	14.600		2.207		48.162		3.487		1.790		9.077		5.261		6.915	
Sig. Fc	.000		.111		.000		.015		.168		.000		.022		.000	

be used together in a multivariate analysis. Next, a hierarchical regression analysis was performed to test a possible order effect of the main predictors (see Table 6). First, students' three goal orientations were entered as predictors of state anxiety (Model 1). The results showed that mastery orientation and performance-avoidance orientation were not significant predictors of state anxiety but performance-approach was marginally significant.

Table 6. Hierarchical regression analysis for state anxiety of the first testing occasion with goal orientations, test anxiety and attitude towards mathematics as predictors.

Predictors / Model	Model 1 (goal orientations)		Model 2 (test anxiety)		Model 3 (attitude towards mathematics)	
	Beta	Sig.	Beta	Sig.	Beta	Sig.
	Model 1					
Mastery goal orientation	-.01	.77	.03	.41	.12	.01
Performance-approach goal orientation	.08	.05	.05	.20	.06	.14
Performance-avoidance goal orientation	.03	.30	-.03	.41	-.05	.16
	Model 2					
Test anxiety			.34	.00	.31	.00
	Model 3					
Attitude towards mathematics					-.15	.00
R^2	.010		.119		.130	
R^2c	.010		.119		.011	
Fc	2.982		106.167		11.294	
Sig. Fc	.031		.000		.001	

In the next model (Model 2), in addition to the three goal orientations, test anxiety was entered. In this model only test anxiety was a significant predictor. In Model 3 the attitude towards mathematics was added. As can be seen in Table 6, attitude towards mathematics predicted state anxiety negatively, but test anxiety and mastery goal orientation predicted state anxiety positively as in the initial hierarchical regression analysis. Finally, in another regression analysis only test anxiety and the attitude towards mathematics were entered as predictors of state anxiety. In this regression the attitude towards mathematics was not significant predictor. The above results indicate that the attitude towards mathematics was not a significant predictor of state anxiety when entered together with test anxiety alone, but was significant when entered together with goal orientations. Furthermore, mastery goal orientation was not a significant predictor when entered together with the other two goal orientations alone or together with test anxiety, but became significant when entered together with attitude towards mathematics.

One possible explanation could be that there was an interaction effect between mastery goals and attitude towards mathematics. To test this possibility the mastery goal orientation and attitude towards mathematics variables were centered (creating two new variables by subtracting out the mean of each variable) and a new variable was created (an interaction term) by computing the product of attitude towards mathematics and mastery goal orientation. Mastery goal orientation, attitude towards mathematics and the new product term of the two were used as predictors of state anxiety. The effect of the interaction term was not significant, thus indicating that there was no interaction of mastery goal orientation and attitude towards mathematics.

After ruling out all of the above explanations, one possible explanation that might be evoked is that mastery goal orientation acted as suppressor variable. In this case a variable that does not predict the dependent variable alone does so if entered together with another predictor. The suppressor variable correlates with the source of error of another predictor and, by doing that, the suppressor variable helps purify that predictor and enhances its predictive power (Pedhazur, 1982). A suppressor variable is identified as a variable that may have a near zero correlation with the dependent variable but yet is a significant predictor in the regression model and is correlated with one or more of the predictor variables (Pedhazur, 1982). Indeed, mastery goal orientation correlated with attitude towards mathematics ($r = .65$), but had a very low nonsignificant correlation with state anxiety ($r = .01$).

With respect to Hypothesis 3 the regression analysis showed that neither mastery nor performance instructions had a significant effect on state anxiety, contrary to what had been predicted, nor did they play any mediational role with respect to students' goal orientations. Hypothesis 4 was confirmed as regards the role of negative EF in the increase of state anxiety; however, this effect was fully mediated by ME, as Hypothesis 5 predicted.

The above findings regarded the predictors of state anxiety in the first testing occasion. To investigate the predictors of state anxiety in the second testing occasion, a similar hierarchical regression analysis was applied as in the first testing occasion (see Table 7).

The final model predicted 25.1% of the variance of state anxiety and 7 out of the 8 models were significant. As previously, the contribution of students' cognitive ability in mathematics and self-concept in mathematics to the explained variance of state anxiety was not significant, whereas that of test anxiety was, as Hypothesis 1 predicted. However, the addition of goal instructions in the predictors resulted in significant change, unlike in the first testing occasion. Both types of goal instructions were positively related to state anxiety, contrary to Hypothesis 3, which predicted that only performance instructions would. This finding supports the notion that mastery goal orientation (the student's or the teacher's) does not safeguard against state anxiety.

The effect of EF was in the expected direction as predicted by Hypothesis 4, but these effects were fully mediated by ME, as predicted by Hypothesis 5. In the final model the addition of ME increased the explained variance by 8%. Moreover, ME also mediated the effect of task performance on state anxiety. It should be noted that it was the estimate of effort rather than feeling of difficulty that predicted positively state anxiety this time. Feeling of confidence predicted negatively state anxiety, as in the first testing occasion. Compared to the findings of the first testing occasion, it should be noted that mastery goal orientation was again a positive predictor, but the attitude towards mathematics was not a significant predictor anymore. Therefore, in the second testing occasion, important differences were observed as compared to those of the first one.

Table 7. Hierarchical regression analysis for state anxiety of the second testing occasion.

Predictors / Models	M1 (control variables)		M2 (cognitive ability and self-concept)		M3 (person factors)		M4 (goal orientations)		M5 (goal instructions)		M6 (extrinsic feedback)		M7 (task performance)		M8 (metacognitive experiences)	
	Beta	Sig.	Beta	Sig.	Beta	Sig.	Beta	Sig.	Beta	Sig.	Beta	Sig.	Beta	Sig.	Beta	Sig.
					Model 1		Model 2		Model 3		Model 4		Model 5		Model 6 ... Model 7 ... Model 8	
Age	.06	.06	.05	.17	.03	.43	.03	.48	.03	.46	.02	.51	.02	.63	-.07	.05
Gender	.12	.00	.12	.00	.09	.01	.09	.09	.09	.09	.08	.01	.08	.01	.06	.07
Cognitive ability in mathematics			-.05	.18	-.01	.79	-.01	.77	-.01	.83	-.02	.61	.01	.73	.00	.92
Self-concept in mathematics			-.04	.30	-.04	.41	-.07	.11	-.07	.10	-.07	.11	-.06	.18	-.02	.66
Test anxiety					.30	.00	.29	.00	.28	.00	.29	.00	.29	.00	.23	.00
Attitude towards mathematics					.05	.25	.00	.95	-.01	.72	-.02	.70	-.02	.75	-.02	.68
Mastery goal orientation							.13	.01	.13	.00	.13	.00	.13	.00	.08	.05
Performance-approach goal orientation							-.03	.49	-.03	.39	-.03	.49	-.02	.57	-.01	.77
Performance-avoidance goal orientation							.05	.22	.05	.19	.06	.13	.05	.16	.06	.12
Mastery instructions									.13	.01	.13	.01	.13	.01	.12	.01
Performance instructions									.24	.00	.23	.00	.25	.00	.22	.00
Negative feedback											.08	.03	.08	.04	.03	.35
Positive feedback											-.08	.04	-.08	.05	-.06	.12
Task performance													-.08	.03	-.04	.34
Liking															.09	.17
Interest															.10	.11
Feeling of difficulty															.01	.90
Estimate of effort															.19	.00
Estimate of solution correctness															.04	.55
Feeling of confidence															-.19	.01
Feeling of satisfaction															-.04	.55
R^2	.020		.025		.106		.115		.143		.160		.165		.251	
R^2c	.020		.005		.081		.010		.027		.018		.004		.086	
Fc	8.637		2.144		38.501		3.134		13.453		8.943		4.478		13.732	
Sig. Fc	.000		.118		.000		.025		.000		.000		.035		.000	

To explore the role of mastery goal orientation in state anxiety formation, a hierarchical regression analysis was applied with students' goal orientations in the first step, attitude towards mathematics in the second, and test anxiety in the last step (see Table 8). In Model 1 consistent with goal orientation theory, only performance-avoidance orientation was significant in predicting state anxiety. After entering attitude towards mathematics, again as in the first testing occasion, attitude towards mathematics and mastery goal orientation were significant predictors, but the effect of performance-avoidance goal orientation became nonsignificant. Finally, after entering test anxiety, only mastery goal orientation and test anxiety were significant predictors as in the full hierarchical model. Separate linear regressions revealed that math attitudes and test anxiety individually predicted state anxiety and test anxiety predicted math attitudes. Therefore, the effect of attitudes towards mathematics on state anxiety in the second testing occasion was fully mediated by test anxiety.

Table 8. Hierarchical regression analysis for state anxiety of the 2nd testing occasion with goal orientations, attitude towards mathematics and test anxiety as predictors.

	Model 1 (goal orientations)		Model 2 (attitude towards mathematics)		Model 3 (test anxiety)	
	Beta	Sig.	Beta	Sig.	Beta	Sig.
Model 1						
Mastery goal orientation	.05	.16	.15	.00	.12	.01
Performance-approach goal orientation	-.01	.87	-.00	.96	-.03	.41
Performance-avoidance	.01	.01	.07	.07	.03	.45
Model 2						
Attitude towards mathematics			-.16	.00	-.05	.28
Model 3						
Test anxiety					30	.00
Fc	3.312		11.706		75.334	
R^2	.011		.025		.104	
R^2c	.011		.013		.079	
Sig. Fc	.020		.001		.000	

These additional results reveal again a suppressor role for goal orientations. It seems that attitude towards mathematics explained a large proportion of the variance of the performance-avoidance orientation, so that this goal's contribution to the variance of state anxiety was overlapped by that of the attitude towards mathematics. On the other hand, mastery goal orientation in both testing occasions contributed a unique variance to state anxiety that could be explained as qualitatively different from the variance explained by the attitude towards mathematics. Furthermore, the predictive power of mastery goal orientation remained intact even when test anxiety was added as a predictor after it.

In conclusion, as regards state anxiety, Hypothesis 3 was partly confirmed, because goal instructions affected state anxiety in the second testing occasion. Moreover, goal instructions did not mediate the effect of achievement goal orientations on state anxiety. On the other hand, there was a totally unexpected finding of mastery goal orientation positively predicting state anxiety, although that could have been a function of statistical suppression.

As regards the effect of EF on emotions, Hypothesis 4 was confirmed. Specifically positive EF maintained interest in and liking of the task, whereas negative EF decreased it. Moreover, the effect of negative EF on state anxiety was fully mediated by ME as predicted. Finally, Hypothesis 5 was also confirmed because ME did not mediate the effect of achievement goal orientations on state anxiety.

In what follows there will be a general discussion on the implications of the present study's findings for motivation within the SRL theoretical framework and to the global or local perspective of understanding motivational phenomena.

General Discussion

In this chapter the SRL theoretical framework, following the Zimmerman's (1998) cyclic model, was used in order to answer the question of whether a global approach to understanding motivation is better than a local one. Specifically, we posited that the relations of motivation with performance in a learning situation should be seen in conjunction with students' general person characteristics that operate at the Forethought phase, with situational characteristics, task performance, and students' ME and activity-related emotions that are present at the Performance/Volitional Control phase, as well as with state anxiety. Moreover, these relations should be investigated in repeated SRL cycles.

As we already mentioned, our study simulated learning in a classroom, in which the teacher promotes goal orientations by providing goal instructions and external feedback (EF) on students' task performance thus shaping the learning situation. Moreover, the learning situation was repeated (as in the two testing occasions of the present study) producing cycles of SRL. In such a complex situation, it is clear that there is an interaction of general person characteristics with situational ones. In what follows we shall discuss our findings in relation to the issues posited in the Introduction, namely (a) the relations between components of SRL phases, within a phase and across phases, (b) the role of affect in the SRL process, and (c) the interaction of general student characteristics with situational ones, taking into consideration that there are cycles of SRL.

Relations between Components of SRL Phases

The present study showed, first of all, that students' motivational, cognitive, and affective characteristics, namely achievement goal orientations, cognitive ability, self-concept, test anxiety, and attitude towards the learning domain (specifically mathematics), at the Forethought phase are interrelated. These are relations within a phase. Yet, there are effects of test anxiety and achievement goal orientations on state anxiety, which is an affective reaction at the situational level, that is, at the Performance/Volitional Control phase. This implies that components of the Forethought phase have relations or effects not only within that phase but also with components of other phases.

Affect and SRL

The present study showed that the learning situation (i.e., goal instructions and EF) differentiated not only task performance, but also activity-related emotions (i.e., interest in and liking of the task), state anxiety, as well as the ME at the Performance/Volitional Control phase. These findings are in line with the SRL cyclic model that predicts relations between cognition and metacognition in the Performance/Volitional Control phase. They also showed that affect is present in this phase as in the Forethought phase, but in a different form. At the Forethought phase affect was present in the form of attitude towards mathematics, test anxiety, and self-concept, whereas in the Performance/Volitional Control phase in the form of emotions or ME. Moreover, in the Performance/Volitional Control phase metacognitive feelings, such as feelings of difficulty and feeling of confidence, mediated the effects of EF on state anxiety. These findings imply that there are local dynamics that develop during the Performance/Volitional Control phase, and affect is an integral part of these dynamics.

Situational Effects on the SRL Process

Before discussing the interaction of student general person characteristics with the learning situation, it is important to point out another aspect of SRL, namely the continuity of the SRL process in time; that is, as soon as one cycle of SRL is concluded another one starts. We found that situation-specific factors, such as goal instructions and EF, which play a role in one cycle of SRL (e.g., the first testing occasion of the present study) may have effects on the next SRL cycle (i.e., the second testing occasion of the present study), that is, SRL in a similar learning situation. This was evident in our finding that goal instructions did not have a significant effect on state anxiety during the first testing occasion but did have during the second testing occasion. This finding supports the idea that the SRL process is continuous and that there can be cumulative effects of situational factors from one SRL cycle to the next. Thus, the cycle of SRL that follows a specific learning situation integrates situational effects of the previous cycle of SRL but, at the same time, maintains a certain level of stability as well. Stability is maintained because students' general person characteristics, such as achievement goal orientations, have effects that can transcend specific learning situations. This was particularly evident in our findings denoting a similar pattern of effects of mastery goal orientation on state anxiety in both testing occasions.

These findings suggest that if we look at SRL as a complex continuous process that involves person characteristics, as well as cognition, metacognition, and affect within specific learning situations, then we can identify both general and situation-specific effects of motivation. In what follows, we shall discuss the interaction of students' general person characteristics between them and with situational factors in light of an unexpected finding of the present study that pertains to achievement goal orientations.

Mastery, but not Performance, Goal Orientation Predicts State Anxiety

The present study showed that two person characteristics, that is, test anxiety and mastery goal orientation directly contributed to state anxiety in both testing occasions, independently from situational factors. Contrary to extant theory, performance-approach and performance-avoidance goal orientations did not predict state anxiety. Moreover, the effect of mastery goal orientation was positive contrary to normative achievement goal orientation theory and the findings of Chen et al. (2000) and Elliot and McGregor (1999).

To understand these discrepant findings, we need to take into consideration the interactions between person characteristics. Specifically, if we look at the correlations between achievement goal orientations and state anxiety we can see that they are in line with normative theory: mastery goal orientation was not related to state anxiety while performance-approach and performance-avoidance goal orientation were positively related to it. Moreover, positive attitude towards mathematics was highly related to mastery goal orientation, moderately to performance-approach goal orientation, and negatively to performance-avoidance goal orientation. These relations proved to be very important because when attitude was entered in the regression analysis then the picture changed: mastery goal orientation was found to be a significant predictor of state anxiety whereas performance-approach and performance-avoidance were not. These findings suggest a suppressor effect; the relation was possibly there but it was not revealed because the effect of attitude towards mathematics was not taken into consideration. Of course, considering the correlational nature of the study and the possible multicollinearity effects, further research is needed to reveal the generality of the finding and the mechanism underlying it.

It needs to be also pointed out that attitude towards mathematics was a significant negative predictor of state anxiety in the first testing occasion but not in the second, whereas the effect of mastery goal orientation on state anxiety was persistent across the two testing occasions. This finding suggests that situational factors interacted with the attitude towards mathematics (i.e., an affective characteristic), but not with mastery goal orientation (i.e., a motivational characteristic). This finding is also consistent with other findings of the present study, namely that there were situational effects on ME, interest, liking, and state anxiety.

Obviously, all the above findings need to be replicated before their theoretical implications are further explored. However, it seems plausible that situational factors impact the affective components of SRL but not students' general person characteristics, such as achievement goal orientations.

The finding that mastery goal orientation was predictive of state anxiety has also practical implications for classroom interventions. Specifically, based on the normative theory of achievement goal orientations, it is often assumed that mastery instructions or a mastery-oriented classroom environment will promote learning and/or achievement and, at the same time, will reduce state anxiety. According to our findings, this is true only when mastery instructions to students are accompanied by positive EF. On the contrary, performance instructions lead to high achievement not only in the presence of positive EF but also in the absence of EF. Negative EF had detrimental effects on students' achievement, particularly in the case of mastery instructions.

Contrary to our expectations, goal instructions did not mediate the effect of achievement goal orientations on state anxiety; nor did goal instructions moderate the effect of test anxiety on state anxiety. These findings are in line with those of Linnenbrink (2005) who did not find beneficial effects of mastery goal condition on anxiety. But if goal instructions do not mediate the effects of person factors on state anxiety, do they have an independent direct effect on state anxiety? We found that the effect of goal instructions on state anxiety was not significant in the first testing occasion but became significant in the second. Moreover, both mastery and performance instructions were positive predictors of state anxiety in the second testing occasion. Therefore, goal instructions can have a direct effect on state anxiety. A possible explanation of this finding is that when the learning situation was repeated students took into consideration what happened in the first testing occasion and, particularly, EF and their ME. This entailed that no matter if it were mastery or performance instructions the students relalized that they could fail. If failure is probable, then students' state anxiety is increased, irrespectively of goal instructions. What is important is that mastery instructions do not prevent state anxiety and performance instructions do not necessarily increase it.

State Anxiety and EF

Negative EF was a principal factor in arousing state anxiety, particularly in the context of performance instructions as the ANCOVA showed. However, negative EF was appraised in light of the testing occasion (first or second) and of ME. The ME were the affective responses that mediated the effect of this situational factor, namely negative EF, on state anxiety in both testing occasions. Therefore, it is not negative EF per se that is important but how it influences students' ME and possibly other affective responses in the learning situation. Feeling of difficulty and/or estimate of effort contributed positively to state anxiety, because they denote lack of fluency in task processing and possible failure, as negative EF also denotes. Feeling of confidence, on the other hand, was negatively related to state anxiety in both testing occasions; the higher feeling of confidence students had the less their state anxiety. This finding suggests that negative EF can be counteracted by feeling of confidence, which acts as a subjective indicator of response correctness and can support the student in appraising the significance of situational factors, such as negative EF. Thus, a significant link in the motivation-emotion mechanism is ME but only in relation to EF and not to goal instructions.

State Anxiety and Activity-Related Emotions

It should be noted that positive activity-related emotions, namely interest in and liking of the tasks, did not have any effect on state anxiety. This finding argues in favor of the theory which distinguishes positive from negative affect (Watson & Tellegen, 1985), and can possibly explain the seemingly contradictory finding that students in the mastery instructions group reported high interest and liking even in the second testing occasion although mastery goal instructions contributed to state anxiety in the second testing occasion.

Conclusion

Our findings argue in favor of a model of SRL which takes into consideration, at the same time, both the general person characteristics (including motivational ones) and the situational factors. In such a model, an important component is ME that connect EF with students' representation of the learning situation and of their competence and, consequently, of their self-concept as shown by Efklides and Tsiora (2002). However, there are situational factors, such as goal instructions, that do not act through ME but possibly through other ways; this is an issue for further investigation. Moreover, goal instructions may have immediate effects on students' affective reactions in a learning situation, or effects that show up later on when the students come up with similar situations. Whether or not these situational effects have a bearing on students' long-term motivation (i.e., on achievement goal orientations) needs to be also investigated in the future. Once the students develop their achievement goal orientations then these goals can act in a general manner, not tied to specific learning situations.

The findings of the present study, however, should be seen in relation to the age of the participants, who were students of junior high school in a transition period, when their goal orientations are still being formed, contrary to the studies of Chen et al. (2000) and Elliot and McGregor (1999) who worked with university students. Therefore, this is a limitation of the study that requires further research.

Appendix A. Measures of the Study in the Two Testing Occasions

First testing occasion

A. Mathematical ability
    Self-concept in mathematics
    Attitude towards mathematics
    Test anxiety (trait)
    Students' goal orientation (mastery, performance-approach, performance-avoidance)

B1. Mathematical Task 1 (easy)
    ME and activity-related emotions
    Solving of Task 1 (Task 1 performance)
    Extrinsic feedback (EF)—No EF
    ME and activity-related emotions
B2. Mathematical Task 2 (moderate difficulty)
    ME and activity-related emotions
    Solving of Task 2 (Task 2 performance)
    Extrinsic feedback (EF)—No EF
    ME and activity-related emotions
B1. Mathematical Task 3 (difficult)
    ME and activity-related emotions
    Solving of Task 3 (Task 3 performance)
    Extrinsic feedback (EF)—No EF
    ME and activity-related emotions

Second testing occasion

1. Mathematical Task 1 (easy)
   ME and activity-related emotions
   Solving of Task 1 (Task 1 performance)
   Extrinsic feedback (EF)—No EF
   ME and activity-related emotions
2. Mathematical Task 2 (moderate difficulty)
   ME and activity-related emotions
   Solving of Task 2 (Task 2 performance)
   Extrinsic feedback (EF)—No EF
   ME and activity-related emotions
3. Mathematical Task 3 (difficult)
   ME and activity-related emotions
   Solving of Task 3 (Task 3 performance)
   Extrinsic feedback (EF)—No EF
   ME and activity-related emotions

Appendix B. Instructions and EF Given to Students

Mastery-Positive group and Mastery-Negative group
"The aim of this study is to investigate the way in which students solve mathematical problems. Specifically, we are interested in giving students an opportunity to solve mathematical problems and see how they apply their knowledge to these tasks. The experience and knowledge that someone obtains while s/he is dealing with a task are very important, independently of whether the person succeeds or fails to solve the task. Please, try to solve these problems and try to find out what you can learn from this experience. When you are finished with each problem you will be informed about the mathematical knowledge required."
The feedback provided by the Experimenter was the following:
• Positive EF: "You seem to have the knowledge required."
• Negative EF: "You seem not to have the knowledge required."

Performance-Positive group and Performance-Negative group
"The aim of this study is to investigate the way in which students solve mathematical problems. Specifically, we want to compare the performance of students and find out how many of them are going to achieve high scores. A higher score means that someone has high ability in mathematical thinking. Please, try to solve these problems correctly and without errors. When you are finished with each problem you will be informed about how you achieved as compared to the mean of students of your age."
The feedback provided by the Experimenter was the following:
• Positive EF: "You achieved higher than the mean of students of your age."
• Negative EF: "You achieved lower than the mean of students of your age."

Mastery-No EF group and Performance-No EF group
The last sentence of the respective goal instructions was omitted in the case of the groups that did not receive EF.

Control Group
"The aim of the study is to investigate the way in which students solve mathematical problems. Please try to solve the problems you are given."

References

Aiken, L. R. (1996). *Rating scales and checklists: Evaluating behaviour, personality, and attitudes.* London: Wiley.

Allison, P. D. (1999). *Logistic regression using the SAS system: Theory and application.* Cary, NC: SAS Institute.

Ames, C. (1984). Achievement attributions and self-instructions under competitive and individualistic goal structures. *Journal of Educational Psychology, 76*, 478-487.

Ames, C. (1992). Classrooms: Goals, structures, and student motivation. *Journal of Educational Psychology, 84*, 261-271.

Barron, R. M., & Kenny, D. A. (1986). The moderator-mediator variable distinction in social psychological research: Conceptual, strategic, and statistical considerations. *Journal of Personality and Social Psychology, 51*, 1173-1182.

Birenbaum, M., & Nasser, F. (1994). On the relationship between anxiety and test performance. *Measurement and Evaluation in Counseling and Development, 27*, 293-301.

Boekaerts, M. (1999). Self-regulated learning: Where we are today. *International Journal of Educational Research, 31*, 445-457.

Chen, G., Gully, S. M., Whiteman, J.-A., & Kilcullen, R. N. (2000). Examination of relationships among trait-like individual differences, state-like individual differences and learning performance. *Journal of Applied Psychology, 6*, 835-847.

Demetriou, A., Platsidou, M., Efklides, A., Metallidou, Y., & Shayer, M. (1991). Structure and sequence of the quantitative-relational abilities from childhood to adolescence. *Learning and Instruction, 1*, 19-44.

Dermitzaki, I., & Efklides, A. (2000). Aspects of self-concept and their relationship with language performance and verbal reasoning abilty. *American Journal of Psychology, 113*, 621-638.

Dina, F. (2000). *The interactions between cognitive and affective factors during the solution of lectical mathematical problems under the influence of positive and negative feedback to students of the 5th grade.* Unpublished diploma thesis, School of Psychology, Aristotle University of Thessaloniki, Greece.

Dina, F. (2006). The effect of feedback as a function of task, motivation, self, and affect. Unpublished doctoral dissertation, School of Psychology, Aristotle University of Thessaloniki, Greece.

Dweck, C. S., & Elliott, E. (1983). Achievement motivation. In E. M. Hetherington (Ed.), P. H. Mussen (Series Ed.), *Handbook of child psychology: Socialization, personality, and social development* (Vol. 4, pp. 643-691). New York: Wiley.

Efklides, A. (2001). Metacognitive experiences in problem solving: Cognition, affect, and self-regulation. In A. Efklides, J. Kuhl, & R. Sorrentino (Eds.), *Trends and prospects in motivation research* (pp. 297-323). Dordrecht, The Netherlands: Kluwer.

Efklides, A. (2002). Feelings as subjective evaluations of cognitive processing: How reliable are they? *Psychology: The Journal of the Hellenic Psychological Society, 9*, 163-184.

Efklides, A. (2006). Metacognition and affect: What can metacognitive experiences tell us about the learning process? *Educational Research Review, 1*, 3-14.

Efklides, A., & Dina, F. (2007). Is mastery orientation always beneficial for learning? In F. Salili & R. Hoosain (Eds.), *Culture, motivation and learning: A multicultural perspective* (pp. 131-167). Greenwich, CT: Information Age Publishing.

Efklides, A., & Petkaki, C. (2005). Effects of mood on students' metacognitive experiences. *Learning and Instruction, 15*, 415-431.

Efklides, A., & Tsiora, A. (2002). Metacognitive experiences, self-concept, and self-regulation. *Psychologia: An International Journal of Psychology in the Orient, 45*, 222-236.

Elliot, A. J., & Church, M. A. (1997). A hierarchical model of approach and avoidance achievement motivation. *Journal of Personality and Social Psychology, 72*, 218-232.

Elliot, A. J., & McGregor, H. A. (1999). Test anxiety and the hierarchical model of approach and avoidance achievement motivation. *Journal of Personality and Social Psychology, 76*, 628-644.

Graham, S., & Golan, S. (1991). Motivational influences on cognition: Task involvement, ego involvement, and depth of information processing. *Journal of Educational Psychology, 83*, 187-194.

Harackiewicz, J. M., Barron, K. E., Pintrich, P. R., Elliot, A. J., & Thrash, T. M. (2002). Revision of achievement goal theory: Necessary and illuminating. *Journal of Educational Psychology, 94*, 638-645.

Jagacinski, C. M., & Strickland, O. J. (2000). Task and ego orientation: The role of goal orientations in anticipated affective reactions to achievement outcomes. *Learning and Individual Differences, 12*, 189-208.

Kavussanu, M. (2007). The effects of goal orientations on global self-esteem and physical self-worth in physical education students. *Hellenic Journal of Psychology*, 4, 111-132.

Linnenbrink, E. A. (2005). The dilemma of performance-approach goals: The use of multiple goal contexts to promote students' motivation and learning. *Journal of Educational Psychology, 97*, 197-213.

McGregor, H. A., & Elliot, A. J. (2002). Achievement goals as predictors of achievement-relevant processes prior to a task engagement. *Journal of Educational Psychology, 94*, 381-395.

McLeod, C., & Mathews, A. (1988). Anxiety and allocation of attention to threat. *Quarterly Journal of Experimental Psychology: Human Experimental Psychology, 40*, 653-670.

Metallidou, P., & Efklides, A. (2001). The effects of general success-related beliefs and specific metacognitive experiences on causal attributions. In A. Efklides, J. Kuhl, & R. Sorrentino (Eds.), *Trends and prospects in motivation research* (pp. 325-347). Dordrecht, The Netherlands: Kluwer.

Meyers, L. S., Gamst, G., & Guarino, A. (2006). *Applied multivariate research: Design and interpretation.* Thousand Oaks, CA: Sage.

Midgley, C., Kaplan, A., Middleton, M., Maehr, M. L., Urdan, T., Lynley, H. A., Anderman, E., & Roeser, R. (1998). The development and validation of scales assessing students' achievement goal orientations. *Contemporary Educational Psychology, 23*, 113-131.

Midgley, C., & Urdan, T. (2001). Academic self-handicapping and achievement goals: A further examination. *Contemporary Educational Psychology, 26*, 61-75.

Newman, R. (1998). Students' help-seeking during problem-solving: Influences of personal and contextual goals. *Journal of Educational Psychology, 90*, 644-658.

Nicholls, J. G. (1984). Achievement motivation: Conceptions of ability, subjective experience, task choice, and performance. *Psychological Review, 91*, 328-346.

Pedhazur, E. J. (1982). *Multiple regression in behavioral research.* Austin, TX: Holt, Rinehart and Winston.

Pekrun, R., Elliot, A. J., & Maier, M. A. (2006). Achievement goals and discrete achievement emotions: A theoretical model and prospective test. *Journal of Educational Psychology, 98*, 583-597.

Pekrun, R., Goetz, T., Titz, W., & Perry, R. P. (2002). Academic emotions in students' self-regulated learning and achievement: A program of quantitative and qualitative research. *Educational Psychologist, 37*, 91-106.

Pintrich, P. R., & DeGroot, E. (1990). Motivational and self-regulated learning components of classroom academic performance. *Journal of Educational Research, 47*, 586-622.

Rajecki, D. W. (1982). *Attitudes: Themes and advances.* Sunderland, MA: Sinauer.

Sarason, I. G. (1975). Test anxiety, attention, and the general problem of anxiety. In C. D. Spielberger & I. G. Sarason (Eds.), *Stress and anxiety* (Vol. 1, pp. 165-188). Washington, DC: Hemisphere.

Spielberger, C. D. (1980). *Manual for the State-Trait Anxiety Inventory.* Palo Alto, CA: Consulting Psychologists Press.

Tauer, J., & Harackiewicz, J. M. (1999). Winning isn't everything: Competition, achievement orientation, and intrinsic motivation. *Journal of Experimental Social Psychology, 35,* 209-238.

Turner, J. C., Thorpe, P. K., & Meyer, D. K. (1998). Students' reports on motivation and negative affect: A theoretical and empirical analysis. *Journal of Educational Psychology, 90,* 758-771.

Urdan, T., & Mestas, M. (2006). The goals behind performance goals. *Journal of Educational Psychology, 98,* 354-365.

Watson, D., & Tellegen, A. (1985). Toward a consensual structure of mood. *Psychological Bulletin, 9,* 219-235.

Zeidner, M. (1995). Adaptive coping with test situations: A review of the literature. *Educational Psychologist, 30,* 123-133.

Zimmerman, B. J. (1998). Developing self-fulfilling cycles of academic regulation: An analysis of exemplary instructional models. In D. H. Schunk & B. J. Zimmerman (Eds.), *Self-regulated learning: From teaching to self-reflective practice* (pp. 1-19). New York: Guilford.

On a Differential Explanation of Self-Direction in Motivating Learning Environments

Peter Nenniger, Katja van den Brink, & Dirk Bissbort

Introduction

In higher as well as in vocational education self-directed or self-regulated learning has turned out to be a framework that explains effective learning. Self-directed learning brings cognitive, motivational, emotional, social and contextual perspectives of learning together with autonomy and independence of the learner. Research in this field aims at improving understanding of learning and finding practical methods in order to enhance its quality according to the demands of the educational, the economical, and the societal systems; it also seeks to promote instruction and learning in different educational and working-life environments (Beck & Krumm, 2001; Boekaerts & Rozendaal, 2007; Nenniger, 1997).

Nevertheless, despite the fact that research in this area is widespread, in its majority it represents snapshots rather than integrative views. Self-directed or self-regulated learning is studied within specific conditions or contexts, and there is no comprehensive explanation of the mechanisms behind it. There are only partially coherent theories that mostly focus on selected aspects of learning such as metacognition, use of strategies, mainly achievement-oriented motivation, evaluative processes and attributions (for overviews see Boekaerts, Pintrich, & Zeidner, 2000; Puustinen & Pulkkinen, 2001; Zimmermann & Schunk, 2001).

In this state of affairs, educational theory tends to concentrate on self-direction in the initiation and continuation of ongoing and life-long learning whereas psychology emphasises self-regulation within the learning process. However, the distinction between self-direction and self-regulation is not so easy to be made, because the two conceptualisations share a lot of characteristics. From the viewpoint of self-direction, self-directed learners learn strategically by actively selecting, structuring and creating learning environments that support their learning. Thus, learners show an enhanced level of self-efficacy and intrinsic motivation and they monitor the progress of their learning by learning activities that mainly include extensive and autonomous planning, organising and self-evaluating. From the viewpoint of self-regulation, learning is described in terms of cognitive, emotional, motivational, volitional and metacognitive processes (Boekaerts & Nenniger, 1999; Efklides, 2004; Schiefele & Pekrun, 1996; Schunk, Zimmerman, Winne, & Alexander, 2006; Zimmerman, 1989; Zimmerman & Martinez-Pons, 1988). Therefore, a closer look at the processes underlying self-direction and self-regulation makes it clear that despite the disciplinary differences in the description of learning, a more comprehensive view of self-directed learning can be achieved. Following Luhmann's (1984) distinction between different levels of system complexity, self-direction seems to be located at the meso-level, whereas self-regulation is located at the micro-level of learning. For this reason, in the subsequent argumentation, self-direction (primarily describing the course of learning) is considered to include self-regulation (with the associated cognitive, emotional, motivational, volitional and metacognitive processes). Consequently, our understanding of self-directed learning includes self-regulated learning. However, even in this conceptualization of self-directed learning the quality of the learning processes in terms of depth in understanding and significance of content are still neglected. For this reason the above conceptualization of self-directed learning needs to include content-related aspects of understanding as well as intentions to understand such content. This perspective on learning is represented by research on approaches to learning.

On this background the present chapter aims at a more comprehensive explanation of the course and process of learning that includes content and the intention to understand it; thus, from a preferentially motivational perspective, an attempt will be made to bring in higher coherence to the still obscure picture of self-directed learning. For this purpose the chapter is organised as follows: first, a theoretical framework that encompasses significant concepts from the research paradigms of self-directed learning and approaches to learning will be offered. On this foundation and on findings from extant empirical research, research questions are presented that serve as guideposts for the subsequent section describing an empirical study that tested the proposed theoretical framework. The chapter ends with an outlook on future theoretical developments and methodological requirements for a comprehensive studying of self-direction in learning.

Theoretical Framework

As already mentioned self-directed and self-regulated learning usually refer to a complex conglomerate of internal, learning-related, and of environmental factors. The defining characteristic of self-directed learning, however, is that the learner shows an active involvement concerning different aspects of his/her learning (Boekaerts & Cascallar, 2006; Brocket & Hiemstra, 1991; Candy, 1991; Pintrich, 2003). In the majority of definitions of self-directed learning (Brockett & Hiemstra, 1991; Candy, 1991; Knowles, 1975) emphasis is given on the learners' motivation and direction of their learning processes within a certain learning situation with the aim of achieving the goals set. Some authors also underscore the importance of scaffolding (Renninger, 2005) so that learners integrate domain-specific knowledge in the learning field with metacognitive abilities that promote reflection on, as well as planning, designing and implementation of the learning project.

Similar emphasis on cognitive, metacognitive and motivational processes is found in accounts of self-regulated learning. Corno (1994) defined self-regulated learning as active participation in goal setting as well as control over learning strategies and learning processes while involved in the learning tasks. Kuhl (1983, 1985) emphasised action control and the use of strategies for the self-regulation of motivation as well as of other processes so that attainment of one's goal can be ensured. Already Pintrich & DeGroot (1990) and later on Pintrich (2000a, 2003, 2004) also stressed motivation in self-regulated learning along with the use of cognitive and metacognitive strategies; in this context motivation is conceived in terms of self-efficacy and achievement goal orientation. Finally, additional constructs related to motivation and self-regulation were introduced by the self-determination theory (Deci & Ryan, 2002) and by the theory on interest (Hidi & Ainley, 2008; Hidi, Renninger, & Krapp, 2004).

In perhaps the most integrative view of self-regulated learning that encompasses motivation as well as cognitive regulation as a complex, interactive process, Boekaerts (1997, 1999) originally described in her Six-Component Model of Self-Regulated Learning two types of self-regulation (cognitive and motivational) that function at three levels, namely the level of (a) goals, (b) metacognition, and (c) domain-specific knowledge, thus resulting in (2 x 3) six components that need to be available or currently accessible by the learner, if self-regulated learning is to occur. In this model the six components of self-regulated learning show interdependence so that, for example, deficits in knowledge can impede self-regulation of goals. Building on her original views, Boekaerts and Cascallar (2006) suggested that self-regulated learning is taking place at three levels: (a) regulation of the self (choice of goals and resources), (b) regulation of the learning process (use of metacognitive knowledge and skills to direct one's learning), and (c) regulation of the modes of information processing (choice of information-processing strategies).

With respect to self-directed learning a number of models extended Knowles' (1975; see also Long, 1989) description of the course of self-directed learning by adding components in which the learner takes the initiative for learning with (or without) the help of others. These components are (a) diagnosing his or her own needs concerning learning, (b) establishing learning goals, (c) identifying the necessary human and material resources, (d) choosing and implementing appropriate learning strategies, and (e) evaluating the learning outcomes. In Nenniger and Straka's Two-Shells Model of Motivated Self-Directed Learning (Nenniger, 1999; Straka & Nenniger, 1995; Straka, Nenniger, Spevacek, & Wosnitza 1996; Straka & Schaefer, 2002), self-directed learning is described in terms of two "shells" (an exterior and an interior) and explanatory components (denominated as "concepts" including several subordinated "constructs"). According to this model, the exterior shell of the model includes the motivational aspect of self-directed learning. The exterior shell influences the interior shell that includes the volitional part of self-directed learning where learners actively exercise the learning process. As the interior shell is embedded in the exterior shell, the evaluated learning experience from the interior shell recursively affects students' future learning and studying and thus directs learning on a next level in the outer shell. Therefore, recursivity in the course of self-directed learning is not thought as a circular sequence, but as an evolving spiral that distinguishes – analogously to Boekaerts (1997) layers of self-regulation – between different levels of the course of self-directed learning.

Even if in a comprehensive understanding of the course of learning and of its associated processes (as described in the models of Boekaerts and Nenniger) the influences of the perceived and the objective environment are taken into account, there is still no explicit conceptualisation of content understanding or of initial interest. The latter do not only refer to the learners' capacity for knowledge acquisition, but also to an actualised stable relation towards the content of learning (Nenniger, Straka, Spevacek, & Wosnitza,

1996). Thus, the quality of the learning processes, beyond measures of achievement, does not seem to attract attention. Self-regulated learning assumes that there is intention to understand, but does not explicitly operationalise understanding in terms of content; yet, if a person learns content successfully, this does not necessarily mean that this person also learns in a self-regulated manner.

A research paradigm that explicitly includes the intention to understand content has been developed during the last three decades under the label of Approaches to Learning and Studying. It has its origins in the phenomenographic research of Marton and Säljö (1976a), has its roots in Husserl's (1923/24) principle of intentionality. According to this principle, experiences like understanding or perceiving cannot be separated from what is understood or perceived and thus are to be described as they appear to people. Consequently, any derivation of general principles of learning independently of its context and content is not acceptable: The way students learn is a consequence of how they perceive the learning environment (learning task, learning material, etc.) and the learning process. In this perspective, Marton and Säljö (1976a, 1976b) categorised the ways in which students handle a learning situation into "deep" (with focus on the meaning underlying the learning material, on what is significant) and "surface" (with focus restricted to learning material as such) and assigned them to different levels of processing. Later on, this categorisation to deep and surface processing was subsumed under the conceptualisation "approaches to learning", which simultaneously involves intention and process. In the last two decades several research groups (Biggs, 1999; Entwistle, 2000) extended the initial methodology of phenomenography in order to include quantitative or mixed design studies, self-report instruments (Entwistle & McCune, 2004; Richardson, 2004) and applied them to further investigate issues related to the approaches to learning (Biggs, 1993; Entwistle, 2000; Entwistle & Tomlinson, 2007; Prosser & Trigwell, 1997a, 1997b).

A closer look at the approaches-to-learning theoretical tradition suggests that it can provide insights into self-directed academic learning. For example, in predicting outcome variables of academic learning, Diseth and Martinsen (2003) observed remarkable common variance of variables related to self-regulatory aspects of learning and different approaches to learning. In an attempt to conceptualise distinctive styles of academic learning, Entwistle and McCune (2004) identified an overlapping between the use of specific approaches to learning and modes of self-regulation in learning with respect to level of processing and use of self-regulating strategies. In addition, they found similarities between scales measuring approaches to learning with components of questionnaires on learning styles (Vermunt, 1996), and on self-regulated learning as measured by the Motivated Strategies for Learning Questionnaire (MSLQ; Pintrich, Smith, Garcia, & McKeachie, 1991). In contrast, Richardson (2004) found that the deep approach, which represents learning strategies for understanding, is clearly different from strategies on the self-regulation of study that require effort and concentration.

With respect to motivational aspects of approaches to learning, there seems to be an interaction of learning approaches with learning environments. For example, there are relationships between students' approaches to learning, achieved grades and further qualitative outcomes, but also specific dependence on the mode of assessment (Tait, Entwistle, & McCune, 1998). Furthermore, a number of studies have shown that the students' approaches to learning influence and are influenced by their perceptions of the learning content. Specifically, Entwistle and Ramsden (1983) found that depending on the domain of one's studies different approaches to academic learning were used. Finally, Meyer (2000) showed that a broad overall pattern describing approaches to learning may not necessarily apply to all groups of students. As some qualitative studies have revealed, students with fair results or particular problems in academic learning may have confusing or even lack self-determined approaches to learning. Meyer, Parsons and Dunne (1990) also found that in failing students the relationships between learning contents and approaches to learning were disintegrated or, at best, randomly associated. In this respect, McCune (2004) came to the conclusion that because of the partially idiosyncratic and dynamic aspects of learning, quantitative studies can only provide limited insight into the development of learning skills; for the relations of learning skills with approaches to learning, qualitative studies are needed to sufficiently describe students' learning within specific academic discourse and content.

The above findings make clear that the research paradigm of self-directed learning (self-regulation included) is essentially a top-down one inspired by information-processing theories (see also critiques by Biggs, 1993). On the contrary, the research paradigm of approaches to learning is a bottom-up one and stresses the effects of different contents of learning on approaches to learning and their associated strategies. Yet, because of their differences, the research paradigms associated with the two theoretical perspectives (i.e., self-direction and approaches to learning) offer the possibility for a broader and more differentiated view of self-direction in learning as well as a more functional view of the conditions that pave the way for the choice of a specific learning approach. As a first attempt in this direction, research on the intersection of self-directed learning with learning approaches is meaningful, because it can uncover the extent to which there is overlap and coherence between the main concepts of each theoretical perspective.

Research Questions

Any attempt to integrate concepts of self-directed learning with concepts from approaches to learning is faced with the following situation:

First, although the two theoretical perspectives have been developed within different research paradigms, they provide sufficient conceptual ground for understanding students' learning strategies, metacognition, and motivation. However, they describe different types of learning strategies and of motivation. Specifically, the approaches-to-learning perspective refers to different forms of motivation (intrinsic, instrumental, achievement motivation, relatedness to others) as well as to different strategies (deep elaborative strategies, surface strategies, intention to understand, repetition and memorisation strategies, achievement strategies) (cf. Printrich, 2004); the two approaches to learning, namely the deep and the surface approach, are associated with different strategies depending on the type of students' motivation (intrinsic, extrinsic, achievement motivation) and intention (intention to understand versus the intention to memorise). In contrast, the self-directed-learning perspective does not distinguish qualitatively different types of self-directed learning, nor categorises the different regulatory components of motivation and learning strategies into homogenous groups. Rather, the various authors focus on different forms of achievement motivation (e.g., mastery or performance motivation) and different forms of learning strategies, as well as metacognitive and achievement strategies.

Second, results from mixed methods studies from both theoretical perspectives suggest that there are relations between their components. For example, the common variance between deep learning strategies and high grades has been found to be up to 10% (Pintrich, 1989, 2000b; Watkins & Hattie, 1990). Furthermore, associations between components of self-directed learning and of approaches to learning have been found (Wild, 1995); specifically, intrinsic motivation, content interest, and use of deep learning strategies tend to be associated, whereas extrinsic motivation is associated with use of surface (memorisation) strategies. Finally, regarding regulatory aspects, DeGroot (2002) showed the interaction of students' motivational orientations with the use of specific learning and metacognitive strategies.

Third, despite the above mentioned associations between motivation and approaches to learning, there are meta-analyses (see Schiefele & Schreyer, 1992) that question the generality of these associations. Based on such findings, Wild (1995) came to the conclusion that intrinsic and extrinsic forms of motivation, associated with an intention to understand, have distinct impact on the use of specific learning strategies. According to Schiefele, Wild, and Winteler (1995), students with intrinsic motivation and a high interest in the subject of the course showed an increased use of deep learning strategies, and students who used deep learning strategies got slightly better grades in examinations than students using surface strategies. Although the above findings suggest that deep learning strategies (which are supposed to lead to more qualitative learning) should result in better performance, there is no general evidence that the employment of deep strategies has an impact on performance in academic examinations, probably because still numerous examinations do not ask for understanding but for retention of knowledge of facts.

Also, from research focussing on regulatory aspects of academic learning, it is not possible to derive a consistent or predominant choice of learning strategies in students who exhibit self-directed learning. Moreover, there is only little research investigating the differentiation between surface self-directed and deep self-directed learning (Silva & Duarte, 2001; Tait, Entwistle, & McCune, 1998; Vermunt, 1996). What we can assume from most of the results available is that self-directed learning could be implemented in a surface as well as in a deep learning mode. In the first case surface self-directed students just try to meet certain needs such as getting acceptable grades or get the task done, and therefore mainly use surface strategies with the only intention to rehearse and memorise material without any intention to understand. In the second case, self-directed students learn along the lines suggested by the "ideal" self-directed learning, according to which students are deeply involved in learning with the intention to understand the learning content. But there might exist a third case, in which students use a mixture of both surface and deep strategies in order to meet their needs (see Entwistle, McCune & Walker, 2001). The above findings and possibilities underscore the necessity for identifying very sensitively the quality of self-directed learning (good, average, poor) and the quality of the learning outcome, implying that self-directed learning has to be conceived as a content-dependent and dynamic process.

It is therefore worthwhile to empirically investigate the relations and possible intersections of the two theoretical perspectives. As any empirical research is limited in scope by its nature, from the multiple theoretical variants of self-directed learning, Nenniger and Straka's conceptualisation of "self-directed learning" related to their Two Shells Model of Motivated Self-directed Learning (Nenniger, 1999) was chosen for the subsequent comparison with approaches to learning. Entwistle's conceptualisation of "approaches to learning" (Entwistle & Tait, 1990) was chosen as the most appropriate to represent the latter theoretical perspective. For a meaningful comparison we have, however, to comply with the following two requirements: first, for each of the two conceptualisations we have to determine the respective concept on the basis of selected constructs assumed to be relevant for comparison and, second, on the basis of the selected constructs we have to identify the structure of each concept. On this basis only, the intersection of the two theoretical conceptualisations can be determined.

The respective research questions, therefore, address the following issues [1]:

1. Which are the constructs and in consequence the concepts that are relevant for the comparison of the Nenniger and Straka's conceptualisation of "self-directed learning" as denoted in the Two-Shells Model of Motivated Self-Directed Learning with Entwistle's conceptualisation of "approaches to learning"?
2. Within each conceptualisation, which is the structure of the respective concept based on the selected constructs relevant for comparison?
3. Which are the characteristics of the intersection of the concepts identified by the comparative analyses with respect to
   (a) the amount of intersection;
   (b) the complexity of intersection;
   (c) the importance of respective constructs of each concept participating in the intersection?

In the following study it was attempted to give a first answer to the above research questions on the basis of analyses of data from several student samples of German universities.

The Present Study

To identify the structure of the concepts within each conceptualisation and the intersection of the two concepts derived from the two conceptualisations, a study was carried out with students from five German universities (for details see van den Brink, 2006). To control possible effects of students' prior expertise in their domain of studies and to ensure the appropriate quality and validity of the instruments we used, a self-report ques-

---

[1] The following explanation may contribute to a better understanding of the terminology used in the present study: On the theoretical level, derived from each conceptualization ("self-directed learning" sensu Nenniger, "approaches to learning" sensu Entwistle) a concept (e.g. "self-directed learning") is defined as a dimensional structure consisting of independent constructs (e.g. "cognitive control") assumed to be relevant for comparison. On the technical level, for each conceptualization a factorial structure (representing a "concept") consisting of several factors (each representing a "construct") is computed by a principal component analysis on the basis of items attributed to each construct in the respective questionnaire.

tionnaire regarding students' prior expertise in their field of study was administered. To analyse the data along the research questions posed, the following steps were performed: First, within each of the two theoretical conceptualisations ("self-directed learning" and "approaches to learning") the factorial structure of the respective concept (consisting of the selected constructs suitable for comparison) was identified by principal component analyses. Second, for each factor (representing a construct), the factor scores were computed for each student. In addition, the reliability of the factor scores (as measures of the constructs) was determined. Third, in several canonical correlation analyses the amount (common variance) and the complexity (number of roots) of concordance between the factorial structures of the two concepts was calculated and the relative canonical weight (representing the importance of the respective construct within the concordance) was assigned to each factor. Finally, the most suitable model that accounted for the findings was determined.

Method

Sample

The sample consisted of 275 computer science students from five public universities in Germany: University of Leipzig (83), Technical University of Berlin (52), Humboldt-University of Berlin (53), Free-University of Berlin (54), and Technical University of Munich (29). The main characteristics of the sample were the following: the mean age was 24 years; 18% were females. They were graduate students in the third, fourth, or fifth year of studies (with 23 % of them having already started another field of study before and 11% having just finished their studies). Of the total sample, 252 students were of German nationality and 23 of other nationalities.

Instruments

BEMSEL-HIS Questionnaire

An adapted version of a questionnaire that consisted of 45 items (response were given in a 6-point Likert-type scale) originally representing four constructs (namely cognition, motivation, metacognition, and evaluation). This version was based on the Bedingungen Motivierten Selbstgesteuerten Lernens – Instrument zur Erfassung an der Hochschule questionnaire (BEMSEL-HIS [Conditions of Motivated Self-Directed Learning – An Instrument for Measurement at Higher Education]; Wosnitza, 2000) for students studying full-time at higher education institutions. The original questionnaire is based on Nenniger's dimensional instrument (Nenniger & Nyberg, 1992) measuring the main components of the "Two-Shells Model of Motivated Self-Directed Learning" (see also Nenniger, Straka, Spevacek, & Wosnitza, 1996), which was partially derived from the original version of the MSLQ (Pintrich et al., 1991).

IPA-u Questionnaire

A version of Duarte's (2000) inventory of conceptions, motivations, and learning strategies (IRA-u) was used. It consisted of 63 items originally referring to the three motivational learning components of approaches to learning (intrinsic, extrinsic, achievement) and to three types of learning strategies (deep, surface, achieving). It was translated, adapted to the German and transformed to a 6-point Likert-type scale. The original Portuguese version (Duarte, 2000) is a 5-point Likert scale self-report instrument of 48 items, based on a critical analysis of Biggs' (1999) and Entwistle's (2000) theoretical framework as well as on an analysis of already existing questionnaires on approaches to learning, namely the "Approaches to Studying Inventory" (Entwistle & Tait, 1995; see also Fung, Ho, & Kwan, 1993), the "Learning Strategy Questionnaire" (Thomas & Bain, 1982), and the "Student Process Questionnaire" (Biggs, 1987b).

Prior Expertise

Additionally, students' prior expertise in the field of their studies (practical informatics, theoretical informatics and practical informatics skills relevant for future work in the field) was measured on a 6-point scale from 1 (excellent) to 6 (poor).

Procedure

After translation, adaptation and pre-tests and technical tests, the data was collected by an internet-based online version of the instruments in December 2003 and between April and July 2004. The online version was constructed based on online investigations using screen-by-screen design (Frey, Balzer, Renold, & Nenniger, 2005).

Results

The results are presented in the order of the research questions stated above. However, before the analyses, the amount of students' prior expertise in the field of studies was tested because it could interfere with the content-related measures of the instruments and in particular with the preference of learning strategies. However, the answers in all items were at a medium range (from 2.4 to 3.0 on a 6-point scale); thus, the student samples were homogeneous in their prior expertise and, therefore, prior expertise was not included in the subsequent analyses.

With respect to the first research question the items from the subscales of BEMSEL – HIS representing the original constructs "cognition", "metacognition", "learning strategies", "motivation", "evaluation" and "attribution" were selected as a basis for the dimensional concept "self-directed learning". As a basis for the dimensional concept "approaches to learning" items of the subscales of the IPA-u questionnaire representing the original constructs "surface strategies", "deep strategies", "achieving motivation strategies", and "motivation" were chosen. As regards the second research question, the factorial structure of each concept derived from each of the two conceptualisations was investigated on the basis of the respective items selected.

Content and Structure of the Concept "Self-Directed Learning"

The principal component analysis of the selected items of the BEMSEL-HIS questionnaire resulted in a rotated ten-factor solution with 64% of explained variance. Eigenvalues ranged between 7.5 and 1.7, communalities of the 45 items between .42 and .80, with 72% of the items above .60 and with 28% between .30 and .60. Reliability was acceptable (alpha-equivalent reliability, taking into consideration eigenvalues, between .52 and .77) for the respective factor scores.

Table 1. Explained variance, mean factor loadings, alpha equivalent, and number of items by each factor of the concept "self-directed learning".

Factor (representing the respective construct)	Explained variance	Mean loadings	Alpha equivalent	Items (n)
Cognitive Control	9%	.51	.71	6
Metacognition and Evaluation Importance	9%	.37	.60	6
Metacognition and Evaluation Trust	8%	.43	.55	7
Evaluation	7%	.51	.71	5
Implementation Strategies	6%	.57	.77	4
Motivational Control	6%	.32	.57	3
Metacognition: Reflection and Regulation	5%	.27	.52	5
Metacognition: Questioning	5%	.48	.69	4
Sequencing Strategies	5%	.54	.74	3
Personal Attribution	4%	.42	.65	2
Total	64%			45

As shown in Table 1, the first factor represents the construct Cognitive Control (i.e., concentration); the second factor represents Metacognition and Evaluation Importance; the third factor represents Metacognition and Evaluation Trust (i.e., trust in own evaluation); the fourth factor represents Evaluation (i.e., evaluation of the learning experience and the degree of achievement of the learning goal); the fifth factor represents Implementation Strategies; the sixth factor represents Motivational Control; the seventh factor represents Metacognition: Reflection and Regulation in terms of self-regulation and self-reflection strategies; the eighth factor represents Metacognition: Questioning in terms of posing questions; the ninth factor represents Sequencing Strategies, and the tenth factor represents the construct Personal Attribution.

Altogether, the majority of the factors mostly represent content assigned to the respective constructs and are distinct from each other. At the same time, the represented constructs are more differentiated as compared to the constructs of the original questionnaire; in particular, "metacognition" did not form one factor but four, thus representing more specialized constructs. Nevertheless, the results are in line with former studies with German students (Nenniger, 1999; Wosnitza, 2000), which showed that self-directed learning is a complex phenomenon that involves many constructs found in various studies

(Boekaerts, 1998; Schunk & Zimmerman, 1998). There was, however, one exception: the factor representing the construct Metacognition: Reflection and Regulation was somewhat problematic and rather ambiguous. Although it was mainly characterised by the metacognition and reflection items, the metacognition and regulation items also loaded moderately on this factor. As this particular constellation of items was stable over all analyses, we kept it as it is as an element for further deliberations.

Content and Structure of the Concept "Approaches to Learning"

The principal component analysis of the selected items of the IPA-u questionnaire resulted in a rotated six-factor solution with 53% of explained variance. Eigenvalues ranged between 7.5 and 1.7, communalities of the 63 items between .23 and .72, with 40% of the items above .60 and with 55% between .30 and .60. Therefore, alpha-equivalent reliability was hardly sufficient for some of the factor scores.

Table 2. Explained variance, mean factor loadings, alpha equivalent, and number of items by each factor of the concept "approaches to learning".

Factor (representing the respective construct)	Explained variance	Mean loadings	Alpha equivalent	Items (n)
Memorisation-Understanding	12%	.32	.57	15
Deep Strategies	9%	.28	.53	17
Extrinsic/Instrumental Motivation	9%	.35	.59	14
Intrinsic Motivation	8%	.49	.70	8
Achievement Motivation and Strategies	8%	.42	.65	5
Surface Strategies (Memorisation)	7%	.50	.73	4
Total	53%			63

The results presented in Table 2 show that items from the original construct deep and surface strategies formed two independent factors, representing the constructs Deep Strategies and Surface Strategies. There was also a third factor representing the construct Memorisation-Understanding, and three factors representing the original construct motivation: the Extrinsic/Instrumental Motivation, Intrinsic Motivation, and Achievement Motivation and Strategy. Four of the original constructs assigned to the concept "approaches to learning" were not found to be independent. Specifically, the original constructs "achievement motivation" and "achieving strategy" were merged into one factor representing now one construct Achievement Motivation and Strategy (which was also the case in the original study of Duarte, 2000) and the original constructs "memorisation" and "understanding" were merged into an additional factor representing a new construct Memorisation-Understanding (which is also the case in the study of Entwistle, McCune & Walker, 2001). Yet, the factors identified correspond to factors found in other studies, even in different cultures (Biggs, 1987a, 1987b, 1999; Duarte, 1996, 2000; Entwistle, 1990, 1998, 2000).

In sum, regarding the constructs representing the concepts of the two conceptualisations "self-directed learning" and "approaches to learning", the results were in most of the cases in accordance with the respective conceptualisations. However, from a structural point of view each of the two concepts was characterized by a more differentiated factorial structure consisting of more specialised constructs than originally assumed. This finding suggests that depending on the interactions between the various constructs of both concepts different forms of self-direction in learning can be found and be associated with different approaches to learning.

The Intersections of the Concepts "Self-Directed Learning" and "Approaches to Learning"

With respect to the third research question regarding the possible intersections of constructs assigned to the factorial structure of each of the two concepts, canonical correlation analysis was applied in order to determine the following structural properties: (a) The amount of intersection between the two concepts in terms of explained common variance of the two sets of constructs consisted of the respective factorial structures, (b) the complexity of intersection terms of independent levels (roots) of concordance and, (c) at each level the impact of each construct to the concordance and thus its location in the area of intersection at each specific level in terms of the respective canonical weight. The results from the canonical correlation analysis showed two significant canonical roots, $\chi^2(70) = 647.69, p < .001$, explaining 76% of the total variance; with 64% ($Rc_1 = .80$) of the total variance significantly ($p < .001$) accounted for the first root (details in Figure 1a) and 12% ($Rc_2 = .33$) for the second root (details in Figure 1b).

The above results reveal considerable amount of intersection of the two concepts and thus of the two conceptualisations related; however, the intersection was in a rather complex manner at two independent levels: at the first level an important intersection of the respective constructs was found, whereas at the second level a rather complementary intersection was found of minor importance.

With regard to the concepts involved the intersection ($Rc = .80$, explaining 64% of variance) at the first level (see Figure 1) represents a kind of intrinsically motivated and controlled, achievement- and implementation-oriented deep approach to self-directed learning. Specifically, in the first set of constructs associated with the concept "self-directed learning", the following ones took notable part in the intersection: Implementation Strategies (.51), Motivational Control (.49), Evaluation (.38), Metacognition and Evaluation Trust (.36), Cognitive Control (-.35), Metacognition and Evaluation Importance (.35), Metacognition: Questioning (.32). In the second set, associated with the concept "approaches to learning", the following constructs took notable part in the intersection: Deep Strategies (.64), Achievement Motivation and Strategies (.60), Intrinsic Motivation (.53), Extrinsic Motivation (-.31) and Memorising-Understanding (.35). The most important constructs of the two concepts that contributed to the intersection were the following: Implementation Strategies and Motivational Control from "self-directed learning" and Deep Strategy, Achievement Motivation and Strategies, and Intrinsic Motivation from "approaches to learning". These constructs appear to be closely linked. Thus, self-direction in learning, characterised by the product of using motivationally controlled implementation strategies, is associated with an approach to learning characterised by an intrinsically motivated use of deep and achievement-oriented strategies.

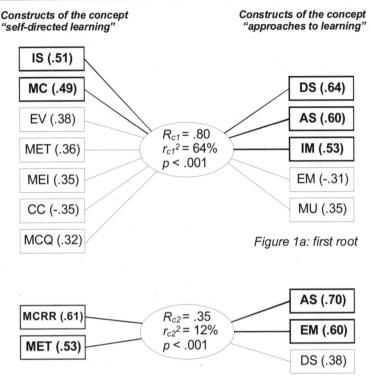

Constructs of the concept "self-directed learning"

Constructs of the concept "approaches to learning"

Figure 1a: first root

Figure 1b: second root

Figure 1. First level (1a) and Second level (1b) areas of intersection of constructs assigned to the concepts "self-directed learning" and "approaches to learning" (first and second root of canonical correlation with canonical weights).

Note: IS (Implementation Strategies), MC (Motivation Control), EV (Evaluation), MET (Metacognition and Evaluation Trust), MEI (Metacognition and Evaluation Importance), CC (Cognitive Control), MCQ (Metacognition: Questioning), DS (Deep Strategies), AS (Achievement Motivation and Strategies), IM (Intrinsic Motivation), EM (Extrinsic/Instru-mental Motivation), MU (Memorisation-Understanding), MCRR (Metacognition: Reflection and Regulation).

The rather complementary intersection ($Rc = .35$, explaining 12% of variance) at the second level (see Figure 2) represents an approach to self-directed learning characterised as extrinsically and achievement-oriented as well as metacognitively reflected, regulated and evaluated. In the first set of constructs, associated with the concept of "self-directed learning", the following ones took notable part in the intersection: Metacognition: Reflection and Regulation (.61) and Metacognition and Evaluation Trust (.53). In the second set, associated with the concept of "approaches to learning", the following constructs took notable part in the intersection: Achievement Motivation and Strategies (.70), Extrinsic Motivation (.60) and Deep Strategies (.38). Considering the most important constructs from the two concepts in this intersection the following picture emerges: self-directed learning is characterised by the use of and trust in metacognitive reflection and regulation, as well as by evaluation strategies that appear to be closely linked with a slightly deep, but extrinsically motivated and achievement-oriented approach to learning.

As a general answer to the third research question regarding the intersection of the two concepts and with regard to the underlying conceptualisations, the findings of the present study can be summarised as follows: Between the constructs of the two conceptualisations there was intersection at two independent levels: at the first level the intersection reveals an intrinsically motivated and controlled, achievement- and implementation-oriented deep approach to self-directed learning; at the second level, the intersection revealed a complementary form of self-directed learning, namely extrinsically and achievement-oriented, metacognitively reflected, regulated and evaluated deep approach to self-directed learning.

Discussion

The issue that motivated the present study was the relations between self-directed learning (including self-regulation) and approaches to learning. These conceptualisations, namely the "self-directed learning" and "approach to learning", have been developed based on different research paradigms that led to two independent theoretical perspectives despite the fact that these two conceptualisations share common motivational and regulatory processes. To identify the possible intersection of the constructs defining the two conceptualisations, an empirical study was carried out. The findings suggest that the two conceptualisations of "self-directed learning" and "approaches to learning" can be understood as encompassing many different constructs. Moreover, the constructs of each conceptualisation intersect at two levels that represent two forms of self-directed learning.

With respect to the basic conceptualisations of self-directed learning (Knowles, 1975; Nenniger, 1999) and the main ideas of self-regulation (Corno & Mandinach, 1983; Kuhl, 1983, 1985; Pintrich & Garcia, 1994; Zimmerman, 1989) the findings of the present study extend Pintrich's (2000b) view of self-regulation but point out that metacognition takes various forms. This finding implies that the construct of "metacognition" requires a more differentiated approach to its understanding (e.g., Efklides, 2004, 2006).

A second issue that emerged from the findings of the present study regards the complexity of the intersection of the two conceptualisations. The fact that there was intersection at two different levels, resulting in two forms of self-directed learning, implies that the association of self-directed learning with deep learning and intrinsic motivation is not always clearcut. Extension of the theorising on self-directed learning as described in the recent versions of Boekaerts' model (Boekaerts, 1997; Boekaerts & Cascallar, 2006; Nenniger, 2005) is probably a good way to go including different content-domains with domain-specific regulatory processes. In addition, an adequate description and explanation of the course of self-directed learning has to take into consideration the multiple interactions and, perhaps non-linear development of its course, which may result in a spiral evolvement rather than in a serial trend. With respect to the approaches-to-learning paradigm, the results confirmed, in the main, the ideas of Marton and Säljö (1976a) but the structure of the basic constructs constituting the selected conceptualisation in this study is less clear cut (see also Biggs, 1993; Duarte, 2000; Entwistle & Ramsden, 1983).

With respect to the importance of the motivational aspect of learning, the findings of the present study underline the limitations of the prevalent explanation of self-direction and of self-regulation in learning if limited to achievement motivation. A more in depth understanding of motivational processes has to include the intentional, content-oriented and a more differentiated view of intrinsic motivation that includes the commitment to the task in order to achieve personal meaning of the content.

However, a real progress in the theory of self-directed learning cannot be achieved unless additional components of self-direction are considered. Emotions closely interact with essential components of self-directed learning such as interest, motivation, strategies of learning and control of learning (Pekrun, Elliot, & Maier, 2006). Emotions represent a complementary component insofar as they trigger, sustain, or reduce academic motivation and related volitional processes and therefore bridge theoretical gaps and offer more coherent explanations of persistence and motivational orientation in the course of self-direction.

A second challenge to the theorising of self-directed learning, as well as of self-regulation, regards the dynamics and the properties of its spiral evolvement. One has to start by asking whether, compared to the initial structure of self-directed learning, the achieved structure at a later point has been extended, or shrunk, or altered, or become more stable or less coherent, etc. A step forward would be the identification of the quality of the dynamics between the components of self-directed learning. Moreover, a complementary *functional* description of the regulatory component of self-direction is needed.

Reviewing the above arguments and looking ahead towards the future, it seems that an expanded and complementary theory regarding the educational paradigm of self-directed learning as well as from the psychological paradigm of self-regulated learning is possible. Such a theory offers a basis for a more general explanation of the phenomenon of self-directed learning which merits to be advanced on a track that includes, on the one hand, multiple approaches to learning combined with the respective regulatory processes and, perhaps via the associated emotions, a dynamic view of its structural evolvement. Thus, the complementary components may fill in some of the empty slots of the complementary pattern of self-directed learning we identified contributing to a more differentiated picture of self-direction and self-regulation in learning. But the glue to fix together such components requires, at the same time, an advanced methodology that allows more adequate descriptions and appropriate analyses of the associated empirical data.

References

Beck, K., & Krumm, V. (Eds.). (2001). *Lehren und Lernen in der beruflichen Erstausbildung* [Instruction and learning in basic vocational training]. Opladen: Leske & Budrich.

Biggs, J. B. (1987a). *Student approaches to learning and studying*. Hawthorn: Australian Council for Educational Research.

Biggs, J. B. (1987b). *The Study Process Questionnaire (SPQ)*. Hawthorn: Australian Council for Educational Research.

Biggs, J. B. (1993). What do inventories of students' learning processes really measure? A theoretical review and clarification. *British Journal of Educational Psychology, 63,* 3-19.

Biggs. J. B. (1999). Western misperceptions of the confucian-heritage learning culture. In D. A. Watkins & J. B. Biggs (Eds.), *The Chinese learner: Cultural, psychological, and contextual influences* (pp. 45-68). Hong Kong: CERC and ACER.

Boekaerts, M. (1997). Self-regulated learning: A new concept embraced by researchers, policy makers, educators, teachers, and students. *Learning & Instruction, 7,* 161-186.

Boekaerts, M. (1998). Do culturally rooted self-construals affect students' conceptualization of control over learning? *Educational Psychologist, 33,* 87-108.

Boekaerts, M. (1999). Self-regulated learning: Where we are today. *International Journal of Educational Research, 31,* 445-475.

Boekaerts, M., Pintrich, P. R., & Zeidner, M. (Eds.). (2000). *Handbook of self-regulation.* San Diego, CA: Academic.

Boekaerts, M., & Cascallar, E. (2006). How far have we moved toward the integration of theory and practice in self-regulation? *Educational Psychology Review, 18,* 199-210.

Boekaerts, M., & Nenniger, P. (1999). Introduction. *European Journal of Psychology of Education, 14,* 3-9.

Boekaerts, M., & Rozendaal, J. (2007). New insights into the self-regulation of writing skills in secondary vocational education. *Zeitschrift für Psychologie, 215,* 164-173.

Brockett, R. G., & Hiemstra, R. (1991). *Self-direction in adult learning. Perspectives, on theory, research, and practice.* London: Routledge.

Candy, P. C. (1991). *Self-direction for lifelong learning: A comprehensive guide to theory and practice.* San Francisco: Jossey-Bass.

Corno, L. (1994). Student volition and education: Outcomes, influences, and practices. In D. Schunk & B. L. Zimmerman (Eds.), *Self-regulation of learning and performance: Issues and educational applications* (pp. 229-254). Hillsdale, NJ: Erlbaum.

Corno, L., & Mandinach, E. (1983). The role of cognitive engagement in classroom learning and motivation. *Educational Psychology, 19,* 88-108.

Deci, E. L., & Ryan, R. M. (Eds.). (2002). *Handbook of self-determination research.* Rochester, NY: University of Rochester Press.

DeGroot, E. V. (2002). Learning through interviewing: Students and teachers talk about learning and schooling. *Educational Psychologist, 37,* 41-52.

Diseth, A., & Martinsen, O. (2003). Approaches to learning, cognitive style, and motives as predictos of academic achievement. *Educational Psychology, 23,* 195-207.

Duarte, A. M. (1996). A relação entre cognição e motivação ao nível da aprendizagem escolar. Uma Análise do modelo das "abordagens à aprendizagem" [About a relation between cognition and motivation on the level of school learning. An analysis of the "approaches to learn" model]. *Psicologia, XI*(1), 127-138.

Duarte, A. M. (2000). *Avaliação e Modificação de Concepções, Motivações e estratégias de Aprendizagem em estudantes do Ensino Superior* [Appraisal and modification of concepts, motivation and learning strategies in students of Higher Education]. Unpublished doctoral dissertation, University of Lisbon, Portugal.

Efklides, A. (2004). The multiple role of metacognitive experiences in the learning process. In M. Wosnitza, A. Frey, & R. S. Jäger (Eds.), *Lernprozess, Lernumgebung und Lerndiagnostik. Wissenschaftliche Beltträge zum Lernen im 21. Jahrhundert* (pp. 256-266). Landau: VEP.

Efklides, A. (2006). Metacognitive experiences: The missing link in the self-regulated learning process. A rejoinder to Ainley and Patrick. *Educational Psychology Review, 18,* 287-291.

Entwistle, N. J. (1990). Student learning and classroom environment. In N. Frederickson & N. Jones (Eds.), *Refocusing educational psychology* (pp. 8-30). London: Palmer.

Entwistle, N. J. (1998). Approaches to learning and forms of understanding. In B. Dart & G. Boulton-Lewis (Eds.), *Teaching and learning in higher education* (pp. 72-101). Melbourne: Australian Council for Educational Research.

Entwistle, N. J. (2000). Approaches to studying and levels of understanding: The influence of teaching and assessment. In J. C. Smart (Ed.), *Higher education: Handbook of theory and research* (Vol. XV, pp. 156-218). New York: Agathon.

Entwistle, N. J., & McCune, V. S. (2004). The conceptual basis of study strategy inventories. *Educational Psychology Review.16,* 325-345.

Entwistle, N., McCune, V. & P. Walker (2001). Conceptions, styles, and approaches within higher education: Analytical abstractions and everyday experience. In R. J. Sternberg & L. Zhang (Eds). *Perspectives on thinking, learning, and cognitive styles* (pp. 103-136). Hillsdale, NJ: Earlbaum.

Entwistle, N., & Ramsden, P. (1983). *Understanding student learning*. London: Croom Helm.

Entwistle, N. J., & Tait, H. (1990). Approaches to learning, evaluations of teaching, and preferences for contrasting academic environments. *Higher Education, 19,* 169-194.

Entwistle, N. J., & Tait, H. (1995). *The revised approaches to studying inventory*. Edinburgh: Centre for Research into Learning and Instruction, University of Edinburgh.

Entwistle, N. J., & Tomlinson, P. (Eds.). (2007). *Student learning and university teaching*. Leicester: British Psychological Society.

Frey, A., Balzer, L., Renold, U., & Nenniger, P. (2005). *Reform der Kaufmännischen Grundbildung: Band 2. Instrumente der Evaluation* [Reform of basic business education: Vol. 2. Instruments of evaluation]. Landau: VEP.

Fung, Y. H., Ho, A. S. P., & Kwan, K. P. (1993). Reliability and validity of the Learning Styles Questionnaire. *British Journal of Educational Technology 24,* 12-21.

Hidi, S., Ainley, M. (2008). Interest and self-regulation: Relationships between two variables that influence learning. In B. J. Zimmerman & D. H. Schunk (Eds.), *Motivation and self-regulated learning: Theory, research, and applications* (pp. 77-109). Mahwah, NJ.: Erlbaum.

Hidi, S., Renninger, K. A., & Krapp, A. (2004). Interest, a motivational construct that combines affective and cognitive functioning. In D. Y. Dai & R. J. Sternberg (Eds.), *Motivation, emotion and cognition: Integrative perspectives on intellectual functioning and development* (pp. 89-115). Mahwah, NJ: Erlbaum.

Husserl, E. (1923/24). *Erste Philosophie: Zweiter Teil. Theorie der Phänomenologischen Reduktion (Husserliana)* [First Philosophy: Second Part. Theory of phenomenological reduction]. Wiesbaden: Kluwer.

Knowles, M. S. (1975). *Self-directed learning*. Chicago: Follett.

Kuhl, J. (1983). Volitional aspects of achievement motivation and learned helplessness: Toward a comprehensive theory of action control. In B. A. Maher (Ed.), *Progress in experimental personality research* (Vol. 13, pp. 99-172). New York: Academic.

Kuhl, J. (1985). Volitional mediators of cognition-behavior consistency: Self-regulatory processes and action versus state orientation. In J. Kuhl & J. Beckmann (Eds.), *Action control: From cognition to behaviour* (pp. 101-128). Berlin: Springer.

Long, H. B. (1989). *Self-directed learning: Emerging theory and practice* . Norman, OK: Oklahoma Research Center for Continuing Professional and Higher Education, University of Oklahoma.

Luhmann, N. (1984). *Soziale Systeme: Grundriss einer allgemeinen Theorie* [Social Systems: Outline of a general theory]. Frankfurt/M.: Suhrkamp.

Marton, F., & Säljö, R. (1976a). On qualitative differences in learning: I. Outcome and process. *British Journal of Educational Psychology, 46,* 4-11.

Marton, F., & Säljö, R. (1976b). On qualitative differences in learning: II. Outcome as a function of the learner's conception of the task. *British Journal of Educational Psychology, 46,* 115-127.

McCune, V. (2004). Development of first-year students' conceptions of essay writing. *Higher Education, 47(3),* 257-282.

Meyer, J. H. F. (2000). The modelling of "dissonant" study orchestrations in higher education. *European Journal of Psychology of Education, 15,* 5-18.

Meyer, J. H. F., Parsons, P., & Dunne, T. T. (1990). Individual study orchestrations and their association with learning outcome. *Higher Education, 20,* 67-89.

Nenniger, P. (1997). Technologie, Wirtschaft und Qualifikation: Zur pädagogischen Analyse des Wandels und seine Konsequenzen für berufsbildendes Lernen [Technology, economy and qualification: An educational analysis of the change and ist consequences for professional learning]. In W. Weber (Ed.), *Abhandlungen der Humboldtgesellschaft: Vol. 14. Spektrallinien: Philosophie, Geschichte, Kunst* (pp. 177-188). Mannheim: Humboldt-Gesellschaft.

Nenniger, P. (1999). On the role of motivation in self-directed learning. The "Two- shells Model of Motivated Self-Directed Learning" as a structural explanatory concept. *European Journal of Psychology of Education, 14*, 71-86.

Nenniger, P. (2005). Commentary on self-regulation in the classroom: A perspective on assessment and intervention. *Applied Psychology, 54*, 239-244.

Nenniger, P., & Nyberg, R. (1992). *Motivated Learning Strategies Questionnaire (MLSQ) (European Adaptation: German, French and Swedish Versions)*. Kiel: Institut für Pädagogik der Universität Kiel.

Nenniger, P., Straka, A., Spevacek, G., & Wosnitza, M. (1996). Zur Mehrdimensionalität selbstgesteuerten beruflichen Lernens: Ergebnisse einer Konstruktvalidierung [On the multi-dimensionality of self-directed vocational learning: Results of a construct validation]. In K.-P. Treumann, G. Neubauer, R. Möller, & J. Abel (Eds.), *Methoden und Anwendungen empirischer pädagogischer Forschung* (pp. 154-169). Münster: Waxmann.

Pekrun, R., Elliot, A. J., & Maier, M. A. (2006). Achievement goals and discrete achievement emotions: A theoretical model and prospective test. *Journal of Educational Psychology, 98*, 583-597.

Pintrich, P. R. (1989). The dynamic interplay of student motivation and cognition in the college classroom. *Advances in Motivation and Achievement, 6*, 117-160.

Pintrich, P. R. (2000a). The role of goal orientation in self-regulated learning. In M. Boekaerts, P. R. Pintrich, & M. Zeidner (Eds.), *Handbook of self-regulation* (pp. 451-502). San Diego, CA: Academic.

Pintrich, P. R. (2000b). Educational psychology at the millennium: A look back and a look forward. *Educational Psychologist, 35*, 221-226.

Pintrich, P. R. (2003). A motivational science perspective on the role of student motivation in learning and teaching contexts. *Journal of Educational Psychology, 95*, 667-686.

Pintrich, P. R. (2004). A conceptual framework for assessing motivation and self-regulated learning in college students. *Educational Psychology Review, 16*, 385-407.

Pintrich, P. R., & DeGroot, E. V. (1990). Motivational and self-regulated learning components of classroom academic performance. *Journal of Educational Psychology, 82*, 33-40.

Pintrich, P. R., & Garcia, T. (1994). Self-regulated learning in college students: Knowledge, strategies and motivation. In P. R. Pintrich, D. R. Brown, & C. E. Weinstein (Eds.), *Student motivation, cognition, and learning: Essays in honour of Wilbert J. McKeachie* (pp. 113-134). Hillsdale, NJ: Erlbaum.

Pintrich, P. R., & Smith, D. A. F., Garcia, T., & McKeachie, W. J. (1991). *The Motivated Strategies for Learning Questionnaire (MSLQ)*. Ann Arbor, MI: The University of Michigan.

Prosser, M. S., & Trigwell, K. N. (1997a). Relations between perceptions of the teaching environment and approaches to teaching. *British Journal of Educational Psychology, 67*, 25-35.

Prosser, M. S., & Trigwell, K. N. (1997b). Using phenomenography in the design of programs for teachers in higher education. *Higher Education Research and Development, 16*, 41-54.

Puustinen, M., & Pulkkinen, L. (2001). Models of self-regulated learning: A review. *Scandinavian Journal of Educational Research, 45*, 269-286.

Renninger, K. A. (2005). The process of scaffolding in learning and development. *New Ideas in Psychology. 23*, 111-114.

Richardson, J. T. E. (2004). Methodological issues in questionnaire-based research on student learning in higher education. *Educational Psychology Review, 16*, 347-358.

Schiefele, U., & Pekrun, R. (1996). Psychologische Modelle des fremdgesteuerten und selbstgesteuerten Lernens [Psychological models of other-directed and self-directed learning]. In F. E. Weinert (Eds.), *Enzyklopädie der Psychologie. Pädagogische Psychologie: Bd 2. Psychologie des Lernens und der Instruktion* (pp. 249-278). Göttingen: Hogrefe.

Schiefele, U., & Schreyer, I. (1992). *Intrinsische Lernmotivation und Lernen. Eine Zusammenfassung theoretischer Ansätze und Metaanalyse empirischer Befunde. (Arbeiten zur Empirischen Pädagogik und Pädagogischen Psychologie, Nr. 24 Gelbe Reihe)*. [Intrinsic learning motivation and learning. A summary to theoretical concepts and a meta-analysis of empirical findings]. München: Universität der Bundeswehr.

Schiefele, U., Wild, K. P., & Winteler, A. (1995). Lernaufwand und Elaborationsstrategien als Mediatoren von Studieninteresse und Studienleistung [Investment in learning and elaboration strategies as mediators of interest and performance in studying]. *Zeitschrift für Pädagogische Psychologie, 9,* 181-188.

Schunk, D. H., & Zimmerman B. L. (1998). Conclusions and future directions for academic interventions. In D. Schunk & B. L. Zimmerman (Eds.), *Self-regulated learning: From teaching to self-reflective practice* (pp. 225-234). New York: Guilford.

Schunk, D., Zimmerman, B. L., Winne, P., & Alexander, P.A. (Eds.). (2006). *Handbook of educational psychology.* Mahwah, NJ: Erlbaum.

Silva, A. L., & Duarte, A. M. (2001). Self-regulation and approaches to learning in Portuguese students. *Empirische Pädagogik, 15,* 251-265.

Straka, G. A., & Nenniger, P. (1995). A conceptual framework for self-drected-learning readiness. In H. B. Long & Associates (Eds.), *New dimensions in self directed learning* (pp. 243-255). Norman, OK: University of Oklahoma.

Straka, G. A., Nenniger, P., Spevacek, G., & Wosnitza, M. (1996). A model for motivated self-directed learning. *Education, 53,* 19-30.

Straka, G. A., & Schaefer, C. (2002). Validating a more-dimensional conception of self-directed learning. In T. M. Egan & S. A. Lynham (Eds.), *Conference proceedings of the Academy of Human Resource Development (AHRD)* (Vol. 1, pp. 239-246). Honolulu, HI: Academy of HR Development.

Tait, H., Entwistle, N., & McCune, V. (1998). ASSIST: A reconceptualisation of the Approaches to Studying Inventory. In C. Rust (Ed.), *Improving students as learners* (pp.262-271). Oxford: Oxford Centre for Staff and Learning Development.

Thomas, P. R., & Bain, J. D., (1982). Consistency in learning strategies. *Higher Education, 11,* 249-259.

Van den Brink, K. (2006). *Conceptual relations between "Self-regulated Learning" and "Approaches to Learning".* Unpublished doctoral dissertation, University of Koblenz-Landau: Landau.

Vermunt, J. D. (1996). Metacognitive, cognitive and affective aspects of learning styles and strategies. A phenomenographic analysis. *Higher Education, 31,* 25-50.

Watkins D., & Hattie, J. (1990). Individual and contextual differences in the approaches to learning of Australian secondary school students. *Educational Psychologist, 10,* 333-342.

Wild, K. P. (1995). *Beziehungen zwischen Belohnungsstrukturen der Hochschule, motivationalen Orientierungen der Studierenden und individuellen Lernstrategien beim Wissenserwerb* [Relations between structures of gratification of the university, motivational orientations of students and individual learning strategies in the acquisition of knowledge] (Arbeiten zur Empirischen Pädagogik und pädagogischen Psychologie, Nr. 34. Gelbe Reihe). Neubiberg: Universität der Bundeswehr München.

Wosnitza, M. (2000). *Motiviertes selbstgesteuertes Lernen im Studium. Theoretische Rahmen, diagnostisches Instrumentarium und Bedingungsanalyse* [Motivated self-directed learning in the academic studies. Theoretical frame, diagnostic instruments and analysis of requirements]. Landau: VEP.

Zimmerman, J. B. J. (1989). A social cognitive view of self-regulated academic learning. *Journal of Educational Psychology, 81,* 329-333.

Zimmerman, J. B. J., & Martinez-Pons, M. (1988). Construct validation of a strategy model of self-regulated learning. *Journal of Educational Psychology, 80,* 284-290.

Zimmermann, J. B. J., & Schunk, D. H. (Eds.). (2001). *Self-regulated learning and academic achievement: Theoretical perspectives.* Hillsdale, NJ: Earlbaum.

Linking Personality to Work Motivation and Performance

Individual Differences Effects

Tanja Bipp

Introduction

Personality, Motivation, and Performance

In several meta-analyses, personality has been consistently shown to predict different indicators of occupational performance (Barrick, Mount, & Judge, 2001). However, only a few attempts have been made to define and test the causal mechanisms behind these empirical correlations. Relatively little is known about when and how personality traits influence, or are expressed in, behavior at work. In the last decade, a growing number of studies have supported models indicating indirect or mediational effects, that is, models linking personality traits indirectly to performance via motivational constructs (Judge & Ilies, 2002). This field of research is nowadays urged to aggregate these (mostly empirical) snapshots into a comprehensive theoretical model explaining the relationships between personality traits and work performance.

To be able to contribute to the specification of a comprehensive explanatory model, first the relationship of personality constructs of high generality (e.g., intelligence, Big Five) to job performance will be examined. However, several motivational constructs (e.g., work orientations, goals) have been shown to be related to individual difference factors. Systematizing the empirical relationships according to a general action model (Rubicon model of action phases) offers a new way of explaining the influence of personality traits on the action process. More specifically, an integration of personality factors into a model of goal-directed action is presented and supplemented by own research data. Therefore, this chapter acknowledges and contributes to the growing body of research regarding explanations how personality affects performance. The fact that goals and associated constructs such as goal orientations can serve as a missing link between personality traits and performance in different settings (e.g., work or learning environments) supports the generalizability of the notion that motivational constructs or self-regulatory processes mediate or transport the effects of personality traits on performance. Yet, it is still unclear which role situational characteristics or cultural factors play in such explanatory models. Therefore, future research directions are outlined in the final section of this chapter.

Personality and Occupational Performance

Since the early 1990s, there has been a renewed interest in personality psychology in various applied settings. Especially in the field of personnel selection, the predictive power of individual differences for work-relevant outcome variables like job performance or job satisfaction has been investigated (Rothstein & Goffin, 2006). General mental ability (GMA) or intelligence measures have been empirically identified as one (if not the most) important predictor for effective learning or work behavior (Kuncel, Hezlett, & Ones, 2004; Salgado et al., 2003). In contrast, early research reviews have not attested personality traits to account for a major percentage of variance in job performance (Schmitt, Gooding, Noe, & Kirsch, 1984). However, in the last two decades several meta-analyses have been conducted that show substantial relations of personality traits to criteria of job or training performance (Barrick & Mount, 1991; Salgado, 2003). Especially the emergence of the *Five-Factor Model* of personality (Digman, 1990) has helped to clarify inconsistent research results so far. There is broad consensus in the scientific community that five (largely independent) personality traits provide a comprehensive taxonomy of personality characteristics, and cross-cultural research supports the construct validity of the "Big Five" (McCrae & Terracciano, 2005). Table 1 contains short descriptions of the Big Five personality traits: neuroticism (sometimes redefined as emotional stability), extraversion, openness to experience, agreeableness, and conscientiousness.

Table 1. The Big Five personality traits.

I. Neuroticism (N)
Neuroticism describes differences between people in their emotional stability or how they experience negative feelings. People scoring high on this dimension tend to be fearful, unconfident, nervous, unstable, timid, and in particular cannot respond properly to stress situations.
II. Extraversion (E)
Extraversion describes people who prefer social situations, and can be described as outgoing, talkative, spontaneous, active, positive, as well as dominant. Warmth, gregariousness, assertiveness, or activity are, for example, postulated lower-order facets of E in hierarchical models.
III. Openness to experience (O)
Openness to fantasy, aesthetics, feelings, actions, ideas and values are part of the construct of openness to experience. People with high scores can be described as creative, curious, intellectual or unconventional. They have a lot of interests and are eager to experience new things.
IV. Agreeableness (A)
Agreeableness describes the quality of social interactions. People with low scores distrust others, are suspicious, arrogant, rude, aggressive, bitter, or show cynicism and sarcasm while interacting with others.
V. Conscientiousness (C)
Conscientiousness describes people who show a high degree of self-discipline and reliability. They tend to be planned, organized, and achievement-oriented, ambitious, dependable, and persistent. The construct of C includes an active component like need for achievement as well as cautiousness aspects.

Establishing the predictive validities of the five personality traits has yielded a clear picture of the personality-performance relationship. Especially conscientiousness is considered to predict indicators of efficient work behavior across different occupations (Barrick et al., 2001) and high scores on neuroticism have been shown to be associated with low job performance or satisfaction (Judge, Heller, & Mount, 2002). Personality traits can predict various indicators of work-relevant behavior, not only at the individual level, but also in the case of leadership or team performance (Peeters, Rutte, van Tuijl, & Reymen, 2006). Besides, there is empirical support for substantial predictive validities of the Big Five regarding expatriate job success or job performance in non-Western cultures (Tyler & Newcombe, 2006). Apart from the fact that the best predictive validities, in general, can be achieved by GMA, personality traits have been shown to have incremental predictive power in performance outcome criteria besides or above mental abilities (McHenry, Hough, Toquam, Hanson, & Ashworth, 1990). Faced with this overwhelming empirical evidence for substantial relations between personality and achievement behavior in different jobs and cultures, research has now come to the point where the role of personality at work is no longer doubted, but the mechanism through which personality influences performance is examined.

Explanatory Models

Although there are explanatory models that outline how cognitive abilities influence job performance (e.g., indirectly via knowledge acquisition or directly via problem-solving skills, Schmidt, 2002), the connection of personality to work-relevant behavior is less clear. Based on components of the construct of job performance (Motowidlo, 2003), there are theoretical models that link personality traits indirectly via motivational processes to job performance. Personality is supposed to influence work behavior primarily through the processes of *arousal, direction,* or *intensity* of behavior, that is, through processes that represent the core of work motivation. Put differently, personality has a substantial influence on what people choose to do and how much effort and time a person devotes to a certain task.

Yet, only a few attempts have been made to simultaneously consider personality variables and motivational constructs to build a comprehensive explanatory model. «Until recently, the status of traits in most work motivation theories has been like that of a distant and not well-liked relative attending a family reunion» (Kanfer & Heggestad, 1997, p. 13). Whereas former research was not able to find proof for a relationship between personality and motivational variables, recent empirical studies have illustrated that variables from different motivation theories or self-regulatory mechanisms can account for the missing link between distal traits, proximal states, and achievement outcomes (Judge & Ilies, 2002; Latham & Locke, 2007). The empirical support for these models is examined in the following section.

Explanatory Models Incorporating Motivational Constructs

Within the field of work motivation, numerous theoretical approaches have been suggested and empirically validated (see Latham, 2007). As they either focus on determinants of behavior within the person (e.g., cognitive approaches) or the work environment (e.g., job design), the various theoretical approaches are not easy to compare, nor is there agreement on a single integrative theory of motivation. Regarding research that links personality to work motivation, internal motivation theories, that claim *cognitive motivational processes* to underlie work behavior, have received a lot of attention. Goals, expectancies, self-efficacy, or cognitive-motivational work intentions have been shown to be associated with dispositional factors on different levels of abstraction.

To be able to explain general job performance, several studies have investigated the mediational role of goals at a relatively high level of abstraction. Based on the hierarchical structure of goals (Cropanzano, James, & Citera, 1993), research has taken into account mid-range or broad goals (such as fundamental motives or motivational orientations) to explain the relationship of personality with job performance. Barrick, Mitchell, and Stewart (2003) proposed a process model in which three fundamental motivational constructs mediate the personality-performance relationship. At least extraversion, agreeableness, and conscientiousness were empirically shown to be connected to cognitive *motivational work orientations* (Barrick, Stewart, & Piotrowski, 2002), which cover not only individual intentions (accomplishment striving) but also deal with aspects of interpersonal motivation (striving for status or communion).

For the building of a general explanatory model, constructs on an even higher level of abstraction have been investigated. Based on extensive research in educational psychology (Dweck, 1986), in the last decades *achievement goal orientations* have become one of the most frequently studied variables in the field of motivation. The original two-dimensional conception of goal orientations, namely learning (or mastery) and performance goal orientations has been further partitioned into approach and avoidance tendencies. The so-called trichotomous goal framework is currently the most widely used in achievement motivation research, which separates learning, performance-approach, and performance-avoidance goal orientations. It has been shown that learning and performance goal orientations are largely independent from each other, and should therefore—contrary to early conceptualizations—not be viewed as two points of a continuum (Pintrich, 2000). Besides a state-oriented approach, goal orientations can also be seen as a relatively stable individual characteristic with an associated preference for particular goals. Current research shows an essential overlap with non-ability-related personality variables, such as the Big Five (Bipp, Steinmayr, & Spinath, 2008). Empirical research has proven an indirect connection of goal orientations to learning performance, for example via personal goals or effort (Chen, Gully, Whiteman, & Kilcullen, 2000; VandeWalle, Cron, & Slocum, 2001). Furthermore, for performance intentions and personality traits it has been shown that achievement motivation can serve as a mediator between them (Zweig & Webster, 2004).

However, these models still seem too broad to explain how personality influences actual behavior in a specific situation. In search for possible explanations at lower levels of abstraction, a number of studies have found evidence for a mediational role of motivational constructs at the *task-specific level.* Judge and Ilies (2002) identified three commonly investigated work motivation theories from which constructs might serve as mediators of the personality-performance relationship: *the goal setting, expectancy,* and *self-efficacy* theory. In a meta-analysis, Judge and Ilies (2002) showed that the Big Five were related to different criteria such as level of personal goal, expectancy for certain outcomes, or self-efficacy ratings for task performance. The meta-analysis showed that neuroticism and conscientiousness were the strongest correlates of performance motivation. Across motivation theories, all five traits reached a strong multiple correlation of .49, which supported the claim that personality variables are a vital source of work motivation. Recently, Judge, Jackson, Shaw, Scott, and Rich (2007) have shown the influence of individual differences on work performance in a more detailed way within social cognitive models, controlling for effects of work experience. In their meta-analysis, intelligence and conscientiousness were positively related to self-efficacy and directly to work performance, whereas extraversion and neuroticism were only related to self-efficacy. Their analysis showed that personality variables were at least as important as self-efficacy for predicting work performance, and therefore did not support a full mediation model.

Personality Traits in the Action Process: The Rubicon Model

To build a common framework that integrates personality traits and motivation in order to explain achievement behavior in a specific task or work setting, it is necessary to systematize the numerous findings from separate empirical studies. We have adopted a new approach by outlining the influences of personality on work motivation within a general model of human action. The *Rubicon model of action phases* (Gollwitzer, 1990; Heckhausen & Heckhausen, 2008) divides the course of goal-directed action into different, consecutive phases. Based on the separation of motivation versus volition (e.g., making a decision vs. initiation of action), the model outlines four distinct phases within the action process (predecisional, preactional, actional, and postactional; see lower part of Figure 1).

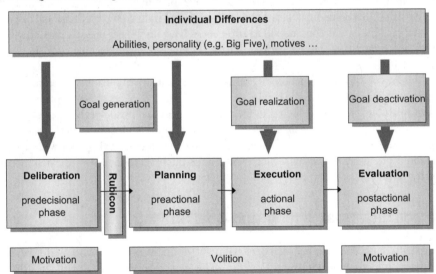

Figure 1. Possible influences of personality traits in the goal-directed action process (Rubicon model).

In the first phase, competing wishes or desires along with their (positive or negative) consequences are weighted up against each other. Once a decision is made and a goal intention has been formed (and, therefore, the river Rubicon is crossed), transition to the preactional phase takes place: while individuals wait for an opportunity to pursue a preferred wish, the action process is anticipated in the planning phase. Plans are being made or strategies developed on how the chosen goal can be accomplished. The initiation of strategies takes place afterwards (actional phase). The individual acts towards goal attainment and has to deal, for example, with implementation problems (e.g., disturbances of action or interference with competing goals). In the final postactional phase, individuals evaluate the results of their actions and look for explanations for certain outcomes (e.g., failures).

In all phases of the model, personality traits may influence the action process (see upper part of Figure 1). Before one starts to work on a task, individual interests or abilities can, for example, have an impact on the selection of goals or formation of intentions that are going to be considered. Research has shown that personality has an impact on the selection of tasks or situations, or that traits influence people's choice for a certain profession, information search or evaluation of alternatives (Barrick, Mount, & Gupta, 2003; Ickes, Snyder, & Garcia, 1997). In the preactional phase personality traits may influence strategy development or selection, and research has confirmed individual differences regarding planning behavior (Heisig, 1995). People with high scores on conscientiousness, for example, are assumed to prefer work-related goals compared to alternative goals (e.g., finishing a due task vs. recreation), or try to rule out possible disturbances before starting to work (e.g., by creating a quiet work environment). A component of conscientiousness in hierarchical models of the Big Five is *deliberation* (Costa & McCrae, 1998), which characterizes people who are thoughtful, systematic, plan their behavior, and act in a reflective way. This component clearly links dispositional traits to the predecisional or preactional phases. In addition, individual differences have an impact on goal pursuit while people work on a task, on feedback seeking or evaluation regarding outcomes (Renn & Fedor, 2001).

Building up on the distinction of goal setting vs. goal striving that had been made by Lewin more than 60 years ago (Lewin, Dembo, Festinger, & Sears, 1944), systematizing extant research findings according to the Rubicon model helps to specify the processes through which personality traits influence work motivation and, consequently, performance. The effects of personality on goal formation compared to goal pursuit will be outlined in depth in the following section, which build the basis for our own research model and hypotheses.

Personality, Goal Setting, and Goal Striving

To specify the connection between personality, work motivation, and work performance, our research focused on constructs from the *goal setting theory* (Locke & Latham, 1990). This theoretical framework was selected because it is «among the most valid and practical theories of employee motivation in organizational psychology» (Locke & Latham, 2002, p. 714). Being around for almost 40 years, it is still one of the most dominant theories in today's work motivation literature. The core mechanism postulated by the theory, namely that specific and difficult goals lead to higher performance compared to easy goals or unspecific goal instructions such as "do your best", has been supported by a vast amount of empirical studies (Latham & Locke, 2007). The effects of conscious goal setting on cognitive and behavioral aspects of performance have been specified in the "high-performance cycle" (Locke & Latham, 2002): Goals have a directive and energizing function; they direct attention to a task, influence effort or persistence, and facilitate strategy development. Several moderators have been found to influence the relationship between goals and performance (ability, task complexity, goal commitment, self-efficacy, and feedback). These mechanisms have been shown to be valid in at least eight different countries (Locke & Latham, 1990, 2002), and this implies a wide generalizability of the theory.

Although the name of the goal setting theory denotes that the theory outlines in detail how goals are being set—and this would position the theory at the predecisional phase—most of the mechanisms stated in the theory can be positioned in the (pre)action phase in the Rubicon model. However, some of the core factors affecting the goal-performance relationship refer to anticipating beliefs (e.g., self-efficacy) and, therefore, can be considered as factors that also affect the generation of action goals. In the following, we will first outline how personality traits affect how people set goals for themselves, and then we shall turn to effects in the action phase.

In several studies, *personal goals* and *self-efficacy* have been shown (at least partly) to mediate the effect of individual difference factors on task performance (Locke, 2001). Personality traits affect how or what goals people set for themselves in achievement settings or their beliefs about their capability to accomplish a certain task (i.e., self-efficacy). Research has shown, for example, that achievement need and self-esteem are related to the level of self-set goals (Matsui, Okada, & Kakuyama, 1982); neuroticism and conscientiousness, in their turn, have been shown to be associated with personal goal setting as well as with self-efficacy beliefs. Thus, people with high scores on conscientiousness tend to set autonomous goals at work (Barrick, Mount, & Strauss, 1993) or report high ratings of self-efficacy (Chen, Capser, & Cortina, 2001). By contrast, high scores on neuroticism are associated with low task-specific or general self-efficacy beliefs, and therefore people with high scores on this personality trait do not set (challenging) goals for themselves (Erez & Judge, 2001). Agreeableness is also negatively associated with goal setting motivation (Judge & Ilies, 2002). For the other Big Five factors, research has shown associations with the level or difficulty of personal goals, at least under specific conditions (Barrick et al., 1993; Klein & Lee, 2006).

With respect to volitional processes in the action phase (i.e., goal realization), personality can also be seen as an antecedent of variables included in the goal setting theory. Besides an impact of individual difference factors on *feedback seeking* and *attention focus* (Derryberry, 2002; Revelle, 1989), several studies have not only related personality to the process of goal pursuit, but also explicitly supported the mediational function of motivational variables. Studies have corroborated, for example, that achievement motivation, locus of control, self-esteem or emotional stability are determinants of *goal commitment* (Erez & Judge, 2001; Klein, Wesson, Hollenbeck, & Alge, 1999). The fact that the effect of conscientiousness on performance is mediated by goal commitment was demonstrated by Barrick et al. (1993) and Klein and Lee (2006). The definition of this Big Five factor and its corresponding lower-order components also suggests that it effects work behavior *via effort* and *persistence*. Kleinbeck, Schmidt, and Carlsen (1985) had already demonstrated that achievement motivation is related to effort and, therefore, indirectly to performance. On the one hand, people with high scores on "hope for success" interpreted in an experimental setting the discrepancy between difficult goals and actual performance as a challenge to increase their effort in a set of repeated trials. On the other hand, people with a dominant "fear of failure" motive favored attributions to stable factors for performance outcomes, for example ability, rather than unstable ones, such as effort (see Weiner, 1974). Thus, when confronted with a series of failures (due to performance goals that were difficult to reach), they did not incorporate goals, and even lowered personal goals and effort during the multiple trial setup. In terms of the Big Five factors, a positive association of conscientiousness with process variables in the action phase has been supported by current research (Yeo & Neal, 2004). The negative association of neuroticism to expectancy beliefs suggests a substantial impact of this factor on the execution of action. It has indeed been shown that people with high scores on anxiety or low scores on self-esteem invest a lower amount of energy while working on tasks (Feather, 1963; Sandelands, Brockner, & Glynn, 1988).

Taken together, research has shown by now that personality traits cannot only explain a substantial amount of variance in motivational process variables (Judge & Ilies, 2002). Moreover, several studies have explicitly demonstrated the meditational role of motivational factors or found support for indirect effects of personality traits on performance (Barrick et al., 1993; Klein & Lee, 2006; Schmitt, 2008). Especially neuroticism and conscientiousness have been shown to be associated with constructs from different work motivation theories. By systematizing the empirical findings in terms of a general motivation theory, a new theoretical approach can be postulated to explain the mechanism through which personality affects work behavior. However, in order to make an important step towards a combined theory of work motivation and individual difference factors, research has to account for interdependencies between single variables and the effects of situational constraints in the motivational process. Whereas in the learning context complex models have already been investigated (Chen et al., 2000; Phillips & Gully, 1997), only a few attempts have been made to transfer these findings to work-relevant settings (Barrick et al., 1993; Gellatly, 1996; Rasch & Tosi, 1992). Hence, the focus of our research was on the analysis of the role of personality traits within the different phases of the action process in work-related settings. To obtain a more comprehensive view, we examined the effects of several dispositional traits and variables derived from the goal setting theory simultaneously on goal-directed behavior under varying work conditions in an experimental setup.

Empirical Evidence for a Model of Indirect Effects

Based on empirical evidence and theoretical considerations in terms of the action process, we specified indirect effects of personality traits on work performance via goal setting and goal realization. Figure 2 shows the theoretical model guiding our research. This model formed the basis to investigate the impact of individual difference factors (such as the Big Five and cognitive ability; see Level 1 in Figure 2) on behavioral outcomes (namely task performance; see Level 4 in Figure 2). Goals and associated constructs from Level 2 and Level 3 in Figure 2 were selected in order to specify effects of personality on work motivation and performance.

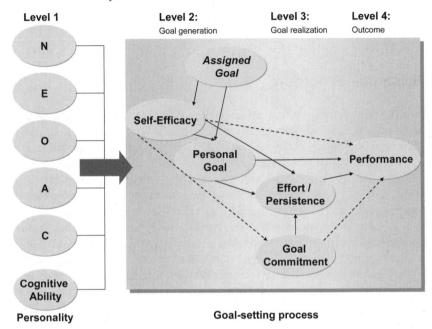

Figure 2. The research model.

In the phase of Goal Generation (Level 2), we predicted relations between personality and task-specific *self-efficacy*, which in goal setting theory is also a determinant of *personal goals*. In goal setting theory, the effects of goals on performance are supposed to be mediated by different factors. Based on our research design and the task we used, we included two mediators: effort/persistence and goal commitment. Because goal setting theory specifies two other mechanisms that have effects on performance, we expected additional direct effects of personal goals and self-efficacy on performance. We were also interested in how external standards like assigned goals may impact the relationship of personality with work behavior. In the process of Goal Realization (Level 3), we put emphasis on the dispositional antecedents of *effort/persistence* and *goal commitment*. Goal commitment in its turn was expected to impact performance directly and indirectly via effort/persistence. Subjective ratings of *effort/persistence* were supplemented by attention aspects. We did not vary other variables from the goal setting framework (feedback or task complexity), and because of the simple achievement task we used, we did not expect strategy use to be a major performance determinant.

Regarding the effects of personality traits, we expected, first of all, the Big Five to be indirectly related to performance, via self-efficacy, personal goals, goal commitment and effort/persistence. Based on previous research, we anticipated conscientiousness to be positively related and neuroticism to be negatively related to variables in the action process (variables from Level 2 and Level 3 in the research model). For example, we expected both of them to be related to goal commitment (cf. Barrick et al., 1993; Erez & Judge, 2001).

Method

Participants – Procedure

To get a clear picture of the effects of personality on goal setting and goal striving, we conducted two correlational lab-studies (see Bipp, 2007). We concentrated our analysis on effects of general mental ability and the Big Five on goal setting and pursuit in a simple achievement task: Participants had to add two rows of five-digit numbers in two consecutive work periods. Demanding highly trained skills, performance was not expected to be mainly predicted by cognitive ability, but by motivational or volitional processes. Participants first performed a 5-minute practice trial, after which they worked for 20 minutes on the task in our first study under the condition of *self-set goals*. Before they started to work on the second trial, students were asked to indicate a personal goal (number of correctly solved problems) for the 20-minute work period. In total, 123 students participated in the study and they received either course credits or a monetary incentive in return for their participation. Complete data was obtained from 115 participants. Seventy four percent of the participants were female, and the average age was 22.80 years ($SD = 4.39$).

Measures

Cognitive ability was assessed with the long version of Cattell's Culture-Free Test 3 (CFT 3; Weiß, 1971), which measures general intelligence (g). In our sample split-half reliability coefficients of both test parts reached a value of .60.

    Big Five were measured by the German version of the NEO-PI-R (Ostendorf & Angleitner, 2004), with 48 items assessing each broad factor. Internal consistency, using Cronbach's alpha coefficient, ranged from .87 to .89.

    Self-efficacy was assessed after the first work period, following a combined operationalization of self-efficacy strength and magnitude suggested by Lee and Bobko (1994). Fourteen different performance levels (50-200 problems) were presented, and participants had to indicate whether they were convinced that they could attain these performance levels (Yes or No) and their degree of confidence on a detailed scale from 0 (totally uncertain) to 10 (totally certain). Cronbach's alpha was .80.

    Goal commitment was assessed with a translation of a self-report scale developed by Klein, Wesson, Hollenbeck, Wright, and Deshon (2001). Responses on the five items were made on a 5-point Likert-type scale and they reached an acceptable value of internal consistency, Cronbach's $\alpha = .82$.

    For *effort/persistence*, to our knowledge, no established measurement instrument exists. For this reason we applied a new operationalization approach. We combined different sources of information into a common index (two subjective rating scales for effort and persistence and an objective measure of persistence, namely average work speed to solve the presented problems). The reliability estimate of the linear combination (see Nunnally & Bernstein, 1994) of those three sources resulted in an acceptable value of .90.

Performance was assessed by the number of correctly solved problems in the second trial. Estimation of test-retest reliability was based on the correlation of performance scores in the two trials ($r = .86$), which indicated that performance was relatively stable over time within the study.

Results

First of all, the zero-order correlations showed a significant correlation with performance only for cognitive ability ($r = .36$), but not for the Big Five. In our data we found nonetheless support for the postulated model by a series of hierarchical regression analyses, linking the Big Five personality traits and intelligence *indirectly* to performance. First, we regressed cognitive ability and the Big Five on performance (see Bipp, 2007). Together with age and gender as control variables, they accounted for 14.9% of the variance in performance directly, $F(8, 108) = 2,32, p < .05$. However, taking motivational variables into account, they are not able to explain an additional amount of variance in performance above those variables. Table 2 displays the results of a hierarchical regression analysis in four steps (or models) predicting performance. After the control variables (Step 1), the potential determinants of performance were entered into the regression starting from proximal to distal factors. Effort/persistence was entered in Step 2, because of the expected direct effect on performance. Afterwards (Step 3) level of personal goal, goal commitment, and self-efficacy beliefs were added to the regression equation, building on their predicted direct and indirect effects on performance. In the last step, cognitive ability and the Big Five were entered.

The prediction model with all twelve variables was significant, accounting for 71% of performance variance (see Step 4). Although age and gender did not play an essential role in explaining performance (R^2 in Step 1 was nonsignificant), adding variables in Step 2 and Step 3 of the regression model accounted for almost 70% of performance variance. Comparing the additional variance explained by variables from Levels 2 and 3, both steps explained a substantial percentage of variance in the explanatory model. In contrast to the significant amount of variance in performance explained directly by proximal variables, entering the Big Five and cognitive ability in the last regression step showed that—besides effort/persistence, level of personal goal, goal commitment, and self-efficacy—distal variables did not predict a significant percentage of variance in performance. Moreover, neither cognitive ability nor any of the Big Five factors did reach a significant regression weight.

Table 2. Hierarchical regression analysis on performance scores.

	β [a]	R^2	F	ΔR^2	ΔF
Step 1					
Gender	-.07				
Age	-.03	.03	$F(2, 112) = 1.53$	--	--
Step 2					
Effort / persistence	.67*	.51	$F(3, 111) = 37.86^{**}$	.48	$F(1, 111) = 107.62^{**}$
Step 3					
Level of personal goal	.33**				
Goal commitment	-.29**				
Self-efficacy	.03	.69	$F(6, 108) = 40.22^{**}$	.18	$F(3, 108) = 21.55^*$
Step 4					
Cognitive ability	.07				
Neuroticism	.11				
Extraversion	-.02				
Openness to experience	-.06				
Agreeableness	.01				
Conscientiousness	.00	.71	$F(12, 102) = 20.94^{**}$	.02	$F(6, 102) = 1.21$

Note: Hierarchical regression in four steps (for each step only the variables that were added to the model are displayed); [a] β values at Step 4; * $p < .05$; ** $p < .01$.

However, further analyses showed that personality traits had a significant impact on variables from Level 2 and 3 in our research model, and therefore had an effect on performance indirectly via motivational variables. Specifically, hierarchical regression analyses demonstrated that the Big Five and cognitive ability accounted for a significant amount of variance of the commitment to personal goals (see Table 3).

Table 3. Hierarchical regression analysis on commitment to personal goals.

	β [a]	R^2	F	ΔR^2	ΔF
Step 1					
Gender	-.03				
Age	.05	.00	$F(2, 112) = .15$	--	--
Step 2					
Level of personal goal	-.13				
Self-efficacy	.19	.03	$F(4, 110) = .74$	.02	$F(2, 110) = 1.32$
Step 3					
Cognitive ability	.18				
Neuroticism	.14				
Extraversion	.17				
Openness to experience	.07				
Agreeableness	.17				
Conscientiousness	.21*	.21	$F(10, 104) = 2.70^{**}$	.18	$F(6, 104) = 3.92^{**}$

Note: Hierarchical regression in three steps (for each step only the variables that were added to the model are displayed); [a] β values at Step 3; * $p < .05$; ** $p < .01$.

Age, gender, self-efficacy, and level of personal goal did not explain a significant percentage of variance in the first two steps of this hierarchical regression. When control variables and variables from the goal setting framework that might also affect goal commitment (level of personal goal/self-efficacy) were taken into account, the Big Five and cognitive ability explained 18% of the variance incrementally (see Step 3). In this last regression step, only conscientiousness reached significance, whereas the beta-weights of cognitive ability and agreeableness were nearly significant ($p < .10$).

Discussion

Linking Personality to Work Motivation and Performance

Our results contribute to the growing number of studies that have investigated the potential mechanism through which personality impacts performance (Barrick et al., 1993; Judge, Bono, Erez, & Locke, 2005; Klein & Lee, 2006). By examining the effects of several personality traits at the same time in the goal-directed action process, our research offered a more comprehensive view of the mechanism compared to former studies. The hierarchical regressions showed that the Big Five and cognitive ability did not have a direct effect on performance when controlling for motivational variables involved in the phases of goal setting and goal realization. Even though the correlations for the Big Five factors and performance were close to zero, indirect effects on performance were found. In our setting the effect on performance was completely indirect, and our data support their role in explaining commitment to personal goals. Although we found a positive effect of conscientiousness on commitment to self-set goals while controlling for effects of all Big Five factors, we found no support for the postulated effect of neuroticism in this phase of the action process.

In addition, further analyses have demonstrated that the effect of some personality traits varies between phases of the action process or work conditions. No single Big Five factor plays the same role for goal generation and realization, nor can effects be transferred to different work settings on a one-by-one basis. Conscientiousness, for example, was not a significant predictor of the level of personal goal in the present study (Bipp, 2007), but the results of a second study with the same task under different work conditions (assigned goals; Bipp & Kleinbeck, submitted) revealed even a negative effect of this personality trait in different action phases. Findings obtained under self-set goal conditions might, therefore, not be easily transferred to other work settings (Whitey, Gellatly, & Annett, 2005).

Although research on the effects of situational constraints or task demands on work motivation has a long tradition (Locke & Latham, 2004; Tett & Burnett, 2003), the role of individual difference factors on motivation under varying work conditions is, at the moment, less clear (e.g., effects of different goal setting conditions, see Kalnbach & Hinsz, 1999). However, to build an integrated theory of personality and work motivation, in particular the interactional effects of personality with situational factors within real-life work settings need to be tested in detail. These results will not only have important implications for theory building but also for human resources management. Based on advanced theories, effective individual interventions might be developed to support goal-directed achievement behavior on a motivational and volitional basis (e.g., by using feedback methods to set realistic goals, or foster goal commitment by incentives).

Global or Specific Explanatory Models?

While there is substantial evidence for indirect effects of personality traits on performance via motivation in work or learning settings, a clear global theoretical perspective in this field is still missing. This seems to be partly due to the various theoretical approaches in the field of work motivation. Cognitive process variables represent only one potential way through which personality can express itself in work motivation or performance. Further relations can be found for variables like mood states or emotions. Personality traits have even been shown to have a substantial relationship with factors specified in external work-motivation models (e.g., equity or reinforcement theory; see Furnham, 1992). Only recently has the field of work motivation acknowledged the findings from other research areas, like social psychology (see Stajkovic, Locke, & Blair, 2006 for the combined effects of subconscious and conscious goals). Moreover, certainly more elaborated research is needed to specify and explain the influence of personality traits (on different levels of abstraction) in all four phases of the Rubicon model to obtain a comprehensive view of the mechanism.

Finally, the importance of situational characteristics for work motivation already raises questions about other possible factors that can have an impact on these relations of personality factors with work motivation and work performance. It is yet not clear, if the postulated explanatory models can, for example, be generalized to different organizational cultures or, even, ethnic ones. The effects of distal factors, like culture or values, on the identified associations have to be tested in detail to sustain the external validity of the postulated explanatory models. When we take a closer look at attempts to formulate an integrated theory of work motivation (see Latham & Pinder, 2005; Locke, 1997), effects of cultural factors can be anticipated for a number of performance-relevant variables. Sanchez-Runde and Steers (2003) outlined, for example, how culturally derived work values or norms influence the way people approach work (e.g., via the individual level, affecting individual needs or values, or indirectly via contextual factors, like organizational culture). That cultural values have an impact on work motivation processes has been supported by recent research (Kurman, 2001; Sue-Chan & Ong, 2002). The combined effects of factors at the individual level (like personality or cognitive ability) and different aspects of culture at the work place (Hofstede, 2001) need to be studied in detail to be able to draw conclusions about a general theory of personality, work motivation, and performance.

References

Barrick, M. R., Mitchell, T. R., & Stewart, G. L. (2003). Situational and motivational influences on trait-behavior relationships. In M. R. Barrick & A. M. Ryan (Eds.), *Personality and work: Reconsidering the role of personality in organizations* (pp. 60-82). San Francisco: Jossey Bass.

Barrick, M. R., & Mount, M. K. (1991). The Big Five personality dimensions and job performance: A meta-analysis. *Personnel Psychology, 44,* 1-26.

Barrick, M. R., Mount, M. K., & Gupta, R. (2003). Meta-analysis of the relationship between the Five-Factor Model of personality and Holland's occupational types. *Personnel Psychology, 56,* 45-74.

Barrick, M. R., Mount, M. K., & Judge, T. A. (2001). Personality and performance at the beginning of the new millennium: What do we know and where do we go next? *International Journal of Selection and Assessment, 9*, 9-30.

Barrick, M. R., Mount, M. K., & Strauss, J. P. (1993). Conscientiousness and performance of sales representatives: Test of the mediating effects of goal setting. *Journal of Applied Psychology, 78*, 715-722.

Barrick, M. R., Stewart, G. L., & Piotrowski, M. (2002). Personality and job performance: Test of the mediating effects of motivation across sales representatives. *Journal of Applied Psychology, 87*, 43-51.

Bipp, T. (2007). *Persönlichkeit - Ziele - Leistung: Der Einfluss der Big Five Persönlichkeitseigenschaften auf das zielbezogene Leistungshandeln* [Personality - goals - performance: Influence of the big five personality traits on goal-oriented achievement behavior]. Doctoral dissertation, University of Dortmund, Germany [Electronic Publication]. Retrieved April 13, 2008, from http://hdl.handle.net/2003/23252.

Bipp, T., & Kleinbeck, U. (submitted). *The influence of personality on goal pursuit: Linking cognitive ability, neuroticism, and conscientiousness to work motivation and performance.* Manuscript submitted for publication.

Bipp, T., Steinmayr, R., & Spinath, B. (2008). Personality and achievement motivation: Relationship among Big Five domain and facet scales, achievement goals, and intelligence. *Personality and Individual Differences, 44*, 1454-1464.

Chen, G., Casper, W. J., & Cortina, J. M. (2001). The roles of self-efficacy and task complexity in the relationship among cognitive ability, conscientiousness, and work-related performance: A meta-analytic examination. *Human Performance, 14*, 209-230.

Chen, G., Gully, S. M., Whiteman, J. A., & Kilcullen, R. N. (2000). Examination of relationships among trait-like individual differences, state-like individual differences, and learning performance. *Journal of Applied Psychology, 85*, 835-847.

Costa, P. T., & McCrae, R. R. (1998). Six approaches to the explanation of facet-level traits: Examples from conscientiousness. *European Journal of Personality, 12*, 117-134.

Cropanzano, R., James, K., & Citera, M. (1993). A goal-hierarchy model of personality, motivation, and leadership. *Research in Organizational Behavior, 15*, 267-322.

Derryberry, D. (2002). Attention and voluntary self-control. *Self and Identity, 1*, 105-111.

Digman, J. M. (1990). Personality structure: Emergence of the Five-Factor Model. *Annual Review of Psychology, 41*, 417-440.

Dweck, C. S. (1986). Motivational processes affecting learning. *American Psychologist, 41*, 1040-1048.

Erez, A., & Judge, T. A. (2001). Relationship of core self-evaluation to goal setting, motivation, and performance. *Journal of Applied Psychology, 86*, 1270-1279.

Feather, N. T. (1963). Persistence at a difficult task with alternative task of intermediate difficulty. *Journal of Abnormal and Social Psychology, 66*, 604-609.

Furnham, A. (1992). *Personality at work.* London: Routledge.

Gellatly, I. R. (1996). Conscientiousness and task performance: Test of a cognitive process model. *Journal of Applied Psychology, 81*, 474-482.

Gollwitzer, P. M. (1990). Action phases and mind-sets. In E. T. Higgins & R. M. Sorrentino (Eds.), *The handbook of motivation and cognition* (pp. 53-92). New York: Guilford.

Heckhausen, J., & Heckhausen, H. (2008). *Motivation and action.* New York: Cambridge University Press.

Heisig, B. (1995). *Planen und Selbstregulation* [Planning and self-regulation]. Frankfurt a. M., Germany: Lang.

Hofstede, G. (2001). *Culture's consequences: Comparing values, behaviors, institutions, and organizations across nations.* Thousand Oaks, CA: Sage.

Ickes, W., Snyder, M., & Garcia, S. (1997). Personality influence on the choice of situations. In R. Hogan, J. Johnson, & S. Briggs (Eds.), *Handbook of personality psychology* (pp. 165-195). San Diego, CA: Academic.

Judge, T. A., Bono, J. E., Erez, A., & Locke, E. A. (2005). Core self-evaluations and job and life satisfaction: The role of self-concordance and goal attainment. *Journal of Applied Psychology, 90*, 257-268.

Judge, T. A., Heller, D., & Mount, M. K. (2002). Five-Factor Model of personality and job satisfaction: A meta-analysis. *Journal of Applied Psychology, 87*, 530-541.

Judge, T. A., & Ilies, R. (2002). Relationship of personality to performance motivation: A meta-analytic review. *Journal of Applied Psychology, 87,* 797-807.

Judge, T. A., Jackson, C. L., Shaw, J. C., Scott, B. A., & Rich, B. L. (2007). Self-efficacy and work-related performance: The integral role of individual differences. *Journal of Applied Psychology, 92,* 107-127.

Kalnbach, L. R., & Hinsz, V. B. (1999). A conceptualization and test of the influences of individual differences in goal-setting situations. *Journal of Applied Social Psychology, 29,* 1854-1878.

Kanfer, R., & Heggestad, E. D. (1997). Motivational traits and skills: A person-centered approach to work motivation. *Research in Organizational Behavior, 19,* 1-56.

Klein, H. J., & Lee, S. (2006). The effects of personality on learning: The mediating role of goal setting. *Human Performance, 19,* 43-66.

Klein, H. J., Wesson, M. J., Hollenbeck, J. R., & Alge, B. J. (1999). Goal commitment and the goal-setting process: Conceptual clarification and empirical synthesis. *Journal of Applied Psychology, 84,* 885-896.

Klein, H. J., Wesson, M. J., Hollenbeck, J. R., Wright, P. M., & DeShon, R. P. (2001). The assessment of goal commitment: A measurement model meta-analysis. *Organizational Behavior and Human Decision Process, 85,* 32-55.

Kleinbeck, U., Schmidt, K.-H., & Carlsen, H. (1985). Veränderungen von Zielsetzungswirkungen auf die Leistung durch leistungsthematische Einflussfaktoren [Change of goal effects on performance depending on achievement thematic factors]. *Zeitschrift für Experimentelle und Angewandte Psychologie, 32,* 263-280.

Kuncel, N. R., Hezlett, S. A., & Ones, D. S. (2004). Academic performance, career potential, creativity, and job performance: Can one construct predict them all? *Journal of Personality and Social Psychology, 86,* 148-161.

Kurman, J. (2001). Self-enhancement: Is it restricted to individualistic cultures? *Personality and Social Psychology Bulletin, 27,* 1705-1716.

Latham, G. P. (2007). *Work motivation.* Thousand Oaks, CA: Sage.

Latham, G. P., & Locke, E. A. (2007). New developments in and directions for goal-setting research. *European Psychologist, 12,* 290-300.

Latham, G. P., & Pinder, C. C. (2005). Work motivation theory and research at the dawn of the twenty-first century. *Annual Review of Psychology, 56,* 485-516.

Lee, C., & Bobko, P. (1994). Self-efficacy beliefs: Comparison of five measures. *Journal of Applied Psychology, 79,* 364-369.

Lewin, K., Dembo, T., Festinger, L., & Sears, P. S. (1944). Level of aspiration. In J. M. Hunt (Ed.), *Personality and the behavior disorders* (pp. 333-378). New York: Ronald.

Locke, E. A. (1997). The motivation to work: What we know. In M. Maehr & P. Pintrich (Eds.), *Advances in motivation and achievement* (Vol. 10, pp. 375-412). Greenwich, CT: JAI.

Locke, E. A. (2001). Self-set goals and self-efficacy as mediators of incentives and personality. In M. Erez, U. Kleinbeck, & H. Thierry (Eds.), *Work motivation in the context of a globalizing economy* (pp. 13-26). Mahwah, NJ: Erlbaum.

Locke, E. A., & Latham, G. P. (1990). *A theory of goal setting and task performance.* Englewood Cliffs, NJ: Prentice-Hall.

Locke, E. A., & Latham, G. P. (2002). Building a practically useful theory of goal setting and task motivation – A 35-year odyssey. *American Psychologist, 57,* 705-717.

Locke, E. A., & Latham, G. P. (2004). What should we do about motivation theory? Six recommendations for the twenty-first century. *Academy of Management Review, 29,* 388-403.

Matsui, T., Okada, A., & Kakuyama, T. (1982). Influence of achievement need on goal setting, performance, and feedback effectiveness. *Journal of Applied Psychology, 67,* 645-648.

McCrae, R. R., & Terracciano, A. (2005). Universal features of personality traits from the observer's perspective: Data from 50 cultures. *Journal of Personality and Social Psychology, 88,* 547-561.

McHenry, J. J., Hough, L. M., Toquam, J. L., Hanson, M. A., & Ashworth, S. (1990). Project A validity results: The relationship between predictor and criterion domains. *Personnel Psychology, 43,* 335-354.

Motowidlo, S. J. (2003). Job performance. In W. C. Borman, D. R. Ilgen, & R. Klimoski (Eds.), *Handbook of psychology: Industrial and Organizational Psychology* (Vol.12, pp. 39-53). Hoboken, NJ: Wiley.

Nunnally, J. C., & Bernstein, I. H. (1994). *Psychometric theory.* New York: McGraw-Hill.

Ostendorf, F., & Angleitner, A. (2004). *NEO-PI-R: NEO-Persönlichkeitsinventar nach Costa und McCrae. Revidierte Fassung. Testmanual* [NEO-PI-R. NEO Personality Inventory - revised form. Manual]. Göttingen: Hogrefe.

Peeters, M. A. G., Rutte, C. G., van Tuijl, H., & Reymen, I. M. (2006). Personality and team performance: A meta-analysis. *European Journal of Personality, 20,* 377-396.

Phillips, J. M., & Gully, S. M. (1997). Role of goal orientation, ability, need for achievement, and locus of control in the self-efficacy and goal-setting process. *Journal of Applied Psychology, 82,* 792-802.

Pintrich, P. (2000). An achievement goal theory perspective on issues in motivation terminology, theory, and research. *Contemporary Educational Psychology, 25,* 92-104.

Rasch, R. H., & Tosi, H. L. (1992). Factors affecting software developers' performance: An integrated approach. *MIS Quarterly, 16,* 395-413.

Renn, R. W., & Fedor, D. B. (2001). Development and field test of a feedback-seeking, self-efficacy, and goal-setting model of work performance. *Journal of Management, 27,* 563-583.

Revelle, W. (1989). Personality, motivation, and cognitive performance. In R. Kanfer, P. L. Ackerman, & R. Cudeck (Eds.), *Abilities, motivation, and methodology* (pp. 297-341). Hillsdale, NJ: Erlbaum.

Rothstein, M. G., & Goffin, R. D. (2006). The use of personality measures in personnel selection: What does current research support? *Human Resource Management Review, 16,* 155-180.

Salgado, J. F. (2003). Predicting job performance using FFM and non-FFM measures. *Journal of Occupational and Organizational Psychology, 76,* 323-346.

Salgado, J. F., Anderson, N., Moscoso, S., Bertua, C., de Fruyt, F., & Rolland, J. P. (2003). A meta-analytic study of general mental ability validity for different occupations in the European Community. *Journal of Applied Psychology, 88,* 1068-1081.

Sanchez-Runde, C. J., & Steers, R. M. (2003). Cultural influences on work motivation and performance. In L. W. Porter, G. A. Bigley, & R. M. Steers (Eds.), *Motivation and work behavior* (pp. 357-374). New York: McGraw-Hill.

Sandelands, L. E., Brockner, J., & Glynn, M. A. (1988). If at first you don't succeed, try, try again: Effects of persistence-performance contingencies, ego involvement, and self-esteem on task persistence. *Journal of Applied Psychology, 73,* 208-216.

Schmidt, F. L. (2002). The role of general cognitive ability and job performance: Why there cannot be a debate. *Human Performance, 15,* 187-210.

Schmitt, N. (2008). The interaction of neuroticism and gender and its impact on self-efficacy and performance. *Human Performance, 21,* 49-61.

Schmitt, N., Gooding, R. Z., Noe, R. D., & Kirsch, M. (1984). Meta-analyses of validity studies published between 1964 and 1982 and the investigation of study characteristics. *Personnel Psychology, 37,* 407-422.

Stajkovic, A. C., Locke, E. A., & Blair, E. S. (2006). A first examination of the relationships between primed subconscious goals, assigned conscious goals, and task performance. *Journal of Applied Psychology, 91,* 1172-1180.

Sue-Chan, C., & Ong, M. (2002). Goal assignment and performance: Assessing the mediating roles of goal commitment and self-efficacy and the moderating role of power distance. *Organizational Behavior and Human Decision Processes, 89,* 1140-1161.

Tett, R. P., & Burnett, D. D. (2003). A personality trait-based interactionist model of job performance. *Journal of Applied Psychology, 88,* 500-517.

Tyler, G. P., & Newcombe, P. A. (2006). Relationship between work performance and personality traits in Hong Kong organizational settings. *International Journal of Selection and Assessment, 14,* 37-50.

VandeWalle, D., Cron, W. L., & Slocum, J. W. Jr. (2001). The role of goal orientation following performance feedback. *Journal of Applied Psychology, 86,* 629-640.

Weiner, B. (1974). *Achievement motivation and attribution theory.* Morristown, NJ: General Learning.

Weiß, R. (1971). *Grundintelligenztest CFT 3 Skala 3. Handanweisung* [Culture Free Intelligence Test CFT 3 Scale 3. Manual]. Braunschweig: Westermann.

Whitey, M .J., Gellatly, I. R., & Annett, M. (2005). The moderating effect of situation strength on the relationship between personality and provision of feedback. *Journal of Applied Social Psychology, 35,* 1587-1608.

Yeo, G. B., & Neal, A. (2004). A multilevel analysis of effort, practice, and performance: Effects of ability, conscientiousness, and goal orientation. *Journal of Applied Psychology, 89,* 231-247.

Zweig, D., & Webster, J. (2004). What are we measuring? An examination of the relationships between the Big Five personality traits, goal orientation, and performance intentions. *Personality and Individual Differences, 36,* 1693-1708.

Mediators and Moderators of Approach-Performance and Avoidance-Performance Relationships in Children

Theoretical and Experimental Aspects

Gunnar Bjørnebekk

Introduction

A central hypothesis of classical motivation theory is that affect underlies motivation and its behavioral manifestations (McClelland, Atkinson, Clark, & Lowell, 1953) and that major self-regulation processes depend on the type of affective response characteristics possessed by the individual (Atkinson & Birch, 1970). Lewin's (1935) theory describes motives as tension systems that do not release their energy until an appropriate goal is attained. In his view, an individual can reflect intensely on an aspired goal state without necessarily performing an appropriate action. In addition to a cognitive representation, some driving force appears to be necessary to propel the individual toward the goal. This theory has, however, been largely ignored during the past twenty years due to the dominance of social cognitivism. As a result, social cognitive processes have been the focus of studies analyzing the factors that determine and maintain performance-related behavior. Achievement goal theory, which emphasizes the cognitive aspects of motivation, has been the primary basis for motivational research. In recent years affect has been "rediscovered", and attempts have been made to combine early writings in psychology and achievement goal theory (Elliot, 1999; Elliot & Church, 1997). According to Elliot and Thrash, goals are vital to self-regulation processes, serving as channels for the general propensities evoked by approach and avoidance dispositions. Goals are believed to have a different function in the motivational process than affective dispositions, and are seen as specific cognitive forms of regulation that give focus and direction to the more general propensities (Elliot & Thrash, 2002). Despite the fact that current social-cognitive models of achievement motivation highlight the centrality of achievement goals to the self-regulation processes, relatively little is known about the achievement goals' function in regulating the motivation of schoolchildren.

Increasingly, emphasis is being placed on the effects of future time perspective (FTP) and future time orientation (FTO) on motivation (e.g., Kaufman & Husman, 2004). FTP is defined as the present anticipation of future goals (Simons, Vansteenkiste, Lens, & Lacante, 2004). Individuals with a rather short FTP set most of their goals in the near future. Conversely, those with a longer FTP set and strive toward goals situated in the distant future. FTP is generally considered to be multidimensional, involving both dynamic and cognitive components (Husman & Shell, 2008). FTO is viewed as a unidimensional construct that describes the stable tendency or individual trait of being oriented toward their future (Gjesme, 1979). Despite the emphasis on the FTO/FTP dimensions in motivational psychology, findings from several earlier studies indicate that the most significant determinant of perceived goal distance in time is the physical distance in time (e.g., Ainslie & Haslam, 1992; Gjesme, 1981). However, recent social-cognitive models of children's motivation have largely disregarded the motivational effect of physical time, which was the focus of early extensions of classical motivation theory (e.g., Gjesme, 1974).

In the present chapter we seek to expand the existing view of motivation in achievement theory by exploring how motivational processes directly and indirectly influence more situation-specific cognition, affect during problem-solving and performance through individual variation in approach and avoidance tendencies, achievement goals and goal distance in time. We will review relevant research and theories, the latter forming the basis for an experimental test whose findings we will discuss in light of motivational theory. The experiment is partly a replication of and partly an extension of earlier experiments in the field (cf. Gjesme, 1974, 1975; Halvari, 1991), and the instruments used have been previously validated and tested in numerous studies under different conditions and in different countries. The design, theoretical grounds and use of instruments are consistent with generalizable principles (conceptual, theoretical and methodological); consequently, certain findings may be of a more basic nature and reflect psychological mechanisms beneath cultural artifacts ("*a global picture*"). The sample consists of Norwegian sixth-graders selected from classes with average or just-above-average scores on national mathematics and reading tests. The age of the participants restricts the range of the variables in the study; thus certain findings may be limited by virtue of context or culture ("*a local picture*").

Motives and Motivation

According to Atkinson's (1964) theory of achievement motivation, the anticipation of failure as a possible outcome of an achievement task arouses the latent motive to avoid failure (M_f). The anticipation of success arouses the latent need for achievement or the motive to approach success (M_s). This implies that in achievement situations two motivational tendencies are situationally stimulated: the tendency to strive for success (T_s) and the tendency to avoid failure (T_f). T_s is an approach tendency that instigates actions directed at achieving success. T_f is an avoidance tendency that directs the individual's behavior away from the achievement task and the possibility of failure.

All individuals are assumed to possess both the motive to approach success (M_s) and the motive to avoid failure (M_f), but the strength of the achievement motives differ from one individual to another (Atkinson, 1957). Furthermore, McClelland posits that a motive is "a strong affective association, characterized by an anticipatory goal reaction and based on past association of certain cues with pleasure and pain" (1955). According to Atkinson (1964), the effects of individual differences in the motive to avoid failure or the motive to achieve success are most pronounced when the task is of intermediate difficulty. When the task appears to be either extremely difficult or very easy, that is, when the probability of success (P_s) is either very high or very low, neither M_s nor M_f is strongly aroused. When P_s is intermediate, both achievement motives are strongly aroused, and the differences in strength of the motives are maximized (Gjesme, 1983). Thus, a pupil may very well have a strong motive to approach success without being motivated to do schoolwork, that is, without having his or her motives aroused in the school situation. This is likely to be the case if P_s is very high or very low (Atkinson, 1964), the psychological distance to goal in time is long (Gjesme, 1974), or the perceived instrumentality of the school activity is low (Raynor, 1974). It therefore becomes important to distinguish between motive and motivation, the former referring to a personality characteristic that may or may not manifest itself in a particular situation, and the latter referring to its manifestation in a specific situation.

Achievement Goals

In the late 1970s and early 1980s, social-cognitive achievement goal theory became the benchmark of motivation psychology (Ames, 1984; Diener & Dweck, 1978). During that period the influence of affect (Linnenbrink & Pintrich, 2002) was largely ignored, or assumed to be predictable, a result of the individual's achievement goal (Dweck & Leggett, 1988). Needs and motive dynamics had long been central in classical motivation psychology. Once cognitivism became dominant, the theory that behavior is motivated by affect-charged needs or desires was replaced by the theory that behavior is an expression of a rational attempt to achieve a specific articulated (or accessible) end or purpose. In the early days, importance was attached to an approach-avoidance distinction (e.g., Nicholls, Patashnick, & Nolen, 1985). Gradually, analysis became focused on two target groups. The first group encompasses individuals who exhibit their own abilities and try to perform better – or at least not worse – than others. The goals of the individuals in this group are called performance goals. The second group is made up of individuals who look upon learning as an objective in itself and seek to improve personal achievement. The goals of the individuals in this group are called mastery goals (Elliott & Dweck, 1988). Early research in achievement goal theory generally associated performance goals with a number of negative processes and consequences. For example, it was assumed that a person who has set a performance goal will give up more easily in the face of difficulty (Dweck, 1986). It was also assumed that performance goals are linked to decreased motivation (Nicholls, 1989) as well as to a tendency to use strategies that promote surface processing of the material, such as rehearsal strategies (Nolen, 1988). Mastery goals on the other hand were considered to be linked to a number of positive processes and consequences. For example, it was assumed that a person who has set a mastery goal will show considerable perseverance when encountering opposition (Dweck & Leggett, 1988), will seek out optimal challenges (Dweck, 1986), and will have a tendency to use strategies that promote deeper processing of the material (Elliot & McGregor, 2001). However, during the mid-1990s the sufficiency of the performance/mastery model had been called into question by a number of research groups on both empirical and conceptual grounds. In their conceptual work, Elliot and his colleagues modified and developed achievement goal theory by drawing on certain aspects of classical motivation psychology (Elliot, 1999; Elliot & Church, 1997). On the empirical front an experiment conducted by Elliot and Harackiewicz in 1996 showed that performance goals can be divided into two categories: performance-approach goals, where an individual demonstrates ability for himself or herself, as opposed to others, and performance-avoidance goals, where an individual avoids demonstrating lack of ability or making a fool of himself or herself. The results of several studies the following year supported these findings (Elliot & Church, 1997; Middleton & Midgley, 1997). More recently, Rawsthorne and Elliot's (1999) meta-analysis of the effect of performance goals found that only performance-avoidance goals showed a negative relation to interest, enjoyment, and free choice. More importantly, performance-approach goals did not undermine intrinsic motivation in terms of self-reported interest and behavioral choice.

Results from later studies suggest that it may be constructive to analyze mastery goals in a similar way because students in the studies not only focused on mastering tasks, learning and understanding, they also focused on avoiding misunderstanding, averting not learning and avoiding not mastering tasks (Elliot & McGregor, 2001). According to Pintrich (2000), mastery-avoidance goals are directed toward avoiding failure and imply a reduction or stagnation of skills and abilities. As an extension of this line of thinking, the hierarchical model developed by Elliot and his associates distinguishes goals along two dimensions that capture the different aims of competence-based striving (for reviews, see Elliot, 2005; Moller & Elliot, 2006). Empirical findings from studies using the 2 x 2 achievement framework indicate that mastery-avoidance goals have antecedents and consequences that are much more similar to performance-avoidance goals than to mastery-approach goals (Moller & Elliot, 2006). In the new achievement goal framework, mastery-approach goals often did not predict performance, whereas performance-approach goals did so on a rather consistent basis (Elliot, 2005). Moreover, findings from several studies suggest that the simultaneous pursuit of the two approach-goals is linked to positive consequences (Barron & Harackiewicz, 2001). This differs significantly from traditional goal theory, which posits that any degree of concern with performance goals may have negative effects.

Toward an Integration of Motives and Achievement Goals

In Murray's (1959) framework, the arousal of an underlying motive disposition provides energy for behavior. Rather than seeking need satisfaction in a diffuse sense, the individual selects and adopts a more concrete, situation-relevant goal that is expected to satisfy the activated need. Since that time, several personality and motivation researchers have developed hierarchical motivation models in which goals are portrayed as specific representations of latent dispositions (Elliot, 1999; Gjesme, 1981). Several motivation theoreticians consider goals to be decisive for the control of action in a given situation because they serve as channels for the energy that is triggered by more general dispositions

(Emmons, 1989). In Elliot and his colleagues' hierarchical model, the motives are presumed to energize behavior, but they do not provide specific guidelines for how an individual can achieve the motive that has been activated (Elliot & Thrash, 2001).

Once an affective disposition is activated, it energizes the individual, ultimately making him or her aware of the possibility of success or failure. According to the somatic marker hypothesis (Damasio, 1994), affect linked to disposition is associated with a system of automatic assessment of assumptions with which the individual – voluntarily or involuntarily – evaluates extremely different future scenarios. According to Damasio, affect influences behavior in several ways. Indirectly, affect influences motivation by influencing judgment components involved in conscious behavioral choices and self-regulation, such as goal setting and self-efficacy. Damasio considers emotions to be a permanent and integral part of rationality. Feelings also influence behavior directly, in ways that are not mediated by discrete choice processes involving beliefs or judgments. Moreover, it is normally individuals with high arousability or younger children who cannot control their emotional reactions with the use of cognitive self-regulatory processes (LeDoux, 1996). Although Elliot and his associates have managed to bring affect back into focus, their approach may be too cognitive-oriented to explain self-regulation processes related to motivation in individuals with high arousability or in children.

Distance to Goal in Time

Time is a critical component of motivated behavior, and several theories on the effect of time on behavior have been developed (e.g., Ainslie, 1992; Trope & Liberman, 2003). A key concept shared by the various theories is that the value of outcomes is diminished as the temporal distance from the outcomes increases (Ainslie & Haslam, 1992; Gjesme, 1996). Moreover, distance in time is shown to follow a hyperbolic function; that is, as the distance in time to an outcome increases, the decline in the value of the outcome is initially steep before becoming moderate (e.g., Steel & König, 2006).

Miller's (1944) theory of approach-avoidance conflict postulated that the tendency to approach or avoid a goal is stronger the "nearer" the subject is to it. Later, Gjesme (1974) applied Miller's theory to motivation in a study of goal distance in time and its effects on the relations between motives and performance. Gjesme posited that the term "nearness" may be defined by varying the goal's distance in time and that the approach and avoidance tendencies (which should be based on Miller's concept of "drive") may be represented by motives. Motives are viewed as capacities to anticipate pleasure and pain, respectively, in achievement situations. This implies that motives are to a certain extent *directed toward future achievement goals and activities* (Gjesme, 1974). Further research has provided a basis for the assertion that future-oriented motivation is related to intrinsic motivation (Maderlink & Harackiewicz, 1984), energy exertion during physical activity (Halvari, 1991), the number of problems attempted in cognitive tasks (Gjesme, 1974), and task engagement and persistence (Lens, Simmons, & Dewitte, 2001). There is also evidence that when there is frequent and exaggerated concern and worry about the future, as is the case with individuals high in M_f, this may not provide positive preparation for future problem-solving. Instead, it may lead to high stress, cognitive interference and preoccupation. Accordingly, in the case of certain individuals, a decrease in the distance to goal may lead to an inability to cope with problems. Conversely, the performance of individuals high in the motive to achieve success will supposedly be enhanced when a distant goal approaches in time due to the effect of temporal distance on arousing motivational affects. In summary, it appears that temporal distance accentuates the effect of motives and reinforcement on learning and performance.

Overview of the Present Study

Achievement motives and achievement goals are some of the most important motivational factors for predicting academic performance and well-being (Elliot, 1999). There appears to be growing interest in extending combinations of classical achievement theory and achievement goal theory and integrating them into models of schoolchildren's motivation. Unfortunately, the participants in the studies conducted by Elliot and his colleagues were undergraduates enrolled in introductory-level psychology courses, and the experiments were not carried out in real school classes. Their findings cannot therefore be directly applied to schoolchildren in their classrooms. It also appears that Elliott and his associates have ignored the motivational effect of physical time. If the relationship between the affective dispositions, the distance to the goal in time, the achievement goals and their effect on well-being during problem solving and performance could be measured and found in a youth population it would be a valuable addition to the existing literature and could promote further research on the development of these relationships in school settings.

Hypotheses

The following hypotheses were derived on the basis of the above-mentioned theories:

(1) The motive to avoid failure is positively related to the avoidance goals (both mastery and performance) and negatively related to task well-being, task-efficacy and performance.

(2) The motive to approach success is positively related to the approach goals (both mastery and approach), task-efficacy, task well-being and performance.

(3) Achievement goals mediate or moderate the links between motives and subjective well-being/performance.

(4) The level of performance increases for pupils high in the motive to achieve success as the goal approaches in time.

(5) The level of performance decreases for pupils high in the motive to avoid failure as the goal approaches in time.

(6) The slope of the goal gradient for performance is a hyperbolic function of time.

Method

The sample consists of 661 sixth-graders in 31 classes selected from schools in Oslo that achieved the same scores on nationwide tests in mathematics and reading. The total sample comprised 335 boys (51 %) and 326 girls (49 %). In the present sample the average mathematics and reading scores were 57 and 60, respectively. The average scores in Oslo schools were 53 and 54, respectively. The raw scores have been converted to standardized T-scores on a national basis: $M = 50$ and the $SD = 10$. As we can see, the participants in the present study scored above average on the nationwide tests.

Questionnaires

Motives. The Achievement Motives Scale (AMS) (Gjesme & Nygård, 1970) was used to assess motives. The AMS is based on achievement motivation theory, and is comprised of: a) items referring to positive affect and negative affect, respectively, and b) items focusing on situations that supposedly arouse approximately the same degree of uncertainty as to the possibility of success. To illustrate, the following item is intended to measure M_s: "*I feel pleasure at working on tasks that are fairly difficult for me*", while the following item is meant to measure M_f "*I become anxious when I meet problems I don't understand at once*". The AMS consists of 30 statements about affect experienced in connection with achievement situations. The scales are therefore explicit rather than implicit measures of motives. The statements were coded on a scale from 1 (not at all true of me) to 4 (very true of me). Results regarding the reliability and validity of the scales as applied to middle-school pupils are summarized in Christophersen and Rand (1982). In the present sample a principal factor analysis with varimax rotation showed that six factors had eigenvalues greater than one. However, inspection of the scree plot supported the expected two-factor solution (the first six eigenvalues were, respectively, 6.15, 3.85, 1.70, 1.51, 1.31, 1.08). The two-factor solution accounted for 29 % of the total variance. All items loaded satisfactory on their primary factor (i.e., > 35). M_s and M_f showed alphas of .82 and .88, respectively.

Achievement goals. Elliot and McGregor's (2001) achievement goals questionnaire was used to assess participants' achievement goals for the problem-solving tasks. Three items measure each goal construct (mastery-approach: e.g., "*I want to learn as much as possible*"; performance-approach: e.g., "*It is important for me to do better than the other pupils*"; mastery avoidance: e.g., "*I'm afraid that I may not understand the content as thoroughly as I'd like*"; and performance-avoidance: e.g., "*My goal is to avoid performing worse than the other pupils*"). Participants indicated the extent to which they believed each item to be true of them on a scale from 1 (not at all true of me) to 7 (very true of me). Cury, Elliot, Fonseca and Moller's (2006) empirical studies have documented the reliability and validity of using achievement goal questionnaires for middle-school children. Following the procedure of Elliot and McGregor (2001), an EFA was conducted on the 12 achievement-goal items using principal-component extracting with varimax rotation. This analysis yielded four factors with eigenvalues over one, and the factor solution accounted for 66 % of the total variance. All items loaded satisfactory on their primary factor (i.e., > 40). However, the performance-avoidance item *"My fear of performing poorly is what motivates me"* also loaded substantially on the mastery-avoidance factor (.48). Reliability for the performance-avoidance, performance-approach, mastery-avoidance, and mastery-approach goals was .64, .77, .75 and .74, respectively.

Unpleasant Affect (UA) and Pleasant Affect (PA). Norwegian core affect scales for children were used to assess UA and PA. These scales were constructed using the terms from the schematic model presented by Yik, Russell and Feldman Barrett (1999) as guidelines. Three core affect items for each eight octants were collected to systematically sample and cover each region of the circular structure of affect (Bjørnebekk, 2007a). The Pleasant Affect factor consists of the octants "pleasant" and "pleasant activated", and the Unpleasant Affect factor consists of the octants "unpleasant" and "unpleasant activated". Each factor comprises six specific core affect-related adjectives, rated on a five-point scale from "very slightly/not at all" to "very much". The adjectives in the UA scale are "nervous", "discontented", "sad", "unwell", "irritable", "uneasy", and in the PA scale "happy", "contented", "excited", "engaged", "interested", "delighted". The Unpleasant Deactivated and Pleasant Deactivated, the Deactivated, and the Activated factors have been omitted in the present study. In the instructions to the scales in the study, participants were asked to indicate *"to what extent did you feel this way during the problem-solving session"*. Bjørnebekk's (2007b) empirical study has documented the reliability and validity of using the UA and PA factors to assess Norwegian middle-school pupils. A principal factor analysis with varimax rotation showed as expected that only two factors had eigenvalues greater than one (the first three eigenvalues were 4.39, 2.06, .89, respectively). The two-factor solution accounted for 54 % of the total variance. All items loaded satisfactory on their primary factor (i.e., > 50). UA and PA showed alphas of .79 and .84, respectively.

Satisfaction During Problem-Solving (SDPS). This scale is a five-item state version constructed for the present study to measure the overall satisfaction with the experience of taking part in the problem-solving session (the cognitive judgmental aspect). Responses were rated on a scale from 1 (not at all true of me) to 4 (very true of me). A principal factor analysis showed as expected that only one factor had eigenvalues greater than one. All items loaded satisfactory on the SPDS factor (i.e., > 40). The factor accounted for 58 % of the total variance. Reliability for the scale was .81.

Task Well-Being (TWB). The concept of subjective well-being has been operationalized as comprising three separable components: positive affect, negative affect, and life satisfaction (Diener & Lucas, 1999). In line with the SWB concept, the TWB factor is determined by combining the two well-being dimensions: the affective dimension and the cognitive dimension. In other words, on the one hand using activated pleasant affect, activated unpleasant affect, and their balance and on the other the satisfaction factor. Thus, well-being during problem-solving was calculated with the following formula: TWB = SDPS + APA – AUA.

Task-efficacy. Bandura's "guide for constructing self-efficacy scales" (2006) was used to construct a five-item task-efficacy scale. The items focus on pupils' judgment of their confidence in their skills to perform the problem-solving tasks. Pajeres, Britner and Valiante's (2000) empirical studies have documented the reliability and validity of using self-efficacy questionnaires for middle-school pupils. A principal factor analysis showed as expected that only one factor had eigenvalues greater than one. All items loaded satisfactory on the task-efficacy factor (i.e., > 40). The factor accounted for 66 % of the total variance. Reliability for the scale was .87.

Tasks. There were three different types of verbal problems and four different types of numerical problems. The verbal problems were as follows: first, there were anagram problems of four to seven letters that were to be put together to make nouns. Second, there were verbal analogies with one pair of related words and another unpaired word. The pupils were asked to choose one word from among four that had the same relationship to the unpaired word as the first pair. Third, there were six words, one of which was the antonym of a word written in capital letters. The pupils were asked to underline the antonym.

The numerical problems were as follows: first, there were nine or ten two, three and four-digit numbers spread out within a square, and the pupils were asked to draw a ring around the number that was twice as great as another number in the square. Second, there were two lines of numbers, and the pupils were asked to draw a ring around the number on the second line that could be subtracted from a number in the first line to achieve a sum of 25. Third, there were eight numbers, of which two were to be added together to achieve a sum of 1,000. The pupils were instructed to draw two rings around those numbers. Fourth, there were four numbers that were to be added together in each task-square. A pre-test had revealed that the tasks were considered fairly easy by a sample from the same population as the present, although the "real" probability of success was around .60.

Experimental Conditions

The experiment was carried out in a group testing session. The participants were randomly assigned to five different distances to goal conditions. The pupils' motive dispositions were assessed in a session preceding the experimental procedures. Each class received the instructions for the condition to which it was assigned. Then the pupils received a booklet of problem-tasks and were told the following: *"The pages in this booklet contain tasks that are fairly easy. The tasks are, however, different from those you usually work at in school. On the blackboard, I will show you examples of all the types of tasks you will find in this booklet"*. The booklet contained 40 problems. The pupils under all five conditions received a test booklet containing identical sets of tasks. After the pupils had received the booklets, and examples of all the types of tasks had been illustrated, they were given specific instructions for the experimental conditions.

Experimental condition 1 (goal). The pupils were told: "Now you will *take a test* in which you will solve tasks like the ones I have shown you on the blackboard."

Experimental condition 2 (one week). The pupils were told: "Today you will receive a booklet in which you will solve tasks like the ones I have shown you on the blackboard. I will return in about *one week*. You will then take a test with tasks of exactly the same type and which are just as easy to solve as the tasks you have practiced today. Everybody can take the test next week regardless of how many problems they were able to solve today."

Experimental condition 3 (one month). Under this condition the pupils were given exactly the same instructions as under condition 2, except that they were told that I would return in one month instead of one week.

Experimental condition 4 (one year). Under this condition the pupils were given exactly the same instructions as under condition 2, except that they were told that I would return in one year instead of one week.

Experimental condition 5 (two years). Under this condition the pupils were given exactly the same instructions as under condition 2, except that they were told that I would return in two years instead of one week.

Under all these conditions the pupils were given 22 minutes to work with the booklet. Before starting the tasks, the pupils were asked to answer some questions about their *self-efficacy and achievement goals*. When finished, *the instructions were repeated*. After the participants performed the anagram problems they answered the well-being scales. The instructions concerning the test to come were entirely fictitious. The pupils were debriefed following the conclusion of the experiment.

The intention of the instructions. We illustrated examples of all the types of tasks on the blackboard to make the measurement of achievement goals and self-efficacy task-specific. The experimental procedure employed is supposed to induce a so-called noncontigent condition (Raynor, 1974), since success at an immediate task is not required for continuing on to the future test (*the goal*). This procedure was chosen in order to examine the possible effects of a future event that approaches in time on the present arousal of achievement motives, regardless of immediate practice. The effect of temporal distance was expected to be, at best, moderate to low. Therefore, in the test situation it was essential to minimize the occurrence of any other achievement-related cue in order to make possible the effect of temporal distance. This is the reason why no standard for good performance was introduced and why fairly easy tasks were employed. Moderately difficult tasks would have probably increased the general level of arousal of motives and thereby overshadowed a weaker effect of time (Gjesme, 1975).

Results

The time to goal groups were dummy coded by a set of four variables. All interaction product terms were constructed using mean-deviated main effects. Significant interaction effects were interpreted by generating predicted values from the regression equations using scores of one standard deviation above (high) and one below (low) the mean for the continuous variables (Aiken & West, 1991). Hierarchical regression analyses were conducted with the motive to achieve success (M_s) and the motive to avoid failure (M_f) in the first step. The goal distance in time variables (both linear and quadric relationships) was tested in the second step, task-efficacy in the third step and the four achievement goals in the fourth step. In the fifth step, the two-way interactions were added and in the sixth step the three-way interactions were added. We also examined potential mediation (Baron & Kenny, 1986) by performing a Sobel test. Descriptive statistics and correlations between the variables are presented in Table 1.

Table 1. Correlations, means, and standard deviations for all variables in the study.

N = 661	M	SD	1	2	3	4	5	6	7	8	9	10
1. M_s	43.9	6.5	1									
2. M_f	29.2	8.1	-.19**	1								
3. GDT	-	-	-.01	.03	1							
4. Self-Eff	25.1	6.0	.30**	-.13**	-.03	1						
5. Perf. App.	11.2	4.7	.27**	.07	.04	.37**	1					
6. Mast. App.	16.0	3.9	.38**	.02	.05	.45**	.43**	1				
7. Perf. Avoi	11.3	4.6	.13**	.24**	.02	.16**	.40**	.29**	1			
8. Mast. Avoi	10.3	4.4	.20**	.31**	.03	.08*	.39**	.37**	.38**	1		
9. Perf. Tot	22.6	8.5	.18**	-.23**	-.10**	.20**	.09*	.05	.02	-.03	1	
10. TWB	21.6	13.4	.33**	-.23**	-.01	.34**	.12**	.24**	-.00	-.04	.25**	1

Note. *$p < .05$; ** $p < .01$ (2-tailed). Ms = Motive to achieve success; Mf = Motive to avoid failure; GDT = Goal Distance in Time; Self-Eff = Self-Efficacy; Perf. App. = Performance-approach goals; Mast. App. = Mastery-approach goals; Perf. Avoi = Performance-avoidance goals; Mast. Avoi = Mastery-avoidance goals; Perf. Tot. = Performance Total; TWB = Task Well-being.

Motives as Predictors of Task-Efficacy

In the first step, M_s was shown to be a positive predictor of task-efficacy, $F_{1, 659} = 67.10$, $p < .0001$, $R^2 = .09$, whereas M_f was shown to be a negative predictor in the second step, $F_{1, 658} = 4.39$, $p < .05$, R^2 change $= .01$. Thus, the results clearly support the hypothesis regarding the link between the motives and task-efficacy.

Motives, goal distance in time and task-efficacy as predictors of achievement goals

Regressing performance-approach goals on the proposed antecedents yielded a significant effect for the overall model, $F_{7, 653} = 22.20$, $p < .0001$, $R^2 = .19$. In the first step, M_s was documented as a positive predictor, $F_{1, 659} = 49.81$, $p < .0001$, $R^2 = .07$, whereas M_f predicted an additional proportion of variance in the second step, $F_{1, 658} = 10.29$, $p < .001$, R^2 change $= .014$. In the fourth step, task-efficacy also made a contribution to performance- approach goal adoption, $F_{1, 653} = 77.39$, $p < .0001$, $R^2 = .10$.

M_s was shown to be a positive predictor of mastery-approach goals in the first step, $F_{1, 659} = 109.30$, $p < .0001$, $R^2 = .14$. In the second step, M_f was revealed as a positive predictor, $F_{1, 658} = 5.86$, $p < .05$, but the additional proportion of variance predicted was rather minor, R^2 change $= .016$. Moreover, the correlation between M_f and mastery-approach goal adoption was not significant, $r = .02$, $p = .70$. In the fourth step, task-efficacy predicted an additional proportion of mastery-approach goal adoption, $F_{1, 653} = 119.02$, $p < .0001$, $R^2 = .13$.

Regressing performance-avoidance goals on the proposed antecedents yielded a significant effect for the overall model, $F_{7, 653} = 18.68$, $p < .0001$, $R^2 = .11$. In the first step, M_s predicted a significant proportion of the variance, $F_{1, 659} = 13.11$, $p < .001$, $R^2 = .016$. M_f predicted an additional proportion of variance in the second step, $F_{7, 653} = 50.74$, $p < .0001$, R^2 change $= .07$. In the fourth step, task-efficacy also made a contribution to performance-avoidance goal adoption, $F_{1, 653} = 15.67$, $p < .0001$, $R^2 = .02$.

Regressing mastery-avoidance goals on the proposed antecedents yielded a significant effect for the overall model, $F_{7, 653} = 19.25$, $p < .0001$, $R^2 = .17$. In the first step, M_s was documented as a positive predictor, $F_{1, 659} = 27.58$, $p < .0001$, $R^2 = .04$, whereas M_f predicted an additional proportion of variance in the second step, $F_{1, 658} = 96.59$, $p < .0001$, R^2 change $= .12$. Task-efficacy was unrelated to mastery-avoidance adoption. In all four models, regression of achievement goals on the overall model indicates that distance to goal in time is unrelated to goal adoption.

The results clearly support the hypothesis regarding the link between the motives/task-efficacy and the adoption of approach goals. The results also support the hypothesis regarding the links between the motives and the adoption of avoidance goals, with the exception of the unexpected relationship between M_s and the mastery-avoidance goal. The relationship between M_s/task-efficacy and performance-avoidance was also unexpected, but these links were minor.

Basic Model for Predicting Performance

Regressing total performance on the proposed antecedents yielded a significant effect for the overall model, $F_{14, 646} = 7.95, p < .0001, R^2 = .14$. In the first step, M_s predicted a significant proportion of the variance, $F_{1, 659} = 21.67, p < .0001, R^2 = .032$, whereas M_f predicted an additional proportion of variance in the second step, $F_{1, 658} = 29.22, p < .0001$, R^2 change $= .04$. The distance to goal in time predicted an additional proportion of variance in the third step, $F_{4, 654} = 1.92, p < .05$, one-tailed, R^2 change $= .01$. The contribution of a quadratic model of temporal distance to increased amount of explained variance above the linear effect was non-significant. In the next step, task-efficacy made a contribution to performance, $F_{1, 653} = 12.36, p < .0001, R^2 = .02$. None of the achievement goals predicted performance above and beyond the main effects of the motives, the goal distance in time and task-efficacy. Only performance-approach goals were positively related to performance, $r = .09, p < .05$. However, in terms of the interactions, both the two-ways between M_s and the adoption of approach goals were significant: M_s x mastery-approach goal adoption, $F_{1, 648} = 5.64, p < .05, R^2 = .008$, performance-approach x mastery-approach goal adoption, $F_{1, 648} = 6.10, p < .05, R^2 = .01$, and M_s x performance-approach goal adoption, $F_{1, 648} = 4.38, p < .05, R^2 = .008$. More importantly, the three-way interactions M_s x M_f x mastery-approach goal adoption, $F_{1, 643} = 5.92, p < .01, R^2 = .008$, and M_s x M_f x performance-approach goal adoption, $F_{1, 643} = 4.34, p < .05, R^2 = .006$, were significant as well. As depicted in Figure 1, only when M_s is high and M_f is low (the *success-oriented* individual in classical motivation theory) is the adoption of mastery-approach goals associated with increased performance.

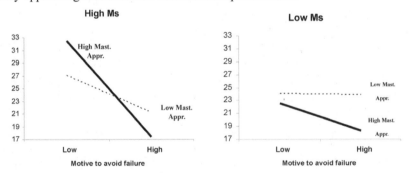

Figure 1. Performance as a function of combinations of the motive to approach success (M_s), the motive to avoid failure (M_f) and mastery-approach goal adoption (Mast. Appr.).

As depicted in Figure 2, performance-approach goal adoption is linked to enhanced performance in success-oriented individuals (High Ms - Low M_f). In contrast, performance-approach goal adoption is linked to a decline in performance in indifferent individuals (Low M_s - Low M_f). Moreover, the interaction between the approach-goals indicates that when a pupil scores high on performance goals, the adoption of a mastery goal is related to decreased performance (Low mastery – High performance $\hat{Y} = 24.70$; High Mastery – High performance $\hat{Y} = 21.26$).

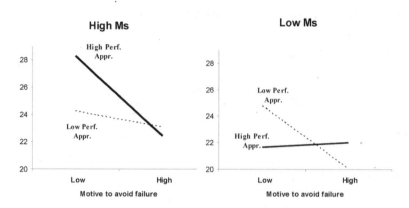

Figure 2. Performance as a function of combinations of the motive to approach success: (M_s), the motive to avoid failure (M_f) and performance-approach goal adoption (Perf. Appr.).

The Slope of the Goal Gradient for Performance

For the mean values of total problems solved correctly, the points on the line for the goal distance in time effect on total performance appear to be scattered around a falling straight line (i.e. they have a more linear form). As we have seen, it is only the linear model of temporal distance that predicts a significant contribution to total performance. The cause of the latter relationship is the pupil's low mean score on verbal performance in the goal condition (see Table 2.). The contribution of a linear model of temporal distance to verbal performance was non-significant. The quadratic models contribution was, however, significant above and beyond the main effects of the motives and the linear model, $F_{1, 656} = 4.45$, $p < .05$, $R^2 = .008$. A visual inspection of the curve and the observation that b1 = 0 and b2 negative (- .28) suggest that the relationship between time to goal and verbal performance is an inverted U-shaped function (Aiken & West, 1991). For mean values of performance as a function of goal distance in time, see Table 2.

Table 2. Mean values of performance as a function of goal distance in time.

Condition	Total Performance	SD	Numeric Performance	SD	Verbal Performance	SD
Goal	23.48	8.52	13.48	4.85	10.01	5.73
1 week	23.69	8.39	12.53	5.05	11.15	5.80
1 month	22.32	8.62	11.95	5.54	10.36	5.60
1 year	22.31	8.93	11.68	5.41	10.62	5.71
2 years	21.06	7.53	11.82	4.78	9.23	5.17
Total	**22.63**	**8.46**	**12.33**	**5.17**	**10.31**	**5.64**

However, for numeric performance the quadratic distance to goal in time model predicted an additional proportion of variance in the fourth step, $F_{1, 656} = 3.32$, $p < .05$, one-tailed, R^2 change = .005. As depicted in Figure 3, the effect of distance to goal in time on numeric performance becomes progressively less steep (going from left to right, it is negatively accelerated). Moreover, the fact that b1 is negative and b2 is positive indicates a hyperbolic curve function of time.

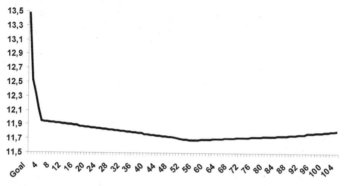

Figure 3. Mean values of numeric performance as a function of goal distance in time.

The two-way interaction of the motive to achieve success and goal distance in time was significant in relation to total performance, $F\ 2,\ 545 = 2.46,\ p < .05$, one-tailed, and almost significant in relation to verbal performance, $F\ 2,\ 545 = 2.09,\ p = .06$, one-tailed. As depicted in Figure 4 the level of performance of pupils high in M_s increases as the goal approaches in time.

As depicted in Figure 4, the curves for pupils high in the motive to achieve success and for pupils low in the motive to achieve success are similar to the curves in Gjesme, Halvari and Thomassen's earlier experiments (see e.g., Gjesme, 1974, Thomassen, Halvari, & Gjesme, 2001).

The performance of pupils high in the motive to avoid failure did not differ significantly as a function of goal distance in time (see Table 4).

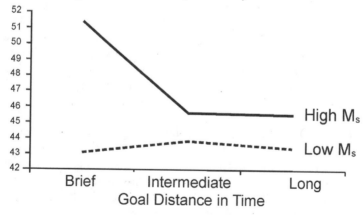

Figure 4. Link between the motive to approach success (Ms) and performance as a function of goal distance in time.

Table 3. Mean values of performance as a function of goal distance in time and the motive to approach success (M_s).

	Distance to Goal in Time	Total Performance		Numeric Performance		Verbal Performance	
		M	SD	M	SD	M	SD
High M_s	Brief	25.7	8.33	14.2	5.53	11.5	6.00
	Intermediate	22.8	7.63	12.7	5.14	10.1	4.97
	Long	22.7	8.50	12.0	5.47	10.7	5.43
Low M_s	Brief	21.5	8.04	11.8	5.11	9.7	5.45
	Intermediate	21.9	9.47	11.3	5.84	10.6	6.16
	Long	21.8	9.51	11.3	5.35	10.5	6.10

Table 4. Mean values of performance as a function of goal distance in time and the motive to avoid failure (M_f).

Motive Level	Distance to Goal in Time	Total Performance		Numeric Performance		Verbal Performance	
		M	SD	M	SD	M	SD
High M_f	Brief	22.2	8.13	12.3	4.96	9.9	5.57
	Intermediate	20.5	8.43	11.3	5.49	9.2	5.37
	Long	20.5	8.95	10.4	5.58	10.0	5.70
Low M_f	Brief	25.0	8.55	13.7	4.90	11.3	5.93
	Intermediate	23.7	8.58	12.4	5.57	11.2	5.67
	Long	24.2	8.59	12.9	4.99	11.2	5.70

Basic Model Predicting TWB

Regressing TWB on the proposed antecedents yielded a significant effect for the overall model, $F_{7, 653} = 24.80$, $p < .0001$, $R^2 = .21$. In the first step, M_s predicted a significant proportion of the variance, $F_{1, 659} = 81.27$, $p < .0001$, $R^2 = .11$, whereas M_f predicted an additional proportion of variance in the second step, $F_{1, 658} = 23.40$, $p < .0001$, R^2 change $= .03$. The goal distance in time was unrelated to TWB. Moreover, the contribution of task-efficacy, $F_{1, 657} = 47.81$, $p < .0001$, $R^2 = .06$, indicates that the higher the task-efficacy, the higher the TWB. In the next step, the achievement goals also made a contribution, $F_{4, 653} = 2.34$, $p < .05$, $R^2 = .01$. However, only the mastery-approach goal, $\beta = .11$, $t_{7, 653} = 2.37$, $p < .05$, and mastery-avoidance goal adoption, $\beta = -.09$, $t_{7, 653} = -2.15$, p $< .05$, yielded a significant unique contribution. As seen in Table 1, it is only mastery-approach goal adoption ($r = .24$) and performance-approach goal adoption ($r = .12$) that show a significant correlation with TWB. Furthermore, the M_s x M_f x performance-approach goal adoption interaction, $F_{1, 650} = 4.94$, $p < .05$, $R^2 = .01$, indicates that it is only when M_s is high and M_f is low that performance-approach goal adoption is associated with increased TWB. Thus, the results indicate that, among the achievement goals, mastery-approach goal adoption is the central predictor of TWB.

The results do not provide support for a hierarchical model with performance-approach, performance-avoidance or mastery-avoidance goal adoption mediating the relationship M_s/M_f and TWB because the avoidance goals did not predict TWB and the relationship between performance-approach goal adoption and TWB is too low. However, the utilization of Sobel's procedure for testing the significance of indirect, mediational relationships substantiated a partial mediation process of mastery-approach goal adoption on the relationship between M_s and TWB (see Figure 5).

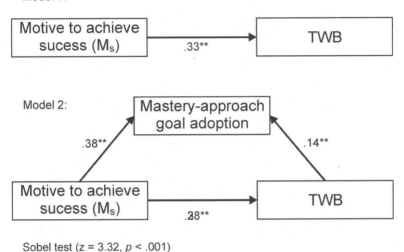

Sobel test (z = 3.32, p < .001)

Figure 5. Mastery-approach goal as a mediator of the positive influence of the motive to achieve success on task well-being.

Discussion

The results of this study strongly support certain predictions of classical motivation theory. The motive to avoid failure was a positive predictor of avoidance goal adoption (both performance and mastery) and a negative predictor of task-efficacy, performance and task well-being. Conversely, the motive to achieve success was a positive predictor of approach goal adoption (both mastery and performance), task-efficacy, performance and task well-being. M_s was, however, also positively related to mastery-avoidance goal adoption. This was unexpected and is difficult to explain. It may be related to a greater susceptibility to response tendency in children.

The assumed mediation of achievement goals on the relationship between motives and performance in the hierarchical social-cognitive model was not independently substantiated since achievement goals did not predict performance. However, in line with the hierarchical model, the relationship between performance-approach goals and performance was significant, although rather minor. A hierarchical model with mastery-approach goal adoption (partially) mediating the relationship between M_s and task well-being was supported. The influence of motives and task-efficacy on TWB was not mediated by any other type of achievement goal. The results regarding how children's goal adoption moderates the effect of the achievement motives were also important. Due to the fact that most research on achievement goals has been conducted on younger adults (i.e., undergraduates) or is related to sports and exercise, the results from studies of schoolchildren in classrooms situations are of great value to the field. The results show that adoption of mastery-approach goals is associated with increased performance only when M_s is high and M_f is low (the success-oriented individual in classical motivation theory). Furthermore, performance-approach adoption is related to enhanced performance in success-oriented individuals (High M_s - Low M_f). In contrast, performance-approach goal adoption is related to a decrease in the level of performance in indifferent individuals (Low M_s - Low M_f). It is important to note that regulation through approach goals in children seems to have no effect – or negative effect – for all motive constellations, with the exception of the success-oriented. It therefore appears that the achievement approach goals have a similar moderating effect on the relationship between motives and performance as perceived intrinsic instrumentality had in classical motivational theory (Atkinson, 1964). In summary, the results strongly support a hierarchical model of approach achievement motivation, in which M_s gives rise to mastery approach and performance approach goals and the combination of M_s and the adoption of approach goals seems to be the combination that best predicts task well-being and performance. The results also indicate that in children the motive to achieve success not only has an indirect effect on the motivational outcomes but a direct effect as well. Although the relationships between M_f and the achievement goals and M_f and task-efficacy were as expected, the hierarchical avoidance model was not supported since the avoidance goals predicted neither task well-being nor performance. These results suggest that there is more to motivation than cognitive contents such as achievement goals and task-efficacy. Furthermore, based on the results, it may be suggested that success-oriented children should be encouraged to adopt both types of approach goals. For indifferent children and children high in M_f, however, this strategy may have an unwanted effect.

The level of performance of pupils high in the motive to achieve success increased as the goal approached in time. The performance of pupils high in the motive to avoid failure did not, however, differ significantly as a function of goal distance. As mentioned above, the results also revealed a positive link between M_s and task-efficacy and a negative link between M_f and task-efficacy. A possible explanation of the non-significant M_f x distance in time interaction might be that for individuals high in M_f the tasks appeared to be of intermediate difficulty. According to Atkinson's theory of motivation (1964), the motives should be most aroused in these situations. The increased level of avoidance motivation (T_f) may thereby overshadow the effect of temporal distance. The strong main effect of M_f at all distances in time support this explanation. Conversely, for pupils high in M_s the tasks appear to be relatively easy. This implies that for individuals high in M_s motives are not activated when the goal is at some distance in time. This might explain the M_s x distance in time effect on performance. Further investigations along this line must take into account differences in task-efficacy (or P_s) among individuals high in M_s and individuals high in M_f.

A main effect of distance in time is that performance increases as physical time distance decreases. Furthermore, the effect of goal distance in time follows a hyperbolic type function with regard to numeric performance, but not verbal performance.

In summary, the findings appear to indicate the following: the functional significance of achievement goals is overemphasized in children; nearness to goal augments performance for pupils high in the motive to approach success; the slope of the goal gradient for numeric performance is hyperbolic as the goal approaches in time; and high M_s, high task-efficacy and low M_f predict high performance and high task well-being at all distances from a goal.

It should be noted that the experiment was partly a replication and partly an extension, of earlier experiments in the field, and the instruments used have previously been validated and tested in a number of studies under different conditions and in different countries. The design, theoretical grounds and use of instruments are therefore consistent with generalizable principles (conceptual, theoretical and methodological). Certain findings in the present study might therefore be of a more basic nature and reflect psychological mechanisms beneath the cultural artifacts ("*a global picture*"). There are, however, certain features related to the sample and the setting that constrain the generalizability of the results. The sample consists of sixth-graders from schools in Oslo with average or just-above-average scores on national mathematics and reading tests. In this respect the findings might be limited by virtue of context or culture ("*a local picture*").

References

Aiken, L. S., & West, S. G. (1991). *Multiple Regression: Testing and interpreting interactions*. Newbury Park, CA: Sage.

Ainslie, G. (1992). *Picoeconomics: The strategic interaction of successive motivational states within the person*. New York: Cambridge University Press.

Ainslie, G., & Haslam, N. (1992). Hyperbolic discounting. In G. Loewenstein & J. Elster (Eds.), *Choice over time* (pp. 57-92). New York: Russell Sage Foundation.

Ames, C. (1984). Achievement attribution and self-instruction under competitive and individualistic goal structures. *Journal of Educational Psychology, 76*, 478-487.

Atkinson, J. W. (1957). Motivational determinants of risk-taking behavior. *Psychological Review, 64*, 359-372.

Atkinson, J. W. (1964). *Introduction to motivation*. New York: Van Nostrand.

Atkinson, J. W., & Birch, D. (1970). *The dynamics of action*. New York: Wiley.

Bandura, A. (2006). Guide to the construction of self-efficacy scales. In F. Pajares & T. Urdan (Eds.), *Self-efficacy beliefs of adolescents* (Vol. 5, pp. 307-337). Greenwich, CT: Information Age Publishing.

Baron, R., & Kenny, D. (1986). The moderator-mediator variable distinction in social psychological research: Conceptual, strategic, and statistical considerations. *Journal of Personality and Social Psychology, 51*, 1173-1182.

Barron, K. E., & Harackiewicz, J. M. (2001). Achievement goals and optimal motivation: Testing multiple goal models. *Journal of Personality and Social Psychology, 80*, 706-722.

Bjørnebekk, G. (2007a). *Motivation and distance to goal in time: Their effect on cognitive and affective manifestations*. Unpublished doctoral dissertation, University of Oslo, Norway.

Bjørnebekk, G. (2007b). Reinforcement sensitivity theory and major motivational and self-regulatory processes in children. *Personality and Individual Differences, 43*, 1980-1990.

Christophersen, K.-A., & Rand, P. (1982). Factor structure of the achievement motives scale (AMS): two factors – two samples. *Scandinavian Journal of Educational Research, 26*, 13-28.

Cury, F., Elliot, A., Fonseca, D. D., & Moller, A. C. (2006). The social-cognitive model of achievement motivation and the 2 x 2 achievement framework. *Journal of Personality and Social Psychology, 90*, 666-679.

Damasio, A. R. (1994). *Descartes' error*. New York: Grosset/Putnam.

Diener, C. I., & Dweck, C. S. (1978). An analysis of learned helplessness: Continuous changes in performance, strategy and achievement cognitions following failure. *Journal of Personality and Social Psychology, 36,* 451-462.

Diener, E., & Lucas, R. E. (1999). Personality and subjective well-being. In D. Kahneman, E. Diener, & N. Schwarz (Eds.), *Well-being: The foundations of hedonic psychology* (pp. 213-229). New York: Russell-Sage.

Dweck, C. S. (1986). Motivational processes affecting learning. *American Psychologist, 41,* 1040-1048.

Dweck, C. S., & Leggett, E. L. (1988). A social-cognitive approach to motivation and personality. *Psychological Review, 95,* 256-273.

Elliot, A. J. (1999). Approach and avoidance motivation and achievement goals. *Educational Psychologist, 34,* 169-189.

Elliot, A. J. (2005). A conceptual history of the achievement goal construct. In A. J. Elliot & C. S. Dweck (Eds.), *Handbook of competence and motivation* (pp. 52-72). New York: Guilford.

Elliot, A. J., & Church, M. A. (1997). A hierarchical model of approach and avoidance achievement motivation. *Journal of Personality and Social Psychology, 72,* 218-232.

Elliot, A. J., & Harackiewicz, J. M. (1996). Approach and avoidance achievement goals and intrinsic motivation: A mediational analysis. *Journal of Personality and Social Psychology, 70,* 461-475.

Elliot, A. J., & McGregor, H. A. (2001). A 2 x 2 achievement goal framework. *Journal of Personality and Social Psychology, 80,* 501-519.

Elliot, A. J., & Thrash, T. M. (2001). Achievement goals and the hierarchical model of achievement motivation. *Educational Psychology Review Volume,13,* 139-156.

Elliot, A. J., & Thrash, T. M. (2002). Approach-avoidance motivation in personality: Approach-avoidance temperaments and goals. *Journal of Personality and Social Psychology, 82,* 804-818.

Elliott, E. S., & Dweck, C. S. (1988). Goals: An approach to motivation and achievement. *Journal of Personality and Social Psychology, 54,* 5-12.

Emmons, R. A. (1989). The personal striving approach to personality. In L. A. Pervin (Ed.), *Goal concept in personality and social psychology* (pp. 87-126). Hillsdale, NJ: Erlbaum.

Gjesme, T. (1974). Goal distance in time and its effects on the relation between achievement motives and performance. *Journal of Research in Personality, 8,* 161-171.

Gjesme, T. (1975). Slope of gradients for performance as a function of achievement motive, goal distance in time, and future time orientation. *Journal of Psychology, 91,* 143-160.

Gjesme, T. (1979). Future time orientation as a function of achievement motives, ability, delay of gratification, and sex. *Journal of Psychology, 101,* 173-188.

Gjesme, T. (1981). Is there any future in achievement motivation? *Motivation and Emotion, 2,* 115-138.

Gjesme, T. (1983). Motivation to approach success (Ts) and motivation to avoid failure (Tf). *Scandinavian Journal of Educational Research, 27,* 145-164.

Gjesme, T. (1996). Future-time orientation and motivation. In T. Gjesme & R. Nygård (Eds.), *Advances in motivation* (pp. 210-222). Scandinavian University Press.

Gjesme, T., & Nygård, R. (1970). *Achievement related motives: Theoretical considerations and construction of a measuring instrument.* Unpublished report, University of Oslo.

Halvari, H. (1991). Effects of goal distance in time on relation between achievement motives and energy consumption by aerobic processes during 1500 m running. *Perceptual and Motor Skills, 72,* 1143-1165.

Husman, J., & Shell, D. F. (2008). Beliefs and perceptions about the future: A measurement of future time perspective. *Learning and Individual Differences, 18,* 166-175.

Kauffman, D. F., & Husman, J. (2004). Effects of time perspective on student motivation: Introduction to a special issue. *Educational Psychology Review, 16,* 1-7.

LeDoux, J. (1996). *The emotional brain. The mysterious underpinnings of emotional life.* New York: Simon & Schuster.

.

Lens, W., Simmons, J., & Dewitte, S. (2001). Student motivation and self-regulation as a function of future time perspective and perceived instrumentality. In S. Volet & S. Järvelä (Eds.), *Motivation in learning contexts: Theoretical advances and methodological implications* (pp. 233-248). Amsterdam; New York: Pergamon.

Lewin, K. (1935). *A dynamic theory of personality: Selected papers.* New York: McGraw-Hill.

Linnenbrink, E. A., & Pintrich, P. R. (2002). Achievement goal theory and affect: An asymmetrical bidirectional model. *Educational Psychologist, 12,* 69-78.

Manderlink, G., & Harackiewicz, J. H. (1984). Proximal versus distal goal setting and intrinsic motivation. *Journal of Personality and Social Psychology, 47,* 918-928.

McClelland, D.C. (1955) 'Notes for revised theory of motivation'. In D.C. McClelland (Ed.), *Studies in motivation* (pp. 226–234). New York: Appleton-Century-Crofts.

McClelland, D. C., Atkinson, J. W., Clark, R. A., & Lowell, E. L. (1953). *The achievement motive.* New York: Appelton-Century-Crofts.

Middelton, M. J., & Midgley, C. (1997). Avoiding the demonstration of lack of ability: An under explored aspect of goal theory. *Journal of Educational Psychology, 89,* 710-718.

Miller, N. E. (1944). Experimental studies of conflict. In J. McV. Hunt (Ed.), *Personality and the behavior disorders (Vol. 1,* pp. 431-465). New York: Ronald Press.

Moller, A. C., & Elliot, A. J. (2006). The 2 x 2 achievement goal framework: An overview of empirical research. In A. V. Mitel (Eds.). *Focus on educational psychology* (pp. 307-326). Nova Science Publishers.

Murray, H. A. (1959). Preparations for the scaffold of a comprehensive system. In S. Koch (Ed.), *Psychology: A study of a science. Formulation of the person and the social context* (Vol. 3, pp. 7-54). New York: Knopf.

Nicholls, J. G. (1989). *The competitive ethos and democratic education.* Cambridge, MA: Harvard University Press.

Nicholls, J. G., Patashnick, M. & Nolen, S. (1985). Adolescents' theories of education. *Journal of Educational Psychology, 77,* 683–692.

Nolen, S. (1988). Reasons for studying. Motivational orientation and study strategies. *Cognition and Instruction, 5,* 269-287.

Pintrich, P. R. (2000). The role of goal orientation in self-regulated learning. In M. Boekaerts, P. R. Pintrich & M. Zeidner (Eds.), *Handbook of self-regulation* (pp. 451-502). San Diego: Academic Press.

Pajeres, F., Britner, S. L., & Valiante, G. (2000). Relation between achievement goals and self-beliefs of middle school students in writing and science. *Contemporary Educational Psychology, 25,* 406-422.

Rawsthorne, L., & Elliot, A. (1999). Achievement goals and intrinsic motivation: A meta-analytic review. *Personality and Social Psychology Review, 3,* 326-344.

Raynor, J. O. (1974). Relationships between achievement-related motives, future orientation, and academic performance. In J. W. Atkinson & J. O. Raynor (Eds.), *Motivation and achievement* (pp. 173-180). Washington, D. C.: Winston & Sons.

Simons, J., Vansteenkiste M., Lens W., & Lacante, M. (2004). Placing motivation and future time perspective theory in temporal perspective. *Educational Psychology Review, 16,* 121-139.

Steel, P., & König, C. J. (2006). Integrating theories of motivation. *Academy of Management Review, 31,* 889-913.

Thomassen, T. O., Halvari, H., & Gjesme, T. (2001). Experimentally induced effects of goal distance in time on the relations between achievement motives, future time orientation and indication of performance in sport. In A. Efklides, J. Kuhl, & R. Sorrentino (Eds.), *Trends and Prospects in Motivation Research* (pp. 47-63). The Netherlands: Kluwer Academic Publishers.

Trope, Y., & Liberman, N. (2003). Temporal construal. *Psychological Review, 110,* 403-421.

Yik, M. S., Russell, J. A., & Feldman Barrett, L. (1999). Structure of the self-reported current affect: Integration and beyond. *Journal of Personality and Social Psychology, 77,* 600-619.

Interest and Efficacy Beliefs in Self-Regulated Learning

Does the Task Make a Difference?

Mary Ainley, Sarah Buckley, & Joanne Chan

Interest and self efficacy are variables that have been shown to be associated with the development of self-regulated learners (Zimmerman, 2002), but there are many unanswered questions concerning how they operate to support learning. This can be investigated at a number of levels. We can take a global perspective and explore how interest and self-efficacy typically operate. To do this effectively requires large representative samples of students and a range of representative learning tasks and contexts. If we shift the focus from the global level to the individual student we can investigate students' typical behaviour. From this perspective, interest is treated as a trait-like characteristic or predisposition that describes what you might expect to see in students' behaviour across a range of learning tasks and contexts. The focus can be shifted again to the local level of a specific task at a particular point in time and within a particular learning context. At this level the questions concern identifying interest and self-efficacy as sets of interconnected processes linked to specific types of tasks or to specific contexts. Hence, to understand what self-regulated learning means, global statements about the general functioning of self-regulatory processes need to be complemented with knowledge of local task and context effects. Teachers are often encouraged to give attention to development of both interest and efficacy beliefs in their students (e.g., Alfassi, 2003) but how this can be achieved is not always clear. Interest and self-efficacy do not necessarily contribute in similar ways across learning tasks and contexts. In this chapter we examine a number of critical questions concerning how interest and self-efficacy interact in relation to students' behaviour on specific tasks from different learning domains. Findings of three of our studies will be presented to illustrate the ways that interest and self-efficacy operate at the local level of three different tasks.

It has been frustratingly clear throughout the history of education that curriculum activities judged by teachers to be interesting are not necessarily perceived in that way by their students. Over the last 50 years, development and introduction of new technologies into classrooms has been heralded with the promise that technology would take care of student motivation. This was true for the Skinnerian teaching machines in the 1960s (Skinner, 1968) and also when microcomputers were introduced in education in the early 1980s. Curiosity, interest, excitement and enjoyment were cited as the basic motivation that would underpin enhanced learning with microcomputers. However, research that followed often showed that the motivational effects observed were more likely to be temporary responses to the novelty of the technology rather than engagement with the substantive learning (Lepper, 1985; Lepper & Chabay, 1985). *Catching* students' interest and *holding* students' interest is not the same thing. As Mitchell (1993) demonstrated in his mathematics classrooms, computer tasks were effective in triggering students' interest but did not keep students engaged with the mathematical content.

It is often difficult for teachers to apply the findings of educational research to their classroom practice. One of the difficulties lies in the difference between trait-level knowledge of the relationships between motivation and learning, and what students do in the localized time and space of a specific classroom task where a range of task and contextual variables are also part of the equation. For the purposes of this chapter we will put to one side the influence of broader contextual variables, such as relationships with classroom peers, and focus on interest and self-efficacy as on-task processes. In particular, we explore two questions concerning how interest and self-efficacy function in order to provide some answers that may be informative for researchers and for those engaged in curriculum design and delivery. Firstly, *at what point(s) in the self-regulated learning sequence do interest and self-efficacy make a significant contribution?* In answering this question we will highlight the importance of distinguishing clearly between different forms of interest, the more general predisposition of individual interest, and the local task specific situational interest. Secondly, *do interactions between interest and self-efficacy vary between tasks from different subject domains?* Before addressing these questions we give a brief overview of the variables that are central to this investigation: interest and self-efficacy.

Interest and Self-Efficacy

Interest has been shown to have a powerful facilitative effect on cognitive performance and affective experience across individuals, knowledge domains and subject areas (Hidi & Harackiewicz, 2000; Hidi & Renninger, 2006). Whether approached as individual interest, which refers to a predisposition to engage with contents from the relevant domain (Renninger, 1998; Schiefele, 1991), or situational interest, which refers to interest generated by specific features of the environment or task (Hidi & Berndorff, 1998; Schraw & Lehman, 2001), interest has been shown to predict learning and achievement outcomes.

Recent literature on interest has shifted the focus to considering interest as an active state (e.g., Ainley, 2007; Hidi, Renninger, & Krapp, 2004; Krapp, 2002; Sansone & Thoman, 2005). This perspective highlights that interest, as a psychological state, involves positive affect and focused attention. It has been described as the mobilization of energy for engagement and interaction with specific objects, activities, or events (Izard & Ackerman, 2000). As we have suggested elsewhere (Ainley, Corrigan, & Richardson, 2005), interest serves an activation function that supports approach, inspection, exploration, and acquisition of further information about the object or problem. Interest involves positive affect and often occurs in combination with other positive feelings such as enjoyment. It may also occur in combination with negative feelings such as anxiety or anger.

Self-efficacy has been shown to be an important motivational factor in self-regulation (Pajares & Schunk, 2001). Self-efficacy is about self-beliefs and the judgment of personal capability to organize and execute actions to attain a certain level of prospective performances. Bandura (1997) postulated four principal sources of self-efficacy information; enactive mastery experiences, vicarious learning, verbal persuasion, and, physiological and psychological feedback. Existing evidence supports the proposal that each of these four sources independently predicts academic self-efficacy with enactive mastery experiences being the most influential source of efficacy information (Usher & Pajares, 2006). Self-efficacy affects people's level of motivation, affective states, actions, thought patterns and resilience (Pajares, 1996). Experiences of success raise self-efficacy and experiences of failure lower self-efficacy. The more efficacious the individual feels, the greater the effort and persistence he or she will invest, especially in the face of setbacks (Bandura, 1989).

Interest and self-efficacy are self-regulatory processes that support learning and a wide range of research findings point to a positive association between them. Both are associated with similar aspects of students' performance, such as increased effort, persistence, and positive emotional reactions (Bandura, 1997; Hidi & Ainley, 2007; Hidi & Renninger, 2006; Zimmerman, 2000).

Some of the earliest evidence on the relationship between interest and self-efficacy was reported in research on vocational interests. According to Social Cognitive Career Theory (Lent, Brown, & Hackett, 1994), vocational interests develop as a function of self-efficacy. Focusing on the development of vocational interests in late elementary school children, Tracey (2002) found that interest and self-efficacy ratings predicted each other equally across a twelve-month interval. This suggests that while self-efficacy can affect one's subsequent interest in an area, interest in that area may also affect subsequent self-efficacy. In relation to specific learning domains, positive associations between interest and self-efficacy have been reported across a range of areas with considerable attention being given to academic domains such as writing and mathematics (e.g., Pajares, 2003; Pajares & Graham, 1999; Pietsch, Walker, & Chapman, 2003). However, it is important in this research to distinguish between the types of interest being investigated. For example, the distinction between individual interest, situational interest, and interest as a psychological state, needs to be articulated more clearly in reporting research on interest and self-efficacy relationships if the findings are to be informative for practice. Individual interest and interest conceptualized as a psychological state (i.e., that which is localized to a particular event) may influence task behaviour in different ways. Hidi, Berndorff and Ainley (2002) reported positive correlations when their study examined the relationship between individual interest for different genres of writing and students' self-efficacy in relation to specific writing tasks. The same result was reported in a later study (Hidi, Ainley, Berndorff, & Del Favero, 2007) when self-efficacy and interest as an on-task state were examined. Both individual interest and interest measured as an on-task state produced positive correlations with self-efficacy for these writing tasks. Yet it is unclear whether the same pattern applies for other domains. Results from our studies using three different types of task are examined in this chapter as a step toward addressing this gap in our knowledge.

At what Point(s) in the Self-Regulated Learning Sequence do Interest and Self-Efficacy make a Significant Contribution?

Self-regulated learning typically refers to a learning sequence or episode that includes a number of phases, for example, Zimmerman and Schunk (2001) referred to phases of forethought, performance, and self-reflection. On the other hand, Pintrich (2004) distinguished four phases: forethought, planning and activation; monitoring; control; and reaction and reflection. These models differ in the roles ascribed to interest and self-efficacy, principally in the phase at which the effects are located. In Zimmerman's (2000) model interest and self-efficacy are driving forces in the forethought phase of self-regulated learning and are conceptualized as self beliefs. Pintrich (2004) also proposed that both interest and self-efficacy play a role at the first phase of self-regulation, the forethought, planning and activation phase. On the other hand, Bandura's (1997) work on the sources of self-efficacy suggests an important function that occurs at the reflection phase of self-regulated learning. Bandura highlighted the role of enactive mastery experiences in the development of self-efficacy. Hence, students' sense of achievement or reflection on their performance when the task has been completed also plays an important role.

Models that have located the contribution of interest to the initial phase of self-regulated learning have predominantly been referring to individual interest. In contrast, Sansone and colleagues (Sansone & Harackiewicz, 1996; Sansone & Thoman, 2005) focus on interest arising from the activity itself (the state). Interest is then seen as a potential mediator between the goals that initiate achievement activities and the strategies and outcomes that result from task engagement. Thus, interest, as psychological state, is triggered by activity and functions throughout the task (performance phase) to maintain behaviour.

The cycle we are considering spans the whole self-regulation sequence. It begins in the forethought phase and is complete in the reaction and reflection phase following task completion. Conventionally, self-efficacy has been measured prior to the designated task with participants providing a rating of confidence in their prospective performance. However, according to Pajares (1996), it is also important to provide opportunities for micro-analytical evaluations of self-efficacy while students are engaged in a task. For example, Lodewyk and Winne (2005) kept track of students' self-efficacy for learning as well as self-efficacy for performance while working on a task. Significant discrepancies between the two aspects of efficacy were observed particularly at the beginning and in the middle of the task. Hence, an important consideration is the changes in levels of interest and self-efficacy that may occur as part of any learning activity. Niemivirta and Tapola (2007) reported reciprocal changes in interest and self-efficacy from a simulated medical laboratory task where students explored the effect of drugs on chemicals in the human body. These results imply a dynamic relationship between the two constructs. In another study (Hidi et al., 2007), self-efficacy beliefs at the forethought phase significantly predicted self-efficacy at the reflection phase and ratings of interest in the task topic were significantly related to pre-task self-efficacy. Of particular significance in this study was the contribution of interest measures to the prediction of self-efficacy at the reflection phase.

Students' reports of their interest in the task[1], recorded at the reflection phase significantly increased the explained variance in students' reflections on their post-task self-efficacy. Therefore, one way that we might expect interest and self-efficacy to interact (corresponding to models proposing that interest operates at the forethought phase of self-regulation) is for initial levels of interest and self-efficacy together to predict how students are likely to feel about their task competence at the end of a task. A second way they may interact is that interest during the task (the performance phase) contributes to feelings of efficacy on task completion.

In the specific research examples that follow interest and self-efficacy have been measured at different points in the task. With multiple measures of both interest and self-efficacy we are able to separate the contributions of these different processes to students' task behaviour. Prior to beginning the task we recorded ratings of individual interest for the task domain. In line with both Zimmerman and Pintrich's models we measured self-efficacy and interest at both forethought and reflection phases of specific learning activities. Consistent with Sansone's position we measured on-task interest by recording students' state of interest mid-way through the task. Individuals who are interested in a task may spend more time on that task and thus develop confidence in their competencies because of the time invested. Successful experience during an activity is an important factor leading to increases in self-efficacy. Therefore, when students are performing an individual problem task it is likely that on-task experiences of interest (states of interest) play an important role in the relationship between initial self-efficacy and self-efficacy at the end of the task. Interest and self-efficacy measures recorded at successive points as students work on open-ended problem tasks can identify how interest and self-efficacy contribute at different phases of self-regulated learning.

Do Interactions between Interest and Self-Efficacy Vary between Subject Domains?

When investigating the character of the relationship between interest and self-efficacy, it is important to consider whether the nature of the observed relationships changes across subject domains. The form of interaction between interest and self-efficacy may vary between, for example, writing on science topics and mathematics. As demonstrated by Stodolsky (1988; Stodolsky & Grossman, 1995) in her work with elementary school students, tasks from different domains are approached differently and these approaches reflect differences not only in the structure of the domain content but characteristic teaching styles in these domains. Stodolsky reported that teaching patterns and classroom lessons were more rigid in mathematics, emphasizing correct procedures and correct solutions, while social studies allowed more room for flexibility. This suggests that the local character of specific problem tasks, for example, task difficulty, is likely to impact on the way

---

[1] Note: In the Hidi et al. 2007 study, the rating of task interest recorded at the end of the task is referred to as a measure of situational interest. Measured as a state this represents the level of interest from the combined sources of students' individual interest and interest triggered by task content and context.

self-efficacy and interest interact.

Task difficulty may also be an important factor in the relationship between interest and self-efficacy because at the local task level self-efficacy may serve as an indicator of the difficulty level of the task (Lodewyk & Winne, 2005). For example, Silvia (2003) investigated participants' ratings of interest in relation to activities of varying difficulty and reported that as self-efficacy increased so did task interest. However, once self-efficacy became very high levels of interest declined. Silvia suggested that in the presence of high levels of self-efficacy and low levels of perceived difficulty, tasks become boring. The complexity of these relationships suggests that understanding the association between self-efficacy and interest also implicates students' perceptions of task difficulty. Thus, in the results described, we have included studies that use a similar task form but with content from different domains.

Interest and Self-Efficacy for Three Problem Tasks

The three studies we describe involved secondary students who were working on problem tasks using *BTL* software. This software provides a vehicle for the presentation of problem issues designed to identify how students use information to address an open-ended problem (e.g., Ainley et al., 2005; Ainley, Hidi, & Berndorff, 2002). Specific problems have ranged from the social impact of technology to problem scenarios that require use of mathematical skills. Each version of the software poses a problem task and provides students with information to help them arrive at an answer. As demonstrated by Lodewyk and Winne (2005), open-ended tasks encourage greater use of students' self-regulatory skills. Study 1 consisted of a writing task where the participants were asked to develop a perspective concerning the impact of technology on modern society (see Ainley & Chan, 2006). The resource information provided them with examples of new technologies, press stories on issues of privacy and modern technology, and information about applications of new nanotechnologies. This study was conducted at approximately the same time as the data was collected for Hidi et al. (2007) where it was clear that on-task interest added to students' sense of efficacy on task completion. Appropriate measures of interest and self-efficacy were therefore included in further studies presenting different types of problem content. The task for Study 2 was a novel investigative problem inviting students to assume the role of a detective investigating a fantasy crime (*Who killed Precious Perseus?*). The information presented included character profiles, forensic exhibits, weather maps, location layout, coroner's reports, and a range of press articles presenting different perspectives on likely causes of death. Students had to identify the murderer, reconstruct the crime, and present evidence to support their answer. In contrast, Study 3 consisted of a mathematical problem (see Buckley, Ainley, & Pattison, 2007). Students were asked to assume the role of a television executive who had to decide which of four programs would fill a vacant slot in prime viewing time. To arrive at a decision students had access to an algebraic formula for estimating cost, statistical information concerning the viewing habits of different age groups, results of program preference polls, and a table of anticipated program success percentages. In sum, the problem task for each study represented a different type of activity; writing, investigation, and mathematical problem solving.

Findings from this set of studies are presented here to explore relationships between interest and self-efficacy and whether these differed across task domains. Do interest and self-efficacy interact across a range of tasks in ways that are consistent with models proposing that interest operates at the forethought phase of self-regulation? If this is the case the evidence will show that the initial state of interest combines with pre-task self-efficacy to predict the level of self-efficacy at the end of the task. A second form of association predicts that interest recorded later in the task makes a further contribution to the prediction of students' self-efficacy at the end of the task. A finding of this nature would demonstrate the importance of processes occurring at performance phases in self-regulated learning, as well as the forethought phase. The final form of association considered was that on-task interest might contribute to self-efficacy at the end of a task by mediating the effects of students' pre-task self-efficacy.

Method and Measures

BTL software used in these studies involves participants being presented with a problem and relevant resource information. Participants have an electronic notepad on which they are able to record notes as they work through the resource information. The recorded notes are then available to assist with the presentation of an answer outlining their solution to the problem with supporting evidence, or their argument in response to a writing task. For each of the three studies students completed the *BTL* task during normal class time. General instructions were given to each class and then participants completed the *BTL* program individually. Class sizes varied between 10 and 35 students according to the specific arrangements in the participating schools.

All of the measures were embedded in the software and were logged automatically as students worked through the task. Interest, self-efficacy, and task difficulty were measured as single item ratings. Each rating was made using a five-point Likert-type scale with the end points clearly labelled. Support for using single-item measures comes from psychological medicine and occupational psychology research (see Ainley & Patrick, 2006) as well as recent work comparing single-term measures of academic emotions with questionnaire measures (Goetz, Frenzel, Pekrun, & Hall, 2006).

The pre-task self-efficacy question asked students to rate how confident they were that they could produce a good answer and post-task asked for a rating of how confident they were that they had produced a good answer (1 = not at all confident; 5 = very confident). On-task interest was recorded three times as students progressed through the task (pre-task, mid-task and post-task). At each measurement point, participants were asked to rate how they were feeling at that moment (1 = not at all interested; 5 = very interested). Perceptions of task difficulty were measured at the beginning of the task in Study 1 and both at the beginning and after task completion in Studies 2 and 3. For the pre-task difficulty ratings participants recorded how difficult they expected the task would be (1 = not at all difficult; 5 = very difficult). When post-task ratings were included participants indicated how difficult the problem was. These sets of ratings from the three problem tasks provided a vehicle for testing whether a general pattern of association existed between interest and self-efficacy irrespective of the type of achievement task considered. Specifically, we were interested in assessing how both interest and self-efficacy contributed to students' efficacy beliefs on task completion as this is an important source of their ongoing self-efficacy (Usher & Pajares, 2006).

Study 1: Interest and Self-Efficacy when Writing on the Impact of Technology

For Study 1 the participants were 81 Year 8 female secondary school students aged between 12 and 15 years ($M = 13.73$, $SD = 0.46$). The overall pattern of their responses indicated that they responded positively to the task of writing about the impact of technology on society. As students commenced the task there was a moderate level of interest, their self-efficacy level was strong, and the task was rated moderately difficult (see Table 1). Self-efficacy was not as strong at the end of the task [$t(79) = 2.47$, $p<.05$] while interest increased [$t(79) = -3.61$, $p<.001$].

The major objective of our analysis was to determine which variables contributed most to students' efficacy beliefs on task completion. Table 1 presents the zero-order correlations between the main variables in the analysis. The significant correlations confirm the predicted link between interest measured as an on-task state and self-efficacy. Significant correlations are shown between pre- and post-task self-efficacy ratings and self-efficacy ratings and all three on-task measures of interest (pre-, mid- and post-). The three successive on-task interest states were also highly correlated. As expected self-efficacy and task difficulty were negatively correlated.

Table 1. Pearson's Correlations among measures of interest, self-efficacy and task-difficulty for Study 1.

	Pre-I	Mid-I	Post-I	SE1	SE2	Pre-D
Pre-task Interest (Pre-I)		.51**	.45**	.33**	.27*	
Mid-task Interest (Mid-I)			.58**	.48**	.41**	
Post-task Interest (Post-I)				.25*	.53**	
Pre-task efficacy (SE1)					.40**	-.32**
Post-task efficacy (SE2)						
Pre-task Difficulty (Pre-D)						
Mean	2.95	3.02	3.42	3.50	2.86	3.16
SD	.96	1.04	1.06	.86	1.00	1.00

Note: Only significant correlations ($p<.05$) are presented: * $p<.05$, ** $p<.01$.

To assess the contribution of on-task interest to the predictive relationship between pre-task self-efficacy and students' reported sense of efficacy when the task was completed, a series of multiple regressions were completed. Post-task efficacy was the criterion variable and at the first step in the analysis pre-task self-efficacy and task difficulty were entered as predictors. Although inclusion of the pre-task interest variable increased the amount of variance explained, it did not make an independent contribution. Self-efficacy was the only significant independent predictor. In each of the successive steps in the analysis one of the three on-task interest ratings was added. The results are shown in Table 2.

Table 2. Prediction of post-task self-efficacy for Study 1: Regression statistics.

Predictors	β	F	df	R^2
Step 1		6.95	(2,77)	.15**
SE1	**.37****			
Pre-D	-.06			
Step 2		5.50	(3,76)	.18**
SE1	**.31***			
Pre-D	-.09			
Pre-I	.17			
Step 3		7.06	(3,76)	.22***
SE1	.23			
Pre-D	-.07			
Mid-I	**.29***			
Step 4		13.78	(3,76)	.36***
SE1	**.26***			
Pre-D	-.08			
Post-I	**.46****			

Note: *p<.05, **p<.01, ***p<.001; Significant predictors in **bold**.

Task difficulty did not add to the prediction of post-task efficacy at any stage in the analysis. The contribution of the interest variables increased as students progressed through the task. At the mid-task stage, the interest rating was the only significant predictor and by the end of the task when the amount of variance explained had increased from an initial 15% to 36%, post-task interest was the strongest predictor. The contribution of self-efficacy was reduced suggesting a mediation effect. This was tested separately using the Sobel test which confirmed that the predictive effect of the pre-task self-efficacy rating was partially mediated by post-task interest (Sobel = 2.14, p<.05). The same pattern was observed at the third step in the series of regressions where mid-task interest mediated the self-efficacy effect (Sobel = 2.22, p<.05).

For the students writing on the impact of technology the pattern of relationships was very similar to that reported by in the study by Hidi et al. (2007), also a writing task. In both studies pre-task interest and self-efficacy were correlated and inclusion of measures of interest across the performance phase of the task added to the prediction of self-efficacy on task completion. So, despite the differences in the specific writing topic, the country in which the study was conducted, and the gender composition of the participants in the two studies, a similar pattern of relationships was observed between the self-efficacy and on-task interest variables. Self-efficacy and interest jointly contributed to students' self-efficacy on task completion with some evidence that on-task interest partially mediated the effects of pre-task self-efficacy. What about other types of tasks? How far can this finding be generalized to tasks from different domains? To explore the influence of local task character on the interaction between interest and self-efficacy different types of tasks need to be considered.

Studies 2 and 3: Self-Efficacy and Interest under Different Task Conditions

For Study 2 participants were 133 Year 9 secondary school students (63 female and 70 male students), aged between 13 and 16 years ($M = 14.41$, $SD = 0.43$). The same pattern of strong positive correlations as was observed in Study 1 between the three on-task interest ratings was evident in the Study 2 responses (see Table 3). Pre-task self-efficacy and post-task efficacy were positively correlated. However, the interest and efficacy relationships showed some differences. The pre-task self-efficacy rating was significantly correlated with only two of the on-task interest ratings (pre- and post-) and the strength of these associations was lower than those observed in Study 1. In contrast, all three on-task interest measures were positively correlated with post-task efficacy and, as was the case for Study 1, the post-task correlation was the strongest. The same negative correlation between pre-task self-efficacy and pre-task difficulty was observed but there was no significant efficacy and post-task difficulty correlation. The pre- and post-task difficulty ratings were significantly correlated.

Table 3. Pearson's Correlations among measures of interest, self-efficacy and task-difficulty for Study 2.

	Pre-I	Mid-I	Post-I	SE1	SE2	Pre-D	Post-D
Pre-task Interest (Pre-I)		.60**	.65**	.18*	.35**		.21*
Mid-task Interest (Mid-I)			.60**		.28**		.19*
Post-task Interest (Post-I)				.18*	.51**		
Pre-task efficacy (SE1)					.44*	-.45**	
Post-task efficacy (SE2)							
Pre-task Difficulty (Pre-D)							.47**
Post-Difficulty (Post-D)							
Mean	3.20	3.27	3.23	3.40	3.15	3.39	3.33
SD	1.16	1.16	1.20	1.02	1.14	.96	1.05

Note: Only significant correlations ($p<.05$) are presented: * $p<.05$, **$p<.01$.

Inspection of the mean scores for the Study 2 task variables indicated that the on-task interest level was relatively strong and was maintained across the task. Efficacy and task difficulty ratings were both relatively high as the task commenced. This level was maintained for the task difficulty estimate but, as was the case in Study 1, students' confidence in their ability to produce a good answer decreased significantly [$t(131) = 2.44$, $p<.05$].

The same form of regression analysis as used with Study 1 was applied to these data (see Table 4) with the difference that the post-task difficulty rating was added in the last step of the regression. Again inclusion of the on-task interest variables added to the amount of variance in post-task efficacy explained by pre-task self-efficacy. Pre-task difficulty did not add to the predictive power of the variable set but post-task difficulty did. Each of the on-task interest variables added to the prediction but the relationship with pre-task self-efficacy was an additive contribution rather than mediation. As with the writing studies the interest students experienced while doing the task contributed to self-efficacy levels on task completion.

Table 4. Prediction of post-task self-efficacy for Study 2: Regression statistics.

Predictors	β	F	df	R^2
Step 1		16.86	(2,129)	.21***
SE1	.50***			
Pre-D	.12			
Step 2		16.21	(3,128)	.28***
SE1	.43***			
Pre-D	.07			
Pre-I	**.27****			
Step 3		15.53	(3,128)	.27***
SE1	.47***			
Pre-D	.10			
Mid-I	**.25****			
Step 4		27.50	(3,128)	.39***
SE1	.39***			
Pre-D	.05			
Post-I	**.44*****			
Step 5		23.92	(4,127)	.43***
SE1	.40***			
Pre-D	.16			
Post-I	**.46*****			
Post-D	**-.22****			

Note: *$p<.05$, **$p<.01$, ***$p<.001$; Significant predictors in **bold**.

Study 3 was completed by 126 year 8 male and female secondary students (72 female and 54 male students) aged between 12 and 14 years ($M = 13.78$, and $SD = 0.38$). All three on-task interest variables were strongly and positively correlated as in the previous studies (see Table 5). Pre-task efficacy was significantly and negatively correlated with pre-task difficulty.

Study 3 showed some important differences in the pattern of correlations between interest, efficacy and difficulty. On-task interest variables were significantly and positively correlated with post-task difficulty ratings but were not significantly correlated with pre-task self-efficacy. Mid- and post-task interest ratings were significantly correlated with post-task efficacy. Unlike Study 2 there was a significant negative correlation between pre-task difficulty and post-task difficulty ratings suggesting a mismatch between expectations and task reality. However, there was a significant positive correlation between post-task efficacy and pre-task difficulty ratings suggesting that students who were confident about their performance on task completion were more likely to have initially perceived the task as difficult. In addition, there were some important features of the overall level of students' responses. Moderate levels of on-task interest were reported which showed a slight decrease from pre- to mid-task and then a significant increase at the post-task stage [$t(125)$ = -3.20, $p<.01$]. Efficacy ratings decreased significantly from pre- to post-task [$t(125)$ = 3.38, $p=.001$] and difficulty ratings increased substantially across the task [$t(125)$ = -6.26, $p<.001$].

Table 5. Pearson's Correlations among measures of interest, self-efficacy and task-difficulty for Study 3.

	Pre-I	Mid-I	Post-I	SE1	SE2	Pre-D	Post-D
Pre-task Interest (Pre-I)		.50**	.44**				.26**
Mid-task Interest (Mid-I)			.60**		.18*	.22*	.30**
Post-task Interest (Post-I)					.26**		.28**
Pre-task efficacy (SE1)					-.25**	-.41**	.48**
Post-task efficacy (SE2)						.38**	
Pre-task Difficulty (Pre-D)							-.23*
Post-Difficulty (Post-D)							
Mean	3.29	3.10	3.42	3.49	3.00	2.94	3.85
SD	1.06	1.21	1.27	.90	1.16	1.08	.99

Note: Only significant correlations ($p<.05$) are presented: * $p<.05$, ** $p<.01$.

The same regression analyses were completed for these data (see Table 6) as for Study 2. Whereas in the previous studies pre-task difficulty had not played a significant role, for Study 3 pre-task difficulty consistently predicted post-task efficacy and on-task interest only made a significant contribution at the post-task stage. Consistent with the negative correlation between pre-task self-efficacy and both pre-task difficulty and post-task efficacy, the contribution of pre-task self-efficacy to the prediction of post-task efficacy was not independent of the stronger positive contribution of pre-task difficulty.

In sum, analyses of the interrelationships between interest, efficacy, and difficulty in Studies 2 and 3 suggested that associations between these variables were task dependent. For the investigative task in Study 2, interest added to the prediction of post-task efficacy consistently throughout the task, as did pre-task self-efficacy. That is, interest and self-efficacy together contributed to students' confidence in their performance. On the other hand, for the mathematical problem in Study 3 interest only made a significant contribution to efficacy at the post-task stage, and, in direct contrast to Study 2, pre-task difficulty was the variable that significantly contributed to post-task efficacy throughout the task. Hence, for the mathematical problem task it appears that students' initial expectation concerning the difficulty of the task was especially critical for confidence in their performance at the end of the task. These findings raise a number of questions concerning the importance of specific features of task content for the way that variables such as interest and self-efficacy function.

Table 6. Prediction of post-task self-efficacy for Study 3: Regression statistics.

Predictors	β	F	df	R^2
Step 1		11.35	(2,123)	.16***
SE1	-.11			
Pre-D	**.34*****			
Step 2		7.57	(3,122)	.16***
SE1	-.11			
Pre-D	**.34*****			
Pre-I	.03			
Step 3		7.70	(3,122)	.16***
SE1	-.12			
Pre-D	**.32****			
Mid-I	.06			
Step 4		11.76	(3,122)	.22***
SE1	-.17			
Pre-D	**.30****			
Post-I	**.27****			
Step 5		8.84	(4,121)	.23***
SE1	-.19			
Pre-D	**.31****			
Post-I	**.26****			
Post-D	.05			

Note: *p<.05, **p<.01, ***p<.001; Significant predictors in **bold**.

For the writing task in Study 1 and the investigative task in Study 2 the combination of pre-task self-efficacy and on-task interest contributed to the prediction of students' sense of mastery after they had submitted their answer. These findings are consistent with those reported by Hidi et al. (2007). In Study 2 which included both pre- and post-task difficulty ratings the pattern was the same and post-task difficulty was a negative predictor. However, for the mathematical problem presented in Study 3, there was a substantial mismatch between the expected difficulty level (pre-task rating) and what many students experienced as they worked through the task. This finding is important in light of the nature of the scenario that was presented. The scenario asked the student to take on the role of the program director of a major television network who was required to decide on the most appropriate program to air at a prime viewing time. Although the task involved using mathematical information to determine and to justify answers to the problem, it was possible that some students interpreted this as a task about their television preferences rather than a task that required the use of mathematical skills.[2] For some students their immediate response to the subject-matter, a scenario deliberately designed to engage their interest, may have overshadowed the pointers to the substance of the task goal which was to create an argument to support their choice of television program using mathematical information. In this respect the problem scenario could be considered analogous to the situations where 'seductive details' have been shown to interfere with students' performance (Schraw & Lehman, 2001). This would explain the negative relationship between pre- and post-task difficulty ratings and the negative correlation between pre-task self-efficacy and post-task difficulty. Another factor that needs to be considered here is that it is not common practice in mathematics classrooms for students to be asked to put together an argument using mathematical evidence. On the other hand students would be more likely to perceive constructing an argument to support their answer as more consistent with the usual demands of the writing and investigative tasks.

The contrasting relationships between the sets of variables across study 2 and study 3 suggested that an index of students' confidence in their ability to handle the task relative to their estimation of the difficulty of the task would provide further insight into how students related to the task than either of the efficacy or difficulty ratings alone.

Task Expectancies and Self-Evaluations of Performance

To effectively represent the complex variations in students' expectations concerning task performance we explored students' estimates of confidence in relation to their estimates of task difficulty. For this purpose, a 'self-confidence in relation to task difficulty' or self/task index was calculated. This self/task index was calculated by first standardizing each of the confidence and difficulty ratings and then subtracting the standardized difficulty score from the corresponding standardized confidence (or self-efficacy) score. A positive self/task score indicated that students' confidence was higher than their estimate of task difficulty. A negative score indicated that students' estimate of the difficulty of the task was higher than their confidence in their own performance. Pre- and post-task scores were treated separately resulting in a pre-self/task score and a post-self/task score for each participant in Study 2 and in Study 3.

The new self/task scores were then used to develop path models for the sequence of relationships representing students' overall response to the task. By comparing these path models for Studies 2 and 3 it was expected that the importance of the task-specific relationship between students' confidence and perceptions of task difficulty would be highlighted. Each of the studies included a number of more general motivation variables. The most relevant to the questions being considered here were included in the path models to provide an indication of how personal orientations and predispositions might add to the models. For Study 2, which involved an investigative task, depth-of-interest curiosity was

---

[2]"Channel 3 has some useful mathematical data on each of the four TV programs… You must make your decision based on the maths information given to you."

included. At the beginning of the *BTL* task participants completed the 18-item short form of the Two Factor Curiosity Scale (see Ainley, 1998) from which the depth-of-interest score was calculated. Students also completed ratings of their individual interest in three schooling domains; reading, science, and mathematics. Ratings for individual interest domains were in the form of five-point Likert-type scales. Of the three individual interest domains, interest in reading had the highest correlations with the on-task variables and so along with depth-of-interest curiosity, was also included in the path model. For Study 3, an 18-item survey that assessed motivation towards mathematics was included at the beginning of the *BTL* program. One of the constructs measured was interest/enjoyment in mathematics (Attitudes Towards Mathematics Inventory - Tapia & Marsh, 2004). Students' scores on this scale were used as an index of individual interest in mathematics.

Due to the high correlations between the on-task interest variables (see Tables 3 and 5) only pre- and post-task interest, that is, initial and final levels of interest, were included in the path analyses. Also, to avoid the danger of multicollinearity, post-task interest was the only on-task interest variable included as an independent variable in the final step of the regression (see Figure 1). Hence, the variables included in the path analyses for Study 2 were depth-of-interest, interest in reading, pre-self/task scores, pre-task interest, post-task interest, and post-self/task scores. The path model for Study 3 involved the same variables except that the general motivational variable was individual interest in mathematics. For Study 2 data the final regression of the path model accounted for 26% of the variance in the post-self/task score. For Study 3 data, which included interest in mathematics as the individual interest variable, the final regression of the path model accounted for 32% of the variance in the post-self/task score. Path models for both Study 2 and 3 are shown in Figure 1.

The Study 2 path shows that neither depth-of-interest curiosity nor interest in reading predicted pre-self/task scores in the first step of the regression. However, depth-of-interest curiosity significantly predicted pre-task interest, showing that higher levels of curiosity were associated with higher levels of initial interest in the task. Post-task interest was predicted by pre-task interest which mediated the effect of more general depth-of-interest curiosity. Post-self/task scores were significantly and positively predicted by pre-self/task scores and by post-task interest. Thus, students whose initial confidence exceeded their initial estimate of task difficulty were more likely to respond in the same way when they had completed the task. On-task interest added to the prediction of their post-task self-evaluation.

The predictive paths for Study 3 shown in Figure 1 are consistent with our earlier argument that there was considerable mismatch for many students between their expectations concerning the substance of the task; there was a negative prediction to post-self/task scores from the pre-self/task scores. Initial estimates of task difficulty exceeding personal confidence were predictive of self evaluations at the end of the task where confidence exceeded task difficulty. This suggests that those who initially saw the task as demanding or challenging had the strongest sense of mastery on task completion. Students whose initial estimate rated the task as well within their competence were more likely to have reversed these estimates at the end of the task. Interest in mathematics and pre-task interest predicted post-task interest but did not contribute significantly to the prediction of the self/task score on task completion.

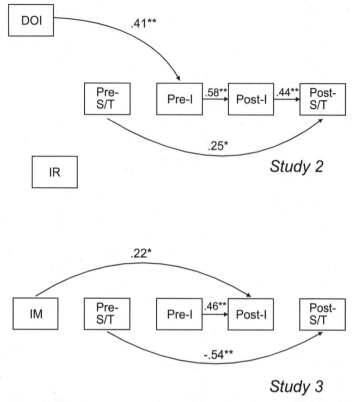

Figure 1. Significant regression coefficients within path analyses for Study 2 and 3.
Note: *p<.01; **p<.001 DOI=depth-of-interest curiosity; IR=individual interest in reading;
Pre-S/T=pre-self/task; Pre-I=pre-interest; Post-I=post-interest; Post-S/T=post-self/task;
IM=individual interest in mathematics. Final regression model did not include Pre-I as an
independent variable for reasons of multicollinearity.

Self-efficacy, Interest and Difficulty: The Task Matters

The results of these studies have been presented to examine three forms of interaction
between interest and self-efficacy. The first, consistent with models proposing that interest operates at the forethought phase of self-regulation, predicted that interest and self-
efficacy at the beginning of a task would together predict students' sense of mastery at the
end of the task. The findings from the three studies presented indicate that interest is an
important process contributing to students' sense of mastery and self-efficacy on task
completion. Interest needs to be considered as part of performance phases in self-
regulated learning and not only a component of the forethought phase. Furthermore, these
findings support a model of self-regulation that proposes a functional role for the state of
interest throughout the whole learning activity.

Across the three tasks the point at which interest added to the prediction of post-task self-efficacy ratings varied. For Study 1, a writing project, interest became a significant independent predictor of post-task self-efficacy at the mid-task stage. For Study 2, a fantasy detective investigation, from the beginning of the task interest significantly added to the contribution of self-efficacy; and for Study 3, a problem task requiring use of mathematical understanding, interest did not make a substantial contribution until the end of the task.

Inclusion of individual interest variables in a series of path analyses demonstrated that the contribution of generalized, personal interests also varied across tasks. Depth-of-interest, a curiosity style representing a general level of interest in new and puzzling phenomena, significantly predicted the level of initial interest students reported in Study 2, the investigative problem. The effects of depth-of-interest on students' final self evaluation in relation to the task at the end, was then mediated through on-task interest. On the other hand, for the mathematics task in Study 3, individual interest in mathematics was predictive of students' interest in the task on completion. As previously suggested this finding for the mathematics task could be the result of an initial misinterpretation of the presented problem. Details intended to engage students may have drawn attention away from the mathematics required to successfully solve the problem. Hence, general interest in mathematics was not associated with levels of interest at the outset of the task. However on task completion, when mathematical information had been processed (or avoided), interest in mathematics was a significant predictor of interest but not predictive of students' final self evaluation in relation to the task.

It is also clear that the specific content of the tasks used in these studies was an important factor in the observed relationships between interest and self-efficacy. Of particular significance was the finding for the mathematics problem in Study 3 that the interactive effects of interest and judgments of task difficulty represented the dynamic of this task rather than an interaction between interest and self-efficacy. Mathematics is likely to be associated with more habitual classroom procedures which foster a relatively narrow set of learning strategies in contrast to the flexible and personal character of student expression in social studies (Stodolsky, 1988). This is supported by Pajares and Miller (1997) who found that students' judgments of self-efficacy in a mathematics task were better calibrated with their performance when a traditional multiple-choice format was used as opposed to an open-ended test. Our results demonstrate that there are complex interactive relationships between self-efficacy, interest and perceived task difficulty that depend, in part, on the local effects of the task.

Findings from our three studies illustrate that the nature of the task is important. The problem scenarios used were all developed in collaboration with teachers. They were designed to represent the types of open-ended tasks used to encourage students' development of problem solving skills. Clearly the content and type of problem scenario is important for generating different expectancies concerning personal competencies and how well these competencies match task demands. The general, functional relationships between interest, self-efficacy, and difficulty perceptions are not independent of tasks characteristics. Nor can they be separated from students' expectancies regarding their competencies in those domains. Silvia has argued that if the goal is to increase feelings of interest in an activity, increasing self-efficacy might not always be appropriate as heightened self-efficacy can make the task look boring (Silvia, 2003). In the same way, the vehicle for making the task interesting (e.g., the television program decision) can deflect attention from the basic skills and competencies required and engender inappropriate evaluations of self-efficacy.

The studies we have presented are not without limitations. The samples of students completed the tasks within their normal classrooms. While increasing the likelihood of students' responses representing how they go about classroom tasks, not all students returned consent forms and so samples have their own selective biases. In addition, because we are looking at how students engage with a specific task rather than their report of how they generally go about specific tasks, the background contextual variability that goes with every day's school experience and with students' multiple peer relationships (see Buckley et al., 2007) is part of the mix of factors contributing to students' responses. Some of this will be able to be factored into the analysis in more recent studies where the same students have completed multiple problem tasks or where peer relationships have been monitored.

Conclusion

Models such as those of Zimmerman (2000), Pintrich (2004) and Sansone and Thoman (2005) point to a range of ways that specific processes such as interest and self-efficacy combine in self-regulated learning. We have identified several ways that interest and self-efficacy function across a problem task. Students' interest and self-efficacy at the outset of a task may combine and together contribute to the sense of efficacy on task completion. On-task interest may add to the prediction of self-efficacy on task completion or may function as a mediator of the influence of initial self-efficacy on the mastery experiences which shape on-going efficacy beliefs. However, our analysis of comparable groups of Year 8 and 9 students responding to different tasks pointed to the necessity to also take into account students' estimates of task difficulty. When the task required mathematical procedures and students' initial estimates of task difficulty did not match what was encountered when working with the task, perceptions of task difficulty were more predictive of how students evaluated their performance at the end of the task. Self-regulated learning is about the dynamics of students monitoring and adjusting their performance in a way that gives due consideration to personal skills and competencies and to the interest triggered. A large body of knowledge has been accumulated concerning dimensions of self-regulated learning such as interest and self-efficacy. There is strong evidence in this literature of a positive relationship between interest and self-efficacy that supports learning. However, direct application of these findings to classroom practice will not always be rewarded with improved outcomes. The nature of the task matters and a range of local task factors may over-ride the more general positive interactive effects of interest and self-efficacy. The one we have presented in this chapter concerns students' perceptions of task difficulty. Other local factors that we are exploring concern networks of peer relationships. We know something of how peer relationships impact on students' behaviour in the school environment generally, but help-seeking networks and popularity or status networks can also have specific influences on task performance within particular learning domains. Global perspectives on how these variables generally function need to be supplemented with the local character of the specific task requirements opening a wide research agenda for the future.

Acknowledgements

Parts of the research reported in this chapter were funded by an Australian Research Council Linkage Grant (No. LP0455559) awarded to the first author.

References

Ainley, M. (1998). Interest in learning and the disposition of curiosity in secondary students: Investigating process and context. In L. Hoffmann, A. Krapp, K. A. Renninger, & J. Baumert (Eds.), *Interest and learning: Proceedings of the Seeon Conference on gender and interest* (pp. 257 - 266). Kiel, Germany: IPN.

Ainley, M. (2007). Being and feeling interested: Transient state, mood, and disposition. In P. Schutz & R. Pekrun (Eds.), *Emotions and Education* (pp. 147-163). Burlington, MA: Academic Press.

Ainley, M., & Chan, J. (2006). *Emotions and task engagement: Affect and efficacy and their contribution to information processin during a writing task.* Paper presented at the Meetings of the American Educational Research Association, San Francisco, California.

Ainley, M., Corrigan, M., & Richardson, N. (2005). Students, tasks and emotions: Identifying the contribution of emotions to students' reading of popular culture and popular science texts. *Learning and Instruction, 15*(5), 433-447.

Ainley, M., Hidi, S., & Berndorff, D. (2002). Interest, learning and the psychological processes that mediate their relationship. *Journal of Educational Psychology, 94*, 545-561.

Ainley, M., & Patrick, L. (2006). Measuring self-regulated learning processes through tracking patterns of student interaction with achievement activities. *Review of Educational Psychology, 18*, 267-286.

Alfassi, M. (2003). Promoting the will and skill of students at academic risk: An evaluation of instructional design geared to foster achievement, self-efficacy and motivation. *Journal of Instructional Psychology, 30*, 28-40.

Bandura, A. (1989). Human agency in social cognitive theory. *American Psychologist, 44*, 1175-1184.

Bandura, A. (1997). *Self-efficacy: The exercise of control.* New York: Freeman.

Buckley, S., Ainley, M., & Pattison, P. (August, 2007). *Exploring the relationships between the social context, motivation, and anxiety in mathematics: Innovative methodologies and analytic techniques.* Presentation at the European Association for Research in Learning and Instruction (EARLI), Budapest, Hungary.

Goetz, T., Frenzel, A., Pekrun, R., & Hall, N. C. (2006). The domain specificity of academic emotional experiences. *Journal of Experimental Education, 75*, 5-29.

Hidi, S., & Ainley, M. (2007). Interest and self-regulation: Relationships between two variables that influence learning. In D. H. Schunk & B. J. Zimmerman (Eds.), *Motivation and self-regulated learning: Theories research and applications* (pp. 77-109). Mahwah, NJ: Lawrence Erlbaum and Associates.

Hidi, S., Ainley, M., Berndorff, D., & Del Favero, L. (2007). The role of interest and self-efficacy in science-related expository writing. In S. Hidi & P. Boscolo (Eds.), *Motivation and interest in writing* (pp. 203-217). Amsterdam: Elsevier.

Hidi, S., & Berndorff, D. (1998). Situational interest and learning. In L. Hoffmann, K. A. Krapp, K. A. Renninger, & J. Baumert (Eds.), *Interest and learning: Proceedings of the Seeon Conference on gender and interest* (pp. 74-90). Kiel, Germany: IPN.

Hidi, S., Berndorff, D., & Ainley, M. (2002). Children's argument writing, interest and self-efficacy: An intervention study. *Learning and Instruction, 12*, 429-446.

Hidi, S., & Harackiewicz, J. M. (2000). Motivating the academically unmotivated: A critical issue for the

21st. century. *Review of Educational Research, 70,* 151-179.

Hidi, S., & Renninger, K. A. (2006). The four-phase model of interest development. *Educational Psychologist, 41,* 111-127.

Hidi, S., Renninger, K. A., & Krapp, A. (2004). Interest, a motivational variable that combines affective and cognitive functioning. In D. Y. Dai & R. J. Sternberg (Eds.), *Motivation, emotion and cognition: Integrative perspectives on intellectual functioning and development* (pp. 89-115). Mahwah, NJ: Lawrence Erlbaum Associates.

Izard, C. E., & Ackerman, B. P. (2000). Motivational, organisational and regulatory functions of discrete emotions. In M. Lewis & J. M. Haviland-Jones (Eds.), *Handbook of emotions* (2nd ed., pp. 253-264). New York: Guilford Press.

Krapp, A. (2002). An educational-psychological theory of interest and its relation to SDT. In E. L. Deci & R. M. Ryan (Eds.), *The handbook of self-determination research* (pp. 405-427). Rochester: University of Rochester Press.

Lent, R. W., Brown, S. D., & Hackett, G. (1994). Toward a unifying social cognitive theory of career and academic interest, choice, and performance. *Journal of Vocational Behavior, 45,* 79-122.

Lepper, M. R. (1985). Microcomputers in education: Motivational and social issues. *American Psychologist, 40,* 1-18.

Lepper, M. R., & Chabay, R. W. (1985). Intrinsic motivation and instruction: Conflicting views on the role of motivation processes in computer-based education. *Educational Psychologist, 20,* 217-230.

Lodewyk, K. R., & Winne, P. H. (2005). Relations among the structure of learning tasks, achievement and changes in self-efficacy in secondary students. *Journal of Educational Psychology, 97,* 3-12.

Mitchell, M. (1993). Situational interest: Its multifaceted structure in the secondary school mathematics classroom. *Journal of Educational Psychology, 85,* 424-436.

Niemivirta, M., & Tapola, A. (2007). Self-efficacy, and task performance: Within-task changes, mutual relationships, and predictive effects. *Zeitschrift für Pädagogische Psychologie, 21,* 241-250

Pajares, F. (1996). Self-efficacy beliefs in achievement settings. *Review of Educational Research, 66,* 543-578.

Pajares, F. (2003). Self-efficacy belief, motivation and achievement in writing. *Reading and Writing Quarterly: Overcoming Learning Difficulties, 19,* 139-158.

Pajares, F., & Graham, L. (1999). Self-efficacy, motivation constructs, and mathematical performance of entering middle school students. *Contemporary Educational Psychology, 24,* 124-139.

Pajares, F., & Miller, M. D. (1997). Mathematics self-efficacy and mathematical problem-solving: Implications of using different forms of assessment. *The Journal of Experimental Education, 65,* 213-228.

Pajares, F., & Schunk, D. H. (2001). Self-beliefs and school success: Self-efficacy, self-concept, and school achievement. In R. J. Riding & S. G. Rayner (Eds.), *International perspectives on individual differences: Self-perception* (Vol. 2, pp. 239-266). Westport, CT: Ablex Publishing.

Pietsch, J., Walker, R., & Chapman, E. (2003). The relationship among self-concept, self-efficacy, and performance in mathematics during secondary school. *Journal of Educational Psychology, 95,* 589-603.

Pintrich, P. R. (2004). A conceptual framework for assessing motivation and self-regulated learning in college students. *Educational Psychology Review, 16,* 385-407.

Renninger, K. A. (1998). The roles of individual interest(s) and gender in learning: An overview of research on preschool and elementary school-aged children/ students. In L. Hoffmann, A. Krapp, K. A. Renninger & J. Baumert (Eds.), *Interest and learning: Proceedings of the Seeon Conference on interest and gender* (pp. 165-175). Kiel, Germany: IPN.

Sansone, C., & Harackiewicz, J. M. (1996). "I don't feel like it": The function of interest in self-regulation. In L. L. Martin & A. Tesser (Eds.), *Striving and feeling: Interactions among goals, affect, and self-regulation* (pp. 203-228). Mahwah, NJ: Lawrence Erlbaum Associates.

Sansone, C., & Thoman, D. B. (2005). Interest as the missing motivator in self-regulation. *European Psychologist, 10,* 175-186.

Schiefele, U. (1991). Interest, learning and motivation. *Educational Psychologist, 26,* 299-323.

Schraw, G., & Lehman, S. (2001). Situational Interest: A review of the literature and directions for future research. *Educational Psychology Review, 13*, 23-52.

Silvia, P. (2003). Self-efficacy and interest: Experimental studies in optimal incompetence. *Journal of Vocational Behavior, 62*, 237-249.

Skinner, B. F. (1968). *The technology of teaching*. New York: Appleton-Century-Crofts.

Stodolsky, S. (1988). *The subject matters: Classroom activity in math and social studies*. Chicago: University of Chicago Press.

Stodolsky, S., & Grossman, P. L. (1995). The impact of subject matter on curricular activity: An analysis of five academic subjects. *American Educational Research Journal, 32*, 227-249.

Tapia, M., & Marsh, G. E. (2004). An instrument to measure mathematics attitudes. *Academic Exchange Quarterly, 8*, 16-22.

Tracey, T. J. G. (2002). Development of interests and competency beliefs: A 1-year longitudinal study of fifth- to eighth-grade students using the ICA-R and structural equation modeling. *Journal of Counseling Psychology, 49*, 148-163.

Usher, E. L., & Pajares, F. (2006). Source of academic and self-regulatory efficacy beliefs of entering middle school students. *Contemporary Educational Psychology, 31(2), 125-141*.

Zimmerman, B. J. (2000). Self-efficacy: An essential motive to learn. *Contemporary Educational Psychology, 25, 82-91*.

Zimmerman, B. J. (2002). Achieving self-regulation: The trial and triumph of adolescence. In F. Pajares & T. Urdan (Eds.), *Academic motivation of adolescents* (pp. 1-27). Greenwich, CT: Information Age Publishing.

Zimmerman, B. J., & Schunk, D. H. (2001). Reflections on theories of self-regulated learning and academic achievement. In B. J. Zimmerman & D. H. Schunk (Eds.), *Self-regulated learning and academic achievement: Theoretical perspectives* (2nd ed., pp. 289-307). Mahwah, NJ: Lawrence Erlbaum Associates.

The Impact of Goal and Feedback Treatments on Self-Determined Motivation and Situational Interest in a Computer-Based Learning Context

Doris Lewalter & Katrin Scholta

Introduction

The impact of different learning contexts on motivational processes is increasingly recognized and consequently integrated in contemporary research approaches (Volet & Järvelä, 2001). Influences of context features can be analyzed on different levels (macro, meso and micro level; e.g., Volet, 2001). On all these levels of investigation, research endeavors mainly focus on the identification of those factors that have an influence on motivational variables. On a macro level, the impact of cultural aspects on motivational processes, among other things, is analyzed. On a meso level, research may focus on the effects of characteristics of different educational institutions within one country. The central point of studies conducted on a micro level is the investigation of the impact of specific characteristics of a learning environment on motivational processes. For instance, in experimental field studies, the influence of specific aspects of a learning situation is frequently investigated, whereas the underlying impact of the particular educational setting, or even possible cultural aspects, are only seldom considered. Considering each of the above mentioned research perspectives, different aspects can be analyzed, reaching from a more global to a more local point of view.

The experimental field study presented here is situated on the micro level, as it is concerned with investigating the impact of specific situational characteristics of a learning environment on motivational processes. Nevertheless, it can be assumed that the learning environment analyzed is part of an educational institution, which influences the findings as well. More concretely, our study focuses on the impact of design characteristics of a computer-based training program (CBT), which was embedded in a university lecture, on motivational variables. Furthermore, we investigate whether a potentially unattractive topic can gain attractiveness depending on the arrangement of the learning material, and the extent to which it is possible to enhance the students' learning motivation. For our investigation we analyzed different versions of a CBT, bearing in mind the specific learning environment of a university. The design characteristics we consider are varieties of goal instruction and feedback. The motivational variables accounted for in our study are self-determined motivation (Deci & Ryan, 1985, 2002) and situational interest (e.g. Hidi, 2000; Hidi & Renninger, 2006; Krapp, 2000; Lewalter & Geyer, in prep.). While self-determined motivation is a rather general motivational variable, situational interest is more sensitive to content factors.

Theoretical Background

This section outlines the theoretical background of the study and the main research questions.

Motivational variables: In general, one can differentiate between extrinsic and intrinsic qualities of motivation. The former refers to motivational qualities which are primarily based on aims located beyond the learning activity itself. The motivation to learn is rooted, for example, in the wish to attain good grades, outperform others, or avoid punishment. On the other hand, intrinsic motivation is based on the joyfulness of the learning activity itself and/or the individual appreciation of the learning content. Upon closer examination of theoretical concepts dealing more or less with intrinsic qualities of motivation, it is noticeable that within these concepts, it has been suggested that a purely cognitive-rational model for describing the course of motivational development is too limited, and therefore, affective processes have to be taken into account (e.g., Boekaerts, 2003; Csikszentmihalyi, 1990; Deci & Ryan, 1985, 1991; Krapp, 1999; Lewalter, 2002; Nuttin, 1984; Renninger, 2000).

Within our study, we focus on theoretical concepts dealing with intrinsic motivational qualities, namely self-determinated motivation and situational interest (Deci & Ryan, 1985, 1991; Hidi, 1990; Hidi & Renninger, 2006; Krapp, 1999; Lewalter, 2002). These foci were chosen mainly because the findings of numerous studies show that these motivational qualities have a positive influence on the quality of learning processes and learning outcomes (e.g. Deci & Ryan, 2002; Hidi, 1990; Krapp, Hidi, & Renninger, 1992; Lewalter, 2002; Prenzel, Kramer, & Drechsel, 2002; Schiefele & Schreyer, 1994; Schiefele & Wild, 2000).

Within self-determination theory, Deci and Ryan (1985, 1993, 2000, 2002) focus on the variation of motivational qualities depending on the degree of self-determination. The authors distinguish between different levels of self-determined motivation, ranging from intrinsic motivation, which is the most explicit form of self-determined motivation, to external regulation, which describes a specific kind of extrinsic motivation characterized by the absence of self-determination or self-regulation. The different forms of motivation distinguished in this theory reflect the degree to which the regulation of the (learning) behavior has been internalized and integrated (Ryan & Deci, 2000). Focusing on learning outcomes, the most desirable motivational qualities are strongly self-determined forms of motivation (integrated regulation and intrinsic motivation; Deci & Ryan, 2002).

In the cognitive evaluation theory (CET), a sub-theory of the self-determination theory, Deci and Ryan (1985, 2002) point out that internalization and integration, which enhance both intrinsic and self-determined motivation, are supported by the fulfillment of three fundamental psychological needs. The so called "basic needs" encompass the need for autonomy, competence, and relatedness. Compared to the experience of competence and relatedness, the experience of autonomy is particularly important for motivational processes (Ryan, 1993). Following deCharms' (1968) theory of personal causation, the concept of autonomy is closely connected to the idea of an internal perceived locus of causality. The need for autonomy refers to a person's desire to be self-initiating and act in accordance to one's own sense of self (Deci, 1998). This description comprises two components of autonomy. The first one specifies the literal definition of the term autonomy, which means "self-governing", and it implies that behaviour is regulated by a person's self. The second component focuses on the relation between the self and the action. Based on these theoretical considerations, a distinction can be made between two facets of autonomy, which can be distinguished from one another on an empirical basis (Lewalter, 2002, 2005):

(1) the experience of self-determination while dealing with a task (autonomy-SD)
(2) the experience of the accordance between a person's desires and goals and the requirements implied in the learning situation (autonomy-PDG).

The second motivational concept we account for is interest, which is characterized by a certain content-specificity, and which is also closely connected to self-determined motivation (e.g., Hidi, 2000; Hidi & Renninger, 2006; Hidi, Renninger, & Krapp, 2004; Krapp, 2000; Lewalter & Geyer, in prep.; Mitchell, 1993). In general, interest can be described as a specific relationship between a person and an object. It can be examined and theoretically reconstructed on two different levels: a context-based situational interest and a longer-lasting individual interest. In our research project, we focus on situational interest as a motivational construct (e.g., Hidi, 2000; Hidi & Anderson, 1992; Hidi & Renninger, 2006; Krapp, 2000; Lewalter & Geyer, in prep). Situational interest can be conceptualized as the first stage of the development of interest. It is primarily roused by conditions or incentives of the learning situation, and it is developed in a particular learning situation. Consequently, it is mainly based on both specific contextual factors and the interestingness of the subject matter (e.g. Hidi, 1990, 2000; Hidi & Berndorff, 1998). It also conforms to the idea that a person's attention can be guided towards a particular topic. When situational interest is developed, learning contents are perceived as personally relevant. In this context, students are willing to engage in activities and deal with learning contents in a concrete learning situation. They want to know more about a certain subject area. Considering different context factors, which can facilitate the development of situational interest, the perceived content relevance is particularly important. Students need to experience the usefulness of the acquired knowledge and skills, as well as their relevance for both themselves and for the learning goals they want to reach. Furthermore, the quality of experience during an activity is essential for the development of situational interest. Here, major ideas from CET (Deci &Ryan, 1985) and similar ideas from Nuttin's (1984) relational theory of behavioural dynamics are taken into consideration: Situational interest develops best in those learning environments that facilitate the satisfaction of the need for autonomy, competence, and relatedness.

Influence of the learning environment on motivational variables: Possibilities for supporting the development of self-determined motivation and (situational) interest are investigated in numerous studies conducted in various learning environments (for an overview see Deci & Ryan, 2000, 2002; Lewalter, 2002). Within these studies, the mediating function of the experience of autonomy, competence, and relatedness for motivational processes is often examined. Furthermore, the impact of different situational characteristics on the basic needs and/or the motivational variables is analyzed. The findings illustrate that situational factors can indeed have a facilitating or constraining effect on the basic needs, and consequently, on self-determined motivation and interest (e.g. Geyer, 2008; Kunter, 2005; Lewalter, 2002, 2005; Lewalter & Krapp, 2004; Prenzel, Kramer, & Drechsel, 2002; Rakoczy, 2006). Considering the need for autonomy, research has shown that, among other things, choice, informative feedback, opportunities for self-direction, and the existence of learning goals that accord to one's own sense of self, support the experience of autonomy, and consequently, enhance self-determined motivation and interest (e.g. Cordova & Lepper, 1996; Deci & Ryan, 1985; Geyer, 2008; Kunter, 2005; Lewalter, 2002; Lewalter, Krapp, Schreyer, & Wild, 1998; Prenzel, Kramer, & Drechsel, 2002; Ryan, 1993). In contrast, tangible rewards, surveillance, pressured evaluation, and imposed goals diminish the feeling of autonomy by conducing an external perceived locus of causality and supporting the experience of control (e.g., Deci, Koestner, & Ryan, 1999; Deci & Ryan, 1987, 2000; Kunter, 2005; Lewalter, 2002). Among other things, the experience of competence appears to be strongly influenced by informative feedback and the fit between the requirements of the task and a person's abilities (e.g., Cordova & Lepper, 1996; Deci, Ryan, & Williams, 1996; Kunter, 2005; Lewalter, 2002).

With regard to CBT, the range of influencing factors is restricted to its program features. Therefore, we focus on two aspects which can be realized in CBT programs: The supply of goal and feedback treatments. While there are numerous studies that identify feedback treatments as quite influential with regard to motivational processes, the research regarding intrinsic goal framing, which has been used to design goal treatments, is quite new.

Goal treatments: The influence of a person's goals on his or her behavior is investigated on the basis of varying theoretical concepts and in a multitude of different contexts (e.g., Dweck & Leggett, 1988; Linnenbrink, 2005; Locke & Latham, 1990, 1994; Nicholls, 1989). Currently studies frequently focus on goals as a part of the motivational system of a person, for example, goal orientations (e.g., Ames, 1992; Harackiewicz, Barron, Pintrich, Elliot, & Thrash, 2002; Linnenbrink & Pintrich, 2000). However, within this paper the term "goal" refers to the concept of goal content (intrinsic vs. extrinsic), which is quite different from the concept of goal orientations focused on the reasons why a person pursues particular goal contents (Urdan, 1997).

With respect to the goal content, learning situations can differ considerably; for example, goal contents can be provided or mentioned explicitly by the teacher or through the learning material. Additionally, it is also possible that goal contents are not mentioned at all, but rather the formulation of individual goal contents is consequently left to the learners themselves. In this case, goal contents are implicit factors of influence on the learning behavior and the motivational process. Furthermore, learners can also be asked to set up their own learning goal contents and express them explicitly.

Explicitly provided goals can be used as an experimental manipulation of the goal contents that students are pursuing (cf. Vansteenkiste, Lens & Deci, 2006a). It can be assumed that intrinsically versus extrinsically formulated goals can have a different impact on both the motivational and learning processes within a learning action. Therefore, Vansteenkiste and colleagues examined the extent to which framing a learning activity in terms of both future intrinsic and future extrinsic goals affected different learning variables in a series of studies (Vansteenkiste et al., 2006a; Vansteenkiste, Lens, Soenens, & Luyckx, 2006b; Vansteenkiste, Simons, Lens, Sheldon, & Deci, 2004a; Vansteenkiste, Simons, Soenens, & Lens, 2004b). It seems that the direction in which goals are formulated has an effect on how students learn. Different findings revealed that future intrinsic goal framing resulted in deeper engagement in learning activities, better conceptual learning, and a higher persistence when compared to the impact of future extrinsic goal framing.

Regarding the learning situation in which students are explicitly asked to formulate their own learning goal contents, following self-determination theory, we assume that students will most likely have a greater internal perceived locus of causality (deCharms, 1968). In case of an intrinsic goal content, this will possibly have an enhancing effect on self-determined motivation, mediated by the feeling of autonomy.

Research on situational interest exposes the importance of formulating one's own goal contents as well. Mitchell (1993) points out the possibility of stabilizing situational interest by enabling learners to integrate the meaningfulness of the learning content into their own goal systems. This is in accordance with Schraw, Flowerday and Lehman (2001), who suggest involving learners in the learning process by giving them the opportunity to identify what they want to learn, which in turn will enhance situational interest. For example, the authors suggest allowing learners to formulate personal goal contents before reading a text. Consequently, the perceived relevance of the learning content will be increased, or, in Mitchell's terminology (1993), relevant themes become integrated into the own goal system. These authors consequently suggest that an optimal learning environment should include the possibility of formulating personal goal contents before engaging in the learning activity.

In sum, a growing body of research supports the idea that motivational processes are influenced by the goal contents that frame a learning situation. Nevertheless, we assume that the impact of goal contents also depends on the learning situation and will vary from person to person. The extent to which students prefer setting their own goal contents or accepting provided goal contents depends on their personalities (e.g., individual interest, self-efficacy) and previous experiences. Hypothetically, students who were rarely allowed to formulate their own goal contents will most likely have difficulties in doing so.

Feedback: Feedback is an instructional tool widely used and investigated in different educational settings. It is regarded as an essential component of a durable, successful learning process (Musch, 2000). Assigning marks to students is a common form of feedback. It is perhaps the one most familiar and frequently used in learning settings and hence shows a great effect size in the meta-analysis of Lysakowsky und Walberg (1982). More standardized forms of feedback are often used in computer-based learning, such as "Knowledge of Result" (KOR), "Knowledge of correct result" (KCR), "Answer Until Correct" (AUC), and "Elaborated Feedback" (e.g., Kulhavy & Stock, 1989).

Based on self-determination theory, the relation between basic needs and feedback has been investigated in different experimental studies, which consistently show that the kind of feedback given is decisive. Feedback that only conveys whether an answer is right or wrong is experienced as controlling and therefore leads to a decrease in the feelings of competence and autonomy, which in turn results in a decrease in self-determined motivation (Deci, Ryan & Williams, 1996). Research results also reveal that feedback that has an informative function supports the feelings of competence and autonomy, independent of the quality and the results of the learning performances (Cordova & Lepper, 1996; Deci et al., 1996). Feedback is regarded as informative when it offers learners precise information referring to the correctness of the results and when it also provides clues for proceeding further. Accordingly, feedback is motivating when it contains information about the learner's progress, independent of a positive or negative result. In the case of so-called informative feedback, the need for competence is fulfilled, and consequently enhances self-determined motivation and situational interest, regardless of the learning result itself (Cordova & Lepper, 1996; Deci et al., 1996). Furthermore, according to CET, "people must not only experience competence or efficacy, they must also experience their behavior as self-determined for intrinsic motivation to be in evidence" (Ryan & Deci, 2000, p.70).

It can be supposed that the ways in which students cope with feedback depends to a great extent on the students' personalities and previous experiences. Therefore, it can be expected that motivation will not only depend on the feedback itself, but also on the context in which it is given.

In sum, it is likely that providing intrinsic goals, as well as formulating (personal) goals, can have a supportive effect on motivational processes. This supportive function is expected to occur for both situational interest and self-determined motivation. Questions remain concerning the strength of such an impact on each of the motivational variables and the role of the basic needs within the motivational processes. Furthermore, we expect a positive relation between informative feedback on the one hand, and the motivational variables in question on the other. Once more, the strength of the impact on each of the motivational variables and the role of the basic needs within the motivational processes are left unspecified. Furthermore, our analysis of a CBT covering a potentially unattractive topic must be considered. The possible impact of such a thematic factor is rarely investigated in empirical studies. We expect that this factor especially influences the situational interest as a content-sensitive variable. However, it is still unclear whether the missing attractiveness of the topic in question leads to an intensification or a reduction of the expected effects.

Nevertheless, we assume that a generalization of the research results outlined so far must be carried out carefully, as these results are limited to specific contexts. We assume that a person's way of handling goals and feedback depends on both the situation in question and previous experiences in similar learning contexts. Therefore the learning context of our study - the computer-based learning activity embedded in a university lecture course - must be respected. In sum our study consequently addresses the following problem statements:

(1) To what extent will different goal and feedback treatments affect the amount of self-determined motivation and situational interest?

(2) Which role does each of the basic needs play for the development of self-determined motivation in different learning situations?

Method

Design of the Study and Learning Material

The study was conducted within a lecture covering topics of educational research. During one meeting, the students were asked to work on a learning program dealing with a topic taken from the domain of statistics.

A CBT was chosen as learning material because it is appropriate for individual learning. Each learner is able to work in a self-determined manner in his/her own time and manner. In contrast to conventional classroom learning, students do not have to keep up with the learning speed enforced by the teacher, but rather can determine the speed and manner of learning themselves (Weidenmann, 2000).

Hence, computer-based learning material can be expected to support the need for autonomy, and consequently raise self-determined motivation. Additionally, this particular learning environment may be able to influence the motivation to learn something about an unpopular topic in a positive way.

The CBT used in our study ("Koralle") was developed and applied within the scope of other research purposes (Krause, Stark, & Mandl, 2004; Tyroller, 2005). The program deals with correlations and consists of three content sections treating the relevant aspects *linearity, outliers* and *heterogeneous sub-groups* (see Figure 1). The learning program was adapted for our purposes by implementing a general introduction to the program, which connected the topic of the program to a relevant job related field of activity of the students: the students should imagine that they are working as a teacher who has to deal with an evaluation project in school. Through this, we designed the program more realistic and relevant for our target group. We also added multimedia elements in order to make the program more attractive.

Each of the three sections begins with a rather theoretical introduction to the individual topic. This introduction is followed by a model task students have to work on. Afterwards, the correct solution of the problem is revealed. At the end of each section, students were given a brief multiple-choice comprehension test. This test contains one or two examples (in terms of problems stated or illustrated graphics), together with two to five related multiple-choice questions that must be answered by selecting the correct solutions. Working on the sections *linearity* and *outliers* was obligatory; the final section, *heterogeneous sub-groups*, was optional.

Treatments

To analyze the effects of context variables, six versions of the basic learning program were designed. These versions differ with regard to the implemented goal treatment (three versions) and the feedback treatment (two versions). Accordingly, the study was conceptualized as a field experiment with a 3 (goals) by 2 (feedback) factorial design. Participants were randomly assigned to one of the six experimental conditions.

Goal treatment: After a general introduction to the learning program, the goal treatments were applied. Depending on randomly assigned conditions, participants either read "provided intrinsic goal contents", formulated their own goals ("individually formulated goals"), or started to work on the program immediately ("no-goals"). The provided intrinsic goal contents offer a personal future value to the subject matter to be learned, by giving the students a reason why it is important for them - as a future teacher - to be familiar with the topic. This version is inspired by the "intrinsic goal framing theory" (Vansteenkiste et al., 2006 a,b). Within the second possible treatment ("individually formulate goals"), students were asked to write down their own goals for the upcoming learning task. This version follows theories emphasizing the importance of setting one's own goals (e.g. Bandura, 1986; Locke & Latham, 1990).

Feedback treatment: Following the multiple-choice test at the end of each content section, the treatment "informative feedback" versus "no feedback" was randomly applied. If feedback was given to the participants, it was designed in the following way: after the students had answered the multiple-choice questions on the test, they received the correct solution to each question in terms of fully written-out explanations. In order to compare personal answers and correct answers, students within the informative feedback treatment additionally received a memory-aid containing their answers given to the questions.

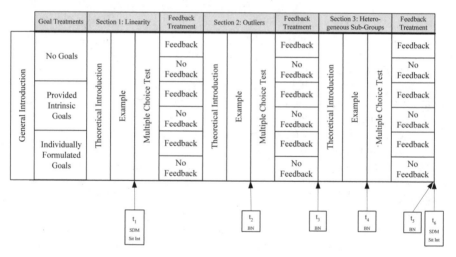

Figure 1. Sequential structure of the learning program.
Note: SDM = self-determined motivation, Sit Int = situational interest; BN = basic needs.

Sample

The study was conducted with a sample of 242 education students (39%) and teacher students (61%) of the RWTH Technical University Aachen in Germany. On average, the participants were 22.8 years (*SD*=3.95) old. The age ranged from 19 to 49 years. 27% of the participants were male, 73% were female.

Variables and applied instruments

The motivational variables under consideration are self-determined motivation (e.g., Deci & Ryan, 1985, 1993, 2002) and situational interest (Hidi, 2000; Hidi & Renninger, 2006; Krapp, 2000; Lewalter & Geyer, in prep.). Both variables are assessed by questionnaires applied twice during the learning process (t_1 and t_6, see Fig. 1) by means of a 5-point Likert-Scale (ranging from 1 = "not at all" to 5 = "very much"). Self-determined motivation is assessed by a 3-item scale developed by Prenzel, Drechsel, Kliewe, Kramer, and Röber (2000). Cronbach's alpha of the scale ranges from .84 (t_1) to .89 (t_6). In order to assess the students' situational interest during the learning process, a reduced version of a scale developed by Lewalter and Geyer (in prep.) is used. Sample items: "To which extent did parts of the learning program spark your curiosity?" "To which extent did you find the subject matter of this learning program personally important?" Cronbach's alpha of the 6 items scale ranges from .92 (t_1) to .95 (t_6).

Furthermore, the basic needs are measured by single items each (Lewalter, 2002). To access the experience of autonomy, both facets (autonomy-SD and autonomy-PDG) are included, and each facet is assessed by a single item (Lewalter, 2002, 2005). Sample items: To what extent … "… do you feel competent (I can understand it)"; "…do you feel related to the fellow students"; "…do you feel self-determined (I can actively influence the learning process)"; "… does the learning process correspond to your desires and goals for this learning situation".

Person related variables are measured as well. For example, self-efficacy is assessed by a 3-item scale adapted from Lewalter (Lewalter, 1997; Cronbach's alpha .66). Initial statistical analyses revealed that, in our data, self-efficacy was not distributed equally over the sub-samples of the goal treatments. Therefore, self-efficacy was consequently applied as a confounder within different analyses of covariances. Finally, at the end of the learning program (t_6), the students had the opportunity to give written comments on the learning program.

The assessment of the variables mentioned is integrated into the learning program (see Fig. 1). Self-determined motivation and situational interest were measured after the introduction of the first content section dealing with linearity and at the end of the learning program. The experiences of autonomy (both facets), competence and relatedness were measured four times: subsequent to the second and the third content section and immediately after the learning tests of each section.

Results

The Influence of Different Goal and Feedback Treatments on Self-Determined Motivation

Goal treatments: In order to examine the influence of different goal treatments on self-determined motivation, the data was analyzed using separate paired samples t–tests for each goal treatment. Table 1 illustrates means and standard deviations of self-determined motivation at the first (t_1) and last point of measurement (t_6) for each of the individual goal treatments.

The results indicate a significant decline of self-determined motivation from the first to the last point of measurement in all sub-groups (see Table 1). Nevertheless, the findings tend to result in a compensatory effect of both treatments, especially for the "provided intrinsic goal treatment". It is possible that the treatments helped to reduce the decline of self-determined motivation between the two points of measurement in question. This is especially true for students who formulated intrinsic goals when asked to formulate their own goals for the learning action. The results of this sub-sample (N=47) revealed no significant changes in self-determined motivation from t_1 to t_6 ($M_{(t1)}$ =2.87, SD=1.05; $M_{(t6)}$ =2.78, SD=.94; T-value = .68, n.s.).

Looking at self-determined motivation at t_1 in more detail, covariance analyses show that the different treatments positively influenced self-determined motivation. However, the goal treatments did not increase self-determined motivation strongly enough for the mean differences at t_1 to be significant.

Similar analyses conducted for self-determined motivation at t_6 reveal a significant difference between the treatments "no goals", "individually formulated goals" and "provided intrinsic goals" (F = 3.7; df = 2,21; p < .05). The lowest mean value of self-determined motivation was found in the control group ("no goals"), followed by the subgroup of students who formulated their goals individually. Learners who were provided with intrinsic goals showed the strongest degree of self-determined motivation. Post hoc comparisons applying Bonferroni correction revealed a significant difference between the group of students who were provided with intrinsic goals and the control group (p < .05). The results indicate a more explicit effect of the "intrinsic goals treatment" at the end of the learning process, after working on two (respectively three) units of the program for about 45 minutes. This effect could not be found at the first point of measurement, which took place immediately after the goal treatment. In this particular learning situation, intrinsic goals tend to need a certain amount of time to develop their impact.

Table 1. Means and standard deviation of self-determined motivation, number of subjects and t-value in dependence for the goal and feedback treatments.

Treatments	Self-determined motivation						
	First point of measurement (t_1)			Last point of measurement (t_6)			
	M	SD	N	M	SD	N	T
No goals	2.73	1.09	82	2.39	0.93	82	3.40***
Individually formulated goals	2.83	1.03	78	2.63	0.94	78	2.07*
Provided intrinsic goals	2.95	1.08	76	2.76	0.93	76	2.09*
No Feedback	2.74	1.04	120	2.59	0.98	120	1.93
Informative Feedback	2.94	1.09	116	2.59	0.91	116	4.29***

Note: Significant at the *p<.05; ***p<.001 level.

Feedback treatments: The influence of informative feedback on self-determined motivation was analyzed in a second step. The first feedback treatment took place after self-determined motivation was assessed for the first time (t_1), and accordingly, the differences between "informative feedback" and "no feedback" cannot have any influence on the amount of self-determined motivation measured at t_1.

Table 1 illustrates the impact of the feedback treatment on the development of self-determined motivation between t_1 and t_6. In both treatment groups, self-determined motivation declined.

In contrast to the goal treatments, which lessen the decline of self-determined motivation, the results concerning the feedback treatment indicate a negative impact of receiving informative feedback on self-determined motivation, which does not correspond to our assumption. Based on our considerations described above, informative feedback was expected to have a positive impact on the development of self-determined motivation.

Corresponding to these analyses, the impacts of the respective treatments on the second motivational variable - situational interest - were investigated as well.

The Influence of Different Goal and Feedback Treatments on Situational Interest

Goal treatments: In order to examine the influence of different goal treatments on situational interest, the data was analyzed using a t-test with paired samples. Table 2 illustrates means and standard deviations of situational interest at t_1 and t_6 for the different goal and feedback treatments.

The results of the analysis of the development of the students' situational interest between t_1 and t_6 show that the second motivational variable also decreases slightly between these two points of measurement. This decline only tends to be significant for those students assigned to the "provided intrinsic goal" sub-group (see table 2). Looking at the sub-sample of students who reported intrinsic goals ($N=47$) when asked to formulate their own goals for the learning action, a marginal increase of situational interest from t_1 to t_6 was found ($M_{(t1)} =2.69$, $SD=.86$; $M_{(t6)} =2.73$, $SD=.87$; T-value = -.38, n.s.).

Covariance analysis of situational interest at t_1 reveals that the goal treatments had no significant influence on the motivational variable in question. Identical analyses calculated for the situational interest at t_6 resulted in similar observations: compared to the control group ("no goals") both goal treatments ("provided intrinsic goals" and "individually formulated goals") lead only to a marginal, non-significant increase in situational interest.

Feedback treatments: In the next step, the impact of feedback on situational interest was analyzed. Knowing that the first feedback treatment took place after the initial assessment of the motivational variables, the differences between "informative feedback" and "no feedback" cannot have any impact on the amount of situational interest at t_1. Table 2 illustrates the influence of the informative feedback treatment on the development of situational interest between t_1 and t_6. In general, the informative feedback treatment also results in a significant decline of situational interest. These findings indicate a negative impact of getting feedback on situational interest in this particular learning context – a result which does not meet our expectations.

All in all, our findings can only indirectly affirm the impact of goal and feedback treatments on self-determined motivation and situational interest. A more detailed analysis concerning the influence of the basic needs on the students' self-determined motivation follows, to get a deeper insight into the processes taking place.

Table 2. Means and standard deviation of situational interest, number of subjects and t-value for each goal and feedback treatment.

	Situational interest						
Treatments	First point of measurement (t_1)			Last point of measurement (t_6)			
	M	SD	N	M	SD	N	T
No goals	2.47	0.97	82	2.41	1.00	82	0.87
Individually formulated goals	2.52	0.93	78	2.45	0.99	78	1.18
Provided intrinsic goals	2.68	0.88	76	2.59	0.93	76	1.97[+]
No Feedback	2.57	0.92	120	2.51	1.00	120	1.09
Informative Feedback	2.54	0.92	116	2.45	0.96	116	2.19[*]

Note: Significant at the [+]$p<.1$; [*]$p<.05$ level.

The Impact of Different Feedback Treatments on the Relation between the Basic Needs and Self-Determined Motivation

In order to gain a differentiated insight into the development of self-determined motivation from the beginning of the learning sequence (t_1) to its end (t_6), the relation between the basic needs and self-determined motivation – in consideration of the different feedback treatments- was examined. To reveal these relations, structural equation modeling (using AMOS 6.0) was applied.[1]

Structural equation models are separately calculated for both treatment versions of the learning program ("informative feedback" vs. "no feedback"). Figure 2 shows the individual path coefficients calculated for the "informative feedback" treatment; the path coefficients for the "no feedback" version are given in parentheses. Both models provide a good fit to the data (CFI = .95, RMSEA = .03).

Looking at the first model (calculated for the sub-sample of students who obtained informative feedback), the path coefficient between self-determined motivation measured at t_1 and t_6 is relatively low, but nonetheless significant ($\beta=.22, p < .001$).

---

[1] In all models which will be presented in the paper, standardized regression coefficients were estimated by using maximum likelihood (ML) fitting function. The models' adequacies of fit were estimated by means of comparative fit indices (CFI) and root-mean-square errors of approximation (RMSEA). For the use and interpretation of the indices see Bentler (1990) and Hoyle (1995).

The model illustrates the mediating function of the basic needs in this learning context: all path coefficients from self-determined motivation (at t_1) to the basic needs (t_2-t_5) are significant, and the impact of the basic needs on self-determined motivation (at t_6) is affirmed: three path coefficients are significant, both coefficients accounting for autonomy (PDG and SD) and the coefficient representing the experience of relatedness. There is no significant effect of the experience of competence on self-determined motivation. Overall, 69% of the variance of self-determined motivation at t_6 can be explained by the included predictors.

The model calculated for the "no feedback" sub-group (values given in parentheses in Figure 2) reveals different results. A higher path coefficient between the two points of measurement of self-determined motivation was found ($\beta = .40$, $p < .001$). Nonetheless, the mediating function of the basic needs is supported as well. The main difference between the "informative feedback" and "no feedback" versions concerns the predictive functions of the individual basic needs: within the specified model for the "no feedback" treatment, the path coefficient between autonomy (PDG) and self-determined motivation (t_6) is significant, and again, this facet bears the strongest predictive function. The coefficient of the second facet of autonomy (SD) is not significant. In contrast to the model calculated for the sub-sample of students who did obtain feedback, now, the experience of competence is revealed to be a significant predictor of self-determined motivation (t_6), whereas the experience of relatedness is not. The finding concerning relatedness indeed corresponds to the expectation that an experience of relatedness in an individual computer-based learning context has no relevant influence on self-determined motivation. With the help of this model, 81% of the variance of self-determined motivation at t_6 can be explained.

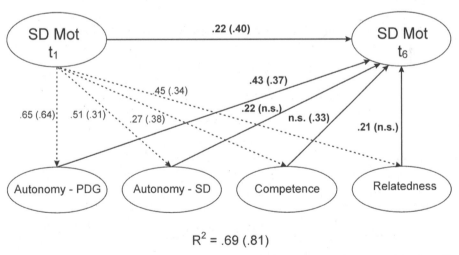

$$R^2 = .69 \ (.81)$$

Figure 2. Structural equation model estimating the predictive function of both self-determined motivation measured at t_1 and the basic needs measured at t_2 - t_5 for self-determined motivation measured at the end of the learning program, for both the treatment informative feedback and (no feedback) (n=120/122); CFI=.95; RMSEA=.03).

All in all, these findings support our assumption that the impact of the experience of autonomy, competence and relatedness on self-determined motivation varies depending on the situational context in which it is analyzed.

Discussion

Bearing in mind the theoretical background and our assumptions, both contradictory and confirmatory results were found. A result which does not correspond to our expectations is that neither the "provided intrinsic goals treatment" nor the "individually formulated goals treatment" was able to raise the students' self-determined motivation while working on the learning program. But nevertheless, the results indicate that both goal treatments had a certain positive impact on self-determined motivation, which can be described as a kind of "protective function" as they reduce the decrease on self-determined motivation. Apparently, for those students who participated in our study, it was helpful either to get an explicit goal-related instruction that illustrated the relevance of the unpopular statistical topic for their future-life, or to be asked to think about and write down their own goals for the upcoming learning activity. With this in mind, the findings concerning the goal treatments correspond to our expectations, for we assumed that different goal treatments have a beneficial impact on self-determined motivation.

With regard to situational interest, our assumptions concerning the positive effect of different goal treatments were not supported by our empirical findings: Situational interest remains stable, and providing intrinsic goals resulted in a significant decline of this motivational variable.

Keeping in mind further investigations, it would be revealing to examine the varying interpretations of the formulations of goal treatments by learners in more detail, in order to be able to explain the established impact of the goal treatments with regard to motivational processes. Here, it can be assumed that local aspects such as the students' former learning experiences and the learning context, as well as more global aspects such as the socio-cultural background of the students, may have an important impact. To gain detailed information about individual differences in the interpretation of varying goal treatments and their background, a qualitative research approach using interviews may be helpful.

Regarding the effects of different feedback treatments, the results also contradict our expectations: feedback explicitly designed as informative actually had a negative impact on self-determined motivation. We suppose that students experienced the feedback as controlling. In relation to this assumption, it is necessary to analyze why informative feedback, which offers learners clues referring to the correctness of the results, is experienced as controlling. More detailed analyses taking into consideration the role of the basic needs provide further information (see below). Presumably, the learning context in which our study was embedded is decisive as well.

Similar to the decrease in self-determined motivation, gaining informative feedback also leads to a decline of situational interest. Consequently, informative feedback negatively influenced the overall motivation of the learners in this study. Feedback, although designed as informative and non–controlling, was probably perceived as controlling.

With regard to this content sensitive motivational variable, the uninteresting topic of the CBT may also have an impact on this negative development. Furthermore, qualitative data gained from an open-ended question asked at the end of the learning program revealed a second verisimilar explanation. Some learners perceived the content of the program as too difficult. As the group of learners was very heterogeneous, it is likely that some of them had severe problems dealing with this particular topic, and therefore, experienced the learning program as too demanding. Further analyses need to show whether individual differences of students regarding the perception of the feedback as controlling can be partly explained by personality characteristics of the students, such as self-efficacy or the topic related self-concept. To get a fuller understanding of the background of varying interpretations of the feedback treatments beneath local factors, the impact of more global factors (e.g. former experiences in a certain learning context such as CBT or universities) have to be taken into account. Based on this information, possibilities can be developed as to how feedback can be given in an informative and non-controlling manner for different sub-samples.

Analyzing the role of the basic needs for the development of self-determined motivation, we found that the situational design of the learning context was decisive. This finding supports our expectation that the relation between self-determined motivation and the basic needs varies, depending on diverse learning circumstances framed through different feedback treatments.

The results show that regardless of different learning contexts, the autonomy facet consisting of personal desires and goals (PDG) is the strongest predictor of self-determined motivation at t_6. This result supports the assumption that the experience of autonomy is particularly important and maintains an outstanding function for motivational processes (Deci & Ryan, 2002; Ryan, 1993).

The autonomy facet SD is only a significant predictor in the feedback condition. This result can be interpreted as an indicator of the positive relation between autonomy and informative feedback, as it is expected on the basis of theoretical considerations (Cordova & Lepper, 1996; Deci et al., 1996; Deci & Ryan, 1993). Furthermore, when informative feedback is included in the learning context, the experience of competence is not a significant predictor of self-determined motivation at t_6. In summary, these results contradict the explanation for the significant decline of self-determined motivation on the assumption that the informative feedback was experienced as controlling. In this case, a negative relation between both basic needs and self-determined motivation at t_6 would have been probable.

It is conceivable that the predictive strength of the feeling of competence was reduced by the informative feedback, as it adjusted the student's experience of competence. For students who have severe problems in understanding the subject matter, this - in combination with the uninteresting topic - may have a negative impact on self-determined motivation. However, the experience of relatedness became important for self-determined motivation at the last point of measurement. Thus, giving feedback adds a certain social component to a rather individual learning situation, which in turn increases the predictive function of the need for relatedness.

Within the learning situation in which students did not gain any feedback, the opposite pattern was detected: the feeling of competence contributes to the explanation of self-determined motivation, while the feeling of relatedness does not. Without gaining feedback, the experience of competence may correspond more to the self-determined motivation. Taking this specific learning context into consideration, the results with regard to relatedness were expected: in a computer-based learning situation, students have to work on the program individually and unrelated to the whole group of learners. In summary, the model specified for the "no feedback" treatment seems to be more in line with our expectations concerning the relation between the basic needs and self-determined motivation in computerized learning situations.

Our empirical findings correspond to some extent with the assumptions of self-determination theory, but when investigating the specific learning context in more detail, they also reveal additional important aspects.

Firstly, a question that remains open concerns the extent of the impact of the uninteresting topic of the CBT on motivational processes. According to our results, it seems that motivation will most likely be even more context sensitive when working with topics deemed as unattractive.

Secondly, in that context, the possibility arises that a remarkable portion of the variance of self-determined motivation might be explained by factors lying in the particular learning situation. Furthermore, the broader learning environment (lecture at the university) may have an impact on these results as well. Our findings underline the necessity of analyzing distinct learning situations and the overall learning environment they are part of in more detail, because the influences of situational factors, especially on motivationally relevant experiences, is stronger than assumed. Consequently, and in line with other findings, (Boekaerts, 1999; Järvelä & Volet, 2004; Pintrich, 2003), future research in motivation will have to investigate assumptions of motivational theories in different learning situations (computer-based learning, classroom settings, constructivist oriented versus conventional teaching and learning, different topics and themes etc.) in much greater detail. To achieve a profound understanding of motivational processes in real-life learning settings, the characteristics of these contexts have to be taken into account more intensely, and comparative studies in different educational settings are necessary. Therefore, research programs combining more local and global focuses of investigation, seem to be promising to get a fuller understanding of the complex ways in which motivational processes in a concrete learning action are affected by personal and situational characteristics on different levels. This insight will again be helpful in refining theoretical assumptions and concepts in the context of motivation.

References

Ames, C. (1992). Achievement goals and the classroom motivational climate. In D. H. Schunk & J. L. Meece (Eds.), *Students perceptions in the classroom* (pp. 327-348). Hillsdale: Erlbaum.

Bandura, A. (1986). *Social foundations of thought and action: A social cognitive theory.* Englewood Cliffs, NJ: Prentice-Hall.

Bentler, P. M. (1990). Comparative fit indexes in structural models. *Psychological Bulletin, 107,* 238-246.

Boekaerts, M.. (1999). Self-regulated learning. *International Journal of Educational Research, 31,* 445-551.

Boekaerts, M. (2003). Towards a model that integrates motivation, affect and learning. *British Journal of Educational Psychology. Monograph Series II, Part 2 (Development and Motivation: Joint Perspectives)*, 41-55.

Cordova, D. I., & Lepper, M. R. (1996). Intrinsic motivation and the process of learning: Beneficial effects of contextualisation, personalization, and choice. *Journal of Educational Psychology, 88*, 715-730.

Csikszentmihalyi, M. (1990). *Flow.* New York: Harper & Row.

deCharms R. (1968). *Personal causation: The internal affective determinants of behavior.* New York: Academic Press.

Deci E. L., & Ryan R. M. (1985): *Intrinsic motivation and self-determination in human behavior.* New York.Verlag: Academic Press.

Deci, E. L., & Ryan, R. M. (1987). The support of autonomy and the control of behavior. *Journal of Personality and Social Psychology, 53*, 1024-1037.

Deci, E. L., & Ryan, R. M. (1991). A motivational approach to self: Integration in personality. In R. Dienstbier (Ed.), *Nebraska Symposium on Motivation: Perspectives on Motivation* (Vol. 38, pp. 237-288). Lincoln, NE: University of Nebraska Press.

Deci, E. L., & Ryan, R. M. (1993). Die Selbstbestimmungstheorie der Motivation und ihre Bedeutung für die Pädagogik.[Self-determination theory and its meaning for education]. *Zeitschrift für Pädagogik, 39*, 223-238.

Deci, E. L., & Ryan, R. M. (2000). Intrinsic and extrinsic motivations: Classic definitions and new directions. *Contemporary Educational Psychology, 25*, 54-67.

Deci, E. L., & Ryan, R. M. (2002). *Handbook of self-determination research.* Rochester: Rochester University Press.

Deci, E. L. (1998). The relation of interest to motivation and human needs: The self-determination theory viewpoint. In L. Hoffmann, A. Krapp, K. A. Renninger, & J. Baumert (Eds.), *Interest and learning. Proceedings of the Seon conference on interest and gender* (pp. 146-162). Kiel: IPN.

Deci, E. L., Ryan, R. M., & Williams, G. C. (1996). Need satisfaction and the self-regulation of learning. *Learning and Individual Differences, 8*, 165-183.

Deci, E. L., Koestner, R., & Ryan, R. M. (1999). A meta-analytic review of experiments examining the effects of extrinsic rewards on intrinsic motivation. *Psychological Bulletin, 125*, 627-668.

Dweck, C. S., & Leggett E. L. (1988). A social-cognitive approach to motivation and personality. *Psychological Review, 95*, 256-273.

Geyer, C. (2008). *Museums- und Science Center-Besuche im naturwissenschaftlichen Unterricht aus einer motivationalen Perspektive. Die Sicht von Lehrkräften und Schülerinnen und Schülern.* [Museum and science centre visits in natural science lessons. The perspective of teachers and students]. Berlin: Logos.

Harackiewicz, J. M., Barron, K. E., Pintrich, P. R., Elliot, A. J., & Thrash, T. M. (2002). Revision of achievement goal theory: Necessary and illuminating. *Journal of Educational Psychology, 94*, 638-645.

Hidi, S., & Anderson, V. (1992). Situational Interest and its impact on reading and expository writing. In K. A. Renninger, S. Hidi, & A. Krapp (Eds.), *The role of interest in learning and development* (pp. 215-238). Hillsdale, NJ.: Erlbaum.

Hidi, S., & Berndorff, D. (1998): Situational interest and learning. In L. Hoffmann, A. Krapp, K. A. Renninger, & J. Baumert (Eds.): *Interest and learning. Proceedings of the Seon-Conference on Interest and Gender* (pp. 74-90). Kiel: IPN.

Hidi, S., & Renninger, K. A. (2006). The four-phase model of interest development. *Educational Psychologist, 41*, 111-127.

Hidi, S. (1990). Interest and its contribution as a mental resource for learning. *Review of Educational Research, 60*, 549-571.

Hidi, S. (2000). An interest researcher's perspective: The effects of extrinsic and intrinsic factors on motivation. In C. Sansone & J. M. Harackiewicz (Eds.), *Intrinsic and Extrinsic Motivation* (pp. 309-339). San Diego: Academic Press.

Hidi, S., Renninger, K. A., & Krapp, A. (2004). Interest, a motivational construct that combines affective and cognitive functioning. In D. Y. Dai, & R. J. Sternberg (Eds.), *Motivation, emotion and cognition. Integrative perspectives on intellectual functioning and development* (pp.89-115). Mahwah, NJ: Erlbaum.

Hoyle, R. H. (1995): The structural equation modeling approach : basic concepts and fundamental issues. In R. H. Hoyle (Ed.), *Structural equation modeling: Concepts, issues, and applications* (pp. 1-15). Thousand Oaks: Sage.

Järvelä, S., & Volet, S. (2004). Editorial: Motivation in real-life, dynamic, and interactive learning environments: Stretching constructs and methodologies. *European Psychologist, 9*, 193-197.

Krapp, A. (1999). Interest, motivation and learning: An educational-psychological perspective. *European Journal of Psychology in Education, 14*, 23-40.

Krapp, A. (2000). Interest and human development during adolescence: An educational-psychological approach. In J. Heckhausen (Ed.), *Motivational psychology of human development* (pp. 109-128). London: Elsevier.

Krapp, A., Hidi, S., & Renninger, K. A. (1992). Interest, learning and development. In K. A. Renninger, S. Hidi & A. Krapp (Eds.), *The role of interest in learning and development* (pp. 3-25). Hillsdale, NJ: Erlbaum.

Krause, U.-M., Stark, R., & Mandl, H. (2004). Förderung des computerbasierten Wissenserwerbs durch kooperatives Lernen und eine Feedbackmaßnahme [Support of computer-based learning outcome by cooperative learning and feedback]. *Zeitschrift für Pädagogische Psychologie, 18*, 125-136.

Kulhavy, R. W., & Stock, W. A. (1989). Feedback in written instruction: The place of response certitude. *Educational Psychology Review, 1*, 279-308.

Kunter, M. (2005). *Multiple Ziele im Mathematikunterricht [Multiple goals in Mathematic classes]*. Münster: Waxmann.

Lewalter, D., & Geyer, C. (in prep.) *Die Skala zum Situationalen Interesse.* [The scale on situational interest]

Lewalter, D. (1997). *Lernen mit Bildern und Animationen.* [Learning with pictures and animations] Münster: Waxmann.

Lewalter, D. (2002). *Emotionales Erleben und Lernmotivation. Theoretische und empirische Analysen des Zusammenhangs von Emotion und Motivation in pädagogischen Kontexten.* [Emotional experiences and learning motivation. Theoretical and empirical analyses of the relation between emotion and motivation in educational contexts] Unveröffentlichte Habilitationsschrift, Universität der Bundeswehr, München.

Lewalter, D. (2005). Der Einfluss emotionaler Erlebensqualitäten auf die Entwicklung der Lernmotivation in universitären Lehrveranstaltungen. [The impact of emotional experiences on the development of learning motivation in university courses] *Zeitschrift für Pädagogik, 51*, 642-655.

Lewalter, D., & Krapp, A. (2004). The role of contextual conditions of vocational education for motivational orientations and emotional experiences. *Educational Psychologist, 9*, 210-221.

Lewalter, D., Krapp, A., Schreyer, I., & Wild, K.-P. (1998) Die Bedeutsamkeit des Erlebens von Kompetenz, Autonomie und sozialer Eingebundenheit für die Entwicklung berufs-spezifischer Interessen [The importance of the experience of competence, autonomy, and relatedness for the development of job related interest]. In K. Beck & R. Dubs (Eds.), Kompetenzentwicklung in der Berufserziehung - Kognitive, motivationale und moralische Dimensionen kaufmännischer Qualifizierungsprozesse (pp. 143-168). Stuttgart: Steiner.

Linnenbrink, E. A. (2005). The dilemma of performance-approach goals: The use of multiple goal contexts to promote students' motivation and learning. *Journal of Educational Psychology, 97*, 197-213.

Linnenbrink, E. A., & Pintrich, P. R. (2000). Multiple pathways to learning and achievement: The role of goal orientation in fostering adaptive motivation, affect, and cognition. In C. Sansone & J. M. Harackiewicz (Eds.), *Intrinsic and extrinsic motivation* (pp. 195-227). San Diego: Academic Press.

Locke, E. A., & Latham, G. P. (1990). *A theory of goal setting and task performance. Englewood Cliffs.* NJ: Prentice Hall.

Locke, E. A., & Latham, G. P. (1994) Goal setting theory. In H. O'Neil & M. Drillings (Eds.), *Motivation: Theory and research* (pp. 13-29). Hillsdale, NJ: L. Erlbaum.

Lysakowski, R. S., & Walberg, H. J. (1982). Instructional effects of cues, participation, and corrective feedback: A quantitative synthesis. *American Educational Research Journal, 19*, 559-578.

Mitchell, M. (1993). Situational interest: Its multifaceted structure in the secondary school mathematics classroom. *Journal of Educational Psychology, 85*, 424-436.

Musch, J. (2000). Die Gestaltung von Feedback in computergestützten Lernumgebungen: Modelle und Befunde. [The Design of feedback in computer-based learning environments. Models and findings] *Zeitschrift für Pädagogische Psychologie, 13*, 148-160.

Nicholls, J. (1989). *The competitive ethos and democratic education.* Cambridge, MA: Harvard University Press.

Nuttin, J. (1984). *Motivation, planning, and action.* Hillsdale, NJ: Erlbaum

Pintrich, P. R. (2003). A motivational science perspective on the role of student motivation in learning and teaching contexts. *Journal of Educational Psychology, 95*, 667-686.

Prenzel, M., Drechsel, B., Kliewe, A., Kramer, K., & Röber, N. (2000). Lernmotivation in der Aus- und Weiterbildung: Merkmale und Bedingungen. [Learning motivation in education and further education. Characteristics and conditions] In C. Harteis, H. Heid, H., & S. Kraft (Eds.), *Kompendium Weiterbildung. Aspekte und Perspektiven betrieblicher Personal- und Organisationsentwicklung* (pp. 163-173). Opladen: Leske + Budrich.

Prenzel, M., Kramer, K., & Drechsel, B. (2002). Self-determined and interested learning in vocational education. In K. Beck (Ed.), *Teaching – learning processes in vocational education. Foundations of modern training programs* (pp.43-68). Frankfurt: Lang.

Rakoczy, K. (2006). *Motivationsunterstützung im Mathematikunterricht.* [The support of motivation in math lessons] Berlin: Unveröffentlichte Dissertation.

Renninger, K. A. (2000). Individual interest and its implications for understanding intrinsic motivation. In C. Sansone, & J. M. Harackiewicz (Eds.), *Intrinsic and extrinsic motivation* (pp. 373-404). San Diego: Academic Press.

Ryan, R. M., & Deci, E. L. (2000). Self-determination theory and the facilitation of intrinsic motivation, social development, and well-being. *American Psychologist, 55*, 68-78.

Ryan, R. M. (1993). Agency and organization: Intrinsic motivation, autonomy, and the self in psychological development. In J. Jacobs (Ed.), *Nebrasca symposium on motivation: Developmental perspectives on motivation* (Vol. 40, pp. 1-56). Lincoln, NE: University of Nebraska Press.

Schiefele, U., & Schreyer, I. (1994). Intrinsische Lernmotivation und Lernen. Ein Überblick zu Ergebnissen der Forschung. [Intrinsic motivation and learning. An overview on research results] *Zeitschrift für Pädagogische Psychologie, 8*, 1-13.

Schiefele, U., & Wild, K,-P. (Eds.). (2000). *Interesse und Lernmotivation.* [Interest and learning motivation] Münster: Waxmann.

Schraw, G., Flowerday, T., & Lehman, S. (2001). Increasing situational interest in the classroom. *Educational Psychology Review, 13*, 211-224.

Tyroller, M. (2005). *Effekte metakognitiver Prompts beim computerbasierten Statistiklernen.* [Effective meta-cognitive prompts in computer-based learning on statistics] München, Univ., Diss.

Urdan, T. (1997). Achievement goal theory: Past results, future directions. In M. L. Maehr & P. R. Pintrich (Eds.), *Advances in motivation and achievement* (Vol. 10, pp. 99-141). Greenwich, CT: JAI Press.

Vansteenkiste, M., Lens, W., & Deci, E. L. (2006a). Intrinsic versus extrinsic goal contents in self-determination theory: Another look at the quality of academic motivation. *Educational Psychologist, 41*, 19-31.

Vansteenkiste, M., Lens, W., Soenens, B., & Luyckx, K. (2006b). Autonomy and relatedness among chinese sojourners and applicants: Conflictual or independent predictors of well-being and adjustment? *Motivation and Emotion, 30*, 273-282.

Vansteenkiste, M., Simons, J., Lens, W., Sheldon, K. M., & Deci, E. L. (2004a). Motivating learning, performance, and persistance: The synergistic effects of intrinsic goal contents and autonomy-supportive Contexts. *Journal of Personality and Social Psychology, 87*, 246-260.

Vansteenkiste, M., Simons, J., Soenens, B., & Lens, W. (2004b). How to become a persevering exerciser? Providing a clear, future intrinsic goal in an autonomy-supportive way. *Journal of Sport & Exercise Psychology, 26*, 232-249.

Volet, S., & Järvelä, S. (Eds.) (2001). *Motivation in learning contexts. Theoretical advances and methodological implications.* Amsterdam: Pergamon.

Volet, S. (2001). Understanding learning and motivation in context: A multi-dimensional and multi-level cognitive-situative perspektive. In S. Volet & S. Järvelä (Eds.), *Motivation in learning contexts. Theoretical advances and methodological implications* (pp. 57-82). Amsterdam: Pergamon.

Weidenmann, B. (2000): Medien und Lernmotivation: Machen Medien hungrig oder satt? [Media and learning motivation: Do media make hungry or full?] In U. Schiefele & K.-P. Wild (Eds.), *Interesse und Lernmotivation. Untersuchungen zu Entwicklung, Förderung und Wirkung* (pp. 117-132). Münster: Waxmann.

Specification Issues in the Use of Multilevel Modeling to Examine the Effects of Classroom Context

The Case of Classroom Goal Structures

Tamera B. Murdock & Angela D. Miller

Goal theory has developed into one of the most prominent perspectives on achievement motivation in contemporary educational psychology (Elliott, Hufton, Anderman, & Il-lushin, 2000; Midgley et al., 1998; Pintrich & Schunk, 2002). According to this theoretical framework, students' motivation as measured by a variety of affective, cognitive, and behavioral indicators, is influenced both by students' personal goals as well as by the goal structures that are established in their classrooms and schools. When students pursue learning for its own sake, believe that their intellect can be improved through effort, and strive for mastery of material, they are said to have goals that are mastery or learning oriented (Anderman & Maehr, 1994). In contrast, the pursuit of performance, ego, or ability goals describes students who see intelligence as something that is finite and unmalleable and whose goals are to demonstrate their ability or hide their perceived lack of ability (Midgley et al., 1998; Urdan, Ryan, Anderman, & Gheen, 2002). Paralleling these personal goals are classroom goal structures, created by teachers' attitudes and behaviors in the classroom. Teachers who communicate mastery goal structures recognize effort, downplay social comparisons, and focus students on learning and improvement whereas performance goal structures are seen in teaching practices such as normative grading, highlighting of individual differences and social comparisons, and encouraging students to get things "right" and demonstrate they are smart (Patrick, Anderman, Ryan, Edelin, & Midgley, 2001; Turner & Patrick, 2004).

Numerous articles and books by educational psychologists advise teachers to increase their use of practices that create mastery goal structures and limit those that enforce norms of performance because of their presumed effect on students' personal goals, and hence on a variety of motivation related outcomes (Anderman, Maehr, & Midgley, 1999; Midgley, 2002). This advice is based on empirical evidence that links performance oriented classrooms and personal performance orientations with such maladaptive behaviors as self-handicapping, avoidance of help seeking, and academic dishonesty (Anderman & Midgley, 2004; Murdock, Hale, & Weber, 2001; Murdock, Miller, & Kohlhardt, 2004; Urdan et al., 2002). Theoretically, classroom goal structures are presumed to influence student motivation primarily by affecting the personal goals that students adopt in a given learning context (see Figure 1). In other words, personal goals presumably mediate the relations between classroom goal structures and cognitive and behavioral indices of motivation.

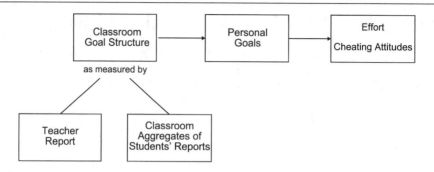

Figure 1. Conceptual model of the relationship between goal structures, goals, and outcomes.

Conclusions about the effects of classroom goal structures versus students' individual goal orientations or personal perceptions of the classroom goal structure are, however, less robust than the one might assume due to several recurring methodological inconsistencies in the literature. First, few of the empirical studies that examine the effects of classroom goal structures actually consider the nested structure of their data, making it impossible to tease out individual difference effects from factors that are truly classroom context effects (see Miller & Murdock, 2007a). Instead, the majority of the studies simply show that there are correlations between a specific individual's outcomes (such as her level of effort) and that same student's perception of the classroom environment.

Multilevel modeling (MLM) affords us the opportunity to achieve better estimates of the effects of classroom goal structures versus the effects of an individual's personal goals, or their individual view of the classroom goal structure (see Kreft & De Leeuw, 1998; Raudenbush & Bryk, 2002).[1] Specifically MLM lets us decompose the variance in student outcomes into the student component, predicted by individual characteristics and cognitions (e.g., personal goals), and that which might be explained by classroom context effects (e.g., the classroom goal structure). To date, however, there are only nine published empirical studies within the motivational literature that use MLM to examine the effects of goal structures on various motivational outcomes (Miller & Murdock, 2007a). These studies typically assess goals and goal structures using the Patterns of Adaptive Learning Survey (Midgley et al., 1998). Beyond this similarity, each study specifies and tests very different conceptual models because of disparities in the source of the data (e.g., teacher versus student), the inclusion or exclusion of "control" variables, and the choice of centering strategies for the level 1 (student-level) variables. More important, the effect of these decisions on the model specification and interpretation of results are rarely detailed allowing readers to assume that the studies are in fact "comparable."

Chapter Aim

The primary aim of this chapter is to elucidate the complexities in trying to tease apart the effects of classroom goal structure by comparing and contrasting the various models that

---

[1] We have chosen the broader term multi-level modeling (MLM) versus Hierarchical Linear Modeling (HLM) because HLM refers to a specific computer program for the analysis of multi-level data.

have been specified and tested in the literature. Our focus is on the implications that four specific methodological decisions have on the model specification and hence, on the meaning of the results. Throughout this chapter, we will illustrate our points using one of our own data sets to examine the links between classroom goal structures, students' personal goals, and two outcome variables that have been consistently shown to be affected by goal structures: students' attitudes about cheating and self-reported effort. Attitudes about cheating refer to students' beliefs that cheating is understandable and justifiable within the context of that classroom. Whereas mastery goals are typically associated with increased effort (Midgley, 2002) they are inversely associated with attitudes towards cheating (Anderman, Griesinger, & Westerfield, 1998; Murdock, Miller, & Goetzinger, 2007).

Four specific issues are addressed: variation in the source of data for the measurement of goal structures, reliability of the goal structure measures, presumed relations between personal goals and classroom goal structures, and the effects of centering decisions. We illuminate how these four decisions affect the meaning of the model that is specified and hence the conclusions one reaches about the importance of personal variables versus classroom contexts. We conclude by delineating the broader implications of these decisions for research on classroom context effects. We limit our discussion to models with two levels, where level 1 refers to student-level effects and level 2 to classroom-level effects.

Issue 1: How to Measure Goal Structures

Although almost all of the nine multilevel studies of goal structure effects assess classroom goal structures using items or adaptations of items from the Patterns of Adaptive Learning Survey (Midgley et al., 1998) the studies are not consistent in the source of the information that is utilized to define the level 2 goal context. Specifically, three rely solely on aggregated student ratings, four use both student aggregates and teacher ratings and two are based exclusively on teacher reports (Miller & Murdock, 2007a). Across these studies it is clear that the source of the data has a large effect on what is actually measured. In studies that utilize teacher and student data, correlations between these ratings are quite small. More important, their relations to student outcomes are not consistent. Of the five studies that relied on teacher reports, only 2 found significant relationships with outcomes: in one study, teacher-rated performance goals were inversely related to students' adoption of mastery goals (Anderman & Young, 1994) and in the other, teacher-rated performance goals were associated with increased self-handicapping (Urdan, Midgley, & Anderman, 1998). In contrast, whereas teacher-reported mastery goals were not associated with any outcomes, students' aggregated mastery goals have been linked to disruptive behavior (Kaplan, Gheen, & Midgely, 2002), self-handicapping (Turner, Midgley, Meyer, Gheen, Anderman, Kang, & Patrick, 2002) and avoidance of help-seeking (Ryan, Gheen, & Midgley, 1998; Turner et al., 2002). Of the three studies that included both student aggregates and teacher self-reports, only one found both measures (of performance goal structures) to predict the same outcome (Urdan, Midgley, & Anderman, 1998).

Although the above studies suggest that teacher reports and student aggregates may not be measuring the same thing, comparisons across studies are difficult because each study uses different dependent variables and includes varying controls at level 1, such as students' personal goals, prior achievement, and self-efficacy. Therefore, to better understand the congruence or lack there of between measures obtained from various sources, we more directly compared teacher, student and observer reports of classroom goal structures in a sample of 689 high school students from 58 independent math and science classrooms (see Miller & Murdock, 2007b). Classroom goal structures were assessed in September or October 2004 and again for 51 classrooms in April or May of 2005 using both student ratings and teacher ratings. A small subset of the classes ($n = 12$) was also observed for goal structure practices by three observers during at least three class sessions.

In the fall of 2004, correlations between student aggregated reports and teacher reports of both performance ($r = .02$) and mastery ($r = .12$) goal structures were not significant. Similar findings were unveiled during the Spring 2005 data collection with non-significant correlations of $r = .18$ for mastery goal structures and $r = -.13$ for performance goal structures.

Based on the observer ratings, we classified the classrooms as high ($n=5$), average ($n=4$) or low ($n =3$) in mastery goal structures. One-way analyses of variance using observer classifications as the IV and student, $F(2,9) = .411$, $p= .67$, and teacher, $F(2,9) = 1.67$, $p=.24$, ratings as the DV revealed no differences between groups, suggesting that observers' perceptions of mastery goal structures differ from both teachers' and students'. The same procedure was followed for observers' ratings of performance goals, yielding four high, six average and two low performance goal classrooms. Again, there were no differences between the high, medium and low performance classrooms, as judged by observers for either student, $F(2,9) = 1.09$, $p = .38$, or teacher, $F(2,9)=1.11$, $p=.37$ ratings of performance goals.

Not only were the classroom goal structure ratings different depending on the rater, the relations between goal structures and students' effort varied based on how goal structures were measured. We examined this in a series of multilevel models first predicting students' self-reported effort and then teacher-rated student effort. In all analyses, self-efficacy, personal mastery and personal performance goals were entered at level 1, followed by classroom goal structures at level 2, measured either based on teacher-reports or on student-aggregates. In both the model for student-rated effort and that for teacher-rated effort, self-efficacy, students' mastery and performance goals were significant predictors. However, at level 2, students' aggregated ratings of mastery goal structures were positive predictors of student-rated effort; whereas teacher ratings of goal structures were unrelated to this outcome. One possible explanation for the disparate finding is the relatively low reliability of the teacher-rated goal structure measures (.62 and .60 for performance and mastery respectively). Neither student-rated nor teacher-rated mastery or performance goals were predictors of teacher-rated effort.

The inconsistencies between teacher and student-rated predictors may also have to do with the content of the items themselves. Whereas two of the four questions on the PALS measure of teacher mastery goals pertain to providing choices among activities of different levels, none of the questions on the student version make reference to this. In contrast, three of the six student items reflect a focus on the importance of understanding versus memorization, but teachers are not asked about this at all. Although this seems like a plausible explanation, other researchers have found similar student-teacher divergence, even after modifying the items to be more parallel.

Issue 2: Reliability of Student Aggregates

Aggregating students' reports of the perceived goal structure within a classroom to form a classroom measure of goal structure presumes that there is a shared consensus among the students about what is going on in that setting. From a technical standpoint, this means that part of what influences the reliability of the aggregate scores is the amount of consistency among respondents within each classroom. Most studies, however, simply report the Cronbach's alpha coefficient, which is only an estimator of the reliability of the responses to items across all of the individuals in the study (Miller & Murdock, 2007c); this is not the correct method of assessing reliability in these cases as it does not factor in information about the level of consistency within the classroom to the construct as a whole. In contrast to a Cronbach's alpha, the calculation of the MLM reliability coefficients at level 2 (classroom level) should be done as follows:

$$\text{Classroom Level} = \frac{\sigma^2_{classroom}}{\sigma^2_{classroom} + \frac{\sigma^2_{student}}{n} + \frac{\sigma^2_{item}}{(p*n)}}$$

where p is the number of items in the scale and n is the average number of students in the classroom.

The variances are 'true' score variances at the classroom, student and item levels. Thus, level 2 reliability is influenced not only by the number of items on the scale but, more importantly, by the number of level 1 units (students) within each level 2 unit (classrooms). A study having on average 4 people per classroom will have aggregates with much greater measurement error than a comparable study with 15 students per classroom. Of the 9 MLM studies which reported classroom size, the average classroom size has ranged from 6 to 18 students.

In our example data, the average classroom size is 12 with a range of 9 to 24 students per classroom. The MLM reliabilities for mastery (.77) and performance (.76) goal structures were slightly lower than the Cronbach's alpha estimates which were .80 for both mastery and performance, but also more than adequate. However, consider that whereas we had an average classroom size of 12 students, previous studies have had class averages as low as 6 students making it reasonable to question the reliability of the classroom aggregates used in the analyses. For example, in our own sample, if we reduce the average classroom size while maintaining the same levels of variances, we see a rapid decline in classroom aggregate reliability; for an average class size of 10, reliability decreases from .77 to .74, average class size of 8 produces a reliability estimate of .68 and average class size of 6 is a reliability estimate of .63. It is also important to note that this marked decline occurs even while maintaining the current levels of variances (e.g., inter-rater reliability); in reality we would also expect the inter-rater reliability to decline with fewer students per classroom and as a result observe an even more severe decline in aggregate reliability. Recall that the reliability calculation is both a function of the number of students in the classroom as well as their level of agreement.

In sum, the use of Cronbach's alpha is not sufficient to assess reliability in MLM studies which include aggregate student perceptions at level 2. It is important to consider both the number of students per classroom as well as their inter-rater agreement. Studies which have small average classroom size are potentially using less than reliable measures of classroom goal structures which adversely impacts the models they are attempting to estimate, most likely underestimating the impact of aggregate student perceptions on outcome variables.

Issue 3: Relations between Personal Goals and Classroom Goal Structures

Conceptually, goal theory specifies that the effects of classroom goal structures on student motivation are mediated by students' personal goals as depicted in Figure 1 (Midgley, 2002). Presumably, classrooms with more mastery oriented teaching practices encourage students to adopt mastery oriented goals for themselves, and these individual personal goals then determine their motivation as measured by various cognitive, affective and behavioral outcomes. Similar processes are presumed to occur with respect to performance oriented teaching practices. From a modeling standpoint, this means that we should test not only direct effects of goal structures on outcomes of interest, but also indirect effects as mediated through personal goals.

An alternative conceptualization of the relations between personal goals, classroom goal structures and student outcomes comes from incremental intelligence theories (Dweck, 1986). Within this theoretical framework, people's goals are considered to be largely a function of their personality attributes, rather than the context of the learning situation. Students who view intelligence as something that is malleable, and can be improved through effort and learning, are said to hold incremental views of intelligence, and are likely to adopt mastery goals; in contrast, students who see intelligence as a fixed entity will concomitantly hold performance goals. In terms of model specification, this would argue that personal goals and classroom goal structures have independent effects: testing this model requires entering personal goals at level 1 and classroom goals at level 2, and reporting the unique contribution of each. Although these perspectives may not be mutually exclusive of one another in a theoretical sense, different variations in the specification of the HLM model more closely represent one of the perspectives or another.

Whereas most of the MLM based research has been conducted by scholars associated with Midgely or Maher and are therefore presumably grounded in the mediational perspective, none of the studies reported in the literature actually test the mediated model. Two studies (Kaplan, Gheen, & Midgely, 2002; Karabenick, 2004) examine the effects of classroom goal structures at level 2 after controlling for students' personal goals at level 1.

However, because we do not know the effects that goal structures have on the outcomes prior to controlling for personal goals (i.e., the direct effect is unknown), we can not estimate the amount of attenuation in the direct effect that occurs with the introduction of the mediator variable (Raudenbush & Bryk, 2002). Any effects of goal structures that occur through their influence on personal goals are not captured. This means that if classroom goal structures actually do influence students' adoption of personal goals, the coefficient for the effects of classroom goals is an underestimate of classroom goal structure effects because the total effect is the sum of the direct effect plus any indirect effect (not estimated) through personal goals. A scholar may therefore conclude that "only personal goals matter" when, in fact, the classroom level did matter through its influence on personal goals.

In our own data, we examined the direct and indirect influence of classroom-level (student aggregated) mastery goals and performance goals on two different outcomes: students' self-reported effort and students' attitudes about cheating (see also Murdock, Miller & Anderman, 2005). To estimate classroom level effects, without any control for personal goals, we ran the model below for both effort and cheating attitudes with G_J standing for the aggregated score of perceived mastery goal structure and H_J for the aggregated score of perceived performance goal structure.

$$\text{Level } 1: Y_{iy} = B_{0j} + r_{ij}$$

$$\text{Level } 2: B_{0j} = \gamma_{00} + \gamma_{01}G_j + \gamma_{02}H_j + U_{oj}$$

$$B_{1j} = \gamma_{10}$$

We subsequently reran the model adding students' personal mastery goals, X, and personal performance goals, Y, both grand mean centered[2], into the level 1 model.

$$\text{Level } 1: Y_{iy} = B_{0j} + B_{1}jX_{ij} + B_{1}jY_{ij} + r_{ij}$$

$$\text{Level } 2: B_{0j} = \gamma_{00} + \gamma_{01}G_j + \gamma_{02}H_j + U_{oj}$$

$$B_{1j} = \gamma_{10}$$

Results for these models are shown in Table 1. Note that when students' personal goals are entered as control variables (columns 3 and 5), the effects of aggregated mastery goal structures at level 2 are statistically significant predictors of both effort and cheating attitudes, but these effects are smaller than when personal goals are not included at level 1 (see columns 2 and 4), suggesting that the effects of mastery goal structures are partially mediated by their effects on students' personal goals. Performance goal structures have no direct or indirect effect on cheating attitudes, but do predict student effort. Once again, these effects appear to be partially mediated by personal goals, given that the size of their influence is attenuated after the effects of students' personal performance goals are added to the model. Together, these results are partially consistent with the model of goal structure effects depicted in Figure 1; however, they also suggest that personal goals are not completely determined by what happens in the classrooms as the magnitude of the per-

---

[2] A discussion of the effects of centering decisions is in the next section of this paper.

sonal goal coefficients are much larger than those for the classroom goal structure effects.

Table 1. Comparison of the direct effects of level 2 goal structures and indirect effects as mediated through personal goals.

	Effort Direct effects model	Effort Indirect effects model	Cheating attitudes Direct Effects model	Cheating attitudes Indirect effects model
Personal mastery goals (level 1)		.49 (.03) $t(753)= 18.37$ $p <.001$		-.38 (.04) $t(752)= -9.06$ $p <.001$
Personal performance goals (level 1)		-.05 (.02) $t(753)= -2.43$ $p <.05$		.08 (.05) $t(752)= 1.45$ $p >.05$
Aggregate mastery goal structure (level 2)	.26 (.06) $t(54) = 4.26$ $p < .001$	.14 (.04) $t(54) = 3.23$ $p < .01.$	-.66 (.07) $t(54) = -9.43$ $p < .001$	-.56 (.07) $t(54) =-7.74$ $p < .001$
Aggregate performance goal structure (level 2)	-.22 (.05) $t(55) = -4.65$ $p < .001$	-.12 (.04) $t(54) = -.79$ $p <.01$	.04 (.11) $t (54) = .35$ $p > .05$	-.04 (.12) $t(54) = -.40$ $p >.05$
Unconditional variance between classes	3.9% $\chi^2(56) =87.43$ $p < .01$	3.9% $\chi^2 (56) =87.43$ $p < .01$	14.17% $\chi^2 (56) =173.80$ $p < .001$	14.17% $\chi^2 (56) =173.80$ $p < .001$
Final model variance between classes	1.2% $\chi^2(54) =56.31$ $p >.05$	.05% $\chi^2 (54) = 53.15$ $p > .05$	7.5% $\chi^2 (55) =115.14$ $p < .001$	7.0% $\chi^2 (54) =110.87$ $p < .001$

Issue 4: Centering and Context Effects

As noted earlier, correlational examinations of goal structure effects that do not account for nesting or classroom level effects measure perceived goal structures only at the individual level. In MLM studies, students' perceptions of the goal structure of the classroom can be entered at level 1 of the model, but, unlike basic correlational studies, the calculation of their effects will now account for the grouping of students within classes. At level 2, the aggregated perceptions across the classroom are added as predictors of between classroom variance in the outcome variable. The aggregate is presumed to reflect a more objective assessment of the actual classroom goal structure. However, the meaning of this level 2 coefficient varies depending on whether or not the individual perceptions were included at level 1, and, if so, what method of centering was used.

Centering refers to the practice of adjusting the scale of the given variable such that all scores are reported as deviations around the mean. One of the main reasons we center variables is to ease the interpretation of the coefficients. Recall that in MLM, prediction equations for a given variable with one level 1 and one level 2 predictor assuming that the relationship between the predictors and the criterion is constant across classrooms (i.e., no random variation in slopes) have the following form[3]:

$$\text{Level 1}: Y_{ij} = B_{0j} + B_1 jX_{ij} + r_{ij}$$

$$\text{Level 2}: B_{0j} = \gamma_{00} + \gamma_{01}G_j + U_{oj}$$

$$B_{1j} = \gamma_{10} + U_{1j}$$

In the above example, if Y_{ij} is self-reported effort of student i in classroom j, and X_{ij} is student i's perceptions of the classroom mastery goal structure in classroom j, then B_{1j} is the effect of a one unit increase in perceived mastery goal structure on self-reported effort within that class. The intercept, B_{0j} is the predicted value of effort when a student's perceived mastery goal structure has a value of zero. Because zero is not a possible or meaningful value for perceived mastery goal structure, the value of the intercept, which becomes a dependent variable at level 2, is conceptually obtuse. By rescaling the level 1 predictor so that it is centered around the mean, however, the value of the intercept becomes more easily interpretable, though the interpretation varies as a function of what method of centering is selected.

If individual scores of a given variable are centered around the mean score of all students in the data set, or the *grand mean* (X_{ij} -X), the intercept value represents the predicted level of effort for a given student in classroom j whose level of perceived mastery goal structure is the average of all the students in the study. The variance in B_{0j} is the between-class variation in the dependent variable after these scores have been adjusted for the effects of the level 1 variable. In a model predicting effort with students' assessment of the mastery goal structure as a level 1 grand-mean centered predictor, B_{0j} is the predicted value of student effort in classroom j for a student who has viewed that classroom as "average" in mastery goals; thus, the variance in B_{0j} is the between class variance in effort after controlling for students' personal perceptions of the classroom goal structures. Note that if the average perceived mastery goal structure score is 3 across all the students in the sample, and both Keisha in classroom A and Barb in classroom B view their classroom as average in mastery goals (a score of 0 with grand mean centering), they will both have the same predicted effort score based on the level 1 model.

When predictors of B_{0j} are entered at level 2, the variance being predicted is partly a function of between class variation and partly a function of within class variation. Why? Because while a separate equation was estimated for each classroom j at level 1, B_{0j} was adjusted for students' views of mastery goal structures relative to the students in all of the classrooms (between-groups), not simply within their own classroom. Thus, if aggregated mastery goals are entered as a level 2 predictor G, the effect of γ_{01} is a *context effect*: it is the effect of a one unit increase in aggregated mastery goal structure above and beyond

---

[3] We are limiting our discussion of centering decisions at level 1 to the effects on the interpretation of the intercept and level 2 predictors of the intercept because this is where the ambiguity occurs in most of the published MLM studies of goal structures, and a full discussion of all the effects of centering is beyond the scope of this chapter. However, centering decisions at level 1 also influence the interpretation of the coefficients of level 2 predictors of the slope, B1. A complete discussion of this can be found in Enders & Tofighi., 2007; Hoffman & Gavin, 1998; Kreft, DeLeeuw, & Aiken, 1995.

the effect of the student's relative view of the mastery goal structure. For example, let's assume that although Keisha and Barb both view their classroom as average in terms of mastery goal structures, Keisha is in a classroom where the level 2 aggregate (grand-mean centered) for perceived mastery goals is 3 and Barb is in a classroom where the perceived aggregate is 1. The magnitude of the context effect γ_{01} estimates how much the aggregate view of the classroom influences a given students' effort beyond the effects of the person's own view of that classroom. Because students' personal views of the class-room are both logically and empirically related to the overall view of the classroom, this means that the context effect, γ_{01}, is not a pure estimate of the between class effect of aggregated goal structures on students' outcome. Rather, it is the between class effect minus the within class effect. A true between class estimate of the effect of aggregated mastery goal structure can be found be adding B_{1j} to the level 2 coefficient, (Enders &Tofighi, 2007; Kreft & DeLeeuw, 1998; Kreft, DeLeeuw, & Aiken 1995; Raudenbush & Bryk, 2002).

When level 1 variables are *group mean* centered, a given person's score is now a de-viation from their own classroom mean; the intercept thus represents the expected value of effort for a student in classroom j when he or she has the average within-class view of the classroom mastery practices. In rescaling the scores this way, they have only been adjusted relative to other students in the class; therefore, differences between classes in views of goal structures are not controlled for. The intercept value B_{0j} represents the pre-dicted level of effort for a given student in classroom j whose level of perceived mastery goal structure is the average level in that classroom. The variance in B_{0j} is the unadjusted between class variation in the dependent variable. Thus, when predictors are entered at level 2, such as the aggregated mastery goal structure, the value of γ_{01} represents the ef-fect of a one unit change in aggregate classroom mastery goal structure for students, who in their respective class have the same relative view of the classroom goal structures. For example, Gregg may be in a class where the aggregate mastery goal structure score was 2; his personal group-mean centered view is 2, meaning he viewed the class 2 points higher than average or a score of 4; Marcus is in a class with an aggregate score of 1, but his personal group-mean centered score is 2, meaning he viewed the class 2 points higher than his classmates, or has a score of 3. Based on the level 1 model, we would predict the same amount of effort from both of these students. However, if there is a positive effect of aggregated goals at level 2, then Gregg's effort would be predicted as being higher.

In short, in the first case, the gamma coefficient is giving us what is known as the "context effect," which is the classroom effect after controlling for variation in individual perceptions, whereas in the later case the gamma coefficient gives us a between class effect, without adjusting for differences in perceptions within classrooms. This is the same value of γ_{01} that one would get if no predictors had been included at level 1. In the latter case, the context effect can be derived from the computer output simply by subtract-ing the individual level coefficient from the gamma coefficient. Similarly, when grand-meaning centering is used, the between group effect can be estimated by adding together the individual and the context effect coefficients.

We examined the effects of centering decision in our data (Murdock & Miller, 2006) using both students' self-rated effort and their score on the measure of cheating attitudes as dependent variables (see Table 2). For sake of clarity, we included only perceived mastery goal structure in the analysis. At level 1, the individual's personal perceptions were entered (either group or grand-mean centered); at level 2, the aggregate for the classroom was included. Although centering has no effect on the magnitude of the level 1 variable, it significantly affects the size of the coefficient at level 2. In the case of effort, the aggregate is not significant at level 2 when grand-meaning centering is used, but it is when the level 1 variable is centered around the group mean. Similarly, when cheating attitude is the dependent variable, the level 2 coefficient is much smaller when grand-mean centering was used at level 1. Also, note, that the context effect coefficient, which is the level 2 coefficient when grand mean centering is used can be derived from the group-mean centered model by subtracting the level 1 coefficient from the level 2 coefficient.

Table 2. Comparison of Level 2 Coefficients when the level 2 aggregate is either grand mean or group mean centered at level.

	Effort Level 1 grand mean centering	Effort Level 1 group mean centering	Cheating attitudes Level 1 grand mean centering	Cheating attitudes Level 1 group mean centering
Perceived mastery goal structure (level 1)	.31 (.03) t (755)= 9.19 p <.001	.31 (.03) t (755)= 9.19 p <.001	-.50 (.05) t (755)= -11.14 p <.001	-.50 (.05) t (755)= -11.14 p <.001
Aggregate mastery goal structure (level 2)	-.08 (.07) t(55) = -1.12 p >.05	.22 (.07) t(55) = 3.32 p <.01	-.15 (.07) t(55) = -2.15 p < .05	-.65 (.06) t(55) =-9.54 p < .001
Unconditional variance between classes	3.9% χ^2 (56) =87.43 p < .01	3.9% χ^2 (56) =87.43 p < .01	14.17% χ^2 (56) = 173.80 p < .001	14.17% χ^2 (56) = 173.80 p < .001
Final model variance between classes	3.7% χ^2 (55) =80.33 p < .05.	3.7% χ^2 (55) =80.33 p < .05.	7.5% χ^2 (55) =115.14 p < .001	7.5% χ^2 (55) =115.14 p < .001

Given that both context effects and betweenclass effects can be derived with either form of centering, the issue is not about which centering method to use, but about clarity of reporting and interpretation. Within the goal theory literature, no one specifies whether they are reporting a between class effect or a context effect—they all interpret their coefficient as having the same meaning, when in fact, that is not the case. As such, conclusions about the influence of goal structures are not comparable across studies. The choice of whether one should interpret the between group versus the context effect is a conceptual rather than an empirical question. If we assume that the aggregated score of perceived mastery goals is a valid indicator of classroom practices, then the between class coefficient gives us information about the extent to which variations from teacher to teacher in these mastery goal practices affect students' level of effort. If however, we assume that these aggregated perceptions are a function of both the students who make up the class and the actual behaviors of the teachers, the context effect might be more meaningful. Finally, if one assumes that teacher practices, such as the goal structures they create, influence students' attitudes, cognitions and behaviors through the perception of the goal structure that students' personally construct, then the meaningful analyses to report are those that would test the mediated model, with personal views of the classroom goal structure as mediators between the level 2 measure of goal structure and individual outcomes. Establishing the effects of aggregated goals on student outcomes without the mediator is simply the between group effect, or γ_{01} with group-mean centering. Establishing the effect of the aggregated goals on student outcomes after controlling for personal perceptions is the "context effect" or γ_{01} with group-mean centering. The magnitude of the difference between the group-mean centering and grand-mean centering coefficients represents the extent to which personal perceptions of classroom goals have mediated the effects of aggregated goal structures.

Conclusion and Future Directions

The advent of MLM techniques has advanced our ability to determine the extent to which classroom-level phenomenon, such as goal structures, affect individual students' attitudes, cognitions and behaviors. As with many a new tool, however, the application has outpaced a careful consideration of the conceptual and interpretive consequences that are associated with various decisions in model specification. The lack of clarity as to how and why these decisions are made or the consequences of these decisions may leave many readers to simply accept the interpretation of the findings in the results section, when such conclusions may or may not be warranted.

Although the examples here were specific to the measurement of classroom goal structure and their relationship to students' personal goals, the arguments we present cuts across efforts to capture the effects of variability in classroom context. With any set of constructs, divergence in ratings based on the raters is a potentially large source in the variability of the meaning that can be drawn from any study. Given that the aim of educational research is to improve students use of adaptive learning strategies, decrease reliance on poor strategies, and ultimately increase student learning, debates about the best source of information need to be resolved by finding those classroom context measures that best predict meaningful student outcomes. Moreover, regardless of the construct that is being assessed, documenting classroom effects will require large enough samples of independent classrooms to have sufficient between-class variability and power to detect classroom level differences, as well as enough people within each classroom to insure that student aggregates are reliable. Currently, there are few MLM studies within the motivational literature where the appropriate power and reliability have been reported.

We used our data to demonstrate the importance of specifying the effects of order of variable entry on the meaning of the tested model using the example of the presumed theoretical relationship between the level 1 variable, such as personal goals, and the level 2 variables, such as goal structures. Any investigation of classroom context effects always faces multiple challenges in these areas, as many of the factors that we would enter as predictors at the individual level, such as self-efficacy, interest, or other indicators of personal motivation, are presumably not stable traits, but are themselves influenced by the context of the classroom, and therefore should be specified as at least partial mediators of the classroom effects. Similarly, when centering decisions are made at level 1, regardless of whether one enters the same or a different contextual variable at level 2, the meaning of the level 2 coefficient changes, because group mean centering does not control for the level 1 variable, whereas grand-mean centering does.

Of the four issues we have discussed in this paper, only one is an issue of correct versus incorrect: insuring the reliability of aggregated variables that are entered at level 2 as a measure of context. The remaining issues are all decisions that the researcher needs to make based on their clearly-articulated understanding of the psychological meaning of the constructs they are measuring and the theoretical relationships between them. Advances in our efforts to understand how classroom processes influence motivation and achievement would be significantly improved by more mindful decision-making about the match between the model one intends to test and the mathematical specification of that model that occurs when we analyze our data.

Implications: Local to Global

Technological advances have helped shrink the world we work in, increasing access to cross-cultural research findings and creating more opportunities for collaborative research within and across nations. While this improved level of information exchange affords many opportunities for scholars to learn about the generalizabilty as well as the limits to the generalizabilty of their theories and models, the findings reviewed in this chapter underscore the importance of carefully defining and testing the measures and models that one has adopted.

Among other things, we have demonstrated how the common practice of aggregating measures at the classroom level as indicators of classroom context can only be valid if the researcher first demonstrates that the scores yield reliable data at that specified level, accounting for level of agreement among people nested within the same group, rather than just consistency in responses across items. This same caution needs to be exercised when scholars adopt a measure that was developed for one linguistic or cultural group and then applied to another. Demonstration of the psychometric properties for a measure of a given "contextual" construct should include showing that the aggregated measure yields a reliable within-class score within the population it is going to be used for. One can not assume that a construct viewed as "individual perception," such as perceived teacher expectations in our sample (Miller & Murdock, 2007c) versus those viewed as "characteristic of classrooms" (e.g., goal structure in our sample) will be see in other cultures as operating in the same manner, due to, among other things, differing views of the extent to which our behavior is viewed as autonomous versus interdependent. Disparities in the psychological meaning of a construct would render some aggregates interpretable to some cultures but not others.

Similarly, just as measures of individual perceptions need to provide validity evidence in the culture they will be used, so too is the case with aggregate validity. For example, in our data from the United States we have found that aspects of the classroom we presumed to be unique (goal structures and perceived pedagogical quality), were, in fact, so highly correlated at the aggregate level as to make it impossible to argue that they were measuring different constructs. This type of validity work is needed in any context a measure will be applied in.

Issues related to providing detailed model specification, such as the inclusion of control variables and the choice of centering techniques at level 1, insure that conclusions reached about the similarities and differences in motivation and factors influencing motivation are not contaminated by artifact. Given the extremely high stakes that educational outcomes have in many countries, it is imperative that scholars making cross-cultural comparisons are meticulous about the comparability of the models they are testing. Assuring this level of consistency in model specification will also open up more dialogs among scholars regarding their views of the relations between context, psychological processes and behavior.

Finally, in doing this work we found a lack of consistent relationships between what teachers said about their practices and what observers or students saw in the classroom. Among other things, this lack of consistency was partially due to the relatively small amount of variability in teachers' ratings of their classroom practices. Given the enormous pressure that teachers in the United States currently feel due to the advent of high stakes testing, these above-average ratings may reflect feelings of being continuously challenged at the local and national level. Comparing the variability and predictive validity of these ratings across cultural contexts where different norms of accountability prevail and trying to ascertain the factors that related to more versus less accurate teacher ratings would be a fruitful area for future research.

Acknowledgements

Funds for this project were provided by a research grant to the first author by the Spencer Foundation.

References

Anderman, E.M., Maehr, M.L., & Midgley, C. (1999). Declining motivation after the transition to middle school: Schools can make a difference. *Journal of Research and Development in Education, 32,* 131-147.

Anderman, E. M., Griesinger, T., & Westerfield, G. (1998). Motivation and cheating during early adolescence. *Journal of Educational Psychology, 90,* 84-93.

Anderman, E. M., & Midgley, C. (2004). Changes in self-reported academic cheating across the transition from middle school to high school. *Contemporary Educational Psychology, 29,* 499-517.

Anderman, E. M., & Young, A. J. (1994). Motivation and strategy use in science: Individual differences and classroom effects. *Journal of Research in Science Teaching, 31,* 811-831.

Dweck, C. S. (1986). Motivational processes affecting learning. *American Psychologist, 4,* 1040-1048.

Elliott, J., Hufton, N., Anderman, E., & Illushin, L. (2000). The psychology of motivation and its relevance to educational practice. *Educational & Child Psychology, 17,* 122-138.

Enders, C., & Tofighi, D. (2007). Centering predictor variables in cross-sectional multi-level models: A new look at an old issue. *Psychological Methods, 12,* 121-138.

Hoffman, D.A., & Gavin, M.B. (1998). Centering decisions in hierarchical linear models: Implications for research in organization. *Journal of Management, 24,* 623-641.

Kaplan, A., Gheen, M., & Midgley, C. (2002). Classroom goal structure and student disruptive behaviour. *British Journal of Educational Psychology, 72,* 191-212.

Karabenick, S. A. (2004). Perceived achievement goal structure and college student help seeking. *Journal of Educational Psychology, 96,* 569-581.

Kreft, I., & De Leeuw, J.(1998). *Introducing multilevel modeling.* Thousand Oaks, CA: Sage.

Kreft, I.., De Leeuw, J., & Aiken L.S. (1995). The effect of different forms of centering in hierarchical linear models. *Multivariate Behavioral Research, 30,* 1-21.

Midgley, C. (2002). *Goals, goal structures, and patterns of adaptive learning.* Mahwah, NJ: Lawrence

Erlbaum.

Midgley, C., Kaplan, A., Middleton, M., Maehr, M. L., Urdan, T., Anderman, L. H., Anderman, E., & Roeser, R. (1998). The development and validation of scales assessing students' achievement goal orientations. *Contemporary Educational Psychology, 23*, 113-131.

Miller, A.D., & Murdock, T.B. (2007a). *What do we really know about the effects of classroom goal structures? A review and methodological critique.* Unpublished manuscript.

Miller, A. D., & Murdock, T. B. (2007b). *Perceptions matter – convergence and divergence of teacher, student and observer reports in measuring classroom goal structures.* Paper presented at the Biennial Meeting of the European Association for Research on Learning and Instruction, Budapest, Hungary.

Miller, A. D., & Murdock, T. B. (2007c). Modeling latent true scores to determine the utility of aggregate student perceptions as classroom indicators in HLM: The case of classroom goal structures. *Contemporary Educational Psychology, 32*, 83-104.

Murdock, T. B., Hale, N. M., & Weber, M. J. (2001). Predictors of cheating among early adolescents: Academic and social motivations. *Contemporary Educational Psychology, 26*, 96-115.

Murdock, T. B., Miller, A., & Kohlhardt, J. (2004). Effects of classroom context variables on high school students' judgments of the acceptability and likelihood of cheating. *Journal of Educational Psychology, 96*, 765-777.

Murdock, T. B., Miller, A. D., & Goetzinger, A. A. (2007). The effects of classroom context variables on university students' judgments of the acceptability of cheating: Mediating and moderating processes. *Social Psychology of Education, 10*, 141-169.

Murdock, T. B., Miller, A., & Anderman, E. (2005). *Classroom and individual predictors of between-class variation in perceived cheating: a hierarchical linear model.* Paper presented at the Annual Meeting of the American Educational Research Association, Montreal, Canada.

Murdock, T. B., & Miller, A. D. (2006). *Defining classroom goal structure effects: Competing statistical models applied to academic cheating.* Paper presented at the 10th International Conference on Motivation, Laudau, Germany.

Patrick, H., Anderman, L. H., Ryan, A. M., Edelin, K. C., & Midgley, C. (2001). Teachers' communication of goal orientations in four fifth-grade classrooms. *Elementary School Journal, 102*, 35-58.

Pintrich, P. R., & Schunk, D. H. (2002). *Motivation in Education: Theory, Research, and Applications* (2nd ed.). Upper Saddle River: Merrill Prentice Hall.

Raudenbush, S.W., & Bryk, A.S. (2002). *Hierarchical Linear Models: Applications and data analysis methods.* Thousand Oaks, CA: Sage.

Ryan, A. M., Gheen, M. H., & Midgley, C. (1998). Why do some students avoid asking for help? An examination of the interplay among students' academic efficacy, teachers' social-emotional role, and the classroom goal structure. *Journal of Educational Psychology, 90*, 528-535.

Turner, J. C., Midgley, C., Meyer, D. K., Gheen, M., Anderman, E. M., Kang, Y., & Patrick, H. (2002). The classroom environment and students' reports of avoidance strategies in mathematics: A multimethod study. *Journal of Educational Psychology, 94*, 88-106.

Turner, J. C., & Patrick, H. (2004). Motivational influences on student participation in classroom learning activities. *Teachers College Record, 106*, 1759-1785.

Urdan, T., Midgley, C., & Anderman, E. M. (1998). The role of classroom goal structure in students' use of self-handicapping strategies. *American Educational Research Journal, 35*, 101-122.

Urdan, T., Ryan, A. M., Anderman, E. M., & Gheen, M. H. (2002). Goals, goal structures, and avoidance behaviors. In C. Midgley (Ed.), *Goals, goal structures, and patterns of adaptive learning* (pp. 55-83). Mahwah, NJ: Lawrence Erlbaum Associates.

Motivation Development in Novice Teachers

The Development of Utility Filters

Susan Bobbitt Nolen, Christopher J. Ward, Ilana Seidel Horn, Sarah Childers, Sara Sunshine Campbell, & Karan Mahna

This chapter describes how graduate students in a teacher preparation program develop motivational filters used to make utility judgments in deciding which promoted practices to learn. Preservice teachers enter teacher education programs (TEPs) expecting to learn methods of instruction in their subject area and classroom management techniques from TEP instructors at the university, "in the field" from "real" teachers, or both. Their approach to learning is largely instrumental, with the overarching goal of becoming a competent teacher. We used person-centered ethnographic methods in a longitudinal design to examine how students decide which practices are worth taking up into their own work as teachers, and which to learn well enough for external demands (e.g., to satisfy course requirements).

Most theories treat motivation as an orientation to school learning, a subject area (e.g., science), or a specific learning situation. For example, a student might be described as having a performance-approach orientation (Elliot & Harackiewicz, 1996) in math class, as interested in a subject or activity (Hidi & Renninger, 2006), or as being "internally regulated" when studying (Ryan & Deci, 2000). Simons and her colleagues (Simons, Dewitte, & Lens, 2004) found that internally-regulated students who perceived the utility of what they learned used more adaptive learning strategies and had increased motivation. Similarly, we found evidence that preservice teachers are continually deciding *what* to learn and *how well* to learn specific ideas or practices. At the same time, they frequently asked how a promoted practice or idea might be used in the classroom. Thus, they might be described as self-regulated learners seeking utility information (Zimmerman & Schunk, 2004).

This description is of limited practical use to teacher educators, however, as it does not tell *why* preservice teachers select some promoted practices over others. As novices with restricted opportunities to try out promoted practices, it is important to understand the basis for these utility decisions. Are they matching their instructors' or cooperating teachers' recommendations to their own experience as students (Lortie, 1975)? Are they examining scientific evidence of the effectiveness of possible teaching techniques? Understanding how novices make these decisions could be useful to teacher educators trying to convince their students of the need to learn "best" practices.

Equally important, the variable-centered survey and experimental research that aims at generalizations about individual characteristics and external influences on motivation has difficulty explaining how particular motivations and values arise and develop "in the wild." Even longitudinal studies with conventional self-report measures require construct invariance across time and contexts, an assumption that is based on a view of motivations and values as residing in the individual. Situative and sociocultural perspectives, on the other hand, frame them as co-constructed through negotiation in particular systems of meaning that must be studied at the same time as the individuals that construct them (Nolen & Ward, in press).

Theories of self-regulation have begun to consider the role of others in the social context as important to understanding regulation in classroom settings. Recent research has investigated co-regulation or other-regulation in collaborative learning settings and documented their importance for successful group functioning (Salonen, Vauras, & Efklides, 2005). Some of this research has been informed by the sociocultural theories of Vygotsky and Valsiner, focusing on the channeling, or canalization, of students' interest and activity by self and others. The work of Walker and his colleagues (Pressick-Kilborn & Walker, 2002; Walker, Pressick-Kilborn, Arnold, & Sainsbury, 2004), for example, explores the development of interest over time as a result of social interaction mediated by artifacts and other tools in classroom settings. This longitudinal work in context allows a look at the processes involved in changing interest and values.

Examining the particulars of specific contexts and individuals can provide more than localized "snapshots" of processes. Analysis of observed interactions, negotiations, and enactments of beliefs over time, taking into account the developing semiotic systems within which those events occur, and including comparisons across cases, samples, and contexts, can lead to generalizations about the global processes and mechanisms that underlie motivated action. In this chapter, we will illustrate this claim with data from observations in both university and field settings, along with ethnographic and semi-structured interviews, using a situative theory of motivation.

Our framework is grounded in the assumption that identities and goals develop in social contexts, influencing and influenced by interaction with others in a particular social world (Holland, Lachicotte, Skinner, & Cain, 1998). Our thinking about motivation was informed by several theories, including Future Time Perspective (Simons et al., 2004), Self-Determination Theory (Ryan & Deci, 2000), and Intentional Theory (Nicholls, 1989). In the end, however, we found that general orientations toward learning, even when considered in a situation-specific fashion, were not sufficient to explain interns' motivation to learn specific promoted practices and ideas. Instead, we have developed a situative conceptualization of motivation that deepens our understanding of the complex processes governing students' decisions to learn, how well, and for what purposes. In this chapter, we will use the concept of *motivational filters*, and in particular the utility filter, to describe how preservice teachers' make decisions about learning.

Motivational Filters

In our study of beginning teachers, we observed preservice teacher interns selecting and rejecting ideas and practices promoted by instructors, supervisors, or cooperating teachers, both in conversations and in making teaching decisions. Interns spontaneously self-reported consciously making decisions about which promoted ideas and practices to incorporate into their developing practices and identities as teachers, and which to learn well enough to satisfy evaluators. As Dania[1], a math intern, put it when asked to describe herself as a student:

> I come to class, I pay attention, I don't promise to take notes and I don't promise to have done the reading ahead of time, but at the same time I'm trying to pick up what sounds important. So like Assessment, I may not find it the most interesting of courses but I can see how useful it is. So I'm trying to pay attention to that and actually do some of the reading.
>
> *Dania, Interview 1, Feb 14, 2005*

Through our analysis of observation and interview data across cases and contexts, we developed the notion of motivational filters to describe this form of regulation and its development over time in preservice teachers. Consonant with a situative view of learning (Greeno, 2006), we see motivational filters as lying at the interface between individuals and their social worlds[2]. Specifically, motivational filters are an example of what Holland, et al. (1998) call "tool[s] of agency or self-control and change" that arise out of interactions among persons, cultural resources, and situations in practice and "act as heuristics for the next moment of activity" (p. 40). As our analysis proceeded, we identified a number of potential filters, including relationship filters in which interns' willingness to consider adopting an idea or practice depended on the trustworthiness or perceived expertise of the source, or a perception of shared values; interest filters in which practices that aligned with personal interests (e.g., ways of questioning pupils that matched an interest in understanding others' thinking) were taken up, and "good teacher" filters, in which a practice was compared with interns' conception of good teaching practice. Our focus in this chapter will be on *utility filters*, in which interns evaluated the feasibility of promoted teaching practices and their value as teaching tools.

Interns are in the process of developing into professional teachers, of building new identities as "good teachers." Practices are bound up in their definitions of good teaching, the standards by which they judge other teachers and themselves. Yet the use of a practice signifies different things in different social worlds, and must be negotiated anew with other members of each community of practice in which it is used (Wenger, 1998). Students often discussed promoted practices among themselves or with instructors or cooperating teachers (CTs) who were not themselves the source of a particular practice. Because the novices in our study learned to teach in multiple contexts, we were able to document how their views of the utility of practices developed through these negotiations.

Data Sources

The data we use to illustrate the concept of utility filters comes from a multi-year, case-based ethnography of beginning teachers. We began observations in the first term of par-

---

[1] All names are pseudonyms.
[2] This is similar to the idea of the "experiential interface" proposed by Volet (2001)

ticipants' masters-level teacher education program and continued through the first years of professional teaching. In the preservice phase, 53 interns (novice teachers) participated in the study as we observed them interacting in all of their teacher education program courses (approximately 100 hours). We also observed social events in which some students participated. Using the concept of "figured worlds" from the work of Dorothy Holland and her colleagues (Holland et al., 1998), we called the university context "TEP-world." In the second quarter of the program we selected 8 focal students for in-depth study: four social studies and four math interns, gender balanced but with diversity in ethnicity, age, marital/parental status, socioeconomic background, and teaching experience. These interns were observed teaching in their respective middle or high school field placements ("Fieldworlds") six times, observed in conference with university supervisors and cooperating teachers, and interviewed seven times during the preservice phase, for a total of about 12 hours of field placement observations and 9-12 hours of interviews per intern over 15 months. After graduation, we were able to continue to study seven of the original eight novice teachers in their first year of professional teaching. We conducted three 2-day observations, in which the researcher spent the entire day with the novice teacher, observing classes, informal interactions with colleagues and students, and formal evaluative or instructional interactions with mentors and administrators. Each of these observations was followed by a one- to two-hour semi-structured interview. All interviews in the study began with a request for novice teachers to reflect on the class session(s) observed, followed by a semi-structured protocol with a "past-present-future" structure. In each subsequent interview, the "present" from the previous interview was revisited to check for changes in interns' thinking about their work.

Data were analyzed using a grounded theory approach (Strauss & Corbin, 1998). Initial analysis was generally guided by the larger project's overall research questions: How are the development of interns' motivation to learn and identity related? And what are the processes that govern that development in the multiple contexts in which they learn to teach? Initial steps included identifying statements of motivation or identity and examining the contexts in which they occurred. We used discourse-analytic techniques to code instances of interns positioning themselves or being positioned by others as teachers, identified chains of interactions with or around particular practices, and documented students' negotiations with others around the value or use of these practices in different contexts. As the concept of motivational filters emerged from the data, we began to focus on evidence and counter-evidence related to student employment of filters in regulating their learning.

Dimensions of Utility Filters

Interns commonly used perceived utility as a criterion for determining their level of motivation to take up or try out various promoted practices. The idea of selecting useful practices seems straightforward at first glance, and various theories have emphasized the utility component of value judgments as central to motivation (e.g., Expectancy X Value Theory (Wigfield & Eccles, 2002)). Our work seeks to understand the bases for these judgments and how they develop in the wild. We have found that utility filters are complex, socially-negotiated heuristics. Two principal dimensions of utility were discerned in participants' talk about promoted practices: their *value* for achieving particular goals, and their *feasibility* in "real" classrooms. Both aspects were developed over time through negotiation in TEPworld and Fieldworld with peers, instructors, pupils, cooperating teachers, and supervisors.

Feasibility

Feasibility decisions were based on interns' representations of teaching as a socially-situated activity and on their understanding of the particular practice under consideration. At the beginning of the program, these representations were based on interns' own experiences as pupils, whatever teaching or tutoring experience they had, and cultural representations of teaching and schools from popular culture. Representations developed over time as interns read about, discussed, and participated in teaching contexts as novice teachers.

Representation of the work of teaching. For most interns, representations of the work of teaching (e.g., curriculum requirements, departmental structures, non-teaching responsibilities, characteristics of schools serving low-income pupils, balancing work and home life) were sketchy early in the program. Interns tended to be most familiar with school contexts similar to those in schools they had attended, but from the pupil's perspective rather than the teacher's. Their knowledge of the difficulties of teaching were based in part on reports in the press and popular culture of disinterested parents, assessment policy pressures, limited instructional time, and having to teach large numbers of pupils. In the following example, Gemma is discussing the assessment course, which occurred relatively early in the program, prior to extended experience in Fieldworld. She describes her view of the assessment practices promoted in TEPworld as being unrealistic, and claims this as a general belief of her peers:

> And we knew that, though, like all of us in assessment class or at least in the language arts/social studies. It's like we will never do this in the real world. We will take the ideas and then they will stay in our heads. Like for example, obviously the multiple choice thing did because I was like oh, that's the obvious answer because it's much longer than the rest of them. But I will never sit and plan like I did for that class. There's no - I would have no life outside of school. I would never give any sort of tests or projects because the amount of work that went into it, that's what that class taught me, that the amount of work that goes into assessing is like, who would ever assess anything? And it taught us basic things and I know how to do a rubric and I know that the kids need to know what's going to get them a certain grade and what's not and to give it ahead of time so that everyone is on the same page. But I can't, I could never - the amount of time that we all spent on that class I would never do that ever again.
>
> *Gemma, Interview 2B, May, 2005*

Gemma acknowledged the utility of what she considered the basic ideas of assessment taught in the course. Based on the representation of the work of teaching she held at that point in her development, however, the practice of carefully developing or critically evaluating assessment tools to ensure reliable and valid data for teacher decision-making was not feasible.

Representation of pupils. Interns' representations of pupils arose from their memories of their own student experiences, images in the popular culture, interactions with adolescents in other contexts (e.g., sports teams, health clinics), or from more formal teaching experiences. Early in the program, self-referenced or generalized images of pupils were often used to filter promoted practices in or out on feasibility grounds. In the following excerpt from a large-group discussion in her assessment course on the advisability of using pop quizzes, Gemma argues against a peer who has suggested announcing quizzes in advance:

> *Gemma:* If you announced it a day before, I would have cheated. I was a big cheater in high school (laughs). I'd find someone who did the reading and sit down with them and go through it. So I wasn't doing the reading ever. Is that cheating? It's like I was "playing the game of school." I was learning, but not doing my own reading. I would want my students to actually read.
>
> *Fieldnotes, Assessment, January 26, 2005*

Here Gemma projects her own remembered motives as a high school student onto high school students in general, rejecting the feasibility of the practice. As interns gained additional experience with pupils, their representations changed, influencing their utility filters. For some, representations became deeper and more complex as interns worked to understand and teach students different from themselves.

Sometimes representations changed more dramatically as expectations were violated, leading to the rejection of practices that initially seemed useful. Caitlyn, a math intern, initially planned to adopt the Complex Instruction practices promoted in her math methods course, telling her high school geometry pupils:

> *Caitlyn* (to the class): We want you loud in here and we want you talking. We're going to do a lot of group work in here. We want to create a community in which you'll know each other, where you'll not be afraid to make mistakes, because in math it's easy to make mistakes and you can be guaranteed that others have the same questions as you guys.
>
> *Fieldnotes, August 31, 2005*

However, within a few months Caitlyn had revised her representation of her students, based in part on her unsuccessful attempts to organize the class productively around group work:

> *Caitlyn:* Yeah. It was just…I was finding the kids just weren't mature enough to handle it. And I was like sitting there going like… trying to put kids that I knew didn't work together, trying to separate them, and still they would find a way to, like, talk across the room to each other.
>
> *Interview 3C, December 12*

Caitlyn's interpretation of her difficulties was supported by some of the other math teachers in her high school department. "I get this actually from…I'm getting a lot of agreement among the teachers. Well, one, they say, like, the reason why all the new teachers teach Geometry is because it's so hard….'Because it's such a low level (Interview 3C, December 12)." Convinced that Complex Instruction strategies were not useful with these students, Caitlyn abandoned their use.

Representation of the practice. When making feasibility judgments, an important resource is the individual's representation of the practice itself. When practices are presented and learned outside of the contexts in which they will be used, it is especially likely that these representations will be partial, even sketchy. Those practices that seem to require excessive amounts of time and effort (which may include many practices when they are first taken up) may be particularly likely to be rejected. As described earlier, Gemma based her representation of the labor required if she adopted the promoted assessment practices on her experiences of trying to construct assessments in TEPworld, as a novice with little real classroom experience. Partial representations might also lead to promoted practices slipping through utility filters. To the extent that a practice was believed to be a collection of straightforward procedures that, if followed, would automatically lead to pupil engagement and learning, it would likely pass the feasibility test. Only when recontextualized in a school might the complexities of using the practice become apparent (Horn, Nolen, Ward, & Campbell, in press).

Value of the Practice

Feasibility is only part of the utility filter. For some interns and some practices, initial judgments of feasibility might be suspended or seen as obstacles to be overcome, if the practice was sufficiently valuable. In our analysis, we found two metrics interns used to judge the value of a promoted practice or idea: its usefulness in attaining a particular teaching goal, and its alignment with interns' representation of their disciplines (Wilson, Shulman, & Richert, 1987).

Value in relation to teaching goals. Value judgments occurred when interns considered the usefulness of teaching practices in reaching particular goals. In part, value was judged in relation to the power of the strategy for reaching a goal (e.g., viewing inquiry as a particularly powerful technique for teaching critical thinking), and in part in relation to the importance of the goal itself (e.g., the importance of ameliorating the injustice of unequal educational opportunities). The goals for particular practices developed and were negotiated in the multiple contexts in which these novice teachers learned and practiced (Nolen, Ward, & Horn, 2007), depending on such factors as departmental context, needs of particular students or groups, and interns' changing representations of the practice itself. A practice that might initially be seen as a good way to engage students' interest while delivering content (e.g., Socratic seminars as used by Hilary and Gemma), could come to be seen as valuable for helping students develop important skills. Novices' more general teaching goals (e.g., to promote social justice, to be efficient) were also taken into account in judging the value of specific tasks (Horn, et al., in press).

Representation of the discipline. Interns' representation of their discipline (e.g., mathematics, history) formed part of the value aspect of the utility filter. Mathematics, for example, might be seen as a collection of algorithms, a set of puzzles to be solved, a language in which the universe is written, and/or a gatekeeper to be overcome. One of Brett's central goals at the beginning of the program was to promote social justice by helping his pupils "beat" math and so have access to more education and career options.

He valued practices to the extent that they helped him provide his pupils with tricks and strategies for solving problems on math tests. Early in the program, this position was challenged in his math methods course.

> And so before I would have been like all right, this is the easy way to memorize the formula or whatever, with like - so when I was like doing it last week, I was like what does this mean? Some of the stuff that Lani really hit on, big picture stuff, like why is it important to teach this? What is the big concept here? And thinking of like different representations and deeper meanings…
>
> *Brett, Interview 1, February 10, 2005*

As he began to revise his representation of mathematics as a way of thinking about the world, he began to question his earlier value judgments.

The examples in this section illustrate the dimensions of utility filters that we observed across interns in our sample. Two characteristics of the social contexts of this particular teacher education program facilitated our capture of interns' thinking about promoted practices. First, the TEP emphasizes the critical discussion of ideas through large- and small-group discussion. Interns were invited by their instructors to comment on practices and to think about the evidence supporting their use. Second, participation in our study entailed being asked to reflect on promoted practices, whether taken up or rejected. The fact that discussion of practices was encouraged no doubt made our requests for reflection in the interviews seem more natural, and interns were quite forthcoming. The promotion of reflection itself, however, may well have increased the extent to which interns paid attention to their thinking about teaching practices and so may have influenced the development of various filter components. The evolution of filters via changes in filter components is considered next.

A Situative Account of Filter Development

Change in any of the components of a motivational filter can change which practices are filtered in and out. For all of the interns for whom we have in-depth data, change in utility filters was prompted by challenges to current versions of filter components, something we call "productive friction." Novices learn their craft in social contexts, and those contexts are the sources of frictions that challenge interns' current conceptions. Challenges may come from students who behave in unexpected ways, from cooperating teachers or peers whose views, practices or goals differ, or from instructors and university supervisors who promote unfamiliar practices.

Friction in TEPworld

Filters were often employed in public to test ideas with other members of the community of practice (Wenger, 1998) or "figured world" (Holland, et al., 1998). In the particular context of this TEPworld, students were frequently encouraged to discuss their thinking about promoted ideas and practices in both small groups and whole-class discussions.

This norm supported the social negotiation of students' filters, as ideas were examined, challenged, and defended. The following example comes from the Assessment class, where a group of social studies interns discussed the use of a particular assessment tool promoted by both the textbook and the instructor. Hilary appeals to value as she asserts her view that the process portfolio has utility for her as a teacher of struggling students (Assessment class, small group, March 7, 2005):

> *Hilary:* I'm really interested in the process portfolio, because students don't know how to write reports, and I want to see their process of writing reports.
> *Karl:* But what about "A" students? I think that this is good for struggling students, but for "A" students I don't think that they're doing anything worthwhile.

In this example, Karl uses his representation of pupils to counter Hilary's assertion about the value of process portfolios as a teaching practice. Karl's Fieldworld is in a relatively affluent suburb, while Hilary is student teaching in an urban school serving lower-income pupils. Hilary's school has recently begun to focus on improving pupils' literacy skills across all subjects, which is likely to have contributed both to the representation of pupils and her judgment of the value of the practice. She challenges Karl's assumption that some pupils don't need to be taught writing skills:

> *Hilary:* I think it can help with all students, because even for the A students, there are things they can learn, too. Writing a 5 page paper in high school is different than writing a 20 page research paper in college.
> *Karl:* I don't think it's very practical. I mean, look at the amount of work they [the Instructor and TA] have to do for this class. But I see your point, about being able to write good research papers.

Karl raises another reason for his skepticism about the utility of a process portfolio: feasibility. Elsewhere he had expressed concern that he needed to find ways not to take work home after school, in order to leave time for his other responsibilities and activities. An important factor in utility for Karl, then, was the amount of time and effort required. He coordinated his observations of his TEPworld instructors, combined with his recent Fieldworld experiences in which the teachers primarily assessed through multiple-choice tests and were dismissive of many TEPworld-promoted practices, to construct a negative utility judgment. Nonetheless, he is willing to concede Hilary's view of high school students as needing skills instruction. (In fact, this discussion, along with other experiences and discussions in the ensuing months, likely contributed to Karl's evolving view of the utility of teaching skills to his pupils.) In her final turn, Hilary contrasts her own, valued preparation in private schools to the experiences of her students.

> *Hilary:* I want students to develop a process for doing research and writing. I was lucky to have learned that back in 5th and 6th grade, but what are students' systems for doing research and writing? I want students to have systems for doing these things.

As was especially common for interns early in the program, Hilary refers to her own experiences as a student in judging the value of a particular practice.

Through this kind of negotiation, interns' utility filters influenced and were influenced by the collective norms and images of teaching in Fieldworld and TEPworld. Once a practice had made it through an intern's utility filter, at least provisionally, public actions or tryouts followed in either TEPworld or Fieldworld, or both, subject to negotiation before, during, and after the event. This negotiation, in turn, could influence the social world in which it occurred.

Friction in Fieldworld

In the example above, two students were discussing contradictory views of an assessment practice, views developed in part in their different Fieldworld contexts but negotiated in TEPworld. Hilary's arguments seemed to shift Karl's representation of students somewhat, a view that is supported by evidence that this shift continued through negotiations with his own students during the next extended period in Fieldworld. As he deepened his understanding of students through his interactions with them, his conception of good social studies teaching broadened to include the teaching of skills, practices he had often filtered out in TEPworld courses. By the time he began full-time student teaching in September, he had become, in his words, "the skill guy":

> *Karl:* Now I understand the [assessment] class better, because I was still... living in my own world in a way, wasn't really, compared to reality, how it is here [in my school], about skills and content. So I felt it was all too much about skills but (laughs). And now I'm the skill guy (laughs) compared to the other teachers, also in the meeting on the first day even before when we met the teachers, it was all about the content, what to teach, but there was no talk about how to do good research or how to do group work or how to, you know, any of it.
>
> *Interview 3A, September 7, 2005*

Sometimes Fieldworld itself did not supply sufficient productive friction for growth. Dania, for example, found that her students and cooperating teacher seemed perfectly happy to go along with her teaching strategies. Her university supervisor, however, pushed her to deepen her representation of the practice of questioning to uncover student understandings, a central promoted practice in math methods. Expanding those strategies gained Dania a better sense of her students, reinforcing the utility of this practice even when students appear to be learning.

Resources for Filter Change

Filter change can also be supported by resources in the community of practice. A university supervisor, for example, can help interns respond to frictions in Fieldworld with suggestions for how to modify or extend newly-motivated practices. Supervisors and cooperating teachers can also help the novice interpret classroom events, offering alternative explanations that lead to changes in students' representations of teaching. Although the teachers in Karl's Fieldworld provided minimal support for teaching and assessing skills, his first position as a professional teacher provided a new and more supportive context.

Karl continued to work on scaffolding his students' skill development during his first year as a professional teacher. For example, on the advice of his mentor, he used some of the assessment practices promoted in TEPworld to teach students both important skills and his standards for essay writing. Sharing of resources and ideas can reinforce utility decisions by addressing both value and feasibility components. The departmental culture in this new school was collaborative, and daily lunchtime discussions frequently involved the sharing of ideas and materials as well as discussion of teaching issues. Karl was included in these discussions and positioned as a competent member of the group.

From an initial emphasis on teaching content, Karl's goals for teaching were modified through negotiation with peers, mentors, and pupils to include teaching specific reading, writing, and thinking skills. This change in goals modified his utility filter, and his motivation to learn and employ those strategies also changed. Although this more particular view of the relationship of goals to motivation does not employ the generalized notions of mastery or task orientation or of the relative ability concerns of ego or performance goals, it is consistent with earlier research linking the goals and purposes of learning to the valuing of specific strategies (Nolen, 1988, 1996). The work described here goes beyond the scope of earlier work on goals, however, to investigate the ways in which goals develop through social interaction.

Utility Filters: Relationships to other Theories

Our account of utility filters and their development is consistent with a situative perspective on motivation (Nolen & Ward, in press). By analyzing the interactions of interns with their mentors and with each other, and the activity systems in which they learned to teach, we were able to account for changes in individual interns' filters over time. Even before interns entered their Fieldworlds, their early judgments of feasibility and value were socially constructed through interaction with peers and instructors. Individuals' initial positions were "tried out" and negotiated with others within and outside of TEPworld. Once they entered their Fieldworld, these judgments were tested against the positions of their cooperating teachers, supervisors, and students. As their experience in the classroom grew, their representations of "good teaching" were revised through negotiation, as were other aspects of their utility filters. Feasibility and value were judged in situ, in the activity system in which the promoted practice might be employed.

In contrast to this distributed account of motivational change, sociocognitive theories (e.g., achievement goal theory, expectancy x value theory, or self-regulated learning theory) focus on the general perceptions and beliefs of the individual and the relationships of various environmental factors to those perceptions and beliefs. The decision whether or not to learn or take up a particular promoted practice, from a sociocognitive perspective, might be a result of self-efficacy judgments, the individual's goal orientation, or whether the individual perceived the promoted practice to be valuable. These perspectives do not address the social origins and meanings of those goals and value judgments, nor propose mechanisms for their change over time, nor take into account the social embeddedness of acting on those motives. More recent research on self-regulation has begun to take social context into account in ways closer to what is proposed here. Nancy Perry, for example, investigated how the interactions of teachers and their young pupils led to changes in self-regulated learning (Perry, VandeKamp, Mercer, & Nordby, 2002). In general, however, sociocognitive research on motivation takes the individual as the unit of analysis, with primacy given to individuals' existing motives and their interpretations of environmental variables.

Utility Filters: Implications for Methodology

The concept of utility filters was developed in analyzing the data from a study of novice teacher learning. In this grounded approach to theory development, both the possibilities and limitations of new constructs must be acknowledged. Ethnography provides the data on social processes like negotiation leading to filter development. We can make claims about changes in goals, representations of teaching and practice uptake not only through observations of changed practice and the collection of artifacts, but through the reflections on practice elicited during the ethnographic interview process. Longitudinal data provide opportunities to trace filter development forward and backward through the corpus, triangulating various sources. Cross-case comparisons allow testing of findings across different contexts, leading to more than local "snapshots."

Although the data for this study came from a single teacher education program, the variety of teaching contexts encountered by novices provides an initial indication of the generalizability of our findings to a situative theory of motivation. This work also lays a foundation for exploring the idea of utility filters in other educational settings. The dimensions of feasibility and value of practices might be applicable to a variety of utility judgments, including those studied in investigations of self-regulation (Boekaerts, 1995; Zimmerman, 1989). For example, students being taught metacognitive and cognitive learning strategies might decide whether or not to adopt and employ those strategies based on their utility filters for studying. These filters would develop in the students' specific contexts for studying (e.g., whether or not a course requires generative use of new knowledge or mere rote memorization, the ways in which the knowledge is used and its meaning within the particular social context). The same could be true for instruction in writing, counseling, or any subject in which strategies or approaches to a task are taught.

Understanding the social contexts in which strategies and other practices are employed requires moving beyond laboratory experiments and survey studies. Self-report alone provides only a partial picture of how utility filters and their components are negotiated and changed. Careful use of ethnographic tools is one way to gain a more complete picture of the social processes underlying motivational filters and motivation change. In our study, observation of interns negotiating their practices was essential in understanding their motivation to learn (or to reject) practices promoted in their social worlds. Work currently under way that focuses on the role of social interaction in motivation development (e.g., Turner & Christensen, 2007; Volet, 2007) promises to challenge current theories and expand our understanding of motivation to learn. In the end, then, what we propose is neither a local snapshot nor a global picture, but perhaps a film in which processes of development and change can be documented and analyzed (Niemivirta, personal communication).

Acknowledgments

Preparation of this chapter was supported in part by a Teachers for a New Era grant from the Carnegie Foundation, Ford Foundation, and the Annenberg Foundation to the University of Washington. The analysis on which this chapter is based was a collaborative effort of all authors.

References

Boekaerts, M. (1995). Self-regulated learning: Bridging the gap between metacognitive and metamotivation theories. *Educational Psychologist, 30*, 195-200.

Elliot, A., & Harackiewicz, J. M. (1996). Approach and avoidance achievement goals and intrinsic motivation: A mediational analysis. *Journal of Personality and Social Psychology, 70*, 461-475.

Greeno, J. G. (2006). Learning in activity. In R. K. Sawyer (Ed.), *The Cambridge handbook of the learning sciences* (pp. 79-96). Cambridge: Cambridge University Press.

Hidi, S., & Renninger, K. A. (2006). The role of social context in the development of motivation to write. In S. Hidi & P. Boscolo (Eds.), *Motivation to write* (pp. 241-255). Dordrecht, NL: Kluwer.

Holland, D., Lachicotte, W., Skinner, D., & Cain, C. (1998). *Identity and agency in cultural worlds*. Cambridge, MA: Harvard University Press.

Horn, I. S., Nolen, S. B., Ward, C. J., & Campbell, S. S. (in press). Developing practices in multiple worlds: The role of identity in learning to teach. *Teacher Education Quarterly*.

Lortie, D. (1975). *Schoolteacher: A sociological study*. Chicago: University of Chicago Press.

Nicholls, J. G. (1989). *The competitive ethos and democratic education*. Cambridge, MA: Harvard University Press.

Nolen, S. B. (1988). Reasons for studying: Motivational orientations and study strategies. *Cognition and Instruction, 5*, 269-287.

Nolen, S. B. (1996). Why study? How reasons for learning influence strategy selection. *Educational Psychology Review, 8*, 335-355.

Nolen, S. B., & Ward, C. J. (in press). Sociocultural and situative approaches to studying motivation. In S. Karabenick & T. Urdan (Eds.), *Social psychological perspective on motivation and achievement* (Vol. 15). London: Emerald Group..

Nolen, S. B., Ward, C. J., & Horn, I. S. (2007, August - September). *The social construction of goals & definitions of success in learning contexts*. Paper presented at the Biennial meeting of the European Association for Research on Learning and Instruction, Budapest. Hungary.

Perry, N. E., VandeKamp, K. O., Mercer, L. K., & Nordby, C. J. (2002). Investigating teacher-student interactions that foster self-regulated learning. *Educational Psychologist, 37*, 5-15.

Pressick-Kilborn, K., & Walker, R. (2002). The social construction of interest in a learning community. In D. McInerney & S. Van Etten (Eds.), *Sociocultural influences on motivation and learning* (pp. 153-182). Greenwich, CT: Information Age Publishing.

Ryan, R. M., & Deci, E. L. (2000). Self-determination theory and the facilitation of intrinsic motivation, social development, and well-being. *American Psychologist, 55*, 68-78.

Salonen, P., Vauras, M., & Efklides, A. (2005). Social interaction: What can it tell us about metacognition and coregulation in learning? *European Psychologist, 10*, 199-208.

Simons, J., Dewitte, S., & Lens, W. (2004). The role of different types of instrumentality in motivation, study strategies, and performance: Know why you learn, so you'll know what you learn! *British Journal of Educational Psychology, 74, 343-360*.

Strauss, A., & Corbin, J. (1998). *Basics of qualitative research: Techniques and procedures for developing grounded theory.* (2nd ed.). Thousand Oaks, CA: SAGE.

Turner, J. C., & Christensen, A. (2007, November). *Collaborating with teachers to foster student motivation: Implementing motivational strategies in mathematics instruction*. Paper presented at the Biennial Meeting of the Southwest Consortium on Innovation in Psychology in Education, Phoenix, Arizona.

Volet, S. (2001). Understanding learning and motivation in context: A multi-dimensional and multi-level cognitive-situative perspective. In S. Volet & S. Järvela (Eds.), *Motivation in learning contexts: Theoretical advances and methodological implications* (pp. 57-82). Amsterdam: Elsevier.

Volet, S. (2007, August). *Studying motivational dynamics within and across socially challenging learning activities: Grappling with methodological issues.* Paper presented at the Biennial Meeting of the European Association for Research on Learning and Instruction, Budapest, Hungary.

Walker, R. A., Pressick-Kilborn, K., Arnold, L. S., & Sainsbury, E. J. (2004). Investigating motivation in context: Developing sociocultural perspectives. *European Psychologist, 9*, 245-256.

Wenger, E. (1998). *Communities of practice: Learning, meaning, and identity.* Cambridge: Cambridge University Press.

Wigfield, A., & Eccles, J. S. (2002). The development of competence beliefs, expectancies for success, and achievement values from childhood through adolescence. In A. Wigfield & J. S. Eccles (Eds.), *Development of achievement motivation* (pp. 91-120). San Diego, CA: Academic Press.

Wilson, S. M., Shulman, L. S., & Richert, A. E. (1987). '150 different ways' of knowing: Representations of knowledge in teaching. In J. Calderhead (Ed.), *Exploring teacher thinking.* (pp. 104-124). Sussex, England: Holt, Rinehart & Winston.

Zimmerman, B. J. (1989). A social cognitive view of self-regulated academic learning. *Journal of Educational Psychology, 81*, 329-339.

Zimmerman, B. J., & Schunk, D. H. (2004). Self-regulating intellectual processes and outcomes: A social cognitive perspective. In D. Y. Dai & R. J. Sternberg (Eds.), *Motivation, emotion, and cognition: Integrative perspectives on intellectual functioning and development.* (pp. 323-349). Mahwah, NJ: Lawrence Erlbaum Associates Publishers.

Students' Perceptions of Parental Attitudes toward Academic Achievement

Effects on Motivation, Self-Concept and School Achievement

Francisco Peixoto & Raquel Carvalho

Introduction

Motivation in achievement settings can be conceived of in terms of either the strength or the direction of motivation. People can differ in the level of motivation as well in the orientation of motivation (Ryan & Deci, 2000). Motivational orientations can be conceptualized in diverse ways. In this chapter, motivational orientations are defined as goals that individuals pursue when they engage in various activities. We approach motivational orientations from the viewpoint of achievement goal theory, which has emerged as one of the most prominent frameworks in the conceptualization of motivation (Kaplan & Maehr, 2007). Initial definitions of goal orientations emphasized the situated nature of goals that individuals can adopt. However, these orientations can also be conceived of as cross-situational, that is, as a kind of disposition towards engagement with particular kinds of goals (Bong 2001; Kaplan & Maehr, 2007).

According to the literature on achievement goal theory, in situations where achievement is a prominent factor we can identify two main types of goals. One is usually denoted by terms such as *task orientation, mastery orientation,* or *learning orientation,* whereas the other is denoted by terms such as *ego orientation, performance orientation,* or *ability orientation* (Eccles & Wigfield, 2002; Kaplan, Middleton, Urdan, & Midgley, 2002; Pintrich, 2000; Skaalvik, 1997). Task/mastery/learning goals can be defined as a motivational orientation in which achievement is inherently valuable, meaningful, and satisfying to individuals, since the most important factor is the task and its mastering independently of extrinsic rewards. Students with task orientation will engage in achievement behaviors with the purpose of increasing their competence. Ego/performance/ability goal orientation refers to a focus on the self, ability or performance relative to others. Students with ego orientation seek to maximize favorable evaluations and minimize negative judgments about their own competence. Ego orientation can be conceptualized either as self-enhancing ego orientation or as self-defeating ego orientation. Self-enhancing ego orientation is defined as the goal of demonstrating superior ability and outperforming others. On the other hand, self-defeating ego orientation is defined as the goal of avoiding negative judgments about one's self from others.

Research in achievement goal theory has shown a more adaptive behavioral pattern in students with task orientation than in students with ego orientation. Students with task goal orientation usually exhibit positive learning-related characteristics such as persistence, effort, use of deep strategies, higher levels of self-efficacy and readiness for challenge (Anderman & Wolters, 2006; Kaplan & Maehr, 2007). Despite the consensus that task goal orientation is more adaptive than ego goal orientation, the relationship between these type of goals and academic achievement remains less clear (Anderman & Wolters, 2006; Kaplan & Maehr, 2007). Ego-oriented goals are usually considered as less desirable because of their association with less adaptive outcomes such as self-handicapping or anxiety. However, when the distinction is made between self-enhancing ego orientation and self-defeating ego orientation the picture is quite different. Research that distinguishes between these two types of ego orientations shows that if self-defeating ego orientation is clearly associated with negative outcomes, under certain conditions (e.g., competition settings), self-enhancing ego orientation can be associated with positive outcomes, such as high achievement (Kaplan & Maehr, 2007; Pintrich, 2000).

Among the factors that can have an impact on motivational orientations in academic settings, family characteristics are a less explored field (Gonzalez-DeHass, Willems, & Holbein, 2005). In the past studies on the relations of family characteristics with school achievement, considered motivation as an additional indicator of school adjustment; moreover, they considered motivation as one among a number of variables such as school achievement, attitude towards school, or self-representations (i.e., self-concept and self-esteem). In the following, we will briefly review research concerning the relations between family characteristics and school adjustment. The aim is to point out the importance of (perceived) parental attitudes towards academic achievement for students' academic self-concept, motivational orientations, and school achievement. Next, a study will be reported in which the above relations were investigated. It will be shown that perceived parental attitudes towards learning as a process or as performance (i.e., outcome) have direct and indirect effects on students' motivational orientation and school achievement. In this way, the relative generality of motivation in the academic context will be highlighted.

Family Characteristics and School Adjustment

Research on the relationships between family characteristics and school adjustment shows that parental educational practices, parental beliefs, parental attitudes and parental involvement in their children's schooling are, in one way or another, associated with school-adjustment variables such as motivational orientation, self-concept or school achievement (Antunes & Fontaine, 2003; Eccles, Jaccobs, & Harold, 1990; Eccles, Wigfield, & Schiefele, 1998; Frome & Eccles, 1998; Harter, 1999; Juang & Silbereisen, 2002; Lord, Eccles, & McCarthy, 1994; Oosterwegel & Oppenheimer, 1993; Peixoto, 2003, 2004). During adolescence, dimensions of parenting such as acceptance, emotional support and school involvement are associated with good school adjustment. Thus, students who feel that they are accepted, supported and whose parents are involved in their schooling, have higher levels of self-esteem, of academic self-concept and of academic achievement (Antunes & Fontaine, 2003; Deslándes, Potvin, & Leclerc, 2000; Grolnick & Slowiaczek, 1994; Harter, 1999; Juang & Silbereisen, 2002; Peixoto, 2004; Song & Hattie, 1984).

Among the family-related variables that are linked to school adjustment, parental attitudes towards academic achievement seem to be of particular relevance. As Eccles et al. (1990) have suggested there are two types of parental attitudes that could influence students' self-perceptions: parents' expectations regarding academic performance and parents' expectations related to academic competence. In this field of research, Baião and Peixoto (2001), in a study with 9th graders, found that parental pressure to achieve in school was negatively associated with academic self-concept, global self-esteem and academic achievement. In another study with high-school students, Antunes and Fontaine (2003) found evidence of a negative relationship between parental attitudes emphasizing academic performance and the students' academic achievement, academic self-concept and global self-esteem; on the other hand, parental attitudes emphasizing the learning process were positively associated with these variables.

As regards the association between parental attitudes (or practices) and school achievement, several researchers have suggested that perceived parental support, acceptance and some control over children's activities are strong predictors of academic performance (Antunes & Fontaine, 2003; Desimone, 1999; Fan & Chen, 2001; Grolnick, Ryan, & Deci, 1991; Grolnick & Slowiaczek, 1994; Juang & Silbereisen, 2002; Paulson, 1994; Song & Hattie, 1984; Wang, Wildman, & Calhoun, 1996). However, recent studies show that the relationship between family-related variables and school achievement is mediated by individual variables arising from students, as for example motivation or self-concept (Alomar, 2006; Gonzalez-Pienda et al., 2002; Koutsoulis & Campbell, 2001; Saleiro & Peixoto, 2005; Vallerand, Fortier, & Guay, 1997; Wong, Wiest, & Cusick, 2002).

With respect to motivation, several studies have provided evidence that parental behaviour and school involvement have a crucial impact on a child's motivation (Fontaine, 1988; Gottfried, Fleming, & Gottfried, 1994; Grolnick et al., 1991; Grolnick & Slowiaczek, 1994; Meece, 1994; Repinski & Shonk, 2002; Wentzel, 1998). Research examining the relations between parental involvement and adolescents' intrinsic motivation shows that perceived support from parents and affect are positively related to adolescents' intrinsic motivation (Wentzel, 1998). As Eccles et al. (1998) have concluded, a child's motivation to succeed can be influenced by the balance between parental emotional support, control and challenge. Other studies based on intrinsic academic motivation identify some variables related to parental practices that are negatively associated with the motivational orientation of adolescents. Parental reactions to school-related outcomes, negative control, disengagement, external rewards, punishment, lack of guidance, and parental displays of anger are behaviors that can be negatively associated with intrinsic motivation (Bronstein, Ginsburg, & Herrera, 2005; Ginsburg & Bronstein, 1993; Gottfried et al., 1994). The results of these studies show that parental behaviors exerting pressure on children to achieve specific standards could lead to a decline in intrinsic academic motivation, and consequently, in school achievement.

Few studies have been conducted that focus on the relations between adolescents' perceptions of parental attitudes towards academic learning and achievement and motivational orientations from the perspective of achievement goal theory. Gonzalez, Holbein, and Quilter (2002) in a study of American high school students examined the relationship between perceived parenting styles and students' goal orientations. They found a positive relationship between authoritative parenting styles and mastery orientation and between authoritarian parenting style and performance goals. Chan and Chan (2007) in a study of Hong-Kong university students corroborated these findings. Performance goals were found to be associated with authoritarian and authoritative parenting styles, whilst learning goals were positively associated with authoritative parenting style. Gonida, Kiosseoglou, and Voulala (2007) in another study with Greek students of 7th, 9th, and 11th grades related perceived parental goals to students' achievement goal orientations. The results showed that perceived parental mastery goals predicted students' mastery goal orientation whereas perceived parental performance goals predicted students' performance goal orientation, both performance-approach and performance-avoidance. However, for younger students the pattern was slightly different, with performance-approach goals also being associated with perceived parental mastery goals.

The Present Study

The first aim of the present study was to delimit the relations between perceived parental attitudes towards academic learning and achievement with students' self-representations (i.e., global self-esteem, academic self-concept) and academic achievement. In line with the research reviewed, it was hypothesized that global self-esteem and academic self-concept would be positively related to perceptions of parental attitudes focusing on the learning process and negatively related to parental attitudes focusing on academic performance (Hypothesis 1).

The second aim of the present study was to highlight the relations of perceived parental attitudes towards academic learning and achievement with students' own achievement goal orientations. Previous research findings suggest that there should be positive relations between perceived parental attitudes focusing on the learning process with students' task/mastery goal orientations. However, the relationship between parental attitudes and ego/performance goal orientation is somewhat less clear. Thus, it was expected that adolescents' perceptions of parental attitudes focusing on academic performance, rather than on the learning process, would be positively associated with students' ego/performance goal orientation in all its forms, namely work-avoidance, self-defeating, as well as self-enhancing ego orientations (Hypothesis 2).

Finally, this study aimed to connect students' perceived parental attitudes, with psychological variables (self-esteem, academic self-concept and motivational orientations) and with academic achievement. The assumption was that perceived parental attitudes towards academic performance would predict academic achievement through students' motivational orientation and academic self-concept. Moreover, in contrast to research that directly relates (perceived) parental attitudes or parental achievement goal orientations to students' achievement goals, we hypothesized that this relationship would be both direct and indirect via students' self-representations (i.e., academic self-concept and global self-esteem). This assumption was based on Eccles et al.'s (1990) claim that parents can influence children's self-perceptions through their expectations about academic competence and performance (Hypothesis 3).

Method

Participants

The participants were 302 Portuguese 9th-grade students of two different schools in the south of Portugal. Their age ranged from 14 to 18 years with a mean of 14.6 years. Of them, 136 were boys and 166 were girls. In relation to school failure, 221 had never failed in previous years, 79 had failed at least once, and two did not give information about previous school failure.

Instruments

Data was collected using a scale of perceived parental attitudes towards academic performance (Antunes & Fontaine, 2003), a self-concept and self-esteem scale (Peixoto & Almeida, 1999) and a scale assessing motivational orientations (Skaalvik, 1997).

Perceived Parental Attitudes towards Academic Performance Scale

The scale used to assess perceived parental attitudes towards academic performance (Antunes & Fontaine, 2003) is a 21-item measure that assesses two dimensions of perceived parental attitudes towards academic performance: attitudes focused on the *learning process* (Process dimension) and attitudes focused on *academic performance* (Performance dimension).

In the dimension of process-focused attitudes, the items tap parental emphasis on the learning process, within an atmosphere of parental support, even when students fail to achieve good grades. Sample items include "When I get a lower mark, my parents help me to understand what went wrong", "My parents feel happy when they realize I enjoy learning" and "My parents support me even if my marks were not so good".

In the dimension of performance-focused attitudes, items assess perceived parental emphasis on academic attainment; that is, students feel that their parents exert pressure on them to achieve better grades and are disappointed when students do not meet their expectations. Sample items of the Performance dimension are: "My parents are only happy if my grades are better than everyone else's", "I feel that, for my parents, my grades are never good enough", and "I think my parents give too much value to school marks".

For both dimensions responses were on a 6-point scale[1] from "Strongly disagree" to "Strongly agree". Internal consistency was satisfactory for both dimensions of the scale, with Cronbach's alpha .75 for the Performance dimension and .93 for the Process dimension.

---

[1] Some of the items were reverse scored.

Self-Concept and Self-Esteem Scale

The Self-concept and Self-esteem Scale (Peixoto & Almeida, 1999) was constructed using Harter's Self-Perception Profile for Adolescents as a starting point, but with two main differences. First, for the item format we used one single statement per item instead of the two in Harter's scale; second, we added two new subscales, namely Portuguese Language Self-concept and Mathematical Self-concept. The Self-concept and Self-esteem Scale consists of 51 items distributed among 10 subscales (5 items in each specific dimension of self-concept and 6 items in the Self-esteem subscale), referring to school competence, social acceptance, athletic competence, physical appearance, romantic appeal, behavioral conduct, close relationships, competence in Portuguese language, competence in mathematics, and self-esteem. This scale is based on the assumption that self-concept is organized hierarchically with the nine specific facets of the self-concept being organized in three second-order factors (Academic self-concept, Social self-concept, and Presentation self-concept). In the present study we used two measures: (a) Academic self-concept (a composite measure including school competence, competence in Portuguese language, and competence in mathematics), and (b) Self-esteem. Sample items included "Some students are fast doing their schoolwork" (School competence), "Some students write easily" (Competence in Portuguese language), "Some students can solve math problems very quickly" (Competence in mathematics), "Some students, most of the time, are happy with themselves" (Self-esteem). Items were assessed on a 4-point scale[1], ranging from "Exactly like me" to "Completely different from me". The reliability of each measure was acceptable, ranging from .68 (Competence in Portuguese language) to .89 (Competence in mathematics).

Scale of Motivational Orientations

The scale of motivational orientations was adapted from Skaalvik (1997). The items were rephrased and new ones were added. The final scale had 27 items organized into four factors: Task orientation (7 items), Self-enhancing ego orientation (7 items), Self-defeating ego orientation (7 items) and Work-avoidance orientation (6 items). In this study, and in order to achieve greater reliability of the measures, we used five items in the Task orientation and in the Self-enhancing ego orientation and four items in each of the remaining two dimensions. Sample items are: "To some students it is important to learn new things at school" (Task orientation), "In class some students feel successful when they do the work better than other students" (Self-enhancing ego orientation), "Some students, when answering questions in class, are worried by how they are perceived by their classmates" (Self-defeating ego orientation), and "In school, some students like to do as little as possible" (Work-avoidance orientation). Responses were on a 4-point scale, from "Exactly like me" to "Completely different from me". Previous work with this scale (Cavaco, 2003; Silva, 2002), using exploratory and confirmatory factor analysis showed a factor structure identical to the one proposed by Skaalvik (1997). In the present study the reliability of each measure was acceptable, with Cronbach's alpha ranging from .75 (Work-avoidance orientation) to .91 (Task orientation).

Academic Achievement

Academic achievement was assessed by asking students to indicate their grades of the last period in six school subjects, namely, Portuguese, Foreign language, Mathematics, Science, Geography, and History. The mean of the school grades on the six school subjects was computed to represent academic achievement (Grade Point Average, GPA).

Procedure

Data was collected at the beginning of the third period of the school year, after the Easter holidays. Respondents were those students whose parents did not oppose their participation in the study. In data collection the presentation order of the questionnaires was counterbalanced.

Results

Perceived Parental Attitudes and Student Characteristics

To accomplish the two first goals of this study we carried out correlation analysis and analysis of variance on two contrasting groups of students: students who perceived their parents mainly as focused on performance and students who perceived their parents as mainly process-oriented.

Correlations between perceived parental attitudes towards academic learning and performance and self-representations showed that attitudes focusing on process were positively correlated with academic self-concept and self-esteem (see Table 1). Perception of performance-focused attitudes was negatively related to self-esteem but it was not related to academic self-concept. Moreover, the correlation was lower than the one between perceived process-focused attitudes and self-esteem. School achievement (i.e., GPA) had a positive, although low, correlation with perceptions of process-focused attitudes.

Table 1. Pearson correlations between the variables of the study.

	Perf	Proc	Task	Avoid	Self-Def	Self-Enh	AcadSC	SE
Perf	1.00							
Proc	-.46***	1.00						
Task	-.06	.23***	1.00					
Avoid	.13*	-.13*	-.35***	1.00				
Self-Def	.17**	-.16**	.04	-.004	1.00			
Self-Enh	.34***	-.08	.24***	-.002	.31***	1.00		
AcadSC	-.03	.19**	.35***	-.26***	-.15**	.16**	1.00	
SE	-.15*	.26***	.31***	-.12*	-.36***	.00	.46***	1.00
GPA	-.11	.15*	.24***	-.16**	-.09	-.03	.52***	.22***

Note: *** $p < .001$; ** $p < .01$; * $p < .05$. Perf = Performance-focused attitudes; Proc = Process-focused attitudes; Task = Task Orientation; Avoid = Work-avoidance orientation; Self-Def = Self-defeating ego orientation; Self-Enh = Self-Enhancing ego orientation; AcadSC = Academic self-concept; SE = Self-esteem; GPA = Grade Point Average.

As regards the relations between perceived parental attitudes towards academic learning, performance, and students' motivational orientations (see Table 1), perceived process-focused attitudes were positively related to task orientation and negatively to self-defeating ego orientation and work-avoidance orientation. Perceived process-focused attitudes were not related to self-enhancing ego orientation. Perceived parental attitudes focusing on academic performance were positively related to ego and work-avoidance orientations. Among these, the stronger relations were with self-enhancing ego orientation.

Effects of Perceived Parental Attitudes

In addition to the correlation analysis we conducted ANOVA contrasting students, who perceived their parents as focused mainly on their academic performance, and students who perceived their parents as mainly concerned with their learning. To constitute the groups, we first split the distribution of the scores on the two dimensions of parental attitudes into three groups, choosing those in the upper third of the distribution for each variable. That is, we chose students who perceived their parents as more process-focused or more performance-focused. Furthermore, we removed students who scored high in both dimensions in order to make sure that we had two distinct groups of students, one that perceived their parents as more concerned with their learning process and, the other, as more concerned with their academic performance.

We performed a MANOVA considering self-representations (academic self-concept and self-esteem) and school achievement (GPA) as dependent variables and perception of parental attitudes toward academic achievement (process-focused or performance-focused) and previous school achievement (failure or not, in previous years) as independent variables. We introduced previous school achievement as an independent variable in order to control for possible interaction effects with parental attitudes. In this sense we focused on the main effects of parental attitudes and on previous school achievement only in the cases when it interacted with the former variable.

The ANOVA on academic self-concept showed a marginally significant main effect of parental attitudes, $F(1, 152) = 3.14$, $p = .08$, partial $\eta^2 = .02$, and no statistically significant interaction with previous school achievement. Figure 1 shows that students who perceived their parents as more concerned with their learning process exhibited slightly higher academic self-concept than their classmates whose parents were perceived as more concerned with their grades. A MANOVA on the specific dimensions of academic self-concept marginally supported this tendency, Pillai's trace $= .044$, $F(3, 150) = 2.29$, $p = .08$, partial $\eta2 = .04$. Univariate analyses showed a statistically significant main effect of perceived parental attitudes on school competence, $F(1, 152) = 5.54$, $p = .02$, partial $\eta^2 = .04$, and marginally significant main effect on Portuguese language competence, $F(1, 152) = 3.47$, $p = .064$, partial $\eta^2 = .02$. In both cases students who perceived their parents as more concerned with their learning process exhibited higher self-perception(s). However, the effect sizes were low to very low.

As regards self-esteem, the respective ANOVA showed a main effect of perceived parental attitudes, $F(1, 152) = 11.23$, $p = .001$, partial $\eta^2 = .07$, and no interaction effects between perceived parental attitudes and previous school achievement. Students who perceived their parents as more performance-focused had lower self-esteem (see Figure 1). As regards GPA, perceived parental attitudes did not have a significant main effect, nor was there any interaction with previous school achievement.

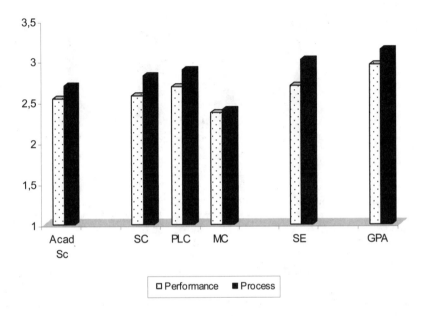

Figure 1. Means for self-representations and GPA as a function of parental attitudes.
Note: AcadSC = Academic self-concept; SC = School competence; PLC = Portuguese language competence; MC = Mathematical competence; SE = Self-esteem; GPA = Grade Point Average.

The MANOVA on motivational orientations corroborated the results obtained in the preliminary correlation analysis. There was a main effect of perceived parental attitudes, Pillai's trace = .136, $F(4, 149) = 5.87, p < .001$, partial $\eta^2 = .14$, and no interaction of this variable with previous school achievement. Univariate analyses showed that perceived parental attitudes affected task orientation, $F(1, 152) = 6.75, p = .01$, partial $\eta^2 = .04$, self-defeating ego orientation, $F(1, 152) = 5.35, p = .02$, partial $\eta^2 = .03$, and self-enhancing ego orientation, $F(1, 152) = 8.57, p = .004$, partial $\eta^2 = .05$. Students who perceived their parents as being more concerned with the learning process were more task oriented, whereas students who considered their parents as being more focused on their grades were more ego-oriented (both in terms of self-enhancing and self-defeating) and slightly more work-avoiding (see Figure 2). However, the effect sizes of the univariate analyses were low.

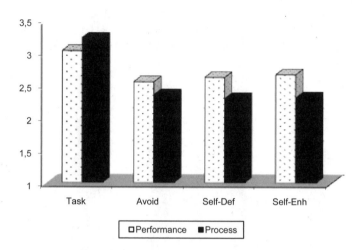

Figure 2. Means for motivational orientations as a function of parental attitudes.
Note: Task = Task orientation; Avoid = Work-avoidance orientation; Self-Def = Self-defeating ego orientation; Self-Enh = Self-enhancing ego orientation.

The Theoretical Model

To test the theoretical model specified in Hypothesis 3 regarding the relationships between perceived parental attitudes, motivational orientations, self-concept, and academic achievement we performed a path analysis using AMOS 7.0 (Arbuckle, 2006).

The theoretical model posited that the relationship between perceived parental attitudes and school achievement (GPA) is mediated by students' academic self-concept, self-esteem and motivational orientations (see Figure 3).

Five indices were used to examine the model's goodness of fit: χ^2, χ^2/df, Bentler's comparative fit index (CFI), Tucker-Lewis index (TLI), and root mean square error of approximation (RMSEA). The following criteria for satisfactory model fit were used: $\chi^2/df \leq 3$; CFI and TLI $\geq .90$ and RMSEA $\leq .07$ (Browne & Cudeck, 1993; Hair, Tatham, & Black, 1995; Kline, 1998; Loehlin, 1998).

The fit indices of the theoretical model were not good, $\chi^2(14, N = 302) = 86.76$, p < .001, $\chi^2/df = 6.2$, CFI = .855, TLI = .628, and RMSEA = .131. In order to achieve a better fit we modified the model through the elimination of paths that were not significant (p > .10), and by the addition of paths suggested by the Modification Indices. These suggestions included the correlations of the residuals of task orientation with the residuals of work-avoidance orientation and self-enhancing ego orientations; also, the correlation of the residuals of self-defeating ego orientation with self-enhancing ego orientation. These correlations can be theoretically supported (Bong, 2001; Martin & Debus, 1998; Nichols & Utesch, 1998; Skaalvik, 1997; Skaalvik & Skaalvik, 2005), and this is why they were added to the model. The correlation between the error terms of Task Orientation and Work-avoidance orientation was negative, -.29, whilst the other two were positive, .20

between the error terms of task orientation and self-enhancing ego orientation and .31 between the two dimensions of ego orientation.

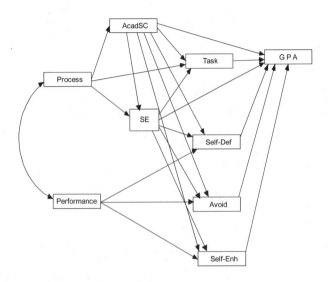

Figure 3. The model submitted to path analysis.
Note: AcadSC = Academic self-concept; SE = Self-esteem; Task = Task orientation; Work-Avoid = Work-avoidance orientation; Self-Def = Self-defeating ego orientation; Self-Enh = Self-enhancing ego orientation; GPA = Grade Point Average.

The modified model fits the data very well: $\chi^2(17, N = 302) = 18.6$, $p = .35$, $\chi^2/df = 1.1$, CFI = .997, TLI = .993, and RMSEA = .018. The results of the path analysis are displayed in Figure 4 (it includes the path coefficients and the R^2).

The paths drawn by broken lines represent negative relations. All values are significant at $p < .05$ except the relationship between Task Orientation and GPA ($p = .08$)
The results of the path analysis showed that perceived parental attitudes are differentially related to the variables considered. Thus, performance-focused attitudes were positively related with self-enhancing ego orientation, self-defeating ego orientation, and work-avoidance orientation, whereas process-focused attitudes were linked to academic self-concept, self-esteem, and to task orientation.

The path analysis showed no direct effects of perceived parental attitudes on academic achievement (GPA). Despite the positive (although low) correlation between process-focused attitudes and school achievement (Table 1), the direct path from process-focused attitudes to GPA was not statistically significant. However, the path analysis showed that this relation was mediated by academic self-concept and task orientation. The total effect of process-focused attitudes on school achievement was .11. Also, performance-focused attitudes had indirect effects on school achievement, through self-enhancing ego orientation. Nevertheless, the total effect of performance-focused attitudes on GPA was negative and nonsignificant.

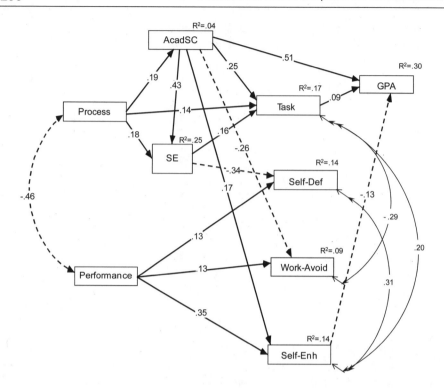

Figure 4. The modified model.
Note: AcadSC = Academic self-concept; SE = Self-esteem; Task = Task orientation; Avoid = Work-avoidance orientation; Self-Def = Self-defeating ego orientation; Self-Enh = Self-enhancing ego orientation; GPA = Grade Point Average.

The variables considered in the model accounted for 30% of the variance of GPA. Among these, academic self-concept was the variable with stronger association with school achievement. Perceived parental attitudes, namely process-focused attitudes, explained only a small percentage of academic self-concept variance, $R^2 = .04$. This means that academic self-concept was influenced by variables other than the perceived parental process-focused attitudes, which were not considered here. Besides the direct effect on school achievement academic self-concept also had indirect effects through motivational orientations (i.e., task orientation and self-enhancing ego orientation) and through self-esteem, which positively predicted task orientation.

Looking now at the relationship between motivational orientations and school achievement (GPA), the findings show that the pattern is somewhat different when the variables are considered alone (Table 1) or when they are considered within a network of relationships. Thus, when motivational orientations were considered alone, significant relationships with GPA appeared for task orientation and work-avoidance orientation. However, when parental attitudes and self-representations were introduced, the significant association between work-avoidance orientation and school achievement disappeared, and the path from self-enhancing ego orientation to GPA became significant.

Discussion

The present study aimed at delimiting the relationships between perceptions of parental attitudes towards academic learning and achievement and indicators of school adjustment such as self-representations, motivational orientations, and academic achievement. The findings presented here support the assumption that different perceptions of parental attitudes are differentially related to student individual characteristics. Thus, perceptions of parental attitudes focusing on the learning process were positively related to academic self-concept, self-esteem, school achievement and task orientation and negatively related to work-avoidance orientation and self-defeating ego orientation. Performance-focused attitudes, on the other hand, were negatively related to self-esteem and positively related to work-avoidance orientation, to self-defeating ego orientation and, primarily, to self-enhancing ego orientation.

In relation to self-representations, students who perceived their parents as more focused on the learning process tended to have slightly higher academic self-concept, and higher self-esteem. These results support our first hypothesis and corroborate findings from other research that showed positive associations between perceived parental attitudes focusing on the learning process and academic self-concept and self-esteem (Antunes & Fontaine, 2003). Here, it is important to stress that the association of process-focused attitudes with self-esteem was higher than with academic self-concept. We can speculate that process-focused attitudes are related to more supportive family dynamics and to a high degree of acceptance that contributes to the construction of positive self-representations and a sense of self-worth (Deslandes et al., 2000; Grolnick & Slowiaczek, 1994; Harter, 1999; Juang & Silbereisen, 2002; Peixoto, 2004). In contrast, parental attitudes focusing on academic achievement emphasize the grades that students must achieve, putting more pressure on the shoulders of adolescents. There is also the possibility that when standards that parents impose are not achieved, this can lead students to feel useless and unworthy. In short, adolescents who receive feedback from parents who are supportive, and probably with higher levels of school involvement, are more likely to develop positive feelings of competence, which contributes to higher academic self-concept and self-esteem, than those who receive feedback largely focused on the grades that they (must) achieve.

As regards motivational orientations, students who perceived their parents as more focused on their academic performance were more ego-oriented (both in terms of self-enhancing and self-defeating ego orientation), had a greater tendency to avoid school work and were less task-oriented. This result confirms our second hypothesis and is in line with research that points to positive associations between parental practices or attitudes that exert more pressure over students and extrinsic motivation or performance goals (Bronstein et al., 2005; Chan & Chan, 2007; Gonida et al., 2007; Gonzalez et al., 2002). One possible explanation is that when parents are mainly concerned with academic performance they probably stress competition and processes of social comparison. Thus, it is not surprising that self-enhancing ego orientation was the dimension with stronger associations with perceived performance-focused attitudes, since social comparison is at the core of ego orientation. As a consequence when students feel that they can not achieve the standards that their parents pose, they are worried about public exposure of failure. This can explain the higher levels of self-defeating ego orientation presented by students who perceive their parents as mainly concerned with academic performance. The findings presented here also point to differences in task orientation if students perceive their parents as more process-focused. This finding is in line with previous research (Bronstein et al., 2005; Chan & Chan, 2007; Gonida et al., 2007; Gonzalez et al., 2002). One possible interpretation for the differences found in task orientation is that parents focusing on the learning process emphasize the usefulness of the learning tasks with which students are confronted. Moreover, we can speculate that in the acquisition process of task orientation students become aware of their parents being happy when they see them interested in the learning tasks and this leads to the reinforcement of this type of motivational orientation.

As regards academic achievement, despite the significant correlation between perceived parental process-focused attitudes and GPA, students who perceived their parents mainly as process-focused did not differ from those who perceived their parents as primarily concerned with their academic performance.

The results from path analysis enable us to see the patterns of relationships between perceived parental attitudes towards academic achievement and self-representations, motivational orientations and school achievement more clearly. First, and following previous research (Koutsoulis & Campbell, 2001; Saleiro & Peixoto, 2005; Vallerand et al., 1997; Wong et al., 2002), effects of perceived parental attitudes on school achievement are not direct but through students' self-representations and motivational orientations. Moreover, the effects on school grades are mainly from process-focused attitudes and through academic self-concept. That is, perceived parental process-focused attitudes contribute positively to students' self-representations (both academic self-concept and self-esteem), and self-representations positively influence academic performance, both directly (as in the case of academic self-concept) and indirectly through task orientation. Second, the path analysis showed clearly that perceived parental attitudes were differentially related to motivational orientations. Thus, process-focused attitudes were related to task orientation whereas performance-focused attitudes were associated with ego and work-avoidance orientations. These findings are in line with other research that shows a positive association between perceived parental mastery goals (which presumably underlie parental attitudes focusing on the learning process) and more adaptive outcomes from students such as motivational orientations (mastery/task orientation) or school achievement (Friedel, Cortina, Turner, & Midgley, 2007; Gonida et al., 2007).

An interesting finding arising from the path analysis is the negative relationship between self-enhancing ego orientation and GPA. Some authors argue that performance-approach goals can contribute, under certain conditions, to positive outcomes, namely in competitive contexts and for older students (Kaplan & Maehr, 2007; Pintrich, 2000). However, this was not the case here, since self-enhancing ego orientation (which can be considered similar to performance-approach goals) was negatively related to school achievement. A possible explanation is that the participants in this study were younger than those in the studies in which positive associations were found between performance-approach goals and achievement. Furthermore, the participants of our study were at the end of compulsory schooling which does not seem to induce much competition, and also, probably some of them would leave school at the end of the school year. A different picture could occur for older students in more competitive situations, as for example at the end of secondary education with the possibility of access to the university and the competition for best marks. A further explanation could be that the negative relationship between self-enhancing ego orientation and GPA is due to the inclusion, in the model, of self-representations. When self-representations are excluded from the model, then the only significant relationship between motivational orientations and GPA that remains significant is with task orientation. This is in line with findings from previous research showing positive relationships between task/mastery/learning goals and academic achievement (Anderman & Wolters, 2006; Kaplan & Maehr, 2007). In order to better understand the relationships between self-representations and achievement goals more research is needed, namely longitudinal studies that can clarify the role of self-representations on motivational orientations.

The results presented here showed that the relations between perceived parental attitudes and academic adjustment variables are weak. A possible explanation could be the developmental phase in which these students are, namely middle adolescence. Developmental research shows that adolescence is characterized by quest for autonomy, with adolescent seeking to progressively separate themselves from parents (Coleman & Hendry, 1999; Collins & Repinski, 1994; Peixoto, 2003). This may imply that parental behaviours or attitudes are not as influential as in younger ages, thus leading to low correlations between perceived parental attitudes and the adolescents' academic adaptation outcomes. The observed weak correlations between perceived parental attitudes and students' motivational orientations also suggest that much of the variability in motivational orientations is due to non-familial factors: contextual factors linked to the learning settings probably have prominent role in this. In order to clarify the role of perceived parental attitudes on motivational orientations more research is needed, namely research that combines parental, student and learning environment variables.

Finally, it needs to be also stressed that perceived parental attitudes is not the same as actual parental attitudes or behaviours. Thus, part of the relations found in the study might be explained by students' representations of their parents' attitudes which are based not only on parental behaviours but also on students' own goal orientation and previous achievement. This is also an issue for future research.

Global or Local Motivation?

A final remark about the implications of the findings presented here: Our results clearly show that perceived performance-focused parental attitudes can have the opposite effect of that desired by parents. Focusing on school performance and stressing the importance of grades does not necessarily contribute to better grades (correlations between perceived performance-focused attitudes and school achievement were not significant) and can even be negatively related to school achievement. Moreover, perceived parental attitudes focusing on performance can promote less desirable motivational orientations (ego and work-avoidance orientations) which are usually related to less adaptive outcomes such as less involvement in school work or higher use of self-handicapping strategies (Anderman & Wolters, 2006; Elliot & Covington, 2001; Kaplan et al., 2002). However, it is not clear if parental attitudes are influenced by children's school-related behaviours and achievement. It is possible that there is a loop from parental behaviours to children's motivation and achievement and vice versa. Nevertheless, we can speculate that what starts at the family context as a series of snapshots related to students' everyday school adjustment and school achievement forms the basis for generalized students' perceptions of parental attitudes towards learning as well of themselves as learners, and these perceptions have an impact on their dispositional achievement goal orientations and academic achievement. Thus, from specific and local events related to their learning, students develop more global motivational orientations that can become trait-like characteristics. From this point of view the dilemma is not between local and global motivation, but how local gets transformed to global motivational dispositions that can have an impact on behaviour across different contexts and situations.

Acknowledgments

This research was supported by grants from the Science and Technology Foundation (POCI 2010). The authors would like to thank Lourdes Mata and João Maroco for their helpful comments on an earlier version of this paper. The authors would also like to thank Anastasia Efklides for her comments, which greatly helped to improve this paper.

References

Alomar, B. O. (2006). Personal and family paths to pupil achievement. *Social Behavior and Personality, 34,* 907-922.

Anderman, E. M., & Wolters, C. A. (2006). Goals, values, and affect: Influences on student motivation. In P. A. Alexander & P. H. Winne (Eds.), *Handbook of educational psychology* (2nd ed., pp. 369-389). Mahwah, NJ: Erlbaum.

Antunes, C., & Fontaine, A. M. (2003, August). *Adolescents' perceptions of their parents' attitudes towards academic performance: Their relation with academic performance, academic self-concept and global self-esteem.* Paper presented at the Biennial Meeting of the European Association for Research on Learning and Instruction, Nicosia, Cyprus.

Arbuckle, J. L. (2006). *Amos (Version 7.0).* Chicago: SPSS.

Baião, G., & Peixoto, F. (2001, Novembro). *Autoconceito, auto-estima e pressão familiar para o sucesso académico em adolescentes* [Self-concept, self-esteem and parental pressure to academic achievement in adolescents]. Poster presented at the IIth Congress "Família, Saúde Mental e Políticas Sociais", Lisboa, Portugal.

Bong, M. (2001). Between- and within-domain relations of academic motivation among middle and high school students: Self-efficacy, task-value, and achievement goals. *Journal of Educational Psychology, 93,* 23-34.

Bronstein, P., Ginsburg, G. S., & Herrera, I. S. (2005). Parental predictors of motivational orientation in early adolescence: A longitudinal study. *Journal of Youth and Adolescence, 34,* 559-575.

Browne, M. W., & Cudeck, R. (1993). Alternative ways of assessing model fit. In K. A. Bollen & J. S. Long (Eds.), *Testing structural equation models* (pp. 136-162). Newbury Park, CA: Sage.

Cavaco, P. (2003). Estudo das *relações existentes entre autoconceito académico e orientações motivacionais em alunos com sucesso e insucesso escolar* [Relationships between academic self-concept and motivational orientations in good achievers and underachievers]. Unpublished master's thesis. Lisboa: ISPA.

Chan, K., & Chan, S. (2007). Hong Kong teacher education students' goal orientations and their relationship to perceived parenting style. *Educational Psychology, 27,* 157-172.

Coleman, J. C., & Hendry, L. B. (1999). *The nature of adolescence* (3rd ed.). London: Routledge.

Collins, W. A., & Repinski, D. J. (1994). Relationships during adolescence: Continuity and change in interpersonal perspective. In R. Montemayor, G. R. Adams, & T. P. Gullotta (Eds.), *Personal relationships during adolescence* (pp. 7-36). Thousand Oaks, CA: SAGE.

Desimone, L. (1999). Linking parent involvement with student achievement: Do race and income matter? *Journal of Educational Research, 93,* 1-30.

Deslandes, R., Potvin, P., & Leclerc, D. (2000). Les liens entre l'autonomie de l'adolescent, la collaboration parentale et la réussite scolaire [The relationship between adolescent autonomy, parental collaboration and school achievement]. *Canadian Journal of Behavioural Science, 32,* 208-217.

Eccles, J. S., Jaccobs, J. E., & Harold, R. D. (1990). Gender role stereotypes, expectancy effects and parents socialization of gender differences. *Journal of Social Psychology, 46,* 183-201.

Eccles, J. S., & Wigfield, A. (2002). Motivational beliefs, values, and goals. *Annual Review Psychology, 53,* 109-132.

Eccles, J. S., Wigfield, A., & Schiefele, U. (1998). Motivation to succeed. In N. Eisenberg (Ed.), *Handbook of child psychology* (5th ed., Vol. 3, pp. 1017-1095). New York: Wiley.

Elliot, A. J., & Covington, M. V. (2001). Approach and avoidance motivation. *Educational Psychology Review, 13,* 73-92.

Fan, X., & Chen, M. (2001). Parental involvement and students' academic achievement: A meta-analysis. *Educational Psychology Review, 13,* 1-22.

Fontaine, A. M. (1988). Práticas educativas familiares e motivação para a realização dos adolescentes [Parental practices and achievement motivation in adolescents]. *Cadernos de Consulta Psicológica, 4,* 13-30.

Friedel, J. M., Cortina, K. S., Turner, J. C., & Midgley, C. (2007). Achievement goals, efficacy beliefs and coping strategies in mathematics: The roles of perceived parent and teacher goal emphases. *Contemporary Educational Psychology, 32,* 434-458.

Frome, P. M., & Eccles, J. S. (1998). Parents' influence on childrens' achievement-related perceptions. *Journal of Personality and Social Psychology 74(2),* 435-452.

Ginsburg, G. S., & Bronstein, P. (1993). Family factors related to children's intrinsic/extrinsic motivational orientation and academic performance. *Child Development, 64,* 1461-1474.

Gonida, E. N., Kiosseoglou, G., & Voulala, K. (2007). Perceptions of parent goals and their contribution to students' achievement goal orientation and engagement in the classroom: Grade level differences across adolescence. *European Journal of Psychology of Education, 22,* 23-39.

Gonzalez-DeHass, A. R., Willems, P. P., & Holbein, M. F. D. (2005). Examining the relationship between parental involvement and student motivation. *Educational Psychology Review, 17,* 99-123.

Gonzalez-Pienda, J. A., Nunez, J. C., Gonzalez-Pumariega, S., Alvarez, L., Roces, C., & Garcia, M. (2002). A structural equation model of parental involvement, motivational and aptitudinal characteristics, and academic achievement. *The Journal of Experimental Education, 70,* 257-287.

Gonzalez, A. R., Holbein, M. F. D., & Quilter, S. (2002). High school students' goal orientations and their relationship to perceived parenting styles. *Contemporary Educational Psychology, 27,* 450-470.

Gottfried, A. E., Fleming, J. S., & Gottfried, A. W. (1994). Role of parental motivational practices in children's academic intrinsic motivation and achievement. *Journal of Educational Psychology, 86,* 104-113.

Grolnick, W. S., Ryan, R. M., & Deci, E. L. (1991). Inner resources for school achievement: Motivational mediators of children's perceptions of their parents. *Journal of Educational Psychology, 83,* 508-517.

Grolnick, W. S., & Slowiaczek, M. L. (1994). Parents' involvement in children's schooling: A multidimensional conceptualization and motivational model. *Child Development, 65,* 237-252.

Hair, J. F., Anderson, R. E., Tatham, R. L., & Black, W. C. (1995). *Multivariate data analysis with readings* (4th ed.). Englewood Cliffs, NJ: Prentice-Hall.

Harter, S. (1999). *The construction of the self: A developmental perspective.* New York: The Guilford.

Juang, L. P., & Silbereisen, R. K. (2002). The relationship between adolescent academic capability beliefs, parenting and school grades. *Journal of Adolescence, 25,* 3-18.

Kaplan, A., & Maehr, M. L. (2007). The contributions and prospects of goal orientation theory. *Educational Psychology Review, 19,* 141-184.

Kaplan, A., Middleton, M. J., Urdan, T., & Midgley, C. (2002). Achievement goals and goal structures. In C. Midgley (Ed.), *Goals, goal structures and patterns of adaptive learning* (pp. 21-53). Mahwah, NJ: Erlbaum.

Kline, R. B. (1998). *Principles and practice of structural equation modeling.* New York: Guilford.

Koutsoulis, M. K., & Campbell, J. R. (2001). Family processes affect students' motivation, and science and math achievement in Cypriot high schools. *Structural Equation Modeling, 8,* 108-127.

Loehlin, J. C. (1998). *Latent variable models: An introduction to factor, path and structural analysis* (3rd ed.). Mahwah, NJ: Erlbaum.

Lord, S. E., Eccles, J. S., & McCarthy, K. A. (1994). Surviving the junior high school transition, family processes, and self-perceptions as protective and risk factors. *Journal of Early Adolescence, 14,* 162-199.

Martin, A. J., & Debus, R. L. (1998). Self-reports of mathematics self-concept and educational outcomes: The roles of ego-dimensions and self-consciousness. *British Journal of Educational Psychology, 68,* 517-535.

Meece, J. L. (1994). The role of motivation in self-regulated learning. In D. H. Schunk & B. J. Zimmerman (Eds.), *Self-regulation of learning and performance* (pp. 25-44). Hillsdale, NJ: Erlbaum.

Nichols, J. D., & Utesch, W. E. (1998). An alternative learning program: Effects on student motivation and self-esteem. *The Journal of Educational Research, 91,* 272-278.

Oosterwegel, A., & Oppenheimer, L. (1993). *Self-system: Developmental changes between and within self-concepts.* Hillsdale, NJ: Erlbaum.

Paulson, S. (1994). Relations of parenting style and parental involvement with ninth-grade students' achievement. *Journal of Early Adolescence, 14,* 250-267.

Peixoto, F. (2003). *Auto-estima, autoconceito e dinâmicas relacionais em contexto escolar* [Self-esteem, self-concept and relational dynamics in school context]. Unpublished doctoral dissertation, University of Minho, Braga, Portugal.

Peixoto, F. (2004). Qualidade das relações familiares, auto-estima, autoconceito e rendimento académico [Quality of family relationships, self-esteem, self-concept and academic achievement]. *Análise Psicológica, 22,* 253-244.

Peixoto, F., & Almeida, L. S. (1999, October). *Escala de auto-conceito e auto-estima* [Self-concept and self-esteem scale]. Paper presented at the Conference "Avaliação Psicológica: Formas e Contextos", Braga, Portugal.

Pintrich, P. R. (2000). An achievement goal theory perspective on issues in motivation terminology, theory, and research. *Contemporary Educational Psychology, 25,* 92-104.

Repinski, D. J., & Shonk, S. M. (2002). Mothers' and fathers' behavior, adolescents' self-representations and adolescents' adjustment: A mediational model. *Journal of Early Adolescence, 22,* 357-383.

Ryan, R. M., & Deci, E. L. (2000). Intrinsic and extrinsic motivations: Classic definitions and new directions. *Contemporary Educational Psychology, 25,* 54-67.

Saleiro, F., & Peixoto, F. (2005, August). *Quality of family relationships and school achievement: Relationships with self-esteem, academic self-concept and goals orientations in 12th grade students.* Paper presented at the Biennial Meeting of the European Association for Research on Learning and Instruction, Budapest, Hungary.

Silva, I. (2002). *Relações entre orientações motivacionais, auto-conceito e género em estudantes portugueses: Adaptação da escala de objectivos motivacionais de Skaalvik* [Relationships between motivational orientations, self-concept and gender in Portuguese students: Adaptation of Skaalvik's scale of motivational goals]. Unpublished master's thesis, ISPA, Lisboa.

Skaalvik, E. M. (1997). Self-enhancing and self-defeating ego orientation: Relations with task and avoidance orientation, achievement, self-perceptions, and anxiety. *Journal of Educational Psychology, 89,* 71-81.

Skaalvik, S., & Skaalvik, E. M. (2005). Self-concept, motivational orientations, and help-seeking behavior in mathematics: A study of adults returning to high school. *Social Psychology of Education, 8,* 285-302.

Song, I. S., & Hattie, J. (1984). Home environment, self-concept and academic achievement: A causal modeling approach. *Journal of Educational Psychology, 76,* 1269-1281.

Vallerand, R. J., Fortier, M. S., & Guay, F. (1997). Self-determination and persistence in a real-life setting: Toward a motivational model of high school dropout. *Journal of Personality and Social Psychology, 72,* 1161-1176.

Wang, J., Wildman, L., & Calhoun, G. (1996). The relationships between parental influence and student achievement in seventh grade mathematics. *School Science and Mathematics, 96,* 395-399.

Wentzel, K. R. (1998). Social relationships and motivation in middle school: The role of parents, teachers and peers. *Journal of Educational Psychology, 90,* 202-209.

Wong, E. H., Wiest, D. J., & Cusick, L. B. (2002). Perceptions of autonomy support, parent attachment, competence and self-worth as predictors of motivational orientations and academic achievement: An examination of sixth-and-ninth, grade regular education students. *Adolescence, 37,* 255-266.

Influencing Students' Motivation for School

The Case of First-Year Students from Different Ethnic Backgrounds in the Netherlands in the Lowest Level of Secondary School

Thea Peetsma & Ineke van der Veen

Introduction

Motivation theories are often regarded as globally applicable. For instance, students' goals and expectations are broadly accepted as motivators for putting effort in learning behaviour. A decline of school motivation from the start of secondary school is a well-known phenomenon in educational research, which has been found in different countries and different types of schools (Midgley, Feldlaufer & Eccles, 1989; Peetsma, Hascher, Van der Veen & Roede, 2005).

Specifically, the motivation for school of students in the lowest school level in the Netherlands has been reported to be low and the percentage of early school leavers is three times higher than in the higher levels (Dutch Inspectorate of Education, 2005). This might be a result of different levels of student motivation as well as different school contexts and family background. Special for these schools is the absence of an option to attend a lower type of school where the student population includes more students with learning and behavioural difficulties. The students themselves have usually belonged to the lower achieving group in elementary education, which made it more likely they had been advised to attend the lower level school. Their fear of failure was found to be higher than in than in the higher school levels (Peetsma, 1996). Relatively many of them come from migrant families with a non-Dutch speaking background. Their parents who are mainly educated quite low themselves are hardly able to help their children with school work.

Observations of the difficult development in students' motivation in the lowest level of secondary school in the Netherlands led to the study presented here. This study focuses on enhancing the motivation for school of students starting in the lowest level of secondary school. Increasing the motivation of these students to engage in their school work at an early age may improve their chances of a successful future career. An intervention was developed to tackle the motivation in that specific situation. As students in the lower level of secondary school appear to have less of a long-term perspective on school and professional career than students in more academic schools (Peetsma, 1992), future time perspectives theory was the starting point for developing an intervention. In order to do this, on the one hand, global applicable theories have been utilized. While on the other hand, results from an intervention of the difficulties in the specific situation of the lower level schools suggested promising opportunities for a broader application of the intervention.

Theoretical Background

In motivation research a distinction can be made between motivated (self-regulated) learning behaviour and motivational factors. Zimmerman (2000) underlined the cyclical nature of self-regulation, assuming that students use feedback from prior learning experiences to make adjustments for subsequent efforts. Motivated behaviour, including personal investment and academic achievement, are positively influenced by motivational factors (Stoel, Peetsma & Roeleveld, 2003; Van der Veen & Peetsma, 2005).

Concerning motivational factors, a distinction can be made between three components: value, expectancy and an affective component (Peetsma, et al., 2005). The value component concerns students' reasons for doing a task or taking a course (task value). It includes students' goals and beliefs about the importance of the course. Concerning this component a number of distinctions have been made, including the distinction between mastery (learning/task) and performance (/ego) goals (e.g., Schunk, 1996). Mastery-oriented students compare their achievement with their own prior achievement and focus on mastery of the task or learning, while performance-oriented students compare their results with those of others and are concerned about demonstrating ability. An increase in mastery-orientation has been found to lead to an increase in self-regulated learning and higher achievement (e.g., Urdan & Midgley, 2000). Performance goals have been linked to less adaptive outcomes (e.g., Pintrich & Schunk, 1996). Nevertheless, (approach) performance goals, when coupled with mastery goals, have been found to be just as adaptive as mastery goals alone (Pintrich, 2000) or even more so (Van der Veen & Peetsma, 2005). The expectancy component includes students' beliefs about their ability to perform a task or their academic self-efficacy. Bandura (1993) found that a belief in one's competence is the guiding force behind thought and action. The affective component concerns students' feelings or emotional reactions to the task. For example, students' well-being in the course they are doing or at school in general. In her dual processing self-regulation model, Boekaerts describes how learning goals interact with well-being goals. Students try to maintain their well-being during the learning process (Boekaerts, 1993).

Future Time Perspective

The concept of future time perspective is generally described as a representation or conceptualisation of a particular life domain in terms of time, or the anticipation in the present of future events (Nuttin & Lens, 1985). Perspective refers to the representation of certain events or objects in the near or more distant future. The perspective is characterized by 'extension' and 'valence' (see e.g., Gjesme, 1975; Lens, 1986). Extension indicates the degree of remoteness of the representation in time. For students, both 'the time after finishing school' and 'the current school year' seem to be meaningful terms in time. The valence of the time perspective indicates the appreciation expressed by a person with respect to a certain life domain in the future, which plays an essential role in defining the concept of future time perspective as a motivational variable.

Simons, Dewitte & Lens (2000) describe future time perspectives in terms of instrumentality and distinguish three types of instrumentality. In the first type (E-E) the future task extrinsically motivates and externally regulates present activities. For instance a student puts a lot of effort into learning for a test, as he wants to earn a lot of money in future. He does not enjoy learning but wants to avoid being poor. In the second type (E-I) the future goal extrinsically motivates and internally regulates present activities. In this case the student in the example puts a lot of effort into learning for the test, as he wants to be able to develop himself (intrinsic). The learning itself is not a motivator, but rather the ultimate goal of self-enhancement. In the third type (I-I) the future goal intrinsically motivates and internally regulates present activities. In this case the student in the example puts a lot of effort into learning for the test, as he wants to acquire skills that he sees to be useful later in life. Students of the first type (E-E) appeared to have a lower task motivation than students of the other two types (E-I and I-I). Simons et al. argued that students' motivation can be enhanced if E-E is changed into E-I when the personal relevance of the extrinsic motives is highlighted.

Peetsma (1992; 2000) regards the concept of time perspective as an attitude to a certain life domain viewed in time with three components (affection, cognition and behavioural intention). Cognition consists of ideas or expectations with regard to the future, and of knowledge of personal and social realities. Affection is interpreted as an expression of feeling or affection towards a particular life domain in the future. Nowadays, far more importance is attached to social and affective aspects of school life than to cognitive aspects (e.g., Mayring & Von Rhoeneck, 2003). In the context of future time perspective, 'behaviour' is first seen as 'behavioural intention'. Defined like this, time perspective is broader than the concept of instrumentality, as it includes an affective component, while instrumentality is mainly cognitive in nature. Time perspective on school and professional career proved indeed to be a better predictor of students' school investment than did perceived instrumentality for their future, here operationalized as usefulness and necessity of education for the future (Peetsma, 1992). Students in the lowest level of secondary school appear to have less of a long-term perspective on school and professional career than students in higher levels (Peetsma, 1992).

Shifts in the relevance of life domains in the future time perspective of secondary school students might explain a decrease in motivation for school (Peetsma, 1997; Peetsma & Van der Veen, 2007). These authors found that students' time perspective on school became less important while perspectives on other domains of life, like leisure time, grew in importance or stayed stable. It seems that the perspectives on other domains of life interfere with their motivation for school. For instance, the long-term perspective on leisure time was found to correlate negatively with school investment.

Intervention

To develop a potentially successful intervention to enhance students' motivation based on future time perspectives theory, we should focus on highlighting the personal relevance of extrinsic motives, thus changing E-E into E-I, and on their perspectives on the life domain school and/or a later professional career. This perspective comprises the three attitude components (affection, cognition and behavioural intention) towards the school and professional career on a short or longer term in time. Furthermore, the intervention should lead to a decrease in students' perceived relevance of 'concurrent' life domains, like leisure time. Further useful information for changing E-E in E-I, can be found in the literature on academic delay of gratification and on possible selves.

Academic delay of gratification refers to students' postponement of immediately available opportunities to satisfy impulses in favour of pursuing chosen important academic rewards or goals that are temporally remote but ostensibly more valuable (Bembenutty & Karabenick, 1998, p. 330). Bembenutty and Karabenick showed that academic delay of gratification can be viewed as an aspect of self-regulated learning behaviour. They argued that teachers could help children enhance their learning behaviour by making them more aware of their future goals, including postive and negative outcomes associated with these goals (Benbenutty & Karabenick, 2004). Awareness of future goals might help students resist immediate gratification, like going out with friends, in order to reach valuable long-term goals, thus choosing to study instead of the immediately attractive alternative.

Possible selves refer to possible futures people can visualize for themselves. According to Oyserman, Bybee, Terry & Hart Johnson (2004), possible selves can serve to guide and regulate behaviour, providing a roadmap connecting the present to the future. Interventions based on possible selves aimed at stimulating students' commitment to school emphasize the relevance of students' actions at school for their later career. In schools this is often neglected (Oyserman, Terry & Bybee (2002). Oyserman et al. (2002) developed a successful intervention based on possible selves. They were able to increase students' commitment to school by stimulating the development of elaborated and plausible possible selves through a series of activities and by teaching students skills that are needed to accomplish this. The following characteristics of their intervention appeared to be essential for its success. Firstly, having possible selves alone is not enough: the more plausible and realistic strategies students have to achieve these possible selves, the better. Secondly, it is important not only to consider what should be done to achieve a possible self, but also what should be avoided. Answers to what should be done and what should be avoided, have to be in balance. Thirdly, students should attach importance to the possible selves. Fourthly, the steps that have to be taken to achieve the future goal (possible self) should be small.

This Study

In this study we wanted to design an intervention with the above-mentioned characteristics.

- A condition was that the intervention would not take more than one lesson. The reason was that we wanted to develop an intervention that could be fitted into the general teaching timetable in order to provide schools with an intervention fitting well in their timetable.
- We chose an indirect intervention (via two non-school topics—athletics and

music—and via two imaginary classmate) being aware of the need to be careful. Making students more aware of future goals might also lead to an unintended decrease in motivation, especially for students with less favourable school experiences in the past, which presumably lowered their expectation that school can be instrumental for their future.

As the intervention on students' school motivation focussed on highlighting the personal relevance of extrinsic motives, thus changing external motives in internal (E-E in E-I), and on the perspectives on the life domain school and/or a later professional career, as well as on a decrease in students' perceived relevance of 'concurrent' life domains, we expected that, if successful, the intervention would:

- increase the importance students attach to future prospects on school and a professional career,
- decrease the importance they attach to future perspectives on leisure time, and
- increase mastery goals, self-efficacy, well-being at school, and students' self-regulated learning behaviour (because time perspective on school and professional career is found to be positively related to this).

Method

Instruments

The Intervention

The intervention in the form of two separate assignments/role plays lasting about 45 minutes each was developed. Both assignments consisted of three parts and involved one interviewer and one student. In the *first part* of the first assignment students were asked to read a short text on high jumping. In the text the student was asked to imagine taking part in this athletics discipline. The student was presented with the following goals: 'surviving' the selection competition at the end of the year in order to be able to take part in the final competition in two years and to do well at this competition. The student was then asked to imagine the following:

- being good at high jumping, even though practice is needed to be able to jump higher (cognition),
- liking high jumping, dreaming about it a lot and getting a good feeling (affection),
- developing a training program with the trainer (behavioural intentions),
- not missing any training sessions, not only because this leads to missing necessary practice, but also because otherwise the trainer assumes the student is not taking high jumping seriously and may not want to train him/her anymore (behavioural intentions – possible selves), and
- how to handle distractions (high jumping practice comes first) (delay of gratification – behavioural intentions).

The text was summarized for the student. Then the student was asked (and given time) to imagine her/himself in that situation with these high jumping goals. The student was encouraged to make up things to supplement the text. The student was interviewed and the interviewer made sure the student was asked about the following aspects:

- affect: feelings toward the goals and activity,
- cognition: knowledge about and opinion on reaching the goals,
- behaviour (intentions): including small and big steps to be taken to reach the goal(s), and
- distractions in the areas of affect, cognition and behaviour: what to do about distractions like bad weather, frustration during practice, unpleasant training partner, etc.

In the *second part* of the assignment, students were asked to imagine a classmate who wants to continue to the next year and graduate. This classmate was a good enough learner to achieve this but sometimes felt insecure about his/her ability. The students were asked what they would recommend their classmate to do to achieve the goals, bearing in mind what they had talked about concerning high jumping. Again, the interviewer made sure the four aspects (affections, cognitions, behavioural intentions and distractions) came up in the interview.

In the *third part* of the assignment the students were asked whether they recognized themselves in the (imaginary) classmate and why (or why not). Again, the interviewer made sure the four aspects came up in the conversation. The interviewer encouraged and influenced the student, for instance, by suggesting alternatives.

The second assignment was similar to the first, but was on another subject. Instead of high jumping, this assignment was on playing in a band and "surviving" a selection procedure in order to be able to play in a festival. The student was asked to imagine a different classmate in this assignment: although having the same goals, this classmate thought he/she could easily achieve this. This classmate often fails to learn because he/she overestimates his/her ability, and in practice, this 'imaginary' student often fails tests.

Self-Report Questionnaire

To investigate whether the intervention has any effect, a self-report questionnaire was administered four times: in September 2004, February 2005, May 2005 and in September 2005. A number of items/scales, used for subject –specific concepts, were worded to have students focus on mathematics lessons, other items on school in general. Mathematics was chosen because all students study this subject and it is regarded as important. The questionnaire included the following scales (range 1-5)

- Four scales from the Future Time Perspective Questionnaire (Peetsma, 1992). The components of the future time perspective concept in the questionnaire are life domain (school and professional career / leisure time), extension (short term: this school year / long term: later after this school) and valence. These three components (domain, extension and valance) were systematically alternated in the questionnaire by using a facet-like approach. In the items the perspective was operationalized by cognitions, affections or intentions towards a life domain over a period of time.

- Students' self-efficacy, students' belief that they are able to cope with school-work and that they are responsible for their own performance, is measured by the subscale academic efficacy from the Patterns of Adaptive Learning Scales (PALS, Midgley et al., 2000).
- Two scales from the Goal Orientation Questionnaire by Seegers et al. (2002) are used. The first scale used is task orientation and measures mastery approach goals (a focus on mastery of the task). The second scale used is self-enhancing ego-orientation and assesses performance approach goals (orientation to a concern for ability and performance relative to others).
- In addition, general well being at school is measured. The students are presented with a scale developed by Peetsma et al. (2001), consisting of five items.

Self-Regulated Learning Behaviour is Assessed Using Three Scales:

- Firstly the school investment questionnaire (Roede, 1989) was used. School investment is operationalized by (1) the onset of students' behaviour; (2) the degree of intensity in doing something, and (3) their perseverance in doing something. Total scores for onset, intensity and perseverance are calculated for each scale. The scale for students' investment in mathematics work in the classroom is used.
- Secondly, from the 'self-regulation' scale developed by Pintrich & De Groot (1990) only six items for meta-cognitive strategy use, are used in order not to overlap with Roede's scale.
- The third scale assessing learning behaviour is a short version of the 'academic delay of gratification' scale developed by Bembenutty & Karabenick (1998).

See table 1 for example items, number of items per scale and reliabilities (Cronbach's alpha for internal consistency of the scales).

Design of Data-Analysis

The questionnaire was filled in four times by 765 first-year students from 13 schools for lower vocational education: 58% were boys and 42% girls. At the first measurement, the students were asked about their parents' ethnic origins. Ethnic background was based on the father, unless this was unknown in which case it was that of the mother. 77% were from Dutch background and 23% from ethnic minorities. At the first measurement the average sample was 12 years old and at the last 13 years old.

Intervention

30 students were selected randomly from the group of students with scores ≤ 4 (maximum was 5) on both the long and short term future time perspective on school and professional career at measurement 1. The reason for selecting students with scores ≤ 4 was that for them there was no need or point in influencing students with already very positive future time perspectives concerning school and professional career. As we could only include a limited number of students in the intervention, it would be more difficult to find

effects when also these students were included.

The 30 students participated in both assignments of the intervention: the first time in the intervention on high jumping a day before questionnaire measurement 2 and the second time in the intervention on the music festival a day before measurement 3.

Table 1. Example items, number of items, and reliabilities for the scales in this study.

Scale	Example item	n items	average reliability m1-m4
well-being at school	At school I feel at home	5	.68
short-term future perspective regarding school and professional career	I am pleased that I will learn a lot of new things this year.	6	.85
long-term future perspective regarding school and professional career	It does not matter too much to me what I study, or what kind of work I will be able to do after finishing school.	7	.66
short-term future perspective regarding leisure time	I enjoy my leisure time and holidays very much now.	6	.80
long-term future perspective regarding leisure time	In future, leisure time will mean a lot to me.	5	.73
self-efficacy	Even if the work is hard, I can learn it.	6	.79
task orientation	I feel satisfied when I have learned something in maths that makes sense to me.	5	.84
self-enhancing ego orientation	I enjoy getting a better grade in maths than my classmate.	6	.89
Scales for self-regulation			
meta-cognitive strategies	I ask myself questions to make sure I know the material I have been studying.	6	.81
maths investment	I put a lot of effort into maths.	5	.81
academic delay of gratification	I do my homework before I meet with my friends.	3	.85

Interview-Control Group

A control group of 25 students was selected randomly from the total sample. These students were interviewed face-to-face (twice) on the subjects in the self-report questionnaire at the same time as the assignment of the intervention took place. They were asked about their motivation and self-regulated learning (self-efficacy, mastery orientation, etcetera, see all the scales in the self-report questionnaire above) and about possible developments herein. By selecting this control group, we could investigate whether only giving attention to students' motivations and perspectives already was enough to enhance their motivation.

Analyses

We investigated the short and long(er)-term effects of the intervention by making two group comparisons. Firstly we compared the developments in motivation and motivated behaviour of the intervention group (group 1) with the students who only filled in the self-report questionnaire and (also) had scores ≤ 4 on the short and long term future time perspectives on school and the professional career at measurement 1 (group 2). This showed whether the intervention appeared successful. By restricting the scores of the non-intervention group, we prevented that effects of regression toward the mean could be attributed to the intervention. Secondly, if we did find an effect of the treatment in the first comparison, we compared students in the control (interview) group (group 3) with all students who only filled in the questionnaire (group 4). This comparison showed to what extent this effect could be attributed to only giving attention to students' motivation for school. Table 2 below shows the number of students in the four groups and the questionnaire response by the four measurements.

Table 2. Number of respondents and response by the different groups.

		M1	m1	M2	m3	m4
		N	%	%	%	%
comparison 1	Group 1: Intervention	30	100	97	93	100
	Group 2: No intervention/interview	174	100	89	91	85
comparison 2	Group 3: Interview	25	100	96	92	96
	Group 4: No intervention/interview	710	100	91	93	88

Although not all students participated in all four measurements, the total response is quite high. We analyzed the differences between the groups by performing repeated measures analysis. Univariate repeated measures analysis requires homogeneity of covariance, an assumption that is often violated in this type of analysis, as correlations between repeated measurements of a dependent variable are often higher the closer they are in time. The best solution is performing a trend analysis, because with this type of analysis it is not possible to violate this assumption (Tabachnick & Fidell, 1996). Results of this analysis indicate whether the trends in the development of the dependent variables are different for students in the different groups and whether this difference is linear, quadratic or cubic. In the analyses we controlled for gender and ethnic background. Furthermore by including interactions of gender and ethnic background with the intervention we checked whether effects of the intervention were different for Dutch background students and students from ethnic minorities and for girls and boys. We did not have specific hypotheses on this, however, when the intervention is successful for one group and not for another, no main effect may be found, as the positive and negative effect may cancel each other out.

Results

First, we present the mean scores on the four measurements for the different dependent variables by the four groups. Then the test results of the trend analyses are displayed. In the case effects were found, a graph of the mean scores on the four measurements will be shown.

Table 3 shows that the scores of the students in the intervention group (1) and their comparison group (2) are less favourable than that of the students in the other comparison (interview (3) and no intervention/interview group (4)). This could be expected, as we restricted the scores on the future time perspectives on school and professional career of the students in the first comparison group (intervention) and not of the students in the second comparison group (interview). In Table 4 we show whether and which differences are significant. Effects in the shaded rows concern the intervention.

Table 3. Comparison of intervention group & non-intervention/interview group and of interview group & non-intervention/interview group in the development of motivational variables.

		Comparison of intervention group 1 & non-intervention/interview group 2					Comparison of interview group 3 & non-intervention/interview group 4			
		m1	m2	m3	m4		m1	m2	m3	m4
short term future time persp.	1	3.4	3.8	3.7	3.7	3	4.4	4.4	4.1	4.1
on school/prof. career	2	3.3	3.7	3.6	3.5	4	4.2	4.1	4.1	3.9
long term future time persp.	1	3.4	3.7	3.8	3.8	3	4.0	4.2	4.1	4.2
on school/prof. career	2	3.5	3.7	3.8	3.8	4	4.0	4.1	4.1	4.1
short term future time persp.	1	4.1	4.0	4.2	4.1	3	4.2	4.3	4.1	4.3
on leisure	2	4.0	4.1	4.2	4.1	4	4.2	4.2	4.3	4.2
long term future time persp.	1	3.7	3.6	3.9	3.7	3	3.5	3.6	3.6	3.5
on leisure	2	3.6	3.8	3.9	3.8	4	3.6	3.7	3.8	3.8
self-efficacy	1	3.5	3.6	3.9	3.8	3	3.9	3.9	4.2	4.1
	2	3.5	3.7	3.7	3.7	4	3.7	3.9	3.9	3.9
mastery goals	1	3.3	3.5	3.4	3.6	3	4.0	4.2	4.0	4.1
	2	3.3	3.4	3.3	3.3	4	3.8	3.8	3.8	3.7
performance goals	1	2.6	2.6	2.6	2.9	3	2.9	2.7	2.7	2.9
	2	2.8	2.8	2.8	2.8	4	3.0	2.9	2.9	2.9
well-being at school	1	3.9	3.8	3.8	3.8	3	4.1	4.1	4.1	3.9
	2	3.8	3.7	3.6	3.6	4	4.0	3.9	3.8	3.7
maths investment	1	3.3	3.1	3.1	3.4	3	3.7	3.4	3.5	3.6
	2	3.2	3.1	3.0	3.0	4	3.6	3.4	3.3	3.3
meta-cognitive	1	3.0	2.8	2.8	3.2	3	3.3	3.2	3.3	3.4
strategy use	2	2.8	2.8	2.9	2.9	4	3.2	3.1	3.1	3.1
academic delay	1	3.5	3.2	2.9	3.2	3	3.9	3.5	3.6	3.8
of gratification	2	3.2	2.7	2.5	2.7	4	3.7	3.1	3.0	3.0

Table 4 shows that except for the long term future time perspectives, the development in scores is different for the intervention (group 1) and non-intervention/interview group (group 2).

To study the significant differences more closely, graphs are shown for these differences. Furthermore, next to the just mentioned significant differences, if significant, we display graphs for the difference between the interview and non-interview/intervention group. Below we display and discuss the graphs per variable. First significant differences are shown for the comparison between the intervention group (1) and the group of students who had no interview and no intervention (2). If significant, a comparison is displayed between the interview group (3) and the group of students who had no interview and no intervention (4). If this second effect is found, then it was not an effect produced by the intervention it self, but possibly by attention to motivation for school.

Table 4. Trend analyses for the motivational variables by the two comparison groups.

	ftp school&prof. career short		ftp school&prof. career long		ftp leisure short		ftp leisure long	
	comp1	comp2	comp1	comp2	Comp1	comp2	comp1	Comp2
Factor	Q**	Ns	L**	ns	Ns	ns	ns	Ns
Factor * interv.	ns	Ns	ns	ns	L***	ns	ns	Ns
Factor * gender	ns	Ns	ns	ns	Ns	L*	ns	Ns
Factor * ethn. min	ns	Ns	ns	ns	Ns	ns	ns	Ns
Factor * interv * gender	Q*	Ns	ns	ns	L**	ns	ns	Ns
Factor * interv * ethn. min.	ns	Ns	ns	ns	L**	ns	ns	Ns

	self-efficacy		mastery goals		performance goals		well-being at school	
	comp1	comp2	comp1	comp2	comp1	comp2	comp1	Comp2
Factor	L***	L***	L*	Ns	Ns	ns	ns	L*
Factor * interv.	C***	Ns	ns	C*	L*	L*	ns	Ns
Factor * gender	ns	Q*	ns	Ns	Ns	ns	ns	Ns
Factor * ethn.min	Q**	Ns	L*	Ns	Ns	ns	ns	Ns
Factor * interv * gender	C*	Q**	C**	Ns	Ns	ns	ns	Ns
Factor * interv * ethn. min.	C**	Ns	ns	Ns	L*	L*	C*	Ns

	maths invest- ment		metacogn. strategy use		acad. delay of gratification			
	comp1	comp2	comp1	comp2	comp1	comp2		
Factor	Q*	Q*	Q**	Ns	L,Q***	L*,Q***		
Factor * interv.	L*	Ns	Q***	Ns	Ns	L*		
Factor * gender	ns	L*	ns	Q*	Ns	ns		
Factor * ethn.min	ns	L*	Q*	C**	Ns	ns		
Factor * interv * gender	ns	Ns	ns	Ns	C*	ns		
Factor * interv * ethn. min.	ns	Ns	Q**	C**	Q*	Q*		

Note: factor = development in scores on the four measurements; comp1 = comparison between intervention group (1) and non-intervention/interview group (2); comp2 = comparison between interview group (3) and non-interview/intervention group (4); * $p < .05$, **, $p < .01$, *** $p < .001$; L: significant linear trend, Q: significant quadratic trend, C: significant cubic trend.

Short Term Future Time Perspective on School

Figure 1 shows the mean scores for the significant interaction effect of the intervention with gender.

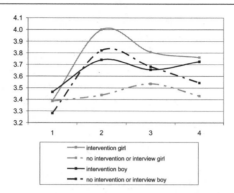

Figure 1. Development in short term future time perspective on school by intervention (group 1) and no intervention/interview (group 2) and by gender.

Girls, but not boys appear to have benefited from the intervention. The interaction effect for the interview was not significant, which indicates that indeed the intervention itself was successful for girls. The difference between the intervention (group 1) and comparison group (group 2) at measurement 3 is still present at measurement 4, indicating a longer term positive effect on the short term future time perspective on the school career. As we did not find a main effect of the intervention, it appears that the effects for girls and boys cancel each other out.

Short Term Future Time Perspective on Leisure.

Table 4 shows significant scores of the intervention, and also for the interaction effects of the intervention with gender and ethnic background. In Figure 2 the corresponding mean scores are displayed. As we expected leisure to be a competitive life domain for the domain school and professional career, we expected that the intervention would lead to a decline or smaller increase in the short term future time perspective on leisure.

Overall, from measurement 1 to 4 the short term future time perspective on leisure decreased for the intervention group (1), while it increased for the comparison group (2). Thus, the intervention seems to have had the intended effect. The other graphs in the figure show that especially for ethnic background students and girls the intervention had the expected effect. Differences were still present (even larger) at measurement 4, indicating that, four months after the second assignment of the intervention the effect of the intervention was still present. These effects were not found for the interview-comparison, indicating that the intervention itself appears to have been successful, not "just" speaking with students on motivational subjects.

Self-Efficacy

Table 4 showed significant effects of the intervention on self-efficacy and furthermore of the interaction effects of the intervention with gender and with ethnic background. There was also a significant interaction effect of the interview with gender. Figure 3 shows the related mean scores, starting with the development in self-efficacy for both the intervention group 1 and non-intervention/interview group (2).

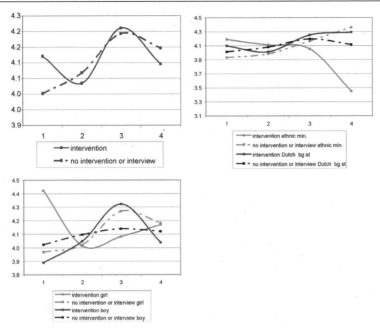

Figure 2. Development in short term future time perspective on leisure by intervention (group 1) and no intervention/interview (group 2), by gender and by ethnic background.

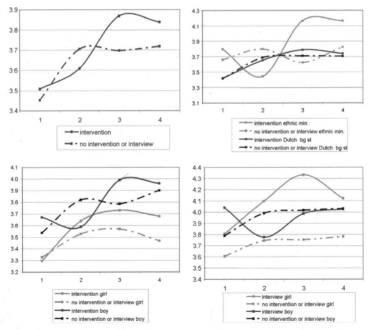

Figure 3. Development in self-efficacy by intervention (1) and no intervention/interview (2) and by interview (3) and no intervention/interview (4), and by ethnic background and gender.

Overall, the self-efficacy of students who participated in the intervention (group 1) increased more than that of students in the comparison group (group 2). Only the second assignment of the intervention (measurement 3) seems to have had an effect, which was still present at the fourth measurement. The second figure shows that this pattern is mainly the case for students from ethnic minorities. We did not find these effects for the interview-group (3), indicating that the intervention itself was successful, especially for students from ethnic minorities. The graphs show that the intervention was successful for girls, not so much for boys. However, a similar effect was found for the interview, indicating that for girls just paying attention to motivational aspects is 'enough' to increase their self-efficacy towards school.

Mastery Goals

Table 4 shows a significant different effect of the intervention on mastery goals for boys and girls. Figure 4 shows the development in mastery goals for boys and girls in the intervention group (1) and non-intervention/interview group (2).

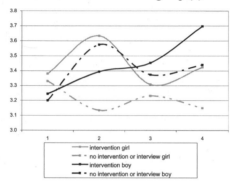

Figure 4. Development in mastery goals by intervention (1) and no intervention/interview (2) and by gender.

Although the patterns are indeed different for boys and girls, the graph shows that both boys and girls seem to have benefited from the intervention, even though not at all measurement occasions: boys not at the second (intervention assignment 1), girls not at the third measurement occasion (assignment 2). As we did not find a main effect of the intervention, the developmental patterns of boys and girls seem to cancel each other out. We did not find an effect of the interview, indicating that the intervention itself had an effect. All in all the intervention effect is not a very clear one.

Performance Goals

The results in Table 4 showed an effect of the intervention and a different effect of the intervention for students from ethnic minorities and Dutch background students. These effects were found for the interview as well. The figure below shows the corresponding mean scores on performance goals at the four measurements.

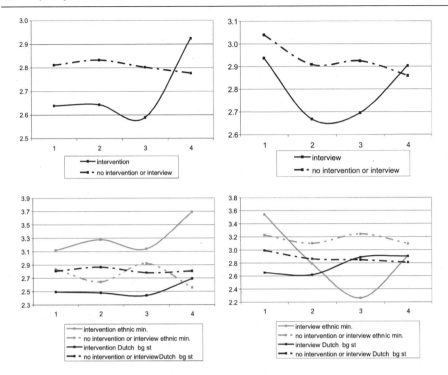

Figure 5. Development in performance goals by intervention (1) and no intervention/interview (2), and by interview (3) and no interview/intervention (4), and by ethnic background.

Although we found an effect of the intervention on performance goals, the effect of the interview appears to be similar: for both groups (1&3) there is a clear increase in scores on performance goals from the third to the fourth measurement. This increase mainly occurs for students from ethnic minorities who participated in the intervention, while the scores for students who were interviewed overall decreased. Although we could conclude that the intervention itself led to an increase in performance goals of students from ethnic minorities, we should be careful drawing this conclusion, as the interventions took place a day before the second and third measurement, not close to the fourth measurement where the increase in scores was found.

General Wellbeing at School

Table 4 shows a different effect of the intervention for students from ethnic minorities and Dutch background students. Figure 6 shows the development in general well being at school for the both students from ethnic minorities and Dutch background in the intervention group (1) and non-intervention/interview group (2).

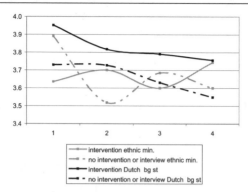

Figure 6. Development in general well-being at school by intervention (1) and no intervention/interview (2) and by ethnic background.

The graph shows that only for students from ethnic minorities the development in well being of students in the intervention group (1) is more favourable compared to the non-intervention/interview group (2). As this difference is not found for the interview comparison, this does seem to be an effect of the intervention itself. Four months after the second assignment of the intervention the effect is still present. We did not find a positive main effect of the intervention, so we can assume the effects for ethnic minority and Dutch background students cancel each other out.

Maths Investment

Table 4 shows an effect of the intervention on maths investment. Figure 7 shows this development for students in the intervention group (1) and non-intervention/interview group (2).

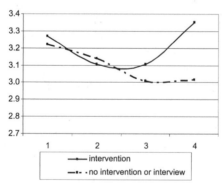

Figure 7. Development in maths investment by intervention (1) and no intervention/interview (2).

Since the second assignment of the intervention (measurement 3), students who took part in the intervention (group 1) put more effort in maths schoolwork than students who did not (2). As the interview-comparison was not successful, this seems to be an effect of the intervention itself, not just of talking with students on motivational subjects.

Meta-Cognitive Strategy Use

As we found significant effects of the intervention and different effects of the intervention and interview for students from ethnic minorities and Dutch background (Table 4), the corresponding development in mean scores for meta-cognitive strategy use are shown in Figure 8.

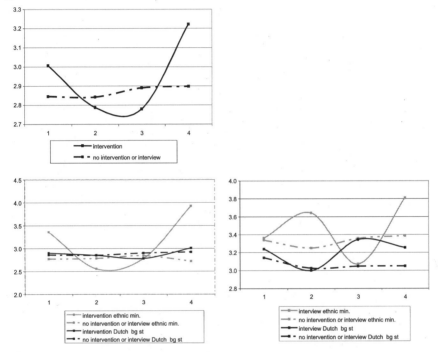

Figure 8. Development in meta-cognitive strategy use by intervention (1) and no intervention/interview (2), and by ethnic background and interview (3) versus no interiew/intervention(4) by ethnic background.

Looking at the development patterns of the first graph, we see lower scores at the second and third measurement and higher scores at the first and fourth measurement for the intervention group (1) compared to the non-intervention/interview group (2). The graph for the interaction effect of the intervention with ethnic background shows that only students from ethnic minorities have this developmental pattern. We could conclude that the assignments of the intervention (measurement 2 and 3) made students more aware of meta-cognitive strategies, lowering their perception of use of it, eventually leading to an increased use at measurement 4. Nevertheless, the interview comparison shows developmental patterns for students from ethnic minorities that are not very different, so the conclusion the intervention itself did not lead to an increased use of meta-cognitive strategies seems more plausible.

Academic Delay of Gratification

Table 4 showed a different effect of the intervention for students from ethnic minorities and Dutch background students. Figure 9 shows the development in academic delay of gratification for both students from ethnic minorities and Dutch background in the intervention (1) and non-intervention/interview group (2) and in the interview (3) and non-interview/intervention group (4).

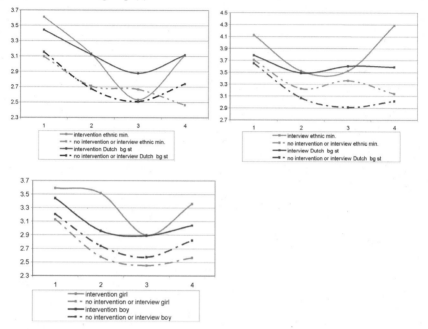

Figure 9. Development in academic delay of gratification by intervention (1), interview (3) and no intervention/interview (2 & 4) and ethnic background.

The graph shows a more beneficial development for students from ethnic minorities (group 1) compared to the non-intervention/interview group (2) than for students from Dutch background. Nevertheless, the same (even more positive) pattern is shown for students from ethnic minorities who participated in the interview (group 3). Therefore, we cannot conclude that the intervention itself led to an increase in the ability of students to delay academic gratification.

Furthermore, we found a different growth pattern for boys and girls: girls seem to have benefited from the intervention, while boys did not. There seems to have been an effect of the first assignment of the intervention (measurement 2), which had disappeared at the third measurement. Although we did not find this interaction effect with gender for the interview comparison, we cannot conclude that the interventions had a clear and lasting effect (for girls).

Conclusions

In the research we tried to enhance the motivation for school of first-year students from different ethnic backgrounds in the lowest level of secondary school in the Netherlands. We can conclude that the results are promising in positively influencing students' motivation for school with two applications of an intervention of just 30-45 minutes each. Furthermore these effects do not seem to be temporary as they remained four months after the second intervention. Maybe the hoped-for effect of a pebble stone scattering ripples in a pond?

First of all, effects on short term future time perspectives were found. The results indicated that girls' short term future time perspective on school was positively influenced by the intervention and their short term future time perspective on leisure, negatively influenced. The latter was also the case for students from ethnic minorities. These effects were still present four months after the second assignment of the intervention. No influences on the long term perspectives were found. This is not surprising, as most students wanted a good education and job in the future. Making students more aware of present actions and beliefs for acquiring this future is more likely to influence present beliefs than beliefs concerning the (already positively valued) future.

Furthermore we found an effect on the expectancy component of motivation. Ethnic minority students' self-efficacy was positively influenced, mainly by the first assignment of the intervention. Seven months after this intervention this effect appeared to be still present. That we found a positive effect of the first assignment of the intervention could be expected, as the second part of this assignment of the intervention was on a student with too low self-efficacy. The second part of the second assignment of the intervention was on an over-confident student.

Although we did find some effects on the value component of motivation, these effects were not clear. We found some indications that the mastery goals of students who participated in the intervention increased somewhat.

Regarding the affective component of motivation only for students from ethnic minorities a positive effect of the intervention on general well-being at school was found. Four months after the second assignment of the intervention this effect was still present. ·

Finally, concerning students' self-regulated learning behaviour, only a positive effect on maths investment was found, mainly of the second assignment of the intervention. Four months later, this effect was still present.

We expected that influencing the future perspectives would influence goals, which in turn would influence learning behaviour. We did indeed find an effect for all students in learning behaviour (maths investment), but a less clear effect on mastery goals. In future research this should be studied further.

The intervention of motivation via students' time perspectives includes a combined influence of the cognitive, affective and behavioural intention aspects of time perspective, together with the distraction aspect from delay of gratification. It is not possible in this study to analyze which of the three aspects cognition, affection and intention, was most effective, as the three components establish the time perspective and are interrelated.

In the intervention 'possible selves' were used in an indirect way, in order to avoid a not intended decrease in motivation instead. The intervention was indirect in two ways:

using a classmate instead of the student itself as target and using possible selves in sports and music instead of learning for school. Only via sports and music activities was the comparison with learning made. This indirect intervention can have caused a weaker effect than might have been produced by a direct intervention. On the other hand, to be directly didactical, might have had an unintended opposite effect.

Although we could conclude that the intervention itself led to an increase in motivation, in some cases this conclusion needs to be made with care. As the intervention took place a day before the second and third measurement, and not close to the fourth measurement where, in these cases, the increase in scores was visible.

Regarding the effects of the two assignments of the interventions, via sports music respectively, it is difficult to conclude which of the two works better. In some cases, the second one on music seems most fruitful, but this might be an effect of addition of treatments. Or students understand better what is going on after getting used to the intervention. At least we can say that only one assignment of the intervention will not be that fruitful.

In this study we included a control group that was interviewed on motivational subjects. This proved to be successful, as otherwise we would have wrongfully attributed some results to the intervention. Nevertheless we could not directly compare the three groups of students (intervention, interview and non-intervention/interview) as we restricted the scores of students who were in the intervention group. We did not include students with very high scores on the future time perspectives on school and professional career, as for them there was no need or point in influencing already very positive perspectives. As we could only include a limited number of students in the intervention, it would be more difficult to find effects when these students were also included. However, when far more students participate in the intervention, there will be no need for the restriction with the advantage of being able to compare the three groups in one analysis. We already indicated that our aim is to design an intervention that can be included in the general teaching timetable or coaching activities. When we succeed in this, the number of participants in the intervention should be high enough to do this. Nevertheless, more research is necessary before we will be able to develop an intervention suitable for inclusion in general school activities.

The intervention to enhance students' motivation was based on time perspectives theory, which can be regarded as an addition to the quite global goal-theory. We focussed on highlighting the personal relevance of the extrinsic motives, thus changing external in internal motives, and on the perspectives on the life domain school and/or a later professional career. Furthermore, the intervention had to lead to a decrease in students' perceived relevance of 'competing' life domains, particularly leisure time. As migrant students and girls seem to profit most from the intervention, it seems that a potentially global theory works out different for students of different gender and different ethnical background. Nevertheless, the theory seems to apply for all students.

This study can be regarded as an attempt to tackle a difficult motivational situation of students in the lower levels of secondary education in the Netherlands. Global theories were utilized for this. Nevertheless, the results of the intervention in this specific type of education seem to offer promising results for a more global use in dealing with difficulties in student motivation.

References

Bandura, A. (1993). Perceived self-efficacy in cognitive development and functioning. *Educational Psychologist, 28,* 117-148.

Bembenutty, H., & Karabenick, S. A. (1998). Academic delay of gratification. *Learning and Individual Differences, 10,* 329-346.

Bembenutty, H., & Karabenick, S. A. (2004). Inherent association between academic delay of gratification, future time perspective, and self-regulated learning. *Educational Psychology Review, 16,* 35-57.

Boekaerts, M. (1993). Being concerned with well-being and with learning. *Educational Psychologist, 28,* 149-167.

Dutch Inspectorate of Education (2005). *Onderwijsverslag 2003/2004* [Dutch Education in 2003/2004]. Utrecht: Dutch Inspectorate of Education.

Gjesme, T. (1975). Slope of gradients for performance as a function of achievement motives, goal distance in time and future-time orientation. *Journal of Psychology, 91,* 143-160.

Lens, W. (1986). Future time perspective: A cognitive-motivational concept. In D. R. Brown & J. Veroff (Eds.), *Frontiers of motivational psychology* (pp. 173-190). New York: Springer-Verlag.

Mayring, P., & von Rhöneck, C. (Eds.) (2003). *Learning Emotions – The influence of affective factors on classroom learning.* Bern: Lang.

Midgley, C., Feldlaufer, H., & Eccles, J. S. (1989). Student/teacher relations and attitudes toward mathematics before and after the transition to junior high school. *Child Development, 60,* 981-992.

Midgley, C., Maehr, M. L., Hruda, L. Z., Anderman, E., Anderman, L., Freeman, K. E., Gheen, M., Kaplan, A., Kumar, R., Middleton, M. J., Nelson, J., Roeser, R., & Urdan, T., (2000). *Manual for the Patterns of Adaptive Learning Scales (PALS),* Ann Arbor, MI: University of Michigan.

Nuttin, J.R., & Lens, W. (1985). *Future time perspective and motivation, theory and research method.* Leuven / Hillsdale, NJ: Leuven University Press / Erlbaum.

Oyserman, D., Bybee, D., Terry, K., & Hart Johnson, T. (2004). Possible selves as roadmaps. *Journal of Research in Personality, 38,* 130-149.

Oyserman, D., Terry, K., & Bybee, D. (2002). A possible selves intervention to enhance school involvement. *Journal of Adolescence, 25,* 313-326.

Peetsma, T. T. D. (1992). *Toekomst als motor. Toekomstperspectieven van leerlingen in het voortgezet onderwijs en hun inzet voor school.* [The future as an incentive? Secondary education students' perspectives concerning their future and their investment in school](Academic dissertation). Amsterdam: Stichting Centrum voor Onderwijsonderzoek, Universiteit van Amsterdam.

Peetsma, T. T. D. (1997, August). *Decline in pupils' motivation during secondary education.* Paper presented at the Biennial Meeting of the European Association for Research on Learning and Instruction. Athens, Greece.

Peetsma, T.T. (2000). Future time perspective as a predictor of school investment. *Scandinavian Journal of Educational Research, 44,* 177-192.

Peetsma, T.T.D. (1996). Pupils' fear of failure in secondary education. In L.A. Bakken, C.L. Jacobson, & K.L. Schnare (Eds.) Upgrading of the social sciences for the development of post-socialist countries (pp. 287-294). Kaunas: Kaunas University of Technology.

Peetsma, T.T.D., Hascher, T., Veen, I. van der, & Roede, E. (2005). Relations between adolescents' self-evaluations, time perspectives, motivation for school and their achievement in different countries and at different ages. *European Journal of Psychology of Education, 20,* 209-225.

Peetsma, T., & Veen, I. van der (2007, August-September). *The developments in students' future time perspectives on different life domains, school investment and achievement.* Paper presented at the Biennial Meeting of the European Association for Research on Learning and Instruction. Budapest, Hungary.

Peetsma, T. T. D., Wagenaar, E., & Kat, E. de (2001). School motivation, future time perspective and well-being of high school students in segregated and integrated schools in the Netherlands and the role of ethnic self-description. In J. K. Koppen & I. Lunt & C. Wulf (Eds.) *Education in Europe, cultures, val-*

ues, institutions in transition (Vol. 14, pp. 54-74). Münster, New York: Waxmann.

Pintrich, P. R., & De Groot, E. V. (1990). Motivational and self-regulated learning components of classroom academic performance. *Journal of Educational Psychology, 82*, 33-40.

Pintrich, P. R., & Schunk, D. H. (1996). *Motivation in education: Theory, research, and applications.* Englewood Cliffs, NJ: Prentice Hall.

Pintrich, P.R. (2000). An achievement goal theory perspective on issues in motivation terminology, theory, and research. *Contemporary Educational Psychology, 25*, 92-104.

Roede, E. (1989). *Explaining student investment, an investigation of high school students' retrospective causal accounts of their investment in school.* (Academic dissertation) Amsterdam: Stichting Centrum voor Onderwijsonderzoek, Universiteit van Amsterdam.

Schunk, D. H. (1996). Goal and self-evaluative influences during children's cognitive skill learning. *American Educational Research Journal, 33*, 359-382.

Seegers, G., van Putten, C. M., & de Brabander, C. J. (2002). Goal orientation, perceived task outcome and task demands in mathematics tasks: Effects on students' attitude in actual task settings. *British Journal of Educational Psychology, 72*, 365-384.

Simons, J., Dewitte, S., & Lens, W. (2000). Wanting to have vs. wanting to be: The effect of perceived instrumentality on goal orientation. *British Journal of Psychology, 91*, 335-351.

Stoel, R., Peestma, T., & Roeleveld, J. (2003). Relations between the development of school investment, self-confidence, and language achievement in elementary education: A multivariate latent growth curve approach. *Learning and Individual Differences, 13*, 313-333.

Urdan, T., & Midgley, C. (2000, May). *Developmental changes in the relations among goal structures, motivational beliefs, affect, and performance.* Paper presented at the 7th WATM, Leuven.

Tabachnick, B.G., & Fidell, L.S. (1996). *Using multivariate statistics.* New York: HarperCollins College Publishers.

Veen, I. van der, & Peetsma, T. (2005). *The development in self-regulated learning behaviour of first-year students in the lowest type of secondary school in the Netherlands.* Paper presented at the EARLI conference, Nicosia, Cyprus.

Zimmerman, B. J. (2000). Self-efficacy: an essential motive to learn. *Contemporary Educational Psychology, 25*, 82-91.

Normative vs. Non-Normative Performance Goals

Effects on Behavioral and Emotional Regulation in Achievement Situations

Georgios D. Sideridis

Introduction

Achievement goal theory has provided the means to understand achievement and achievement-related cognitions and behaviors in achievement situations. This comprehensive framework has enhanced our understanding of motivated behavior by using trait dispositions, situation-specific cognitions, and affect (Ames, 1992; Dweck & Leggett, 1988; Pekrun, Elliot, & Maier, 2006). Elliot (1997, 1999) made a successful attempt in linking global motive dispositions — such as the motive to achieve (Atkinson, 1964) — with task-specific dispositions (e.g., goal orientations). Elliot's (1997, 1999) analysis placed motive dispositions (global perspective) as antecedents of task-specific motives (local perspective) with a tight link between them. For example, individuals with the *need to achieve* are likely to pursue performance goals (approach form), whereas those with the *need to avoid failure* are likely to endorse performance goals of avoidance form. Elliot (1999) suggested that the link between global and specific forms of motivation is based on "explicit congruence", that is, both motives operate on the same source of valence (e.g., the need to avoid failure and performance avoidance goals focus on avoiding negative end states).

The aim of the present chapter is to deal with motives at the task level and test the proposition that performance-approach goals, which represent situation-specific motives, can be further bifurcated into normative vs. non-normative components (Grant & Dweck, 2003). This proposition was tested across two studies using the methodology of the Emotional Stroop task (William, Mathews, & MacLeod, 1996) as well as performance instructions along the dimension of valence (desire to outperform others, desire to be excellent). Initially, there is a review of the literature regarding the different types of goals that originate in goal theory, followed by two studies in which the Emotional Stroop task (MacLeod, 1991; Schiller, 1966) was used to test the proposed hypotheses.

Achievement Goal Theory

Since the pioneering work of Dweck (1986) and Nicholls (1984; see also Jagacinski & Nicholls, 1984, 1987), two distinct approaches to motivated behavior have been identified: (a) the orientation to *perform*, which is based on normative evaluative standards, and (b) the orientation to learn, *master*, and acquire a skill, which is based on internal standards of success. In the latter case engagement with the task is derived from pleasure and interest. According to Elliot and McGregor (2001) goal selection is a function of one's perception of competence and his/her value system. If one judges competence given *normative standards* then s/he values grades and normative evaluations and is more likely to espouse performance goals in achievement situations. If one uses *absolute standards* of competence, s/he may judge ability based on attainment of skills and competencies, and is likely to pursue mastery goals. Recently, however, Grant and Dweck (2003) suggested that performance goals may be further distinguished into various forms of performance goals with differential focus. One crucial distinction pertains to the differentiation between performance goals having or not a normative evaluation focus. This proposition is the focus of the present chapter. Below there is a brief historical account of how performance goals developed over time followed by two studies in which performance normative and non-normative goals are contrasted in order to provide evidence whether their differentiation is meaningful and empirically validated.

A Historical Account of Performance Goals

Performance goals originated in the achievement motive tradition (Atkinson, 1964, 1974; McClelland, 1951) and the need to achieve compared to the need to avoid failure (Schmalt, 1982; Teevan & McGhee, 1972). However, the achievement motive operated at the level of the need (global type of motivation) and, thus, being more biologically determined, it was a motive that was not malleable. The pioneer work of Dweck, Nicholls, and Ames provided a more situational function of this motive to reflect task-specific demands and functions. These situational-specific, task-specific, motives were termed goal orientations. Initially, goal orientations were described by a dichotomy (mastery/learning vs. performance/ego), and with the exception of mastery/learning goals, which were associated with adaptive behavioral outcomes (Meece & Holt, 1993), the effects of performance goals were mixed.

Elliot and Harackiewicz (1996) suggested that the mixed findings with regard to performance goals were due to the fact that there was a confounding of two distinct but also opposing motivationally forces, the motive to achieve and the motive to avoid failure. Thus, they proposed and tested a dichotomization of performance goals into approach and avoidance forms, that is, "to do better than others" or "strive to not fail" (for a discussion on approach-avoidance motivation see Elliot, 1999). This dichotomization provided evidence that the early negative effects of performance goals could potentially be attributed to the avoidance component (efforts to move away from failure) and, thus, performance-approach goals were proposed to be positive correlates of achievement outcomes. This new line of research contributed unequivocal findings (positive, null, or negative), complicating the picture further as regards the regulation from adopting performance-approach goals compared to mastery goals. Given, however, the consistent direct positive effects between performance-approach goals and achievement, Harackiewicz, Barron, Pintrich, Elliot, and Thrash (2002) suggested a revision of goal theory, which would clearly state the adaptive functioning of performance approach goals, although others were against that proposition (Kaplan & Middleton, 2002; Midgley, Kaplan, & Middleton, 2001).

Since then, the construct of performance goals has been the object of great debate and a large amount of controversial and conflicting findings (Elliot & Moller, 2003; Rawsthorne & Elliot, 1999; Sideridis, 2007; Utman, 1997). More recently, Urdan and Mestas (2006) proposed that performance goals can be bifurcated based on appearance or competition. The authors suggested that appearance performance goals (i.e., appearing able or not) and social comparison goals (i.e., trying to do better than others) comprise different motivational mechanisms with the former acting as a distracter of the latter (Urdan, 2000). Urdan and Mestas added that the desire to outperform others is not necessarily associated with low achievement, which is likely accountable for some of the positive effects reported in performance approach goals (Harackiewicz et al., 2002; Sideridis, 2005). Thus, Urdan and Mestas (2006) proposed a 2 x 2 taxonomy of performance-approach goals, although their qualitative study revealed eight classes of goals representing interpersonal standards of competence, five classes representing intrapersonal standards of what success is, and three classes of goals not being classified (termed ambiguous). The authors concluded that individuals pursue performance goals for a wide variety of reasons, certainly many more than their conceptualization entails. Thus, the picture with regard to what exactly performance goals encompass was complicated using this study's findings.

Using a similar methodology, Sideridis and Mouratidis (2008) reported that endorsing performance goals (approach or avoidance) was associated with a very broad network of motives with constructs from self-determination theory, expectancy-value theory, or social learning theory. Thus, social goals (Elliot, Gable, & Mapes, 2006; Mouratidis & Sideridis, in press; Ryan & Shim, 2006) and other classes of goals were simultaneously operative suggesting a multi-motive presence with regard to performance approach goals. The findings from such qualitative studies suggest that performance goals may be further bifurcated to different classes of strivings.

Normative vs. Non-Normative Performance Goals

Grant and Dweck (2003) pointed to the fact that performance goals should be further distinguished based on both valence and outcome focus. One of the major differentiations was with respect to the presence or not of normative evaluations (i.e., a focus on outcomes). Grant and Dweck (2003) stated that "t would be interesting to find that normative and non-normative performance goals do indeed differ, particularly if these differences could illuminate discrepancies in the reported effects of performance goals on motivation and performance"(p. 542).

Is this differentiation viable? Let's consider the difference between performance normative goals and performance non-normative goals. One student may be interested in doing well and achieving good grades and another on doing well in order to outperform others. Both goals have the component of performance built in, but one has intrapersonal standards of what success is and the other interpersonal. One question of interest then is the following: If we take out the normative component, are these still "performance" goals or can they be considered mastery goals? Performance non-normative goals focus on performing well using intrapersonal standards of success. Mastery goals target at learning, understanding, and improving a skill. Thus, performing well in tests and achievement situations is not the focus of mastery goals. For example, a mastery-oriented student could be potentially absorbed into an interesting and challenging activity and could fail an achievement situation because the focus of his/her strivings is not on performing well in terms of outcomes (i.e., earning good grades) but on learning and understanding the material in hand. In other words, mastery goals do not reflect approaching achievement but rather approaching desirable end states from being involved with an activity. This is why mastery goals correlate so strongly with intrinsic motivation (Harackiewicz, Barron, Carter, Lehto, & Elliot, 1997; Harackiewicz, Barron, Tauer, Carter, & Elliot, 2000) — because they have such a strong basis on intrinsic interest (Hidi, 1990, 2001; Hidi & Harackiewicz, 2000; Van Yperen, 2003).

Yet, other authors have claimed that performance goals cannot be defined in the absence of normative evaluative standards (Elliot & Harackiewicz, 1996), showing how heavily performance goals rely on interpersonal evaluative standards. As described above, performance-approach goals without a normative component are different from mastery goals. Also, the normative component is likely salient enough to discriminate the two performance goals as, once again, the focus of mastery goals is not on performance per se but on learning. Empirical evidence will be the judge in favor of, or against the hypothesis that performance goals can be further bifurcated based on a focus or not on normative evaluations.

It is also likely that performance goals without a normative component are strongly related to non-linear combinations of goals such as a combination of mastery goals with other types of goals having or not a performance component or approach versus avoidance tendencies (Sideridis, 2008; Wentzel, 1993). Having multiple goals operative is an important direction of research (Barron & Harackiewicz, 2001) that may enhance our understanding of goals and their regulation.

Regulation of Students' Behavior and Affect by Adopting Various Goals

The relevant literature has pointed to the fact that achievement goals, particularly mastery, have adaptive effects on students' learning and achievement, type of processing, and well-being, whereas performance-avoidance goals have the most detrimental effects (Karabenick, 2004; Rawsthorne & Elliot, 1999). Findings related to the effects of performance-approach goals have been mixed (Harackiewicz et al., 2002; Linnenbrink, 2005) and have in essence clouded the picture regarding the regulation of behavior, that is, the outcome from adopting these goals.

What is less known is how goal orientations influence or are influenced by affect (Ntoumanis & Biddle, 1999; Pekrun et al., 2006). This is a very important question, given the salient role of emotions, mood, and metacognitive experiences for achievement and well-being (Efklides, 2006; Efklides & Petkaki, 2005; Pekrun et al., 2006; Sideridis,

2005). Only recently the influential works by Pekrun and colleagues shed light on the relationship between goals and emotions (Meinherdt & Pekrun, 2003; Pekrun et al., 2006) and there is no evidence to the fact that different types of performance goals may exert different effects on the emotional experience during achievement strivings with the exception of one recent study. Pekrun et al. (2006) developed a series of predictions regarding goals and affect positing that mastery and performance-approach goals would relate positively to positive affect, given their approach propensities. The opposite would be true for performance-avoidance goals. These predictions were confirmed in two studies using German and U.S.A. samples. Specifically, mastery goals were related positively to enjoyment and negatively to boredom and anger. Performance goals, which are the focus of the present chapter, were unrelated to affect, although tested in the absence of their avoidance component. This finding, however, is in accordance with similar findings in the Sideridis (2005) study. As expected, performance-avoidance goals were positive predictors of anxiety, hopelessness, and shame (trends only emerged for the latter two). Interestingly, the authors found that mastery goals were associated with competence-based emotions (e.g., pride), a finding that raises the question whether the valence in mastery goals entails a broader taxonomy of motives than initially thought (e.g., as in the multiple goal perspective, Barron & Harackiewicz, 2001; Pintrich, 2000). Their finding agrees with recent contributions of qualitative studies that have broadened the classes of motives that belong to each goal orientation (Dowson & McInerney, 2001, 2003; Sideridis & Mouratidis, 2008; Urdan & Mestas, 2006).

The aim of the present chapter is to provide empirical evidence that normative performance goals are associated with unique and differential effects on achievement compared to non-normative performance goals. The prediction formed from the literature was that normative performance goals would have more deleterious effects with regard to achievement and affect, compared to non-normative performance goals because a focus on outcomes and normative comparisons is more likely to elicit anxiety and feelings of apprehension, particularly when ego-threats are involved (which are very likely in achievement situations). Evidence of that kind will support the bifurcation of performance goals as normative vs. non-normative by means of focusing on outcomes (Grant & Dweck, 2003). Both studies presented herein evaluate the existence of differences between the two goal conditions on affect and achievement. Below there is an analytic description of each study.

Study 1

Method

Participants

Participants in Study 1 were 324 elementary-school students. All students attended Grades 5 and 6 and came from elementary schools in the Greek part of Cyprus. Because all assessments were conducted during the Spring semester of the academic year, 5th graders were around 11 years of age and 6th graders around the age of 12 years. As regards gender distribution, there were 152 boys and 172 girls. A computerized Emotional Stroop Task was implemented using the Genov, Shay, and Boon (2002) software.

Measures

The Emotional Stroop Task, which is a modification of the original Stroop task (Kuhl & Kazen, 1999; MacLeod & Rutherford, 1992; Stroop, 1935), was implemented. In the original Stroop task, participants are required to match the color of the ink in which a word is written to the actual color the word denotes (e.g., word "blue" in blue color vs. word "blue" in green color) (see also MacLeod & Rutherford, 1992). Based on how information is organized in one's memory, the prediction is that individuals will delay, or make significantly more errors, in the color-naming of words in which there is a mismatch (e.g., word "blue" written in red color). The Emotional Stroop Task represents an extension of the classical paradigm in that prolonged latencies are expected whenever the written words represent a source of concern to individuals compared to words having neutral content. This "delay" in responding has been termed as "interference" and reflects attention and information biases towards particular sets of stimuli. As Mogg and Bradley (1998) stated «output from the valence evaluation system feeds into a goal engagement system, which in turn determines the allocation of resources for cognitive processing and action» (p. 817). Thus, they suggested that goal engagement is a function of valence, which is an important component of goals.

Assessment of cognitive interference. Lists of emotional stimuli related to success, failure, persistence, anxiety, positive affect, negative affect, calmness, positive self-esteem, and negative self-esteem were examined as linear combinations of underlying latent states and were assessed at a computerized environment using the Genov Modified Stroop Task (GMST; Genov et al., 2002; see Figure 1 for a description of the computerized environment). The GMST is a computerized version of the Emotional Stroop Task and presents words in the centre of a circular 20-color palette. The colored words appear in the middle of the color circle. After the word is presented, the respondent has to select the correct color from the palette by use of a mouse. Subsequently, the respondent has to click on a small circle in the center of the screen to initiate the presentation of the next word. For example, as soon as the word "excellent" appears on the screen, the student has to select the color in which the word is written. Time is running with the onset of each word stimulus. The software accurately records participants' reaction time between the presentation of the word and the selection of the corresponding color. It also records the actual color selected by the respondent (to identify correct matching). Each time the GMST is run, the word – color pairs are presented in a different, random order. Thus, the order of the words is counterbalanced per person, in essence accounting for serial position effects due to fatigue or word characteristics.

Initially, simple analyses of variance were run to ensure equivalence of words in terms of length, number of syllables, and frequency of usage in the Greek language (as appeared in the Hellenic National Corpus of the Greek Institute for Language and Speech Processing; http://hnc.ilsp.gr/statistics.asp). There were no significant differences between word lists as regards length, $F(9, 32) = 0.432$, $p = .91$, number of syllables, $F(9, 32) =$

1.069, $p = .41$, or frequency of usage (per million occurrences), $F(9, 32) = 1.883$, $p = .09$ (see also Sideridis, in press). Recent empirical evidence suggests that the computerized version of the Emotional Stroop Task is valid for the evaluation of cognitive interference (Karademas, Kafetsios, & Sideridis, 2007; Karademas, Sideridis, & Kafetsios, 2008).

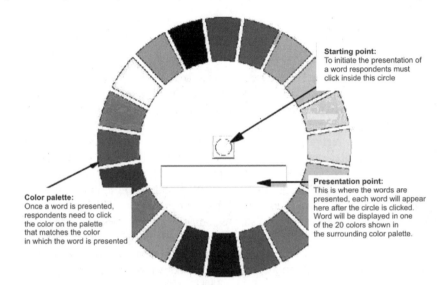

Figure 1. Computerized environment for the assessment of cognitive interference using the Emotional Strop Task (screen shot).

Procedure

Participants were randomly assigned into a mastery-goal condition, a normative perform-ance-goal condition and a non-normative performance-goal condition in order to avoid potential participant biases. The following scenarios were implemented in order to elicit different goal conditions.

Mastery condition. This scenario was modified from the original Dweck and Leggett (1988) study: "With this exercise we would like to see how kids your age distinguish colors and the ways they use to accomplish that. We want to see how you go about learn-ing various complex color sequences. So, every time you see a word on the PC, you should choose the color that matches the color in which the word is written. It is more important to find the color correctly than to go quickly and make errors." Sixty two stu-dents were randomly assigned to this condition.

Normative performance-goal condition. "With this exercise we would like to see the ability of kids your age to distinguish complex color sequences. So, every time you see a word on the PC, you should choose the color that matches the color in which the word is written and do that as quickly as possible. In the end of this exercise we will make a list with the names of the participants, from most to least successful. I want you to try to out-perform everybody else." Sixty one students were randomly assigned to this condition.

Non-normative performance-goal condition. "With this exercise we would like to see the ability of kids your age to distinguish complex color sequences. I would like you to give your best. So, every time you see a word on the PC, you should choose the color that matches the color in which the word is written. I want you to try and do the matching correctly but also as quickly as possible." Two hundred one students were randomly assigned to this condition.

Results

The main effect of goal condition, tested within a factorial analysis of variance, was indicative of several significant effects. As shown in Figure 2, students in the normative performance-goal condition spent significantly more time to match the correct pair of stimuli compared to the non-normative performance-goal condition. There were no significant effects with regard to the amount of errors. Those effects favored the non-normative performance-goal condition with regard to stimuli related to the classes of positive affect (beta = -.294), negative affect (beta = -.311), failure (beta = -.339), negative self-esteem (beta = -.227), calmness (beta = -.303), and neutral stimuli (beta = -.345). All these effects exceeded conventional levels of significance ($p < .05$).

When comparing the mastery-goal vs. the normative performance-goal condition, no significant effect was observed. Considering that the normative performance-goal condition emphasized speed in response, the presence of null effects between the two conditions is likely indicative of interference effects for the normative performance-goal condition. Let's see how this can be the case: In the mastery-goal condition students were not striving to complete the associations quickly compared to the normative performance-goal condition in which directions explicitly guided the students to complete the associations as quickly (and accurately) as possible. Thus, comparable effects between these two conditions are indicative of an interference effect for students in the normative performance-goal condition. In other words, the absence of significant effects suggests the presence of interference for the students in the normative performance-goal condition because, by definition (scenario), these students *likely* tried to complete the task as quickly as possible.

When comparing the mastery-goal vs. the non-normative performance-goal condition, several significant differences emerged that were in the expected direction given the fact that each goal condition was associated with different scenarios as regards speed. That is, in the non-normative performance-goal condition students were instructed to complete the associations quickly and correctly while that was not the case with the mastery-goal condition, in which only correctness was emphasized. Consequently, it took students in the mastery goal condition significantly longer to complete the correct matching and this was true in relation to words on negative affect (beta = .228), anxiety (beta = .317), negative self-esteem (beta = .259), and also the neutral ones (beta = .336).

Conclusion

Thus, the findings from Study 1 pointed to the fact that cognitive interference was evident in the normative performance-goal condition compared to the non-normative one. These

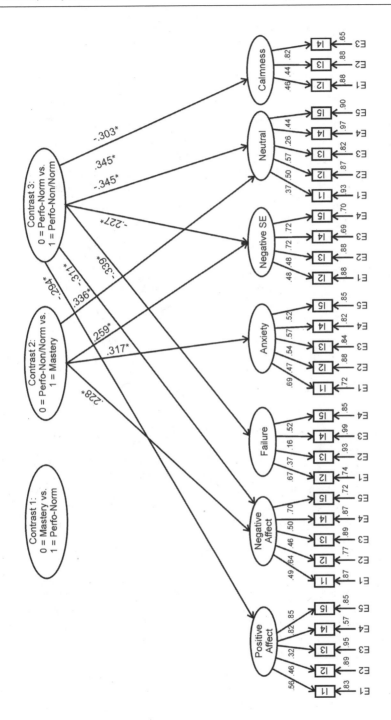

Figure 2. Simple main effects (multiple contrasts) at the latent level between goal conditions.
Note: Only significant effects are shown at $p < .05$, for simplicity. MG condition = Mastery-goal condition. NORM-PG condition = Normative performance-goal condition; N-NORM-PG condition = Non-normative performance-goal condition; SE = self-esteem.

findings provided preliminary evidence regarding the different effects these goal orientations exert on achievement. These interference effects may have implications for students' learning because they likely get in the way of skill acquisition or, generally, in their learning experience.

Study 2

The aim of Study 2 was to replicate the effects of Study 1, regarding the differentiation of normative performance-goal condition from mastery-goal and non-normative performance-goal conditions, with an independent sample of elementary school students. Also, Study 2, extended the findings of Study 1 by involving different ability students (with low or high language skills), thus, introducing the variable ability in the function of goal orientations as well.

Method

Participants

Participants were 239 elementary school students from Grades 5 and 6 ($n = 102$ and $n = 137$, respectively), drawn from elementary schools in Crete and Athens, Greece. Because all assessments were conducted during the fall semester, students were between 11,5 and 12,5 years of age. There were 113 boys and 126 girls.

Measures

Students were given the Color Trailing Task (CTT; D'Elia & Satz, 1996) that requires participants to connect consecutive numbers having different color (see Figure 3) without lifting their pen. The task has two parts (CTT1 and CTT2) as well as increased difficulty along school grades. It was implemented to evaluate differences in achievement (as reflected by correct sequences, amount of time, and amount of errors).

Procedure

Students were randomly assigned to a mastery-goal condition ($n = 75$), a normative performance-goal condition ($n = 78$), and a non-normative performance-goal condition ($n = 86$) as in Study 1. They were also classified as having low or high scores on word fluency based on a median split of correct words read aloud per minute in low and high ability group. The same goal scenarios that were used in Study 1 were also implemented in Study 2.

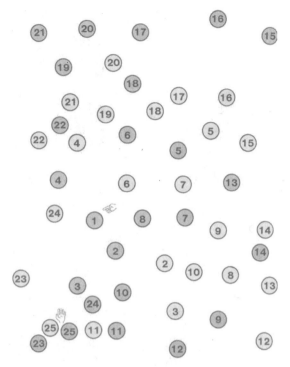

Figure 3. Color Trailing Task employed in Study 2 (CTT) (screen shot).

Results

As regards the effects of goal conditions the results pointed to the existence of significant differences. Specifically, students in the normative performance-goal condition spent significantly less time with the task compared to the mastery-goal condition, $F(2, 233) = 5.126$, $p < .01$, partial $\eta^2 = .04$, although the effect size was low (see Figure 4). In other words, students in the normative performance-goal condition tried to complete the exercise as quickly as possible in order to outperform every other student. This finding was in the expected direction in that students in the normative performance-goal condition were explicitly instructed to complete the task as quickly as possible. However, this finding is contrary to what was found in Study 1 in which no such difference was found.

   Given that there were no significant differences between the normative vs. non-normative performance-goal conditions on time spent to complete the task, it is concluded that with regard to this dependent variable, the two performance motives are not differentiated. Had there been no differences in the amount of errors emitted by students, the overall conclusion would be that of null effects as a function of the normative component in performance goals. However, this was not the case. Students in the normative performance-goal condition emitted significantly more errors compared to students in the non-normative performance-goal condition, especially when they had high achievement levels in fluency (see Figure 5).

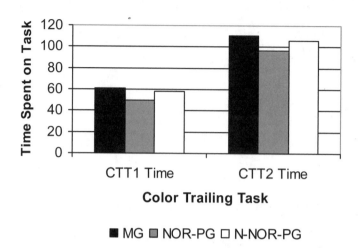

Color Trailing Task

■ MG ▨ NOR-PG ☐ N-NOR-PG

Figure 4. Differences in goal conditions on amount of time needed to complete the task in Study 2.
Note: MG condition = Mastery-goal condition; NOR-PG condition = Normative perform-ance-goal condition; N-NOR-PG condition = Non-normative performance-goal condition.

Because of the moderating role of ability suggested earlier (Dweck & Leggett, 1988), two groups of students were formed with regard to their word fluency (Kelly, Best, & Kirk, 1989). Thus, a two-way interaction was tested with ability grouping and goal condition being the between groups factors. Results indicated that there was a significant interaction with regard to the amount of errors emitted, $F(2, 233) = 3.298$, $p = .04$, partial $\eta^2 = .03$, although the effect size was low. When testing interaction contrasts using the LMatrix, high ability students in the normative performance-goal condition emitted significantly more errors compared to the same group in the non-normative performance-goal condi-tion, $F(1, 233) = 4.197$, $p = .04$, partial $\eta2 = .03$, although the effect size was low. The amount of errors emitted suggests that high ability students in the normative perform-ance-goal condition, in their effort to go quickly and outperform their fellow students, emitted significantly more errors compared to those in the non-normative performance-goal condition. With regard to low ability students, no significant effects emerged. This finding points to the existence of another salient difference between the two performance-goal conditions, a difference in errors and not on actual achievement, a finding that could only be revealed with the high ability students. The effects of this factorial analysis of variance are shown in Figure 5.

Conclusion

In summary, the detrimental effects of normative performance goals were evident in the high ability group only, but may be indicative of a pattern that needs to be investigated in the future. Future studies need to test the validity of Study 2 finding as well as those of Study 1. The same regards the difference found between mastery-goal and normative performance-goal conditions. It seems that high ability students in their effort to outperform others in speed made more errors.

Thus, Study 2 provided additional evidence with regard to the differentiation of normative performance goals from non-normative ones.

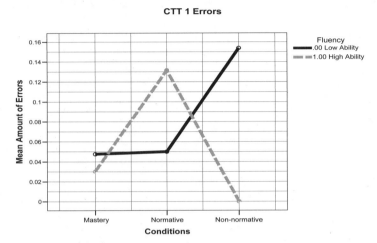

Figure 5. Findings linking amount of errors emitted by differential ability students on the three goal conditions on the Colour Trail Task.

Discussion

Is there Enough Evidence to Suggest Another Dichotomization of Performance Goals?

The answer to this question, as evidenced by the empirical findings of the present studies, is yes. As demonstrated in the two studies described herein, performance goals with an emphasis on normative comparisons were associated with significantly different effects compared to the same goals without a focus on normative evaluations. Specifically, there were significant differences in the processing of information related to stimuli often encountered in an achievement situation (Study 1). Particularly, with respect to positive and negative affect, salient differences pointed to how affective constructs are associated with normative vs. non-normative performance goals. These findings corroborate with the idea that performance goals involve several reasons for engaging with a task than their operationalization suggests (Urdan & Mestas, 2006) and that the presence of both evaluative and intrapersonal standards of performance likely confounds the picture of performance approach goals.

The differentiation of performance goals, as suggested by Grant and Dweck (2003), was supported by the present studies' findings although the original authors failed to find such effects. For example, in Grant and Dweck's (2003) studies no significant differences emerged between normative and non-normative performance goals on both engagement with a task and vulnerability for helpless responding, although the authors expected effort withdrawal, helplessness (Klein, Fencil-Morse, & Seligman, 1976) and self-regulation failure (Dweck, 1986; Dweck & Leggett, 1988).

The findings from the first study suggested that normative performance goals were consistently more positive predictors of cognitive interference compared to non-normative performance goals. In other words, students in the normative performance-goal condition displayed the worst regulatory profile compared to mastery-goal and non-normative performance-goal conditions. When encountering stimuli related to self-esteem, positive affect, negative affect, failure, and calmness, even to neutral ones, they were preoccupied by these thoughts and delayed significantly their action. These decrements in processing time were substantial and may have implications about how one approaches achievement situations. For example, what would happen if students attempt to take national entrance or other examinations with the goal of outperforming others? There are good chances that they will achieve less than what they expect. However, considering the results of Study 2, normative performance goals seem to be detrimental for high ability students whereas non-normative performance goals are detrimental for low ability students (although not significantly more detrimental). Thus, these findings qualify Brophy's (2005) views on the importance of performance goals and adds to the relevant literature which has pointed to the negative effects of performance-approach goals (Kaplan & Middleton, 2002; Midgley et al., 2001) or earlier of a generalized performance orientation (Dweck & Leggett, 1988).

Implications of the Present Findings for Practice

Performance goals with a focus on normative evaluations were clearly maladaptive using the present findings. The differences in achievement were evident, contrary to the findings from previous studies (Elliot & Church, 1997; Harackiewicz, Barron, & Elliot, 1998). Thus, regardless of the presence of high stakes testing, it is suggested that teachers use different motivators for their students than cultivating performance goals using normative evaluative standards. The fact that performance goals with a normative component can be maladaptive suggests immediate intervention as teachers are likely unaware of their negative functioning. Of course, performance goals cannot be avoided in classroom settings; yet, their emphasis can change. Emphasizing different outcomes (rather than interpersonal) and reinforcing those outcomes is important and is strongly recommended. Certainly, more studies need to replicate the present findings and verify the present claims.

Limitations of the Studies

The present studies are limited for several reasons. First, as a thoughtful reviewer suggested, there was no control for prior goal orientations. That is, the effects could have been more pronounced for a student with performance-approach goal orientation (based on self-reports) who was assigned to a normative performance-goal condition compared to whether a student was mastery-goal oriented. In the present studies random assignment of students onto conditions has probably counterbalanced the effect of personal goal orientations. However, this has to be further investigated in the future. Second, in Study 1, there was an unequal number of students assigned to a mastery-goal condition compared to the other two and this fact may have represented a larger amount of measurement error for the two performance goal conditions. However, in all conditions, the numbers were not at all small but rather moderate to large to allow for between groups differences (given some adjustments due to the unequal group sizes). Additionally, the effects of task difficulty may have been differential across participants. These individual differences were not controlled for (Efklides, Samara, & Petropoulou, 1999) and the same may have been true with traits or states (e.g., Jansson & Lundh, 2006).

Conclusions

In the future it would be interesting to further test whether the two types of performance goals differ on other aspects as well. For example, differences between the two performance-goal conditions on well-being or self-handicapping may be at least two dependent variables in which one would expect to find differences (due to apprehension or ego threats). As a thoughtful editor suggested, it would be interesting to verify and ascertain the role/regulation of performance-avoidance goals given the present dichotomization. How performance-avoidance goals would relate to the new forms of performance goals would be an interesting new direction of research. Certainly more studies are needed to accumulate evidence on whether the proposed differentiation is valid and meaningful and how the bifurcated motives relate to other, established ones. Nevertheless, the present two studies suggest that at the "local" level of motivation, there may be a need to further bifurcate goals in order to evaluate self-regulation of behavior in achievement situations from their adoption. It would then be important to attempt and link those goals to more "global" motivational forces. For example, what are the needs behind adoption of normative versus non-normative performance goals? Need for achievement, fear of failure, need to belong or other?

Acknowledgments
I would like to thank my students Maria Shiakali, Maria Georgiou, Ioanna Irakleous, Ioanna Tsigourla, and Eirini Fragiadaki who assisted in the data collection of Study 1. Similarly, I would like to thank Aggelos-Militadis Krypotos, Christina Avgerinou and Christina Louka who assisted in the data collection of Study 2. Also, appreciation is extended to Drs. Konstantinos Kafetsios and Evangelos Karademas who provided information on the computerized version of the Emotional Stroop Task and Maarten Vansteenkiste for his constructive feedback with regard to Study 1 findings. Last, I would like to acknowledge the assistance of all the students and teachers from Greece and Cyprus who took part in the present studies.

References

Ames, C. (1992). Classrooms: Goals, structures, and student motivation. *Journal of Educational Psychology, 84,* 261-271.

Atkinson, J. (1964). *An introduction to motivation.* New York: VNR.

Atkinson, J. W. (1974). The mainsprings of achievement oriented activity. In J. Atkinson & J. Raynor (Eds.), *Motivation and achievement* (pp. 13-41). New York: Wiley.

Barron, K., & Harackiewicz, J. (2001). Achievement goals and optimal motivation: Testing multiple goal models. *Journal of Personality and Social Psychology, 80,* 706-722.

Brophy, J. (2005). Goal theorists should move on from performance goals. *Educational Psychologist, 40,* 167-176.

Dowson, M., & McInerney, D. M. (2001). Psychological parameters of students social and work avoidance goals: A qualitative investigation. *Journal of Educational Psychology, 93,* 35-42.

Dowson, M., & McInerney, D. M. (2003). What do students say about their motivational goals? Towards a more complex and dynamic perspective on student motivation. *Contemporary Educational Psychology, 28,* 91-113.

Dweck, C. S. (1986). Motivational processes affecting learning. *American Psychologist, 41,* 1040-1048.

Dweck, C. S., & Leggett, E. L. (1988). A social-cognitive approach to motivation and personality. *Psychological Review, 95,* 256-273.

D'Elia, L. F., & Satz, P. (1996). *The color trailing task.* Lutz, FL: Psychological Assessment Resources.

Efklides, A. (2006). Metacognition and affect: What can metacognitive experiences tell us about the learning process? *Educational Research Review, 1,* 3-14.

Efklides, A., & Petkaki, C. (2005). Effects of mood on students' metacognitive experiences. *Learning and Instruction, 15,* 415-431.

Efklides, A., Samara, A., & Petropoulou, M. (1999). Feeling of difficulty: An aspect of monitoring that influences control. *European Journal of Psychology of Education, 4,* 461-476.

Elliot, A. J. (1997). Integrating the 'classic' and 'contemporary' approaches to achievement motivation: A hierarchical model of approach and avoidance achievement motivation. In M. L. Maehr & P. R. Pintrich (Eds.), *Advances in motivation and achievement* (Vol. 10, pp. 143-179). Greenwich, CT: JAI.

Elliot, A. J. (1999). Approach and avoidance motivation and achievement goals. *Educational Psychologist, 34,* 169-189.

Elliot, A. J., & Church, M. A. (1997). A hierarchical model of approach and avoidance achievement motivation. *Journal of Personality and Social Psychology, 72,* 218-232.

Elliot, A. J., Gable, S., & Mapes, R. R. (2006). Approach and avoidance motivation in the social domain. *Personality and Social Psychology Bulletin, 32,* 378-391.

Elliot, A. J., & Harackiewicz, J. M. (1996). Approach and avoidance achievement goals and intrinsic motivation: A mediational analysis. *Journal of Personality and Social Psychology, 70,* 461-475.

Elliot, A. J., & McGregor, H. A. (2001). A 2 x 2 achievement goal framework. *Journal of Personality and Social Psychology, 80,* 501-519.

Elliot, A. J., & Moller, A. (2003). Performance approach goals: Good or bad forms of regulation? *International Journal of Educational Research, 39,* 339-356.

Genov, A., Shay, I., & Boone, R. T. (2002). *Genov modified Stroop task (GMST)* [Computer software and manual]. Retrieved September 7, 2005, from *http://facpub.stjohns.edu/~booner/GMSTsite/index.htm.*

Grant, H., & Dweck, C. S. (2003). Clarifying achievement goals and their impact. *Journal of Personality and Social Psychology, 85,* 541-553.

Harackiewicz, J. M., Barron, K. E., Carter, S. M., Lehto, A. T., & Elliot, A. J. (1997). Predictors and consequences of achievement goals in the college classroom: Maintaining interest and making the grade. *Journal of Personality and Social Psychology, 73,* 1284-1295.

Harackiewicz, J. M., Barron, K., & Elliot, A. J. (1998). Rethinking achievement goals: When are they adaptive for college students and why? *Educational Psychologist, 33,* 1-21.

Harackiewicz, J. M., Barron, K. E., Pintrich, P. R., Elliot, A. J., & Thrash, T. M. (2002). Revision of achievement goal theory: Necessary and illuminating. *Journal of Educational Psychology, 94,* 638-645.

Harackiewicz, J. M., Barron, K. E., Tauer, J. M., Carter, S. M., & Elliot, A. J. (2000). Short-term and long-term consequences of achievement goals: Predicting interest and performance over time. *Journal of Educational Psychology, 92,* 316-330.

Hidi, S. (1990). Interest and its contribution as a mental resource for learning. *Review of Educational Research, 60,* 549-571.

Hidi, S. (2001). Interest, reading, and learning: Theoretical and practical considerations. *Educational Psychology Review, 13,* 191-209.

Hidi, S., & Harackiewicz, J. (2000). Motivating the academically unmotivated: A critical issue for the 21st century. *Review of Educational Research, 70,* 151-179.

Jagacinski, C. M., & Nicholls, J. G. (1984). Conceptions of ability and related affects in task involvement and ego involvement. *Journal of Educational Psychology, 76,* 909-919.

Jagacinski, C. M., & Nicholls, J. G. (1987). Competence and affect in task involvement and ego involvement. *Journal of Educational Psychology, 79,* 107-114.

Jansson, B., & Lundh, L. G. (2006). The interactive role of worried mood and trait anxiety in the selective processing of subliminally presented threat words. *Personality and Individual Differences, 41,* 1195-1204.

Kaplan, A., & Middleton, M. J. (2002). Should childhood be a journey or a race? Response to Harackiewicz et al. (2002). *Journal of Educational Psychology, 94,* 646-648.

Karabenick, S. A. (2004). Perceived achievement goal structure and college student help seeking. *Journal of Educational Psychology, 96,* 569-581.

Karademas, E., Kafetsios, K., & Sideridis, G. D. (2007). Optimism, self-efficacy, and information processing of threat and well-being related stimuli. *Stress & Health, 23,* 285-294.

Karademas, E., Sideridis, G. D., & Kafetsios, K. (2008). Health-related information processing and recent health problems: Evidence from a modified Stroop task. *Journal of Health Psychology, 13,* 28-38.

Kelly, M. S., Best, C. T., & Kirk, U. (1989). Cognitive processing deficits in reading disabilities: A prefrontial cortical hypothesis. *Brain and Cognition, 11,* 275-293.

Klein, D. C., Fencil-Morse, E., & Seligman, M. E. P. (1976). Depression, learned helplessness, and the attribution of failure. *Journal of Personality and Social Psychology, 85,* 11-26.

Kuhl, J., & Kazen, M. (1999). Volitional facilitation of difficult intentions: Joint activation of intention memory and positive affect removes stroop interference. *Journal of Experimental Psychology: General, 128,* 382-399.

Linnenbrink, E. A. (2005). The dilemma of performance-approach goals: The use of multiple goal contexts to promote students' motivation and learning. *Journal of Educational Psychology, 97,* 197-213.

MacLeod, C. M. (1991). Half a century of research on the Stroop effect: An integrative review. *Psychological Bulletin, 109,* 163-203.

MacLeod, C., & Rutherford, E. M. (1992). Anxiety and the selective processing of emotional information: Mediating roles of awareness, trait and state variables, and personal relevance of stimulus materials. *Behavioral Research & Therapy, 30,* 479-491.

McClelland, D. (1951). *Personality.* New York: Holt, Rinehart & Winston.

Meece, J. L., & Holt, K. (1993). A pattern analysis of students' achievement goals. *Journal of Educational Psychology, 85,* 582-590.

Meinhardt, J., & Pekrun, R. (2003). Attentional resource allocation to emotional events: An ERP study. *Cognition and Emotion, 17,* 477-500.

Midgley, C., Kaplan, A., & Middleton, M. (2001). Performance-approach goals: Good for what, for whom, under what circumstances, and at what cost? *Journal of Educational Psychology, 93,* 77-86.

Mogg, K., & Bradley, B. P. (1998). A cognitive-motivational analysis of anxiety. *Behavior Research and Therapy, 36,* 809-848.

Mouratidis, A., & Sideridis, G. D. (in press). On social achievement goals: Their relations to peer acceptance, classroom belongingness and perceptions of loneliness. *Journal of Experimental Education.*

Nicholls, J. G. (1984). Achievement motivation: Conceptions of ability, subjective experience, task choice, and performance. *Psychological Review, 91,*328-346.

Ntoumanis, N., & Biddle, S. J. H. (1999). Affect and achievement goals in physical activity: A meta-analysis. *Scandinavian Journal of Medicine and Science in Sports, 9,* 315-332.

Pekrun, R., Elliot, A. J., & Maier, M. A. (2006). Achievement goals and discrete achievement emotions: A theoretical model and prospective test. *Journal of Educational Psychology, 98,* 583-597.

Pintrich, P. R. (2000). Multiple goals, multiple pathways: The role of goal orientation in learning and achievement. *Journal of Educational Psychology, 92,* 554-555.

Rawsthorne, L., & Elliot, A. J. (1999). Achievement goals and intrinsic motivation: A meta-analytic review. *Personality & Social Psychology Review, 3,* 16-25.

Ryan, A. M., & Shim, S. O. (2006). Social achievement goals: The nature and consequences of different orientations toward social competence. *Personality and Social Psychology Bulletin, 32,* 1246-1263.

Schiller, P. H. (1966). Developmental study of color-word interference. *Journal of Experimental Psychology, 72,* 105-108.

Schmalt, H. (1982). Two concepts of fear of failure motivation. In R. Schwarzer, H. van der Ploeg, & C. Spielberger (Eds.), *Advances in test anxiety research* (Vol. 1, pp. 45-52). Hillsdale, NJ: Erlbaum.

Sideridis, G. D. (2008). Feeling obliged to "do well" or "not to fail"? The distinction between approach and avoidance dimensions in oughts. *Learning and Individual Differences, 18,* 176-186.

Sideridis, G. D. (2007). Persistence of performance approach individuals in achievement situations: An application of the Rasch model. *Educational Psychology, 27,* 753-770.

Sideridis, G. D. (2005). Goal orientations, academic achievement, and depression: Evidence in favor of revised goal theory. *Journal of Educational Psychology, 97,* 366-375.

Sideridis, G. D. (in press). Assessing cognitive interference using the emotional Stroop task in students with and without attention problems. *European Journal of Psychological Assessment.*

Sideridis, G. D., & Mouratidis, A. (2008). Forced-choice versus open-ended assessments of goal orientations: A descriptive study. *International Review of Social Psychology,* 21, 219-248.

Stroop, J. R. (1935). Studies of interference in serial verbal reactions. *Journal of Experimental Psychology, 18,* 643-662.

Teevan, R. C., & McGhee, G. (1972). Childhood development of fear of failure motivation. *Journal of Personality and Social Psychology, 21,* 345-348.

Urdan, T. (2000, April). *The intersection of self-determination and achievement goal theories: Do we need to have goals?* Paper presented at the Annual Meeting of the American Educational Research Association, New Orleans, LA.

Urdan, T., & Mestas, M. (2006). The goals behind performance goals. *Journal of Educational Psychology, 98,* 354-365.

Utman, C. H. (1997). Performance effects of motivational state: A meta-analysis. *Personality and Social Psychology Review, 1,* 170-182.

Van Yperen, N. W. (2003). Task interest and actual performance: The moderating effects of assigned and adopted purpose goals. *Journal of Personality and Social Psychology, 85,* 1006-1015.

Wentzel, K. R. (1993). Motivation and achievement in early adolescence: The role of multiple classroom goals. *Journal of Early Adolescence, 13,* 4-20.

Williams, J. M. G., Mathews, A., & MacLeod, C. (1996). The Emotional Stroop Task and psychopathology. *Psychological Bulletin, 120,* 3-24.

Incentives and Flow Experience in Learning Settings and the Moderating Role of Individual Differences

Julia Schüler & Stefan Engeser

Introduction

Motivation psychology aims to understand why people behave they way they do. Various approaches to the conceptualization of the reasons explaining the variability of human behavior can be traced (see Heckhausen & Heckhausen, 2008). In this chapter we focus on the role of incentives in human strivings. Following classical conceptualizations, we define incentives as affective states people expect to experience after or while performing a certain behavior. In this sense incentives are anticipated affects that motivate goal-directed behavior (see Beckmann & Heckhausen, 2008; Schmalt, 1996). In a learning context an incentive may be, for example, the anticipated pride (affective goal state) regarding a good performance in an exam. This anticipation is likely to lead to revising for this exam (goal-directed behavior). Depending on the positive (e.g., pride after passing the exam) or negative (e.g., disappointment after failing the exam) value of the antici-pated affective state, people develop approach or avoidance tendencies towards the exam situation.

Interestingly, the incentive concept has its origin in experiments with animals. Hull (1943) studied the food-searching behaviour of rats using variables of the organism itself and argued that behaviour can be predicted by the rats' drive (aroused hunger drive) and their habits (number of previous food-searching actions). Later, he improved the model to predict motivated behaviour of rats by additionally considering the quality of the incen-tive (amount of food). The rats ran the fastest when their drive and habit were strong and when additionally the incentive was attractive. Also for human beings the necessity of incentives to explain behavior is unquestioned, in both classical (e.g. Atkinson, 1957) as well as modern approaches (Beckmann & Heckhausen, 2008; McClelland, 1985; Schnei-der & Schmalt, 2000).

At first sight, motivated behavior such as the preparation for an exam may seem to be a holistic action unit. Because theoretically the motivational process consists of different components such as incentives, motives, needs and goals, we first need to introduce and differentiate the incentive concept from related concepts.

We will explore the nature of incentives in more depth and will then propose an ap-proach that distinguishes activity-related from purpose-related incentives. Then, we will have a closer look at the flow experience (Csikszentmihalyi, 1990) that can be seen as a specific activity-related incentive. We will introduce the conditions that lead to flow experience and report on moderators of the relationship between flow experience and the challenge-skill balance, which is the most important condition for flow experience. We will conclude by discussing theoretical considerations and empirical results regarding practical implications in learning settings.

With respect to the topic of this volume, we start with a global perspective on the functioning of incentives and proceed with a more local one. Our approach to incentives is rooted in motivation psychology, which aims at finding general mechanisms that predict human behavior. In this respect, incentives are constructs that explain individual behavior regardless of gender, age, culture, or other individual dispositional characteristics. This represents a *global* approach to incentives in the sense that what is important to understand is the mechanism through which incentives influence behavior. A different approach in the study of incentives is the one that focuses on how individual differences and situational characteristics influence incentives and, particularly, flow experience. An individual difference approach emphasizes the persons' motive dispositions (Atkinson, 1957; McClelland, 1985; Schneider & Schmalt, 2000). Motive dispositions are defined as individual preferences for particular local conditions and situations (Schneider & Schmalt, 2000). Following such a local perspective, one and the same situation may evoke different motivational tendencies in different individuals. For example, an upcoming examination may evoke fear in individuals with a high fear-of-failure motive. Such individuals may therefore avoid examinations. In individuals with a high hope-of-success motive the same examination will evoke confidence and approach behavior. We argue that there are individual differences in motive dispositions, which are related to flow experience. We argue that not only global mechanisms (e.g., challenge-skill balance), but also local conditions, such as the interaction of situations with motive dispositions (e.g., achievement motive) must be taken into account in order to predict the flow experience.

Incentives

As already mentioned, incentives are anticipated affective goal states that stimulate goal-directed behavior in order to reach this valued affective state (Beckmann & Heckhausen, 2008; Schmalt, 1996); for example, a person is doing something just for feeling good, or for feeling good while working for his/her end goal, or for feeling good after achieving his/her end goal (i.e., the desired performance outcome). One and the same situation can activate different anticipated affective goal states, depending on personal characteristics. Incentives are conceptually related to the motivational concepts of motive, need, and goal, but they also show some critical differences.

The Differentiation between Incentives, Motives, Needs, and Goals

One characteristic that differs between individuals is one's motive (McClelland, 1985; Schneider & Schmalt, 2000). Motives are defined as a preference or recurrent concern for special incentives (Heckhausen & Heckhausen, 2008; McClelland, 1985; Schneider & Schmalt, 2000). For example, for individuals with a high achievement motive the mere anticipation of feeling proud after a sport contest will elicit goal-directed behaviour, such as practising (McClelland, Atkinson, Clark, & Lowell, 1953). In contrast, an individual with a low achievement motive will be less attracted to the same achievement situation and will not show goal-directed behavior. Therefore, a situation offers incentives to the extent there is a general preference of individuals for such a situation. Similarly, individuals high in affiliation or power motive may anticipate affective goal states such as the feeling of belonging or the feeling of being strong and influential in situations like a party or an influential political position. On the other hand, individuals low in these motives may not find any benefit in the same situations (for affiliation see McAdams, Healy, & Krause, 1984; Sokolowski & Heckhausen, 2008; for power see McClelland, 1975; Schultheiss, 2007). Thus, according to McClelland (1985) incentives emerge from the interaction of the person (motive) with the environment (situational stimuli). Hence, motives and incentives describe different aspects of the motivational process. Incentives are the apparent reason for action and they emerge from the interplay of situational stimuli and a persons' motive.

The concept *need* is often used interchangeably with *motive* and is, therefore, also assumed to vary among individuals. Sometimes the term need describes the fundamental and evolution-based desideratum which is innate to every human being. The latter perspective is taken in the Self-Determination Theory (SDT) of Deci and Ryan (1985). The authors assume that the need for autonomy (see also DeCharms, 1968), the need for competence (see also White, 1959) and the need for social relatedness are innate human needs and that basic need satisfaction leads to well-being whereas frustration of basic needs results in unhappiness (Deci & Ryan, 1985; Ryan & Deci, 2000). According to the SDT, the basic needs can be satisfied in various situations provided they offer the opportunity to feel autonomous, competent, or socially related. The incentives for the person are derived from the interaction of the three basic needs with situational or personal variables. For example, the incentive to feel proud in sports is based on the human need for competence and on the individual interest for sports. The reason why people get involved in sport activities or not lies in the expected feeling of being proud or not being proud in this case.

Most theorists conceptualize *goals* as cognitive representations of desired future states; for example, there are personal goals (Brunstein, Schultheiss, & Grässmann, 1998) or achievement goals (Dweck, 1996; Elliot, 2005). Goals are *manifestations* of motives or "individualized instantiations" of higher-order motives (Emmons, 1989, p. 95). They are an intermediate step that links the abstract motive (e.g., achievement motive) with concrete behaviour (e.g., practicing for a sport contest) (Brunstein et al., 1998; Elliot & Thrash, 2001) and therewith contribute to motive satisfaction. One could argue that both incentives and goals are *results of an interaction process* between motives and situational stimuli. But it is important to note that both constructs capture different aspects of the motivational process. A goal is a desired end state that normally has various incentives. A student may strive for a good grade (goal) because s/he wants to achieve (motive) and because achievement will make him/her proud of him/herself, or because s/he needs it for job applications, or because s/he wants to avoid negative appraisal from his parents (incentives). These incentives are the reason why the person strives for this goal. The goal again can be seen as a means to reach the incentives.

Incentives in Classic Approaches to Motivation

A classical approach to motivation is to consider motives and needs and to analyze their interplay with incentives. According to this classical approach incentives are at the core of the motivation process and the reason for action. Another approach stresses the role of expectancies in the motivation process (Bandura, 1997). Yet, another approach considers incentives as well as expectancies (e.g., expectancy-value models; see Eccles & Wigfield, 2002). In this section, we introduce the Risk Taking Model (Atkinson, 1957) and the Expanded Cognitive Model of Motivation (Rheinberg, 2008). The Risk Taking Model is influential in research on achievement motivation (see Brunstein & Heckhausen, 2008) and will be used later on when we present and discuss findings from research on flow experience. We also refer to the Expanded Cognitive Model of Motivation because it distinguishes two types of incentives that are located at different points within the motivational process.

Atkinson's (1957) Risk Taking Model is making predictions about the choice of task difficulty. According to the model the choice depends on incentives related to the task achievement and on the expectancy that the task can be achieved. Incentives and expectancies are interrelated in the achievement context. For an easy task in which achievement is very probable (high expectancy) the incentive is low. There is less reason for being proud when having achieved a task that everybody else would have achieved easily. Vice versa, for a difficult task the incentive is high, but the probability to manage the task is low (low expectancies). By considering expectancies and incentives simultaneously (expectancy x value), the model predicts that very easy and very difficult tasks will not be chosen. In contrast, for moderately challenging tasks both the probability of success as well as the incentive are on a moderately high level, which will make the choice of such tasks more likely (see Brunstein & Heckhausen, 2008). According to this, moderately challenging tasks evoke the highest motivation to work on them. This assumption is analogous to the flow model by Csikzentmihalyi (1990) and fits with the idea that students should be confronted with challenging tasks in order to be motivated.

The Risk Taking Model further postulates that the choice of the task also depends on the person's achievement motive. For an individual with a high achievement motive the incentive of success is strong (feeling very proud) and this person will therefore be highly motivated by challenging tasks. Because success and failure are equally probable, tasks of moderate difficulty are suitable to determine one's level of competence. People with a high achievement motive typically find it attractive to compare themselves with standards of excellence and seek feedback about their performance. Apart from the approach form of the achievement motive (hope-of-success) Atkinson claimed that people differ in their fear-of-failure. Some people feel especially ashamed when failing. They fear to fail a standard of excellence and thus try to avoid feedback about their anticipated incompetence. Therefore, they feel uncomfortable with moderately challenging tasks and prefer easy or difficult tasks for which failure is either very unlikely (easy tasks) or can be attributed to external reasons (difficult tasks). With these considerations, Atkinson (1957) incorporated individual differences in the achievement motive taking an expectancy-value approach.

The Expanded Cognitive Model of Motivation (Heckhausen & Rheinberg, 1980) also contains expectancy and incentive components. The original model captured the motivational aspects of a whole behavior episode (see Figure 1; without dotted lines).

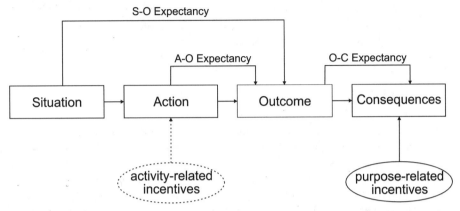

Figure 1. The Extended Cognitive Model (see solid lines, adapted from Heckhausen & Rheinberg, 1980) and its revision by Rheinberg (see below; dotted lines, adapted from Rheinberg, 1989).
Note: S-O = situation-outcome; A-O = action-outcome; O-C = outcome-consequence.

The model assumes that an individual has various action alternatives in any given situation. Every action will lead to an outcome, which subsequently leads to several consequences. Some of these consequences function as incentives. As noted above, a goal or a performance outcome can have several incentives. The incentives that lie in the consequences of an action are called purpose-related incentives. *Purpose-related incentives* can be very diverse. Examples of incentives in the case someone is preparing for an exam in school range from self-evaluative incentives (e.g., being proud, feeling good if someone understands things and proves it), to being approved by the teacher, or to getting money from parents (for details see Rheinberg, 1989; see also Eccles & Wigfield, 2002).

Apart from incentives, three different types of expectancies are influential at several steps in the Extended Cognitive Model. The *situation-outcome (S-O) expectancy* accounts for the possibility that an outcome can ensue without a person's active engagement. For example, a student may expect that an exam will be so easy that he does not have to study. With the *action-outcome (A-O) expectancy* the model captures the subjective belief about how likely it is that an action will be taken and will influence the outcome. High action-outcome expectancies enhance an action tendency. The separation into outcomes and consequences, and with this the *outcome-consequence (O-C) expectancy*, is based on a basic assumption of the Valence-Instrumentality-Expectancy model (VIE; Vroom, 1964). Here it is assumed that an action result, as for example a good grade in an exam, may not necessarily lead to the desired consequences. The model captures the fact that the relationship between outcomes and consequences is not always certain and therefore the expectancy that the outcomes will lead to the desired consequences varies. For example, the anticipated compliment of the parents may not come or the career chances may not be enhanced as the person might have expected. High outcome-consequence expectancies enhance an action tendency. But if high action-outcome and outcome-consequence expectancies come together with low situation-outcome expectancies, an action will not be initiated unless the incentives are highly valuable.

The Expanded Cognitive Model of Motivation and the Risk Taking Model have in common that they conceptualize incentives as being associated with the outcome of an activity. According to these models, the source of incentives lies in the result of the action.

Activity-Related Incentives

Rheinberg (1989, 2008) and Csikszentmihalyi (1990) stated that not every behavior can be explained by incentives that lie in the result of an action. For a broad variety of behaviors, such as painting pictures, doing sports, or learning without external rewards, the result of the action often is irrelevant. Thus, the Extended Cognitive Model of Motivation (Heckhausen & Rheinberg, 1980) could predict whether or not students prepare for an examination (Engeser, Rheinberg, Vollmeyer, & Bischoff, 2005; Rheinberg, 1989), but failed to correctly predict the learning behavior of some individuals. According to Rheinberg (1989), the reason for this lies in the fact that the model does not capture the important aspect that activities themselves can be the source of valued experiences: people learn because they like the learning activity; for example, students get absorbed by writing a computer program, musicians make music because they enjoy getting totally involved in the music, athletes do sports because they enjoy the movement, and children play because of the fun they have during the game. A variety of other academic or leisure activities such as reading, writing, chatting and singing are done irrespective of the consequences. Some activities such as risk sports or spending time and money on skiing or diving are performed although the consequences even have negative incentives. These considerations prompted Rheinberg (1989, 2008) to suggest a revision of the Extended Cognitive Model by adding activity-related incentives as a second source of incentives. As represented by the dotted lines in Figure 1, the activity-related incentives are associated with the activity itself. Considering both activity-related as well as purpose-related incentives enhances the prediction of learning behavior (preparation for an exam, e.g., Rheinberg, 1989), given that both are essential to understand motivation.

The differentiation into activity- and purpose-related incentives may remind of the differentiation into intrinsic and extrinsic motivation. Following a suggestion by Rheinberg (2008) we used the terms *activity-* and *purpose-related incentives* because in the literature the terms *intrinsic* and *extrinsic* are often used inconsistently. The term "intrinsic motivation" has been used to describe the need for self-determination and competence (Deci & Ryan, 1980, 1985), but was also used in the sense of a correspondence between means and ends (Heckhausen, 1989; Shah & Kruglanski, 2000). Individuals were also described as intrinsically motivated "when their behavior is motivated by the actual anticipated, or sought experience of interest" (Sansone & Smith, 2000, p. 343). By using the term "activity-related incentive" we refer to an early conceptualization of intrinsic motivation in the sense that the motivation lies "in the activity itself". According to Bühler (1922) and Groos (1899) incentives in the pursuit of an activity are intrinsic, whereas incentives that occur only when the activity has been completed are extrinsic.

Besides their different location in the behavior episode, activity- and purpose-related incentives differ regarding another aspect. As illustrated in Figure 1, the three different expectancy types can easily interfere with behavior that is driven by purpose-related incentives. Thus, if the situation-outcome expectancy is high or if either the action-outcome or the outcome-consequence expectancy is low, purpose-related incentives lose their motivating power. Activity-related incentives, however, are much more straightforward, because they do not require special expectancies. Thus, behavior that is driven by activity-related incentives is less easy to be disturbed and more robust.

Integrating activity- and purpose-related incentives in one model further has the advantage that both of them can be considered simultaneously. This is of special interest when the two types of incentives are of different direction, that is, one is positive and the other negative. In pedagogical settings, students often have purpose-related incentives to engage in learning activities as, for example, to get a good grade in an upcoming exam. But although most students highly desire a good grade they often show different learning behaviors. This is probably due to differences in activity-related incentives. If the learning activity is associated with fun and interest (positive activity-related incentive) then students will be involved in it with pleasure. However, if the learning activity is a boring or even aversive experience (negative activity-related incentive), students will not get involved or engaged with the desired learning activity. Finally, if a student has strong activity-related incentives and "loses" himself in the learning material without considering the action results, s/he might fail to prepare target-oriented contents for the exam.

Flow Experience

Rheinberg (1993, 2008) interviewed motor cyclists, windsurfers and musicians and described incentive profiles of these different activities. Apart from some common activity-related incentives of all activities, such as feeling physically fit or feeling strong and leaving worries behind, Rheinberg (1993, 2008) identified specific incentives for different activities. For example, playing music was associated with being creative and expressing fantasy, whereas windsurfing was characterized by the incentive of being alone and fighting with nature. Unlike Rheinberg, Csikszentmihalyi (1975) mainly focused on common characteristics of activities which are done for their own sake. He found that such activities share a positive and enjoyable subjective experience quality that is mainly characterized by an intense experiential involvement in moment-to-moment activity. Because this involvement was described as if a current carries a person along effortlessly, Csikszentmihalyi (1975) called this phenomenon "flow experience". It is as "[…] a subjective state that people report when they are completely involved in something to the point of forgetting time, fatigue, and everything else but the activity itself" (Csikszentmihalyi & Rathunde, 1992, p. 59). Besides experiential involvement, flow experience has additional characteristics (Csikszentmihalyi, 1975; see also Csikszentmihalyi, Abuhamdeh, & Nakamura, 2005): The person is absolutely concentrated on the activity (*concentration on the task at hand*) and therefore everything else in the environment and all self-reflective processes are barred from consciousness. The separation between actor and action is faded and action and awareness seem to merge (*action and awareness merge*). When experiencing flow, individuals feel that they can control the action perfectly (*sense of control*). No doubts or anxiety about losing control intrudes into awareness. During flow experience time seems to pass faster (*altered sense of time*).

It is important to note that flow experience is a multifaceted phenomenon including the multiple characteristics described above, and that it is associated with a positive affective experience. This notion partly overlaps with research by Pekrun (2000, 2006) who addressed the role of affective experience qualities in achievement emotions. In line with Rheinberg's (1989) activity- and purpose-related incentives, Pekrun (2000, 2006) distinguished between positive and negative emotions experienced while studying (e.g., enjoyment or frustration) and outcome-related emotions (e.g., hope, pride in case of success, as well as shame and anger in case of failure). Stressing the similarities of both approaches one could say that the achievement emotions in Pekrun's model are anticipated before an action is initiated. Thus, achievement emotions can become the reason for goal-directed behaviour (e.g., learning because the activity or its consequences promise to be associated with enjoyment or pride). In this case, they are like incentives according to the classical definition of incentives as anticipated affects (Beckmann & Heckhausen, 2008; Schmalt, 1996) and therewith are also in accordance with Rheinberg's (1989, 2008) concept of activity- and purpose-related incentives. In case achievement emotions occur without being anticipated and therefore are not the main reason for the initiation of the goal-directed behavior, they might be an accompaniment of a complex learning process while being conceptually different from the incentive concept.

A further research domain that overlaps with research on flow experience is the analyses of task involvement and of its effects on learning activities (Harackiewicz & Sansone 1991). Task involvement is defined as "[...] the degree to which an individual concentrates on or becomes cognitively immersed in an activity" (Elliot & Harackiewicz, 1996, p. 463) and was found to be an important condition of intrinsic motivation (Harackiewicz & Sansone, 1991). According to this definition, task involvement highlights a phenomenological relation to the intrinsically rewarding experiential involvement which is so characteristic of flow experience (Csikszentmihalyi et al., 2005). Flow experience also shares characteristics with some conceptualizations of interest. For example, Sansone and Smith (2000) described interest as a positively charged cognitive and affective experience that is characterized by a deep involvement into the activity. However, the educational theory of interest (Krapp, 1999) interpreted the purpose of interest-driven learning as an engagement with an object (e.g., being interested in biology). The motivated student is eager to learn more about that object. Because knowledge is the outcome of an activity, interest in this sense is strictly speaking extrinsic or purpose-related but not intrinsic or activity-related.

The research fields described above support the importance of emotions and task for learning activities. The unique feature of research on flow experience is that it comprises multiple characteristics such as cognitive phenomena (e.g., deep involvement in an activity) as well as affective experience qualities. This multifaceted character of flow brings along a broad variety of consequences such as enhanced motivation, high performance and well-being. Thus, because of its positive affective quality, "the phenomenological experience of flow is a powerful motivating force" (Csikszentmihalyi et al., 2005, p. 602) working as a reward that enhances the likeliness to perform the rewarded activity again and the competences in performing the activity further improve. Additionally, some characteristics of flow experience, such as high concentration and high sense of control, directly foster performance. Several studies confirmed that flow experience predicts academic or work performance (Eisenberger, Jones, Stinglhamber, Shanock, & Randall, 2005; Engeser et al., 2005), learning behavior (Cskiszentmihalyi, Rathunde, & Whalen, 1993; Lee, 2005) and creativity (Perry, 1999; Sawyer, 1992). For example, Engeser et al. (2005) measured the flow experience of students at the beginning of a semester during a lesson of a foreign language course and an elementary statistics course and found that it predicted exam performance at the end of the semester, even when skill was controlled for. Also studies in the domain of sport revealed associations between flow experience and sports performance (Jackson & Roberts, 1992; Jackson, Thomas, Marsh, & Smethurst, 2001; Pates, Karageorghis, Freyer, & Maynard, 2003; Stein, Kimiecik, Daniels, & Jackson, 1995).

Apart from having a positive effect on motivation and performance, Moneta and Csikszentmihalyi (1996, p. 277) stated that flow is a psychological state "[...] in which the person feels simultaneously cognitively efficient, motivated and happy" and Csikszentmihalyi (1999; Csikszentmihalyi et al., 1993) added that repeated experience of flow has a pervasive incremental effect on positive mood. Empirical research confirmed that flow experience is associated with positive affect during a working day (Csikszentmihalyi & LeFevre, 1989) and in an academic learning context (Schüler, 2007). Given the importance of flow for motivation, performance and well-being, it is interesting to have a closer look at its antecedents.

The Antecedents of Flow Experience

Antecedents of flow experience can be analyzed by either taking a "global" perspective by assuming that conditions are generally valid for all individuals or by taking a "local" perspective arguing that some conditions are valid for some individuals under some circumstances, but not for others. We will discuss both perspectives separately and will then outline how global and specific conditions can be considered simultaneously.

"Global" Antecedents of Flow Experience

Three global conditions are of key importance for the flow experience (Csikszentmihalyi et al., 2005). The first is the *clarity of the goal*. At first sight this does not seem compatible with the conceptualization of flow as an activity-related incentive, because a goal is in essence a focus on the action result. But taking a closer look it seems plausible: Clear goals direct behavior and help to focus attention on goal-relevant behavior. This again facilitates getting absorbed by the action and focussing all energy and attention that otherwise would get lost. Goals structure the activity without being the only or the actual reason for performing the activity, and by this, they foster flow (Rheinberg, Manig, Kliegl, Engeser, & Vollmeyer, 2007). The second global condition is *clear and immediate feedback*. Feedback signals whether a course of action is still on its way to the desired end-state or whether correction of the action is necessary. Without clear feedback the individual is not informed about how well s/he is progressing and doubts may arise about whether the present course of action should be maintained. The third global condition is the *challenge-skill balance*. Because it is assumed to be the most important condition for flow experience (Csikszentmihalyi, 1975, 1990), it is described in more detail in the following paragraph.

The challenge-skill balance is the subjective perception of a balance between the challenge of a task and the perceived own skills which can be used in order to cope with the challenge. Later, Csikszentmihalyi postulated that the challenge and the skill must both be on a high level to arouse flow experience (see quadrant model, Csikszentmihalyi & Csikszentmihalyi, 1991). If the challenge and the skills are balanced but low, this could result in boredom instead of flow experience. On the other hand, a challenge that is too high for a person's skills could arouse anxiety. If the skills exceed the demands of a task, people feel relaxed.

If there is a causal relation between the challenge-skill balance and flow experience, as Csikszentmihalyi expected, then variations of the challenge-skill balance must lead to variations in flow experience. This idea was the basis of an experimental study conducted by Rheinberg and Vollmeyer (2003). Undergraduate students were asked to play a computer game for which the level of difficulty could be easily manipulated. As expected, the authors found that flow was most likely experienced when the difficulty was at a level that participants perceived as a challenge-skill balance. At difficulty levels that were rated as too low or too high for their skills less flow was reported. This curvilinear trend indicates that the balance between the challenge and the skill indeed is a precondition for flow experience, whereas an imbalance is a predictor of low scores of flow experience.

Engeser and Rheinberg (in press) identified moderators that were important in the relationship between challenge-skill balance and flow experience. The authors hypothesized that it depends on aspects of the task, whether or not the challenge-skill balance leads to flow experience. They suggested instrumentality to be such a relevant aspect and argued that tasks have a high instrumentality when success or failure has important consequences (important purpose-related incentives). In this case individuals should experience flow when their skills exceed the challenge of the task. In other words, here individuals prefer an imbalance of the challenge and their skills. Tasks have a low instrumentality when their consequences are not important. With such tasks flow should best be experienced when a challenge-skill balance is given. To test this hypothesis, the authors asked for the perceived instrumentality in three different activities: learning for a final examination in a statistics course, playing a computer game, and learning French in a non obligatory course. The results confirmed the hypothesis. When the instrumentality of task was perceived to be high, participants experienced the highest amount of flow when their skills exceeded task difficulty. When the perceived instrumentality was low, flow experience was most likely when individuals felt that their skills and the challenge were balanced. This moderating role was found in all of the three activities. The results showed that the effect of the challenge-skill balance on flow experience is moderated by the instrumentality of the task and that this moderation holds for all different activities. Later in this chapter we will suggest that the relationship between challenge-skill balance and flow experience is also moderated by individual characteristics.

"Local" Antecedents of Flow Experience

In this section we take a "local" perspective on flow antecedents by considering individual differences. We will discuss the *autotelic personality, motivational competence, self-concept,* and *self-regulation skills.*

Csikszentmihalyi showed that individuals generally differ in the intensity and frequency with which they experience flow (Csikszentmihalyi & Csikszentmihalyi, 1988). Csikszentmihalyi and Rathunde (1992) suggested that an autotelic personality might explain these individual differences. "An autotelic person is one who finds intrinsic motivation and flow in everyday life [...], who finds enjoyment in activities that would make others bored or anxious" (Csikszentmihalyi & Rathunde, 1992, p. 88). A longitudinal study with talented teenagers revealed that students who scored high on the personality factors achievement motive, endurance, sentience and understanding reported more flow during the week. Csikszentmihalyi and Rathunde (1992) suggested that those personality factors are similar to the autotelic qualities of being energetic and capable, and being open to new challenges (Csikszentmihalyi & Rathunde, 1992). In order to specify Csikszentmihalyi's description of an "autotelic personality", Kimiecik and Jackson (2002, p. 515) defined the autotelic person as an individual who generally does things for their own sake, rather than to achieve some later external goals. They studied flow experience in sportsmen and sportswomen and suggested that dispositional factors constitute an autotelic personality. They suggested that task orientation (rather than ego orientation), high perceived ability, low trait anxiety, and high intrinsic motivation (operationalized by a high need for autonomy according to Deci & Ryan, 1985) are related to flow experience (Jackson, Kimiecik, Ford, & Marsh, 1998). However, the authors critically mentioned that their "[...] findings lend credence to the notion that something akin to autotelic personality may exist" (p. 517), but that "we have a long way to go, however, in figuring out the role of personality factors in understanding optimal experience in sport" (p. 517).

Another personal feature that can explain individual differences in flow experience is "motivational competence" that is defined as the ability to reconcile current and future situations with activity preferences enabling the individual to function efficiently, without the need for permanent volitional control. The most important component of motivational competence is an accurate sense of one's own implicit motives (Rheinberg, 2008). Knowing one's implicit motives enables to bring one's motivational self-concept (or explicit motive, see McClelland, Koestner, & Weinberger, 1989) into agreement with the implicit motives. This facilitates the setting of goals that fit to both motive systems. Goal-striving which is based on motive congruence guarantees the absence of volitional control and the presence of activity-related incentives, which are both beneficial for the experience of flow. In contrast, if the implicit and explicit motive systems are incongruent, individuals are likely to set goals that do not fit their implicit motives and thus hinder flow during goal-striving. Empirical support for the *flow hypothesis of motivational competence* (see Rheinberg, 2008) was provided by Clavadetscher (2003) who was interested in the flow experience of voluntary workers and found that individuals with congruent implicit and self-reported motives reported a higher amount of flow experience than individuals with incongruent motives. Engeser et al. (2005) showed that students of a statistics course whose implicit achievement motive was high and congruent with a high self-attributed achievement motive could better self-regulate their behavior. They could better identify themselves with their actions and were more likely to feel absorbed by the action. Thus, individual differences in motivational competence revealed to be an important determinant of flow experience.

Jackson et al. (2001) investigated flow experience in sports. They focused on the *athletic self-concept* and *self-regulation skills* as personal determinants of flow experience. A positive athletic self-concept (e.g., regarding mental competence, overall performance and skills) was expected to be a flow predictor, due to the enhanced confidence in one's actions. In an earlier study the related construct of perceived ability was shown to be positively associated with flow experience (e.g., Jackson & Roberts, 1992). Self-regulation skills (e.g., emotional control, relaxation, self talk) should also be connected to flow experience, because their effective use means a greater control over one's thoughts and emotions. Hence, concentration on the sport activity itself should be facilitated. Jackson et al. (2001) studied athletes of different competitive sports and found that the athletic self-concept as well as the self-regulation skills was associated with flow experience.

The Consideration of Global and Local Perspectives on Flow Antecedents

The previous paragraphs showed two perspectives that can be taken to analyze antecedents of flow experience. On the one hand, there is the perspective of global (i.e., universally valid) antecedents, as for example, unambiguous feedback or the clarity of goals. On the other hand, flow experience is to some extent determined by individual differences in the preference for situations that can bring about flow experience, such as personality characteristics and motivational competences. This paragraph simultaneously considers a local and a global perspective.

As mentioned above, Csikszentmihalyi (1975, 1999; Csikszentmihalyi et al., 2005) postulated that the challenge-skill balance is an important determinant of flow experience. The balance of challenges and skills is associated with flow experience, whereas the imbalance leads to negative experience (anxiety, boredom). This relationship between challenge-skill balance, on the one hand, and flow experience, on the other, was formulated as global regularity that was assumed to be valid for all individuals. Empirical evidence, however, showed that this regularity does not always hold. Studies investigating the relationship between challenge-skill balance and flow experience yield inconsistent results (Ellis, Voelkl, & Morris, 1994; Engeser & Rheinberg, in press; Schüler, 2007; Stoll & Lau, 2005). Rheinberg (2008; see also Stoll & Lau, 2005) suggested that these inconsistencies might be explained by moderator variables.

A moderator that might explain why some individuals experience flow when there is a challenge-skill balance, whereas others do not, is the achievement motive (Engeser & Rheinberg, in press; Rheinberg, Vollmeyer, & Engeser, 2003; Schüler, 2007). With Atkinson's (1957) Risk Taking Model we already introduced a theoretical framework linking the achievement motive to the challenge-skill balance and its consequences. The Risk Taking Model assumes that individuals with hope of success and fear of failure both have the desire "to overcome obstacles, to exercise power, to strive to do something difficult as well and as quickly as possible" (Murray, 1938, pp. 80) and want to surpass personal standards of excellence (McClelland et al., 1953). The main difference between individuals motivated by hope of success and fear of failure is that the former prefer moderately difficult tasks whereas individuals with fear of failure feel more comfortable with tasks that are either too easy or too difficult. The link between Atkinson's conceptualization of task difficulty and Csikszentmihalyi's challenge-skill balance follows a clear rationale. A moderately difficult task which is preferred by individuals motivated by hope of success can be interpreted as a task where the challenges of the situation can be faced with adequate personal skills. Analogously, tasks that are either too difficult or too easy (preferred by individuals motivated by fear of failure) are characterized by an imbalance of challenge and skill. Integrating both theories, a challenge-skill balance should lead to higher motivation only for individuals who are high in hope of success, whereas it does not arouse higher motivation for individuals with fear of failure. For the latter, being in a challenge-skill balance arouses anxiety that is known to hinder flow experience (Csikszentmihalyi, 1990; Jackson, 1995). Thus, only individuals with hope of success are assumed to experience flow when a perceived challenge-skill balance is given; individuals motivated by fear of failure are expected to report the absence of flow experience when they are in a challenge-skill balance situation.

Eisenberger et al. (2005) applied Csikszentmihalyi's (1990) flow theory to the workplace and found support for the moderating role of the achievement motive. They found that among employees with a high need for achievement the experience of high skills and challenges of a job task was related to a better mood, task interest, and organizational spontaneity. Employees with a low need for achievement, however, showed no such correlation. Although it could be criticized that flow experience was only measured indirectly by assessing task interest, the findings are generally consistent with the assumption of the achievement motive as a moderator of the challenge-skill balance and a motivational state comparable to flow experience.

Schüler (2007) found evidence for the moderating function of the achievement motive in an academic learning setting. In two studies the hope-of-success motive and the fear-of-failure motive were measured among undergraduate students using the Multi-Motive-Grid (MMG; Sokolowski, Schmalt, Langens, & Puca, 2000) which was proven to be a highly economic, reliable and valid measurement of motives (Gable, Reis, & Elliot, 2003; Sokolowski et al., 2000). In an elementary course in psychology the students were asked whether the challenge of course contents was either too low for their skills, too high for their skills, or whether it fitted their skills. Then, participants' experience of flow during the course lectures was registered by administering the Flow Short Scale (Flow Kurz Skala, FKS; Rheinberg et al., 2003), which showed high reliability and validity in several studies (see Rheinberg et al., 2003). Items included "My thoughts run fluidly and smoothly", "I am totally absorbed in what I am doing" and "I am completely lost in thought" and were rated using a 7-point scale (from "not at all" to "very much"). As expected, participants whose challenges and skills were in a balance and who additionally had a high score in hope of success reported high amount of flow experience. Students with high scores in fear of failure experienced the lowest amount of flow experience when a challenge-skill balance was given.

Engeser and Rheinberg (in press) extended previous research by using a direct measurement of flow in longitudinal studies. Assuming that flow is a transient state occurring during the activity itself, the authors measured students' flow experience directly while the learning activity was performed. The flow measurement at the end of the semester was expected to be predicted by the hope-of-success measure (Picture Story Exercise; Pang & Schultheiss, 2005) and the fear-of-failure measure (German Version of the Achievement Motives Scale; Dahme, Jungnickel, & Rathje 1993), which were administered at the beginning of the semester. As expected, when the challenge of the task was rated "just right" — an example item is "I think that my competence in this area is 1 (too low) / 5 (just right) / 9 (too high) — flow experience was high for highly in hope-of-success motivated individuals. In contrast students with fear of failure reported low scores of flow experience in a situation with challenge-skill balance. Again, the relationship between the challenge-skill balance and flow experience was moderated by individual differences in the achievement motive.

The results of the cited studies strongly recommend considering a local perspective on motivation (individual differences in interaction with special situations) when analyzing the relationship between a global predictor (challenge-skill balance) and flow experience. Further research that considers a global as well as a local perspective on flow-experience antecedents will be needed to enhance the understanding of the interplay of global and specific conditions.

Summary and Practical Implications

In this chapter, we elaborated the concept of incentives by introducing the distinction into activity-related and purpose-related incentives (Rheinberg, 1989, 2008). We then focused on flow experience which constitutes a prominent representative of an activity-related incentive and examined its antecedents and consequences.

The theoretical separation into activity-related and purpose-related incentives as well as a detailed knowledge of flow conditions has important practical implications for educational settings. Assuming that alongside purpose-related learning incentives (e.g., compliments and grades) a second source of incentives exists provides the opportunity to enhance the incentive intensity of a learning context. Because activities with only purpose-related incentives are much easier to disrupt than activities done for their own sake, it is helpful to enrich learning settings with activity-related incentives. It is crucial to note that this does not mean that purpose-related incentives are unimportant. Even if activity-related incentives yield a more robust form of motivation the most robust form is when activity- and purpose-related incentives are both given simultaneously. An example is a high enjoyment while preparing for an exam and additionally being proud after achieving a good grade.

In what follows we speculate about some starting points and general advices for the enhancement of the activity-related incentive of flow experience. With flow, a robust form of motivation is created, which remains present even if the control by external demands or rewards (e.g., exam grades, controlling teachers) is missing and even if the persons' expectancies to achieve a goal state are low (see above: activity-related incentives do not need any outcome expectancies!).

Csikszentmihalyi (1990) proposed that the clarity of the goal, clear immediate feedback, and challenge-and-skill balance are critical preconditions for flow experience. The new conceptualization provided by our research is that the relationship between the challenge-skill balance and flow experience is moderated by a personal variable (the achievement motive) and by a more situation-specific variable, that is, the instrumentality of an activity. Herewith we differentiated between a global perspective on flow antecedents (e.g., clear goals and feedback) and a local perspective (e.g., achievement motive, instrumentality).

Our results showed that individuals with hope of success, but not with fear of failure, experienced flow when they were in an achievement situation characterized by challenge-skill balance. In contrast, individuals with fear of failure experienced flow when the task was either too difficult or too easy for their skills. For educational settings these results mean that in order to evoke flow experience in students, either the challenge-skill balance can be adapted to students motive or the motives can be changed in that way that they fit with the challenge-skill balance condition. It is important to note that both ways are just theoretical speculations unless empirical evidence for their efficacy is supplied, but nevertheless they might inspire a new view on educational settings.

Adapting the challenge-skill balance condition to a person's motive would be a new strategy that has not been used so far within the achievement motivation research. With this strategy it would be possible to motivate students. Facilitating flow experience in students with fear of failure is a desirable pedagogical aim but, on the other hand, providing a student with too easy or too difficult tasks (which are optimally flow-arising for students with fear of failure) is in conflict with the increase of competences and knowledge. The increase of competence and knowledge depends on realistic demands that are not given for individuals in a challenge-skill imbalance situation. Therefore, in the long run, it makes much more sense to make a student feel comfortable with challenge-skill balanced tasks. This second implication requires modifying a students' motive in a way that it interacts optimally with challenge-skill balance.

Changing motives is a complex procedure, because motives are conceptualized as characteristics, which, once they are developed, are relatively stable across the life span and that are difficult to influence by the social environment (McClelland, 1985). Nevertheless, sophisticated intervention programs showed that it is still possible to change motives to some degree. Intervention programs that have been proven to be highly effective mostly reduce fear of failure (rather than enhance hope of success); for example by training realistic goal setting and teaching beneficial attributions for success and failure (Krug & Hanel, 1976; for an overview see Rheinberg & Engeser, in press; Rheinberg & Krug, 2005). With effective motive modification programs, fear of failure with its negative consequences (e.g., the negative consequences on flow experience in case of a challenge-skill balance situation) can be reduced so that again the development of students' skills and well-being are enhanced.

Considering the instrumentality of a task as a moderator within the challenge-skill balance and flow relationship could also have interesting practical implications. Regarding Engeser and Rheinberg's (in press) results, challenge-skill balance is optimal to experience flow in activities of low instrumentality, whereas for high instrumentality tasks the skill should be higher than the challenge of the task. Transferred to teaching practice, it would be best to challenge students with skill-fitting tasks that are not evaluated by the teacher, do not influence a grade and do not have other important consequences (= low instrumentality). For example, such a task could be learning a new topic without being directed towards an important purpose such as an examination or solving complex math problems that are not evaluated. This can evoke flow experience and thus learning motivation and performance can be enhanced and will help to improve students' competences. To deal with the fact that grades and evaluations are part of most pedagogical school systems, teachers could lower the task challenges when tasks have a high instrumentality such as a statistics test or other kinds of examinations. This could be done, for example, by letting students practice already well handled operations (e.g., routine tasks) during the preparation for an examination. With this procedure, flow can be maintained even in necessary exam preparation periods. Additionally, the students can perform on a high level due to high competences they achieved by low instrumentality tasks they performed before. Teachers may decide whether adapting task challenges to different periods of learning (learning new things without being evaluated vs. preparing for an examination) is practical in their teaching work.

References

Atkinson, J. W. (1957). Motivational determinants of risk taking behavior. *Psychological Review, 64*, 359-372.

Bandura, A. (1997). *Self-efficacy: The exercise of control.* New York: Freeman.

Beckman, J., & Heckhausen, H. (2008). Motivation as a function of expectancy and incentives. In H. Heckhausen & J. Heckhausen (Eds.), *Motivation and action* (pp. 99-136). Cambridge, UK: Cambridge University Press.

Brunstein, J. C., & Heckhausen, H. (2008). In H. Heckhausen & J. Heckhausen (Eds.), *Motivation and action* (pp. 137-183). Cambridge, UK: Cambridge University Press.

Brunstein, J. C., Schultheiss, O. C., & Grässmann, R. (1998). Personal goals and emotional well-being: The moderating role of motive dispositions. *Journal of Personality and Social Psychology, 75*, 494-508.

Bühler, K. (1922). *Die geistige Entwicklung des Kindes* [The mental development of the child]. Jena, Germany: Fischer.

Clavadetscher, C. (2003). *Motivation ehrenamtlicher Arbeit im Verein Mahogany Hall, Bern [Motivation for voluntary work in the association Mahogany Hall, Bern].* Bern: Abschlussarbeit NDS BWL/UF, Hochschule für Technik und Architektur.

Csikszentmihalyi, M. (1975). *Beyond boredom and anxiety.* San Francisco: Jossey-Bass.

Csikszentmihalyi, M. (1990). *Flow: The psychology of optimal experience.* New York: Harper & Row.

Csikszentmihalyi, M. (1999). *Das Flow-Erlebnis: Jenseits von Angst und Langeweile.* [Flow experience: Beyond Anxiety and Boredom]. Stuttgart, Germany: Klett-Cotta.

Csikszentmihalyi, M., Abuhamdeh, S., & Nakamura, J. (2005). Flow. In A. J. Elliot & C. S. Dweck (Eds.), *Handbook of competence and motivation* (pp. 598-608). New York: Guilford.

Csikszentmihalyi, M., & Csikszentmihalyi, I. (1988). *Optimal experience: Psychological studies of flow in consciousness.* Cambridge, UK: Cambridge University Press.

Csikszentmihalyi, M., & Csikszentmihalyi, I. S. (1991). *Die aussergewöhnliche Erfahrung im Alltag: Die Psychologie des Flow-Erlebens* [Extraordinary experience in everyday life: Psychology of flow experience]. Stuttgart, Germany: Klett-Cotta.

Csikszentmihalyi, M., & LeFevre, J. (1989). Optimal experience in work and leisure. *Journal of Personality and Social Psychology, 56*, 815-822.

Csikszentmihalyi, M., & Rathunde, K. (1992). The measurement of flow in everyday life: Toward a theory of emergent motivation. In R. Dienstbier & J. E. Jacobs (Eds.), *Nebraska Symposium on motivation* (pp. 57-97). Lincoln, NE: University of Nebraska Press.

Csikszentmihalyi, M., Rathunde, K., & Whalen, S. (1993). *Talented teenagers: A longitudinal study of their development.* New York: Cambridge University Press.

Dahme, G., Jungnickel, D., & Rathje, H. (1993). Güteeigenschaften der Achievement Motives Scale (AMS) von Gjesme und Nygard (1970) in der deutschen Übersetzung von Göttert und Kuhl: Vergleich der Kennwerte norwegischer und deutscher Stichproben [Psychometric indices of the Achievement Motives Scale by Gjesme and Nygard (1970) in the German version by Goettert and Kuhl: A comparison of Norwegian and German samples]. *Diagnostica, 39,* 257-270.

DeCharms, R. (1968). *Personal causation.* New York: Academic.

Deci, E. L., & Ryan, R. M. (1980). The empirical exploration of intrinsic motivational processes. In L. Berkowitz (Ed.), *Advances in experimental social psychology* (pp. 39- 80). New York: Academic.

Deci, E. L., & Ryan, R. M. (1985). *Intrinsic motivation and self-determination in human behavior.* New York: Plenum.

Dweck, C. (1996). Capturing the dynamic nature of personality. *Journal of Research in Personality, 30,* 348-362.

Eccles, J. S., & Wigfield, A. (2002). Motivational beliefs, values, and goals. *Annual Review of Psychology, 53,* 109-132.

Eisenberger, R., Jones, J. R., Stinglhamber, F., Shanock, L., & Randall, A. T. (2005). Flow experiences at work: For high need achievers alone? *Journal of Organizational Behavior, 26,* 755-775.

Elliot, A. J. (2005). A conceptual history of the achievement goal construct. In A. J. Elliot & C. S. Dweck (Eds.), *Handbook of competence and motivation* (pp. 52-72). New York: Guilford.

Elliot, A. J., & Harackiewicz, J.M. (1996). Approach and avoidance achievement goals and intrinsic motivation. A mediational analysis. *Journal of Personality and Social Psychology, 70,* 461-475.

Elliot, A. J., & Thrash, T. M. (2001). Achievement goals and the hierarchical model of achievement motivation. *Educational Psychology Review, 13,* 139-156.

Ellis, G. D., Voelkl, J. E., & Morris, C. (1994). Measurements and analysis issues with explanation of variance in daily experience using the flow model. *Journal of Leisure Research, 26,* 337-356.

Emmons, R.A. (1989). The personal striving approach to personality and subjective well-being. In L. A. Pervin (Ed.), *Goal concepts in personality and social psychology* (pp. 87-126). Hillsdale, NJ: Erlbaum.

Engeser, S., & Rheinberg, F. (in press). Flow, performance, and moderators of challenge-skill balance. *Motivation and Emotion.*

Engeser, S., Rheinberg, F., Vollmeyer, R., & Bischoff, J. (2005). Motivation, Flow-Erleben und Lernleistung in universitären Lernsettings [Motivation, flow experience and performance in learning settings at university]. *Zeitschrift für Pädagogische Psychologie, 19,* 159-172.

Gable, S. L., Reis, H. T., & Elliot, A. J. (2003). Evidence for bivariate systems: An empirical test of appetition and aversion across domains. *Journal of Research in Personality, 37,* 349-372.

Groos, K. (1899). *Die Spiele des Menschen* [Human games]. Jena, Germany: Fischer.

Harackiewicz, J. M., & Sansone, C. (1991). Goals and intrinsic motivation: You can get there from here. In M. L. Maehr & P. R. Pintrich (Eds.), *Advances in motivation and achievement* (Vol. 7, pp. 21-49). Greenwich, CT: JAI Press.

Heckhausen, H. (1989). *Motivation und Handeln* (2. Auflage) [Motivation and Action (2nd ed.)]. Berlin: Springer.

Heckhausen, H., & Rheinberg, F. (1980). Lernmotivation im Unterricht, erneut betrachtet [Learning motivation in the classroom reconsidered]. *Unterrichtswissenschaft, 8,* 7-47.

Heckhausen, J., & Heckhausen, H. (2008). Motivation and action: Introduction and overview. In J. Heckhausen & H. Heckhausen (Eds.), *Motivation and action* (pp. 1-9). Cambridge, UK: Cambridge University Press.

Hull, C. L. (1943). *Principles of behavior.* New York: Appleton-Century-Crofts.

Jackson, S. A. (1995). Factors influencing the occurrence of flow state in elite athletes. *Journal of Applied Sport Psychology, 7,* 138-166.

Jackson, S. A., Kimiecik, J., Ford, S., & Marsh, H. W. (1998). Psychological correlates of flow in sport. *Journal of Sport & Exercise Psychology, 20,* 358-378.

Jackson, S. A., & Roberts, G. C. (1992). Positive performance states of athletes: Toward a conceptual understanding of peak performance. *The Sport Psychologist, 6,* 156-171.

Jackson, S. A., Thomas, P. R., Marsh, H. W., & Smethurst, C. J. (2001). Relationships between flow, self-concept, psychological skills, and performance. *Journal of Applied Sport Psychology, 13,* 129-153.

Kimiecik, J. C., & Jackson, S. A. (2002). Optimal experience in sport: A flow perspective. In T. S. Horn (Ed.), *Advances in sport psychology* (Vol. 2, pp. 501-527). Champaign, IL: Human Kinetics.

Krapp, A. (1999). Intrinsische Lernmotivation und Interesse [Intrinsic learning motivation and interest]. *Zeitschrift für Pädagogik, 45,* 387-406.

Krug, S., & Hanel, J. (1976). Motivänderung: Erprobung eines theoriegeleiteten Trainingsprogramms [Motive modification: Testing a theory-based training program]. *Zeitschrift für Entwicklungspsychologie und Pädagogische Psychologie, 8,* 274-287.

Lee, E. (2005). The relationship of motivation and flow experience to academic procrastination in university students. *The Journal of Genetic Psychology, 166,* 5-14.

McAdams, D. P., Healy, S., & Krause, S. (1984). Social motives and patterns of friendship. *Journal of Personality and Social Psychology, 47,* 828-838.

McClelland, D. C. (1975). *Power: The inner experience.* New York: Irvington.

McClelland, D. C. (1985). *Human motivation.* Glenview, Ill.: Scott and Foresman.

McClelland, D. C., Koestner, R., & Weinberger, J. (1989). How do self-attributed and implicit motives differ? *Psychological Review, 96,* 690-702.

McClelland, D. C., Atkinson, J. W., Clark, R. A., & Lowell, E. L. (1953). *The achievement motive.* New York: Appleton-Century-Crofts.

Moneta, G. B., & Csikszentmihalyi, M. (1996). The effect of perceived challenges and skills on the quality of subjective experience. *Journal of Personality, 64,* 274-310.

Murray, H. A. (1938). *Explorations in personality.* New York: Oxford University Press.

Pang, J. S., & Schultheiss, O. (2005). Assessing implicit motives in U.S. college students: Effects of picture type and position, gender and ethnicity, and cross-cultural comparisons. *Journal of Personality Assessment, 85,* 280-294.

Pates, J., Karageorghis, C. I., Fryer, R., & Maynard, I. (2003). Effects of asynchronous music on flow states and shooting performance among netball players. *Psychology of Sport and Exercise, 4,* 415-427.

Pekrun, R. (2000). A social cognitive, control-value theory of achievement emotions. In J. Heckhausen (Ed.), *Motivational psychology of human development* (pp. 143-163). Oxford, England: Elsevier.

Pekrun, R. (2006). The control-value theory of achievement emotions: Assumptions, corollaries, and implications for educational research and practice. *Educational Psychology Review, 18,* 315-341.

Perry, S. K. (1999). *Writing in flow.* Cincinnati, OH: Writer's Digest Books.

Rheinberg, F. (1989). *Zweck und Tätigkeit. Motivationspsychologische Analysen zur Handlungsveranlassung.* [Goal and activity. Motivational psychology analyses of action initiation]. Göttingen, Germany: Hogrefe.

Rheinberg, F. (1993). *Anreize engagiert betriebener Freizeitaktivitäten. Ein Systematisierungsversuch* [Incentives of dedicated leisure activities: A suggestion for systematization]. Unpublished manuscript.

Rheinberg, F. (2008). Intrinsic motivation and flow-experience. In H. Heckhausen & J. Heckhausen (Eds.), *Motivation and action* (pp. 323-348). Cambridge, UK: Cambridge University Press.

Rheinberg, F., & Engeser, S. (in press). Motive training and motivational competence. In O. C. Schultheiss & J. C. Brunstein (Eds.), *Implicit motives.* New York: Oxford University Press.

Rheinberg, F., & Krug, S. (2005). *Motivationsförderung im Schulalltag* [Motivation promotion in everyday school life]. Göttingen, Germany: Hogrefe.

Rheinberg, F., Manig, Y., Kliegl, R., Engeser, S., & Vollmeyer, R. (2007). Flow bei der Arbeit, doch Glück in der Freizeit: Zielausrichtung, Flow und Glücksgefühle [Flow during work but happiness during leisure time: goals, flow-experience, and happiness]. *Zeitschrift für Organisationspsychologie, 51,* 105-115.

Rheinberg, F., & Vollmeyer, R. (2003). Flow-Erleben in einem Computerspiel unter experimentell variierten Bedingungen [Flow experience in a computer game under experimentally controlled conditions]. *Zeitschrift für Psychologie, 211,* 161-170.

Rheinberg, F., Vollmeyer, R., & Engeser, S. (2003). Die Erfassung des Flow-Erlebens [The assessment of flow experience]. In J. Stiensmeier-Pelster & F. Rheinberg (Eds.), *Diagnostik von Selbstkonzept, Lernmotivation und Selbstregulation* (pp. 261-279). Göttingen, Germany: Hogrefe.

Ryan, R. M., & Deci, E. L. (2000). Self-determination theory and the facilitation of intrinsic motivation, social development, and well-being. *American Psychologist, 55,* 68-78.

Sansone, C., & Smith, J. L. (2000). Interest and self-regulation: The relation between having to and wanting to. In C. Sansone & J. M. Harackiewicz (Eds.), *Intrinsic and extrinsic motivation* (pp. 343-372). San Diego: Academic.

Sawyer, K. (1992). Improvisational creativity: An analysis of jazz performance. *Creativity Research Journal, 5,* 253-263.

Schmalt, H. D. (1996). Zur Kohärenz von Motivation und Kognition [The coherence of motivation and cognition]. In J. Kuhl & H. Heckhausen (Eds.), *Enzyklopädie der Psychologie. Motivation, Volition und Handeln* (pp. 241-273). Göttingen, Germany: Hogrefe.

Schneider, K., & Schmalt, H. D. (2000). *Motivation* [Motivation]. Stuttgart, Germany: Kohlhammer.

Schüler, J. (2007). Arousal of flow-experience in a learning setting and its effects on exam-performance and affect. *Zeitschrift für Pädagogische Psychologie, 21,* 217-22.

Schultheiss, O. C. (2007). A biobehavioral model of implicit power motivation. In P. Winkielman & E. Harmon-Jones (Eds.), *Social neuroscience: Integrating biological and psychological explanations of social behavior* (pp.176-196). New York: Guilford Press.

Shah, J. Y., & Kruglanski, A. W. (2000). The structure and substance of intrinsic motivation. In C. Sansone & J. M. Harackiewicz (Eds.), *Intrinsic and extrinsic motivation* (pp. 105 – 127). San Diego: Academic.

Sokolowski, K., & Heckhausen, H. (2008). Social bonding: Affiliation motivation and intimacy motivation. In H. Heckhausen & J. Heckhausen (Eds.), *Motivation and action* (pp. 184 - 201). Cambridge, UK: Cambridge University Press.

Sokolowski, K., Schmalt, H.-D., Langens, T. A., & Puca, R. M. (2000). Assessing achievement, affiliation, and power motives all at once – The Multi-Motive Grid (MMG). *Journal of Personality Assessment, 74,* 126-145.

Stein, G. L., Kimiecik, J. C., Daniels, J., & Jackson, S. A. (1995). Psychological antecedents of flow in recreational sport. *Personality and Social Psychology Bulletin, 21,* 125-135.

Stoll, O., & Lau, A. (2005). Flow-Erleben beim Marathonlauf – Zusammenhänge mit Anforderungspassung und Leistung. [Experiencing „flow" during a marathon – Association with the fit between demand and ability]. *Zeitschrift für Sportpsychologie, 12,* 75-82.

Vroom, V. H. (1964). *Work and motivation.* New York: Wiley.

White, R. W. (1959). Motivation reconsidered: The concept of competence. *Psychological Review, 66,* 297-333.

Striving for Personal Goals

The Role of Negative Mood and the Availability of Mood-Regulation Strategies

Thomas A. Langens

Introduction

Personal goals are defined as consciously accessible and personally meaningful representations of objectives people pursue in their everyday live (Brunstein, 1993; Klinger, 1977). One can hardly imagine a person who does not pursue at least a single personal goal; quite to the contrary, most individuals pursue many personal goals at the same time (Emmons, 1986; Klinger, 1977), which may be related to education (e.g., getting good grades in college), profession (advancing in a professional career), close relationships (finding a romantic partner or maintaining the relationship to a significant other), friendship (getting to know other people or keeping in touch with old friends), sport and fitness (conserving a high level of physical fitness), health (keeping up a healthy diet) and hobbies. Personal goals are often a central part of a person's self-concept, defining for oneself and others the person one is (e.g., "I am a psychology major") and wants to become in the future (e.g., "I'll be a competent clinical psychologist") (Brunstein & Gollwitzer, 1996; Wicklund & Gollwitzer, 1982).

Motivation psychology has already identified some of the factors which predict whether a person will be more or less likely to attain his or her personal goals. For example, high *goal commitment* (the willingness to invest effort and time in the pursuit of a goal), high levels of *self-efficacy* (high expectations of being able to achieve an intended outcome), and availability of *skills* necessary for goal pursuit (such as learning strategies) all predict higher levels of future goal attainment (Bandura, 1998; Brunstein, 1993; Zimmerman, 1998). In the present chapter, I'd like to add two factors to this list, suggesting that successful goal striving jointly depends on a person's mood and his or her ability to regulate mood. In a nutshell, the main argument is that high levels of negative mood tend to impair long-term goal striving because negative mood-relevant thought interferes with the processes necessary for successful goal pursuit. This tendency, however, can be counteracted by employing mood-regulation strategies which effectively lead to a sustained reduction in negative mood. Since the processes and mechanisms involved are conceptualized to apply to people of different ages and cultures, the chapter is representative of a global approach to motivational processes. To substantiate this claim, I will also discuss the role of cultural factors in mood and mood-regulation in the final section.

Mood, Self-Regulation, and Goal Striving

Affective states (such as "sadness") can take the form of either emotions or moods. While emotions are typically a response to a specific object or situation and tend to subside when this object or situation is no longer present, moods can be characterized as diffuse and global and may persist for extended periods of time (Frijda, 1994; Morris, 1989; Parkinson, Totterdell, Briner, & Reynolds, 1996). According to Siemer (2005a, 2005b), mood-relevant thought constitutes an essential part of the phenomenal experience of mood, such that "being in a sad mood" is partly identical with "thinking sad thoughts." As such, moods "reflect general conditions of feeling good or bad which pervade our reactions to a wide variety of situations" (Parkinson et al., 1996, p. 8).

A host of studies have shown that mood states tend to be moderately stable over time, with retest-correlations of negative mood ranging from .61 over a two-year period (Suh, Diener, & Fujita, 1996) to .43 for a ten-year period (Costa, McCrae, & Zonderman, 1987). While the relative stability of mood is attributed to personality characteristics like extraversion and neuroticism (Costa et al., 1987), trait positive and negative affect (Watson, 2000), and carry-over effects (feeling sad today predicts feeling sad tomorrow; see Ormel & Rijsdijk, 2000), mood may be modulated by recent positive and negative life experiences (Headey & Wearing, 1989; Ormel & Schaufeli, 1991; Suh et al., 1996). For the present purpose, it is important to note that mood is stable enough to exert an influence over processes of goal pursuit which may cover a period of days, weeks or even months.

Several approaches have explored the role of negative mood in motivational processes. First, negative mood may arise as a *consequence* of unsuccessful or slow goal pursuit. In their control theory of self-regulation, Carver and Scheier (1990, 1998) argue that goals serve as reference values for feedback loops guiding human motivation. Emotional states are conceptualized as indicators of the rate of discrepancy reduction. Whereas positive affect occurs if discrepancy reduction exceeds a personal standard (i.e., a goal can be approached more rapidly than expected), negative affect is likely to arise if discrepancy reduction falls short of the standard (i.e., goal progress is slower than expected). Hence, high levels of negative mood may result if a person repeatedly encounters set-backs or problems in goal-pursuit or completely fails to attain a highly valued goal (see also Klinger, 1977).

Second, negative mood may *prospectively* impair successful striving for personal goals. For example, negative mood and the capacity to down-regulate states of negative mood have been implicated in an individual's capacity to adopt and pursue self-concordant goals. To account for differences in the ability to regulate mood, Kuhl (1983, 2001) introduced the concept of action vs. state orientation. As contrasted with action-orientated people, state-oriented individuals are characterized by an inability to down-regulate negative mood states[1]. Kuhl (2001) further proposes that state-oriented individu-

---

[1] More precisely, failure-related state orientation is associated with the inability to down-regulate negative emotional states, whereas prospective state-orientation is related to an inability to generate positive emotions (Kuhl, 1983, 2001). The present discussion focuses on failure-related state orientation.

als have limited access to their emotional and motivational preferences and are therefore prone to adopt goals which do not fit their motivational self-system. In accord with this suggestion, Kuhl and Kazén (1994) found that state-oriented individuals were more likely to think that they themselves chose a goal that was actually assigned to them by another person. This inability to differentiate self-chosen from assigned goals was absent among action-oriented individuals. In a study focussing on personal goals, Brunstein (2001) found that action-oriented individuals were committed to goals that were attainable and matched their implicit motivational needs. State-oriented individuals, on the other hand, tended to pursue unrealistic goals which did not match their motives. Since there is evidence that people invest more effort and are more successful at pursuing goals which are concordant with their motivational needs and values (Deci & Ryan, 1991; Sheldon & Elliot, 1999), we may expect people who are unable to regulate high levels of negative mood (i.e., state-oriented individuals) to be less persistent and less successful at goal pursuit.

Another model which stresses the potential debilitating effect of negative mood on goal pursuit and task performance is Gendolla's Mood Behavior Model (MBM; Gendolla, 2000; Gendolla & Brinkmann, 2005), which states that mood has an impact on motivation by moderating the subjective demand of a task. In a negative (as compared to a positive) mood, people tend to judge a task as more difficult and demanding, and rate the likelihood of success as well as their own subjective ability as lower (Gendolla, Abele, & Krüsken, 2001). As a consequence, a negative mood may prompt an individual to invest more effort to tackle an *easy* task, because the task – while still appraised as attainable – is subjectively more demanding in a negative (as compared to a positive) mood. In contrast, when people in a negative mood face a *difficult* task, then the task is likely to be appraised as unsolvable (due to reduced expectancies of success), prompting people in a negative (but not in a positive mood) to disengage from the task. These predictions have been generally confirmed in laboratory studies (Gendolla & Krüsken, 2001, 2002). According to the MBM, then, negative mood may lead to a motivational deficit on difficult tasks and, most probably, on challenging long-term goals, because negative mood diminishes the subjective probability of success (for a full account of the MBM, see Gendolla, 2000).

The approaches summarized so far suggest that negative mood can be a result of thwarted attempts to pursue a goal and that negative mood can prospectively impair goal striving by (a) prompting individuals to commit to goals which are not compatible with their motivational and emotional preferences and (b) by lowering expectations of being able to actually attain a difficult goal. In the present chapter, I will suggest that there is yet another process which may account for the debilitating effect of negative mood on goal striving. In essence, I will suggest that negative mood impairs motivational processes because it drains attentional resources which are needed for the pursuit of complex personal goals.

Mood states have been shown to exert an influence over a wide range of psychological processes (Parkinson et al., 1996). Of central importance for the present research, there is evidence that negative mood induces cognitive changes with respect to attentional capacity (cf. Kahneman, 1973) and working memory (Baddeley, 1990). Ellis and Ashbrook's (1988) resource allocation model of mood posits that mood reduces the amount of attentional capacity that can be allocated to a given task by increasing the amount of task-irrelevant processing. To illustrate, a sad mood is characterized by thoughts related to recent failures or losses, an anxious mood is associated with thinking about possible threats to one's health or self-esteem, and an angry mood is related to thoughts about possible revenge (Oatley & Johnson-Laird, 1987). In each case, mood-congruent thought requires a fair amount of working memory and will therefore impair performance on tasks which require at least a minimum amount of attentional capacity.

Empirical research has yielded support for the resource allocation model, demonstrating that negative mood is related to a greater proportion of task-irrelevant thoughts and lower performance on memory tests (Ellis, Moore, Varner, Ottaway, & Becker, 1997; Seibert & Ellis, 1991) and, more generally, that negative mood seems to impair working memory (Ikeda, Iwanaga, & Seiwa, 1996; Kensinger & Corkin, 2003; Spies, Hesse, & Hummitzsch, 1996). Of central importance for the present research are studies which investigated the effect of mood on *prospective memory*, which is defined as the ability to remember to perform an intended activity in the future (Brandimonte, Einstein, & McDaniel, 1996), such as remembering to attend a meeting or post a letter. Prospective memory is impaired in anxious individuals (Harris & Cumming, 2003; Harris & Menzies, 1999) as well as in clinically depressed adults (Rude, Hertel, Jarrold, Covich, & Hedlund, 1999). In a study by Kliegel et al. (2005), induction of a sad mood (vs. a neutral mood) was related to decreased performance on an experimental task assessing prospective memory (remembering to press a target key at 1 min. intervals while working on another task). In sum, these studies suggest that the initiation of a planned action may be impaired by high levels of negative mood.

This research suggests that negative mood may also impair the ability to strive for and finally attain long-term goals because the pursuit of long-term goals seems to depend on the availability of attentional capacity. When pursuing a personal goal, individuals benefit from becoming closed-minded to irrelevant information while processing goal-relevant information and planning the concrete actions which are necessary to advance toward the goal (Gollwitzer & Bayer, 1999; Gollwitzer, Fujita, & Oettingen, 2004). Since the pursuit of long-term goals is often interrupted and has to be put on hold until a favorable opportunity to proceed occurs, long-term goals can only be attained if a person manages to detect opportunities and flexibly initiates goal-directed actions (Kuhl, 2001). Individuals who experience high levels of negative mood can be expected to ruminate about mood-related yet goal-irrelevant thoughts ("why do I feel this way, and what can I do about it?") which interfere with processes required for goal-pursuit, such as processing goal-related information, planning goal pursuit as well as detecting and seizing on opportunities to advance toward a goal. This reasoning yields the hypothesis that, all other things being equal, individuals who experience high levels of negative mood over an extended period of time may be less successful in advancing toward personal goals than those who experience low levels of negative mood.

Mood Regulation

As noted before, people do not only differ in their susceptibility to experience states of negative mood, but also in their ability to "get a grip" on their moods and emotions

(Koole & Jostmann, 2004; Kuhl, 2001; Larsen, 2000), that is, to effectively down-regulate a state of high negative mood. As a consequence, factors that give rise to chronic negative mood (personality, carry-over effects, recent life events) can be expected to impair long-term goal striving if and only if a person fails to employ efficient strategies to regulate negative mood. Among the broad range of mood-regulation strategies which can be distinguished (Larsen & Prizmic, 2004; Parkinson & Totterdell, 1999), some seem to be more effective in reducing negative mood than others (Langens & Mose, 2006). For example, strategies like substance use, denial, self-blame and behavioral disengagement may offer some short-term relief, such as a release of negative affect and/or an immediate reduction in negative mood, but may lead to even higher levels of negative mood in the long run, that is, when they are rigidly employed over several weeks or months (Lazarus & Folkman, 1984; McKenna, Zevon, Corn, & Rounds, 1999; Suls & Fletcher, 1985). On the other hand, mood regulation strategies like confrontation, planning, problem-solving, and positive reframing are related to a sustained, long-term reduction in negative mood, because they foster a new understanding of events which gave rise to negative mood or serve to neutralize the "root" cause of negative mood (Larsen & Prizmic, 2004; Matheny, Aycock, Pugh, Curlette, & Canella, 1986; Mullen & Suls, 1982; Schwarzer & Leppin, 1991).

According to the present theoretical framework, using effective (rather than ineffective) mood-regulation strategies should neutralize the debilitating effect of negative mood on goal striving. Instructing individuals who experience high levels of negative mood to employ effective mood-regulation strategies should have a multi-tiered effect: First, and most obviously, they should experience a sustained reduction in negative mood in the following weeks and months. As a consequence, they may also be expected to show increased attentional capacity and, in turn, may be more successful in advancing toward their personal goals. One of the challenges in testing this hypothesis is to identify an intervention which has proved to reliably reduce negative mood in the long run.

In the studies to be described shortly, an intervention originally designed by Pennebaker (1997; Pennebaker & Beall, 1986) was employed as a way to test the effect of mood-regulation on long-term goal striving. In this program of research, Pennebaker and Beall (1986) found that writing about highly emotional experiences in an emotional way (which will also be called "written emotional expression" hereafter) has beneficial effects on physical health and emotional well-being. In their seminal study, Pennebaker and Beall (1986) had participants write about the most stressful experience of their life for 15 minutes a day over the course of 4 days and found that students who elaborated stressful experiences both cognitively *and* emotionally subsequently reduced the number of health-center visits. A meta-analysis of writing studies conducted subsequently (Smyth, 1998, see also Lepore & Smyth, 2002) demonstrated that written emotional expression also has beneficial effects on blood markers of immune functions, general functioning, and subjective emotional well-being. In addition, there is evidence that written emotional expression enhances working memory capacity (Klein & Boals, 2001a).

Discussions of the mechanisms which may be responsible for the effects of emotional expression (Pennebaker & Seagal, 1999; Smyth, 1998) typically highlight the importance of forming a narrative and developing a new understanding of upsetting events. According to Pennebaker and Seagal (1999), writing about stressful events can help to integrate upsetting experiences into a coherent narrative which may render the traumatic experience more meaningful. Once a person has developed a new understanding, the event can "be summarized, stored, and forgotten more efficiently" (Pennabeker & Seagal, 1999, p. 1248). Written emotional expression may be especially helpful for individuals who experience chronic high levels of negative mood because it may help to mute mood-related cognitions ("Why do I feel this way?", "What can I do about it?"), thereby releasing attentional capacity and increasing working memory (cf. Klein & Boales, 2001a), and clearing the way for a vigorous pursuit of one's personal goals.

In sum, then, the present research was guided by the following hypothesis: (a) High negative mood will be prospectively related to lower levels of attainment of personal goals. The relationship between mood and goal attainment should be evident even after accounting for other factors which influence goal pursuit (such as goal commitment), and may be mediated in part or fully by working memory capacity: people high in negative mood may be less able to pursue their personal goals because they are preoccupied by mood-congruent thought which is irrelevant for current goal pursuit. (b) Using effective strategies to regulate negative mood should neutralize the effects of mood on goal-striving. Mood-regulation strategies are expected to facilitate goal striving because they free working-memory from mood-congruent thought which may interfere with successful goal pursuit. Note that employing mood-regulation strategies should have beneficial effects on goal-striving only among participants who actually experience a high level of negative mood, while having no effect for participants who report low levels of negative mood.

In what follows, I will present three studies which put these hypotheses to an empirical test. I will then present an integrative model which outlines the effects of mood on goal striving, the mediating role of attentional processes, and the moderating effect of mood-regulation strategies. Finally, I will discuss how cultural beliefs and values shape emotional experiences as well as mood-regulation strategies.

Exploring the Empirical Relationships between Mood and Goal Striving

Study 1: Negative Mood and Goal Advancement

An initial study sought to explore the relationship between negative mood and subsequent goal striving in a sample of first-year university students. Pilot testing (Langens & Schmalt, 2002) had revealed that first-year university students typically pursue at least three goals: achieving progress in their studies (which will be called the *academic goal*), keeping in touch with old friends (*friendship goal*), and getting to know their fellow students (*peer goal*). Goal commitment was assessed by employing scales developed by Brunstein (1993), which asked participants to rate their determination (e.g., "No matter what happens, I will not give up this goal") and their willingness to invest effort in the pursuit of their goals (e.g., "Even if it means a lot of effort, I will do everything necessary to accomplish this goal"). In addition, chronic mood (Matthews, Jones, & Chamberlain,

1990) was assessed by asking participants to rate how they had been feeling the last weeks. Goal attainment for the three goals was assessed six weeks later using scales taken from Brunstein (1993), which directly asked participants how successful they were in advancing toward their goal. It was predicted that high levels of negative mood will be related to lower levels of goal attainment at the end of the study even after controlling for initial goal commitment. The central results are depicted in Table 1. In accord with previous research (e.g., Brunstein, 1993), the data showed that goal commitment significantly predicted goal attainment six weeks later. Importantly, further analyses revealed that negative mood, at the beginning of the study, was negatively related to future goal attainment for each of the three goals after controlling for initial goal commitment.

Table 1. The relationship between initial goal commitment and negative mood with goal attainment assessed six weeks later.

	Goal attainment		
	Academic goal	Friendship goal	Peer goal
Goal commitment	.28*	.22 ns	.32*
Negative mood	-.48**	-.27*	-.38*

Note: Correlations between negative mood and goal attainment are controlled for goal commitment: * $p < .05$; ** $p < .01$.

Study 2: Mood Regulation, Depressive Symptoms, and Goal Advancement

Although Study 1 provided some suggestive evidence that negative mood prospectively impairs goal advancement, the lack of experimental control yields this conclusion vulnerable to several alternative interpretations (e.g., assuming that a third variable like neuroticism affected both initial mood and subsequent goal striving). While it seems neither possible nor feasible to directly manipulate mood over a long period of time, it can be hypothesized that negative mood may be influenced indirectly by asking participants to take part in an intervention – like written emotional expression – which has proved to lead to a sustained reduction of negative mood. By decreasing negative mood, written emotional expression may enable people to successfully advance toward their long-term goals.

To investigate this hypothesis, data from a study (Study 2) by Langens and Schüler (2005) were reanalyzed. In this study, participants were asked in an initial session (Time 1, T1) to rate commitment for the goals also examined in Study 1 and to provide measures of chronic negative mood. Next, half of the participants were instructed to write about highly emotional autobiographical experiences that had occurred in the past once a week for a total of eight weeks. Participants in the control condition did not write about emotional experiences. Thirteen weeks (Time 2, T2) after the onset of the study, participants were contacted again and asked to provide measures of depressive symptoms and to rate goal attainment for the goals investigated in this study. For the statistical analyses, ratings of goal commitment at T1 and goal attainment at T2 were averaged across the three goals. According to Pennebaker (1997), writing in an emotional way about personally meaningful events should lead to a sustained reduction in negative mood, and we expected this effect to be most pronounced among participants who had high levels of negative mood at the onset of the study. According to the main hypothesis presented in the introduction, a reduction in negative mood associated with written emotional expression should then lead to more successful goal striving.

The results were generally in accord with these predictions. Replicating the results of Study 1, there was a significant negative relationship between initial negative mood and goal attainment assessed at T2 in the control condition, which was still significant after controlling for initial goal commitment (see Figure 1, left panel). In contrast, the relationship between negative mood and goal attainment was not significant among participants who wrote about highly emotional experiences. Notably, the intervention was effective in facilitating goal attainment only among participants initially reporting high levels of negative mood, who reported higher levels of goal attainment than their counterparts in the control condition. Among participants low in negative mood, the intervention had no effect on goal attainment. Further analyses revealed that written emotional expression led to a reduction in depressive symptoms (Figure 1, right panel). While initial negative mood was positively associated with depressive symptoms thirteen weeks later in the control condition, this relationship was not significant in the experimental condition. Most importantly, writing led to a reduction in depressive symptoms among participants who initially reported high levels of negative mood, but not among participants low in negative mood.

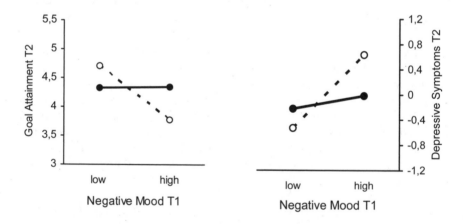

Figure 1. Goal attainment (left panel) and depressive symptoms (right panel) 13 weeks after the onset of the study (T2) as a function of initial negative mood (T1) and the experimental conditions. The solid line represents the experimental condition (written emotional expression), the dashed line represents the control condition (Study 2).

An additional mediation analysis confirmed that the effect of initial negative mood and the experimental conditions on goal attainment was mediated by a reduction in depressive symptoms (see Figure 2), which suggests that written emotional expression helped people who initially reported high negative mood to attain their goals because the intervention reduced depressive symptoms.

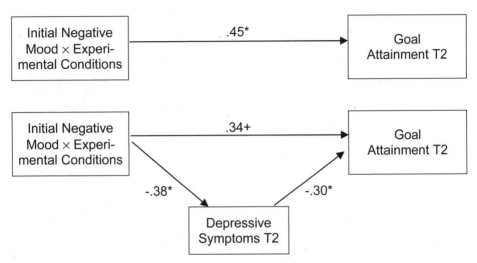

Figure 2. Path analyses testing the mediating role of depressive symptoms in the relationship between initial negative mood and the experimental conditions (written emotional expression vs. control condition) and subsequent goal attainment (Study 2).

Study 3: Mood Regulation, Working Memory, and Goal Advancement

Study 3 (Langens, 2007) was conducted to test the hypothesis that negative mood impairs goal striving by blocking working-memory capacity, and that written emotional expression facilitates goal-striving by increasing working-memory capacity. Data for Study 3 were collected in three phases. At Time 1 (T1), participants completed measures of chronic mood, provided descriptions of the two most important personal goals they were currently pursuing, and completed a measure of working memory. To assess working memory, we administered a test based on Turner and Engle's (1989) arithmetic operation-word memory task. In each trial of this task, an arithmetic equation, e.g., $(5 \times 3) - 1 = 16$, is presented on a computer screen along with a one-syllable word (e.g., ring). Participants are asked to indicate verbally whether the equation is correct or incorrect and to read the word out aloud. After sets of 3 to 7 problems, participants are prompted to write down as many of the words of the preceding set as possible. To master this task, participants have to actively rehearse the words presented on previous trials while simultaneously solving the arithmetic equations. Klein and Boals (2001a, 2001b) demonstrated that having experienced stressful events is associated with decreased working memory (possibly because of intrusions interfering with good performance) and that written emotional expression increases performance longitudinally. Following this initial session, participants were randomly assigned to the experimental condition in which they were asked to write about negative emotional experiences, or the control condition, in which participants planned activities for the following day. In both conditions, participants completed writing assignments for four consecutive days (see Pennebaker, 1997). Six weeks later

(Time 2, T2), participants were again invited to the lab where they were again tested for their working memory and rated goal attainment for the goals they provided at T1.

Looking at goal attainment at T2, we found a similar pattern of results as in Study 2: negative mood was negatively related to goal attainment in the control condition, while this relationship was not significant in the experimental condition (see Figure 3, left panel). Again, writing about negative experiences (as compared to planning activities for the following day) was related to more successful goal striving only among participants who reported high levels of negative mood at the beginning of the study. For participants low in negative mood at T1, the intervention had no significant effect.

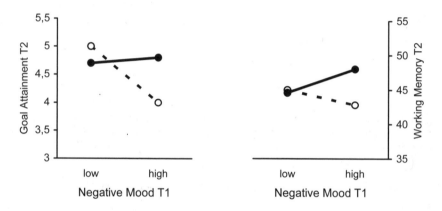

Figure 3. Goal attainment (left panel) and working memory (residualized change scores, right panel) at the end of the study (T2) as a function of initial negative mood (T1) and the experimental conditions. The solid line represents the experimental condition (written emotional expression), the dashed line represents the control condition (Study 3).

The next set of analyses was conducted to explore the role of working memory in mood and goal striving. In accord with the resource allocation model of mood, the results showed that negative mood was significantly related to lower levels of working memory capacity at T1, although not very strongly so, $r = -.22, p < .05$. Replicating the finding of Klein and Boals (2001a), it was also found that written emotional expression (as compared to the control treatment) significantly increased working memory capacity from T1 to T2. Most importantly, though, we found that the increase in working memory in the experimental condition was most pronounced among participants who had high negative mood at T1 (see Figure 3, right panel). Among participants who reported high levels of negative mood at T1, those who employed written emotional expression showed a sizeable increase in working memory, while working memory stagnated for participants high in negative mood in the control condition. In contrast, written emotional expression did not have an effect on working memory for participants low in negative mood.

An additional mediation analysis confirmed that the effect of initial negative mood and the experimental conditions on goal attainment was partly mediated by a change in working memory (see Figure 4). Hence, participants who initially reported high levels of negative mood were more successful in advancing toward their personal goals when writing about negative experiences because written emotional expression (as compared to planning) increased working memory capacity.

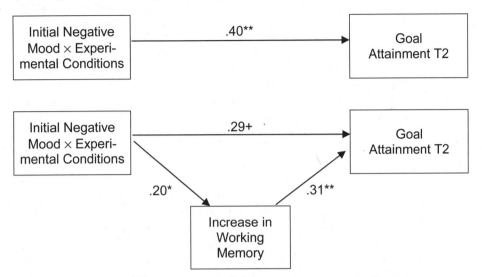

Figure 4. Path analyses testing the mediating role of working memory capacity in the relationship between initial negative mood and the experimental conditions (written emotional expression vs. control condition) and subsequent goal attainment (Study 3).

Mood and Goal Striving: An Integrative Model

The results of the present studies suggest that (a) negative mood prospectively impairs advancement toward personal goals, (b) the relationship between negative mood and impaired goal striving is mediated in part by decreased working-memory capacity and (c) that an effective mood-regulation strategy neutralizes the effect of negative mood on goal striving by increasing working-memory. Although the results are generally in accord with the resource allocation model of mood, the results may be explained by alternative approaches to the relationship between mood and goal striving.

For example, negative mood may have impaired goal striving because people who experience sustained high levels of negative mood tend to adopt goals which are not integrated in their self, conceptualized as an implicit network of emotional and motivational preferences (cf. Kuhl, 2001). Such discordant goals are typically pursued less vigorously and less successfully (Sheldon & Elliot, 1999). In support of this notion, negative mood tended to be negatively correlated with initial goal commitment in all three studies (correlations ranged from -.14 to -.38). Note, however, that negative mood predicted long-term goal attainment *after controlling for initial goal commitment*. Hence, other factors than reduced goal commitment stemming from initial negative mood seem to mediate the relationship between negative mood and subsequent goal striving.

Also, the results of the present studies may be explained in terms of the Mood Behavior Model (MBM; Gendolla, 2000; Gendolla & Brinkmann, 2005). Let us presume that the personal goals described by the participants in the studies reported here were mostly complex and difficult to attain. The MBM predicts that people in a negative mood tend to disengage from difficult goals because negative mood reduces perceived likelihood of success, transforming an objectively difficult goal into a subjectively unattainable one. Again, we may note that initial negative mood was only weakly related to goal commitment and that mood predicted goal advancement over and beyond goal commitment.

The best way to integrate the present findings with existing approaches to the relationship between mood and motivation may be to suggest that there is more than one mechanism which renders negative mood states detrimental for long-term goal pursuit. As already noted, people in a negative mood may select the wrong goals (goals which are discordant with their motives) or may tend to prematurely disengage from goal pursuit. The present studies suggest that a reduction of working memory capacity by negative mood-relevant thought is yet another process which accounts for detrimental effects of negative mood on goal pursuit.

Since this discussion exclusively focused on the debilitating effects of negative mood on goal striving, it may be worthwhile to add some speculations on the role of *positive mood* states like joy and happiness on goal pursuit. First and foremost, there is little evidence that a positive mood is related to impairment in working memory, which is easily explained given that people only tend to ruminate about possible causes and consequences of negative mood, but not about the origins and effects of positive mood ("Why do I feel so good? What can I do about it?"). In addition, there is evidence that positive emotionality is at the core of a motivational approach system which sensitizes individuals for desirable stimuli and induces a behavioral tendency toward such stimuli (Elliot & Thrash, 2002). Thus, in a positive mood, people seem to be acutely aware of the positive affective consequences related to the attainment of long-term personal goals (such as joy and satisfaction stemming from a job well done) and are therefore more likely to seek out and seize opportunities to advance toward their personal goals. In addition, the MBM suggests that positive mood has the same effect on effort intensity as high ability beliefs, which should support the striving for personal goals (Gendolla & Brinkmann, 2005). These approaches suggest that mood-regulation strategies aimed at lifting positive mood, such as self-reward, engaging in pleasant activities, or moderate exercise (cf. Larsen & Prizmic, 2004), may be successful in *facilitating* long-term goal pursuit.

The model depicted in Figure 5 integrates these speculations with the results of the research presented above. It suggests that both positive and negative mood states influence long-term goal striving by directing attention either to mood-relevant thought or goal-relevant thought. Chronic states of negative mood tend to shift attention toward negative mood-relevant thought (related, for example, to failure, threat, or revenge), which preoccupy working memory and interfere with advancement toward personal goals. Note that people who experience high levels of negative mood may be perfectly able to carry out behavioral routines and tackle easy tasks which do not require complex planning. However, they should be less able to advance toward complex goals which depend on working memory capacity, such as preparation for exams or advancing in their professional career. Chronic states of positive mood, on the other hand, should induce an attentional bias toward incentives associated with attaining a personal goal and opportunities to advance in goal pursuit, which should increase the likelihood to implement goal-related actions.

The model further assumes that people may act on their chronic mood states, which may result from uncontrollable factors like temperament and life events, by deliberately employing mood-regulation strategies aimed at up-regulating positive mood or down-regulating negative mood. Strategies which are effective in changing chronic mood may then indirectly promote goal pursuit by altering attentional processes. Hence, although a person may have a high propensity to experience high levels of negative mood or low levels of positive mood, he or she may nonetheless terminate possible debilitating effects on goal striving by employing effective strategies to change mood. Note, however, that the model in its present form does not account for cultural factors which modulate both mood and mood regulation. This issue will be addressed in the following section.

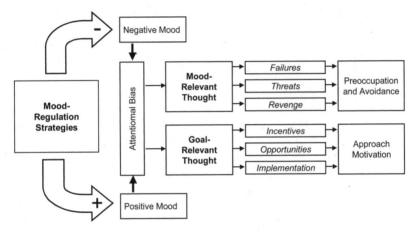

Figure 5. An integrative model of the effects of mood and mood-regulation strategies on long-term goal striving.

Cultural Influences on Mood Regulation

There is now overwhelming evidence that psychological processes do not unfold in a social vacuum, but are highly attuned to a culture's predominant beliefs and values (Kitayama, 2002). Therefore, it is necessary to explore how culture may modulate the effects of mood on goal striving. In doing so, I will focus on a central dimension of cultural differences which concerns the construal of the self as either independent or interdependent (Markus & Kitayama, 1991; Triandis, 1989). *Independence*, which is promoted in North America as well as in Western Europe, is characterized by seeking personal accomplishment and distinction from others as well as an expression of the individual self. In contrast, *interdependence*, which is fostered in many Latin-American, African, Asian cultures (including Japan) as well as in many Southern European cultures, is associated with the desire to fit in and belong, to promote social harmony, to engage in appropriate action and to subject individual aspirations to common aims and goals. There is conclusive evidence that this orientation permeates many facets of individual experience, including emotional and motivational processes (Markus & Kitayama, 1991). Thus, it seems worthwhile to investigate how the model depicted in Figure 5 can accommodate the different cultural construals of the self.

In a first step, it seems important to ask whether the link between negative mood and goal striving, which was evident in the studies reported above, is specific for predominantly independent cultures like Western Europe. To be sure, there is conclusive evidence that the emotional life of people in interdependent cultures differs substantially from those living in independent cultures (Kitayama, Markus, & Kurokawa, 2000; Mesquita & Karasawa, 2002). As suggested by Kitayama, Karasawa, and Mequita (2004), independent cultures promote the expression of socially disengaging emotions such as pride and feelings of self-esteem as well as anger and frustration. In contrast, interdependent cultures promote the expression of socially engaging emotions, like feelings of closeness and respect as well as guilt and feelings of indebtedness. As a result, individuals in independent cultures tend to experience socially engaging emotions more frequently and with higher intensity than socially disengaging emotions, while the reverse is true for interdependent cultures. Moreover, general levels of well being – such as chronic emotional well-being vs. feelings of depression and dejection – seem to depend more strongly on disengaging emotions in independent cultures and engaging emotions in interdependent cultures. Thus, individuals in independent cultures tend to become depressed because they failed to achieve personal accomplishments and to stand out from the rest, whereas people in an interdependent culture experience chronic negative mood because they failed to fulfill the expectations of significant others, especially their family (Kitayama, Mesquita, & Karasawa, 2006).

Although the origins of chronic positive and negative mood depend on cultural factors, we might still expect a chronic negative mood to reduce working memory capacity in both interdependent and independent cultures. Note that negative mood decreases working memory because negative mood elicits mood-relevant thoughts (Ellis & Ashbrook, 1988), which may well differ by culture: people in independent cultures may tend to ruminate more about personal failures, whereas individuals in interdependent cultures are more strongly preoccupied by thoughts related to not living up to others' expectations. Still, working memory is decreased in both cases and hence not available for long-term goal pursuit. Thus, we may expect a chronic negative mood to impair goal striving in both independent and interdependent cultures. In a related vein, although positive mood may have different origins in independent and interdependent cultures, we may still suggest that a positive mood facilitates goal striving in both, since the mechanism underlying the link between positive mood and goal striving – i.e., priming a motivational approach system which sensitizes a person to incentives and opportunities – should be unaffected by the source of positive mood.

So far, I have stressed the universal aspects of the model depicted in Figure 5. However, cultural factors do seem to play a central role in how people go about regulating their emotions and moods. Applied to mood-regulation strategies, the concept of *cultural reinforcement* (Kitayama et al., 2004) (which states that each culture praises and encourages certain acts while punishing, discouraging, or disparaging others) suggests that cultures promote certain strategies of mood regulation more than others. More specifically, cultures seem to afford and reinforce mood-regulation strategies which are in accord with their overarching values and beliefs (Mesquita & Albert, 2007). Thus, while Western cultures seem to encourage mood-regulation strategies which are based on expressing mood-relevant thought and venting negative emotions, Asian cultures are more prone to promote private and less imposing strategies (Markus & Kitayama, 1991; Mesquita & Albert, 2007).

As an example, participants in a study by Mesquita, Karasawa, Haire, and Izumi (2002, as cited in Kitayama et al., 2004) were asked how they would respond to an offense from another person. While a large majority of American participants reported to blame the offender, which is perfectly in accord with independent values, the responses by Japanese participants were geared toward adjustment, engagement and interdependence: they either reported doing nothing in response to the offense, took responsibility, or tried to seek closeness to the offender, all of which promote social harmony. Another line of research has demonstrated that suppressing negative emotions has a host of detrimental consequences among North American and European individuals, including heightened physiological activation and, ultimately, further increases in negative mood (Gross, 2002; Wegner, 1994). Interestingly, though, these effects are attenuated or absent among individuals expressing interdependent values (Butler, Lee, & Gross, 2007), suggesting again that mood-regulation strategies are effective to the extent that they are attuned to cultural values and beliefs.

Summary and Conclusion

The present chapter introduced the hypothesis that advancement toward personal goals depends on a person's chronic mood and his or her ability to regulate mood. While a negative mood seems to distract people from the pursuit of their goals, making goal advancement less likely over time, a positive mood seems to remind them of the incentives associated with successful goal pursuit, sometimes providing the extra edge needed to tackle the complex and demanding tasks ahead. While mood is often triggered automatically by inner states or external events beyond their control, people may try to act on their mood by employing mood-regulation strategies. However, regulating negative mood is by no means an easy task. People sometimes resort to mood regulation strategies which offer some immediate relief (like alcohol use, behavioral disengagement or denial) while increasing negative mood and impairing health in the long run (Langens & Mose, 2006). In addition, there is evidence that mood regulation strategies have to be attuned to the basic beliefs and values of a culture in order to have a sustained effect (Kitayama et al., 2004). An important goal for subsequent research is to further investigate and identify mood regulation strategies which help people to effectively regulate their mood in the long run within their cultural context. In this way, we may be able to provide people with the means to exploit the central source of well-being which is associated with striving for and attaining personal goals. From a theoretical point of view, although the effects of mood and mood-regulation on goal striving can be explained by a general global mechanism, the situational or local aspect is also present, as cultural effects on goals pursued and strategies adopted suggest.

Acknowledgements

Parts of the research summarized in this chapter were supported by the Deutsche Forschungsgemeinschaft grant LA 1155/4-1. I would like to thank Jennifer Fett, Aneta Kozlowski, Tatjana Schlaht, and Lisa Warmbier for their help in data collection.

References

Baddeley, A. D. (1990). *Human memory: Theory and practice.* Hillsdale, NJ: Erlbaum.

Bandura, A. (1998). *Self-efficacy* (2nd ed.). New York: Guilford.

Brandimonte, M. A., Einstein, G. O., & McDaniel, M. A. (1996). *Prospective memory: Theory and applications.* Mahwah, NJ: Erlbaum.

Brunstein, J. C. (1993). Personal goals and subjective well-being: A longitudinal study. *Journal of Personality and Social Psychology, 65,* 1061-1070.

Brunstein, J. C. (2001). Persönliche Ziele und Handlungs- versus Lageorientierung: Wer bindet sich an realistische und bedürfniskongruente Ziele? [Personal goals and action versus state orientation: Who builds a commitment to realistic and need-congruent goals?]. *Zeitschrift für Differentielle und Diagnostische Psychologie, 22,* 1-12.

Brunstein, J. C., & Gollwitzer, P. M. (1996). Effects of failure on subsequent performance: The importance of self-defining goals. *Journal of Personality and Social Psychology, 70,* 395-407.

Butler, E. A., Lee, T. L., & Gross, J. J. (2007). Emotion regulation and culture: Are the social consequences of emotion suppression culture-specific? *Emotion, 7,* 30-48.

Carver, C. S., & Scheier, M. F. (1990). Origins and functions of positive and negative affect: A control process view. *Psychological Review, 97,* 19-35.

Carver, C.S., & Scheier, M.F. (1998). *On the self-regulation of behavior.* Cambridge: Cambridge University Press.

Costa, P. T., McCrae, R. R., & Zonderman, A. B. (1987). Environmental and dispositional influences on well-being: Longitudinal follow-up of an American national sample. *British Journal of Psychology, 78,* 299-306.

Deci, E. L., & Ryan, R. M. (1991). A motivational approach to self: Integration in Personality. In R. Dienstbier (Ed.), *Nebraska Symposium on Motivation* (Vol. 38, pp. 237-288). Lincoln, NE: University of Nebraska Press.

Elliot, A. J., & Thrash, T. M. (2002). Approach-avoidance motivation in personality: Approach and avoidance temperaments and goals. *Journal of Personality and Social Psychology, 82,* 804-818.

Ellis, H. C., & Ashbrook, P. W. (1988). Resource allocation model of effects of depressed mood states on memory. In K. Fiedler & J. P. Forgas (Eds.), *Affect, cognition, and social behavior* (pp. 25-43). Toronto, CA: Hogrefe.

Ellis, H. C., Moore, B. A., Varner, L. J., Ottaway, S. A., & Becker, A. S. (1997). Depressed mood, task organization, cognitive interference, and memory: Irrelevant thoughts predict recall performance. *Journal of Social Behavior and Personality, 12,* 453-470.

Emmons, R. A. (1986). Personal strivings: An approach to personality and subjective well-being. *Journal of Personality and Social Psychology, 51,* 1058-1068.

Frijda, N. H. (1994). Varieties of affect: Emotions and episodes, moods and sentiments. In P. Ekman & R. J. Davidson (Eds.), *The nature of emotions: Fundamental questions* (pp. 59-67). New York: Oxford University Press.

Gendolla, G. H. E. (2000). On the impact of mood on behavior: An integrative theory and a review. *Review of General Psychology, 4,* 378-408.

Gendolla, G. H. E., Abele, A. E., & Krüsken, J. (2001). The informational impact of mood on effort mobilization: A study of cardiovascular and electrodermal responses. *Emotion, 1,* 12-24.

Gendolla, G. H. E., & Brinkmann, K. (2005). The role of mood states in self-regulation. *European Psychologist, 10,* 187-198.

Gendolla, G. H. E., & Krüsken, J. (2001). Mood state and cardiovascular response in active coping with an affect-regulative challenge. *International Journal of Psychophysiology, 41,* 169-180.

Gendolla, G. H. E., & Krüsken, J. (2002). Mood, task demand, and effort-related cardiovascular response. *Cognition and Emotion, 16,* 577-603.

Gollwitzer, P. M., & Bayer, U. (1999). Deliberative versus implemental mindsets in the control of action. In S. Chaiken & Y. Trope (Eds.), *Dual-process theories in social psychology* (pp. 403-422). New York: Guilford.

Gollwitzer, P. M., Fujita, K., & Oettingen, G. (2004). Planning and the implementation of goals. In R. F. Baumeister & K. D. Vohs (Eds.), *Handbook of self-regulation: Research, theory, and applications* (pp. 211-228). New York: Guilford.

Gross, J.J. (2002). Emotion regulation: Affective, cognitive, and social consequences. *Psychphysiology, 39,* 281-291.

Harris, L. M., & Cumming, S. R. (2003). An examination of the relationship between anxiety and performance on prospective and retrospective memory tasks. *Australian Journal of Psychology, 55,* 51-55.

Harris, L. M., & Menzies, R. G. (1999). Mood and prospective memory. *Memory, 7,* 117-127.

Headey, B., & Wearing, A. (1989). Personality, life events, and subjective well-being: Toward a dynamic equilibrium model. *Journal of Personality and Social Psychology, 57,* 731-739.

Ikeda, M., Iwanaga, M., & Seiwa, H. (1996). Test anxiety and working memory system. *Perceptual and Motor Skills, 82,* 1223-1231.

Kahneman, D. (1973). *Attention and effort.* Englewood Cliffs, NJ: Prentice Hall.

Kensinger, E. A., & Corkin, S. (2003). Effect of negative emotional content on working memory and long-term memory. *Emotion, 3,* 378-393.

Kitayama, S. (2002). Cultural psychology of the self: A renewed look at independence and interdependence. In C. von Hofsten & L. Bäckman (Eds.), *Psychology at the turn of the millennium. Social, developmental, and clinical perspectives* (Vol. 2, pp. 305-322). Florence, KY: Taylor & Frances/Routledge.

Kitayama, S., Karasawa, M., & Mesquita, B. (2004). Collective and personal processes in regulating emotions: Emotion and the self in Japan and the United States. In P. Philippot & R. S. Feldman (Eds.), *The regulation of emotion* (pp. 251-273). Mahwah, NJ: Erlbaum.

Kitayama, S., Markus, H. R., & Kurokawa, M. (2000). Culture, emotion, and well-being: Good feelings in the Japan and the United States. *Cognition and Emotion, 14,* 93-124.

Kitayama, S., Mesquita, B., & Karasawa, M. (2006). Cultural affordances and emotional experience: Socially engaging and disengaging emotions in Japan and the United States. *Journal of Personality and Social Psychology, 91,* 890-903.

Klein, K., & Boals, A. (2001a). Expressive writing can increase working memory capacity. *Journal of Experimental Psychology: General, 130,* 520-533.

Klein, K., & Boals, A. (2001b). The relationship of life event stress and working memory capacity. *Applied Cognitive Psychology, 15,* 565-579.

Kliegel, M., Jäger, T., Phillips, L. H., Federspiel, E., Imfeld, A., Keller, M., & Zimprich, D. (2005). Effects of sad mood on time-based prospective memory. *Cognition and Emotion, 19,* 1199-1213.

Klinger, E. (1977). *Meaning and void. Inner experience and incentives in people's lives.* Minneapolis, MN: University of Minnesota Press.

Koole, S. L., & Jostmann, N. B. (2004). Getting a grip on your feelings: Effects of action orientation and external demands on intuitive affect regulation. *Journal of Personality and Social Psychology, 87,* 974-990.

Kuhl, J. (1983). *Motivation, Konflikt und Handlungskontrolle* [Motivation, conflict, and action control]. Berlin: Springer.

Kuhl, J. (2001). *Motivation und Persönlichkeit* [Motivation and Personality]. Göttingen, Germany: Hogrefe.

Kuhl, J., & Kazén, M. (1994). Self-discrimination and memory: State orientation and false self-ascription of assigned activities. *Journal of Personality and Social Psychology, 66,* 1103-1115.

Langens, T. A. (2007). *Written emotional expression, working memory, and goal advancement.* Unpublished data, University of Wuppertal, Germany.

Langens, T. A., & Mose, E. (2006). Coping with unemployment: Relationships between duration of unemployment, coping styles, and subjective well-being. *Journal of Applied Biobehavioral Research, 11,* 189-208.

Langens, T. A., & Schmalt, H. D. (2002). Emotional consequences of positive daydreaming: The moderating role of fear of failure. *Personality and Social Psychology Bulletin, 28,* 1725-1735.

Langens, T. A., & Schüler, J. (2005). Written emotional expression and emotional well-being: The moderating role of fear of rejection. *Personality and Social Psychology Bulletin, 31,* 818-830.

Larsen, R. J. (2000). Toward a science of mood regulation. *Psychological Inquiry, 11,* 129-141.

Larsen, R. J., & Prizmic, Z. (2004). Affect regulation. In R. F. Baumeister & K. D. Vohs (Eds.), *Handbook of self-regulation: Research, theory, and applications* (pp. 40-61). New York: Guilford.

Lazarus, R. S., & Folkman, S. (1984). *Stress, appraisal, and coping.* New York: Springer.

Lepore, S. J., & Smyth, J. M. (2002). *The writing cure: How expressive writing promotes health and emotional well-being.* Washington, DC: American Psychological Association.

Markus, H. R., & Kitayama, S. (1991). Culture and self: Implications for cognition, emotion, and motivation. *Psychological Review, 98,* 224-253.

Matheny, K. B., Aycock, D. W., Pugh, J. L., Curlette, W. L., & Cannella, K. A. S. (1986). Stress coping: A qualitative and quantitative synthesis with implications for treatment. *Counseling Psychologist, 14,* 499-549.

Matthews, G., Jones, D. M., & Chamberlain, A. G. (1990). Refining the measurement of mood: The UWIST Mood Adjective Checklist. *British Journal of Psychology, 81,* 17-42.

McKenna, M. C., Zevon, M. A., Corn, B., & Rounds, J. (1999). Psychosocial factors and the development of breast cancer: A meta-analysis. *Health Psychology, 18,* 520-531.

Mesquita, B., & Albert, D. (2007). The cultural regulation of emotions. In J. J. Gross (Ed.), *Handbook of emotion regulation* (pp. 486-503). New York: Guilford.

Mesquita, B., & Karasawa, M. (2002). Different emotional lives. *Cognition and Emotion, 16,* 127-141.

Morris, W. N. (1989). *Mood: The frame of mind.* Berlin: Springer.

Mullen, B., & Suls, J. (1982). The effectiveness of attention and rejection as coping styles: A meta-analysis of temporal differences. *Journal of Psychosomatic Research, 26,* 43-49.

Oatley, K., & Johnson-Laird, P. N. (1987). Towards a cognitive theory of emotions. *Cognition & Emotion, 1,* 29-50.

Ormel, J., & Rijsdijk, F. V. (2000). Continuing change in neuroticism during adulthood – structural modeling of a 16-year, 5-wave community study. *Personality and Individual Differences, 28,* 461-478.

Ormel, J., & Schaufeli, W. B. (1991). Stability and change in psychological distress and their relationship with self-esteeem and locus of control: A dynamic equilibrium model. *Journal of Personality and Social Psychology, 60,* 288-299.

Parkinson, B., & Totterdell, P. (1999). Classifying affect-regulation strategies. *Cognition and Emotion, 13,* 277-303.

Parkinson, B., Totterdell, P., Briner, R. B., & Reynolds, S. (1996). *Changing moods. The psychology of mood and mood regulation.* London: Addison Wesley.

Pennebaker, J. W. (1997). *Opening up: The healing power of expressing emotions* (2nd ed.). New York: Guilford.

Pennebaker, J. W., & Beall, S. K. (1986). Confronting a traumatic event: Toward an understanding of inhibition and disease. *Journal of Abnormal Psychology, 95,* 274-281.

Pennebaker, J. W., & Seagal, J. D. (1999). Forming a story: The health benefits of narrative. *Journal of Clinical Psychology, 55,* 1243-1254.

Rude, S. S., Hertel, P. T., Jarrold, W., Covich, J., & Hedlund, S. (1999). Depression-related impairments in prospective memory. *Cognition and Emotion, 13,* 267-276.

Schwarzer, R., & Leppin, A. (1991). Social support and health: A theoretical and empirical overview. *Journal of Social and Personal Relationships, 8,* 99-127.

Seibert, P. E., & Ellis, H. C. (1991). Irrelevant thoughts, emotional mood states, and cognitive task performance. *Memory and Cognition, 19,* 507-513.

Sheldon, K. M., & Elliot, A. J. (1999). Goal striving, need satisfaction, and longitudinal well-being: The self-concordance model. *Journal of Personality and Social Psychology, 76,* 482-497.

Siemer, M. (2005a). Mood-congruent cognitions constitute mood experience. *Emotion, 5,* 296-308.

Siemer, M. (2005b). Moods as multiple-object directed and as objectless affective states: An examination of the dispositional theory of moods. *Cognition and Emotion, 19,* 815-845.

Smyth, J. M. (1998). Written emotional expression: Effect sizes, outcome types, and moderating variables. *Journal of Consulting and Clinical Psychology, 66,* 174-184.

Spies, K., Hesse, F. W., & Hummitzsch, C. (1996). Mood and capacity in Baddeley's model of human memory. *Zeitschrift für Psychologie, 204,* 367-381.

Suh, E., Diener, E., & Fujita, F. (1996). Events and subjective well-being: Only recent events matter. *Journal of Personality and Social Psychology, 70,* 1091-1102.

Suls, J., & Fletcher, B. (1985). The relative efficacy of avoidant and nonavoidant coping strategies: A meta-analysis. *Health Psychology, 4,* 249-288.

Triandis, H. C. (1989). The self and social behavior in differing culturalcontexts. *Psychological Review, 96,* 506-520.

Turner, M. L., & Engle, R. W. (1989). Is working memory capacity task dependent? *Journal of Memory and Language, 28,* 127-154.

Watson, D. (2000). *Mood and temperament.* New York: Guilford.

Wegner, D.M. (1994). Ironic processes of mental control. *Psychological Review, 101,* 34-52.

Wicklund, R. A., & Gollwitzer, P. M. (1982). *Symbolic self-completion.* Hillsdale, NJ: Erlbaum.

Zimmerman, B. J. (1998). Academic studying and the development of personal skill: A self-regulatory perspective. *Educational Psychologist, 33,* 73-86.

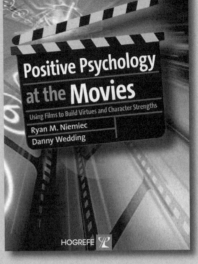
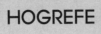

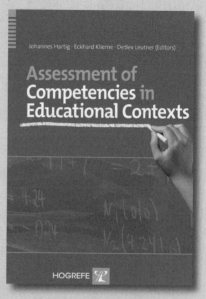
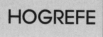

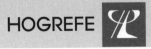